ENTREPRENEURSHIP

Strategies and Resources

FOURTH EDITION

Marc J. Dollinger

Kelley School of Business
INDIANA UNIVERSITY

MARSH PUBLICATIONS
Lombard, Illinois U.S.A.

In memory of Ken Marino, a great teacher, a wonderful colleague, and a true friend.

EDITOR   Libby Rubenstein
COPYEDITOR   Shelia Whalen
TYPESETTER   Phoenix Graphics, LLC
EDITORIAL SUPPORT   Barbara Burwold, Thomas Serb
MANUFACTURER   Sheridan Books, Inc.

Library of Congress Cataloging-in-Publication Data

Dollinger, Marc J.
   Entrepreneurship : strategies and resources / Marc J. Dollinger. — 4th ed.
      p. cm.
   Includes bibliographical references and index.
   ISBN 978-0-9713130-6-4
   1. New business enterprises. 2. Entrepreneurship. I. Title.
   HD62.5.D65 2008
   658.4'21—dc22

                    2007022574

Manufactured in the United States of America

10   9   8   7   6   5   4   3   2   1

∞ PRINTED ON ACID-FREE PAPER

Contents

Cases

Preface

Since the publication of the first edition of *Entrepreneurship: Strategies and Resources*, the field of entrepreneurship has grown even faster than I would have predicted. There are more courses and schools teaching entrepreneurship than ever. The major business periodicals, *Business Week, Fortune,* and *The Wall Street Journal* continue expanding their coverage of entrepreneurs and their companies. There are a number of publications that rank graduate and undergraduate entrepreneurship programs. Business plan competitions at the graduate and undergraduate level continue to proliferate and the prizes get larger and larger. International interest in new venture creation has grown exponentially. Programs in the United States and overseas have partnered to provide cross-cultural and multinational entrepreneurial courses for their students. I personally participated in one such effort between Indiana University and City University of Hong Kong. The technology enabled us to form joint ventures between students in the United States and Hong Kong for the purpose of starting businesses. It was marvelous.

In this fourth edition of *Entrepreneurship: Strategies and Resources*, I have tried to improve upon the foundation set in the first three editions. This book is intended to be friendlier to the user, beginning with its new design and soft cover. A number of features will help make the text easier to read and understand. Dozens of new examples and minicases, called "Street Story," have been added. International examples and applications are integrated throughout the book.

ORGANIZATION OF THE BOOK

Entrepreneurship: Strategies and Resources is organized into three parts. Part I introduces the major themes and theory of the book. Chapter 1 describes the roles that new venture creation plays in the international economy, defines entrepreneurship, and shows how three factors—individuals, environments, and organizations—come together to create the entrepreneurial event. I also make a point of explaining that studying entrepreneurship cannot be done in a formulaic, by the numbers fashion.. It requires judgment.

Chapter 2 sets this textbook apart from others because it casts entrepreneurial phenomena in terms of the predictive theory of the resource-based framework. In this chapter, I present the basic concepts and model of the resource-based theory. There are six types of resources in our theory: financial, physical, technological, human, organizational, and reputational. The theory says that entrepreneurs can create sustainable competitive advantage for their ventures when they possess or can acquire and control resources that are rare, valuable, hard to duplicate, and nonsubstitutable. Here I emphasize the importance of human resources, especially the entrepreneur. I then explain how these resources are a source of profit and rent for the entrepreneur, and how the new venture needs to protect these rents and profits through isolating mechanisms and first-mover advantages. The chapter also has an appendix that introduces the basics of creativity as I believe that this is a personal resource that can be further developed in all of us.

Part II of *Entrepreneurship: Strategies and Resources* describes the environment for entrepreneurship. It presents the tools and techniques for analyzing business and competitive conditions, and for evaluating entrepreneurial opportunities. It is comparable to the strategy formulation phase of corporate strategic management. The purpose of this section is to show how the environment affects, directs, and impinges on the strategy formulation problem in new venture creation. It does this in two ways that can be expressed by the resource-based model: The environment helps determine what is rare, valuable, imitable, and substitutable *and* it is the source of resources that possess these four attributes. The strategy formulation problem in new venture creation can be stated as follows: What configuration of resources will provide the new firm with the best chances of achieving a competitive advantage?

Chapter 3 covers the aspects of the macro- and microenvironment that affect entrepreneurship and new venture creation. I present a process model for environmental analysis and then describe a six-element model of the macroenvironment: political, stakeholder, economic, technological, sociodemographic, and ecological. . Next I offer the elements of the competitive environment. I incorporate the Porter model (five-forces model) into the analysis. I begin by asking two questions of utmost importance to the entrepreneur in the early stages of new venture creation:

1. Is the industry the entrepreneur is about to enter an attractive one?
2. What are the best ways to compete to increase the chances of creating a high profitability venture?

To address the first question, the chapter depicts an industry's profitability as a function of buyer and supplier power, the threat of substitutes, entry barriers, and the state of interfirm rivalry. Students are shown how to do this analysis in sufficient depth and with limited data by resorting to the basics of microeconomic theory. To address the second question, I discuss the ways that the possession and acquisition of the four-attribute resource base provide the entrepreneur with tools to overcome strong industry forces and exploit weak industry forces. The resource-based model is incorporated into this discussion by demonstrating its applicability as a screening device for new venture ideas. I create and describe a resource-based implementation matrix—the four attributes of sustainable competitive advantage by the six types of resources: financial, physical, technological, reputational, human, and organizational resources.

Chapter 4 presents types of new venture strategies and examines different positions that entrepreneurs take regarding the resources required for their firms. I present the basic entry wedges available to the new venture and develop the set of resource-based strategies. I introduce the concepts of strategy for businesses-producing information-type products. I look at how the industry life cycle influences strategy choice. New ventures can be created successfully across the life cycle, but each poses its special challenges. The chapter concludes with an overview of strategic postures and orientations that entrepreneurs can take.

Chapter 5 presents the major tool for formulating and creating new ventures: the business plan. It offers an in-depth outline for a business plan, including all the key sections and tips on how to structure the plan and the financial proposal for maximum effectiveness. The chapter continues with a discussion of the criteria and techniques for evaluating business plans. At the end of the chapter, there are proven tips for the format and presentation, writing, and editing of successful business plans. A complete business plan follows the chapter.

Part III of *Entrepreneurship: Strategies and Resources* makes the transition from the formulation of entrepreneurial strategy to the implementation stage. The section covers marketing, financing, and organizational issues. The final chapter in the book covers some special topics that students might need as they work their way through the course. These are intrapreneurship and franchising.

Chapter 6 is the marketing chapter. It introduces the basics of marketing for a new venture. I cover customer orientation, selection of segments and the basics of segmentation, the primary marketing activities, and the special problems of marketing on the Internet. The chapter concludes with a treatment of the problems and issues of sales forecasting. The appendix to Chapter 6 offers an example of sales forecasting using the market potential/sales requirements technique.

Chapter 7 introduces the elements of entrepreneurial finance. It discusses how financial resources can and cannot be a source of advantage for the new venture. Then we show how the venture can determine its financial and cash flow needs. After reviewing the types and sources of potential financing, I present three methods of new venture valuation. The chapter has an appendix: a brief introduction into the process of going public.

Chapter 8 shows how entrepreneurs actually obtain investors and structure the financial deal. It looks at the characteristics of various types of investors and how to appeal to their needs. The basic elements of the deal structure are presented, and then more advanced elements, such as phased financing and the use of options, are introduced. I have a new section on negotiation skills in this chapter. The chapter concludes with a review of the legal and tax issues raised by seeking outside investors. This chapter has three appendices: an outline of a term sheet, a description of a typical investment agreement, and a description of the negotiable terms to a financial agreement.

Chapter 9 examines the creation and development of the organization. It begins with a discussion of the top management team and provides guidelines for effective top management processes. I do the same for boards of directors. Then I discuss the design of the new venture, including alliances and partnerships. I offer the research and recommendations from Collins and Porras's *Built to Last*. I feel that the time to begin to think about building an enduring organization is right at the start of the venture, and the *Built to Last* concepts provide great insight into the entrepreneurial problem. I also offer an introduction to the dimensions of the *balanced scorecard*. I explore these in the context of entrepreneurial performance and show that performance is not just financial, but a set of indicators across four dimensions. The *balanced scorecard* can be a system of management for the entrepreneurial TMT. Last, I offer a vision of the entrepreneurial workplace. I discuss how culture, ethics, and personnel practices can help make organizations unique and therefore provide a competitive advantage.

Chapter 10 discusses intrapreneurship—the factors that lead to successful intrapreneurship and those that hinder large corporations from being entrepreneurial. This topic may be assigned if students require an introduction to it to enable them to do their projects, or if the course has a corporate component. I cover the issues of Innovator Dilemma and Innovator Solutions. A new addition to this chapter reviews the basic concepts of *Blue Ocean Strategy*. This important new book offers a method and process for evaluating the current situation for corporate products and a process to find less competitive but profitable positions. The chapter concludes with an appendix that covers the foundations of franchising. Again, this can be assigned if the student projects need a basic treatment of the subject or if the instructor has a franchising component in the class design.

Note from the author. I recently read a very good book: Deirdre McCloskey, *The Bourgeois Virtues* (Chicago: University of Chicago Press, 2006) and came across this quote in it.

"Courage plus prudence yields enterprise."

I think this sums up my approach in the book. Entrepreneurs require courage. They require the courage of their convictions, of their assumptions and the courage to risk money and time to pursue their ventures. But courage without prudence is too dangerous to encourage. Prudence requires thoughtful analysis, getting information, asking the views of others, and weighing the gains available against the costs incurred.

I wish you all both courage and prudence.

PEDAGOGIC FEATURES

The fourth edition of *Entrepreneurship: Strategies and Resources* provides several features that are designed to aid the learning process:

- **Chapter outlines** at the beginning of each chapter inform the students of what they should know about entrepreneurship when they complete the reading.
- **Chapter objectives** are a blueprint of concepts the student should understand upon completion of the chapter.
- **Theory-based text** enables the student to analyze, evaluate, and predict the prospects for various business concepts and plans, and make recommendations that increase the venture's chances.
- **Practical applications and guidelines** are offered in all the chapters to show the student how to deal with the real world of entrepreneurs, markets, and competitors.
- **Street Story** is the name of our boxed series of minicases. Each chapter contains these real-life examples drawn from the pages of the business press. Each Street Story illustrates the application of good theory to everyday new venture creation.
- **Tables and figures** throughout the book help illustrate difficult points and summarize the material for the student.
- **Extensive references** at the end of each chapter provide documentation for all of the arguments offered and enable the student to follow up with additional reading.
- **End-of-chapter case and questions** provide the basis for stimulating discussion. Adapted from real situations described in the business press, these short cases are provocative illustrations of what can go right and what can go wrong in the process of new venture creation.
- **Key terms** are listed at the end of each chapter so that the student can be familiar with the language used in the field of entrepreneurship.

- **Chapter discussion questions** can provide the basis of classroom debate and be used for written assignments.
- **Chapter exercises** are designed for two purposes. The first is to aid the student in the development of his or her own business plan. The exercises guide the students to complete the portion of their plan covered in the chapter. Chapter exercises can also be used to complement the classroom experience by having the student go out into the business community to observe entrepreneurship first hand.
- **End-of-text cases** provide an in-depth learning exercise for the student. I have prepared 10 cases for analysis. The cases deal with the problems and opportunities of new venture creation, of securing resources, of building reputations, and of operating in a competitive market. The instructor's manual offers a comprehensive teaching note for each case.
- **Name and subject indexes** at the end of the book aid in finding topics and key people and companies.
- **State-of-the-art design** makes the book more readable and enhances learning.

ACKNOWLEDGMENTS

First I wish to thank my new publishers, Libby Rubenstein and Stephen Ferrara of Marsh Publications. Their support and encouragement has been very much appreciated. They are consummate professionals and best of all, have become my friends.

I have been fortunate to work for a very understanding dean, Dan Smith, and a number of department chairs: Patricia McDougall, James Wimbush, and Idalene Kesner, who have supported my efforts. I would also like to acknowledge the fine professors who teach in the entrepreneurship program at Indiana University: Jeff Covin, Joe Denekamp, Don Kuratko, and Dean Shepard.

The most important thank you goes to my wife and partner Mimi. She contributed a great deal to the book and helped with the organizing, writing, editing, and proofreading. She had great enthusiasm for the project and that kept me going.

Finally, I would like to thank my students and the many reviewers and adoptors of this edition and the past editions. I offer a special thank-you to the following reviewers of this edition, whose incisive comments about the manuscript were invaluable to me as I revised the book:

- Eugene F. Fregetto, University of Illinois at Chicago
- Lindle Hatton, California State University at Sacramento
- Patrick Kreiser, Ohio State University
- Richard Arend, University of Nevada at Las Vegas
- Frederick Crane, Northeastern University

I have tried to incorporate all of your many helpful suggestions and comments. All errors of commission and omission are my own alone.

Marc Dollinger
Indiana University
March 2007

ENTREPRENEURSHIP

Strategies and Resources

CHAPTER 1 A Framework for Entrepreneurship

"Twenty years ago students who dared to say they wanted to start their own companies would be sent for counseling. Today entrepreneurship is the fastest-growing course of study on campuses nationwide."
—Jerome Katz, professor of management, St. Louis University

OUTLINE

LEARNING OBJECTIVES

After reading this chapter, you will understand

- how entrepreneurship may affect *your future*, whether you're an employee, a venture creator, or a consumer.
- how to define *entrepreneurship*.
- that entrepreneurship is a *worldwide phenomenon*.
- how the concept of a *new entrepreneur* has emerged.
- that entrepreneurship is a *multidimensional concept*.
- the *paradoxes* of entrepreneurship.

Entrepreneurship with a Purpose

She was well on her way to the top of the corporate game—a senior vice president for a high-tech firm with a successful 14-year career including stints at 3Com (formerly U.S. Robotics) and IBM.

But Cheryl Mayberry McKissack wasn't happy; in fact, she was stressed out. McKissack realized that what she really wanted was a job in Chicago with flexible hours that would also give her an opportunity to work with other African-American women. "It was clear to me that it would be difficult, if not impossible, to craft the perfect job, unless I did it myself," McKissack says. "I really wanted to use my technological expertise, but in a different way than I had before. And I wanted it to have a community element that I hadn't had the opportunity to pursue."

McKissack came up with not one, but two interrelated entrepreneurial solutions. Both of them take their names from *nia*, the Swahili word for "purpose." In 2000, McKissack founded Nia Enterprises, a market research and services firm that uses Web-based tools to provide online consumer research, delivering insights into the buying habits and consumer preferences of the U.S. ethnic group with the largest buying power: African-American women and their families. The firm's corporate clients include General Motors, Sears, Disney, American Airlines, Revlon, and State Farm Insurance.

That same year McKissack and Bonita K. Coleman, an automotive marketing and brand executive, also created an online community for African-American women with a Web site called NiaOnline™. They structured the site to become the premier Internet destination for African-American women by offering articles on women's health, careers, fashion, relationships, travel, and entertainment topics, with a special focus for their target audience. In addition, the site featured columns with

"empowering advice" from other African-American women. The site claims to reach an online community of more than 100,000 black household members.

More important, NiaOnline is the vehicle for much of Nia Enterprises' market data collection. Web site users can "opt-in" to sample and evaluate products provided by manufacturers. They can voice their opinions through simple quick-response surveys. Or they can register for the Consumer Advisory Panel, where they agree to take surveys or participate in online focus groups, and are then rewarded with points that can be redeemed for merchandise, such as photo albums or briefcases.

McKissack, who received an MBA from Northwestern's J. L. Kellogg School of Management, got some help for starting her ventures from Springboard Enterprises, a national not-for-profit that educates, showcases, and supports women entrepreneurs trying to start high-growth potential enterprises. One of Springboard's most effective programs has been their Women's Venture Capital Forum, which gives fledgling women entrepreneurs access to sources of equity funding while providing an environment where they can refine their business strategy. McKissack was one of the 25 women selected for the first Springboard Forum in January 2000 at the Kellogg School. Since that time more than 350 women entrepreneurs have presented at more than 15 additional forums across the country, where they have raised over $3 billion for their ventures.

While McKissack notes that minorities are "frequently left out of the networks that provide the best advancement opportunities," she has obviously bridged the gap in her own career. Her marketing firm and Web site have helped her to reach her personal goal while she achieves her purpose of helping other African-American women. In addition to starting these businesses, McKissack has co-written three "Nia guide" books on careers, balance, and health, and serves on several corporate boards. She also shares what she has learned with aspiring entrepreneurs by teaching at the Kellogg School of Business at Northwestern University in Chicago.

SOURCE: Adapted in part from Louise Witt. "What's the Right Time to Become an Entrepreneur?" *Fortune Small Business*,, 2005. Retrieved from the Web February 1, 2005. http://www.fortune.com. Also, Cheryl Mayberry McKissack, "Practice: Funding and Hiring for Women and Minorities: The Challenges of Access and Inclusion," *Kellogg World Alumni* magazine, Winter 2004. Retrieved from the Web May 8, 2006. http://www.kellogg.northwestern.edu.

ENTREPRENEURSHIP AND THE FUTURE

I N the new millennium, the ideas, talents, skills, and knowledge that promote entrepreneurship are evident in people all around the globe, but especially in today's generation. This new direction is a change from previous times when the forces for economic growth tended to favor more established businesspersons from the corporate world. But the face of the world economy has shifted, and young people today are well suited for entrepreneurial activity. For instance:

- The aspiring entrepreneurs of today are technologically precocious. They are comfortable with new technologies and are not fearful of change and the radical shifts that new technology can bring. Younger people are at home with computers and all sorts of consumer electronics. Over 80 percent of homes with children have computers and access to the Internet. A Carnegie Mellon study found that children and young adults are the authority on computer technology in the home.[1] Adults take a back seat to the kids. Even beyond their technical competency, young people are immersed in technology and have internalized its power.
- "It's a great time to be an entrepreneur," especially an Internet one. Compared to ten to fifteen years ago, hardware is 100 times cheaper, infrastructure software is free, there is easy access to global labor markets, and SEM (search engine marketing) has changed distribution and selling tactics.[2]
- This generation is passionate, inquisitive, and challenging. They welcome change and embrace the idea of progress. They have seen the improvement of information technology, new medical and biotech processes and products, and radical changes in the way people communicate and work. They believe that continued improvement and even revolutionary change await them in the future.
- They think differently. As *Fast Company* puts it, "Forget the experience curve. The most powerful force in business today is the inexperience curve. Young companies, born on the right side of the digital divide, are running circles around their older, richer, and slower rivals. If one wants his or her company to think outside the box, why not learn by working with people who don't know there is a box?"[3] For example, Youtube.com began business without "knowing" it was a business. The founders created a Web site for videos, which developed into a business. Recently, the founders sold their interests for well over $1 billion.
- They are independent. More and more people starting out in professional business careers consider themselves free agents. They have portable skills and will take them

wherever they can do the most good or make the most money. These workers are international free agents and show little loyalty to companies that continue to make strategic mistakes or fall behind the market.

How Does the New Entrepreneurship Add Up?

The sum of these trends is more entrepreneurship and business start-ups for younger people. Many new ventures will be technology based. The traditional career path may become a rarity.[4]

Today's younger people are more entrepreneurial than those of any previous generation. More and more people are striking out on their own. According to the Opinion Research Council, 54 percent of 18- to 24-year-olds are highly interested in starting a business, compared with 36 percent of 35- to 64-year-olds.[5] A US News survey found that "entrepreneur" was the preferred career of Generation X.[6] A Newsweek poll asked "millenials" (people who have come of age within a few years of the millennium) to name their hero, and more than half named Bill Gates, the founder of Microsoft.[7]

In fact, most teenagers entering college know more about business than their parents ever did. Many more teenagers work today than their parents did at their age. According to the Bureau of Labor Statistics, more than half the teens in the United States have jobs and over 90 percent have summer jobs.[8] Many high school students belong to investment clubs and Junior Achievement and help raise money for charities through a variety of businesslike activities. Ever buy a Girl Scout cookie? Harvard University recently struck down a long-standing ban on operating businesses out of dorm rooms because they feared losing student entrepreneurs to Stanford or Columbia. *Vanity Fair* magazine has coined a new word—"enfantrepreneurs."[9]

Today's students and their peers (entrepreneurs or enfantrepreneurs) will take us into the future. It is only a matter of time before their entrepreneurial activity brings the innovations that will shape the new millennium. The spirit of entrepreneurship—the notion of human progress, development, achievement, and change—motivates and energizes people.

Innovations in the way we work and play, travel and eat, start our families, and raise our children all create opportunities for entrepreneurs to build businesses and organizations that will exploit new technology and trends. We can also say that entrepreneurship is a self-perpetuating phenomenon: If a society has it, more is likely to come. For example, Hong Kong is often cited as an example of a very entrepreneurial place. Even after the handover of Hong Kong to the mainland Chinese in 1997, it has remained entrepreneurial. However, most of western and central Europe has not been entrepreneurial throughout history and many years of government programs designed to correct this have not proved effective. In the United States, we have vast and growing entrepreneurial resources, as demonstrated by the tremendous increase in supply and demand for entrepreneurship classes and programs on campus.

An estimated 2,000 two- and four-year colleges now have entrepreneurship courses or programs. Universities and business schools have discovered that the entrepreneurship program has enormous potential for raising the school's profile and visibility, promoting economic activity and job creation, serving highly motivated students (who may be wealthy alumni one day), and engaging already rich and successful alumni.

Look at Mark Cuban, for example. He is the billionaire owner of the Dallas Mavericks basketball team and co-owns HDNet (high definition TV). He took his first entrepreneurship class at Indiana University's Kelley School of Business and says it was one of the best classes he ever took. "It really motivated me. There is much more to starting a business than just understanding finance, accounting and marketing. Teaching kids what has worked with startup companies and learning about experiences that others have had could really make a difference. I know it did for me."[10]

Michael Guerrieri would agree. He is a recent graduate of the University of Chicago Graduate School of Business. Guerrieri went back to school to change careers. He credits his MBA experience with giving him the confidence to start his own business, the quantitative skills needed for advanced analysis, and the network of people who gave him advice. He has two ventures in progress: a private label health food snack line, and a medical services business that will automate refilling prescriptions. "It is one thing to dream and another to execute it," he says.[11]

Of course, not every entrepreneur is made in the classroom. Some believe entrepreneurs are born with special personalities and characteristics that distinguish them from ordinary folks. Many feel that entrepreneurship cannot be taught at all, or that successful entrepreneurship is a function of luck or congenital "smarts." "I don't think in a million years you can teach it in the classroom," said Paul Fleming, founder of P. F. Chang's China Bistro.[12] But the fact is that students who take entrepreneurship classes have more successful business start-ups than those who don't. They also make fewer business mistakes and earn higher annual incomes. Moreover, the business and social networks that schools create and sustain to put students and entrepreneur-alumni together help the nascent entrepreneurs make connections. And school is a safe place to learn: Missteps in a classroom setting can cause a little embarrassment and affect one's grade, but they will not likely result in years of hard work, money, and loss of personal reputation.[13]

A former best-selling book, *Workplace 2000*, argued that entrepreneurship not only affects our lives through innovation but also represents the working future for many of us.[14] As large corporations continue to lay off middle managers to realize their goals of flatter, more responsive organizations, these middle managers must "go"—and the place they will go is into business for themselves. What will they do? They will fill the niches and markets of servicing their former employers—providing consulting, aftermarket service, and other support functions. These former middle managers will operate small entrepreneurial firms that provide high quality and value to their customers in a way that working inside the bureaucracy of a large corporation makes impossible.

There are other entrepreneurial alternatives as well. In a business environment where large corporations try to stay flat, lean, and responsive, a burst of growth is occurring in "micro-business" firms—firms with four or fewer employees. Some of these will be started by former middle managers and executives who have been let go. Some are started by current managers trying to beat the clock to the next wave of layoffs. Many are created by people who have never and will never work for *Fortune* 1000 companies. In addition to micro businesses, there are more corporate-backed ventures: spin-offs, joint ventures, intrapreneurial (corporate-based new ventures) units, and partnering arrangements. Although these types of ventures originate in larger organizations, they are being formed now specifically to stay small and entrepreneurial, to avoid bureaucracy, and to maintain their innovative edge.

Older people are also participating in a great wave of entrepreneurship. These people are the "silver entrepreneurs." Many corporate middle managers have left the ranks of the white collared to join the self-employed (voluntarily and through redundancy). Some are previously retired. A recent *Business Week Online* special report called "Second Acts" described the action. Tom Washburn was a researcher for a financial services company. After a year of study, he opened his own ice cream shop, which he named Moxley's after the family dog. Today he has three Baltimore locations and an award-winning ice cream brand. "My dream came true," he says. Amy Hilliard left a 20-year career as a marketing executive focused on consumer brands. She took a big risk as a single mother of two (she also has a Harvard MBA) to invest $300,000 in a cake-baking business. (Have a look at her business at http://www.comfortcake.com.) Hilliard concludes, "I didn't realize how hard it would be. Food is a very complex business. But it is gratifying to create something from scratch. It is never boring. Every day is something new, and I'm using all of my cylinders at once."[15]

Not all older entrepreneurs are constrained by technology and to entering the food and beverage industry. Many have discovered eBay, and they dig long and deep for treasure to be sold online. Selling on eBay helps these silver entrepreneurs earn extra cash and clean out their closets too. Marcia Cooper and Harvey Levine started an eBay selling business as 60-somethings. It was a low entry barrier situation because all they needed was a computer and an Internet connection. They went through the eBay training program and decided to specialize in event tickets. Then they expanded to sell just about anything, indiscriminately. Now they focus on quality items that yield a minimum of $100 in commissions.[16]

We really do not need to be a futurist, however, to see that entrepreneurship plays a large and increasing role in the future of our nation's and our individual working lives. The nature of organizations, work, and employment has changed, and individuals who recognize these changes and prepare for them will be best able to succeed in the new environment. Therefore, most people will encounter entrepreneurship through the marketplace, in new products, services, or technologies, or through their own employment. The better they understand the marketplace, the better they will be able to survive and thrive in the new entrepreneurial environment. Entrepreneurship is and will remain a normal, regularly occurring opportunity in everyone's professional career.

Before beginning our journey through the entrepreneurial adventure, let's listen closely to someone who has already been through the process—more than once. Steve Jobs gave a commencement address to Stanford University's graduates in the spring of 2005, and Street Story 1.1 summarizes his words and thoughts.

WHAT IS ENTREPRENEURSHIP?

There have been almost as many definitions of entrepreneurship as there have been writers on the subject. Translated from the French, entrepreneur literally means "one who undertakes." An entrepreneur is a doer. But what does this mean with respect to the businessperson? Some suggest that trying to define entrepreneurship may be fruitless because the term is too vague and imprecise to be useful.[17] Table 1.1 provides a short selection of definitions that have been offered.

STREET STORY 1.1

Lessons for the Hungry and Foolish

Steve Jobs, CEO of Apple Computer and Pixar Animation Studios, began his commencement address at Stanford University by admitting he was a college dropout.

Jobs not only confessed that he dropped out of Reed College after just six months, but added that he doesn't regret it. In fact, when he looks back on his diverse but connected experiences (which explain how he got where he is now), Jobs sees leaving school as "one of the best decisions" he ever made. Doing so enabled him to stop spending his adoptive parents' carefully saved money on education at a time when he had no idea how he might use that education, and allowed him to informally sit in on courses that interested him instead of enrolling in required courses that bored him.

One of the courses that interested Jobs was calligraphy. Learning how to create beautiful letters didn't seem like a very practical skill at the time, but ten years later, when he was developing the first Macintosh computer, Jobs drew on that calligraphy experience to incorporate multiple typefaces and proportionally spaced fonts as two of the Mac's most distinctive features. His competitor, Microsoft, was then quick to add those elements to its Windows operating system.

As Jobs reflected in his Stanford speech, "If I had never dropped out, I would have never dropped in on this calligraphy class, and personal computers might not have the wonderful typography that they do." The life lesson he extracts from this experience is that individuals must be willing to trust their gut instincts when they make choices, and believe that those choices (or "dots") will somehow connect to their future.

A second experience that Jobs shared with Stanford grads that day was that after building Apple into a $2 billion enterprise in just ten years, he was fired by the company's board of directors. While he was understandably dev-astated at the time, Jobs now calls this "the best thing that could ever have happened to me" because it "freed me to enter one of the most creative periods of my life." Within five years Jobs started both the NeXT company and Pixar Animation Studios. Apple purchased NeXT, and Jobs returned to the company that had fired him. He now oversees what he calls Apple's current renaissance, based on the NeXT technology.

Jobs calls this a "love and loss" life lesson; he continued to do the things he loved after he lost his job, and that passion enabled him to reach a new pinnacle in his career. Jobs' advice to grads is also appropriate for aspiring entrepreneurs. He said that "work is going to fill a large part of your life, and the only way to be truly satisfied is to do what you believe is great work. And the only way to do great work is to love what you do. If you haven't found it yet, keep looking. Don't settle."

The third life lesson Jobs spoke about that day is what he calls a death lesson. In 2004 he was diagnosed with pancreatic cancer, and told he had three to six months to live. Then the doctors discovered that his tumor was actually a rare form of the disease that is curable by surgery. Now that he is cancer free, Jobs wants everyone to "have the courage to follow your heart and intuition. Our time on earth," he reminds us, "is limited."

In his closing remarks, Jobs reminisced about *The Whole Earth Catalog,* a publication from the 1960s and 1970s, which he described as a kind of "Google in paperback." The catalog's farewell advice, printed on the back cover of the final issue, was "Stay Hungry. Stay Foolish." Jobs says this is something he has always wished for himself, and something he would wish for new college graduates.

It's a good motto for entrepreneurs, too.

SOURCE: Jobs' commencement address was reprinted in *Fortune,* September 5, 2005: 31–32.

TABLE 1.1   Definitions of Entrepreneurship

Source	Definition
Knight (1921)	Profits from bearing uncertainty and risk
Schumpeter (1934)	Carrying out of new combinations of firm organization—new products, new services, new sources of raw material, new methods of production, new markets, new forms of organization
Hoselitz (1952)	Uncertainty bearing...coordination of productive resources... introduction of innovations and the provision of capital
Cole (1959)	Purposeful activity to initiate and develop a profit-oriented business
McClelland (1961)	Moderate risk taking
Casson (1982)	Decisions and judgments about the coordination of scarce resources
Gartner (1985)	Creation of new organizations
Stevenson, Roberts, & Grousbeck (1989); Barringer & Ireland (2006)	The pursuit of opportunity without regard to resources currently controlled
Hart, Stevenson, & Dial (1995)	The pursuit of opportunity without regard to resources currently controlled, but constrained by the founders' previous choices and industry-related experience
Shane & Venkataraman (2000)	A field of business seeks to understand how opportunities create something new...
Kuratko & Hodgetts (2004)	A dynamic process of vision, change and creation...
Allen (2006)	A mindset or way of thinking that is opportunity focused, innovative and growth-oriented. Can be found in large corporations and socially responsible not-for-profits...

SOURCE : F. Knight, *Risk, Uncertainty and Profit* (Boston: Houghton Mifflin, 1921); J. Schumpeter, *The Theory of Economic Development* (Cambridge, MA: Harvard University Press, 1934); B. Hoselitz, "Entrepreneurship and Economic Growth." *American Journal of Economic Sociology,* 1952; A. Cole, *Business Enterprise in Its Social Setting* (Cambridge, MA: Harvard University, 1959); D. McClelland, *The Achieving Society* (New York: John Wiley, 1961); M. Casson, *The Entrepreneur* (Totowa, NJ: Barnes and Noble, 1982); W. Gartner. "A Conceptual Framework for Describing the Phenomenon of New Venture Creation," *Academy of Management Review* 10, 1985:696–706; H. Stevenson, M. Roberts, and H. Grousbeck, *New Business Venture and the Entrepreneur* (Homewood, IL: Irwin, 1989); M. Hart, H. Stevenson, and J. Dial, "Entrepreneurship: A Definition Revisited," Babson Frontiers of Entrepreneurship Research, 1995; S. Shane and S. Venkataraman, "The Promise of Entrepreneurship as a Field of Research," *Academy of Management* Review 25, 2000:217-226; D Kuratko,and R. Hodgetts, *Entrepreneurship,* 6th ed. (Mason, Ohio: Thompson-Southwestern, 2004); B. Barringer and D. Ireland, *Entrepreneurship* (NJ: Prentice-Hall, 2006) and K. Allen, *Launching New Ventures* (Boston: Houghton Mifflin, 2006).

Within these definitions, we might find the following common elements and characteristics:

- Creativity and innovation
- Resource identification, acquisition, and marshaling
- Economic organization
- Opportunity for gain (or increase) under risk and uncertainty

Entrepreneurship, then, is the control and deployment of resources to create an innovative economic organization (or network of organizations) for the purpose of gain or growth under conditions of risk and uncertainty.[18] What are the implications of this definition?

Creation and Innovation

The term **creation** implies a founding and an origin. Therefore, technically speaking, the purchase of an existing firm or its transfer to new owners does not represent entrepreneurship. As one group of authors point out, if founding was the only criterion for entrepreneurship, then neither Tom Watson of IBM nor Ray Kroc of McDonald's would qualify.

It is rare for an organization to change ownership without a change in its management and resource configuration; however, the degree of change and innovation determines whether entrepreneurship is present. To see how large a change is needed, we can rely on Schumpeter's categories of "new combinations."[19] Is:

- A new product or service offered?
- A new method or technology employed?
- A new market targeted and opened?
- A new source of supply of raw materials and resources used?
- A new form of industrial organization created? (This is, perhaps, the rarest of all innovations.)

Now we can see how Watson and Kroc can reapply for membership in the entrepreneur's club.

Control and Deployment of Resources

The foundation for this book is the resource-based theory (or view) of sustained competitive advantage.[20] This theoretical framework originally derives from the viewpoint of a large corporation.[21] The resource-based theory is the most appropriate to understand new venture creation because it best describes how entrepreneurs themselves build their businesses from the resources and capabilities they currently possess or can realistically acquire. Successful entrepreneurship is not simply an analytical exercise. Industry and competitor analysis—the application of the theory of industrial organization economics—alone is insufficient. The resource-based theory argues that the choice of which industry to enter and what business in which to be is not enough to ensure success. The theory says that the nature and quality of the resources, capabilities, and strategies the entrepreneur possesses and can acquire can lead to long-term success. In fact, one can argue that choosing the resources for a firm, configuring these resources into a consistent strategy, and deploying the resources (implementation) are the quintessential entrepreneurial acts.[22]

Economic Organization

The term **economic organization** means an organization whose purpose is to allocate scarce resources. An economic organization can be a firm, a business unit within a firm, a network of independent organizations, a social network, or a not-for-profit organization (NPO).[23] Though it may seem paradoxical, even governments can create entrepreneurial organizations under the right conditions.

The business organization can, of course, pursue gain and growth as its motivations. In fact, some firms use both profit and size as their main objectives.[24] Other businesses do not seek growth, which distinguishes entrepreneurial firms from small businesses.[25] Do NPOs seek gain and growth? You bet they do. Although NPOs may be prohibited by law from making profits for stockholders, they are allowed to accumulate surpluses in their accounts. NPOs certainly seek growth: More members, more services performed, more clients served—the list may be endless. Our collective agreement that all of these organizations can be examples of entrepreneurship illustrates the ubiquitous nature of entrepreneurship and contributes to its vague and imprecise definitions.

A relatively new phenomenon in entrepreneurship is the creation of the **virtual organization.** A virtual organization is a network of independent organizations fulfilling core functions "as if" they were operating within the framework of a single company. For example, let us say that we are starting a company to manufacture and distribute canoes. But our primary expertise is in designing the boats—like Walden Kayaks. We could raise the money and recruit the top managers to do everything in-house. Or we could contract with a manufacturer, a distributor, a marketing organization (for promotion), an accounting firm, and a legal firm. None of these other organizations is within our absolute control, yet each will perform "as if" it were because of its contracts and incentives. This is a virtual organization. The advantages are that everyone does what they are best at. The disadvantages are that there are extra communication and control costs, and each organization carries its own overhead.[26]

Risk and Uncertainty

Entrepreneurship exists under conditions of risk and uncertainty. The two terms are not the same. **Risk** refers to the variability of outcomes (or returns); if there is no risk, the returns are certain. A firm operating in a risk-free environment would continue to expand forever, because a negative outcome could not occur. Therefore, risk is a limit to ever-expanding entrepreneurship.[27] Risk can also be measured quantitatively by using statistics that measure dispersion, like the variance and the standard deviation.

Uncertainty refers to the confidence entrepreneurs have in their estimates of how the world works—their understanding of the causes and effects in the environment. If there is no uncertainty, the environment and future can be perfectly known. If the future can be known, then everyone can know it (at least for a price), and it will not be a source of lasting profit for anyone. Uncertainty is what makes markets and poker games. Who would continue to place bets on a hand if all the cards were face up?

There are three types of uncertainty.

1. State uncertainty is the lack of knowledge about current conditions. The world is a big place and no one can know all the information of all the elements in it. There is uncertainty about which technologies will prevail. Demand for a new product is highly uncertain. Sometimes there are simply no data. For example, in China there is currently a lack of statistical information about employment, income, growth rates, entrepreneurial start-ups, and productivity gains. No one has this data. It has never been collected and even if it existed, it would likely be a government secret.

2. Effect uncertainty is the lack of knowledge of cause and effect. Even if we can somehow identify and know all the elements in a complex situation, we frequently will not understand the cause and effect relationships. Which comes first, the chicken or the

egg? Is a business successful because it has targeted psychologically satisfied customers, or are the customers satisfied because the business is successful? In a laboratory situation, we can do experiments to determine causality, but in the messy real world these experiments are impossible. We often just substitute correlation for causality—but this is a logical error.

3. Response uncertainty is not knowing what the response will be to some action. Related to effect uncertainty, here we have uncertainty about what kind of responses our actions will provoke. In some business cases, expanding the product line will cause competitors to expand theirs as well. In other cases, the competitors might simply ignore the expansion. They may think that the core business is suffering and that any new offerings are a desperate attempt to save the business. With response uncertainty present, it is hard to predict competitor and customer reaction. Similarly, we are frequently uncertain how regulators will view a firm. Will its products pass regulatory scrutiny, will licenses be forthcoming, and will legal challenges be met?

These uncertainties are barriers to entrepreneurship for some people, because they greatly increase anxiety about the future. But entrepreneurs bear this uncertainty. They can manage it as well as the concurrent risks.[28]

Entrepreneurs definitely take risks, which means that they engage in activity that leads to very variable outcomes. For example, a study of Canadian inventor-entrepreneurs showed that of 1,091 inventions, only 75 reached the market. Six of these earned returns above 1400 percent while 45 others lost money. (All of the non-commercial inventions lost money for the inventors as well.) William Baumol, famed economist of both Princeton and New York Universities, believes that people who take risks like this must have a "touch of madness." Baumol has spent decades trying to integrate the entrepreneur into a theory of rational economics, but madness and rationality are incompatible so far.[29] Entrepreneurship is "economics with imagination."[30]

WHERE IS ENTREPRENEURSHIP?

Two conditions must exist for entrepreneurship to flourish. First, there must be freedom—freedom to establish an economic venture, and freedom to be creative and innovative with that enterprise. Second, there must be prosperity—favorable economic conditions that give an entrepreneurial organization the opportunity to gain and grow.

Economic Growth and Freedom

Entrepreneurship is a global phenomenon. Therefore, it is vital that the prospective entrepreneur understand the relationship between the country in which the business will be located and the climate for business success. The Heritage Foundation and *The Wall Street Journal* publish an annual "Index of Economic Freedom." The index examines the trade policies, taxation levels, government intervention and regulation, monetary policies, and six other categories of over 150 countries. Data from all the years that these rankings have been made are available online at http://www.heritage.org/research/features/index/. The 2007 rankings show that once again Hong Kong is number one despite the 1997 return of Hong Kong to the People's Republic of China under the "one country–two systems" formula. Other countries in the top of the rankings of "free" economies are (in order): Singapore, Australia, United States, New Zealand, United Kingdom, Ireland, Luxembourg, Switzerland, and Canada. The seven countries with the lowest rankings and categorized as "repressed" were: North Korea, Cuba, Libya, Burma and Turkmenistan.

Data collected by the index support several conclusions that are important for entrepreneurs and the study of entrepreneurship. First, the study indicates the strong correlation between a high level of economic and political freedom and a high standard of living. Second, a comparison of data over several years indicates that as wealthy countries become richer, they often impose fiscal restrictions that reduce economic freedom, such as higher taxation and social welfare programs. This is why the relatively well-off countries in Scandinavia and Western Europe are mostly missing from the top 10 list. The poorest countries are poor because of the lack of economic freedom, not because of a lack of aid from richer countries or a lack of natural resources.[31] Some of these poor countries are now the targets of social entrepreneurs who are trying to jumpstart economic growth from the perspective of feeding the poor or treating and preventing AIDS.

Two examples from formerly communist economies illustrate how important economic freedom can be to entrepreneurship. After years of exile in France, Anoa Dussol-Perran returned to her native Vietnam to open a passenger-helicopter service in Hanoi. To avoid a possible three-year wait for government approval, Ms. Dussol-Perran attempted to smuggle her first helicopter into Vietnam without filing the proper paperwork. The helicopter was discovered and impounded by the Vietnamese government. It was released to Ms. Dussol-Perran only after a long wait, followed by a grueling six-hour interview. When the time came to add a second helicopter to her service, Ms. Dussol-Perran elected to fly the new equipment from Paris to Hanoi herself rather than risk importing another machine.[32]

In contrast, Jake Weinstock and his two partners have enjoyed relatively smooth sailing as they set up Gold's Gym franchise in Moscow. Although Russia (#122) is still ranked as mostly unfree in the Index of Economic Freedom, it did place 20 slots above Vietnam (#142) in the 2006 survey. Weinstock was able to avoid customs problems with his imported equipment—reportedly the toughest hurdle for new businesses in Russia—by letting his Russian partner, a former athlete and sporting goods trader, handle those negotiations. He was also able to avoid the organized crime threats that plague other foreign businesses. "We built up many relationships and alliances, which meant we were less susceptible to shakedowns," explains Weinstock. "We made sure important people were interested in our success."[33]

Yet even in the "free" United States, entrepreneurs can run into problems concerning their economic freedom. . Consider the case of Andrew Beebee. Beebee is an Internet entrepreneur who started his dot.com in the largely Hispanic Mission district of San Francisco. He signed a five-year lease for five floors of a nine-story building when his business began to skyrocket. When Beebee moved in, his landlord told many of the other tenants that they would not have their leases renewed due to asbestos removal and because the building was going high-tech. These tenants, however, had their freedoms too. Over the next several months they conducted sit-ins, acts of civil disobedience, and picketing to protest what they saw as the gentrification of the area. Mr. Beebee was stymied and his company hemmed in by political activity and zoning ordinances. "Aqui estamos, y no vamos" ("Here we are, and we are not going") chanted the demonstrators.[34]

Another indicator of "where" entrepreneurship flourishes is found in the ease of starting a business. The World Bank has a global index for this indicator. Table 1.2 presents a top-10 list of best countries in which to start a business. Note there are other business indicators on the list as well.

WHO IS THE NEW ENTREPRENEUR?

Ask any group of businesspeople today if they consider themselves entrepreneurs. According to Bill Sahlman, professor and senior associate dean at the Harvard Business School, "most of them will raise their hands. That doesn't mean that they are entrepreneurial, but they would certainly not like you to think they aren't."[35] If entrepreneurship is one of the hot labels today, it is because the concept of being an entrepreneur has changed.[36] Fifteen years ago, an entrepreneur might have been described as a business version of a John Wayne cowboy (tough, gutsy, and male), who steered his business through the rodeo of commerce without the help of training or education and without the assistance of bankers or other experts. Entrepreneurs were once seen as small business founders with a strong independent streak and perhaps a flair for the dramatic. Entrepreneurs were thus born, not made.

Things are different now (see Table 1.3). A class of *professional entrepreneurs* is emerging today who rely more on their brains than their guts—and who have been trained to use both methods and technology to analyze the business environment. Some of the firms created have been named **gazelles**.[37] A gazelle is a fast-growing, innovative company that creates buzz and jobs. Gazelles are distributed in all industries and environments. It is estimated that of the more than 18 million small businesses in the United States, there are only about 340,000 gazelles. They even have their own Web site: http://gazellesInc.com.[38]

A look at Table 1.3 reveals some significant trends. First, there is increased emphasis on leadership. Leadership is a complex phenomenon and although most of us have some capacity for it, the pundits agree that outstanding leadership is always in short supply. The entrepreneur has to lead his or her organization and its people. He or she needs to be a motivator and a model for behavior. He or she must be out in front inspiring people to follow.

A second trend is better management. The days of building a better mousetrap and leaving it at that are gone. The entrepreneur must be a manager—planning, monitoring the business's achievements, controlling the flow of work and information through the organization, and staffing the venture with other leaders and competent managers.

According to Bill Wetzel, professor emeritus at the University of New Hampshire, the difference is like night and day. Wetzel says that the old-style entrepreneur or business founder was thought primarily to be concerned with earning a living, while today's

TABLE 1.2 **World Bank Economic Rankings**

Economy	Ease of Doing Business	Starting a Business	Dealing with Licenses	Employing Workers	Registering Property
Singapore	1	11	8	3	12
New Zealand	2	3	18	10	1
United States	3	3	22	1	10
Canada	4	1	32	13	22
Hong Kong, China	5	5	64	16	60
United Kingdom	6	9	46	17	19
Denmark	7	14	6	15	36
Australia	8	2	29	9	27
Norway	9	21	14	109	6
Ireland	10	6	20	83	80
Japan	11	18	2	36	39
Iceland	12	16	30	42	8
Sweden	13	20	17	94	7
Finland	14	18	35	111	15
Switzerland	15	27	38	24	11
Lithuania	16	48	23	119	3
Estonia	17	51	13	151	23
Thailand	18	28	3	46	18
Puerto Rico	19	8	91	33	46
Belgium	20	37	48	23	158

SOURCE: Adapted from the World Bank, "Doing Business Economy Rankings," 2006. Retrieved from the Web May 1, 2006. http://www.doingbusiness.org/EconomyRankings/Default.aspx?direction=asc&sort=2

entrepreneur "has the intention of building a significant company that can create wealth for the entrepreneur and investors."[39]

Street Story 1.2 describes the start-up process for Jeremiah Hutchins. He has built a significant company by being prepared, doing some commonsense research, and using technology to his advantage.

The new entrepreneurs come from different backgrounds too. Many of them are corporate-track dropouts, pushed out by downsizing or lured out by the quest for status, big money, or control of their personal lives. Globalization has promoted an entrepreneurial spirit in both big and small companies, while information technology now enables many small start-ups to compete against big business.

Academia has also contributed to the creation of this new professional entrepreneur class. Harvard Business School, which once had three or four professors teaching courses about small business, now has 17 full-time faculty members in its entrepreneurial-studies program. Staffing at other colleges and universities reflects the same trend. The content of much finance, marketing, and other business courses has also been adjusted to reflect new venture concerns and development methods. The new entrepreneurs don't just do; they understand what they're doing.[40]

TABLE 1.3 Entrepreneurs

Then	Now
Small-business founder	True entrepreneur
Boss	Leader
Lone Ranger	Social and business networker
Secretive	Open
Self-reliant	Inquisitive
Seat of the pants	Business plan
Snap decisions	Consensus
Male ownership	Mixed ownership (In 1993, women owned one-third of all sole proprietorships, up from one-quarter in 1980.)
Idea	*Execution*
In 1982, 80% of the CEOs of the *Inc.* 500 companies believed their companies' success was based on novel, unique, or proprietary ideas.	1992, 80% of the CEOs of *Inc.* 500 companies said that the ideas for their companies were ordinary, and that they owed their success to better business models.
Knows the Trade	*Knows the Business*
Eastern, one of the first airlines in the United States, was founded by pilot Eddie Rickenbacker.	Federal Express, an overnight delivery service using airplanes, was developed from a business plan written by Fred Smith while he was studying for his MBA at Yale.
Automation	*Innovation*
Technology lets business automate the work people had always done	Technology lets people do things never done before.

SOURCE: Adapted from Tom Richman, "The Evolution of the Professional Entrepreneur," *Inc.'s* the State of Small Business Special Issue, 1997: 50–53.

DIMENSIONS OF ENTREPRENEURSHIP

New Venture Creation

This book is concerned with entrepreneurship as the formation of a new business enterprise—most often called simply **new venture creation**. It contains theory and research about, and descriptions of, practice and techniques of entrepreneurship. We take an economic and managerial approach to entrepreneurship and new venture creation, although at times we borrow important material from other disciplines. Much has been written about the phenomenon of entrepreneurship and new venture creation from the economic and managerial perspectives. There have been numerous descriptive studies and some valuable empirical research, but no textbook, including this one, can offer prospective entrepreneurs advice that will ensure their success. There is no "rule for riches" as we will see in the next chapter. Not enough is known about entrepreneurship (or business

STREET STORY 1.2

Peace of Mind Goes Digital

Jeremiah Hutchins says he had many ideas for new business ventures while driving his truck along the highways of California. None of his ideas, including one to digitize business cards on miniature CD-ROMs, ever got off the ground.

But a radio alert report about a missing child inspired Hutchins to make the entrepreneurial leap to actually starting a business. Hutchins, the father of two small girls, wondered whether his mini-CD idea might be used to store identification data for children.

Within 24 hours, Hutchins had networked with a local police investigator to get some feedback on his idea. The investigator liked his concept, and supplied Hutchins with a list of the kinds of information, such as a physical description, blood type, scars, and distinctive habits, that the police want to have when a missing-person report is filed. Hutchins also searched the Internet to see if anyone else offered a similar product, and decided he had discovered a niche with an unmet need.

Over the next ten days, Hutchins took a leadership role as he and his partner, a security guard at the trucking firm where Hutchins worked, did more groundwork. They created and registered a Web-site domain name (www.safekidscard.com), and then tested digital cameras, ink, CD burners, and other equipment in preparation for creating a prototype of a digital ID card.

The idea of parents collecting information about their children as a safety measure is certainly not unique to Jeremiah Hutchins. But the technology he used to collect and store that data into a compact database was innovative. When Hutchins showed local police how he could use a computer to collect child identification information and then store it in a convenient form, they were impressed. They invited him to set up a booth at a community safety fair the following week. Just three weeks after he first had this idea,

Hutchins and his partner had sold 150 ID cards and grossed $3,000.

Hutchins' primary product today is a do-it-yourself, Windows-compatible CD-ROM that holds three digital color photos and a digital thumbprint, along with personal, medical, and contact information. Slightly larger than a credit card, the mini CD can be carried in a parent's wallet, and can be easily shared with police or hospitals in the event of an emergency. Hutchins' Web site also markets ID cards for adults and pets, along with a variety of related products, including child ID bracelets, dental impression kits, shoe labels, personal safety books, and DVDs.

Hutchins has also been innovative in expanding his company. In 2002, he began selling franchises, and by 2005, he had 43 functioning franchises producing ID CDs on site at schools, day-care centers, and other locations. Several Web sites now recommend Safe Kids Card as a good example for people who want to launch low-cost, home-based businesses.

According to the company Web site, the franchisee fee is less than $20,000, including equipment. Safe Kids Card also sells economical distributorships to people who want to market the do-it-yourself ID kits in their area.

In 2006, Safe Kids Card began a partnership with the National Troopers Coalition in which a portion of the proceeds troopers receive from selling kits benefits state trooper programs. In the future, Hutchins also hopes to works with businesses that will offer customers a discount or gift certificate for the ID kits as a service or appreciation gift.

This entrepreneur has done a good job of using technology to benefit both himself and society.

SOURCE: Adapted in part from Gwendolyn Bounds, "You Have a Great Idea. Now What?" *The Wall Street Journal Online*, May 9, 2005. Retrieved from the Web May 2, 2006. http://www.online.wsj.com.

in general) for the field to be considered a "sure thing." In fact, any guidance obtained from a book is probably of little long-term value to a potential entrepreneur.[41] However, the insights a reader gains by comparing personal experience with the material in this book may be invaluable.

One thing we do know is that ventures that employ resources and capabilities that are valuable, rare, hard to copy, and have no good substitutes, in favorable industry conditions, provide sustainable competitive advantage.[42] Choosing the appropriate resources is ultimately a matter of entrepreneurial vision and intuition. The creative act underlying such vision is a subject that has so far not been a central focus of resource-based theory. This book extends the theory and views of entrepreneurship within the context of the resource-based theory of the firm.[43]

Opportunity Analysis

A second dimension of entrepreneurship focuses on **opportunity analysis**. *Opportunity* is the confluence of personal preparation, external circumstances, and sensitivity to change. Different people may have different opportunity analyses. Some may feel the time window of opportunity is open and that they are ready to begin the new venture creation process. Others may feel they are not yet personally well prepared or that the external circumstance is not yet right or has passed them by. People might well agree on both preparation and circumstances, but have different levels of sensitivity. Some people are first-movers and others are, more cautiously, later movers. Chapters 2, 3, and 4 are devoted to processes and models for venture opportunity analysis. Chapters 6, 7, 8, and 9 will emphasize lower-level opportunity analysis in marketing, finances, and organizations, respectively.

Where do entrepreneurial opportunities come from? How does one get business ideas? One approach to the answer is "change." Changes in the business environment offer opportunities for entrepreneurs. Existing firms have their resources, strategy, and organization structure geared for the past or current environment. When a change occurs, the new firm frequently has an easier time spotting it and configuring a set of resources and an organization to meet the new needs and the new realities than an existing organization. Change can occur from market disequilibrium, factors that enhance production possibilities, and the opportunities created from earlier acts of entrepreneurship. Entrepreneurship builds on itself and is a virtuous[44] cycle of economic activity.[45]

According to the late management guru, Peter Drucker (who firmly believed that entrepreneurship could be taught), there are seven sources of opportunity to look for in the environment.[46]

The Unexpected. When current businesses are surprised by an unanticipated event, they are often unable to adapt quickly enough to take advantage of that event. The event can be an unexpected success (good news) or an unexpected failure (bad news). For example, if war breaks out where it is unexpected, it changes the economics and demand structure of the warring parties and their populations. The war can provide opportunity if it is ethically pursued. Similarly, a breakthrough in a peace negotiation can also provide opportunity, because it can change the economies of the former combatants. For example, if the Israeli and Palestinian conflict can be resolved, the beachfront property in the Gaza strip (now a dormant resource) would become one of the premier vacation resorts in the world.

Sometimes the unexpected happens directly to the company; The shock can be fatal or it can be the source of new opportunities. For example, in August of 2000, the Walt Disney Company released a movie called "Coyote Ugly" about a wild and raucous bar in New York. The movie was not especially believable and the reviews were bad. It faded from mainstream consciousness, but then an unexpected event occurred: the movie became a cult hit. Sudddenly, the real Coyote Ugly bar received a great rush of interest and publicity. The owner, Lilliana Lovell, had a hit business on her hands. "What business ever anticipates getting $40 million in free national advertising? We decided to take advantage of it," she said. So she cleverly imitated all the details of the movie set and now has 13 bars and is a millionaire. "Most people have to build a business to get the brand and name recognition, she did it in reverse. There has never been a woman to build a [national] chain of bars, period," remarked Morris Reid, a branding specialist.[47]

The Incongruous. Incongruity is dissonance, something that "ought to be" but is not. Incongruity creates instability and opportunity. For example, it is incongruous for a growing industry with increasing sales not to be profitable, but such a scenario is possible and is taking place now on the Internet. Some key to the industry's economics has yet to be discovered. When reality and conventional wisdom collide, incongruity exists. Listen for "expert old-timers" who use the words *never* and *always* to explain how things should be. These unexamined assumptions may have once been right, but may now be wrong and therefore may provide opportunities for the responsive entrepreneur.

The Process Need. The process need has its source in technology's inability to provide the "big breakthrough." Technicians often need to work out a way to get from point A to point B using some process. Currently, researchers are making efforts in the areas of superconductivity, fusion, interconnectivity, and the search for a treatment and cure for AIDS. Thomas Edison and others knew that in order to start the electric energy industry, they needed to solve a process need—to develop a light bulb that worked. Process need opportunities are often addressed by program research projects, which are the systematic research and analysis efforts designed to solve a single problem, such as the effort against AIDS.

Industry and Market Structures. Changes in technology, innovation, and invention alter market and industry structures by altering costs, quality requirements, and volume capabilities. This alteration can potentially make existing firms obsolete if they are not attuned to it and are inflexible. Similarly, changes in social values and consumer tastes, as well as demographics, shift the economics of industries to a new equilibrium. The markets of firms that do not adapt to these changes are fair game for the entrepreneur.

Demographics. Demographic changes are changes in the society's population or subpopulations. They can be changes in the size, age, structure, employment status, education, or incomes of these groups. Such changes influence all industries and firms by changing the mix of products and services demanded, the volume of products and services, and the buying power of customers. Some of these changes are predictable, because people who will be older are already alive, and birth and death rates stay fairly stable over time. Other changes are not predictable and are caused by natural disasters, war, social change, and immigration. Population statistics are available for assessment of demographic changes, but opportunities can be found before the data are published if the entrepreneur observes what is happening in the street and being reported in the newspaper.

Changes in Perception. Is the glass half full or half empty? The two perceptions are logically equivalent but reflect significantly different attitudes and behaviors. People hold different perceptions of the same reality, and these differences affect the products and services they demand and the amounts they spend. Some groups feel powerful and rich; others, disenfranchised and poor. Some people think they are thin when they are not; others think they are too fat when they are not. The entrepreneur can sell power and status to the rich and powerful, and sell relief and comfort to the poor and oppressed. Whether people are rich or poor, if they perceive that they are middle class, they will demand education for their children, good housing for their families, and travel for their vacations.

New Knowledge. New knowledge is often seen as the "superstar" of entrepreneurial opportunity. However, it can be "temperamental, capricious, and hard to manage."[48] Having new knowledge is not enough: entrepreneurs must also find a way to make products from this knowledge and to protect the profits of those products from competition as the knowledge is spread to others. In addition, timing is critical. It frequently takes the convergence of many pieces of new knowledge to make a product. For example,

> A number of knowledge bases came together to make possible the computer. The earliest was the binary theorem, a mathematical theory going back to the 17th century that enables all numbers to be expressed by two numbers only: one and zero. It was applied to a calculating machine by Charles Babbage in the first half of the nineteenth century. In 1890, Hermann Hollerith invented the punch card, going back to the invention in the early 19th century by Frenchman J. M. Jacquard. The punch card makes it possible to convert numbers into "instructions." In 1906 an American, Lee de Forest, invented the audion tube, and with it created electronics. Then, between 1910 and 1913, Bertrand Russell and Alfred North Whitehead, in the *Principia Mathematica*, created symbolic logic, which enables us to express all logical concepts as numbers. Finally, during World War I, the concepts of programming and feedback were developed, primarily for the purposes of anti-aircraft gunnery. By 1918, in other words, all the knowledge needed to develop the computer was available. The first computer became operational in 1946. (P. Drucker, *Innovation and Entrepreneurship*. NY: Harper and Row, 1985)

Three additional dimensions or lenses are used to study entrepreneurship: individuals, environments, and organizations. These are required to flesh out the arguments and examples.[49] The interactions among individuals, environments, and organizations make each new venture unique and must be considered.

The Individual

The role that individuals play in entrepreneurship is undeniable. Each person's psychological, sociological, and demographic characteristics contribute to or detract from his or her abilities to be an entrepreneur. Personal experience, knowledge, education, and training are the accumulated human resources that the founder contributes to the enterprise. The personal integrity of the entrepreneur and the way the entrepreneur and the new venture are viewed by others are captured in the person's reputation. The risk profile of the entrepreneur determines the initial configuration of the venture—for example, financing, product offerings, and staffing. Although it is common to speak of the individual entrepreneur, frequently the entrepreneur is not alone. Entrepreneurs rely on a network of other people, other businesspeople, and other entrepreneurs. These contacts are personal resources that help the entrepreneur to acquire additional resources and start his or her business. It is true that "who you know" and "who knows you" are sometimes very valuable resources in new venture creation.

One of the individual entrepreneur's most important responsibilities is to establish an ethical climate for the new venture. Business **ethics** has been defined in many ways by many people. One definition of ethical behavior is: any business decision that creates value for the customer by matching quality and price. Why is this so? Ethical decisions (1) provide the customer with valid data about the product and service, (2) enable the customer to make a free and informed choice, and (3) generate customer commitment to the product and the organization that provides it. Violations of these three rules produce unethical behavior— invalid and false data, coerced and manipulated decisions, and low integrity and poor reputation for the firm.[50] How important are ethics and a good reputation? According to one advertising executive, "The only sustainable competitive advantage any business has is its reputation."[51]

Entrepreneurs are sometimes placed in situations where ethical decision making appears hard. It is tempting to cut corners, look for the edge by shading the truth, and adopt a *caveat emptor* ("let the buyer beware") attitude. If entrepreneurs see themselves as outsiders, underdogs, overworked, and underappreciated, they may make decisions based on the premise that the ends justify the means. Caution is advised. The means will become known, and if the means fail the tests for ethical conduct, the fine reputation of the product and the entrepreneurial team will be irreparably tarnished.

• The role of the individual founder or team changes over time. We can imagine that at the founding of the business, the imprinting of the individual/team characteristics on the business represents the primary way of identifying the firm. The venture is made in the image of its makers. But over time the importance that this initial imprinting has on the firm decreases. While the imprinting is always present in some form, the business develops its own personality and characteristics. New leaders and managers come aboard. Product and service mixes change and new management makes organizational changes. Eventually the business develops its own identity, although the ethos and the values of the original entrepreneurs may remain.

The Environment

The environment poses both opportunities (see above) and threats for new venture creation. The opportunities come in the form of change and resources—money, people, technology. The entrepreneurial challenge is to acquire resources from the environment, combine them with other resources already possessed, and configure the new venture into a successful organization. The threats, or constraints, imposed by the environment

Sam Walton's 10 Best Rules

Sam Walton was born in 1918 and died in 1992. In his lifetime, he built the largest, most successful retail organization in the world and became America's richest person. His chosen path to empire was either "overlooked or underestimated by his rivals."

After graduating from the University of Missouri, Walton went right to work for J.C. Penney in 1940 for $75 per month. He loved retailing and its competitiveness. He bought his own store, a Ben Franklin, when he was mustered out of the Army in 1945. However, he did not open the first Wal-Mart until 1962.

Between 1940 and 1962, "Mr. Sam" developed many of the habits and garnered the experience that was to serve him so well later. He says his big lesson came early when he found that if he "bought an item for 80 cents . . . and priced it at a dollar, [he] could sell three times more of it than by pricing it at $1.20. I might have made only half the profit per item but because I was selling three times as many, the overall profit was much greater."

In the early 1960s, Mr. Sam discovered that others were beginning to develop large discount stores and chains. He did his homework and spent many nights on the road visiting these other merchants' stores. He admits that he "borrowed" quite a bit from Sol Price, founder of Fedmart. He finally decided that the future was in discounting, and proceeded to open the first Wal-Mart. In 1962, Wal-Mart's first year, the first Kmart, Target, and Woolco stores were also opened.

Ten years after the opening of the first Wal-Mart, the scoreboard read: Kmart, 500 stores and $3 billion sales; Wal-Mart, 50 stores and $80 million sales. In addition, the four leading retailers of the first half of the century—Sears, J.C. Penney, Woolworth, and Montgomery Ward— were still flourishing,

and every urban area had a regional department store or chain with which to compete. Many had resources far in excess of Walton's. So how did Mr. Sam become number one?

In a book written shortly before his death in 1992, Mr. Sam was asked about his rise to prominence. He said that the keys were (1) going head to head with Kmart, because the pressure of the competition made everyone a better retailer and encouraged innovation and change; (2) going small town (under 50,000 people), because this was an underserved niche; (3) employee profit sharing, because everyone was then an owner directed toward the same goal; and (4) communication and sharing information with all people inside the organization, because doing so empowered people and pushed responsibility for decision making down. Sam wouldn't say this, but a fifth factor was his tireless and unceasing dedication to keeping costs down and spirits up. His leadership was unparalleled by any of his competitors.

Clearly, Mr. Sam possessed personal experience, values, vision, and dedication in heroic proportions; he was unequaled by any of his rivals. But were his business decisions so unique that they cannot or could not be duplicated by another firm? When asked this question, Mr. Sam came up with his 10 rules to follow, rules that worked for him. If you follow these rules, can you be the next Sam Walton?

Rule 1: Commit to your business and believe in it.
Rule 2: Share your profits with your partners (employees).
Rule 3: Motivate your partners, challenge them, and keep score.
Rule 4: Communicate everything.

Rule 5: Appreciate your associates with well-chosen words.
Rule 6: Celebrate your successes.
Rule 7: Listen to everyone and get them talking.
Rule 8: Exceed your customers' expectations.
Rule 9: Control your expenses.
Rule 10: **BREAK ALL THE RULES**. Swim upstream. Go the other way.

Rule 10 is a doozy (as well as a paradox). It suggests that rules 1 through 9 may not be for everyone. It also suggests that Mr. Sam himself knew that by following everyone's

advice on everything, you could never achieve much more than everyone else. Just as Mr. Sam visited as many Kmarts as he could, everyone who paid attention could have visited all the Wal-Marts and copied what they did. You could easily duplicate rules 1 through 9, but you could never duplicate precisely the decisions that were made following rule 10. This is the unique and idiosyncratic aspect of Mr. Sam that made him the world's greatest merchant.

SOURCE: *Fortune*, March 23, 1992:113–114, and June 29, 1992:98–106.

are those inherent in any competitive marketplace. The entrepreneur can overcome these constraints, or protect against their worst effects, by developing strategies that exploit the firm's resources. The key elements of the environment are the government and politics, the economy, technology (i.e., innovation and invention), sociodemographics, and the ecosystem. Because the environment is characterized by change, uncertainty, and complexity, entrepreneurs must continually monitor events and trends and make adjustments to their organizations and strategies.

The Organization

The result of nearly all entrepreneurial start-ups is the creation of a new organization. This organization has a form and structure. It has a strategy that enables it to penetrate or create a market (entry wedges) and protect its position (isolating mechanisms). It possesses resources that it transforms into value for its customers.

However, an organization can be even more than this. An organization is made up of people who have skills and talents, values and beliefs, and maybe the recognition that by working together they can create something special. For example, the organization can have a culture that supports high performance and high quality. We will take a few minutes to look more closely at the concept of quality.

Quality is a difficult concept to grasp, yet it is critical to success. It is a way to differentiate the firm and provide it with a degree of protection from competitors. Quality is part of the entrepreneur's strategy. We will address strategy again in Chapter 4, but it is important to get a handle on this issue early.

Garvin identified five different approaches to the concept of **quality**: transcendent, product based, user based, manufacturing based, and value based.[52]

The Transcendent Approach. The transcendent approach to quality is philosophical and asks questions about the nature of things. With this approach, quality is considered "innate excellence."[53] Some experts dismiss this approach as being of little practical value for the businessperson, but we believe it can offer some guidance. A product's or service's quality concerns the function that it is intended to serve. Anything that inhibits that function detracts from quality. For example, consider quality in terms of a restaurant meal. Its quality includes its nutritional value, premium ingredients, taste, aroma, presentation, and timeliness. A poor-quality meal lacks what is necessary and also has other qualities attached, such as slow service, foreign ingredients, poor presentation, and careless preparation. The high-quality meal is distinguished from the poor-quality meal because it has only the elements it should and none of the detracting elements.

Product-Based Approach. The product-based concept of quality focuses on an attribute of the product that is held in high regard—for example, the high butterfat content in ice cream, the tightness and intensity of evenness (consistency) of stitches in a garment, or the durability of a washing machine. Quality of this sort can be ranked because it lends itself to quantitative measurement. Because the assessment of these attributes can be made independently of the user, product-based quality is sometimes referred to as "objective" quality.[54]

User-Based Approach. User-based quality is "subjective"—it exists in the eye of the beholder. Customers have different preferences, wants, and needs and therefore judge a product's quality by its usefulness to them. Are firms who meet these needs, but do so in nonquantitative ways (perhaps through advertising or superior product distribution), producing quality products? And when "subjective" quality competes with "objective" quality, is "good enough" really enough? For example, Toyota continues to have among the highest customer ratings for its automobiles despite the objective fact that many of Detroit's slow-selling cars are every bit as good. The car-buying public makes Toyota the higher quality product by how it perceives the brand.

Manufacturing-Based Approach. Manufacturing-based quality, or process quality, concerns the attention to detail in the construction and delivery of the product or service. It is linked to customer wants and needs and to objective quality because it presumes that someone defined *conformance standards* for the product or service. *Quality* is defined as the degree to which the product conforms to a set standard or the service to set levels and times. In other words, high reliability and zero manufacturing defects are important. The problem with this definition is that the link between standards and customer preferences was established in the past, perhaps long ago, and is not responsive to changes in the environment. Manufacturing-based quality shifts attention internally to how things are done. At its worst, it leads to taking the wrong steps but taking them very well.

Garvin's last category of quality is value based. This approach takes the concept of quality farther than the previous definitions. **Value** looks at quality in terms of price, and price is what customers consider when they decide whether to buy a product or service. If money were not scarce, nothing would be valuable, not even quality, because everyone could buy anything—but this is, of course, not true. Therefore, in business where prices are signals and money is scarce, value, not pure quality, is critical.

Which is the correct perspective on quality and value for the entrepreneur? We believe that entrepreneurs should understand all these perspectives and be able to make decisions based on their current situations. The ability to understand many facets of quality improves the entrepreneur's decision making. It enables an entrepreneur to meet the challenges posed by complex problems. It highlights the importance of the individual in new venture creation.

Figure 1.1 illustrates the dimensions of entrepreneurship and new venture creation.

PARADOXES OF ENTREPRENEURSHIP

The resource-based theory of entrepreneurship also helps explain two of the paradoxes of entrepreneurship in ways that other theories cannot.

Intelligence Paradox

The first paradox is often stated as, "If you are so smart, why aren't you rich?" Certainly professors and researchers can testify that there are a great many more smart people than rich people. A good theory of entrepreneurship needs to explain why intelligence does not always lead to success in business. Common logic seems to dictate that the better we understand a phenomenon such as new venture creation, the more likely we are to be successful in its practice. Textbook presentations of entrepreneurship that provide facts without examining cause and effect may make the student smarter (in some narrow sense), but these approaches are unlikely to make anyone (except the authors) richer.

The resource-based approach acknowledges that keen analysis (strategy formulation) and fact accumulation are necessary but insufficient tasks for entrepreneurs. Also, the resource-based theory holds that some aspects of entrepreneurship cannot be analyzed; they are hard to copy because no one, including the founders, quite understands how or why they work. This inability to be duplicated or explained is actually a business advantage because competitors cannot copy the entrepreneur's strategy if they can't understand it. In simple language, what is known (or knowable) to all is an advantage to none. We can get smarter without getting richer if the knowledge we possess lacks any of the four characteristics (valuable, rare, hard to copy, or no substitutes).[55]

Entry Barrier Paradox

The second paradox is summed up by the old line, "You wouldn't want to belong to any club that would have you as a member."[56] The parallel application of this adage to new venture creation is that "you wouldn't want to enter any industry that would have you" (low-entry barriers) because if you could get in, then anyone could. Therefore, the opportunity will appear unattractive. This is the traditional economic analysis that examines the height of the entry barriers and weighs the cost of entry against the profit potential (margins) of firms in the industry, and the probability of retaliation by incumbents.[57] One implication of this analysis is that, for the vast majority of economic organizations, existing firms have the edge. Yet, experience indicates that certain individuals create businesses in industries with seemingly insurmountable barriers, and these individuals achieve superior and sometimes spectacular results. Analysis of industry structure fails to explain this phenomenon because it cannot explain why everyone cannot follow suit. The resource-based theory can explain the likes of Sam Walton, founder of Wal-Mart (see Street Story 1.3), Ted Turner of Turner Broadcasting, and Dave Thomas of Wendy's

FIGURE 1.1   Dimensions of New Venture Creation

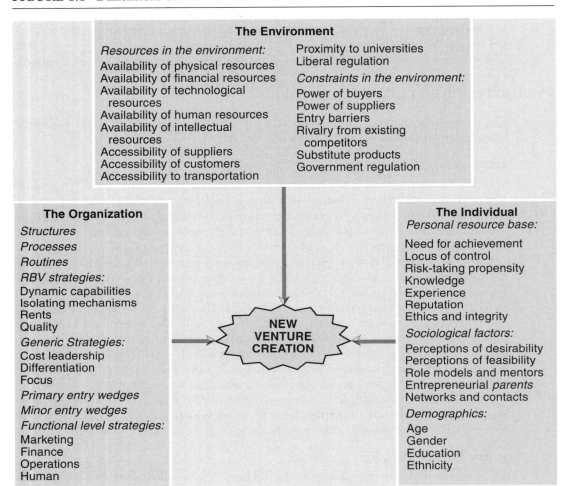

The Environment

Resources in the environment:
Availability of physical resources
Availability of financial resources
Availability of technological
   resources
Availability of human resources
Availability of intellectual
   resources
Accessibility of suppliers
Accessibility of customers
Accessibility to transportation

Proximity to universities
Liberal regulation
Constraints in the environment:
Power of buyers
Power of suppliers
Entry barriers
Rivalry from existing
   competitors
Substitute products
Government regulation

The Organization
Structures
Processes
Routines
RBV strategies:
Dynamic capabilities
Isolating mechanisms
Rents
Quality
Generic Strategies:
Cost leadership
Differentiation
Focus
Primary entry wedges
Minor entry wedges
Functional level strategies:
Marketing
Finance
Operations
Human

NEW VENTURE CREATION

The Individual
Personal resource base:

Need for achievement
Locus of control
Risk-taking propensity
Knowledge
Experience
Reputation
Ethics and integrity
Sociological factors:
Perceptions of desirability
Perceptions of feasibility
Role models and mentors
Entrepreneurial *parents*
Networks and contacts
Demographics:
Age
Gender
Education
Ethnicity

SOURCE: Adapted from W. Gartner, "The Conceptual Framework for Describing the Phenomenon of New Venture Creation," *Academy of Management Review* 10, 1985: 696–706.

as individuals with unique personal resources. They were able to enter industries that appeared to have powerful predatory competitors and go against the odds to build major influential organizations.

ORGANIZATION OF THE BOOK

Chapter 1 provides the framework for the study of entrepreneurship, beginning with the theme that entrepreneurs succeed because of the resources that they possess and acquire and the strategies they employ. This resource-based theory is described in greater detail in Chapter 2, where we also examine different types of resources and capabilities, and explore the relative importance of each.

Chapter 3 explains the environment for entrepreneurship as having two interrelated components: (1) a remote environment that cannot be controlled by the entrepreneur, and (2) a competitive environment in which the entrepreneur executes his or her strategies and plans. The importance of environmental scanning and a model for scanning are also presented in this chapter. Chapter 4 details exactly how entrepreneurs go into business by looking at the strategies they pursue. We will also introduce the Information Rules strategies that are critical to the success of ventures based on information. Chapter 5 explains the basics of writing the business plan. The plan is required for all new ventures and it signifies the transition from planning to implementation. We offer an example of a business plan as the appendix to Chapter 5.

After Chapter 5, we make the transition from the formulation of venture strategy to the implementation phase. Chapter 6 examines the marketing-entrepreneurship interface. We examine how the success of the venture is enhanced with effective marketing. We also cover many of the marketing, sales, and pricing strategies that are critical for the new venture. The advent of electronic commerce and the Internet has changed forever the nature of starting a business for those who incorporate technology into their operations and products. We will focus on information-related businesses and see how the combination of having rare, valuable, and hard-to-copy information and the Internet provide new opportunities for entrepreneurs.

Chapter 7 describes the foundations of entrepreneurial financing, including debt, equity, and cash flow. Chapter 8 continues the discussion of financial issues by looking at how investors and entrepreneurs view each other, and describes how they are likely to want to structure a financial deal. The chapter also covers legal and taxation issues.

Chapter 9 explores the new venture's organization. We will look at how some organizations are strong from the start and have characteristics that enable them to persevere through many business cycles. Our discussion is based on Collins and Porras's book, *Built to Last*. Chapter 10 describes corporate venturing and intrapreneurship. We see how large organizations try to keep fresh so they can remain innovative and entrepreneurial. In this final chapter, we introduce the *Balanced Scorecard* concepts.

The 10 chapters are followed by a selection of cases drawn from real situations and business plans. These cases illustrate the possibilities and opportunities facing entrepreneurs.

A FINAL WORD

Not everyone will succeed as an entrepreneur, and sometimes the people who do succeed do so only after a number of painful attempts. As the introductory quote illustrates, studying entrepreneurship and being an entrepreneur are two different things. The odds of success are quite different in these two endeavors, and the outcomes are evaluated by different criteria. However, the student of entrepreneurship should realize that he or she can be a successful entrepreneur. Previous academic achievement is not a requirement.

Many of the students who excel in accounting, marketing, or finance will spend most of their careers working for entrepreneurs—people who were better at seizing opportunity than taking classroom examinations.

Entrepreneurship students should try not to be too concerned about their grades. Consider the story of Fred Smith, founder of Federal Express. It is said that when he took the entrepreneurship course in which he proposed a nationwide delivery system for packages that would compete with the U.S. Post Office, he received a grade of "C" for his efforts, suggesting that at times teachers of entrepreneurship have limits to their vision as well. The true test of entrepreneurial potential is in the marketplace, not in the classroom.

SUMMARY

The future is full of entrepreneurial opportunities, and new venture creation and entrepreneurship are changing the face of the world's businesses and economies. Historically, entrepreneurship has taken many different turns. In today's market-based economies, new venture creation is the key to technological and economic progress. Through entrepreneurship, people will continue to live better, longer, and more rewarding lives.

We have defined *entrepreneurship* as the creation of an innovative economic organization (or network of organizations) for the purpose of gain or growth under conditions of risk and uncertainty. This definition enables us to make distinctions between entrepreneurship and other wealth- and income-generating activities.

Although entrepreneurs and entrepreneurship have been studied from many different perspectives, we take an economic and managerial perspective in this book. The guiding framework for our discussion and analysis of entrepreneurial opportunities is the resource-based theory of sustainable competitive advantage. This theory enables us to understand what is unique about the new venture and how the new enterprise will create value for its customers and subsequently its founders. The managerial dimensions of entrepreneurship are individuals, environments, and organizations. These dimensions provide us with a useful organizing framework with which to view the complex forces and interactions that produce entrepreneurial activity.

—————————————— DISCUSSION QUESTIONS ——————————————

1. What would it be like to work for an entrepreneurial firm? Compare this to working for a *Fortune* 500 firm. Give examples from your own experience.
2. What are Schumpeter's definitions of an entrepreneurial new venture? Give examples of businesses you know that meet these criteria. How are these firms regarded in our society? By the media?
3. What kinds of uncertainty do you have in your life? Are these uncertainties comparable to the types faced by entrepreneurial firms? What are your coping strategies?
4. What kinds of changes might have to occur in countries like North Korea or Cuba to make them more accessible to entrepreneurs?

5. What kind of American-style ventures do you think would prosper abroad, especially in those countries with a low level of economic freedom? Provide examples.
6. What are Drucker's seven sources of opportunity? Provide examples of each. Which seem to be the easiest, hardest to find?
7. Why doesn't being smart easily translate into being rich?
8. How do entrepreneurial dimensions of individuals, environments, and organizations interact to produce new ventures?
9. Discuss the different forms of quality. Why is quality important for an entrepreneur?
10. What is value? How is it created? Provide examples of value products that you use and enjoy. What makes these special to you?

KEY TERMS

Creation
Economic organization
Entrepreneurship
Ethics
Gazelles
New venture creation
Opportunity analysis
Quality

Resource-based theory
Risk
Uncertainty
Value
Virtual organization

EXERCISES

1. Search the business press (*Business Week, Fortune, The Wall Street Journal*, and others) to identify future entrepreneurial opportunities. These opportunities may meet any of Schumpeter's criteria. What different options would an entrepreneur have in developing these opportunities? Could you develop these? Distinguish between the opportunities of which you could take advantage and those that you could not, even though others might be able to.
2. Interview an entrepreneur. Find out what "rules" he or she followed to become a successful entrepreneur. Ask your entrepreneur if he or she agrees with Sam Walton's rule 10.
3. Interview a government official in your city or county. How does this person view entrepreneurship? What does the government do to encourage or discourage entrepreneurship? Why do they do this?
4. Read a nonbusiness book or article about entrepreneurship. (Hint: Go to the library.) Or see a video that depicts entrepreneurs in action. How is entrepreneurship treated in this material? How does it complement or add to the economic and managerial approach we take in the business school?
5. Jack Welch, the famous former CEO of General Electric and management guru, recommends in his book, *Winning*, that people entering business consider careers in companies doing business at the "intersection of biology and information technology." What kind of businesses could be created at this intersection? How would these businesses be developed? What role could you play in their development?

6. Construct your own entrepreneurial resume. This resume should emphasize your entrepreneurial experience, skills and abilities. The format should be:

- Name and contact information at the top
- Entrepreneurial objective next
- Body of the resume: List your experience, most recent to earliest in this section. Emphasize things that are entrepreneurial. Words that are entrepreneurial descriptors include: *initiated, founded, developed, designed, created, originated, organized, implemented.*
- References. Show off your connections and list influential people you might know or might know you.

DISCUSSION CASE

Delivering a Powerful Kick

So far her knees feel fine.

But 38-year-old fitness instructor Ilaria Montagnani knows this may not be the case forever. Last year she made $100,000 teaching aerobics classes six days a week. In the future she hopes to increase her earnings while at the same time decreasing her physical effort.

In 1995 Montagnani, who has a black belt in karate, teamed up with fitness and dance trainer Patricia Moreno to create Powerstrike™, a trademarked workout program that blends aerobic routines with martial arts movements. The program has been very successful. Montagnani and a few instructors now offer more than 50 Powerstrike classes each week in the greater New York City area. The program has been demonstrated on television shows like "Today" and "Good Morning, America," and featured in magazines including *Allure, Jane,* and *Shape.* New York magazine named Powerstrike™ the best exercise class in both 1999 and 2001.

But Montagnani has her eye on the future. "I'm at my highest earnings level, and there's only one way to go from here," she says. She knows her options are limited. Some fitness instructors increase the price of their classes as their popularity grows, or even open a private studio. But experts say that health club chains such as Equinox, Crunch, and Bally Total Fitness offer stiff competition to independent gyms. At the same time these clubs are often too reluctant to pay an outside expert to teach a fitness class, preferring to develop their own programs with in-house staff.

As part of the solution, Montagnani has been trying to build her program into a "name" or a brand, much like fitness instructors Jack LaLanne, Richard Simmons, or Billy Banks have done with their exercise routines. To expand in this fashion, she has extended her offerings from one class to six different kinds of classes, including her initial Powerstrike™ Kickboxing, the more intensive Powerstrike™ Kicks, Powerstrike™ Impact (kickboxing with a free-standing bag), Powerstrike™ on Guard for self-defense, Powerstrike™ Forza (also known as Samurai Sword Training, which uses a plastic Japanese-style fitness sword), and an advanced body-sculpting program called Powerstrike Body™ Strikes. Montagnani also

(continued on next page)

has a Web site (www.powerstrike.com) where she sells videos and a DVD, and where she markets a book she wrote about her Forza samurai sword workout.

But the fitness instructor recognizes she needs to be even more entrepreneurial. "If you want to stay in the fitness industry," she says, "the question is, how do you create a continuation of what you do?"

So far, the answer to that question has been to train other fitness instructors. There are approximately 45,000 fitness instructors in the United States who have been certified by the American Council on Exercise. Montagnani now offers one-day training workshops on Powerstrike™ Kickboxing, Impact, and Forza at fitness conventions and other locations across the United States, and even around the world. For a fee of about $250, instructors can learn not only the correct Powerstrike alignment and form, but also the coaching techniques that have made Montagnani's classes so popular. Class size ranges from 10 to 350, and Montagnani esti-

mates she has issued about 6,500 certification certificates to date.

The Powerstrike™ president also has a group of official trainers who recruit students for her certification classes in exchange for a fee, and another group of master trainers who teach her certification programs earning half of the tuition. Now that Powerstrike™ has developed a following, two fitness chains have also paid Montagnani to develop programs for them and train their employees.

Montagnani still has to process all her Web site's e-mail herself, and operate her business out of her one-bedroom apartment. And she still schedules herself to teach at least one class six days a week. But she's taking steps so she won't become a "pathetic 50-year-old jumping around" leading low-paying classes with declining enrollments.

SOURCE: Adapted in part from Gwendolyn Bounds, "Making the Most of Your 15 Minutes," *The Wall Street Journal* Startup Journal, 2006. Retrieved from the Web May 9, 2006. http://www.startupjournal.com and http://www.powerstrike.com.

Case Questions

1. What has Ilaria Montagnani done that qualifies her to be called an entrepreneur? Using Table 1.3, how would you evaluate what she has done so far?
2. What other things do you think Montagnani could do to build her Powerstrike business?
3. What other businesses can you think of that are similar to the fitness industry? What innovative strategies have they used to become successful?
4. Do you think Powerstrike will continue to grow? Why or why not?

CHAPTER 2 Resources and Capabilities

There is nothing as practical as a good theory.
—*Kurt Lewin*

OUTLINE

Identifying Attributes of Strategic Resources
    Valuable Resources
    Rare Resources
    Hard-to-Copy Resources
    Nonsubstitutable Resources

Resource Types
    Physical Resources
    Reputational Resources
    Organizational Resources
    Financial Resources
    Intellectual and Human Resources
    Technological Resources

A Psychological Approach
    Personality Characteristics
    Limits of the Trait Approach

A Sociological Approach
    Impetus for Entrepreneurship
    Situational Characteristics

Summary

Appendix A. Creativity and Idea Generation

LEARNING OBJECTIVES

After reading this chapter, you will understand

- various approaches to and theories of *entrepreneurship*.
- the *resource-based theory of entrepreneurship*, which explains how new firms can obtain and sustain competitive advantage.
- *strategic resources*, and how these resources influence success.
- some of the misconceptions about *personality traits* and the entrepreneurial personality.
- why and how an entrepreneur is the primary *human resource* for a new venture.
- the components of the *entrepreneurial event*, which is the creation of a new venture.
- *creativity techniques* for generating business ideas.

32

Opportunities, Recognition, and Intuition

Having the ability to see an opportunity, obtain resources to exploit that opportunity, and launch the business are critical entrepreneurial capabilities. This profile is about action-oriented and intuitive entrepreneurs who use this process.

Chad and Andy Baker enrolled at Indiana University, intending to major in finance and accounting. Even before they got to college, the twin brothers wanted to start and run their own business; they had been entrepreneurs in their hometown of Nashville, Tennessee, during high school, selling shirts, music CDs, and computer equipment to their classmates. In Indiana, they even operated a gumball vending operation to help cover their tuition expenses. But their college grades were too low for them to enroll as business majors at Indiana University's Kelley School of Business, so they dropped out of school and started pursuing entrepreneurial opportunities.

Their first idea was to place custom advertisements for all sorts of products in the restrooms of restaurants and bars; they thought the ads could be geared to the demographic group that the restaurant served, and specifically targeted to either men or women. But the competition was fierce, and after a few installations they abandoned this effort.

Next, the twins became enamored with rock climbing. They developed a business plan for a company that would build and supply rock-climbing walls to health clubs and free-standing rock-climbing businesses. With a price tag of $30,000 per wall, this business seemed to offer plenty of margin and profit. But because the plan required a big investment, and because the twins were worried that they would be stuck with a big inventory of walls if the fad faded, they rejected this idea in their entrepreneurial search.

Then, at a trade show, the Bakers found what they were looking for. One of the exhibitors was selling a license to manufacture etched Plexiglas signs with a unique LED-illuminated edge. Based on their prior experience with advertising specialties and some fabrication work, the brothers believed they could manufacture custom-made signs easily with this process. They obtained a license and hired someone with artistic skills to help with design. Because the fabrication tasks were easy, they arranged to have the signs made at a facility that employed handicapped people, which saved them money and was good for their community, too.

The signs, which are sold primarily to restaurants and bars, have now led to a new product: the Drink Tower. The tower is a vertical Plexiglas tube with a spigot or tap that dispenses drinks in place of a pitcher. It can be filled with beer or soda or any beverage, and is both portable and fun to use. The Baker twins originally sold towers made in France, but they have now obtained a Small Business Administration loan to manufacture Drink Towers in China.

While the Bakers sell their signs primarily at trade shows, they now have a Web site (www.drinktower.com) to market their newest product in both 100- and 168-ounce sizes. They hope to add more products to the Web site in the future. The sales volume from their businesses now exceeds $500,000, and Andy and Chad have received the Indiana Small Business Administration's "Young Entrepreneur of the Year" award.

Their latest venture is back in their hometown of Nashville. They are flipping houses and providing second mortgages for homeowners with financial emergencies. Real estate financing may turn out to be their future. Or it may not.

SOURCE: Adapted from SBA Young Entrepreneurs Award *Indiana Business* 13, May 2004; "Success Story: Indoor Signs LLC," *Indiana Small Business Development Center Newsletter*, March 23, 2005. Retrieved from the Web May 17, 2006. http://www.isbdc.org/newsletter/001.indoor.htm, www.drinktower.com; and personal interviews.

W HY do entrepreneurs need a theory of entrepreneurship? Because a theory enables its user to be efficient. For the entrepreneur, *efficiency* means economizing on time and effort. The profile of the Baker brothers demonstrates how entrepreneurs, with intuition and a trial-and-error process, approach new venture creation. The Bakers see opportunities and then, because they are action oriented, they throw themselves into creating a business. If it works, fine, but if not, no problem. They just move on to the next opportunity. While this process is fun for the Bakers, it is not particularly efficient. The Bakers are not using a theory to guide their entrepreneurial efforts. They are simply full of energy.

The advantages of having a theory of entrepreneurship are that it saves time and effort. With a theory, we will recognize what kinds of information are helpful. The theory will enable us to translate this raw information into usable data, and to process the data into categories and variables. A good theory tells the user how things and events are related and the probable direction of causality. Finally, a theory tells the user the timing and sequencing of events. Some events occur before others, and these are leading indicators; others occur after, and these are lagging variables. When events happen at the same time, they are concurrent.

An entrepreneur with a good theory of how entrepreneurship works is a practical and efficient person. These traits are crucial because entrepreneurship can be expensive; real-time failures cost money and the irreplaceable time of many people, as well as their hopes and reputations. There are thousands of opportunities for entrepreneurship, but we cannot try them all. Which will we pursue? By using a good theory, we can think about all of the problems and issues of new venture creation without having to start business after business to see what works and what does not.

A caution is in order. A theory is not a law. A theory does not pretend to explain precisely what will happen with absolute certainty in all cases. It deals with hypotheses and propositions—educated guesses about the chances that certain relationships exist and the strength and nature of these relationships. If there were a "law of entrepreneurship," once people knew it, they could apply it and everyone would experience unlimited success. Such a scenario does not make sense in any market-based economy where competition is prevalent. Besides, if everyone could succeed, how would we measure profit? We should be pleased that we have a theory and not a law of entrepreneurship.

Some say that there have been a great many successful entrepreneurs, most of whom did not have a theory. How did they do it? One serious possibility is luck. There are at least two kinds of luck—the "dumb luck" of chance, such as that of people who win the lottery. Other than buying the ticket, winning is completely independent of any action on their part. Their win defies great odds, much greater than the odds against business success.

Then there is business luck. Peter Drucker famously defined luck as "when preparedness meets opportunity." Business luck explains in large part how entrepreneurs create their own good fortune. They develop their own skills and capabilities to take advantage of opportunity, and they have a systematic method for encountering and analyzing opportunity. Lucky things happen to entrepreneurs who start fundamentally innovative and compelling businesses. Lottery luck is therefore different than business luck.

At times, a lucky person will not be able to tell which kind of luck he or she is having. Consider this: If we hold a worldwide competition in coin tossing to find the best heads-or-tails caller in the world, someone will win. We will start out with six billion pairs of tossers, and after the first toss, we will have three billion left. This process will be repeated until we have the final 64. The tournament will be televised and all the players will have coaches, who will be interviewed on their coin-tossing strategy. Eventually, we will get down to the final four, and then two; then the coin-tossing tournament winner will be crowned.

If it was a fair coin and a fair toss, the winner won simply by luck. But ask her about the experience and she (as well as the last 16 or so competitors left) will give you all sorts of explanations about her technique, her decision-making process, her personality, her father's coin-tossing expertise, and how smart she is. People often confuse being smart with being lucky.[2]

A second possibility is that the winner succeeded after many failures, an expensive and time-consuming method. But the most likely explanation is that he or she succeeded as a result of having a tacit, or unspoken, theory of how his or her business and industry operates. Like Sam Walton, the entrepreneur who created Wal-Mart and Sam's Club, and his rules (see Chapter 1, Street Story 1.3), a lifetime of experience can help to summarize the theory, but some pieces remain so complex and intuitive that even the theorist doesn't know them.

This chapter introduces the fundamentals of the **resource-based theory** (often referred to as the **resource-based view, RBV**) of entrepreneurship.[3] The resource-based theory is efficient and practical because it focuses on the strengths, assets, and capabilities of entrepreneurs and their ventures.[4] It incorporates market opportunity, industry structure, and competition, but it emphasizes resources, **skills** and **capabilities** (including the skill and capability to learn new skills and capabilities). The entrepreneur may already control these resources or may be able to obtain them in the future. But without resources with which to exploit a situation, even the best-case scenario cannot create an entrepreneur.[5] As you read through the chapter, note how the examples, the Street Stories, and the end-of-chapter case provide guidance on how entrepreneurs have used an implicit model (they may not have been aware of the theory) of the RBV to make their businesses successful.

IDENTIFYING ATTRIBUTES OF STRATEGIC RESOURCES

What is a resource? A **resource*** is any thing or quality that is useful,[6] tangible or intangible. Another characteristic of a resource is that it is semipermanent or sticky; it adheres to the venture and the entrepreneur.[7] Resources can be property based or knowledge based. Property-based resources give the entrepreneur "rights." If one owns a machine, one has the right to use it. If one has an exclusive long-term contract, that contract protects one's rights. Property-based resources enable a firm to control its environment. Knowledge-based resources are more intangible, like talent or skill. These are protected by their tacit nature. Knowledge-based resources enable the firm to adapt to a changing environment. Miller and Shamsie reported that property-based resources

---

*To improve the readability of this text, at various times we write the terms **resource**, **capital**, and **asset** interchangeably. Alos, we say resource, we include "skill" and "capability." **Capability** and **skill** in this context mean the ability to do something useful.

were associated with higher profits in stable environments, while knowledge-based resources were correlated with higher levels of profitability in uncertain environments.[8]

A **capability** is a socially complex routine that determines the efficiency of the physical transformation of inputs to outputs. Capabilities are ordinarily not traded in factor markets. They are therefore built internally and can be hard to copy. Organizations in general have three types of capabilities:

- Basic **functional capabilities**, such as marketing, finance, operations, and research and development. Firms differ in the content of their capabilities as well as the strength of their management.
- **Dynamic improvement capabilities** that enable the organization to change and be responsive and flexible— the learning and innovation capability. The concept exists that firms can "learn to learn." This concept is sometimes called double-loop learning. Firms with the capability of learning to learn have less need of specific capabilities because they can adapt on the fly.[9]
- **Entrepreneurial capabilities** are those that use the firm's resources and develop new ones strategically.[10]

The ultimate goal—and the one that is very difficult to achieve—is **sustainable competitive advantage (SCA).** SCA occurs when the firm is able to create and capture value, and protect it against erosion from competition. There are limits to the degree to which a capability can be a source of sustainable competitive advantage. Competitors attempt to copy successful products, services, and value-creating strategies. Capabilities are diminished when key people retire, or the chemistry or culture of work groups and departments changes, or another firm develops a better capability.

The Basic Process under the RBV

No two entrepreneurs are alike, and no two new firms are identical. Our resource-based theory of entrepreneurship makes sense for the study of new venture creation because it focuses on the differences between and among entrepreneurs and includes the founding of their companies. Entrepreneurs are individuals who are unique resources to the new firm, resources that money cannot buy. These entrepreneurs can be different based on their personalities and characteristics, their skills, knowledge, and experiences, their sociodemographic backgrounds, their social and business networks, their motivations, and their vision of the world and business. As such, to understand a theory of differences, we must begin with the entrepreneur.

The theory says that firms have different starting points for resources (called *resource heterogeneity*) and other firms cannot get them (called *resource immobility*). Our theory values creativity, uniqueness, entrepreneurial vision and intuition, and the initial conditions (history) under which new ventures are created.[11]

What are the origins of new firms? Economic organizations that have their origins in the entrepreneur's resources, and the assets that the entrepreneurial team controls can potentially acquire and, finally, combine and assemble. Firms usually begin their history with relatively few strategically relevant resources and skills, and each company's uniqueness shows how these resources are expected to perform in the marketplace. Our theory has a rather simple formula.[12]

A. Produce (or acquire) resources and skills cheaply.

B. Transform (the resource or skills) into a product or service.

C. Deploy and implement (the strategy).

D. Sell dearly (for more than was paid).

This formula can be broken down into a two-phase process. The first phase is value creation: The entrepreneur creates "use value," the value that is perceived by the buyer or customer. Points A and B above describe this phase. The second phase of the process is value capture. Entrepreneurs must sell or exchange the value that they create for a customer. Price received is a function of the relative bargaining power between the producer and the buyer.[13] Points C and D above refer to value capture. We will cover bargaining power and the other elements of industry analysis in Chapter 3.

It is possible to create value only if cheap or undervalued resources and skills exist or can be developed at the time of the firm's start-up. Their availability depends on market imperfections and differences of opinion about prices and events. These opinion differences are not limitations, because perfect agreement seldom exists, and the key to an entrepreneur's vision is insight into the future.

Our resource-based theory holds that sustainable competitive advantage (SCA) is created when firms possess and employ resources and capabilities that are:

1. *valuable* because they exploit some environmental opportunity.
2. *rare* in that there are not enough for all competitors.
3. *imperfectly imitable* (most of the time we will refer to this as *hard to copy*) so that competitors cannot merely duplicate them.
4. *nonsubstitutable* with other resources.

These four items are known as the **VRIN** characteristics or indicators of sustained competitive advantage.[14] It is also important to distinguish between **competitive advantage** and sustained competitive advantage. Competitive advantage occurs when the entrepreneur "is implementing a value-creating strategy not simultaneously being implemented by any current or potential competitors."[15] "Value creating" refers to above normal gain or growth. Sustained competitive advantage is competitive advantage with a very important addition: Current and potential firms are unable to duplicate the benefits of the strategy. Although SCA cannot be competed away by duplication, it also cannot last forever. Changes in the environment or industry structure can make what once was SCA obsolete. Important strategic factors in one setting may be barriers to change in another, or simply irrelevant.

Why are these four characteristics so important?[16] When a firm possesses and controls resources with these four characteristics, it can withstand competitive pressures. If the new enterprise can protect these resources and maintain these four qualities, it will have competitive advantage over the long term. New ventures that form with some of these characteristics but not others have short-term or minor advantages. Firms with all these qualities, but not in full measure and without a plan to protect the resources, will have a competitive advantage until other firms are able to copy and imitate them. If the entrepreneur's goal is to achieve SCA for the new venture, then he or she must create a venture that is forgiving, rewarding, and enduring.[17] If the entrepreneur fails to build such a firm, he or she fades into an also-ran whose bundle of resources and skills may soon be depleted by the forces of destructive capitalism. This entrepreneur will eventually go out of business [18]

A recent research study has verified this conclusion. The study sought to identify the criteria that influence the performance of high-tech new ventures. The results indicated that entrepreneurial quality, resource-based capability, and competitive strategy are the critical determinants of the firm's viability and achievement. Successful entrepreneurs develop multiple, resource-based capabilities to sustain multiple strategies that will push their products to market. Furthermore, researchers have concluded that it is not the unique products relative to those of competitors that bring success; rather, it is the firm's ability to meet customers' unique requirements.[19]

In Street Story 2.1, we see how sometimes resources and skills have to be found overseas because they are in short supply locally. The same principles apply to a resource that is underpriced; one can use that resource to generate profit (rent) for a venture.

Street Story 2.1 illustrates that for the tailoring business, master tailors are a strategic resource. Can we generalize to other situations? What are strategic resources? Strategic resources create competitive advantage. There is a distinction between strategic and non-strategic, or common, resources. Not all capital resources and assets are strategically important for the entrepreneur. Many are considered "common" because, while they are necessary for carrying out the firm's usual activities, they provide no specific advantage. Ordinary desks, chairs, and office furniture are examples. Some resources may prevent the formulation and implementation of valuable strategies due to their shoddiness, imperfections, and poor quality. Still others may prevent beneficial strategies by blinding the entrepreneur to alternative possibilities because he or she focuses too narrowly on resources that are already controlled rather than on resources that are potentially controllable.[20]

Valuable Resources

What makes resources valuable? Resources are **valuable** when they help the organization implement its strategy effectively and efficiently, which means that in a "strengths, weaknesses, opportunities, and threats" model of firm performance, a valuable resource exploits opportunities or minimizes threats in the firm's environment. A valuable resource is useful for the venture's operation.[21] Examples of valuable resources and capabilities are property, equipment, people, and skills such as marketing, finance, and accounting. All of these resources are fairly general, however, so we must look at other factors.

Rare Resources

Valuable resources that are shared by a large number of firms cannot be a source of competitive advantage or SCA. Because of their widespread availability, they are not rare. An example might be legal resources, either independent professionals on retainer or staff attorneys. Their major purpose is to minimize threats of lawsuits from a contentious environment. Clearly, these are valuable resources in that they neutralize a threat, but lawyers are not rare. Most, if not all, firms have access to approximately the same legal talent (at a price, of course). Retaining legal counsel or building a corporate

A Strategic Stitch in Time

A famous Islamic parable declares, "If the mountain will not come to Muhammad, then Muhammad will go to the mountain."

The John H. Daniel Company of Knoxville, Tennessee, found a way to transform the proverbial mountain into a rare, valuable, and hard-to-copy resource. The company manufactures high-ticket men's suits, producing more than 75,000 garments, priced between $800 and $2,900 each year, for retailers and independently-owned custom clothiers. Most of its suits are made-to-order garments with handcrafted details sewn by master tailors. Thirty years ago, John H. Daniel was one of 30 firms in the United States producing suits like this; today they are one of the five.

When the company went into business 70 years ago, many of its tailors were Italian immigrants. Thanks to an improved, modern Italian economy, that resource is no longer available. The company was unable to find American workers with the advanced tailoring skills their products demand, but it was also reluctant to close the Knoxville factory and move the company's production offshore and overseas.

Then the Bryan family, who own and operate the company, had an idea. Some of the tailors they had recently lured away from a competitor in New York were immigrants from Turkey, so Benton Bryan, the company's chief operating officer, traveled to Istanbul with one of his new Turkish employees. He found that Turkey had a large number of skilled tailors facing competition from new mass manufacturers. Some of these tailors were willing to move to Tennessee to work for John H. Daniel at an entry wage of $11.50 per hour in a nonunion shop, especially if there were other Turks already on site to ease their transition process. Bryan interviewed more than 100 Turkish *terzi* or tailors, testing their skills

by asking then to stitch a jacket sleeve in place or sew a buttonhole by hand, and found 13 firm prospects.

Nine of those prospects are now living and working in Tennessee. To make that happen, Jackson L. Case IV, the company's general counsel, spends a large chunk of his time negotiating with the State, Labor, and Homeland Security departments to get visas for these Turkish tailors and their families. The visas are issued under the same proviso that allows universities to recruit foreign academics, or high-tech firms to hire skilled programmers.

Part of what makes these tailors a rare, valuable, and hard-to-copy resource is the care and expense this company invests in them. Attorney Case personally oversees the welcome for each new hire to Tennessee. He and an interpreter meet the employee and his family at the Knoxville airport, and drive them to the apartment complex where many of the other Turks live. The company pays the rent on a two-bedroom apartment for the first few months, and purchases new furniture, a television, dishes, pots and pans, towels, and other necessities for the apartment. If the tailor's family includes school-aged children, Case arranges for them to be vaccinated, tested for tuberculosis, and enrolled in the local schools. The company also provides each worker with $1,000 in spending money to get him or her started, and will even make a no-interest loan so their new employee can buy a used car. Case estimates that it costs John H. Daniel about $12,000 to bring each Turkish family to Knoxville.

The daily routine at John H. Daniel now allows time for their new employees, who are all Muslims, to pray at their required *salaah* times during the day. Both the Bryan family and their new *terzi* indicate that this innovative strategic resource arrangement works for them. "The world has changed," Aydin Olcum, one of the company's Turkish tailors, observes. "You're not supposed to live where you're born. You're supposed to live where you can feed your family."

SOURCE: Adapted from Michael M. Phillips, "Why Turkish Tailors Seem So Well-Suited to Work in Tennessee," *The Wall Street Journal*, April 12, 2005: A1, and http://www.johnhdaniel.com.

legal staff cannot be the source of an advantage. Common resources such as these may be necessary under certain conditions and may improve chances for survival, but they are not a source of SCA.

Some resources have inelastic supply, which means that even when there is an increase in the demand for the resource, and a corresponding rise in price, the market takes a long time to respond with additional supply. The lag time provides the firm with an advantage that it can exploit until the competition catches up.[22]

How rare must a resource be to generate a competitive advantage? A unique and valuable resource clearly gives a firm SCA, but does this resource need to be one of a kind? Probably not. A resource may be considered rare when it is not widely available to all competitors. If supply and demand are in equilibrium, and the price of the resource is generally affordable, the resource will cease to be rare. Examples of resources that may be considered rare are a good location, managers who are also considered good leaders, or the control of natural resources like oil reserves (if you are in the oil business). A special case of a rare resource that does not provide SCA can be found in a Bertrand market. A Bertrand market is a duopoly in which both firms have similarly rare resources, giving them the same marginal costs. They will ultimately charge the competitive price based on their marginal costs and neither will therefore have a sustainable competitive advantage. [23]

Imperfectly Imitable (Hard-to-Copy) Resources

Firms with rare and valuable resources clearly have advantages over firms lacking such assets. Indeed, such strategic endowments often lead to innovation and market leadership.[24] However, even rare resources can be obtained at some price. If the price is so high that the firm makes no profit, there is no SCA because the firm has spent its advantage on the resource. Where duplication is not possible at a price low enough to leave profits, the resource is said to be **imperfectly imitable** or **hard to copy**. Four factors make it difficult for firms to copy each other's skills and resources: (1) economic and legal deterrence, (2) unique historical conditions, (3) causal ambiguity, (4) and social complexity.

Economic and Legal Deterrence.   Under certain circumstances, it is illegal for one firm to copy the resources of another. These legal protections take forms such as copyrights, patents, trademarks, service marks, and intentionally proprietary trade secrets. In addition, economic deterrence can prevent copying, as a firm can retaliate in the marketplace as well as in court. For example, the victimized company can cut prices, develop other products that compete closely with those of the offender, or attempt to shut the offender out of the market with long-term contracts and tie-ups.

Unique Historical Conditions. The defining moment for many organizations is their founding. At birth, organizations are imprinted with the vision and purpose of their founders. This emphasis on the founders illustrates the importance of the individual. The initial assets and resources that accompany the organization's origin are unique to that place and time. Firms founded at different times in other places cannot obtain these resources; thus, the resources cannot be duplicated. Examples of unique historical foundings abound, such as starting a company in a great location that was unrecognized by others at the time. Another example might be the creation of a new venture by scientists and engineers whose special knowledge is in companies specializing in genetic engineering or software development.

Ambiguous Causes and Effects. Causal ambiguity exists when the relationship between cause and effect is not well understood or is ambiguous.[25] In business, causal ambiguity means that there is doubt about what caused what and why things happened. When these factors are imperfectly understood, it is difficult for other firms to duplicate them. Even though the pieces may look the same as in the original, the rules of congruence are unknown, so the imitator cannot replicate them. Entrepreneurs themselves often cannot explain their own successes, so how can imitators hope to duplicate their operations? Sam Walton's break-all-the-rules rule shows that he understood that some things simply could not be predicted by an algorithm.

In the context of competencies and skills, two kinds of causal ambiguity exist. One is **linkage ambiguity**, which includes how relationships work together. Linkage ambiguity is related to the complex relationship issue discussed below. For example, companies recognize that training is a good thing, and they spend billions of dollars each year training their employees and managers. However, sometimes much of the training is wasted as people return to their jobs without demonstrating any noticeable change in performance. What is the link between training and performance? Some companies train more successfully than others, but no one really understands why. If we understood, we would make all training the same and it would all be effective. Even copying the way a successful company does its training doesn't work because the capability of transferring skills also has linkage ambiguity.

The other ambiguity is **characteristic ambiguity,** which refers to the lack of knowledge about which competencies are the actual sources of SCA and how they work. Why do some ventures have high-performing teams while others do not? Why is information technology an advantage in one firm and a continual problem in another? The reason is that IT and teams have characteristic ambiguity, that is, we do not know everything there is to know about either IT or teams.

It may seem odd that a firm with high-performance skills and resources has no better idea of why things work than the potential imitator. How is this possible? Economic organizations can be very complex. The relationships among product design, development, manufacturing, and marketing are not subject to complete quantitative analysis. They often depend on the complicated interaction of social, psychological, economic, and technical factors. Even when organizations have all available information about their competitors, they often are unable to answer such questions as:

- What makes one firm's sales force more effective than that of another?
- What makes one firm's production more efficient than that of another?
- Why are one firm's designs more appealing to the customer than that of another?

These are but a few of the ambiguous areas. No one can answer these questions.

What if there is no causal ambiguity? Consider a firm that understands the cause and effect relationship between its resources and its performance. Can it keep that knowledge secret from its competitors? Not in the long run. Competitors have strategies to unearth the information they need, such as hiring workers and managers away from the advantaged organization, and devising schemes to extract the needed information. Competitors may spend time and money, but in the long run, they will know all the firm's vital secrets, as will the entire industry. The entrepreneur who started with an advantage will not be able to sustain it indefinitely.

Complex Social Relationships. Social complexity is the third reason a firm's capabilities and resources may not be easily duplicated. As long as a firm uses human and organizational resources, social complexity may serve as a barrier to imitation. Why? The interpersonal relationships of managers, customers, and suppliers are complex. Someone, for example, could point out that customers like the firm's salespeople, but knowing this is the case does not make it possible for competitors to copy the likability of their salespeople. The competitor can hire away the whole sales force, but even this action may not reproduce the original relationship: The sales force may now work under different conditions, with different managers, and for different incentives.

Perhaps the most complex social phenomenon is **organizational culture.**[26] The new venture's culture is a complex combination of the founder's values, habits, and beliefs, and the interaction of these elements with the newly created organization and the market. The culture might be, among other things, very supportive, highly authoritarian, very aggressive, extremely thrifty, or combinations of all these and more. As organizations grow, subcultures form, adding more complexity. Organizational cultures are difficult to "know" from the outside; they cannot be directly observed and they resist quantitative measurement, which makes them almost impossible to copy.

Despite this hard-to-copy element, strong forces are at work that make organizations appear very similar. These forces are described by a framework known as institutional theory.[27] At its most basic, institutional theory says that the forces for conformity in organizational structure, practice, and culture are very strong. These forces are:

- The shaping nature of the business environment
- The accepted wisdom of how to succeed
- The risk aversion that accompanies the prospect of doing something different
- The lack of diversity among the most powerful decision makers
- Organizational practices like benchmarking

Without doubt, these are powerful forces, which is why, when observing large corporations, we frequently find a great deal of conformity. Many new ventures also have look-alike and me-too aspects, making it nearly impossible to differentiate all aspects of the new venture from aspects of existing firms. Such differentiation is probably undesirable as well, because customers also want the convenience of procuring familiar services and products from the firm. However, for the nascent entrepreneur and new venture creation, which theory, RBV or institutional, is more useful in providing accurate description and prediction?

Nonsubstitutable Resources

Nonsubstitutable resources are strategic resources that cannot be replaced by common resources. For example, let us say there are two firms, A and B. Firm A has a rare and valuable resource, which it uses to implement its strategy. If firm B has common resources that can be substituted for firm A's valuable and rare resources, and these common resources do basically the same things, then the rare and valuable resources of firm A do not confer strategic advantage. In fact, if firm B can obtain common resources that threaten firm A's competitive advantage, then so can many other firms, thereby ensuring that firm A has no advantage.

Very different resources can be substitutes for each other. For example, an expert-system computer program may substitute for a manager. A charismatic leader may substitute for a well-designed, strategic-planning system. A well-designed, programmed-learning module may substitute for an inspirational teacher. Figure 2.1 summarizes the four resource attributes needed for competitive advantage.

RESOURCE TYPES

Our resource-based theory recognizes six types of resources: physical, reputational, organizational, financial, intellectual/human, and technological; they can be called our **PROFIT** factors. These resources are broadly drawn and include all "assets, capabilities, organizational processes, firm attributes, information, and knowledge."[28] Strictly speaking, a list like this one (as is true of many lists in this book) should be exhaustive, and the items on it mutually exclusive. Here, the list is exhaustive. But sometimes, the category types are not mutually exclusive. For example, if the organization has great marketing, does this characteristic reside in the person who is a great marketer or in the marketing department? Sometimes it is tough to tell. From our point of view, it is more important to identify great marketing than to put marketing into the most correct category.

We explore these six resource types and note the special situations in which they may confer a particular advantage or no advantage at all.

Physical Resources

Physical resources are the tangible property the firm uses in production and administration. These include the firm's plant and equipment, its location, and the amenities available at that location. Some firms also have natural resources, such as minerals, energy resources, or land. These natural resources can affect the quality of the firm's physical inputs and raw materials.

Physical resources can be the source of SCA if they have the four attributes described

FIGURE 2.1 Resource Attributes and Competitive Advantage

Creates Competitive Advantage	Resource Dimension	No Competitive Advantage
Exploits opportunity Neutralizes threats	Valuable resources	Not suited to the environment: common
Unique Costly to procure	Rare resources	Readily available Inexpensive
Unique history Causally ambiguous Socially complex	Imitable resources	Ordinary history Causality known Socially simple
Not possible through: Similar modes Different modes	Substitutable resources	Easily possible: Similar modes Different modes

SOURCE: Adapted from J. Barney, "Firm Resources and Sustained Competitive Advantage," *Journal of Management* 17, 1991: 99–120.

above. However, because most physical entities can be manufactured and purchased, they are probably not rare or hard to copy. Only in special circumstances, such as a unique historical situation, will physical resources be a source of SCA. For example, one might believe that in Street Story 2.2, Amanda Knauer's discovery of Argentine leather (a physical resource) is her source of advantage. But read closely. What are the underlying resources and capabilities of Qara Argentine?

The amenities and infrastructure of a locality or region can also promote entrepreneurship. Founders frequently locate wherever they happen to be when the entrepreneurship bug bites, but some areas in the country can give a significant push to entrepreneurial start-ups' success. These geographic areas form the basis of an **entrepreneurial system**.[29] A recent research study shows how effective such a system can be. The system components might include incubator organizations, formal and informal networks, economic and social networks, physical infrastructure such as roads and subsidized industrial space, universities with engineering and entrepreneurship programs and dense high-tech activity. Systems like this exist in legend, such as Silicon Valley and the Massachusetts Route 122 area. Examples of other up-and-coming areas are the Boulder County, Colorado, area for high tech, and the Indianapolis Life and Health Science Initiative region.

Reputational Resources

Reputational resources are the perceptions of the company held by people in the firm's environment. Reputation can exist at the product level as in brand loyalty, or at the cor-

STREET STORY 2.2

It's in the Bag

When 23-year-old Amanda Knauer first arrived in Buenos Aires in 2004, she wasn't sure what she was going to do. The former documentary film assistant thought she wanted to do something involving fashion, but it wasn't until she discovered Argentine leather that she envisioned "drawing luxury from raw materials," and expressing her "dream of crafting a tangible product and creating my own business."

Argentina provides many of the animal skins used to make fine Italian leather. The cowhides that the country has at home are tanned by a less-advanced process than the cowhide it exports, producing more distinctive and natural finished skins. Knauer thought Argentine leather would be perfect for products geared to the 25-to-40-year-old urban man, which she saw as an underserved market. So she used $45,000 in savings to create a company called Qara, using the word for leather from the Quechua language, the Incan dialect still spoken by some indigenous residents of the Andes today.

Knauer credits the physical resource, Argentine leather, as the inspiration for her company, but in fact, she brought many other resources to her new venture. Friends in the United States helped her find a lawyer who assisted her in incorporating her business in America. That lawyer then helped her find an "on-paper-only" Argentine partner to facilitate incorporation in Argentina. The business used established leather manufacturers in Buenos Aires to produce Knauer's designs until a problem forced Knauer to use her analytical skills to reassess the situation. "It didn't occur to them [the leather suppliers] that I was expecting what I asked for," she said. "So I looked at the numbers and realized it made more sense to open my own production facility."

Despite her limited Spanish-language skills, Knauer was able to rent space, purchase secondhand machinery, and hire skilled leather workers. She now has seven employees producing 3,000 items a year, and hopes to buy more sewing machines and hire more workers shortly. Qara currently produces travel bags, messenger bags, totes, wallets, and handbags for both men and women made from leather, calfskin, and horsehair. The items are sold through the company's Web site (http://www.qara.com), as well as in two stores, one in Argentina and one in New York City.

Knauer believes the company will be profitable by the end of its second year, but she is running out of money. She is now using her networking skills to attract new investors, and to help her business expand to U. S. department stores.

"It hasn't been easy recruiting Argentina's best craftsmen, building a workshop, and negotiating in a language not my own," says Knauer. "But it's been worth it." While the physical resource of Argentine leather may make her products distinctive, it is obviously Knauer's own entrepreneurial resources that are making her business a success.

SOURCE: Adapted from Tara Siegel Bernard, "Entrepreneur Heads Far South to Launch Firm," *The Wall Street Journal*, February 21, 2006. Retrieved from the Web February 21, 2006, http://www.online.wsj.com/article_print/SB114048480322778606.html, and http://www.qara.com.

porate level, as in a firm's global image. Although technological resources may be short-lived because of innovations and inventions, reputational capital may be relatively long-lived. Many organizations maintain high reputations over long periods of time. *Fortune* magazine's annual survey of corporate reputation indicates that 7 of the top 10 corporations in any given year have appeared in the top 10 many times. The *Fortune* survey uses the following eight different criteria for its rankings:

- The quality of management
- The use of corporate assets
- The firm's financial soundness
- The firm's value as an investment
- The quality of the firm's products and services
- The firm's innovativeness
- The firm's ability to attract, develop, and retain top people
- The firm's commitment to community and environmental responsibility

Our research indicates that the most important of these criteria are product quality, management integrity, and financial soundness.[30] The value of reputational relationships goes beyond personal relationships, because reputations continue even after the individuals originally responsible for them are no longer around (either in that job or with the firm).

Take a moment and reread the case at the end of Chapter 1. It is about a woman who has her proverbial "15 minutes of fame." This marks the start of her reputation-creating and value-capturing strategy. How she manages this good fortune is the key to her business success.

Organizational Resources

Organizational resources include the firm's structure, routines, and systems.[31] The term ordinarily refers to the firm's formal reporting systems, its information-generation and decision-making systems, and its formal or informal planning.

Organizational resources are what the organization does well. Some of the things that an organization does well reside in a person, and we will include these under the Intellectual and Human Resources section below. But many skills reside in a team or group, a department or a functional area: marketing, operations, finance (see below), and research and development. These are the primary skill areas.

The organization's structure is an intangible resource that can make the difference between an organization and its competitors. A structure that promotes speed can be the entrepreneur's most valuable resource. In the postindustrial economy, organizations will be required to make decisions, innovate, and acquire and distribute information more quickly and more frequently than they have in the past.[32]

Organizational structures that separate the innovation function from the production function speed innovation; those that separate marketing from production propel marketing. The appropriateness of the organizational design depends on the complexity and turbulence in the environment.[33] Organizational resources also manifest themselves as the skills and capabilities of the people within the organization. Different combinations of resources can be associated with the age and life-cycle stage of a business. Depending on where the firm is in its life cycle, certain resources are more vital than others. For example, although human capital and experience are more important early on, organizational resources dominate later.[34]

For new ventures that have emerged from the embryonic stage, or those that are a spin-off or business development effort of an ongoing firm, other intangible resources are available. Collective remembered history (myth) and recorded history (files and archives) may also be considered organizational resources. These are part of the organization's past and, to the extent that past is prologue, organizational history will be incorporated into the culture of the new venture, providing a set of rules, norms, policies, and guides for current and future behavior.

Financial Resources

Financial resources represent money assets. Financial resources are generally the firm's borrowing capacity, its ability to raise new equity, and the amount of cash generated by internal operations.[35] Being able to raise money at below-average cost is an advantage attributable to the firm's credit rating and previous financial performance. Various indicators of a venture's financial resources and financial management skills are its debt-to-equity ratio, its cash-to-capital investment ratio, and its external credit rating.

Although start-up entrepreneurs see that access to financial resources is the key to getting into business (it is certainly a necessary component), most agree that financial resources are seldom the source of sustainable competitive advantage. Why is it, then, that fledgling entrepreneurs see money and financial resources as the key to success while established businesses seldom do so? Table 2.1 summarizes the results of a survey that compares high-tech and service-industry entrepreneurs' perceptions of the sources of sustainable competitive advantage. Financial resources did not rank near the top. In fact, financial resources were named by just 16 percent of high-tech manufacturing firms and 23 percent of service firms. Out of 20 different factors mentioned, financial resources were ranked 12th by manufacturers and 6th by service firms.

TABLE 2.1   Sources of Sustainable Competitive Advantage

Factor	High Tech*	Service
Reputation for quality	38	44
Customer service/product support	34	35
Name recognition/profile	12	37
Good management	25	38
Low-cost production	25	13
Financial resources	16	23
Customer orientation/market research	19	23
Product line depth	16	22
Technical superiority	44	6
Installed base of satisfied customers	28	19
Product innovation	22	18

* The numbers represent the frequency of mention by respondents. Numbers may add up to more than 100 percent.

SOURCE: Adapted from D. Aaker, "Managing Assets and Skills: The Key to Sustainable Competitive Advantage," *California Management Review* 31, Winter l989:91–106. Abridged from a list of 20 factors from a study of 248 California businesses.

Limitations of Financial Resources

Why do entrepreneurs think that financial resources are *not* the most important measure of their success? To shed light on this subject, we will examine financial resources according to the four attributes of resources.

Are Financial Resources Valuable? No doubt about it. Valuable resources enable a firm to lower its costs, increase its revenue, and produce its product or service. Without financial resources—that is, money—no firm can get very far. Start-up incurs real financial costs, even for micro and home-based businesses. The axiom that you have to spend money to make money is true, and the entrepreneur who cannot acquire any financial resources may find that his or her dream never becomes a reality.

Are Financial Resources Rare? Sometimes yes and sometimes no. At various times in the business cycle, credit crunches deter banks and other lending institutions from making loans and extending credit. (However, because banks do not often finance pure start-ups, this rarity applies to going concerns.) Similarly, the economic climate that governs initial public offerings (the IPO market) sometimes favors new issues (when the stock market is high and climbing) and at other times discounts new issues heavily (when the market is low and falling). For firms that must spend money before collecting receipts, financial resources are rarer than for firms who can collect receipts and deposits before expenses are paid. Overall, however, financial resources are not rare. It is estimated that each year as much as $6 billion is available through formal investors and an additional $60 billion through informal investors, or "angels." These funds do not include the money invested by the entrepreneur and the top-management team.[36]

Are Financial Resources Hard to Copy? No. One person's money looks and spends the same as another's. Financial resources lead to competitive advantage in trading markets for large transactions only.[37] For example, the leveraged buyout of RJR Nabisco required about $25 billion in financing. Only a few organizations had the connections and were capable of securing that much money: Shearson-American Express; Kohlberg, Kravis, and Roberts; and Forstmann Little. In such a situation, the absolute size of the financial resource is an advantage. Most deals, however, are settled at amounts below $25 billion, and on a strictly financial basis, money is a perfect copy of itself.[38]

Are Financial Resources Nonsubstitutable with Common Resources?

Once again, the technical answer is no. A few entrepreneurs succeed on the basis of sweat equity, and nothing is more common than sweat. This means that most entrepreneurs start very small, on little capital other than their own hard work and efforts. This is called *bootstrapping*. Through frugality, efficient operations, and reinvestment, they are able to grow their businesses. Eventually, they can cross the threshold that makes them attractive to investors. Under certain circumstances, hard work substitutes for outside financing. Another alternative is a relationship with another firm. Strategic alliances can replace financing because they enable the firm to meet its goals without having to make additional investment by piggybacking on the investment of another firm.

To summarize: Financial resources are valuable and necessary, but because financial resources are not rare, hard to duplicate, or nonsubstitutable, they are insufficient (in most cases) to be a source of sustainable competitive advantage.

However, the *management* of financial resources—the firm's organization, processes, and routines that enable it to use its resources more effectively—*can be a source of SCA*. This is because capable financial management involves complexity and a human element that is valuable, rare, hard to copy, and nonsubstitutable. Thus, although money as a resource is inert and static, the ability and skill to manage money is dynamic, complex, and creative.

Intellectual and Human Resources

Intellectual and human resources include the entrepreneur's knowledge, training, and experience, and his or her team of employees and managers. It includes the judgment, insight, creativity, vision, and intelligence of the individual members of an organization. It can even include the social skills of the entrepreneur.[39] Entrepreneurs often perceive great opportunities where others see only competition or chaos; therefore, entrepreneurial perception is a resource. The entrepreneur's values and his or her beliefs about cause and effect can form the initial imprint of the firm's culture. For example, entrepreneurs who believe in racial and cultural diversity and can build a workforce around these values are even more successful than those who do not practice diversity. A new study indicates that diversity interacts with strategy in three ways to enhance performance: improves productivity, improves return on equity, and improves market performance.[40]

One of the fastest-growing entrepreneurial companies that depends on its intellectual resources is Cognizant Technology Solutions of Teaneck, New Jersey (USA) at http://www.cognizant.com/. Cognizant is a software development company for information-intensive firms and industries. It was recently ranked number eight on *Business Week*'s list of hot growth companies. By visiting its Web site, we find that Cognizant shares a great deal of its expertise and prior work online. The site features case studies of previous clients, descriptions of industry practices, and a complete description of corporate advantages. How can the company be so forthcoming? Because its true advantage is embodied in the people it employs and the knowledge and experience that these folks have. Cognizant even runs its own academy. Here is its description from the Web site:

> Our greatest strength is our people's knowledge and it is our associates and managers who deliver the outstanding projects upon which we have built our reputation. Cognizant is committed to facilitating continuous learning among its associates. This commitment plays an important role in ensuring that the associates keep themselves current with leading-edge technologies and executive communication skills so that they can perform their roles effectively and efficiently. (Retrieved from the Web May 10, 2006, http://www.cognizant.com)

In addition, human capital includes **relationship capital** as a subset. Relationship capital refers not to *what* the organization's members know but rather to *who* the organization's members know and what information these people possess. Networking gives the entrepreneur access to resources without controlling them. This access minimizes the potential risk of ownership and keeps overhead down. Entrepreneurial networking has become standard practice, and the old view of the entrepreneur as a rugged individualist has been modified to reflect the realities of today's complex business environment. [41] There is a perspective called the *relational view* of the firm.[42] We incorporate the relational view theory into the resource-based view.

Frequently, the most important and valuable resource that the new venture has is the founding entrepreneur. These are unique people with their own special characteristics, histories that cannot be duplicated, and complex social relationships.

Technological Resources

Technological resources consist of processes, systems, or physical transformations. They may include labs, research and development facilities, and testing and quality control technologies. Knowledge generated by research and development and then protected by patents is a resource, as are formulas, licenses, trademarks, and copyrights. Technological secrets and proprietary processes are resources as well.

There is a distinction between technological capital and intellectual capital. Intellectual capital is embodied in a person or persons and is mobile. If the person or persons leave the firm, so does the capital. Technological resources are physical, intangible, or legal entities and are owned by the organization.

Can complex physical technology provide a basis for SCA? The answer in general must be no. Technological resources—machines, computer systems, equipment, machine tools, robots, complicated electronics, and so on—cannot be the basis for SCA because they can be duplicated and reproduced. There are enough mobile and capable engineering and scientific human resources to take apart and put together any of this complex technology. A patent, however, might make it illegal for a firm's competition to commercially develop an exact copy. However, complex technology is not worthless as a source of competitive advantage. Although a number of firms may have the same complex technology, one firm may be more adept at exploiting this technology through its human or organizational resources. If the method of exploiting the technology is not easy to copy (assuming it is valuable, rare, and difficult to substitute), then other resources can augment technology to provide SCA.[43]

For example, consider information technology (IT). Many would consider IT a rent-generating resource, but not because of the hardware involved. IT has an infrastructure and systems, and these are complex. IT employs human resources with skills and management capabilities that are hard to copy. IT has enabling intangibles, such as knowledge of customer orientations and synergies. High IT capability can lead to improved profits and lower costs.[44]

One company with outstanding technological resources is Sicor. Sicor (Irvine, California) is a pharmaceutical company specializing in injectable products. It is ranked number 15 in *Business Week*'s 2003 list of hot growth companies. (The company has since been acquired by TEVA.) One of Sicor's sources of competitive advantage is its technological resources. It has mastered the manufacture and testing of hundreds of medical compounds in its labs and facilities, as well as the production of injection instruments, the "packaging" for the product. When we go to Sicor's Web site (http://www.sicor.com/), we see that it is an international firm with facilities all over the world. The site also reveals that in addition to its technological resources, Sicor has enormous relationship capital (alliances), intellectual and human resources (world-class scientists and executives), and superb worldwide labs (physical resources).

Strategic Liabilities

Just as ventures and businesses can have strategic resources, they can also have strategic liabilities. This is especially true with respect to incumbent firms. They have resources and capabilities that may well be obsolete. They have relationships with partners who are no longer central, and they belong to networks that are not as relevant as they once were. They may be wedded to technology that has been surpassed. If an entrepreneur enters a market in which other companies have strategic liabilities, the entrepreneur's strategic assets will be enhanced.

Table 2.2 below summarizes the characteristics of the six resources.

To see an example of the effective acquisition and deployment of strategic resources in action, please review the case at the end of the chapter. Zara is a designer, manufacturer, marketer, and retailer of women's fashion clothing. This is a tough business; many such firms fail. But Zara has been able to capture the imagination and the dollars of both European and American women through its systematic use of very hard-to-copy resources. The Zara story is remarkable and ongoing.

A PSYCHOLOGICAL APPROACH

It seemed clear to researchers that people who became entrepreneurs took extraordinary risks and thought in a different way from people who were not entrepreneurs. The study of personality characteristics and traits emphasized the way that enduring behavioral tendencies influence business start-up.

Personality Characteristics

A critical (some might say *the* critical) resource for the new venture is the entrepreneur or founding team. Therefore, we must consider the characteristics of the entrepreneur

TABLE 2.2 Strategic Resources Summary

Resource	Valuable?	Rare?	Hard to copy?	Nonsubstitutable?
Physical	yes	sometimes	not usually	sometimes
Reputational	yes	yes	yes	yes
Organizational	yes	yes	yes	yes
Financial	yes	sometimes	no	no
Intellectual	yes	yes	usually	sometimes
Technological	yes	sometimes	sometimes	sometimes

in the same way that we consider other resources. What entrepreneurial traits make a person rare, valuable, imperfectly imitable, and nonsubstitutable?

Are there personality characteristics that help us predict who will be an entrepreneur and who will not? Some believe that the drive for entrepreneurship is an inherent part of a person's personality. For example, the inventor of kitty litter, the late Edward Lowe, called the inventive and entrepreneurial spirit **beagleism.** He didn't believe someone could go to school to be an entrepreneur, or simply decide to become one out of the blue. Lowe believed that becoming an entrepreneur was as natural to a person as chasing a rabbit is to a beagle.[45]

Street Story 2.3 tells of one such beagle—Jeff Fluhr, founder of Stubhub, Inc. Fluhr showed entrepreneurial promise early, but not until he dropped out of Stanford University did he create his best venture. Does he have a key personality trait that is responsible for his success, or does his marshaling of resources and capabilities prove decisive?

Who will be a successful entrepreneur and who will not? Over the past few decades, entrepreneurial research has identified a number of personality characteristics that differentiate entrepreneurs from others.[46] Among the most frequently discussed are the need for achievement, locus of control, and risk-taking propensity.

The Need for Achievement. The entrepreneurial need for achievement, or **n Ach,** was first identified as a personality trait by McClelland in his work on economic development.[47] People with high levels of n Ach have a strong desire to solve problems on their own, enjoy setting goals and achieving them through their own efforts, and like receiving feedback on how they are doing. They are moderate risk takers.

However, the link between n Ach and entrepreneurship has not always held up in empirical testing. Researchers who have attempted to replicate McClelland's findings or apply them in other settings have occasionally been disappointed. For example, n Ach is a weak predictor of a person's tendency to start a business, and people specially trained to have high n Ach sometimes perform no differently than a control group that receives no training. The causal link between n Ach and small business ownership has not been proven.[48]

Locus of Control. A second trait often associated with entrepreneurship is **locus of control.**[49] In locus-of-control theory, there are two types of people: (1) **externals,** those who believe that what happens to them is a result of fate, chance, luck, or forces beyond their control; and (2) **internals,** those who believe that for the most part the future is theirs to control through their own efforts. Clearly, people who undertake a new business must believe that their personal efforts will have something to do with the business' future performance.

This theory suggests that internals are more entrepreneurial than externals. Evidence supporting this hypothesis, though, has been inconclusive.[50] Some studies have shown that more internals are entrepreneurs, but others show no difference between entrepreneurs and other people. In fact, we can argue that any good manager must also possess the qualities of an internal, that is, must be a person who believes that efforts affect out-

Ticket Master

One of Jeff Fluhr's classmates from elementary school claims he had entrepreneurial spirit even then. "I can remember him as a kid wanting to buy vending machines, stuff that the average sixth grader was not interested in," recalls David Fisch, who now works in finance for Fluhr's company.

Fluhr's mother remembers that he was reprimanded in junior high school for selling candy out of his locker. She also recalls that after falling in love with a toy he spotted when he was on vacation, he contacted the manufacturer and convinced them to make him a distributor in his home state of New Jersey. "They had no idea they were talking to a 12-year-old," his mother says. Entrepreneurship may be in Fluhr's blood; his mother operates a women's designer clothing resale shop in Manhattan, and her grandfather once owned a resale fur shop.

Fluhr worked for a stockbroker for a short time during high school, and then went on to earn a dual degree in systems engineering and finance at the University of Pennsylvania. After college, he executed large leveraged buyout transactions for The Blackstone Group, and was a founding professional in the private, equity-investing group at Thomas Weisel Partners before he enrolled in Stanford University's Graduate School of Business.

At Stanford, Fluhr and a classmate entered a business plan competition with an idea for a Web site that would auction tickets for sporting events or concerts. Their plan didn't win because Fluhr withdrew it before dropping out of school. In 2000, that business plan evolved into StubHub, a company that is now estimated to have $200 million in sales volume (in a $10 billion market).

If you have tickets you can't use for a football game, or if you want to get tickets to a concert that is sold out, www.StubHub.com may be the place to point your Web browser. Dedicated strictly to tickets, StubHub allows potential sellers to post tickets on its Web site, and then try to sell them by set price, auction, or for a declining price, meaning a price that is lowered as the event approaches. StubHub takes 15 percent from sellers and 10 percent from buyers, and provides prepaid FedEx shipping for delivering the tickets, passing that cost along to the buyers.

While selling tickets, or even reselling them on the Internet, is hardly revolutionary, a few distinctive features contribute to StubHub's success. Fluhr's company charges a commission instead of a listing fee like eBay; StubHub facilitates delivery and guarantees that buyers will receive their tickets on time or receive replacements. The company also reduces risk by offering 24/7 customer service by phone and providing refunds if an event is canceled. Instead of splitting commissions from the sale of extra season ticket holders' tickets, StubHub now pays the team a flat fee in exchange for the team's endorsement.

Fluhr says he continues to spend a large chunk of his time on marketing, business development, and recruiting for StubHub, possibly because this born entrepreneur is preparing for what he sees as the future for online ticket sales—prices that fluctuate according to supply and demand from the moment the tickets go on sale.

Addendum: In January 2007, eBay bought Stubhub for $310 million.

SOURCE: Adapted from Steve Stecklow, "Web Site Conceived in School Is Now a Leader in Hawking Access to Sold-Out Events," *The Wall Street Journal*, January 17, 2005: B1. See also http://www.StubHub.com, and "eBay's Strong Earnings," *The Wall Street Journal*, January 25, 2007:A3.

comes. Thus, while locus of control may differentiate people who believe in astrology from those who do not, it may not make a distinction between potential entrepreneurs and potential managers, or just plain business students.

Risk-Taking Propensity. Are people with a **risk-taking propensity** high entrepreneurial achievers? Because the task of new venture creation is apparently fraught with risk, and the financing of these ventures is often called *risk capital,* researchers have tried to determine whether entrepreneurs take more risks than other businesspeople. This hypothesis has been tested in a number of ways, but the work by Brockhaus has been most incisive.[51]

In Brockhaus' research, the risk-taking propensities of entrepreneurs were tested objectively via a series of decision scenarios. The results obtained from the entrepreneurs were compared with those obtained from a sample of managers. The study concluded that a risk-taking propensity is not a distinguishing characteristic of entrepreneurs.

Dispositional Optimism. Dispositional optimism refers to generalized outcome expectancies that good things, rather than bad things, will happen; pessimism refers to the tendency to expect negative outcomes in the future.[52] Researchers have found that entrepreneurs are much more optimistic than nonentrepreneurs and the population at large.[53] This optimism may be the best distinguishing trait of the entrepreneur. However, further research on the subject is necessary.

Limits of the Trait Approach

Overall, the trait approach has not been successful at providing the decisive criteria for distinguishing entrepreneurs from others. What distinguishes entrepreneurs from nonentrepreneurs is that entrepreneurs start new businesses and others do not.[54]

One researcher described the search for the entrepreneurial trait this way: "My own personal experience was that for 10 years we ran a research center in entrepreneurial history, for 10 years we tried to define the entrepreneur. We never succeeded. Each of us had some notion of it—what he thought was, for his purposes, a useful definition. And I don't think you're going to get farther than that."[55]

The trait approach looks inside the entrepreneur for an answer. What it frequently ignores is that many of these traits are also present in excellent managers, football coaches, and health-care professionals. The traits do not tell us who will be a successful entrepreneur, but they do hint at what qualities might be required for success at any endeavor. Traits are more useful when they are viewed as precursors to behaviors. Entrepreneurship is not a psychological tendency; it is the act of starting a business. Therefore, it would be better to look at someone's skills and actions rather than his or her personality traits.

In a recent anthology of the psychology of the entrepreneur, the authors presented a structural equation model displaying the relationships between traits and behaviors on venture growth (the numerical values represent the relative contribution to venture growth holding the other values constant).[56] Their findings suggest the following *direct* effects on venture growth:

- All psychological traits (together) are related by +.06 to new venture growth.

- Communicated vision is related by +.22.
- Goal setting is related by +.26.
- Self-efficacy (the ability to produce the desired effect) is related by +.34.

It is true that traits help to explain behavior, but it is behavior that is related to the venture growth variable.

Our resource-based theory suggests that actions and competencies (what one can do; skills) are much more important than psychological traits. To understand entrepreneurship, we must look for capabilities and circumstances that produce differences, not similarities. To do so, we turn to a sociological framework that emphasizes personal history and the uniqueness of an individual's path to new venture creation.

A SOCIOLOGICAL APPROACH

How else are entrepreneurs unique? Each has a unique background, history, and biography. The sociological approach tries to explain the social conditions from which entrepreneurs emerge and the social factors that influence their decisions to start new ventures. A sociological model is presented in Figure 2.2.[57] It depicts the decision to become an entrepreneur as a function of two factors: the impetus factor and the situational factor. It is a supply model of entrepreneurship because it indicates the sources of entrepreneurial spirit and activity. The model is multiplicative: A zero on either of the causes means a failure to produce the entrepreneurial event.

Impetus for Entrepreneurship

What propels entrepreneurs toward self-employment? There are four factors: negative displacement, being between things, positive push, and positive pull. A recent study proposed that pull entrepreneurs may perform better than push entrepreneurs, and those that can be classified as both push and pull may be the most motivated of all.[58]

Negative Displacement

Figure 2.2 begins with the notion that people who find themselves displaced in some negative way may become entrepreneurs. **Negative displacement** is the alienation of individuals or groups of individuals from the core of society. These individuals or groups may be seen as "not fitting in" to the main flow of social and economic life.

Some recent survey analysis supports the negative displacement factor (see also below, "between things"). In a 2004 study by the "Global Entrepreneurship Monitor," researchers collected data on U.S. entrepreneurs and their level of education. This information appears in Figure 2.3.

The figure illustrates that being between things (not finishing a complete degree) or having negative displacement (being a high school dropout) are significant factors for many entrepreneurs. Indeed, college dropouts are better represented among entrepreneurs than college graduates. But there is often a difference in the types of businesses founded. High school dropouts engage in "necessity-based" entrepreneurship (3.6%). They start a business because they have limited opportunities for employment; they have to be self-employed. The group with the highest educational level has the least necessity-based entrepreneurship (6%).

FIGURE 2.2   The Supply of Entrepreneurship

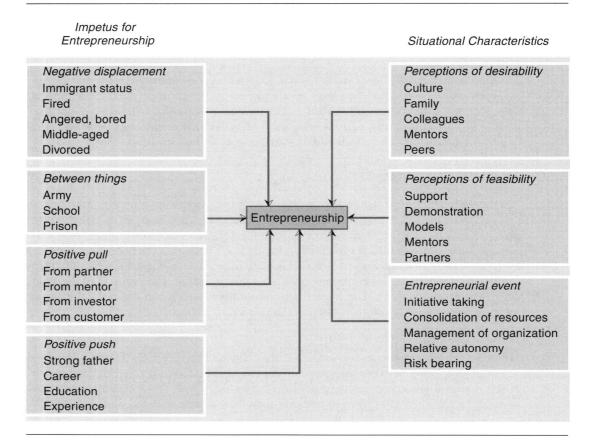

FIGURE 2.3   Percentage of U.S Entrepreneurs by Level of Education

Tech/professional school/business school	17.8%
Post high school/no degree	13.7
College degree	12.8
High school dropout	12.0
Post college experience	11.4
High school graduate	10.4
Grade school	6.2

SOURCE: Kauffman Foundation, Babson College. Reported in *The Wall Street Journal*, September 7, 2004: B4.

Recent immigrants and refugees are also affected by negative displacement. Because they are on the outer fringes of the economy and of society, they are sensitive to the allure of self-employment; having no one to depend on, they depend on no one. In societies where economic rights are more easily exercised than political rights, immigrants turn to entrepreneurship. Throughout the world, for example, Asian and Jewish immigrants, wherever they have settled, have gone into business for themselves. Recent trends in the United States demonstrate high levels of entrepreneurship in the Hispanic, Vietnamese, and Korean populations. One statistical estimate of Korean immigrants in the New York City area concludes that 65 percent of Korean families own at least one business.[59] Take the example of Jung Pack, a Korean who immigrated to the United States in 1982. Jung works 16 hours a day in his own grocery business even though he has a college degree in business administration and was in construction management back in Korea. Jung says he left Korea because it was too rural; he wanted to live in a big "cosmopolitan" country. However, when he arrived in the United States, downward mobility forced him to give up his vision of a white-collar career as a self-employed shopkeeper. His career in the United States has been blocked by the language barrier and skepticism about the value of his academic degree. But Jung can probably expect his two children, who will be U.S. citizens, to pursue either professional careers or entrepreneurial opportunities in business services like data processing or management consulting. Meanwhile, Jung says he still dreams of "a better life."

Other negative displacements result from being fired from a job or being angered or bored by one's current employment. Many bored managers and stifled executives in large corporations are leaving their white-collar jobs and looking for challenges and autonomy. According to Harry Levinson, a Harvard psychologist who specializes in career and life-cycle issues, "The entrepreneur, psychologically speaking, has a lot more freedom than anybody in a big corporation."[60] Consider the case, for example, of Philip Schwartz, who was an executive with Olin Corporation and Airco Inc. Schwartz left his middle-level managerial career to start a business as a wholesaler of packaging materials and cleaning supplies and to find out "who and what I am." He reports that he enjoys the autonomy and action of drumming up business and interacting with customers. He enjoys putting his own personal stamp on his company. Having only four employees, he can create a family atmosphere, relaxed and friendly. He imprints his own values of honesty and dependability on the business, something that no middle-level corporate managers can do.[61]

Middle age or divorce may also provide the impetus for new venture creation. In an unusual example, one entrepreneur recreated his business because of a midlife crisis. Tom Chappell cofounded a personal-care and health-products business, Tom's of Maine, Inc. A number of years ago, Chappell realized that he was not happy running this business even though he was successful. He went back to school and obtained a master's degree from Harvard Divinity School. His studies led him to examine his values and his motivation for managing his own firm. He changed the company's goals, making its mission to "address community concerns, in Maine and around the globe, by devoting a portion of our time, talent and resources to the environment, human needs, the arts and education."[62]

"Between Things"

People who are between things are also more likely to seek entrepreneurial outlets than those who are in the middle of things. Like immigrants, people who are between things are sometimes outsiders. The model in Figure 2.2 gives three examples of this state:

between military and civilian life, between student life and a career, and between prison and freedom.

Positive Pull

Positive influences also lead to the decision to investigate entrepreneurship; these are called **positive pull** influences. They can come from a potential partner, a mentor, a parent, an investor, or a customer. The potential partner encourages the individual by sharing his or her experience, helping with the work, and spreading the risk. The mentor raises self-esteem and confidence. Mentors and partners can also introduce the entrepreneur to people who are inside the social and economic network for new venture activity.[63] There also appears to be a relationship between a parent's occupation and off-spring entrepreneurship: Many entrepreneurs have a strong self-employed father figure in the family.[64] Investors who provide the initial financing may convince the individual that "there may be more where that came from." The prospect of a potential customer pulling the entrepreneur into business raises some difficult ethical and economic issues.[65] However, having a guaranteed market for products or services is a temptation few can resist.

Positive Push

The final category of situations that provide impetus and momentum for entrepreneurship is **positive push.** Positive-push factors include such things as a career path that offers entrepreneurial opportunities or an education that gives the individual the appropriate knowledge and opportunity.

What types of career choices can people make that put them in a good position to become entrepreneurs? Two types of career paths can lead to entrepreneurship. The first is the **industry path.** A person prepares for a job or career in a particular industry and learns everything there is to know about that industry. Because all industries change over time, entrepreneurial opportunities that exploit that change come and go. A person with a deep knowledge of an industry is in an excellent position to develop a business that fills a niche or gap created by industry change.

People taking the industry path to new venture creation view specialized knowledge as their key resource. That knowledge may be embodied in particular people, a technology, or a system or process. The new firm may be a head-to-head competitor, it may serve a new niche not served by the former employer, or it may be an upstream firm (a supplier) or a downstream firm (a distributor or retailer). Whatever its functional form, a spin-off is a knowledge-based business; its primary resources are its competencies, experiences, networks, and contacts.[66] The challenge for these people is to procure the other resources, financial and physical, that will enable them to make their plan a reality.

A different approach, the **sentry path,** emphasizes money and "the deal." People with careers in sentry positions see many different opportunities in many different industries. They tend to be lawyers, accountants, consultants, bankers (especially business loan officers), and brokers. These people learn how to make deals and find money. They have contacts that enable them to raise money quickly when the right property comes along. The challenge for these people, because they are experts in the "art of the deal" and not part of any particular industry, is to locate and retain good managers.

Situational Characteristics

Once an individual's inclination to become an entrepreneur has been activated, situational characteristics help determine if the new venture will take place. The two situational factors are perceptions of desirability and perceptions of feasibility.

Perceptions of Desirability. Entrepreneurship must be seen as desirable if one is going to pursue it. The factors that affect the perceptions of desirability can come from the individual's culture, family, peers and colleagues, or mentors. For example, the Sikhs and Punjabis, who dominate the service-station business in New York City, also dominate the transportation and mechanics business in their home country. Sometimes religion can spark entrepreneurship and legitimize the perception of desirability. For example, Zen Buddhist communities are historically self-sufficient economically and provide the background for the story of an unusual entrepreneur, Bernard Glassman.

Glassman was born the son of immigrant Jewish parents and trained as a systems engineer; now he is building a better world by combining Zen entrepreneurship with a mission to help people at the bottom of the economic ladder. After Glassman's introduction to Buddhism, he found that meditation alone could not meet his spiritual needs, so he chose the "Way of Entrepreneurship." In 1983, he and his Zen community launched Greyston Bakery in Yonkers, New York, supplying high-priced pies and cakes to wealthy consumers. Glassman received his early training as a baker from another Zen sect in San Francisco. Today his bakery grosses $1.2 million and employs 200 people whom many previously considered unemployable. Many entrepreneurs say that they want to help the poor and needy, but Glassman has made it happen. Through Greyston's profits, he has been able to renovate buildings, provide counseling services, and open a day-care center. However, he still has to pay close attention to the bottom line; the bakery is his mandala and he must concentrate intensely to make it a success.[67]

Perceptions of Feasibility. Entrepreneurship must be seen as feasible if is to be undertaken. Readiness and desirability are not enough. Potential entrepreneurs need models and examples of what can be accomplished. They require support from others— emotional, financial, and physical support. Consider Jessica Rolph. She had worked for the Federal Trade Commission in Washington and had been a political consultant for an Internet company. She wanted to be in business for herself, but as she said, "lacked the one big idea." Enter Shazi Visram. She had a degree in visual arts from Columbia University, and was teaching children how to use the Internet for a nonprofit organization. The two met through mutual friends, and Visram described her idea for "producing and marketing organic food for babies." No one had quite understood the power of this idea until Visram met Rolph. They used their own money to prepare their pitch and raised $500,000 from angels and manufacturers. They even won a $10,000 prize for women-owned businesses. They named their company Nurture Inc. and their frozen baby food is expected on the market any time now. Rolph concludes that the venture was, "a choice between risking your personal security and your personal happiness." Visram says of her partner, "Jessica . . . somehow understood why I was doing what I was doing. She understood the concept of giving back to society."[68]

What happens next? At the end of the process shown in Figure 2.2, the new venture creation process begins. As we will see in the following chapters, the complement to the "resource and capabilities approach" is the "opportunity recognition and analysis" process. In Chapter 3, we will look at the process of opportunity recognition and its dimensions. For now, we can summarize the pre-entrepreneurial conditions that result in the entrepreneurial event, that is, in the creation and management of a new venture. One model of this process comprises five components.[69]

1. *Initiative.* An individual or team, having been brought to the state of readiness by personal factors and by perceptions of desirability and feasibility, begins to act. Evidence of initiative usually includes scanning the environment for opportunities, searching for information, and doing research.
2. *Consolidation of resources.* Levels of resource needs are estimated, alternatives for procurement are considered, and timing of resource arrival is charted and eventually consolidated into a pattern of business activity that can be called an organization.
3. *Management of the organization.* The business' resource acquisition, transformation, and disposal are routinized and systematized. Those elements that are not easily systematized are managed separately. No entrepreneur behaves in an entrepreneurial manner all the time. There are forces acting on the individual that sometimes make entrepreneurial behavior appropriate and at other times make administrative or managerial behavior appropriate.[70]

The management of the new venture is characterized by free choice of strategy, structure, and processes—*autonomous action*. The initiators have put themselves at risk—*risk taking*. They are personally affected by the business' variability of returns and by its possible success or failure. Each entrepreneur assesses the forces pushing for entrepreneurial action and those requiring administrative action, and then makes the choice that is best for the new venture.

SUMMARY

This chapter presents the basic concepts of the resource-based theory, including the four attributes of resources necessary to achieve sustainable competitive advantage: rare, valuable, hard to copy, and nonsubstitutable. Our resource-based theory allows that certain aspects of entrepreneurship are not analyzable: They are causally ambiguous because no one, including the founders, quite understands how or why they work. New ventures created around the possession and controllability of resources with these characteristics have the potential to be rewarding, forgiving, and enduring.

The chapter also describes the six types of resources: physical, reputational, organizational, financial, intellectual/human, and technological. These are the basic profit factors to be used in assessing the potential of the new venture. All of the resources are important for the new venture, but the ones that are most likely to lead to competitive advantage are organizational, reputational, and human resources.

The entrepreneur is the primary human resource for the new venture. Although it is uncertain what, if any, personality traits make the best entrepreneurs, the entrepreneur's life history, experience, and knowledge make each founder a unique resource.

KEY TERMS

Ach (need for achievement)
Beagleism
Capabilities
Characteristic ambiguity
Competitive advantage
Dispositional optimism
Dynamic improvement capability
Entrepreneurial capability
Entrepreneurial system
Externals
Functional capability
Imperfectly imitable (hard to copy)
Industry path
Internals
Linkage ambiguity
Locus of control
Negative displacement

Nonsubstitutability
Organizational culture
Positive pull
Positive push
PROFIT model
Rare resources
Relationship capital
Resource
Resource-based theory
Resource-based view (RBV)
Risk-taking propensity
Sentry path
Skills
Sustainable competitive advantage (SCA)
Valuable resources
VRIN model

DISCUSSION QUESTIONS

1. What are the characteristics of a good theory? What makes a theory practical? How can an entrepreneur use the resource-based theory for his or her advantage?
2. Explain the problems we would have if there was a "law of entrepreneurship."
3. How does each of the four attributes of resources contribute to SCA?
4. What is the difference between competitive advantage and sustainable competitive advantage?
5. How can an organization's culture be a source of SCA?
6. Describe how each of the six types of resources can be a source of SCA. What are the strengths and weaknesses of each type?
7. Why are personality traits not sufficient for evaluating and predicting successful entrepreneurship?
8. Describe the sociological approach to entrepreneurship. How can this approach be used to promote more entrepreneurship within the economy?
9. If immigrants are a major source of entrepreneurship in an economy, why do most countries limit the number of immigrants they allow in each year?
10. How are entrepreneurs behaviorally different from managers? When can we expect entrepreneurs to behave managerially? When can we expect managers to behave as entrepreneurs?

EXERCISES

1. Research a company and inventory its resource base by using the six types of resources discussed in the chapter. Evaluate these resources in terms of the four attributes of resources

necessary for SCA. Does the company have a competitive advantage? A sustainable competitive advantage? What recommendations about resource procurement and development would you make for this company?

2. Interview an entrepreneur. Ask the entrepreneur to describe the keys to successful entrepreneurship. Ask the entrepreneur to estimate how much of his or her success was the result of luck or unknown factors. Do the answers seem to fit the resource-based model?

3. Inventory your personal resource base by using the six types of resources described in the chapter. Evaluate these resources by employing the four criteria. Comment on your individual potential to start a business that has the prospect of achieving SCA.

4. If you are in a group with other students, inventory the group's resources and repeat exercise 3.

5. Assume you have access to your college or university's resources. Redo your inventories (see exercises 3 and 4). How have you increased your potential for competitive advantage?

——————— EXERCISES FOR WRITING A BUSINESS PLAN ———————

Beginning with this chapter, the exercises are designed to prepare the student to develop and write a business plan. These exercises may be done either individually or in a group setting.

1. Exercise envisioning. Sit in a quiet and dark room and begin to think about what kind of business you would like to start. Close your eyes and let your mind's eye see yourself working in that business. What do you see? Is it a manufacturing business, a service or retail outlet, a construction site, or something else? Notice the physical setting and the people. What are they doing? Which are employees and which are customers? Are the people happy? Busy? Confused?

2. Develop 20 ideas for a new business. Make the 20 ideas into 100 ideas, no matter how unusual or apparently strange. Sort the ideas into the 10 best, and make the concepts more original. At the end of the exercise, you should have 20 to 30 truly creative new business ideas.

3. For each of the group or individual's best ideas, do the following short assignment:
   a. Describe the business in 25 words or less. The description should include the product/service, the customer, and the technology employed.
   b. Describe the opportunity that you believe this business exploits. In other words, why do you think this is a great business idea?
   c. Describe the resources you believe you would need to execute this new venture idea. Use the six categories from Chapter 2. Which resource(s) will be the source of competitive advantage?
   d. Estimate how much money it would cost to actually get this business started. The estimate will be very rough, but try to make an educated guess.

A Special Flair for Fashion

Have you ever tried to describe an item you want to a salesperson in a clothing store, and then watched that person shake his or her head and shrug his or her shoulders?

Maybe you should be shopping at Zara. This Spanish chain is now one of the world's fastest-growing retailers of affordable fashion clothing for women, men, and children, and a big reason behind their success is the fact that they listen to what their customers want.

Zara uses point-of-sale terminals to track every purchase in each of their 900 stores, and then uses that data to determine what kind of clothes to make and ship to their stores in the future. In other words, Zara doesn't decide in advance whether to push short skirts or long skirts this season; they wait to see what the customer is buying. The company describes their approach by saying that Zara "is in step with society, dressing the ideas, trends and tastes that society itself has developed." Store managers also use a personal digital assistant to see what designs are available, and then place weekly orders for the items they think will sell best in their store.

While other retailers claim to be responsive to customer demands, Zara adds some oomph to their boast. Most retailers have to order their inventory months in advance, but Zara is able to manufacture and ship replacement garments in two weeks, and create and deliver new garments with a fresh design in just five weeks. (When Madonna recently gave a series of concerts in Spain, fans appeared at her last show wearing a Zara copy of the outfit the pop star wore at her first show.) The company does this by employing 200 designers, including many recent graduates of top design schools, at their head office in northern Spain. Almost all of their merchandise is produced by several hundred sewing cooperatives in the home office area.

When the garments are done they are returned to Zara's huge warehouses where they are checked, ironed, packaged, and sorted for immediate delivery by either truck or air.

Even when an item is a hot seller, Zara produces its slightly updated replacements in relatively small lots. Veteran shoppers know that when they see something they like at Zara they'd better grab it, and they also know that only a limited number of shoppers will be able to buy an identical garment. Small batches means that Zara's inventory always looks new and fresh; the chain introduces about 11,000 different items each year, as compared to the 2,000 to 4,000 items annually introduced by competitors like Gap or H&M. Their lean and mean approach also means that Zara is rarely forced to discount garments, unlike other retailers at the end of a season.

While Zara's approach is based on technology, it is actually the efficient use of relatively simple technology. The company also spends less than 0.3 percent of sales on advertising, while many of its competitors generally spend more than 3 percent. This containment of expenses also contributes to Zara's success. In 2005, the Inditex group, which operates Zara and seven other similar concept soft-good chain stores (including Pull and Bear, Massimo Dutti, Bershka, Stradivarius, Oysho, Zara Home, and Kiddy's Class), posted sales of 6.7 billion euros, equal to 8.6 billion dollars, an increase of 21 percent over its 2004 figures. Since opening its first Zara store in 1975, Inditex has grown to more than 2,800 stores in 64 countries, and the company hopes to expand to more than 4,000 stores over the next three years.

SOURCE: Adapted from "The Future of Fast Fashion," *Economist*, June 18, 2005: 57-58, and www.zara.com and www.inditex.com.

Case Questions

1. Zara is different from other companies. Using Table 2.1, what do you think are the most important factors affecting Zara's SCA, and what are the least important factors?
2. What other industries could use an approach like Zara's?
3. What can Zara do to make sure it maintains its competitive advantage(s) in the future?
4. Do you think a company like Zara could function in the United States? What conditions would make it easier, and what conditions would make it more difficult?

APPENDIX

Creativity and Idea Generation

The famous management and entrepreneurship guru, Peter Drucker, believed that a combination of systematic environmental analysis and creativity could lead businesses and entrepreneurs to find new opportunities for entrepreneurship and innovation. In his book, *Innovation and Entrepreneurship* (New York: Harper and Row, 1985), Drucker details seven sources of ideas for new businesses. These were described in Chapter 1.

How can we use Drucker's sources of change to generate ideas for ourselves? We can do so by combining environmental scanning with creativity techniques. After we read and work through the following sections on creativity, we will be ready to generate some business ideas for our projects.

The Concept of Creativity

Creativity is the initiation of a product or process that is useful, correct, appropriate, and valuable to the task at hand where that task is heuristic rather than algorithmic. A heuristic is an incomplete guideline or rule of thumb that leads to understanding, learning, or discovery. It is a fuzzy map of where we are and where we are going, but the roads are not completely drawn in. Heuristics serve to stimulate a person to learn more; they are similar to determining how to get from A to B on a blurry, indistinct roadmap.

An algorithm, in contrast, is a mechanical set of rules, a preset plan of operations for problem solving, decision making, and conflict resolution. Flipping a coin is an algorithm because the two sides of the coin and the indicators of head and tails predetermine exactly what the outcomes will be after the coin is tossed in the air.

Perhaps a better question than, "What is creativity?" is "Where is creativity?" Creativity occurs at the dynamic intersection of three forces (T. Amabile, *The Social Psychology of Creativity* [New York: Springer Verlag, 1983]). These forces are:

1. The individual, with his or her intelligence, experience and dispositions
2. The domain of knowledge within which the particular individual has chosen to work
3. The field or social context within which the merits of the work or product produced are evaluated and judged

We are now quite familiar with the first force, that of the individual. Some of the attributes of creative people, discussed in the literature on creativity, are curiosity, openness to new experiences, tolerance of ambiguity, independence of judgment, sensitivity to problems, flexibility, and originality. One of the better ways to think of individual tendencies is by using the Kirton Adaptor-Innovator theory (KAI). The KAI postulates that everyone is creative in either one of two ways. Some people are good at figuring out how to "do things better." This is an improvement approach to creativity. People who can do things better find ways to incrementally change what is already in existence. People who are good at the "do-things-differently" approach are creative in finding new and novel solutions to problems. But research has found that this trait approach is insufficient; therefore, we need to consider other variables.

We also need to consider the domain of knowledge. Here we may be referring to arts, like music or painting; sciences, like computer science or biology; or a business area, like finance, marketing, product development, or new venture creation. People can only be creative if they are prepared to be creative, which means they must have some understanding of a knowledge base and some skills at manipulating this base. It is also true that one can know "too much" about a domain of knowledge and uncritically accept all of its forms, premises, assumptions, and values. An individual who accepts all of these things might have a difficult time producing divergent thinking—ideas that modify or substitute for the conventional wisdom.

The last force is the field or social context. For an idea or product to be judged creative (as opposed to simply crazy or weird), it must be considered valuable and meritorious. Who does the judging? In the case of fine art, this work is done by critics, curators, and experts. In the case of business-related creativity, the organization and inevitably the market make these judgments. If an idea sells, it was creative; if it does not sell, it was not creative. This sort of retrospective evaluation is part of the paradox of creativity. If there were rules that one could formulate *a priori,* then one would have developed an algorithm, and its product could no longer be considered creative.

Types of Creative Behavior

All creative behavior can be described in one of three general ways. Creation is the act of pure invention—making something out of nothing. A writer facing a blank page "creates" characters, plot, and action. For example, Beethoven created symphonies from scratch. People generally consider this the only type of creativity. Because we associate it with heroic efforts and classic works of art and science, we tend to believe that creativity is a gift from the gods and is available to only a chosen few. But there are other types of creativity that are just as important and within the reach of mere mortals.

Synthesis is the creative act of joining together two previously unrelated things. It is bringing together the telephone with the computer, or combining a theory of evolutionary biology with economics. Synthesis is the creativity we find in humor, when two incongruous elements are combined to make something appear funny. Synthesis can have a major impact on a market or a product. For example, the Japanese created synthesis when they merged statistical methods, quality control, and systems thinking in the manufacture of automobiles. The synthesis of direct-selling methods with the cosmetics industry created Avon. And the synthesis of the computer with the concept of small and personal led to the creation of Apple Computer (http://www.apple.com). In retrospect, all successful creative acts look logical and predictable through the historical lens because they work. But at the time of the creative act and the birth of the creative product, the creator cannot judge the value of any particular outcome.

Another type of creativity is modification. Modification occurs when a thing or a process is improved or gains a new application. A modification can be quite small—a change in design, a new floor plan for an office, a new way to solder electrical connections along an assembly line. Clearly, no heroic acts are needed for a modification, and therefore creativity is within the reach of all people, and is in fact a natural part of all human experience.

Analogy is the creative act of seeing how one thing is like another. It enables us to take an action or use a product that was originally meant for one purpose, but has other purposes as well. For example, a common screw is also a propeller. A television commercial is like a little movie, and so is a music video. There are many instances of one industry borrowing a practice or product from another and putting it to effective use. The people who think of these transfers are doing so by making an analogy—seeing how the problem they face is like a problem that was faced by others in the past.

Creativity and the Resource-Based Theory

What are the links between creative entrepreneurship and competitive advantage? Because creative ideas are based on imagination, they are hard to duplicate, rare and intuitive, and not easily substituted with expert systems and artificial intelligence. Creativity has always been of interest to researchers and practitioners in the field of new venture creation, not because it is magical and metaphysical, but because economic advantage can be derived from creativity. The requirement that creative behavior be of value (as opposed to simply weird) is clearly in line with our resource-based model. A creative act is not valuable in and of itself unless it is appropriate to the situation; here the situation is the creation of a new product or process. The creative act must therefore in some way contribute to the new venture's objectives of gaining revenues or lowering costs (which encompasses all the nuances and permutations that can be included in the firm's revenue and cost functions).

All humans have creative abilities to some extent; the evidence is in our dreams. But creativity is rare in organizations because organizations have elements that suppress creative thinking, creative behavior, and the use of creative programs and processes. The barriers to innovation and creativity in large organizations are quite real, for the repressing side of "big business" has a decided slant toward uniformity. Inventors and entrepreneurs need longtime horizons, flexibility, incentives, and motivation to succeed. In large organizations, the forces against creativity may be so strong that separate business units may be required.

Creativity is one of the most important resource advantages because it is so difficult to duplicate. Its elusive nature has stumped philosophers and entrepreneurs since the beginning of recorded time. Attempts have been made to stimulate the creative impulse, from meditation techniques to computer simulations. Not only should the entrepreneur covet and encourage creative impulses in him- or herself and others, he or she needs to engender a culture that transforms creative energy into economically (as opposed to psychologically) rewarding forms.

Creativity Techniques

An individual can learn to be more creative by understanding the process of creativity and mastering a few simple techniques. These techniques can be used by a single person working on a problem that calls for a creative solution, or they can applied within a group setting. The key to using these techniques is to overcome the linear thinking and the traditional linkages between things and events, and employ lateral thinking, which encourages innovation by challenging concepts, perceptions, and assumptions, and provoking incongruity (E. De Bono, *Serious Creativity* [New York: Harper & Row, 1992]).

The Creative Pause. Trying to force a creative solution is impossible, but we can make an effort to find one. The creative pause is a deliberate interruption in the routine flow of work in order to concentrate on a point or process. At what point does the pause occur? It doesn't matter. And there need be no particular reason for that pause at that time. This pause is a technique that makes people aware that they are doing something routine, and enables them to question why they are doing it a particular way, or if they should be doing it at all.

Focus. Simple focus is paying attention and concentrating. There need not be a problem to solve. Such focus simply means questioning the linear thinking embedded in any routine. The target of one's focus can be an object, a process, or a policy. When using specific focus, a person has a defined target, such as looking for new ideas to serve customers, or generating creative ways to reduce the cost of handling materials. Although the specific focus technique requires that the user have knowledge of the domain, it is not dependent on increasing the amount of knowledge, but rather on using existing knowledge in new ways.

Challenge. Using the creative challenge, people question why something is done a certain way, and if there are other ways of doing it. We challenge the historical and traditional processes. Such challenge is not meant to be an exercise in criticism. We may challenge something that works quite well while looking for a better way. The creative challenge does not accept the view that there is one best way to do something, or that the current way is the optimal way.

Alternatives. Generating alternatives is the most basic creative response. However, we usually engage in this exercise only when we feel a need or have a problem. Creative alternatives can be generated at any time and applied to anything, even when there is no crisis. Creating alternatives is a two-stage process: (1) We need to find out what alternatives are already available because there is no sense in reinventing the wheel, and (2) We must design new alternatives or ways to do things. The first stage is information gathering, but the second is about being creative.

Provocation. Creative provocations are experiments in thought. Deliberate provocations force a person to consider incongruities, discontinuities, and seemingly impossible events and situations. The key to using the provocation technique is the childlike question, "What if?" and working backward from there, to determine the implications of the question. Einstein asked, "What if I could ride on a beam of light? What would I see?" and from this thought experiment, he derived the conditions of relativity.

Mind Mapping. This is a technique that works through mental and linguistic associations. It enables the user to break through the "wall of rationality" surrounding a proposition. Mind mapping is a multistage process that starts with a clear statement of the problem at hand in order to search for a creative approach to that problem. Free association follows as a map of free associations is generated and some arbitrary limit is reached. Then the map is studied for patterns, novelties, and interesting insights. Above is a mind map that helps illustrate how the process works.

Mind Map Guidlines mind map with branches: Clarity (hierarchy, order, outlines), Center (Start, image of topic, at least 3 colors), Style (personal, develop), Use (Links, Colors), Emphasis (images, codes a b, dimension), Keywords (print case UPPER and lower, lines, organised central thicker more important / outer thinner less important, style organic free flowing, length same as word image), word image alone, for each, connect center radiate out

There is an easy four-part model to help us think about the way creative thought and action are turned into a business. Each of the model's elements begins with the letter *I*, so, this is known as the Four-I model. The four parts are:

1. Imagination—the creative act of originality.
2. Incubation—the time period between the point at which the entrepreneur gets the idea and the time when the breakthrough is discovered.
3. Illumination—the point at which the entrepreneur is able to see how the idea can be turned into a profitable business.
4. Implementation—the transformation of the idea and concept into a physical reality.

3 The Environment for Entrepreneurship

The central task facing an organization which has entrepreneurial aspirations is to take advantage of the opportunities from change that appear in its environment.
—*Sharon Oster*

─────────────────── OUTLINE ───────────────────

─────────────── LEARNING OBJECTIVES ───────────────

After reading this chapter, you will understand

- the components of the *business environment.*
- the *process* of business environment analysis.
- the six segments of the *macroenvironment,* and the issues presented by each of them.
- what changes in the macroenvironment can become *sources of opportunity* for the entrepreneur.
- the five elements of the *industry environment,* and the components that affect each of these segments.

Getting Ideas from Books

Alex Zoghlin never stops learning, never stops scanning, and is always on the lookout for entrepreneurial opportunities. His recognition process is very successful.

Zoghlin is a high school dropout who earned his GED in the U.S. Navy, and then went on to study Mandarin Chinese and statistical economics at the University of Illinois. He is a voracious reader, a master scuba diver, and a black belt in Tae Kwon Do. He goes to work in downtown Chicago dressed in blue jeans, with his hair in a long ponytail hanging down his back, but no one objects because he's the boss.

Diverse interests have, in fact, made Zoghlin into a serial entrepreneur, now working on his fourth new venture. His first enterprise was Internet retailer, Sportsgear LLC. Then, in 1995, he founded Neoglyphics Media Corporation, a Web-site developer whose clients included General Motors, Amazon.com, and Nokia. After selling that company in 1998, Zoghlin, the son of a travel agent, became the number-one employee and chief technology officer of Orbitz.com, the e-ticket-for-consumers site developed by United, Delta, American, Northwest, and Continental Airlines.

While the sale of Orbitz and his earlier ventures have made him a rich man, 36-year-old Zoghlin still appreciates a challenge. His new company, G2 Switchworks, is built on software that makes it easier for travel agents to make travel plans for their customers. Zoghlin claims his product can locate the same information in less than 30 seconds as existing electronic networks like Sabre, Galileo, and Worldspan, which take up to eight minutes and multiple searches. G2 Switchworks has the backing of seven U.S. airlines and two private equity firms.

Zoghlin's opportunity-recognition process is primarily externally driven. He reports that he gets many of his ideas from reading business books. "A lot of people are technically competent, but they don't see how the technology is applied in everyday life or in business. Then you have people who are really good in business and finance, but they don't understand technology. I'm really lucky, I can connect the dots to both."

SOURCE: Adapted from Michael Arndt, "Voices of Innovation, High-Flying Dropout," *Business Week*, March 6, 2006: 22; and "Chicago Dropout Makes Good" Retrieved from the Web May 30, 2006. http://www.businessweek.com/magazine/content/06_10/b3974037.html.

SCHEMATIC OF THE NEW VENTURE'S ENVIRONMENT

W HAT does the world look like to the entrepreneur? What parts of that world are important for making entrepreneurial decisions and finding opportunities for the new venture? Figure 3.1 shows the business environment as it might appear to an entrepreneur—a series of concentric circles. The innermost circle represents the firm and its resources. This is the core of the entrepreneur's world; it holds the least amount of uncertainty for the entrepreneur. The next circle holds all the elements that are part of the firm's industry, but are not part of the firm itself. There is more uncertainty here. The largest circle represents everything that is not part of the firm's industry, but is still important for the new venture. This is the **macroenviron-ment** in which the firm operates. This domain has the most uncertainty. Uncertainty is a barrier to entrepreneurship, but some people are willing to bear this uncertainty.[1] There are six identifiable, though overlapping, segments within the macroenvironment:

1. Politics and government
2. Stakeholders
3. Macroeconomy
4. Technology
5. Sociodemography
6. Ecology

In this chapter, we will describe the characteristics and segments of the macroenvironment, as well as the characteristics and segments of the industry or competitive environment. The distinction between the two environments is somewhat artificial because, ultimately, institutions and organizations use them interchangeably. Indeed, the organizations and institutions themselves are also exchangeable. They come and go as society, technology, and the rules of law dictate. As new industries are created from new technologies or the desires of consumers, resources from deteriorating industries are converted for their use. The purchasing power of a declining industry's customers can be redirected either to a new industry or to another, more stable industry. Thus, the concentric circles representing the business environment appear as broken lines to depict the

FIGURE 3.1   Schematic of the New Venture's Environment

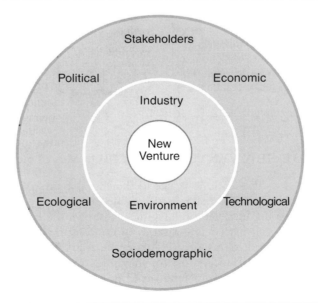

permeability of environmental boundaries and the possibility, indeed the necessity, of flow and exchange.

In the second half of this chapter, we will examine the competitive environment for entrepreneurship. To do so, we will use the model of competitive industry analysis popularized by Michael Porter of the Harvard Business School.[2] We will conclude the chapter by discussing how to perform a competitor analysis, based on our resource-based model, which can exploit industry opportunities and lessen the threats arising from unfavorable industry conditions.

PROCESSES OF BUSINESS ENVIRONMENT ANALYSIS

Most of the time, we think and analyze very quickly, and we are quite unaware that we are doing so. Sometimes, though, we must be more conscious of our thinking, and do our analyzing in systematic ways. This is the case when we are thinking about the environment for entrepreneurship. We want to make sure we are being comprehensive and analytical. Four separate (although sequentially related) tasks are required for a comprehensive entrepreneurial analysis: scanning, monitoring, forecasting, and assessing.[3]

Scanning

How does this comprehensive process begin? It begins by looking around. **Scanning** the environment is the process by which the entrepreneur first identifies the environment's key elements and their characteristics. It is a surveillance system for early detection. The goal of scanning is to detect change that is already underway. Successful scanning catches important changes early, giving the new venture enough lead time to adapt.

The prospective entrepreneur scans innumerable sources of data. *The Wall Street Journal, Business Week,* and the *Economist* are solid sources for obtaining the broad picture. Television provides a general and continual source of data through Cable News Network (CNN), network news, special reports, and documentaries. More specialized business programming is becoming increasingly popular on cable channels like MSNBC. Surfing the Internet has become an important scanning activity. In addition, through "people-to-people" interactive scanning, like Web logs (blogs), entrepreneurs consult with a variety of professionals and experts outside their fields of expertise. Accountants, lawyers, engineers, consultants, and, yes, even professors are available to the entrepreneur for information and advice. Scanning gives the entrepreneur a sensitivity to environmental conditions that sometimes looks like intuition.

Monitoring

Monitoring is the process of tracking the evolution, development, and sequence of critical events that affect the future business' survival and profitability. Data from the scanning process are used in the monitoring process. Specific trends and events are monitored in real time to confirm or disprove predictions about how they will affect the firm. Monitoring is less general and therefore more focused than scanning. The entrepreneur follows specific periodicals, consults select experts, and even convenes focus groups.[4] The result of the monitoring process is a detailed model of how various elements in the macroenvironment influence and affect the firm. The monitoring model, however, is not reality; rather, it is a workable version of cause and effect.

For example, consider Charlie Ayers, also known as Chef Charlie around Google corporate headquarters. Ayers ran the cafeteria at Google for six years. During that time, he carefully monitored the eating habits and the tastes and preferences of the Google workforce. The folks who worked at Google were the future target market for Ayers' own new venture. They were also potential sources of finance: A lot of Google employees became quite rich when the company went public. Ayers honed his recipes and tried new dishes. "I did most of my research on them," he said.[5] His restaurant, Calafia, in Redwood City, California, is a success and has been featured in the *New York Times*.

Forecasting

Forecasting enables the entrepreneur to develop plausible projections for the future. These can be projections for elements such as price level, the direction of interest rates, or future scenarios for cause and effect. For example, a typical forecast might be: If the money supply grows at above-target rates, inflation will occur. Thus, inputs for forecasts are the data collected from monitoring.

Forecasting includes a series of techniques that provide insight into the future. The specific techniques chosen for a task should correspond to the type of data used as input, and the nature of the desired forecast. When forecasting is used to help search for new business opportunities and to uncover potential macroenvironmental constraints on these opportunities, the following five-step process is suggested.[6]

1. *Choose* the macroenvironmental variables that are critical to the new venture. These will probably relate to the firm's resource base. For example, if a business generally hires low-wage, entry-level people, the minimum-wage costs and payroll taxes are critical variables.
2. *Select* the sources of data for the forecast. These will probably be those the entrepreneur has been monitoring. Data sources can be found in many places, including the local university or library. Internet searches can also produce forecasts.
3. *Evaluate* various forecasting techniques. Forecasters use different techniques and therefore sometimes produce different forecasts. For example, a firm might see a forecast that says the stock market is going up, and therefore conclude that this is a good time to go into business. But just how closely linked are the stock market and the firm? And is the stock market a leading indicator (the economy will be getting better) or a lagging indicator (the economy has already topped and may now be heading down)?
4. *Integrate* forecast results into a plan for the creation of the new venture. These results will probably include resource levels, resource availability, and sales forecasts. If sales are predicted to go up 5 percent to 6 percent, the firm must also plan on increased costs.
5. *Keep track* of the critical aspects of the forecast, meaning compare actual results with forecasted results. If and when a gap appears, it is time for another forecast, beginning at step 1. If the forecasts indicate that the industry can expect 3 percent to 4 percent gains for the coming year (as is frequently predicted in the restaurant indus-

try), it can plan for this level of sales increase. If the industry falls short of the forecast, it may have problems with its customer base and product offerings. If the industry achieves higher-than-forecasted gains, it had a good year and might raise its forecast for the following year.

Table 3.1 summarizes the costs and benefits of six quantitative and judgmental forecasting techniques. The criteria of cost and complexity are used. Cost is a useful criterion because it can be evaluated against the expected benefits to see if the activity is justified. Complexity refers to the difficulty of using the technique. This criterion helps us evaluate the risk involved so that we can weigh the cost/benefit analysis. Levels such as low, medium, and high are subjective, and depend on the venture's familiarity with the technique and overall financial position.

Assessing

Assessing the environment is the most difficult and important of the four environmental analysis tasks. Here the entrepreneur has to answer that most difficult of questions: What does it all mean? Interpretation is an art form, and so is assessment. In a poker game, players can agree on what cards are showing, the previous bets made, and the value of the cards they are holding. Some players hold, some fold, and others raise their bets. Because their assessments are different, their behavior is different. In assessing most entrepreneurial opportunities, there are few facts that people would agree can be generalized.

Although the four-part process described in this chapter seems quite analytical, it actually takes place over time in a mode that is more intuitive than rational. It is sometimes called *entrepreneurial insight* or *vision*. In Street Story 3.1, we see that if one is in the retail sector, one will have to scan, monitor, analyze, and forecast, because each year small changes in the environment bring about large changes in the competition.

Another model for opportunity analysis has been offered by Bhave.[7] New business

TABLE 3.1   Quantitative and Judgmental Forecasting Methods for Emerging Industries, New Ventures, and New Products

Method	Description	Complexity	Cost
1. Sales force estimate	A bottom-up approach that aggregates unit demand	Low	Low
2. Juries of executive opinion	Forecasts jointly prepared by experts in a functional area	Low	Low
3. Customer surveys: market research, focus groups	Intentions of potential customers and final users	Medium	Medium
4. Scenario development	Effects of anticipated conditions imagined by forecasters	Medium	Low
5. Delphi method	Expert guide to consensus	Low	Medium
6. Brainstorming	Idea generation in a noncritical group situation	Low	Medium

SOURCE: Adapted from J. Pearce and R. Robinson, *Strategic Management*, 4th ed. (Homewood, IL: Irwin, 1991).

Tweaking the Retail Environment

It looks more like a store selling fine jewelry instead of women's clothing.

It has small, eye-level display windows with dramatic lighting, and a luxurious interior décor. In the center of the store, there is a circular dressing room—no, *fitting salon*—with three-way mirrors and adjustable lighting where salespeople—no, *style consultants*—offer customers complimentary bottled water, and bring them garments from *collections* with names like Allegory and Prize. Forth & Towne is the newest offering from the people who brought us Gap, Old Navy, and Banana Republic, and its target market is women over 35 with money.

Scanning the American retail environment has convinced a number of retailers to focus on middle-to-upper-class consumers, or customers who at least want to look upscale. Macy's has widened its aisles, added plush sofas to its department stores, and replaced coupon advertising with image-building commercials. Wal-Mart is running ads in the fashion magazine, *Vogue*. Chains like Gap and Chico's FAS are unveiling concepts tailored to the fashion dreams of specific age groups; Abercrombie & Fitch now has Little A stores for kids, Hollister for high school students, and Ruehl for college students and older shoppers.

Technological monitoring is enabling retailers to target the customers they want with the products they want to pitch to them. The club cards that grocery stores have been using for years are now spreading to noncommodity stores like Borders bookstores, and retailers are using the data they collect with those cards to offer customers customized discounts on the kind of pet food they buy, or to tell them about an upcoming release from their favorite author. Retailers such as the jewelry chain, Zale Corporation, plan to use the information they collect as a guide for future marketing. Some of today's monitoring methods are rather low tech: Clothing retailers are using private-label house brands to evaluate fashion trends, offering expensive garments to customers at relatively low prices.

Forecasting trends have persuaded some retailers to make physical changes to lure well-heeled shoppers. Enclosed shopping malls are being replaced across the country with lifestyle centers where open-air walkways are lined with smaller boutique merchants instead of big-box stores. The most popular lifestyle-center tenants are those that cater to an upscale good life: stores like Williams-Sonoma, Barnes & Noble, Pottery Barn, and Victoria's Secret. The decline of the mall has motivated traditional shopping center anchors like J.C. Penney and Sears, Roebuck & Co. to experiment with stand-alone stores. Some developers are replacing demolished malls with new retail districts where stores are blended into a mix of office and residential tenants, creating an innovative white-collar neighborhood.

Some of these new retailing trends are too new to produce much assessment, but some retailers have obviously decided that size matters. Once independent department stores Macy's, Bloomingdale's, Filene's, Lord & Taylor and Marshall Field's, are now combined under one umbrella, allowing them to increase their advertising clout and leverage with suppliers on their quest to attract well-to-do shoppers.

SOURCE: Adapted from Kris Hudson, "Upscale Experience, Downscale Prices," *The Wall Street Journal*, November 21, 2005. Retrieved from the Web March 4, 2006, http://www.online.wsj.com/article_print?SB11322509 4874700333.html, and www.forthandtowne.com.

UPDATE: Fourth and Towne announced it would close all its stores in June 2007.

development and entrepreneurship are processes (a series of events and decisions) that lead to a specific outcome (the creation of a new venture). The process begins with opportunity recognition. The sources of opportunities have two points of origin: **internally-stimulated opportunity recognition** and **externally-stimulated opportunity recognition.**

Externally-generated opportunity recognition occurs after the entrepreneur decides to start a business. He or she scans the environment for opportunities, and generates a set of possibilities—but which possibilities should the nascent entrepreneur pursue? The entrepreneur must have some criteria from which to choose. Thus, he or she filters these possibilities, then compares their requirements against his or her skills, resources, experiences, and desires. Usually, but not always, the entrepreneur decides which business opportunity to pursue based on his or her skills, abilities, experiences, and preferences. The exception is when the entrepreneur needs very specialized expertise. Here, he or she may hire outside people.

Once the entrepreneur commits to a suitable idea, he or she refines the idea into a business concept or model. This opportunistic search is the externally driven one. The Chapter 2 profile of the Baker Boys is an example of an externally driven opportunity. The twins looked outward and found ways to make money, regardless of where this path took them.

Internally driven opportunity recognition precedes the decision to start a business. The individual sees a need or a problem related to his or her own experiences at work, a hobby, or some strong belief or value that he or she holds. The individual may be able to solve the problem alone, only afterward realizing that others have the same problem—and are willing to pay to get it solved. Often, the entrepreneur starts to think of the problem and its solution as a business opportunity only after this realization. In other cases, this realization may strike the individual as soon as he or she has identified the problem. In either case, the wish to start a venture comes after the entrepreneur recognizes the problem to be solved, and typically only one "opportunity" is considered. A general advantage of this process is that the entrepreneur will typically do a good job of matching this opportunity with the interests and competencies of the persons pursuing it. Moreover, the entrepreneur will prove at least some level of demand before he or she decides to "go for it." On the downside, we find the fact that people who "stumble" over opportunities related to their personal life in this way may have less motivation and fewer skills needed to successfully start and run a business.

Betty Morris provides an example of internally driven opportunity recognition. The last thing Morris wanted was a career in the toy industry. All she intended that afternoon in her kitchen was to entertain a gaggle of eight-year-old Scouts. She decided that it would be fun and productive to make something, so she found a craft book and studied it for an appropriate activity. She followed the directions on how to make plastic trinkets, and was delighted with the charms she created—Shrinky Dinks. Morris and another mother, Kathryn Bloomberg, decided to invest $1,200 in 1,000 pounds of 8-inch by 10-inch sheets of plastic. The two women formed a partnership, K&B Innovations, and began assembling kits. The toy was introduced at a booth in a mall and received inquiries from 16 different stores. "Companies came out of the woodwork wanting to negotiate some kind of licensing agreement with us," says Morris.[8]

POLITICAL AND GOVERNMENTAL ANALYSIS

Politics is the art of the possible. We could say the same thing about entrepreneurship. Analyzing the political scene will give the entrepreneur a feeling for what is possible, what is probable, and what is unlikely. The political and governmental segment of the business environment is the arena in which different interest groups compete for attention and resources to advance their own interests, establish their own values, and achieve their own goals. It is where particular individuals and groups exercise political power. To a large extent, the individual entrepreneur is forced to accept the current political environment of the new venture. Collectively and over time, however, an organized group of entrepreneurs can influence the political sector. One such group, the National Federation of Independent Business (NFIB), lobbies hard for issues that affect entrepreneurs and small businesses. One can register with the NFIB free of charge, and monitor its Web site at http://www.nfib.com/page/home.

Global and International Issues

Although the entrepreneur may *think* that his or her business is strictly local, this is true of very few businesses. We are all interconnected in a global economy, and events that occur thousands of miles away can influence our businesses. The main global issues are trade barriers, tariffs, political risks, and bilateral and multilateral relationships. All of these issues are interrelated.

Trade Barriers and Tariffs. Trade barriers and **tariffs** hinder the free flow of resources across national boundaries. They are the result of economic interest groups within a country attempting to prevent transnational competition. The trend today is to reduce trade barriers worldwide.

Trade Agreements. Since World War II, and especially since the end of the Cold War, the trend has been toward increased trade agreements. These country-to-country and regional agreements have set the economic rules businesses follow when they are interacting with other businesses within the cosigning group of nations.

Political Risk. The potential for instability, corruption, and violence in a country or region is known as political risk. Political risk is an important variable, because in areas where it is high, resources are difficult and costly to procure, protect, and dispose of. Further, the risk of governmental nationalization and the legal appropriation of firms is always present. (Even in a stable democracy, people can vote to take away other people's money.)

National Issues

Political and governmental analysis at the national level refers to taxation, regulation, antitrust legislation, government spending, and patent protection.

Taxation. The primary political factor facing the entrepreneur is taxation. Governments require large amounts of money to promote the public good and carry out the will of the people (stakeholders). However, taxation reduces the cash available to a firm for reinvestment. Thus, the entrepreneur may invest or reinvest not the economically rational amount, but a somewhat lower amount—his or her after-tax earnings. The outside investor too must calculate returns after taxes, which means that required rates of return must be high enough to cover the government's share. Some new ventures are not able to generate outside financing because their after-tax returns to investors will simply be too low to justify the investment.

Taxation affects not only individual businesses, but also the relationships between businesses, giving some firms advantages over others. Special tax breaks for certain industries, such as depreciation and depletion allowances, benefit the firms that receive them. Capital-intensive companies, such as manufacturers, benefit disproportionately from the tax shield that depreciation affords. On the other hand, service businesses with large investments in training and development cannot depreciate their employees. The differential tax treatment given to interest and dividends under the U.S. Tax Code favors firms that can obtain bank loans and other forms of debt over equity-financed firms that pay dividends and whose investors receive capital gains. Because "bankable" businesses—those that usually receive bank loans—are generally older firms with physical assets than can serve as collateral for a loan, new ventures (especially service businesses) are disadvantaged by the current tax code.

Taxation also has a global effect. Different countries treat dividends, interest, and capital gains in different ways. For example, Japanese firms pay very low dividends relative to their German and U.S. counterparts because dividends are more highly taxed in Japan. Thus, the Japanese investor prefers capital gains, which are not taxed at all, thus enabling Japanese firms to keep more cash for reinvestment.[9]

Regulation. Government agencies control the flow of resources to firms and the property rights of business owners through federal regulation. The government creates these agencies in response to a special-interest group or a group of stakeholders to protect its interests, values, and goals. Regulation is not inherently bad; we all belong to one special-interest group or another. For example, we all eat and take medicine at some time. The Food and Drug Administration, with its regulatory function, helps protect our interests in these matters.

The effects of regulation on business, however, are sometimes negative. Regulatory agencies impose significant costs on firms in forms such as paperwork, testing and monitoring, and compliance. These costs may or may not be recoverable through higher prices. If the industry being regulated has good substitutes for its products, and the substitute industry is less regulated, the firms in the more highly regulated industry must absorb the costs, and profitability suffers. These costs result in less reinvestment and an overall lower output in the regulated industry. If the industry can charge higher prices, the public eventually pays for the protection and services conferred by the regulations.

Antitrust Legislation. Each national government determines the level of antitrust activity it will enforce. The United States has the toughest antitrust laws in the world. The antitrust division of the United States Justice Department was a driving force in the breakup of AT&T, and in Microsoft's change in strategy, from a passive observer of federal legal policy to an active lobbyist. Other countries, most notably Japan, have a different view of antitrust regulation. In these countries, the zeal of regulatory enforcement may be a function of national economic interests (such as balance of trade or currency exchange). When national interests collide with consumer or entrepreneurial interests, national interests have priority. Generally, new ventures are not in danger of violating antitrust laws; they are more likely to be victims of lax antitrust enforcement.

Patent Protection. National governments grant patents and enforce patent laws. A patent is legal property that enables its holder to prevent others from using a product or service for a specified period of time. There are three types of patents:

1. **Utility patents,** which cover new articles, processes, machines, and techniques
2. **Design patents,** which cover new and original ornamental designs for manufactured products
3. **Plant patents**, which cover various forms of life, and genetically-engineered organisms

A patent is a resource and therefore can be analyzed using our resource-based model. In countries where patent enforcement is lax, a firm may need to weigh the costs of publicly divulging its technology against the benefits of having patent protection before applying for one.. In many cases, small changes to a product or design erode patent protection enough to make the patent worthless. In the United States, patents and trademarks are managed from the U.S. Patent and Trademark Office (http://uspto.gov). Here we can find out how to file a patent or trademark, or do patent and trademark searches to ensure that we are not violating someone else's patent or mark.

Recently, businesses have tended to seek patent protection for the *way* they do business, making minor distinctions in the processes they use. These are known as *business process* patents. For example, J. M. Smucker, the Orrville, Ohio, jam maker, attempted to patent its method for making Uncrustables. Uncrustables are round, sealed, crustless sandwiches. Smucker's already had a patent on the sandwich, but wanted to expand the patent to include how the sandwich was made. They argued that they used a compression method versus the "smushed" method employed in making tarts and ravioli. A federal appeals court judge rejected their application, holding that the patent extension failed the test by being "obvious." A spokesperson for Smucker's said, "It wouldn't be fair to let another company simply copy the product and benefit from the hard work our people invested."[10]

Government Spending. In most countries, the national government is the largest purchaser and consumer of goods and services. The government is therefore a large market, and it displays preferences for certain products, services, and suppliers. These preferences are influenced by pressures from the various interest groups, stakeholders, and political organizations that constantly lobby the government. At times, the political winds seem to favor defense spending and new entrants into defense and related industries. At other times, government priorities may work to the benefit of building infrastructure or developing social programs. In the latter case, the beneficiaries would include construction contractors, consultants, and related service industries.

State, Regional, and Local Issues

State, regional, or local tax policies can create opportunities or disadvantages for the entrepreneur. At the state level, three other areas affect business: licensing, securities and incorporation laws, and economic development and incentives.

Licensing.   Licenses are economic privileges granted to individuals and firms that enable them to legally conduct a business. Not all businesses require licenses, but many do. At one time, licenses were valuable franchises and a way of limiting entry and raising quality within a particular industry. Today, however, state and local authorities often consider licenses a revenue source and do little to monitor the performance level of the licensees. The entrepreneur must remain watchful of current licensing regulations and potential changes to upgrade enforcement that could affect the new venture.

Securities and Incorporation Laws.   Many security regulations and incorporation laws are written and enforced by the states. Because the U.S. Constitution does not specifically grant the federal government the power to regulate business incorporation, this is one of the major regulatory roles left to the states. Although the federal government does have an important regulatory role under the Securities Act of 1934, which created the Securities and Exchange Commission, new incorporations are granted and monitored at the state level. Most early financing that the firm receives is covered by state securities regulations. Entrepreneurs need to employ lawyers and accountants to ensure that the firm complies with all state regulations.

Incentives.   State and local authorities control the granting of economic-development incentives and tax abatements to new or old businesses relocating within their jurisdiction. These incentives can be a powerful stimulus for new firms. They may include subsidized job-training programs, real estate improvements and favorable real estate tax treatment, and improved infrastructure (e.g., roads and interchanges, sidewalks, water and sewer improvements). Local governments also control zoning ordinances and laws, which determine how property can be used and developed. Every firm has a local component. Entrepreneurs can scan and monitor these developments, especially when considering where to locate.

State and local agencies also can pose serious barriers and disincentives. For example, in the Philippines, the local government can require that an entrepreneur conduct 11 different procedures to set up a new venture. In the Organization for Economic Cooperation and Development (OECD), the average number of procedures is six. Pablo Planas invented a fuel-savings device for cars and motorbikes. Unfortunately, he invented the device in the Philippines 30 years before he could put it into production. He hassled with the lack of infrastructure and bureaucracy for the longest time, but eventually, he made the device and founded Khaos Super Gas Saver. "I was one of the lucky ones," he said.[11]

At the municipal level, taxation again erodes the firm's ability to finance itself and reward its investors. Local taxes include income and property, sewer, water, and waste disposal. If local taxes can be allocated to particular services that the local government provides for business use, they are not really taxes but fees for service.

In summary, the entrepreneur must be knowledgeable about a variety of political issues, particularly those related to securing, protecting, and disposing of resources. The effect of political power on property rights is of primary concern. Table 3.2 presents the four levels at which political and governmental analysis should be performed.

STAKEHOLDER ANALYSIS

How many different individuals, groups, and interests can influence the survival, development, and profitability of the new venture? Quite a few. In this section, we will discuss **stakeholders** and stakeholder analysis.

Stakeholder analysis helps the entrepreneur identify which groups and interests are friendly to the new venture and which are hostile. It enables the entrepreneur to see whether any groups have an immediate affinity for the product or service, and whether this affinity can be translated into a market. The analysis also reveals trends regarding consumer attitudes and behavior for the new venture's products, competing products, and complementary goods.

Seven Dimensions

Stakeholders' influences can be both positive and negative. Not all stakeholders are alike. Stakeholders may vary along the following seven dimensions[12]:

Resource capability: The degree to which stakeholders have access to resources that help influence businesses or agencies that can be categorized in the same way as described in Chapter 2 (financial, physical, technical, reputational, human, and organizational; rare, valuable, hard to copy, and nonsubstitutable).

Extent of influence: The degree to which the interest group is able to promote its agenda. Some stakeholders are organized as lobbying groups and have enormous influence—for example, the National Rifle Association or Mothers against Drunk Driving.

Degree of organization: The extent to which stakeholders are organized for collective action locally, regionally, and nationally. Some stakeholders are very well organized

TABLE 3.2   Political and Governmental Concerns

Global	National	State and Region al	Local
Trade barriers	Taxation	Taxation	Taxation
Trade agreements	Regulation	Securities law	Zoning
Tariffs and duties	Antitrust legislation	Licensing	
Political risk	Patent protection	Incentives	
	Government spending		

and influential. Others are disorganized or incompetently managed organizations. They do not represent a significant threat to existing firms.

Nature of interest: The type of agenda the interest group has: a specific agenda (e.g., cleaning up toxic waste sites) or a general agenda (e.g., making business responsive to people's needs).

Duration: The length of time the interest group has been active and its potential staying power. Sometimes stakeholders are interested in issues that prove to be fads or of passing interest. This is especially true in areas such as consumer goods, travel, and leisure industries.

Degree of manifestation: The ability of the interest group to take its case directly to the public or to the media.

Bases of influence: The extent to which an interest group can gain support from other interest groups that share an affinity for similar causes.

Kauffman Foundation

The Kauffman Foundation is one of the most important nongovernmental organizations (NGO) to become a stakeholder for entrepreneurs. It is formally known as The Ewing Marion Kauffman Foundation of Kansas City, Missouri (http://www.kauffman.org/). The Kauffman Foundation supports education, research, and community-based action to help promote new venture creation and entrepreneurship. For example, when the foundation became aware of a study showing that minority-owned businesses were growing rapidly but were faced with financial problems, it established a coalition with the National Urban League and other organizations to address the issue. When Hurricane Katrina devastated the Gulf Coast of the United States and New Orleans, the foundation drew up plans to offer entrepreneurs intensive help and free advice.[13]

MACROECONOMIC ANALYSIS

The macroeconomy is the total of all goods and services produced, distributed, sold, and consumed. Where does all of this activity take place? It happens at the global, national, and local levels. Each level has its own macroeconomy, and the sum of all the lower levels is the global economy. These geographic distinctions are important to policy makers because policy makers' power and influence are usually constrained by geographic limits. These geographic distinctions are also important to the entrepreneur because, to a greater or lesser degree, every business is entwined in all three macroeconomies. The entrepreneur should analyze all three macroeconomies, but the time he or she spends on any one of them should be proportional to the potential impact on the firm's performance. Macroeconomic change can occur at any of the three geographic levels discussed previously.[14] There are two types of macroeconomic change: structural change and cyclical change.

Structural Change

Structural changes in the macroeconomy are major, permanent shifts of resources and customers from one sector of the economy to another. As these shifts occur, the financial capital, physical resources, and employees diminish in an industry that is fading, and flow to the emerging industry. An example of recent structural change can be found in the newspaper industry. News-gathering capability, advertising dollars, financial resources, and technological innovation have been transferred from the printed newspaper industry to the Internet and the electronic news and information industry. Some newspapers were able to make the adjustment, such as *The Wall Street Journal,* which has the largest paid Internet subscription base in the United States. Other newspapers have lost business, gone out of business, or been bought by investors looking to milk these cash cows. Without new investment and innovative strategies, this industry may become a dinosaur.[15]

Cyclical Change

The second type of macroeconomic change is **cyclical change**. The macroeconomy enjoys periods of growth followed by periods of contraction. These alternating time periods form what is called the **business cycle**. Business cyclicality is the degree to which the new firm follows the trend of the business cycle. A venture that grows and contracts as the economy does is **procyclical**. An example is the automobile industry and its suppliers. People buy more cars when their wages are high and rising and they feel their jobs are secure. Thus, when the economy is good, car sales are good, and when it is poor, car sales are slow.

A **countercyclical** industry has just the opposite pattern. Sales are better when the economy is poor and wages are down. To a large extent, the fast-food industry is countercyclical because, when people are economizing on eating out, they tend to choose lower-cost restaurants. A venture that is unaffected by the business cycle is **acyclical**. For example, consumer staple industries are frequently acyclical because people need soap and soup, shampoo, and light bulbs regardless of how the economy is performing.

Understanding the new venture's relationship to the business cycle is crucial to the entrepreneur because it is difficult, if not impossible, for the new business to run counter to its natural cyclicality. Thus, if the firm is in a procyclical industry and the current trend in the business cycle is downward, the firm will have a difficult time ignoring this trend by expanding. Clearly, the entrepreneur needs to scan and monitor the economic variables that indicate the direction of economic trends.

TECHNOLOGICAL ANALYSIS

What is technology? **Technology** can be defined as "the branch of knowledge that deals with industrial arts, applied science, and engineering," and "a process, an invention, or a method." The first part of the definition tells us that technological analysis is concerned with the "what" of science. Technological analysis, then, requires scanning and monitoring from the time of basic research through product development and commercialization. The second part of the definition implies that technology is also concerned with the "how" of science. Therefore, a complete technological analysis also includes scanning of operations and manufacturing techniques. Technological change takes place in two ways: (1) through pure invention (and scientific discovery), and (2) through process innovation.

Pure Invention

Pure invention is the creation of something that is radically different from existing technologies or products. Because pure invention is different, it has certain characteristics that are economically interesting. An invention may have no competitors at its birth, thereby giving a monopoly to the individuals who hold its legal rights. The disadvantage at this time is that the invention also has no market. Further, there may never be a market for the commercial version of the invention. The combination of the monopolist upside with the no-ready-market downside makes the economic aspect of invention risky because the outcomes are potentially so variable.

New inventions can create new industries. The invention of the semiconductor created the computer industry in all its forms. The scientific discoveries made by geneticists created the biotech industry with all of its niches and segments. In the initial phase of such technologies and discoveries—the creation of products and markets— entrepreneurs play the most important role. Over the product's life cycle, large organizational units develop to exploit these products and markets as they mature.

Process Innovation

After an invention has been successfully commercialized, the second type of technological change, **process innovation**, becomes dominant. Whereas pure invention is radical and revolutionary, carrying with it the potential to create new industries, process innovation is incremental and evolutionary. Its purpose is to make existing industries more efficient. Process innovation refers to the small changes in design, product formulation and manufacturing, materials, and service delivery that firms make to keep their product up-to-date and their costs down. Table 3.3 presents the ways in which technology and key related variables change over the course of the product life cycle. The table headings show the product life-cycle stages: introduction, shakeout, growth, and maturity. The left-hand column gives the important dimensions for product innovation, such as who is in charge and how the innovation process is organized. For example, we can see that major innovations are most likely in the introduction and shakeout stages, while incremental innovation is more prevalent in the growth and maturity stages. We will discuss the table's bottom line, Organization Structure, in more detail in Chapter 9.

Frequently, process innovation improvements are made by people working for large companies. If these companies are not the best place to fully exploit these improvements, the people who make them may decide to become entrepreneurs. They literally spin themselves and their new product into a new venture.

The critical question for the entrepreneur should be: Which innovations have the best chance of success? An academic study of these factors reported the results of 197 product innovations (111 successes and 86 failures). The researchers found that the successful innovations had some or all of the following characteristics:

1. They were moderately new to the market.
2. They were based on established technology.
3. They saved customers money.
4. They met customer expectations.
5. They supported existing processes and procedures.

TABLE 3.3   Forms of Technological Change Over the Product Life Cycle Stages

	Product Life-Cycle Stage			
	Introduction	*Shakeout*	*Growth*	*Maturity*
Type of innovation	Major product innovation or invention	→ Major product innovation or invention	→ Incremental product or major process innovation	→ Incremental product or process innovation
Location of innovation	Entrepreneur	→ Marketing and R&D	→ Marketing and production	→ Production
Bases of competition	Product, performance, or novelty	→ Product, performance, or novelty	→ Product differentiation or price	→ Price, image, minor differences
Production process	Job shop	→ Batch	→ Islands of automation	→ Assembly line or continuous flow
Dominant function	Entrepreneur	→ Marketing/R&D	→ Marketing/production	→ Production/sales and promotion
Management role	Entrepreneur	→ Sophisticated market manager	→ Administrator and integrator	→ Steward
Modes of integration	Informal communication	→ Informal communication, task forces and teams	→ Informal communication, teams, project manager	→ Formal communication, senior management, committees
Organization structure	Free form	→ Functional organic	→ Project/matrix	→ Functional bureaucratic

SOURCE: Adapted from W. Moore and M. Tushman, "Managing Innovation over the Product Life Cycle." In Tushman and Moore (eds.), *Readings in the Management of Innovation* (Boston: Pitman Press, 1982): 143.

The study concluded that the failures were either too cutting edge or too "me-too"; there were no suggestions for how to improve them. The study also looked at the sources for the innovation and found six of them: need spotting, market research, solution spotting, trend following, mental inventions, and taking advantage of random events. Of these, the greatest number of failures derived from trend following and mental inventions (no basis in the market). Need spotting accounted for twice as many successes as failures, market research four times the successes, and solution spotting seven times the number of successes. What was the best source of ideas? Taking advantage of random events! This process accounted for 13 times more successes than failures. Why? Only the most flexible organization with the best resources can take advantage of serendipity. It is the hardest thing to copy.[16]

SOCIODEMOGRAPHIC ANALYSIS

The sociodemographic phase of business environment analysis has two closely-related aspects: demographics and social trends (sometimes referred to as *lifestyle trends*). The interaction that results when these elements combine is known as *popular culture*. Enormous business opportunities in consumer and durable goods, retailing and services, leisure and entertainment, and housing and construction are found in a society's popular culture.

Demographics

Demographic changes are a major source of long-term social change. **Demography** is the study of trends in human populations: the size of the population and its various subgroups; the population's age structure, geographic distribution, and ethnic and racial mix; and the distribution of income and wealth within the population. Demographic change refers to changes in any of these variables as well as changes in the relationships between them. Demography is destiny, because all of these factors form the essence of consumer demand, industrial capacities, and purchasing power. Markets are created from demographic analysis.

We obtain some of the best demographic data from the census. In the United States, a census is taken every 10 years; the results for the most recent 10-year period (1990–1999) are available at http://www.census.gov. A number of important trends emerged from comparing the last 10-year period with the first 10-year period of the twentieth century.[17]

First, it is clear that we are living longer. The most significant increases in life expectancy are found among older people. During the second half of the twentieth century, life expectancy for people in their 70s grew by an additional 5 years, to age 82. Seniors today are living substantially longer and healthier lives. One of the most studied and targeted demographic segments is the baby boomers. Baby boomers are those born between 1946 and 1960; they represent over 76 million consumers—almost 27 percent of the total population. Table 3.4 provides some key statistics on this group.

We can learn more about the "mature" market and how to target it from Street Story 3.2.

Immigrants are once again an important demographic in the United States. The major new groups of immigrants come from Korea, Haiti, Vietnam, and Mexico. In fact, Hispanics constitute the second-largest ethnic group in the United States (after people of European descent). The Census Bureau considers a Hispanic any person whose national origins are Latin America or Spain (e.g., Cubans, Mexicans, Puerto Ricans, Dominicans).

Entrepreneurs have emerged to serve this market. For example, Bill Kulik started his own radio network to broadcast Boston Red Sox baseball games in Spanish. His company, Spanish Beisbol Network Incorporated, was incorporated in 2002. He is commentator, engineer, and chief marketing person. As the Hispanic market is growing at more than 8 percent per year, and because approximately 30 percent of all major league baseball players speak Spanish, Kulik figured that his network would offer a great way to reach his target market. But he had problems, mostly financial. "Every newspaper article I saw said that the Latin market was booming. But I never expected it to be this hard," he noted. Nevertheless, Kulik seems to have become a cult figure and is working toward becoming a successful entrepreneur.[18]

Third, the population of the United States is moving south and west. California is our largest state, with over 34 million people. Twenty-two percent of Americans live in the West; that percentage would be higher if the Census Bureau counted Texas as a southern state. The South, then, is the largest region, with 36 percent of the total population, which may make the air conditioner the most important invention in the history of U.S. demographics.

The total population of the United States is growing, too. It is now slightly over 300 million people. Only China and India have larger populations,[19] which explains why companies want to sell to these markets.

Social Trends and Values

Social trends refer to the modes and manners in which people live their lives. Lifestyles reflect people's tastes and preferences from an economic standpoint. Lifestyle-related

TABLE 3.4 Targeting the Baby Boomers

Descriptor Variable	Numerical Value
Percentage women	51%
Percentage minorities	16.9%
Number already 50+	32 million
Average annual spending	$45,654
Divorce rate	14.2%
Percentage who never married	12.6%
Percentage who voted in 2000	59%
Percentage who finished high school	88.8%
Percentage with bachelor's degree or higher	28.5%

SOURCE: "Boomers by the Numbers," *The Wall Street Journal*, September 26, 2005: R4. Adapted from Metlife Mature Market Institute data. (http://www.metlife.com).

STREET STORY 3.2

Moving from Boom to Zoom

A senior vice president at Home Depot, Inc. calls them "a really sweet spot." That's why his company recently announced plans to install information kiosks in 80 of its Florida stores to specifically help that sweet spot—50-year-old-plus baby boomers—get advice on making changes to the kitchens, bathrooms, entryways, and hallways of their homes in preparation for postretirement life.

Seniors have become the hot prospect in marketing today, and the hottest of them all are the *zoomers*, meaning those baby boomers born between 1946 and 1955. "They're in high-income years and are still young at heart," says Lois Huff, an executive with the Ohio consulting and research firm, Retail Forward, Inc.

By 2010, about one-third of the U. S. population will be at least 50 years old. The boomers already control an estimated 67 percent of the country's wealth. "They are a big consumer group with a lot of buying power," notes Mitch Rhodes, president and CEO of Safeway.com, an online service for grocery and pharmacy deliveries.

Convenience is one of the keys to attracting this demographic group. Because older shoppers have historically dominated catalog shopping, five years ago a company called Newgistics, Inc. developed a prepaid, preaddressed, bar-coded label for mail-order companies like Lands' End. Customers can use the catalog to return merchandise without standing in line at the post office. "Baby boomers were in mind as a large part of the direct-shopper crowd when the company was born," says a company spokesperson. A 2004 Harris poll found that a convenient return policy was important or very important to shoppers between the ages of 55 and 64, and that more than 90 percent of this group said ease of return was likely to affect their decision to shop with that retailer again.

Novelty items like kayaks and Segway people movers have helped to draw 50-plus vacationers to resorts like Amelia Island Plantation. "It's a gadget," comments Richard Goldman, marketing vice president, on the appeal of the stand-up scooters that older vacationers use for ecology tours. "Baby boomers are big on trying something new." Safeway.com has discovered that upscale goods are important to zoomers, too. The company now has its butchers customcut meat orders for its delivery service instead of having the orders picked from the packaged-meat selection. Safeway has also added party goods like deli trays to their offerings, and has provided its order pickers with additional training to make them more responsive to older shoppers' discerning tastes.

The one thing that doesn't seem to attract this affluent group is the word *senior*. "We're very sensitive about using the 's' word," says Amelia Island's Goldman. To avoid using this word, the resort decided to christen a skin treatment for menopausal women *The Baby Boomer Facial*. "We can use the term because there's a certain amount of affection in it," Goldman says. He reports that the treatment has now become the third most popular facial at the resort.

SOURCE: Adapted from Jeanette Borzo, "Follow the Money," *The Wall Street Journal*, September 26, 2005. Retrieved from the Web February 23, 2006. http://online.wsj.com/article_print/SB112724418267446432.html.

variables that affect new venture creation include household formation, work modes and labor-force participation rates, education levels and attainments, patterns of consumption, and patterns of leisure.

Scanning and monitoring lifestyle changes are relatively easy because many diverse sources of data are available. Much of this data is aggregated and therefore suggests trends. There are both public and private sources for demographic data. The national government, through its agencies, bureaus, and regulatory bodies, collects vast amounts of data. Trade publications and specialist magazines and newspapers contribute demographic analysis. Consumer reports and the annual reports of corporations furnish additional details. One publication, *American Demographics,* is specifically designed to ferret out unusual and important trends.

Social values and social change together form an important component of socio-demographic analysis. "A **value** is a conception, explicit or implicit, distinctive of an individual or characteristic of a group, of the desirable, which influences the selection of available means and ends of action."[20] Simply stated, this statement means that the choices we make reflect our values. The values that individuals and groups hold cluster around the dimensions of the macroenvironment discussed earlier in this chapter. People hold political values relating to the role of government, political participation, and distributive justice.[21] They hold regulatory values concerning issues such as consumerism and energy policy. Their social values reflect their beliefs about work, the relationship between races, and the significance of gender. Their economic values are reflected in the choices they make about growth and taxation. Some of these values are at the core of an individual's belief systems, and others are on the periphery.

Of course, people within the same country may have diametrically opposite values. For example, the United States is one of the largest church-going countries in the world. We could make the case that Americans are a religious and pious people, devoted to serving a higher power. But then what do we make of the mass media, which occasionally borders on the libertine, our vast consumption of tobacco and alcohol, and our high divorce rate? To avoid wrongly characterizing a value held by a group, an analyst must be sure that he or she is investigating the right subgroup.

ECOLOGICAL ANALYSIS

Ecological analysis is the study of the current state of the ecology. The **ecology** pertains to such issues as pollution and waste disposal, recycling of usable materials, protection of wildlife and wilderness preserve areas, workplace safety and hazards, and overall quality of life. Ecological analysis cuts across all the other areas already discussed: politics and government, the macroeconomy, technology, and lifestyle. Ecological issues are bottom-line concerns; the entrepreneur must be as accountable for them as any other businessperson or citizen . Ecological awareness goes beyond simply addressing the manufacturing issues of pollution and waste.

The entrepreneur is part of the world movement toward **sustainable development**, that is, meeting the needs of the current generation without compromising the needs of future generations.[22] Future economic progress must be guided by ecological conservation. The ecosystem and its protection enter into all major entrepreneurial and business-development decisions. For example, product development and design issues take into account the rate of usage and transformation of natural resources and the disposal of waste products. Entrepreneurs should make decisions about these matters in the planning stage of a business, not at the crisis stage. In addition, financial calculations should fully value natural resources for their current worth and their potential value to future generations. Undervaluation of natural resources causes waste and overdemand. The time at which entrepreneurs could run the earth like a business in liquidation has long since passed.[23]

General Electric (GE), one of the largest companies in the world, has an initiative called *ecomagination*. As part of this initiative, GE teams with Dow Jones & Company to promote a competition for the best business plan for an innovative, environmentally friendly venture. The prize is $50,000. The winner in 2006 was Mr. Robert R. Wright. His idea was for potable water, and his plan fit the prize criteria: (1) innovative and beneficial to the environment, (2) a clear path to profitability, and (3) a persuasive and logical presentation. Wright has spent his entire career, over 40 years, working in the field of water management and wastewater. He is an author, consultant, and a partner in his own firm. He cares deeply about the environment, and he knows water.[24]

COMPETITIVE ANALYSIS

The tools of competitive analysis are derived from economics, the so-called dismal science. Jokes are sometimes told to illustrate how deflating economics can be to entrepreneurs. So let us begin with a joke.[25] A student and her economics professor, while walking together across campus, were engaged in a serious discussion concerning the price elasticity of demand for a college education. As they walked, the student's eyes fell on a piece of paper on the pavement ahead of them. As they drew closer, the student could see that the paper was a $20 bill. When they were upon the bill, the student bent down to pick it up. "What are you doing?" asked the economics professor. "There's a $20 bill on the walk," replied the student. "Nonsense," said the professor. "If there were a $20 bill on the ground, someone would have picked it up by now."

This joke demonstrates that a strong belief in the all-powerful, efficient-market model of economics can prevent a person from seeing an opportunity, even when that opportunity is right under his or her nose. The economics professor cannot believe that a $20 bill (an opportunity) would be lying on the walk, because, with the assumptions of the efficient market theory, opportunities disappear instantly.[26] However, current reality and economic history show that there are truly many opportunities for individuals who follow their instincts and act on them intelligently.

Industry Analysis

The purpose of industry analysis is to determine what makes an industry attractive and to decide which segments of that industry are the most attractive. This analysis reveals the appropriate strategies and resources to procure or develop. Industry attractiveness is generally indicated either by above-normal profits or high growth, depending on the resources and cost positions of the firms in the industry. For example, hard-to-replicate efficiency levels (resources) lead to high industry profitability, but also make the industry less attractive for inefficient firms. On the other hand, high-growth industries are generally more attractive for less-efficient firms than for efficient firms.[27] Research has shown that some industries are more profitable over the long run than others. Each year, *Fortune* surveys all major industry groups and publishes the data. The results have been remarkably stable over time: One-year results for an industry might be spectacularly bad or good, but overall profitability within that industry is constrained by the industry's characteristics.

The firm's ultimate objective is to earn above-normal profits. It does this in one of two ways: (1) by developing a product that is so distinctive the customer will be willing to pay a price high enough to produce attractive margins, or (2) with a product identical to the competition's that can be produced at a cost low enough to result in attractive margins and profitability. These two strategies are broadly referred to as **differentiation strategy** and **low-cost strategy**, respectively. When a firm pursues either the differentiation or the low-cost strategy for a subsegment of a market (as opposed to the general market), it is using a **focus strategy**.[28]

A comprehensive analytical tool for determining the attractiveness of an industry is the *model of competitive analysis*.[29] This model describes five forces that determine the price/cost relationships within an industry and therefore define the industry's margins. These forces are:

1. The **bargaining power of buyers**
2. The **bargaining power of suppliers**
3. The **threat of** relevant **substitutes**
4. The threat of new entrants into the industry (presence and height of **entry barriers**)
5. The **rivalry** among existing firms (influenced by the other four factors)

Figure 3.2 is a schematic of the five forces at work. The industry under analysis is referred to as the **focal industry** to distinguish it from the buyer, supplier, and substitute industries that exert pressure on it.

Buyer Power

In perfectly competitive markets, buyers or customers have no power other than to accept or reject the product offered. All products are the same, so there is no shopping around for quality, service, or other characteristics. All have the same price, so no haggling is possible. When we relax this condition, we find that in a number of scenarios the buyer has a great deal of bargaining power. The two issues that are dearest to the buyer in bargaining situations are: (1) decreases in price for the product, and (2) increases in the product's quality.

Both of these buyer bargaining positions decrease the producer firm's margins. Price concessions squeeze margins from the revenue side; increases in quality squeeze margins by increasing the seller's costs.[30]

Once the conditions for perfect competition are relaxed, a buyer group can become powerful in several circumstances.

1. *Buyer Group Concentration.* If there are more sellers selling than buyers buying, the natural tendency is for the sellers to reduce prices to make a sale. Even if they do not reduce prices, they offer additional services to make quality improvements to their products, both of which have the effect of squeezing margins. If the buying group makes large purchases, in an absolute as well as a relative sense, it will bargain for volume dis-

FIGURE 3.2 Elements of Industry Structure

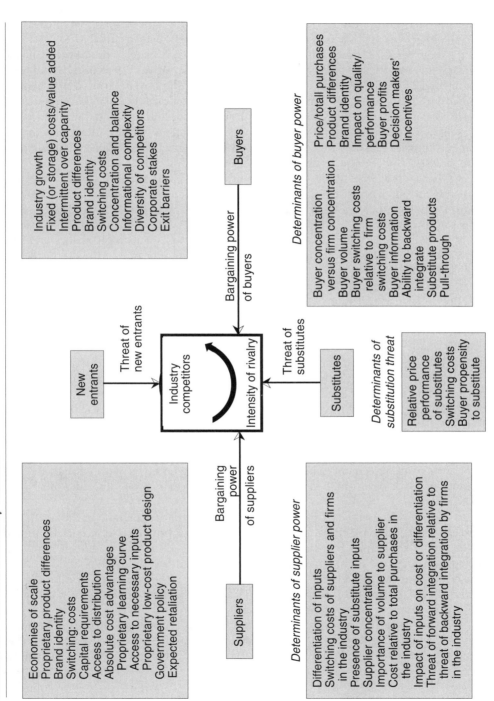

Economies of scale
Proprietary product differences
Brand identity
Switching: costs
Capital requirements
Access to distribution
Absolute cost advantages
 Proprietary learning curve
 Access to necessary inputs
 Proprietary low-cost product design
Government policy
Expected retaliation

Industry growth
Fixed (or storage) costs/value added
Intermittent over capacity
Product differences
Brand identity
Switching costs
Concentration and balance
Informational complexity
Diversity of competitors
Corporate stakes
Exit barriers

Buyer concentration
 versus firm concentration
Buyer volume
Buyer switching costs
 relative to firm
 switching costs
Buyer information
Ability to backward
 integrate
Substitute products
Pull-through

Price/totall purchases
Product differences
Brand identity
Impact on quality/
 performance
Buyer profits
Decision makers'
 incentives

Determinants of buyer power

Determinants of supplier power

Differentiation of inputs
Switching costs of suppliers and firms
 in the industry
Presence of substitute inputs
Supplier concentration
Importance of volume to supplier
Cost relative to total purchases in
 the industry
Impact of inputs on cost or differentiation
Threat of forward integration relative to
 threat of backward integration by firms
 in the industry

*Determinants of
substitution threat*

Relative price
 performance
 of substitutes
Switching costs
Buyer propensity
 to substitute

New
entrants

Threat of
new entrants

Industry
competitors

Intensity of rivalry

Bargaining power
of buyers

Buyers

Threat of
substitutes

Substitutes

Bargaining
power
of suppliers

Suppliers

counts. The bases for these discounts are: (1) the threat to withhold the order and disrupt production, (2) the lower per-unit costs of billing and shipping large orders, and (3) the lower production costs resulting from long production runs.

2. *Buyer's Costs.* If the products represent a significant share of the buyer's total costs or total income, the buyer becomes extremely price sensitive. When purchases are large, small concessions in price produce large benefits for the buyer. Most consumers are familiar with this situation, because bargaining over the price of cars and homes is the primary consumer bargaining experience. The automobile and residential real estate industries allow people to bargain over the prices of these items because they know their customers are price sensitive owing to the size of the purchase. Consumers bargain a little, but they still pay enough to salvage the sellers' margins.[31]

3. *Similar Products.* If the buyer is indifferent among sellers because the products available for purchase are basically alike, the buyer has power. If buyers can procure alternatives, they naturally look for a reason to buy from a particular seller, and one good reason is a lower price. The implication here is that the selling firm may believe it has a product that should command a premium price because of its high quality and special features. If these features are unimportant or not communicated to the buyer, the buyer will still shop on price.

4. *Switching Costs.* If the buyer faces few switching costs and can shop for price or quality without incurring high transaction costs, the buyer is powerful. Switching costs are costs that lock the buyer into an ongoing relationship with the seller. An example is frequent-flyer miles. Travelers will fly higher-priced, less-convenient air routes to accumulate these miles. The cost of switching airlines is the loss of frequent-flyer miles.[32] Sometimes, high transaction costs also result from switching vendors or searching for information. Faced with these costs, the buyer remains in the current relationship, enabling the seller to maintain profitable margins.

5. *Buyer Income.* The buyer whose profits are low or who has a low income is price sensitive. Price sensitivity increases when the buyer is short of funds, either personal income (for consumers) or profits from operations (for industrial buyers). Rich people sometimes haggle over a price, and purchasing agents of profitable companies search for a penny-saving agreement. More often, though, for the buyer with enough funds, the cost of negotiating a tough deal outweighs the minor savings derived from haggling over price.

6. *Threat of Integration.* If the buyer firm chooses not to purchase in the open market and can make a credible threat to fabricate a product or provide a service itself, it increases its power by gaining bargaining leverage over the sellers in the industry. This factor brings into play the classic make-or-buy decision, and it does so on a strategic level. If the buyer firm can provide the entire product itself, that firm then constitutes a credible threat for full **backward integration**. If it can provide some of the input, the process is known as **tapered integration**. The reasons for increased buyer power are as follows: (1) The buyer can make a take-it-or-leave-it offer to the seller with the full knowledge that if the seller "leaves it," the firm can still supply itself; (2) the buyer knows the actual costs of producing the product or delivering the service and can thus negotiate more effectively down to the seller's reservation price. The major offsetting factor for the sell-

er is the credibility of its threat of **forward integration**.

7. *Indifference to Quality.* If the products or services in an industry are not distinguished by quality, cost becomes a determining factor in consumer choice. In the presence of indifference to quality, the major reason buyers distinguish between sellers is price. Increased price sensitivity causes buyers to shop around and negatively affects the industry's margins.

8. *Full Information.* The more information the buyer group has about product prices, manufacturing costs, comparative product attributes, and the negotiating strategies of sellers, the more bargaining leverage it has. In young industries, where buyers and sellers are new at dealing with one another, certain cost and price data can be kept secret, which makes firms in young industries less likely to face pressure on margins. In mature industries, as firms build up long records and files of information on each other, they are more likely to have full information, causing downward pressure on prices.

Seldom do an industry's products have only one type of buyer. Certainly, for consumer products, market segmentation analysis demonstrates that there are many types of buyers. Each segment possesses its own utility functions and is therefore subject to strategic product-positioning tactics. The same is true in industrial marketing, making **buyer selection strategy** a key decision. Firms strive to hold a portfolio of buyers, each with a different degree of bargaining power. If a firm has only weak buyers, its short-term margins may be good, but the firm is not producing high-quality products and is probably not investing enough in the kind of product improvements and innovation that more powerful buyers demand. These deficiencies make the venture potentially vulnerable to an innovative competitor that produces high-quality products or services. If the venture has only strong buyers in its portfolio, it will have low margins and will always be a captive of its customers. Such a firm is vulnerable to the whims of its customers and to their desire to increase their own profits.

Strategies to manage buyer power are particularly critical to new ventures in the retailing industry. Street Story 3.3 reports on the efforts of a pair of entrepreneurs attempting to reach the pinnacle of retailing—successful placement of their product in Wal-Mart.

Supplier Power

Like buyers, suppliers exert bargaining power over an industry in two ways. Suppliers seek to (1) increase the prices they charge for the products and services they sell, or (2) lower the quality of those products and services to current market-clearing prices. Either of these bargaining objectives has the net effect of squeezing the margins in the focal industry and, other things being equal, making the industry less attractive. If the supplier industry is successful in the use of these tactics, it shifts profits from the focal industry to its own industry, capturing the economic power that the focal industry may have with its own buyers and appropriating the gains. Entrepreneurs who concentrate all their energy and analysis on their buyers and none on the supplier industry may well find that profits are quickly eroded by cost-squeeze pressures.

Supplier power is basically the other side of the buyer-power coin. The same prin-

The Write Stuff

For many vendors it represents nirvana: access to 138 million customers every week in 5,300 stores. "They see Wal-Mart and see dollar signs and think they can sell us anything," says Excell La Fayette, Jr., the retailer's director of supplier development. In 2004, 10,000 vendors applied to become new Wal-Mart suppliers, but only 2 percent, or around 200, were selected for trial runs. Approximately one-quarter of those ultimately became official suppliers.

Colin Roche and Bobby Ronsse were two of the lucky ones. In 2001, the former fraternity brothers used $10,000 to found Pacific Writing Instruments, a company that manufactures an ergonomic pen that Roche created when he was in high school. Unlike padded "stick" pens, the PenAgain's wishbone design is powered by the user's index finger, allowing a writer to rest the entire weight of his or her hand between its two prongs. Roche created the pen to combat writer's cramp, but many occupational therapists and physicians now recommend it for patients with arthritis and carpal tunnel syndrome.

Roche and Ronsse have a Web site (www.penagain.com), and have been selling the pen to more than 5,000 independent retailers and to Amazon.com. Their company chalked up sales of $2 million in 2005. But the two entrepreneurs longed to break into national, mass-market distribution, and their attempt to do so provides an interesting illustration of buyer and supplier power—and its pitfalls.

Unfortunately for Pacific Writing Instruments, most of the power during their buyer-supplier negotiations rested with the buyer. Wal-Mart's sheer size provided the group concentration needed to negotiate lower costs. While the PenAgain sells for as much as $12 in some stores, Wal-Mart wanted their almost identical model to retail for $3.76. To produce a product at that price, the supplier had to move production to China. Wal-Mart also required Pacific Writing Instruments to follow specific packaging and labeling guides to help the chain minimize its sorting and display costs.

Wal-Mart, of course, already sells lots of pens, and had previously rejected an instrument similar to the PenAgain. But Roche and Ronsse convinced their chain contact that their pen already had a proven track record, and that they were well on their way to building a brand with name recognition and different versions.

Buyer Wal-Mart kept lowering its costs by granting Pacific Writing Instruments a trial period in which the PenAgain would be stocked in 500 stores, primarily in easy-to-change displays at the ends of aisles, for a period of six weeks. The retailer placed an initial order for 48,000 pens. Even though sales fell short of the 85 percent of stock goal, after 30 days Wal-Mart ordered additional pens for the 150 stores where they sold best.

As a supplier, most of Pacific Writing Instruments' power rests with the fact that their product is relatively unique, and that they have a cadre of users and people who recommend the product who have already purchased 1 million pens during the lifetime of the company. Roche and Ronsse appealed to their e-mail list of 10,000 names to help make their Wal-Mart test successful, and contacted all 150 chapters of their Lambda Chi Alpha fraternity. They also hired a merchant service company to call each of the 500 Wal-Mart department managers and ensure that PenAgain was actually displayed in the aisles. In addition, each day they downloaded sales data for each store from the Wal-Mart vendor site.   Roche and Ronsse even personally visited 50 stores. Wal-Mart's La Fayette says they went "probably above and beyond" the retailer's expectations.

The two entrepreneurs are somewhat concerned about backlash from their existing outlets, and have developed a line of special versions of the PenAgain to sell through those vendors, but their chance to more than double their revenue with the Wal-Mart trial makes this risk worthwhile.

You can follow PenAgain's progress by checking its Web site, and by going to www.Walmart.com.

SOURCE: Adapted from Jeanette Borzo, "Follow the Money," *The Wall Street Journal*, September 26, 2005. Retrieved from the Web February 23, 2006, http://www.online.wsj.com/article_print.SB1127244182674 46432.html, and from Gwendolyn Bounds, "Pen Maker's Trial by Wal-Mart, Part III," *The Wall Street Journal*, July 18, 2006, and www.aipfl.com.

ciples apply, only here the focal industry is the buyer. Suppliers can exert pressure on margins under several conditions.

1. *Supplier Concentration.* When the supplying industry is dominated by a few companies and is more concentrated than the focal industry, suppliers have power.

2. *Role of Substitutes.* Suppliers are powerful when there are few good substitutes for supplying the industry's products. Even large, powerful suppliers cannot maintain high prices and low quality if good substitutes for their products are available.

3. *Purchasing Power.* If the focal industry is not an important customer for the suppliers, the suppliers have power. If the total dollars spent by the focal industry are small relative to the supplying industry's total sales, it will be difficult for the focal industry to obtain price concessions, quality improvements, or extra services such as delivery, warranties, and on-site repair.

4. *Importance of Quality.* When the product or service being purchased is crucial to the success of the industry's product or service, it must be of high quality. Focal industry firms often pay dearly for this high quality. Without substitutes of similar quality, the focal industry can expect cost increases for the product or service, which could severely diminish its profitability.

5. *Switching Costs.* Switching costs prevent buyers from playing suppliers off against each other in an attempt to bargain for price concessions or improvements in quality. These costs are, of course, analogous to the buyer-power conditions mentioned in the preceding section.

6. *Threat of Integration.* Again, the analogy to the buyer-power situation is apparent. If suppliers can do for themselves what the focal industry does, the focal industry cannot expect to exert much bargaining power. For suppliers, this is a use-or-sell decision. They have the option to either sell their input to another firm or use that input themselves to produce a final product. Also, tapered integration, where the supplier uses only some of the input internally, can be used to generate data on costs, which enhances the supplier's bargaining power.

Although there is a tendency to think of suppliers as firms that only sell the entrepreneur goods and services, other supplier industries may require analysis. For example, labor, capital, land, information, and business services are all suppliers. Each can be analyzed using the framework described previously. Every new venture has a portfolio of suppliers—some can be influenced by strategy and some are too powerful to be influenced. **Supplier selection strategy** minimizes the possibility that profits made in output markets will be lost in input decisions.

The Threat of Substitutes

Every industry competes against other industries for customers. Sometimes the competition is fairly direct, as in the case of fiberglass insulation versus rock wool, cellulose, or plastic foam.[33] At other times, the substitute-product rivalry is indirect, though still real. For example, the "eat-at-home" food-processing industry and its distribution chain—grocery stores and supermarkets—compete with the "meals away from home" restaurant industry and all its many segments. At times, it is difficult to tell whether another industry is a factor in determining the pricing power of the company. For example, does the motor home industry compete with the car, truck, and boat industries, or does it compete with motels located along interstate highways and near campgrounds and parks? Clearly, the substitute product is defined by its function, not by the way it looks, how it is produced, or even what it costs.

It is important for the entrepreneur to understand the nature of substitute products for three reasons. First, when entrepreneurs are the first to market a new product or product type, they sometimes believe they have no competition because "we're the first ones doing this." However, competition often exists in function, and a competitive challenge from a substitute industry is likely to surface. Second, substitutes can limit the potential returns to the focal industry by placing a price ceiling on what the industry can charge. A price may be so high that it will force customers to switch from one industry's product to another's. The more attractive the value of the substitute (its price/performance relationship), the lower the price ceiling will be.

Last, existing firms often disparage the threat of substitutes because of psychological factors that block quick action. For the entrepreneur, this can be an advantage. The entrepreneur usually has a period of time in which to maneuver before established firms recognize a threat.

Entry Barriers

Why is the professor of economics so certain that the $20 bill is not there? Because nothing prevents someone else from picking it up first. There are no entry barriers to the "found $20 opportunity." Entry barriers are a crucial factor for entrepreneurs in analyzing industry structure.[34] The entrepreneur must overcome entry barriers as they currently exist, and later attempt to create entry barriers to prevent others from following and diminishing the found opportunity.

This is again the second **paradox of entrepreneurship** (see Chapter 1). If the entrepreneur can find an industry that is easy to enter, it may be similarly easy for others to enter. The second paradox of entrepreneurship sets what may appear to be a lucrative opportunity against the characteristic low profitability of low-entry barrier businesses. If the entrepreneur finds an industry that is difficult to enter (and by implication profitable), all its profit potential might have to be expended in high initial start-up costs to overcome the barriers.[35] The paradoxical conclusion might therefore be: No profit can be made in an industry with low-entry barriers, and no profit can be made in an industry with high-entry barriers (the conclusion is the same for intermediate situations). Therefore no new firms can make profits. The answer to the paradox is that the new entrant's resources and the strategic differences between new firms and existing firms allow entry and success despite high barriers.

Table 3.5 presents the major entry barriers that face a new venture entering an existing industry. There are two general types: (1) **structural barriers**, which result from the industry's history, technology, and macroenvironment, and (2) **retaliatory barriers**, which are a function of current competitors' anticipated reactions to the new entry.

Structural Barriers to Entry. Structural barriers prevent the entrepreneur from getting started; they represent a lost opportunity. For example, capital investment may be high and out of the reach of most entrepreneurs. Or scientific knowledge may be needed and difficult for entrepreneurs to procure. But retaliatory barriers are even more dangerous to the entrepreneur because they can destroy the entrepreneur's chances of success after a large investment of time, money, and resources.

Retaliatory Barriers to Entry. Usually, when a new firm, especially one that is relatively small, enters an industry, there is little response from that firm's large, well-established competitors. Sometimes, however, entry by a new venture provokes a strong response from larger and more powerful firms. Because retaliation becomes an immediate threat to the survival of the new venture, the owners of new firms should understand when they may provoke retaliation. Large, established firms retaliate primarily under the following three conditions:

1. *When they have a reputation to uphold and a history of retaliation.* Firms that are historically known as aggressive competitors do not want to lose that reputation, even if the competition is a new venture of small size. This is the case because that reputation is an asset (rare, valuable, imperfectly imitable, and nonsubstitutable) that helps protect the competitor from other aggressive strategies and tactics. If the reputation is tarnished, other firms may decide to attack. Microsoft is a company with this type of aggressive position.

2. *If the attack is at the core business.* When a newcomer attacks the core business of an established firm, the attacked firm feels the greatest threat and will most likely retaliate. When the Dr. Pepper soft drink threatened Coke's cola business, Coke developed Mr. Pibb, a Dr. Pepper taste-alike that it could promote (a fighting brand) if need be.

3. *If the entry occurs in a slow-growth industry.* When an industry is growing slowly, in terms of total sales dollars and unit volume, each new entrant takes away a small percentage of sales that an established firm was counting on. The slow-growth industry has the elements of a zero-sum game: Sales garnered by one firm are forever lost to all other firms. Segments of the liquor industry are slow growth, and new entrants are targeted. The tobacco industry would be the same if a new entrant emerged.

Price Cutting. Retaliation can be expected in two additional situations: when the product is commodity-like and when the industry has high fixed costs. Both are likely to cause price-cutting retaliation in an attempt to force the new firm out of business. The

TABLE 3.5 Entry Barriers

Structural Barriers	Retaliatory Barriers
Economies of scale	Competitors' reputation
Excess capacity	Industry history
Product differentiation	Attack on competitors' business
Specific assets	Slow industry growth rate
Capital requirements	Competitors with substantial resources
Switching costs	Price cutting
Access to distribution channels	Legal challenges
Cost disadvantages unrelated to size	

presence of either of these conditions drives the industry price level down to the entry-deterring price, the hypothetical price that will just balance the rewards and cost of entry. In other words, it is the product or service price that makes the entrepreneur forecast zero profits for the proposed new venture. When an industry's prices are below the entry-deterring level, no rational entrepreneur would start a new business in that industry. The existing firms will allow prices to rise again when the threat of entry has subsided. If the threat is persistent, these firms will have to use other methods or concede that their industry imposes low-entry barriers and, therefore, other things being equal, is not an attractive industry in which to be.

In some situations, the small, new venture is protected from entry-deterring price cuts. Table 3.6 lists the factors that both encourage and inhibit the use of price cutting as a competitive tactic. The table illustrates that when price cutting is not likely to work—when it is likely to cause major losses for the price cutter and probably provoke large, existing competitors to follow suit—the new firm can operate under the **price umbrella** of the existing competition without fear of price retaliation.

Legal Challenges to New Ventures. New firms can expect retaliation to take forms other than price cutting, especially when larger firms do not see price cutting as an option. Legal attacks have become a common method of retaliation. The basis for a court battle could be patent, copyright, or trademark infringement, violation of a former-employee noncompete clause, claims of defective products, violation of environmental laws, or, in the case of a foreign new venture entrant, claims of dumping and unfair competition. If we try to start a business called Squids "?" Us, we will see legal retaliation. Toys "R" Us™ owns the property rights to all such names; its policy on this subject appears on its own Web site.

Trademarks. Certain trademarks, trade names, service marks, and logos used or displayed on this Web site are registered and unregistered trademarks, trade names, and service marks of Toys "?" Us or its affiliates. Nothing contained on this Web site grants or should be construed as granting, by implication, estoppel, or otherwise, any license

TABLE 3.6   Factors Affecting Retaliatory Pricing

Encouraging Factors	Discouraging Factors
Elastic demand	Inelastic demand
Cost advantages	No cost advantages
Excess capacity	Tight capacity
Small competitors	Large competitors
New competitors	Long-time rivalry
Single-product markets	Market interdependency

or right to use any trademarks, trade names, service marks or logos displayed on this Web site without the written permission of Toys "R" Us, GSI or such other owner.[36]

Rivalry between Firms

An industry with strong buyer power, strong supplier power, good substitutes, and low entry barriers is more competitive than an industry without these forces. Each force, by itself, can cause costs to rise, prices to fall, or both. This cost push or price squeeze reduces the operating margins of the firms in the industry. Reduced margins force less-efficient firms to go out of business (if exit barriers are low),[37] modestly efficient firms to break even, and the most efficient firms to endure low profitability until industry conditions are altered.

The rivalry and competitiveness between firms increase when the other four forces in the model are negative. However, additional conditions lead to rivalry and low industry attractiveness. These conditions focus on the status of the existing firms. Rivalry among firms increases (and, other things being equal, margins and profitability decrease) when the following conditions prevail.

1. *Numerous and Balanced Competitors.* The more competitors there are, the more likely that some of them will "misbehave" by slashing prices and quality. This misbehavior causes problems for everyone. When competitors are balanced and all are about the same size, there is no clear leader in the industry to whom the others can look for direction. An industry leader helps maintain price discipline, and keeps the industry from engaging in destructive price wars.

2. *Slow Industry Growth.* When an industry is growing, there are enough customers to go around and fill most firms' capacity. Slow growth causes firms to compete for customers, either with price decreases or quality increases. Also, as growth slows, the need for advertising may increase, adding an additional expense and hurting margins.

3. *High Fixed Costs.* Firms with high fixed costs have high operating leverage. This means that they need high volumes to break even, but after the break-even point has been reached, each unit they sell adds significantly to their bottom line. Therefore, industries with high fixed costs have strong incentives to fill capacity any way they can.   Filling capacity may lead to price cutting. Examples here are the recent histories of the airline and automobile industries.

4. *Commodity-Type Products.* When the product is a commodity, or is perceived by the public as a commodity because the industry cannot differentiate products, pressures for intense price and service competition grow. The absence of switching costs and increased buyer power are related to this condition.[38] It is time to address the *all things being equal* assumption interspersed in our discussion. All things being equal refers to the firm's resource-based strategies. That is, industries are attractive or unattractive for entry without considering the resources the new entrant may bring to the table. The type of resources and the extent to which they possess the four attributes of competitive advantage do make a difference. An unattractive industry might be a profitable opportunity for a firm with a winning configuration of resources. An attractive industry might produce mediocre results for a firm without any resource advantages.

COMPETITOR ANALYSIS

What is the new entrepreneur to do with all of this analysis? The new entrant in an industry must perform a detailed analysis of its competition. The industry analysis, discussed previously, precedes the competitor analysis and is more general. The data required for the industry analysis are aggregated; in their disaggregated (firm-level) form, these data provide the raw material needed to assess the strategy and resource base of the competition. The competitor analysis will be used in the next chapter to develop the strategy for the new venture.

Identifying the Competition

The first step the firm must take in identifying the competition is to determine who the competition is. This step is the equivalent of asking, What business am I in? and What needs does my product or service fulfill for the customer? The competition consists of firms that fill the same customer needs as the new venture, or have the potential to serve those customers. How can the presence of these competitors be determined?

Current competitors can be identified in a number of ways. A direct method is to ask customers (of existing firms) or potential customers (of new ventures) where else they would consider procuring the product or service. Indirect methods include scanning trade and business directories, reading the *Yellow Pages,* and searching the Internet. To discover the larger competitors, the entrepreneur should check *Value Line, Standard & Poor's* classifications, and the *Disclosure* database that identifies firms by the U.S. government's four-digit Standard Industrial Classification code http://www.sec.gov/info/edgar/sic-codes.htm).[39]

Ranking Competitors

The next step is to evaluate a set of relevant current and potential competitors based on the qualities of their resources. This analysis will give a picture of the competitors' relative strengths and weaknesses and will present a comparative framework, enabling the entrepreneur to position the new venture. Weaker competitors may be attacked head-on. Competitors with characteristics similar to those of the new entrant may be candidates for alliances that would strengthen both firms. Or the entrepreneur may be required to position the new venture around powerful competitors to avoid head-to-head conflict.

A useful tool for competitor analysis is the resource-based grid in Figure 3.3. The grid presents the six types of resources by attribute for each relevant competitor, and requires the entrepreneur to assign a score for each dimension.[40] The entrepreneur's own venture is included in the analysis. In later chapters, we will also use a competitor grid to look at strategies, products, and services.

The initial information derived from the competitor analysis will rank the competitors on each type of resource, producing a grand ranking of all competitors. The next step is to examine how the competitors use their resource bases to confront industry forces. That is, how do the competitors' strategies influence buyer power, supplier power, threats of substitutes, entry barriers, and rivalry among firms? The competitors' strategies are revealed by studying their deployment of resources.[41] This examination enables the entrepreneur to answer the second question posed earlier in the chapter: What is the best way to compete in the industry for the highest profitability? The answer is: *Look for ways to employ one's resource base that reduce the forces threatening firm profitability, and position one's firm for leadership in that area.*

SUMMARY

The business environment can be viewed as a stock of resources: financial, physical, technological, reputational, human, and organizational. The entrepreneur with an effective strategy for acquiring resources can control some of these resources, with others being controlled by competitors and potential competitors. No single entrepreneur can control all the resources. Larger forces are at work, and it is unlikely that the trends in the macroenvironment will be influenced by any single firm.

The entrepreneur must understand the macroenvironment, for it establishes the political, economic, technological, sociodemographic, and ecological rules under which the new firm is created and must operate. The entrepreneur must be able to scan and monitor the macroenvironment and to recognize the contingencies and constraints the macroenvironment imposes. This analysis, however, is not enough for the firm's success.

The entrepreneur must be able to forecast and assess development, using as a knowledge resource the four attributes required for competitive advantage. Also required is the ability to marshal the resources necessary to overcome the constraints or effectively deal with the contingencies.

Understanding the elements and the processes of the competitive market enables us to discover the forces that make an industry attractive to the entrepreneur. These forces are the power of buyers, the power of suppliers, the threat of substitutes, the height of the entry barriers, and the nature of the rivalry between competitors. When buyers and suppliers are powerful, when good substitutes exist for the firm's products, and when entry barriers are low and rivalry is intense, the industry is not attractive because profits are likely to be low.

However, the entrepreneur's resource configuration occasionally enables entry into an unattractive industry. If an entrepreneur can configure his or her resource base and

FIGURE 3.3   Resource-based Competitive Analysis Grid

Instructions: On a scale of 1 through 7, evaluate the competition's resource base. A value of 1 indicates that the firm has absolutely no advantage in the resource area; a value of 4 indicates that the firm possesses about the same resource capabilities as other industry participants. A value of 7 indicates that the firm possesses an absolute advantage in the resource category.

Resource Types and Attributes	*Competitive Analysis Grid*					
		Competitors				
	Own firm	#1	#2	#3	#4	#5
Physical resources						
Rare						
Valuable						
Hard to copy						
Nonsubstitutable						
Reputational resources						
Rare						
Valuable						
Hard to copy						
Nonsubstitutable						
Organizational resources						
Rare						
Valuable						
Hard to copy						
Nonsubstitutable						
Financial resources						
Rare						
Valuable						
Hard to copy						
Nonsubstitutable						
Intellectual/human resources						
Rare						
Valuable						
Hard to copy						
Nonsubstitutable						
Technical resources						
Rare						
Valuable						
Hard to copy						
Nonsubstitutable						
Total scores						

design a strategy that offsets the profit-reducing forces within an industry, the new venture can achieve a sustainable competitive advantage.

Attractive industries provide opportunities for profitability. The forces that determine rivalry in attractive industries are not strong forces, and the rivalry is not cutthroat. Firms compete on the level of product innovations, advertising, brand loyalty, and distribution channels, a level that enables them to differentiate and position their products. There is little pressure on prices, and increased costs are passed along to the customer as increased value. Operating margins are generous and sufficient for reinvestment and shareholder distributions. An industry characterized by high profitability and good returns to investors is attractive for entry, all things being equal.

KEY TERMS

Assessing
Acyclical
Backward integration
Bargaining power of buyers
Bargaining power of suppliers
Business cycle
Buyer selection strategy
Countercyclical
Cyclical change
Demography
Design patents
Differentiation strategy
Ecology
Entry barrier
Externally stimulated opportunity
Focal industry
Focus strategy
Forecasting
Forward integration
Internally stimulated opportunity
Low-cost strategy
Macroenvironment

Monitoring
Paradox of entrepreneurship
Plant patents
Political risk
Price umbrella
Process innovation
Procyclical
Recognition
Retaliatory barriers to entry
Rivalry
Scanning
Stakeholders
Structural barriers to entry
Structural change
Supplier selection strategy
Sustainable development
Tapered integration
Tariffs
Threat of substitutes
Utility patents
Values

DISCUSSION QUESTIONS

1. Perform "thought experiments" on the following businesses using the six dimensions of the macroenvironment: politics, stakeholders, the macroeconomy, technology, sociodemographic forces, and ecology factors.
   a. Video game designer
   b. Pizza restaurant
   c. Manufacturer of women's sweaters
2. What are the costs and benefits of the process model of environmental analysis? How could an "ordinary" entrepreneur set up and manage such a model?

3. Discuss the primary factors in political and governmental analysis. Compare and contrast these factors for the following countries: United States, India, Russia, China, and Nigeria.
4. Identify the stakeholders of the university or college that you attend. Which are the most powerful? Why and when? Which are the least powerful? Why and when?
5. Discuss how technological change creates entrepreneurial opportunities. What are some current technological changes and what opportunities do they create?
6. Discuss how demographic change creates entrepreneurial opportunities. What are some current demographic changes and what opportunities do they create?
7. Discuss how ecological change creates entrepreneurial opportunities. What are some current demographic changes and what opportunities do they create?
8. How does challenging old assumptions and traditions lead to entrepreneurial opportunities?
9. How can the entrepreneur influence the power of buyers and suppliers toward competitive conditions more favorable for the entrepreneur?
10. How do substitutes influence industry attractiveness and profitability?
11. How do entry barriers influence industry attractiveness and profitability?
12. Explain the paradox of entrepreneurship. What can you do about this paradox to help launch your venture?

―――――――――― EXERCISES ――――――――――

1. Here is a list of problems to help students develop a business idea. Perform an environmental analysis on one of these and then develop five business ideas that would help solve the problem.
   a. Traffic in big cities is too heavy during rush hour.
   b. Cyber crime is spreading.
   c. There are so few chances for married people to have some time to themselves.
   d. Older people complain about their aches and pains all the time.
   e. Getting documents (licenses, permits, certificates, etc.) from the government takes for ever.
   f. Public and municipal services are constantly deteriorating.
   g. It is a bother to make a good cup of coffee in the office.
   h. Children play too many violent video games.
   i. Minor surgery is only minor when someone else is having it.
   j. Too many people do not really understand the value of an online degree program.
2. Return to the business treatments and business ideas that you developed in the Chapter 2 exercises.
   a. Set up a system for analyzing the business environment for that business.
   b. Where will the information come from?
   c. How will you assess and evaluate it?
   d. Evaluate the six dimensions for your business.
      Political-government
      Stakeholders
      Macroeconomy
      Technology
      Sociodemographic
      Ecology

3. Return to the business treatments and ideas that you developed in the Chapter 2 exercises. In what ways do these ideas emerge from the business environment? How does the business environment support these ideas? What resources are available from the business environment that will support these business ideas?

4. Scan the business press. Identify an entrepreneurial opportunity using each of the seven sources described in the chapter.

5. Perform an analysis of the industry that you (and your team) are considering for your new venture. Use outside sources for data, such as the library, computer databases, and industry experts.

6. Perform an analysis of the competitors for your new venture. Use Figure 3.3 as a summary sheet to guide you in your research.

7. Go to the U.S Patent and Trademark Office Web page. Do a search on the intellectual property you are using. Company and product names? Technology? Other?

DISCUSSION CASE

Clean, with a Whistle

Two entrepreneurs in New York City have used not one but *two* differentiation strategies to give their new ventures a competitive edge.

Both Deanne Hains and Miguel Zabludovsky have started cleaning businesses; Hains has a home-cleaning business and Zabludovsky a clothes-cleaning business. Both market their businesses as ecologically friendly alternatives to traditional competitors. Even the name Hains' Zen Home Cleaning Service suggests the nontoxic, human-and-pet-friendly products the owner uses. Zabludovsky's Slate NYC cleans clothes with a combination of organic and biodegradable agents instead of the Perclorethylene, or Perc, that is used by many dry cleaners.

Slate NYC's slogan, "We protect the environment from Perc and your reputation from Ms. Rivers," hints at its second differentiation strategy. As the tongue-in-cheek reference to the celebrity fashion commentator suggests, Slate NYC avoids the solvent Perc not only because it is toxic, but also because it damages clothes, makes color fade, and gives garments a chemical smell.

Organic is just one element of the laundry service's pampering approach.   Slate NYC also provides customers with a stylish transport hamper, picks up dirty clothes at a time specified by the customer, and returns the items wrapped in tissue paper and what it describes as uber-trendy packaging.

Convenience is an important part of Slate NYC's luxury service: Customers pay one weekly fee for as many clothes as they can stuff into the company hamper, and then let the company decide whether garments need laundering or dry cleaning. Pickups can be scheduled by phone or Internet, and the weekly fee is automatically charged to the customer's credit card.

Zen Home Cleaning has a few upscale flourishes of its own. It burns jasmine and citrus oils in each room while cleaning, and it sprays the freshly changed beds with lavender water. To support the company's claim that its service is comparable to that of a four-star hotel, the Zen cleaners leave a potpourri sachet and an organic chocolate bar on each bed as a thank-you gift. Customers can sign up on a regular service schedule or book a cleaning with two days' notice; they pay by credit card. In addition to its four-hour general-cleaning service, the company offers more comprehensive spring-cleaning overhauls and professional organizing services for homes that are too cluttered to clean.

Neither of these services is inexpensive: Zen Home Cleaning's rates start at $120 for a regular cleaning, and Slate NYC charges $60 per week. But both firms are located in Manhattan, where there is a large base of professionals who can afford premium prices. "The consumers buying eco products are not very price conscious," observes Zabludovsky. "They are willing and able to pay up to 200 percent premiums."

Both companies became profitable in their first year. Hains is currently exploring franchising opportunities in three locations outside of New York City, while Zabludovsky hopes to build his company to a point at which an investor will buy him out and extend his service to other communities.

SOURCE: Adapted from Riva Richmond, "Two Urban Start-Ups Mix Ecology, Luxury," *The Wall Street Journal*, February 28, 2006. Retrieved from the Web February 28, 2006. http://www.online.wsj.com/article_print/SB1141081937448 84661.html, www.zenhomecleaning.com and www.slatenyc.com.

Case Questions

1. Do you think Hains and Zabludovsky have been successful in developing a differentiation strategy to make their products distinctive? Why or why not?
2. Under the conditions described here, what kind of power do buyers or customers have with these firms? What kind of power do suppliers or businesses have?
3. Are these businesses vulnerable to the threat of substitution? What are some of the different ways in which another firm could compete with them?
4. Are the conditions right for the paradox of entrepreneurship here? What are some of the structural barriers? What might some of the retaliatory barriers be?
5. Would a franchise for either of these companies work in your community? Why or why not?

Profits are not made by differential cleverness, but by differential stupidity.
—*Attributed to David Ricardo,* Economist, *by Peter Drucker*

─────────────────────── OUTLINE ───────────────────────

─────────────────── LEARNING OBJECTIVES ───────────────────

After reading this chapter, you will understand

- how entrepreneurship is related to *strategic management*.
- the value and purpose of a *business model*.
- five different *hierarchies of strategy* that an entrepreneur can employ.
- what an *entry wedge* is, and the different major and minor entry wedges.
- three *resource-based strategies* an entrepreneur can use to achieve sustainable competitive advantage.
- *first-mover advantage and isolating mechanisms.*
- strategies for *information-based* ventures.
- five different *industry environments*, each with its own unique *life cycle*.
- how to craft and evaluate *entrepreneurial strategies*.

PERSONAL PROFILE 4

Tony Hsieh:
Strategy That's A Step Above

His first entrepreneurial success came at the age of 12; Tony Hsieh made pin-on buttons with photos, and then sold a couple of hundred dollars worth to his classmates every month.

At Harvard he sold pizzas in the dorms; his friend Alfred Lin bought some of those pizzas, and resold them by the slice.

Armed with a B.A. in computer science from Harvard, Hsieh went to work for Oracle, but in 1996 he started a banner ad swap program for small Web sites called *Link Exchange*. Hsieh and his former fellow student, Lin, sold that business to Microsoft in 1998 for $265 million. They then used some of the money they received to found Venture Frogs, an Internet start-up incubator and investment company that invested in start-ups including Ask Jeeves, MongoMusic, and Zappos.com.

In the words of one of their customers, Zappos is a "shoe store that comes to you." Its Web site offers more than 500 brands and 90,000 styles for both women and men, and there are almost two million items in stock. Hsieh became interested in Zappos when he learned that only $2 million of the $40 billion in annual shoe sales was attributable to mail order. A 1999 survey reported that only a third of Zappos' customers had purchased shoes by mail order before, but Hsieh believes that in the future 30 percent of all retail purchases will be online. "Over time I saw there was a lot of potential for the company," he says.

Zappos had already hired an experienced shoe buyer from Nordstrom, a department store famous for its selection of shoes, when Hsieh became the company's CEO in 2000. Under Hsieh's leadership, gross merchandise sales grew from $1.6 million in 2000 to $370 million in 2005. After his old friend, Alfred Lin, joined the company as CFO in 2005, Hsieh predicted that Zappos would reach $600 million in sales and become profitable by the end of 2006.

An almost fanatical devotion to customer service distinguishes Zappos from its competitors. In addition to offering a wide selection of shoe styles and sizes, the company provides both free delivery and free return shipping. It warehouses every item it sells under one roof in Kentucky. Because the warehouse is staffed around the clock, seven days a week, customers can often order shoes as late as 11 p.m. and still get next-day delivery. To emphasize its commitment to customers, Zappos locates its customer call center in the same building as the company's corporate headquarters in Las Vegas. These strategies must work; Zappos does very little advertising, and credits repeat business and word-of-mouth recommendations for its phenomenal growth.

Zappos isn't just good to its customers. All employees get a free lunch every day, and the company pays 100 percent of employee health insurance premiums. Suppliers like Zappos, too. "You can't believe how pleasant they are to work with," says a regional manager for Clarks Companies North America.

SOURCE: Adapted from Kimberly Weisul, "A Shine on Their Shoes," *Business Week*, December 5, 2005: 84 http:// www.zappos.com.

W HAT is the most common criticism that entrepreneurs hear about their business ideas and new venture strategies? It is, If that's such a good idea, why hasn't someone else already done it? The answer, implied by David Ricardo in the introductory quote, is that most people never have a good idea, and many who do lack the faintest clue about what to do next. Human intelligence and energy are the scarce resources. There are countless business ideas for creating and operating profitable enterprises, but most of them have not yet been conceived or implemented. The resource-based view of the firm values creativity and intelligence. The strategy and resource configurations can be sources of SCA.

A business idea is not a business.   The design, development, and implementation of a business require that the entrepreneur make certain strategic decisions about the venture's configuration.   These decisions form the initial vision and objectives for the business. Although it is possible to alter the decisions in the future, it is very difficult to change the fundamental economics and structure of the firm.   In this chapter, we will develop the embryonic venture idea into a fully workable business model with a sustainable strategy.

Our view is that there is an interaction between the resources, capabilities, experience, and vision of the entrepreneurs (internal factors) and the remote and operating environment of the industry (external factors) in the formation of new venture strategy.   The entrepreneur must know how to integrate these elements into a cohesive and coherent business plan.

We will also examine some of the strategic choices available to new ventures. We will begin by looking at how strategy, resources, and entrepreneurship intersect. We will then present the concept of the business model followed by a discussion of the strategy choices available to entrepreneurs. Next, we will introduce the industry life cycle and see how the different stages influence new venture strategy. We will also look at the effects of fragmented environments. Then we will introduce two approaches that help entrepreneurs to craft their strategy. At the end of the chapter, we will present a model for assessing entrepreneurial opportunities and evaluating the strategies chosen.

ENTREPRENEURSHIP AND STRATEGY

How are entrepreneurship and business strategy related? Some of the concepts presented in this chapter are borrowed and adapted from the strategic management literature.[1] In this literature, **strategy** is defined as "the patterns of decisions that shape the venture's internal resource configuration and deployment and guide alignment with the environment."[2] This definition has two major implications. The first is that "patterns of decisions" means both **strategy formulation** and **strategy implementation**. Formulation includes planning and analysis. Implementation is the execution and evaluation of the activities that make up the strategy. The second implication is that the entrepreneur has to consider both internal factors such as the firm's resources and capabilities, and external factors such as the market environment. That is what we did in Chapters 2 and 3.

One of the core assumptions of strategic management is that strategy exists on different levels within the firm. In descending order, these are the enterprise, corporate, business, functional, and subfunctional levels. Part of the environment for each level is the level above it; lower and higher levels must be aligned, with the higher levels leading the way. One result of this hierarchy is a cascading effect. Strategy formulation starts at the top of the hierarchy and flows down to each level. As it does, strategy formulation is increasingly replaced by implementation. The cascade effect contributes to consistency and helps hold together organizations that are sometimes large and far-flung.

Enterprise-level strategy is at the top of the hierarchy. It is concerned with the relationships between the firm and society at large. The context for analyzing this strategy was presented in Chapter 3. **Corporate strategy** focuses on the problems of diversification and the management of a portfolio of business. Because the new venture is most often a single business, corporate strategy is not discussed in this book. **Business-level strategy** is oriented toward competing within a single industry. It deals with the acquisition, organization, and employment of resources. Industry analysis was examined in Chapter 3. The strategies that correspond to industry conditions are the subject of this chapter. In other words, this chapter is about business-level strategy. **Functional** and **subfunctional strategies** involve marketing, finance and accounting, and human resource policies, which will be examined in Chapters 6 through 9.

BUSINESS MODELS AND STRATEGY

A **business model** goes beyond the business idea and adds significant detail. A business model is not a strategy, but it is the basis of strategy. It is the story of the business.[3] This model tells the story by answering the following questions.

- Who are the customers?
- What do the customers value?
- How does our business make money?
- What is the underlying economic logic of the venture?

There are two parts to the story. The first part describes how we obtain the resources, people, money, materials, and inputs that we use to produce our product and services. The second part of the story tells who we produce the product for, the conditions of sale and delivery, the marketing process, and the flow of cash back to the business.

We must also include the notion of the **revenue model**. The revenue model tells the story of how the flows of sales and cash revenue will be accumulated. The spreadsheet details the financial narrative of the story. Through the spreadsheet, we are able to do sensitivity analysis that tells us how the story might turn out, given different assumptions, endowments, and starting conditions. This is the financial picture of the story and we will return to it in Chapter 7.

Hambrick and Fredrickson put these pieces together into a framework they called the **strategy diamond**.[4] While their business-model framework has five dimensions, it is similar to the questions raised above. The key difference is that the strategy diamond asks us explicitly to lay out the staging and sequencing of our strategy. Figure 4.1 summarizes the strategy diamond model.[5]

FIGURE 4.1   The Strategy Diamond

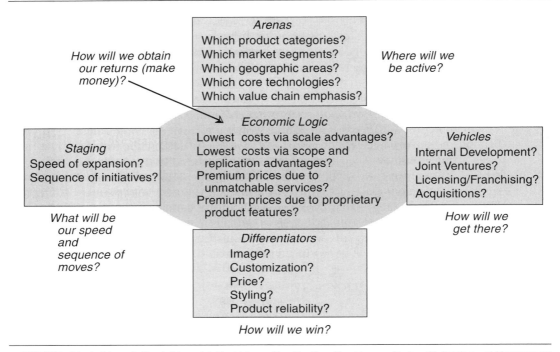

SOURCE: Adapted from D. Hambrick and J. Fredrickson, "Are You Sure You Have a Strategy?" *Academy of Management Executive*, 2001.

The first question to answer is: In which arenas will the venture compete? This is the initial part of the story of the business model. The next question is: What vehicles will we employ? At this point in the text, we have primarily been focused on internal development as the prime vehicle. The other collaborative and cooperative formats will be covered in Chapter 9. Here we note that creating the organization involves a set of strategic decisions.

The third question is: How will we be different? This is where our RBV theory and strategy come into play. We will be looking for resources that have the VRIN characteristics. The fourth question requires the firm to specify the staging of the decisions. In what order will the venture do things and how fast? All of these decisions converge on the center square. This is the revenue model described above.

Another way of looking at a business model was offered by Amit and Zott.[6] They emphasize the transactions and exchange themes of the story. These authors define a business model as "the content, structure and governance of transactions designed so as to create value through the exploitation of business opportunities."

Transaction content refers to the actual goods, services, and information that are being exchanged by the parties, and the resources and capabilities employed to facilitate the exchange. It represents the "what" of the story.

Transaction structure refers to the people or organizations involved in the transactions and how they participate—what their roles are (customer, vendor, and consultant). This represents the "who" of the story.

Governance of transactions refers to the rules, protocols, customs, and methods of exchange used. It is the way in which these transactions are controlled, and may include the legal forms of the businesses and the transactions. It describes the "how" of the story.

Table 4.1 below summarizes a number of e-commerce business models. Some of these were very popular during the boom of the late 1990s; others have been around for many years and can easily be applied to nontraditional businesses.

For example, the mash-up combines the content of other Web-based models and attempts to integrate and add value based on these other sites. One such mash-up, Platial (http://www.platial.com/splash), is a mapping service for people, videos, and stories. All of the content comes from other places, but Platial has the software to integrate the content into a story. The revenue model is aimed at online advertising. But many investors feel that a mash-up like Platial is not strategically defensible because it cannot protect the resources it doesn't own or control. Others are not so sure. Platial received financial commitments from both Kleiner Perkins and Omidyar Networks.[7]

Street Story 4.1 offers us the example of an affiliate business model called Brad's Deals.

TABLE 4.1   Internet Business Models and Stories

Business Model Name	Business Model Story
Business to Business (B2B)	Selling to commercial organizations directly
Business to Customer (B2C)	Selling to final users and consumers directly
Business to Business to Customer (B2B2C)	Selling to commercial organizations and then selling through directly to final users and consumers
Niches (vertical or horizontal)	Selling to a very specific customer segment (vertically through the supply chain) or selling a very specific set of products (horizontally to a variety of customers)
Clicks and Bricks	Selling through both the Internet and traditional business location with a physical presence
Roll-ups	Buying many smaller firms using the same business model (usually in fragmented industries) and then achieving economies of scale or scope
Advertising Models	Selling advertising in a media (cyberspace, newspapers, magazines, etc.) and giving away the content
Pay-for-content Models	Selling the content through information rules type strategies
Affiliate Models	Selling products on a second-party Web site for a fee. Enables the affiliate to piggyback on a more famous Website like Amazon or eBay
Mash-ups	Selling a Web-based application that mixes data from different online sources

---

| STREET STORY 4.1 |

I Can Get It for You (Almost) Wholesale

He works out of a 400-square-foot office with just a couch, fax machine, phone, white board, and a couple of computers. He has two part-time employees. He doesn't manufacture any items or inventory any products, and he doesn't have any special training or unusual skills.

Still, Brad Wilson's company took in over $1 million in revenue in 2005, and Wilson expects to do even better now that his Web site has a new name and some new features.

Wilson's site is an online discount shopping portal for savvy bargain shoppers. He started it when he was a student at the University of North Carolina at Chapel Hill, after negotiating a super low price for a 27-inch flat-screen TV from Amazon.com by combining Amazon's sale price, an e-coupon, and a free shipping offer. Friends and family asked him to find similar online deals for them, so Wilson created dealsdujour.com, an "affiliate" site that referred consumers to vendor sites with sale specials and other good deals in exchange for a fee from the vendor.

The site is now known as BradsDeals (www.bradsdeals.com). Wilson works with more than 700 merchant partners, including clicks and bricks retailers like Gap, Office Depot, Target, and Internet stores like Amazon.com and Overstock.com. Under the trademarked slogan Handpicked Deals™, BradsDeals lists a handful of specials every day. Each item has a brief description explaining why it is such a good deal, and a link to click through so that the shopper can get that low price and Wilson can get his commission. Shoppers can also use the affiliate site to search for deals by vendor or by category (such as apparel, cars, or pets). They can also use the site to access coupons that are good at retailers like Dick's or Kohl's.

Wilson claims that approximately 1.5 million shoppers have spent more than $100 million at the sites of his merchant partners. "We have tried to create a user-friendly site and a complete shopping experience for our visitors," he explains. BradsDeals has been honored by the online marketing industry for helping Internet retailers acquire new customers and increase their revenues.

SOURCE: Adapted from Gwendolyn Bounds, "Finding Good Bargains Is Also a Good Business," *The Wall Street Journal*, January 4, 2005. Retrieved from the Web January 4, 2005. http://online.wsj.com/article_print/O.,SB110479919259915983,00.html, and www.BradsDeals.com.

ENTRY WEDGES

Entry wedges are momentum factors.[8] They are part of the business model story. A wedge is not really a full-blown strategy, but is rather the methods the founders use to get their initial foothold in a business. Because the entry wedge becomes an important part of the firm's unique history, it may, from an RBV perspective, influence later strategic decisions. Unique historical conditions are impossible to copy. Therefore, the entry wedge can be part of the firm's sustainable competitive advantage.

Major Wedges

All new ventures employ one or more of three major entry wedges: new product or service, parallel competition, and franchising.

New Product or Service. A new product or service is one of the most potent entry wedges. Truly new products and services are relatively rare. If they include a new technology as well, they may be hard to imitate. Typically, new products have a lower failure rate than new services, primarily because most service organizations face lower entry barriers. Firms that do use the new-service wedge are likely to offer or introduce a related product if they gain a foothold in the industry. Ventures that initially offer a new product sometimes follow up with a related service, but this is less common.[9]

The new product or new service wedge is what Drucker called the "being first with the most" strategy.[10] This strategy is used to achieve a permanent leadership position either within an existing industry or by creating a new industry. Success with this strategy requires a concentrated effort at being comprehensive and innovative. "Being first," like the first-mover advantage, gives the firm a head start and possibly an insurmountable lead in market share, in low-cost manufacture and supply, and in public awareness and recognition. "With the most" requires that the product or service be comprehensive. If it is missing something (for example, service, warranty, delivery, or functional components that customers require), the door is left open for competitors. This is the high-risk, high-reward entry wedge. Table 4.2 below illustrates some of the types of new products that have been introduced in recent times and are considered award winners. (Students might want to research these companies to see what particular uniqueness they have brought to market.)

Parallel Competition. Parallel competition is a "me too" strategy that introduces competitive duplications into the market. These duplications are parallel, not identical, to existing products or services. They represent an attempt to fill a niche, a small hole in the market. This can be done with a small innovation or a variation in an already well-accepted and well-understood product line or service system. An entrepreneur who notes that a firm's current customers are unhappy and who conceives of a strategy to make them happy would be entering with a parallel wedge strategy. Marginal firms always risk being replaced by others that do basically the same things but do them better.

Most retailing start-ups, for example, enter with the parallel competition wedge. The difference between one retail operation and another might only be location or minor variations in merchandising and marketing. The typical retail store carries the same or similar products from the same suppliers and charges approximately the same markups as its competitors. This type of entry is fairly easy, because entry barriers are low. Firms of this type can produce stable income and profits over a long time if they possess some distinctive competence. More likely, though, these firms are low-sales, low-profit operations. For the entrepreneur, they are alternatives to other jobs and replace income from other employment. Without a distinctive competence, these small retailers quickly become marginal and risk being replaced by another firm using the parallel wedge strategy.

However, if used with creativity and vision, the parallel wedge strategy can lead to superior payoffs. Drucker calls this form of the parallel strategy **creative imitation**.[11] Creative imitation combines the common business configuration of the competition (the imitation part) with a new twist or variation (the creative part). Two types of com-

TABLE 4.2   Innovative New Product Ideas
The Wall Street Journal's 2005 Technology Innovation Award Winners

Company Name	Industry	Winning Product Description
454 Life Sciences*	Biotech-Medical	Low-cost gene-splicing method
Optimyst Systems Inc.	Medical devices	New device for applying eye medicines
Solar Integrated Technologies, Inc.	Energy and Power	Solar roof system designed for large commercial and industrial buildings
MIT team (nonprofit)	Environment	Low-cost water filtration system for developing countries
Ecological Coatings	Materials	Non-toxic, easy-to-use finishes and coatings
Riverbed Technology Inc.	Network/Broadband Internet	Steelhead network appliances that reduce delay between remote offices and servers
ObjectVideo Inc.	Security facilities	Software that monitors multiple-security camera feeds
Fujitsu Laboratories Ltd.	Security network	Network that reads the veins in the palms of hands as alternative to fingerprints
Alien Technology	Semiconductors	Low-cost method for RFID production
Agitar Software Inc	Software	Software that automatically tests programs for bugs and flaws
QinetiQ (UK)	Transportation	Tarsier high-resolution radar system
Freescale Semiconductor Inc.	Wireless	Wireless technology for consumer products that use "ultra wide band"

*Grand Prize Winner

SOURCE: M. Totty, "A Better Idea," *The Wall Street Journal Report: Technology,* October 24, 2005. Retrieved from the Web February 21, 2006. Http://online.wsj.com/article/SB112975757605373586.html.

petitors are susceptible to a new venture's creative imitation: those with weak spots and those with blind spots. Firms with weak spots may have the same resources as others but not employ them well. The new venture, without different assets but knowing how to use the assets it does have, has an advantage. Some entrepreneurs also have blind spots—things they do not see about the market, the competition, or themselves—that make them vulnerable to creative imitation. Examples include:

- The *"not invented here" syndrome.* Firms are sometimes slow to adapt innovations or are reluctant to change because they did not initiate an idea themselves. This syndrome makes the firms easy to target for the new venture that is quick to adopt the new standard. For example, the Polaroid corporation and Kodak waited much too long to adopt digital photography as their core technology. Polaroid is gone and Kodak is much diminished as a result.
- The *"skim-the-market" blind spot.* Here, firms that charge high prices and attempt to capture only the most profitable business are vulnerable. Other firms can

operate under their price umbrella, gain market share, and become close to their customers. The creative imitators learn how to add value by serving the tougher customers. Hertz Corporation and its rental car business is the high-priced provider. There are literally dozens of car rental companies that operate under Hertz's price umbrella. These companies owe their very existence to Hertz's reluctance to discount.

- *Technologcial tunnel vision.* Firms that emphasize product- and manufacturing-based quality to the exclusion of user-based quality have technological tunnel vision. They are vulnerable because they fail to notice minor changes in customer needs and perceptions that are obvious to the imitator. The makers of cell phones have been guilty of this. For many segments of the market, they offer too many features and the phones become more complex with each generation. Apple Corporation is offering the iPhone as a simpler and more integrated product.
- *The maximizer complex.* Firms that try to do too much, that serve all types of customers with all types of products and services, are vulnerable because they may not serve any customers particularly well. A parallel competitor who carves a niche to serve a specialized customer base can succeed here.

Franchising. The third major wedge is franchising. It is a twist on both the new product and me-too wedges. Franchising takes a proven formula for success and expands it. The **franchisor** is the seller of franchises. The franchisor is attempting to create something new and offer it to the market. For the franchisor, franchising is a means of expanding by using other people's money, time, and energy to sell the product or service. These other people are the **franchisees**. In return for a franchise fee and royalties (usually based on sales), they gain the expertise, knowledge, support (training, marketing, operations), and experience of the franchisor, which reduces their risk of failure. The franchisee is pursuing a me-too strategy as one of a potentially large group of franchises. For example, Subway sandwich shops offer the same products through thousands of outlets. For franchising details, see http://www.subway.com.

The key to franchising power is for the franchise system to expand geographically under a license agreement. Geographic expansion enables the franchise system to saturate markets. Saturation gives the franchise the benefits of visibility and recognition, logistical cost savings, volume buying power, lower employment and training costs, and the ability to use the mass media for efficient advertising. The license agreement gives the franchise system a mechanism for standardizing its products or services, incentives for growth, and barriers to entry. All three parties to the franchise system (franchisor, franchisee, and customer) benefit, which explains why franchising has become the most prevalent form of new business start-up. We will return to franchising in Chapter 10.

Minor Wedges

A number of other entry wedges are designated as minor because they can be classified under the three major categories. Four categories of minor wedges, each with several variations, include exploiting partial momentum, customer sponsorship, parent-company sponsorship, and government sponsorship. They can be seen as a way to obtain resources that the new venture can use to compete. Table 4.3 cross-references the major entry wedges with the minor ones. For example, we see that "tapping under-utilized resources" can be part of either a new product/service wedge or a parallel wedge strategy.

Exploiting Partial Momentum. Sometimes the entrepreneur already has sufficient market and product information to indicate that the new venture will be successful. This information acts as the impetus for the launch. The entrepreneur can exploit this existing momentum in three ways: by geographic transfer, by filling a supply shortage, or by putting an underutilized resource to work. A **geographic transfer** occurs when a business that works in one area is started in another. For example, Miho Inagi has opened a bagel bakery and store in Tokyo. She first learned about bagels as a student in New York. She took a job at Ess-a-Bagel (translation: Eat a Bagel) where she learned the business from the floor (sweeping) up (baking). But would Japanese eat hard bread? Most Japanese bakeries focus on soft-bread items and quasi-bread and cake concoctions. Inagi has made few concessions to Japanese tastes, offering mostly traditional, New York-style bagels. Her father (who later helped finance the business) lamented that, "We must have

TABLE 4.3   Major and Minor Entry Wedges

Minor Entry Wedges	Major Entry Wedges		
	New Product/ Service	Parallel Competition	Franchising System
Exploiting partial momentum			
1. Geographic transfer			X
2. Supply shortages		X	
3. Tapping underutilized resources	X	X	
4. Creating or modifying existing channels	X	X	
Customer sponsorship			
5. Customer contract		X	
6. Second sourcing		X	
Parent-company sponsorship			
7. Joint venture	X		
8. Licensing		X	
9. Market relinquishment		X	
10. Spin-off	X		
Government sponsorship			
11. Favored purchasing		X	
12. Rule change	X		
13. Direct assistance	X	X	

SOURCE: Adapted from K. Vesper, *New Venture Strategies* (Upper Saddle River, NJ: Prentice-Hall, 1980).

done a bad job raising you." But Inagi persisted and opened her business, Maruichi Bagel, in August 2004. After a slow start, the store now draws crowds and Inagi makes a modest profit.[12]

Entrepreneurs can launch new ventures by filling market gaps such as **supply shortages**. Sometimes the product or service in short supply must be physically transferred from one area to another. In this case, filling the supply shortage resembles geographic transfer in that the entrepreneur organizes resources to fill a shortage within an area. For example, recent trends indicate that for various tasks at varying times of the year, many firms prefer to hire temporary workers rather than full-time employees. However, there is a shortage of people available for temporary positions because most people prefer to work full time if they can. New ventures have been developed that specialize in personnel services for temporaries. These firms, like Professional Employer Organizations (see www.peo.com), organize the resource that is in short supply (temps) to meet market demand. They also meet the demands of the temporary personnel by scheduling additional work after each temporary assignment expires. For the firm, the shortage is relieved; for the personnel, there is full-time work (in various temporary assignments).

An **underutilized resource** is one with an economic value that is not recognized or one that is not being used to its best advantage. Often people are the most underutilized resource. Hence, entrepreneurs who can more fully realize other people's economic value are considered leaders. The underutilized resource can also be physical, financial, reputational, technological, or organizational. For example, entrepreneurs in the financial sector find ways to better use nonperforming financial assets, such as cash or bonds. Entrepreneurs have helped large organizations with strong positive reputations (for example, Disney and Coca-Cola) gain additional income by licensing their brand names, trademarks, and copyrights. Underutilized physical resources are often somebody's junk, waste, by-product, or worn-out product. These resources constitute the core of the recycling and remanufacturing industries. For example, entrepreneurs are building businesses by finding new uses for the mountains of worn-out tires dumped across the United States. Others are building vending machines that take in aluminum cans for recycling and dispense store and manufacturers' coupons.

Creating or modifying existing distribution channels enables the new venture to take advantage of the momentum that already exists in the value chain. For example, if strong production or inbound logistical areas already exist, finding new channels helps the entrepreneur to reach new markets. Many longtime successful catalog sellers, such as Lands' End, now use their Web sites as surrogate catalogs. They still do most of their business by mail order, but the Web is a new channel for them.

Customer Sponsorship. A new venture's launch may depend on the momentum supplied by the firm's first customers. A customer can encourage an entrepreneur in either of two ways. A **customer contract** can guarantee the new firm sales, and help it obtain its initial financing. Because the customer is not assumed to have altruistic motives, the entrepreneur should seek to expand the customer base once the venture is up and running. Sometimes, customers encourage entrepreneurs to become a **second source**. If the customer has previously had difficulty working with a single supplier, good purchasing practice would suggest that the customer rebid the contract. However, a good alternative for obtaining the product or service is not always available. When this is the case, the customer can encourage and even provide assistance (managerial, technical, and financial) to the entrepreneur who can satisfy the customer's needs. Both customer contract and second-source sponsorships generally lead the firm to use parallel competition as its major wedge.

Parent Company Sponsorship. A parent company can help launch a new venture in four ways. Two of these methods require ongoing parent-company relationships: **licensing** and **joint venturing**. The other two methods may continue the parent–new venture relationship, but are optional: **market relinquishment** and the **spin-off**.

Under a licensing agreement, the entrepreneur contracts with the parent company to produce a product or service or to employ a system or technology. The connection between the entrepreneur and the parent provides momentum for the new venture, because the founders have previous organizational experience with the parent as well as technical experience with the product or technology. The joint venture differs from the licensing format in two significant ways: (1) Resources are commingled when the joint venture is formed, and (2) Ownership rights in a joint venture require negotiation. These differences make the joint venture more difficult to manage, but the benefits of having two (or more) organizational parents can outweigh the cost.

For example, if we wanted to create an Internet business that used Java software, we would license the software from Sun Microsystems, Inc.[13] There would be no need for a joint venture with Sun because all the details of the relationship between the venture and Sun could be handled in the legal document. However, when the major automobile companies wanted to create a common application, using Java, for credit for a car loan, they formed a new company, RouteOne LLC. This company was formed as a joint venture.[14]

Market relinquishment means that the parent company decides to stop serving a market or producing a product. Although its motivation can vary, the parent usually makes such a decision because the firm is not cost-efficient. This is especially likely to be true if the product volume or market niche is small, for a large company's overhead can be high enough to make a small niche unprofitable. However, such a niche may be profitable for a small firm. The most likely candidates to start that small firm are the large firm's former managers of that product/market niche. Therefore, when the larger corporation relinquishes the market, the former managers may have the opportunity to purchase the larger firm's specialized assets and continue in their jobs, but this time as owner/managers instead of simply managers, thus providing the new venture with strong momentum. The change may not be visible to customers and suppliers, but the new firm can be much more profitable (and perhaps strategically more flexible) when it does not have to support the corporate bureaucracy.

One of the most common starting points for new venture creation (based on previously acquired knowledge) is the spin-off. A spin-off is a new firm created by a person or persons leaving an existing firm and starting a new firm in the same industry. The most frequent examples of spin-offs today are in high-tech businesses—biotechnology and life sciences, semiconductors and computers, consulting, law, and medicine (and medical devices). What do these diverse industries have in common? Both emerging and growing industries are prime breeding grounds for spin-offs. In these industries, pockets of information possessed by employees can be disseminated throughout the market. This information is mobile; it is embodied not in a machine or particular location but in individuals, a process, or a technique. Both the knowledge and the individuals can be transferred at very low cost to just about any place on earth.

Government Sponsorship. In Chapter 3, we discussed the impediments and constraints that government often imposes on new ventures. However, the government can also act as a sponsor for new ventures and provide entrepreneurs with launch momentum in the following ways.

1. *Direct assistance.* "They're from the government, how can they help you?" A number of local, state, and federally supported programs can aid the entrepreneur in starting or managing a new business. Most provide managerial or technical assistance; a few, like the Small Business Administration, may also on occasion provide financial assistance. One of the less well-known sources of technical assistance is the federal research laboratory system. At these labs, such as the Oak Ridge National Laboratory in Oak Ridge, Tennessee, scientists and engineers help businesses solve difficult technical problems. Other federal agencies have started programs to help small- and medium-sized businesses. NASA offers free consulting advice in cooperation with state agencies in Tennessee, Mississippi, and Louisiana. The Sandia National Laboratory in Albuquerque, New Mexico, also has a program.[15]

2. *Favored purchasing.* Favored-purchasing rules enable some firms to enter the marketplace with an edge. The federal government's own procurement policies often mandate set-asides and quotas for small businesses, minority and woman-owned firms, and firms started and managed by physically disabled people and veterans of the armed services. Many of these favored-purchasing rules have also been incorporated into procurement policies and practices at other government levels and throughout corporate America.

3. *Rule changes.* As government regulatory practices change and as new laws are implemented, opportunities for new firms arise. One of the most significant areas in terms of changes in government policy in the last decade has been privatization. Over the years, governments frequently found themselves in the business of providing goods and services to people. These have ranged from the provision of rail service to the running of hotels on government-protected lands. Of course, in former communist countries where the government owned all the means of production, privatization has been the way in which these assets have shifted to the hands of entrepreneurs. Even as we begin the twenty-first century, privatization opportunities abound for the sharp-eyed and quick-moving entrepreneur.[16]

RESOURCE-BASED STRATEGIES

How can our resource-based theory help us to create entrepreneurial strategy? We have already discussed the fundamentals of competitive strategy in terms of our resource-based theory. Briefly, resource-based theory says that for firms to have a sustainable competitive advantage, they must possess resources and capabilities that are rare, valuable, hard to copy, and nonsubstitutable (with resources that are neither rare nor valuable). One way of thinking about this issue is from the **payments perspective.** Each resource employed by the firm in the design, manufacture, and delivery of every product must earn a return or a payment. These payments are the rents on the resources. The total payments earned by the firm's resources are equal to its total revenue. The enemies of value and scarcity are imitation and substitution. Therefore, the critical strategy is the coupling of entrepreneurship and isolating mechanisms (see below).[17]

Rent-Seeking Strategies

Strategy in the resource-based framework is rent seeking.[18] There are five types of rents, and the strategies available to obtain them are different. Firms can attempt to capture more than one type of rent simultaneously. The five types of rents are as follows:

• **Ricardian rent**: These are rents derived from acquiring, owning, and controlling a scarce and valuable resource. They are most often derived from ownership of land or natural resources or from a preferred location. These types of rent can be collected as long as ownership and control exist, possibly in perpetuity.

• **Monopoly rent:** These are rents collected from government protection, collusive agreements, or structural entry barriers. Examples of government protection include patents and copyrights, restrictive licenses, and government-granted franchises. Many collusive practices such as price fixing and conspiracies in restraint of trade are illegal in the United States, but enforcement varies by time and place.

• **Entrepreneurial rent:** These are rents accrued from risk-taking behavior or insights into complex and uncertain environments. This type of rent is also known as "Schumpeterian rent," and is the type most closely associated with new venture creation. Schumpeterian rents are not as long-lasting as Ricardian and monopoly rents because of the eventual diffusion of knowledge and competing firms' entry into the market.

• **Quasi-rent:** These are rents earned by using firm-specific assets in a manner that other firms cannot copy. These rents are often based on idiosyncratic capital and dedicated assets. They are derived from a distinctive competence in how to use the resource as opposed to mere control of that resource. These rents can be collected by discovering or estimating the value of combinations of resources. The combinations are more difficult to price than stand-alone resources and therefore add value. The most important implication here is that it is possible to capture value in a tradable, scarce but not unique resource due to complementarities, asymmetrical information, or simply high levels of bargaining skill.[19]

• **Relational rents:** These are rents earned by cooperative-type strategies and interorganizational relationships.[20] They are somewhat similar to quasi-rents but they require that the venture work with another company. These rents may be a result of (1) relationship-specific assets, such as site specificity (co-location); (2) knowledge-sharing routines, such as technology-transfer agreements; (3) complementary resources that are not available or are priced in factor markets; or (4) effective governance, which minimizes transaction costs among organizations.

Resource-based strategies are geared toward rent-seeking behavior. The most prevalent of the five rent-seeking behaviors is the entrepreneurial strategy. Here a firm enters with a new resource configuration or implementation strategy and makes above-average profits until, through technological diffusion and increased knowledge, competitors are able to enter and compete away those profits. This describes the cycle of "destructive capitalism" that constantly redeploys capital to its most economic use.

Ventures with the four attributes required for sustainable competitive advantage are positioned to use strategy to collect one or more of the five types of rents. The more types of rent the firm can accumulate, the better its overall long-term performance will be. Any of the five types of rent described above require that the firm be able to protect its advantage. These protective devices are called *isolating mechanisms*. The absence of isolating mechanisms means that others (workers, investors, customers, competitors, governments) can work out strategies to claim the rents for themselves.

ISOLATING MECHANISMS AND FIRST-MOVER AVANTAGES

An entrepreneur who is fortunate enough to create a new venture must expect that competitors will attempt to retaliate, and protect his or her own positions.[21] Therefore, it is important that the entrepreneur find ways to increase these benefits and cash flows for either future investment or personal incentives. The methods the entrepreneur uses to prevent the rents generated from the new venture leaking out are known as **isolating mechanisms**.

Types of Isolating Mechanisms

Isolating mechanisms can take a number of forms. Most obvious are **property rights**, which consist of patents, trademarks, and copyrights. Any secrets, proprietary information, or proprietary technology also help isolate the firm from competitive attack. These mechanisms, though, will not last indefinitely; therefore, the entrepreneur must be prepared to move quickly and establish a strong position. Some firms establish their position, and work to protect it right from the beginning of the new venture. This is known as **first-mover advantage (FMA)**. First-mover advantage can also be a powerful isolating mechanism when combined with a government rule change that encourages privatization or industry deregulation.[22]

Sources of First-Mover Advantage

First-mover advantages prevent the erosion of the new venture's competitive advantage.[23i] A firm's resources and capabilities are frequently enhanced by its early entry. Examples include:

- Having prime physical locations
- Having technological space
- Having customer perceptual space
- Having an industry with standard setting
- Developing switching costs
- Generating lead time and learning

The first use of a technology, known as **technological leadership**, can provide first-mover advantages. The first mover in a particular technology can, of course, obtain the initial patents, but these are seldom decisive.[24] More important, the first mover builds up a research and development base that can lead to further innovations and improvements, thus keeping the venture ahead of the pack. As production (either *through* the new technology or *of* the new technology) increases, the learning curve is pushed ahead of that of competitors, often conferring cost advantages and economies of scale that can preempt or delay competition. Being the first mover may mean obtaining valuable and scarce resources ahead of others. It may mean getting rights to natural resources, securing the best locations, or crowding distribution channels (distribution space is a valuable and rare resource).[25]

The final source of first-mover advantage is the imposition of switching costs on buyers.[26i] **Switching costs** can be developed through marketing or contractual obligations. When a new venture creates brand loyalty through effective advertising, high buyer learning and evaluation costs, or complementary products, the firm makes it difficult for others to compete away its profit.

To be first, ventures need to be organized for speed and develop the capability to innovate and get to market quickly. Street Story 4.2 provides some examples of these fast-moving companies and some rules for organizing.

First-mover advantages can also be a disadvantage in certain situations. In some cases, the first mover must reveal the underlying business concept, and others may copy this by using different resource combinations. The first mover invests in resolving the technological and production problems that accompany any new venture. Other firms can then benefit from these investments. Also, being first once does not guarantee that the firm will always be first. Indeed, inertia can make the successful first mover resist abandoning a strategy when it is no longer effective. There are no simple prescriptions about first-mover advantages and disadvantages. The magnitude of the first-mover effect varies greatly and will dissipate over time. Later entrants sometimes catch up through advertising and pricing strategies.[27]

Growth Strategies

So far, we have seen how new ventures enter using their wedges, and how they seek to collect rents based on their capabilities and resources. We can also use our resource-based model to account for the rate and direction of a venture's growth strategies. Firms grow in the direction of underutilized resources and toward their areas of expertise. The rate of growth is a step function, not a smooth path, because resources are usually employable only in bulky, discrete increments.[28] Basically, a firm's growth is limited to its resources. Resources determine the industry the firm will enter and the levels of profit it can attain. For example, labor shortages, insufficient access to capital, and technological barriers all limit growth.

In the long run, however, the most important limit of all may be the scarcity of management capacity. There are two demands on managerial capacity: (1) to run the firm at its current size, and (2) to expand and grow. Current managers recruit new managers to increase the growth potential of the venture. However, these new managers need to be trained and integrated into the firm's current activities, which takes time away from existing managers. While incorporating these new managers, the firm's growth slows.

The Fast Track to Profits

It used to take the Nissan Motor Company 21 months to develop a new car model; now they've got it down to half that time. It once took manufacturers like Motorola and Nokia 12 to 18 months to produce a new cell-phone model. Now they do it in six to nine months. AMR Research consultant Bruce Richardson has a terse explanation: "There are two kinds of businesses: the quick and the dead."

Atlanta-based casual food franchiser, Raving Brands, has launched seven different restaurant concepts, including Moe's Southwest Grille and Mama Fu's Asian House, in the past five years. The company doesn't have a central office; its senior directors meet every Monday at a Raving Brand restaurant to solve problems and discuss new ideas, including ideas that come from other restaurants. This get-down-to-business approach has enabled the company to translate ideas from concept to restaurant opening in one year as opposed to the two years needed by other franchisers. Raving Brands also jump-starts its expansion by hosting "tour days" in more than 15 target markets where company representatives present their different restaurant opportunities and meet with potential franchisees.

A speed advantage doesn't always come from the product itself. In 2004, wine producer, Jackson Enterprises, was able to come up with an innovative solution to a worldwide wine glut in just a few weeks. With the help of the product and service design firm IDEO, a team of Jackson employees quickly developed rough prototypes of two packaging concepts that were radically different from those of their traditional Kendall-Jackson brand, including wine in a cardboard container that looked like an elegant perfume box, and wine poured into a screw-top bottle with a drawing of a silly dog on the label. "We absolutely broke all the unspoken rules," reported team

leader Laura Kirk Lee. The wine maker also set up a temporary bottling plant in a parking lot tractor-trailer truck to get the products to market as quickly as possible. While the team's goal was to sell 10,000 cases of each wine concept, they actually sold more than 100,000 cases of both new ideas.

Consumer electronics and appliances have today devolved into a commodity competition based on low prices, which unfortunately means low profits for retailers. But one store has found a way to get a first-mover advantage.

According to Best Buy Company's Executive Vice-President Ron Boire, "We go upstream to find out what the suppliers are doing. It's about speed to market. We know what the customers are looking for, and we have a time advantage in getting it to them." The company meets regularly with tech start-ups in both Silicon Valley and Asia to spot new products it thinks might become best sellers. In 2005 these meetings led to the discovery of Sling Box, a device that allows customers to transfer programs from their home TV to a PC in a different location. The $250 item was a winner for Best Buy, especially since the company was able to stock Sling Box three months before most of its competitors.

When one of Best Buy's Geek Squad service-team members had an idea for a PC external disk drive inside its own protective case (an item that didn't exist at that time), the company was able to find a manufacturer and then place the item in its stores within 120 days. Best Buy is also experimenting with concept stores in a few markets. One concept is *studio d*, a store that combines the latest electronic gadgets with classes to show nontechies how to use them. Another concept is the *eq-life shop*, where customers can attend fitness classes and then purchase the latest fitness gear. If Best Buy succeeds in building customer loyalty through this product-with-training approach, the company may also have an innovative approach to building switching costs.

SOURCE: Adapted from Steve Hamm, with Ian Rowley, "Speed Demons," *Business Week Online*, March 27, 2006.

Retrieved from the Web March 21, 2006. http://www.businessweek.com/priont/magazine.content/06_13/b3977001.htm?chan=gl, and Best Buy: Also see "How To Break Out of Commodity Hell," *Business Week Online*, March 27, 2006. Retrieved from the Web March 21, 2006. http://www.businessweek.com/print/magazine.content/06_13/b3977007.htm?chan=gl, and www.ravingbrand.com.

Once these managers have learned the venture's structure and systems, growth begins again. This implies that "management is both the accelerator and brake for the growth process."[29] This rubber-band process, called the Penrose effect after the theorist who first proposed it, suggests that fast growth in one period will be followed by slow growth in the next period (that is, there is a negative correlation between period growth rates).[30]

Quality as a Strategy

In Chapter 1, we introduced the concepts of quality. Considerable thought, energy, and money have been devoted to making quality a source of sustainable competitive advantage. Hundreds of articles and books have been written on the subject. A prestigious national contest, the Malcolm Baldridge National Quality Award (http://www.quality.nist.gov/), is held each year. Many states now have programs to help companies develop and improve their products' quality. Although the concept of total quality management (TQM) is not new, there are still many programs that emphasize customer satisfaction (user-based quality discussed in Chapter 1). To some, TQM is the number-one priority for the firm, and it has entered the language and curriculum of top-rated business schools.[31] Companies that promote TQM programs are themselves a fast-growing industry. Consultants sell "off-the-shelf" TQM programs based on some simple ideas that can be understood by using the analogy with playing golf:

- **Continuous improvement.** This is the process of setting higher standards for performance with each iteration of the quality cycle. In golf terms, yesterday someone shot a score of 112, so today he or she will try to shoot 111.[32]
- **Benchmarking.** This means identifying and imitating the best in the world at specific tasks and functions. If one believes that Tiger Woods has the best swing, he or she tries to swing like Tiger.
- **Quality circle.** This is a loop of activities that includes planning, doing, checking, and acting. Keep one's head down, keep one's eye on the ball, and don't press. Now, where did it go?
- **Outsourcing.** This means procuring top quality from outside the organization if the firm cannot produce it from within. If she can't hit this shot, can somebody else hit it for her?

The resource-based approach calls into question the efficacy of these quality programs for long-term competitive advantage. If any firm can buy the principles of TQM off the street (so to speak), then it is not rare. Benchmarking, which is neither more nor less than copying, is by definition able to be copied. Outsourcing products from the best-quality vendors is both substitutable by producing in-house, or sourcing from other best-quality vendors. Can TQM be an effective strategy for sustainable competitive advantage? Research indicates that TQM programs are not magic formulas.[33] At best, they were termed a "partial success." The following were among reseachers' general conclusions regarding TQM:

- Copying other firms may mean expending time and money on the wrong things.
- Adopting a TQM program, under certain conditions, can actually make things worse because the program is so disruptive.
- Failing to link the TQM program with bottom-line results may ensue.
- Benchmarking is not effective unless the company already has a comprehensive quality program.
- Lower-performing firms should adopt TQM programs gradually; middle performers are better able to begin full-scale adoption; and high performers benefit the most from TQM.

INFORMATION RULES STRATEGIES

With the advent and popularity of e-commerce, many pundits claimed that the old ways of doing business had ended and the laws of economics should be rewritten.   But two economists from the University of California at Berkeley did not see it that way.   Carl Shapiro and Hal Varian believed that the same principles of economics that applied to the real world of business also apply to the virtual world of business.   To establish their point, they wrote a book called *Information Rules: A Strategic Guide to the Network Economy*.[34] This discussion draws heavily on their ideas.   We can see what their emphasis and focus are by going to their Web site: http://www.inforules.com/.   The site demonstrates that these authors practice what they preach when it comes to offering a digital information product.

The electronic entrepreneur deals with **information**.   Information is anything that can be put into a digital format, for example, photographs, text, catalogs, data, movies, stock quotes, and online MBA classes.   Information is intellectual property and can be protected using copyrights, trademarks, or business-method patents.   Finally, information must be experienced for people to determine its quality and benefits. People usually require a peek or preview before they purchase. Information can be very expensive to generate, but it is almost costless to reproduce.   Therefore, selling information provides great margins—unless it is reproduced and re-sold by others.   Information also has different uses for different people.   Different versions of information can be offered to different customer segments. By segmenting the market, an entrepreneur can extract maximum value—the most profit from his or her property.   E-businesses have many value drivers or ways of creating value through their operations and strategies (see Table 4.1 above). All of these facts about information are embodied in the strategies of e-entrepreneurs.

There are a number of key strategic options that e-entrepreneurs need to consider as they form their businesses and marshal resources and capabilities for their firms.

Value Pricing. Value-pricing strategy is based on the fact that different people value information to different degrees. What pricing strategy should we employ? If we are able to differentiate our product, we can attempt to sell information to each customer for a different price, depending on what the customer can bear. If we cannot differentiate and our information has become a commodity, we can be aggressive but not greedy, as the customer can likely get the same information elsewhere at a better price. We must remember that the information is almost costless to duplicate, and results in large economies of scale. We should also consider offering group sales, as the cost of selling data or information to a group is probably the same as the cost of selling it to a single individual. This strategy is the basis for site licenses for software products.

Versioning. This strategy means producing information in many forms for the customer. Some possibilities are:

- Delay. Sell some information to customers who need it in a hurry and want fresh, up-to-the minute reports (like stock quotes). Sell another version in another format (e.g., a digest of monthly stock movements). Charge the most for the latest data.
- Convenience. This is related to delay. Make it easier for some customers to use the data, and charge them for this privilege.
- Speed of operation. This is also related to delay. Make some information accessible quickly and charge for this service. Make some customers wait for their versions and give them a discount for doing so.
- Image resolution. Some data can be displayed to ultimate effect through enhanced graphics. Charge extra for an enhanced graphics version and offer a version without enhanced graphics (like text only) at a discount.
- Features and functions. Make some versions of the product available with search capability, cross-referencing, and a full line of features and functions. Make other versions with certain functions disabled, and charge less for these versions. Many users will trade up for full functionality. Note that it costs the same to produce the two versions; the firm simply offers less information to the price-conscious consumer. For example, many students may purchase student versions of software such as Windows Office Suite or Bizplan. The student versions are actually the same as the full-feature versions, but with some functionality turned off.

Intellectual Property. Intellectual property strategy is intended to maximize the value of the intellectual property. Many businesspeople think this strategy is the same as one that maximizes the protection for the property. But this is not true. Indeed, carried to its extreme, the maximum protection for the property is not to sell it at all! As we can see from the controversial maximum-protection positions once taken by the film and music industries, we can offend our customers with too much protection. Customers sense that information wants to be free and shared, so we need a strategy that maximizes value, not protection. Because digital technology lowers production and distribution costs, we must be willing to pass these savings on to the consumer. How?

- Give away free samples.
- Offer low-cost versions purchased one at a time.

- Give away indexes, tables of contents, and some graphic images.
- Give away lower-quality product and information.
- Be willing to license use, and employ group sales.

There will always be customers who want the highest quality, the timeliest data, and the product with the fullest functionality, and the one that is easiest to use. These very demanding customers tell us what is most important to them. They help us locate the true value of the property. They are the core of successful intellectual property management.

Lock-in. This strategy keeps the customer loyal to the venture. It is essentially the same concept we discussed earlier under the heading of switching costs. A lock-in strategy raises switching costs for the customer. The entrepreneur who can design a lock-in strategy and engender brand loyalty has the ability to maintain a relatively high price for the product. Further, this strategy reduces the cost of keeping current customers. Table 4.4 offers lock-in strategies and switching cost models.

Network Strategy. This strategy is based on the principle that one telephone is useless, but a million are very useful. The first fax machine was just a toy, but with two such machines, there is communication. A network with a great many users is significant because the more users there are, the more valuable it becomes for any single individual to be a part of that network. We see these principles applied in such successful businesses as eBay (http://ebay.com), Amazon (www.amazon.com), and the Japanese cellular phone company, DoCoMo (http://www.nttdocomo.com). If we find ourselves in a network of this type, it is vital that we recognize this fact. If we are in a network, we must take advantage of the **positive feedback** that exists within that network. If we do not do so, we will incur a large opportunity cost. If competitors take advantage of the positive effects and we do not, we might not survive.

A good example of pure network effects is instant messaging. The more people that are in a particular instant message network, the better it is for all the members. They can have extended buddy lists and contacts. The instant messaging firms compete to have the largest networks.

Cooperation and **Compatibility** Strategy. Many times entrepreneurs try to steer their firms' strategy in an adversarial "win-lose" fashion. But in the digital economy, this strategy is frequently wrong. The entrepreneurial team needs to determine which other firms may be part of its network, actual or potential. Then the team needs to cooperate with these firms to build the size and strength of the network. Often this means making products and technology compatible with each other. The goal is to have the network's standards become the industry standard. Doing so will create a "winner-take-all" situation, and if the network becomes the industry standard, that network wins.

A related way of thinking about how e-businesses create value is to look again at the **drivers** within this type of business. Four drivers emerge: **efficiency, novelty**, **complementarities** and (the now-familiar) **lock-in**.[35]

Some of the value that is created by an e-business results from the use of efficiencies—

TABLE 4.4   Lock-In and Switching Costs for Customers

Types of lock-in	Switching costs
Contracts and subscriptions	Damages for breaking the contract or ending the subscription before it expires
Durable purchases	Replacement of the equipment; switching cost declines as equipment ages
Brand-specific training	Customers have to learn a new system, process or technique; loss of productivity during training period
Information and databases	Data conversion costs, potential for losing data; larger databases equal higher costs of conversion
Specialized suppliers	Search of finding new supplier; new supplier may not have precisely the same capabilities and quality of older supplier
Search costs	Aggregate of buyer and seller costs
Loyalty programs	Lost benefits from program; need to start over with another company's program

reducing the costs of searching, transacting, monitoring, and decision making. These are real costs to the consumer and the consumer will pay to have them reduced or eliminated. In theory, as each consumer might have a different set of costs, a new version of the product or e-business Web site can be created for each consumer.

Novelty is created by bundling the features and benefits of the e-businesses' products and services. Each product or service can have an element of difference or novelty, but even if the product or service lacks such novelty, the bundle can be novel or unique in some way. Because every customer (in theory) will want a different bundle, this type of customization is a value driver.

The value driver, complementarity, is a function of the bundles, but may go further. It may refer to the complementarities of partners or technologies, and include the network effects of complementarity of customers and vendors.

Last, Amit and Zott include the concept of lock-in, which is similar to previous descriptions including brand loyalty, loyalty programs, and dominant technology.

STRATEGY AND INDUSTRY ENVIRONMENTS

Not all ventures enter the same industry. How much difference does the industry itself make in determining strategy? The answer is, "quite a lot." Entrepreneurs can significantly add to the success of their strategies by understanding the industry environment they are entering. A static description of industry structure was presented in Chapter 3. However, industry environments are static only in the short term; over a longer period of time they evolve. This evolution is called the **industry life cycle**. The industry life cycle progresses through four stages: emerging, transitional, maturing, and declining.

The industry life-cycle progression is not the same for all industries. The length of each stage and the timing of the stages are highly variable and difficult to predict. The same is true for product and organizational life cycles. Entry and competition take on different forms, depending on the stage of the life cycle.[36] Figure 4.2 presents a diagram of the industry life cycle. It follows the familiar s-curve of many economic phenomena.[37] The shape of the curve shows that emerging industries are characterized by increasing rates of growth. Transition occurs as growth continues at decreasing rates. In the mature stage, growth rates approach zero. A declining industry is characterized by no growth or negative growth rates, whether measured in total units of production or in dollars.

Emerging Industries

Emerging industries are the newly created networks of firms launched to exploit a new technology, a new market configuration or set of customer needs, or other changes in the macroenvironment.[38] Emerging industries experience high levels of uncertainty, rapid change, and a growing number of organizations (high rates of births). Recent examples of emerging industries are biotechnology and life sciences, the electric automobile industry, products for use on cellular telephones, and the interactive television industry.

Individual firms and entrepreneurs can create or reconfigure entire industries through vision, creativity, and innovation. An innovation strategy can create a customer where none previously existed.[39] How can this be done?

• *By creating utility.* The entrepreneur can change something that is hard for people to do into something that is easy for people to do. For example, there had been "mail" since Roman times, but the mail industry arose with the creation of a postal service in Great Britain, making it easier for people to pay for and send a letter.

• *By creating value.* The entrepreneur can change something that was expensive into something that is inexpensive, and thereby create value through creative pricing. King Gillette did so when he unbundled the razor from the razor blade. Xerox did so when it realized it did not have to sell copiers, just the use of the copiers. It changed a relatively large capital-investment decision into a small operating expense to gain acceptance.

• *By changing the customer's reality.* The entrepreneur can help customers buy products through creative distribution and financing, and help customers use products by simplifying operation and providing training. Entrepreneurs help customers solve problems by selling systems instead of products.

Structural Uncertainty. Even for ventures on the verge of revolutionizing the market, however, entry into emerging industries imposes certain structural conditions and constraints. The most imposing structural condition is uncertainty. There are no traditional ways of doing things, rules of thumb, standard operating procedures, or usual and customary practices. There is only the unknown future and the entrepreneur's will to succeed. Technological uncertainty means that the final configuration of resources, especially technological resources, is still unsettled. Firms, like laboratories, are trying new com-

FIGURE 4.2 The Industry Life-Cycle Curve

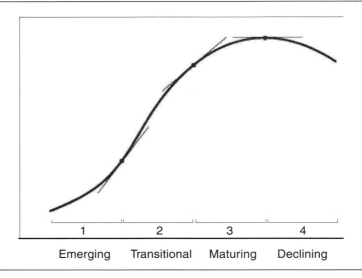

binations of technology, human resources, and organizational systems to discover what works. Successful combinations are adopted by other firms as fundamental, and further experiments are conducted to refine the concepts and practices. Usually a single standard emerges for all firms. Occasionally, two competing standards reach the public at the same time as, for example, video technologies like Beta and VHS. But only one survives.

Strategic Uncertainty. Emerging firms also face a great deal of strategic uncertainty. New ventures in emerging industries are often unaware of who the competition is (or will be), what types of products and processes the competition is working on, and what posture the government will take toward the new industry. Because birth rates are high, new firms are springing up all the time, making it difficult to keep track of who and what they are. Government regulatory agencies at all levels are slow and bureaucratic. They are unlikely to have existing rules to help guide the new ventures.

Resource Uncertainty. Additional uncertainty looms in the firm's input markets. It is often difficult for the new venture to raise capital, because financial sources are unfamiliar with the new industry's risk/reward profile. Although some venture capital firms specialize in supporting investments in emerging industries, most financial institutions shy away from them. Labor is another input that is difficult to procure, especially managerial talent. Managers and executives face a great deal of career risk and economic uncertainty when joining firms in emerging industries. Turnover may be high in an unstable and turbulent industry. Managers and executives may need to be as entrepreneurial as the founders in order to meet the challenge of a new venture in a new industry.

The procurement of raw materials, supplies, and parts may also be difficult during the industry's emergence. If these inputs are also employed by other industries, there may be shortages until the vendors can adjust their capacity. If the inputs are newly created, developed, or engineered, they may be of uneven quality *and* in short supply. In either event, input costs are likely to be at their highest during the emergence stage.

Customer Uncertainty. Uncertainty also plagues the output (customer) market. To a large extent, the customer market is only vaguely understood: buyer needs and wants, income levels, demographic characteristics, psychographic profiles, and buyer behavior characteristics. Prices and the points at which customers will resist high prices are uncertain. There may be quite a bit of instability as firms, producing widely diverse and nonstandard products, come to market with different and nonstandard prices. The customer is also confused by the variety of product offerings, the lack of standardization, the perception of rapid obsolescence, and the erratic quality of some competitors.

Controlling Uncertainty. In the face of difficult structural conditions and constraints, what must the new venture in an emerging industry do to be successful?

> *Look toward developing, generating, acquiring, and controlling resources that have the four attributes (rare, valuable, hard to copy, nonsubstitutable) needed for sustainable competitive advantage.*

The priority in an emerging industry is to acquire resources. Ventures that acquire resources early are more likely to set the rules and standards for industry competition, technological configuration, and product quality. Speeding up decision making, product development and introduction, and organizational systems and processes all have positive effects on firm survival and performance.[40] One industry that is attempting to speed itself up and that represents a typical emerging industry in its early stages is superconductive materials.

The next priority is to employ resources to gain a defendable foothold in the industry on which to build. The early acquisition of a core group of loyal customers is a major accomplishment. It enables the firm to develop experience in production and marketing, evaluate new products and alternative pricing schemes, and provide steady cash flow. From this base, expansion is possible.

Last, because knowledge and information can possess the four attributes of SCA, the new venture must move as quickly as possible to develop an intelligence network to forecast future environmental trends, competitive moves, and technological developments.[41] The initial turbulence and change that made the formation of a new industry possible are not likely to subside once a handful of early new entrants has formed. The turbulence may continue unabated, often for years. While the new entrants sort out the standards, later entrants make their appearance and attempt to capitalize on the efforts of the first movers. Older and larger firms attempt to invigorate their operations by entering new markets or forming joint ventures. Regulators, organized labor, and the government conspire to appropriate and tax the "profits" of new ventures. These so-called profits are in reality the early excess returns, which the founders may need for reinvestment to recoup the firm's up-front investment, encourage future investment, and maintain its technological or marketing advantages. Taxes and other appropriations leave the firm and, in aggregate, the industry underinvested and therefore smaller than it otherwise might have been. The result, of course, is diminished output, innovation, and employment. When this problem is recognized by policy makers, protection can be authorized, such as patent rights, tax abatements and credits, and accelerated depreciation schedules. An intelligence system may not be able to stop these trends, but a forewarned firm is in a good position to protect its assets.

Transitional Industries

Transitional industries—those moving from emergence to stability—have certain recognizable features. At some point, they will experience scarce resources, changes in customer tastes and values, and, finally, a shakeout. The shakeout period is crucial, for many firms go out of business at this time. The new venture can anticipate these developments, although their precise timing is always problematic.

Scarcity of Resources. As new firms enter the industry with an often dazzling array of products, strategies, and configurations, two powerful forces are at work. First, these firms bid up the prices of the resources they need to get started. Physical resources increase in price as they become scarcer. Scientific and managerial expertise costs more as people are lured away from current jobs with higher salaries and perquisites. Financial resources become more expensive as venture capitalists and investors demand higher yields from the later entrants. Overall industry costs rise as demand for industry inputs rises.

Customer Changes. The second force is the changing nature of the output market. Customers become more sophisticated and sure of what they want in terms of value, quality, and product characteristics. They become more powerful as they become more knowledgeable; they have more choices than they had earlier in the industry life cycle; and they are more likely to shop on price. The uncertainty of not knowing who the customer is and how large the market may be starts to fade as experience tells businesses who will buy and who will not. Competition for the existing customer base intensifies. Growth slows at the same time that shoppers become more price sensitive.

Survival Strategies in the Shakeout. What is the result of increasing production costs and decreasing selling prices? Smaller margins for everyone. Only the efficient survive. This is the transition phase, also known as the **shakeout**. Firms whose costs are too high will be forced out of business.[42] Firms that survive will be those that have resources with the four attributes of sustainable competitive advantage. When assets that are rare, valuable, hard to copy, and nonsubstitutable are deployed, the venture will be able to withstand price pressure and/or maintain lower costs than competitors.

The first priority in surviving the shakeout is to rationalize the resource base. This means pruning resources (of all six types) and the products or markets they serve if these resources are not earning rents and profits. During the emerging stage, firms often acquire excess resources, or slack. They do this for two reasons: (1) Because they are uncertain which resources will be the most important, they seek to gain control over as many as possible; and (2) Growth is difficult to absorb, and as resources build, it is not easy to reinvest or deploy them quickly enough. During the shakeout period, as growth slows and margins are squeezed, slack must be wrung from the venture to restore it to agile, lean, and flexible conditions.

The next priority is to get the most out of reputational and organizational resources. These are often the last to develop for the new venture. Reputation is slow to develop because it takes time for the market and other stakeholders to gain experience with the firm. The organization, with its systems, processes, and routines, is also often a late-developing resource; it tends to evolve as the business grows, experimenting along the way. The interaction among the people, work flow, and policies that constitute the organization also tends to evolve as the business grows. This interaction is complex. It takes time for all these components to come together. Even after the components have coalesced, it takes practice and therefore time before that system can be perfected.

Reputation and organization are two of the most difficult resources to copy. As technology becomes more diffuse, as financing becomes more available to entrants, and as physical resources evolve toward commodity-type inputs, reputation and organization (and, by implication, human resources) are the best defense against increased competition and rivalry.

Another potent strategy during the shakeout period is for the firm to buy cheap assets from the losers in the competitive game. As firms go out of business and their investors try to recoup whatever they can by selling the company or liquidating its assets, these assets often come to market at prices below their rent-earning capacity. The surviving firms, with superior human resources and organizational skills, can employ the liquidated physical resources, patent rights, licenses, and newly unemployed workers, managers, and staffers more effectively than their previous owners could. This firm-specific talent enables the survivor to collect a quasi-rent on the loser's former assets.

The strategy of expanding within the same business line by acquiring (by whatever method) other businesses is also known as **horizontal integration**. For example, horizontal integration and resource rationalization are the hallmarks of the shakeout in the biotechnology industry.

Shakeout Pitfalls. Firms must avoid pitfalls to survive this dangerous period. The most important of these is the "uniqueness paradox."[43] The paradox refers to a blind spot that many companies have, especially those that are still relatively young. The uniqueness paradox occurs when people attribute unique characteristics to their own organization, characteristics that are, paradoxically, possessed by many other organizations. Although internal cohesion may strengthen when organizational members differentiate themselves from their competitors by believing they are unique, this practice is bad for strategy. It is bad because it fools the firm into believing that some or all of its resources have the four attributes of SCA when, in fact, they do not. It makes the firm complacent and gives it a false sense of security. The firm is forced to react to outside pressures instead of generating its own proactive activities. The uniqueness paradox spells doom for the firm.

A second pitfall has already been mentioned—keeping slack and excess capacity. The only thing worse than holding onto unused resources and facilities with too much capacity is acquiring new capacity that provides no rent-collecting possibilities. But firms do make the mistake of trying to corner the market on physical capacity even as growth slows.

A final pitfall is simply failing to recognize that the industry environment has changed. Sometimes the founders have difficulty adjusting to these new realities, and the entrepreneur is forced out and succeeded by a less creative but more managerially efficient executive. This scenario is more probable when outside investors control the firm and fear that failure to act will cost them their investments.

Maturing Industries

It seems more appropriate to think of entrepreneurial strategies in the emerging and transitional environments because the most visible and publicized entrepreneurial activity takes place here. Entrepreneurs, though, are not limited by law, economics, or customers to these two phases of the industry life cycle. Entry can take a place in mature industries as well. Some flatly reject the idea that there is such a thing as a mature industry—there are only mature (and poorly run) firms. The argument is over the direction of causation. Does a maturing industry lower firm profitability, or does low firm profitability bring on the mature condition?[44]

Mature industries are characterized by slower growth, little pure innovation, more product and process improvements, more sophisticated customers, and an increasing concentration of producers.[45] The last characteristic means that a few firms may produce 40 percent to 80 percent of the goods and services in the industry. This increased concentration also means that one or two industry leaders have emerged. An industry leader is the one the others look to for price changes and strategic movements. Sometimes mature industries appear to be friendly "clubs" with minimum competition and a general understanding of how to compete. The U.S. auto industry, the beef packers, the television networks, and the beer brewers spend as much time cooperating with each other to fend off attacks from outsiders (the Japanese automakers, the pork lobby, cable TV operators, temperance societies) as they do competing against each other. Street Story 4.3 demonstrates that success in a mature industry can sometimes come from a new-product innovation or twist. It is a gut-wrenching tale.

However, entry is possible in mature industries, although the barriers are high. The computer hardware business is an example.[46] Start-up and entry in this industry are increasingly rare. The business is saturated. Ben Rosen, the venture capitalist who bankrolled Compaq Computer in 1982, says, "In terms of main-line, hard-core computer companies, it's very hard to define an area where you can get to a critical mass of $50 million to $100 million" in sales. Short of that size, the chances of an entrepreneur making big returns and taking the company public are slim. Veterans of the industry are sadly concluding that the heyday is over. "It may not be possible to start a new computer manufacturing company," laments Richard Shaffer, publisher of *Technologic Computer Newsletter.* There are other problems as well:

- Capital costs have soared. "It costs $50 million just to find out if anybody cares."
- Limits on technological innovation are being reached. Firms promising breakthroughs are often disappointed.
- Customers are ordering replacements slowly. Much computer machinery just doesn't wear out.
- The industry's move to standardized parts and operating systems limits the innovation small companies can provide.[47]

A Gripping Experience

Inventor Dan Brown entered the maturing hand-tool market literally with a twist: He introduced a wrench-pliers hybrid with tiny jaws inside its circular head that grasps 16 different sizes of bolts or nuts evenly when you squeeze the tool's ergonomic handles. Known as the Bionic Wrench, this eight-inch tool saves handymen from bringing fixed-head wrenches in multiple sizes to every job, and is quicker to use than traditional adjustable wrenches. It's also particularly effective with nuts and bolts that are "stripped" or worn around the edges, user-friendly for people who don't have a lot of strength in their hands, and it works with both metric and standard-sized equipment.

Brown knows he has a good product. The Bionic Wrench was selected by *Popular Mechanics* magazine to receive its Editor's Choice award for outstanding achievement in new-product design at the 2005 National Hardware Show; it also won a 2006 International Forum Design Award in Germany and an International Industrial and Graphic Design Award from the Chicago Athenaeum.

But accolades may not carry enough weight for the Bionic Wrench to succeed. National retailer, Home Depot Inc., has declined to carry the product. Buyer Billy Bastek explains, "Hundreds and hundreds and hundreds of new products come across my desk every year, and that doesn't even include all the inquiries from our Web site." One factor turned Bastek against the product. "I thought the Bionic Wrench was somewhat of a neat item, but I didn't think it was priced particularly well, and that's kind of it." In contrast, the hand-tool buyer for Ace Hardware was eager to stock the Bionic Wrench in his

2,600 retailer-owned hardware cooperative stores, even at its $32.95 suggested retail price. "There are a handful of items to grab onto for the year, and we said, 'This might be one of them,' and we rolled the dice," says Dan Crane.

Bionic Wrench's price is high because the tool is manufactured in the United States. Brown could produce the item more cheaply by moving production to China, but he says, "I want to show this can be done in the States." Brown has also resisted making deals with chain stores like Sears and Lowe's to produce a version for their Craftsman or Kobalt private label, because he fears the chains would discount the retail price too much. Instead, he promotes the Bionic Wrench on his own Web site (www.logger-headtools.com), under a slogan that promises "a gripping experience." He plans to introduce the wrench in six- and ten-inch sizes, in addition to offering a multi-purpose tool, a Bionic pipe cutter and three additional wrenches.

Bionic Wrench racked up sales of $800,000 in 2005. Now that the wrench is being carried not only by Ace Hardware but also by QVC, Hammacher Schlemmer, Canadian Tire Corporation, and other retailers, Brown hopes to reach a sales volume of $6 to $8 million in 2006. That's pretty good—even if it's not as good as the sales figure for the other guy named Dan Brown, the one who wrote *The DaVinci Code*.

SOURCE: Adapted from Gwendolyn Bounds, "Wrench Wins Awards, but Is It Priced Too High to Be a Hit?" *The Wall Street Journal*, March 21, 2006. Retrieved from the Web March 21, 2006. http://online.wsj.com/article_print.SB114289721659203443.html, and www.loggerheadtools.com

Attacking the Leader. One possible strategy is to attack the industry leader (an imposing task, but not impossible).[48] Industry leaders may become vulnerable when the business cycle is on the upswing and things look good; they may become complacent. Past performance success leads to strategic persistence (inflexibility) even when the environment changes radically.[49] Those industries with unhappy customers can also be attacked; they have grown arrogant and are no longer providing value. When leaders are under antitrust investigation, they are certainly less likely to retaliate, but even here it is never wise to attack an industry leader with an imitative, me-too product or service. The challenger who does so has nothing to defend.

Three conditions must be present for the attacker. First, it must have some basis for sustainable competitive advantage. Some resources must possess the four-attribute qualities that would provide the entrant either a cost advantage or a sustainable difference. Second, the new entrant must neutralize the leader's advantage by at least matching the perceived quality of the leader's product. Third, there must be an impediment (more than one is even better) that prevents retaliation. These impediments are:

- Antitrust problems
- A cash crunch caused by overextension
- A blind spot such as the uniqueness paradox
- An overdiversified portfolio, causing neglect of key areas
- A strategic bind (retaliation would jeopardize another business strategy)

If these three conditions are met, the new entrant has a chance. One tactic for success is to reconfigure the ways of doing business, that is, do something startlingly different. For example, the makers of Grey Poupon mustard reconfigured their marketing by spending more on advertising than the mustard business had ever done in the past. French's, Heinz, and others were forced to give up market share to this upstart.

A second tactic is to redefine the scope of service. A new entrant can focus on a particular niche, serve that customer exceedingly well, and gain a foothold in a mature industry. For example, La Quinta motels concentrated on the frequent business traveler on a small budget. There was little retaliation, lest entrenched competitors ruin their own pricing structure and demean the reputation of their core brands. Last, the challenger can attempt to spend its way to success. It can try to buy market share by offering exceptionally low prices and conducting heavy promotion and advertising. This is risky business and out of the reach of all but the best-financed entrepreneurs.

Specializing. One additional entrepreneurial strategy can be used to enter a mature market. This strategy requires that the new venture do something for a mature business better than the business can do for itself. New firms and small firms can thrive in a mature market if they can take over some specialized activities for a big concern.[50] It is not unusual for a highly specialized small firm to have lower operating costs than large firms. The larger, more mature firms carry more overhead, have older technology, and do not focus on the cost drivers the way a smaller firm can. For example, Ameriscribe operates mailrooms for National Steel; it does so better and more inexpensively than National Steel could. The Wyatt Company, a consulting firm, conducted a survey and found that 86 percent of the nation's largest corporations had cut back on operations and had contracted services to outsiders.

Declining Industries

Declining industries are characterized by end-of-unit sales growth and by flat, constant dollar sales (i.e., sales adjusted for inflation). Ultimately, both of these indicators decrease.[51] Current examples of consumer industries in decline in the United States are tobacco, dial-up services, and hard liquor. Industrial sectors in decline include manufacturers of carburetors for automobiles and producers of bias-ply tires for original equipment manufacturers (OEM). The primary causes of industry decline are technological substitution, shifts in the tastes and preferences of consumers, and demographic factors.

Technological Substitution. When an older technology is replaced by a newer one, the older technology goes into decline. However, it does not immediately disappear. Even after the invention and adoption of the transistor, which replaced vacuum tubes in radios, televisions, and other devices in the late 1950s and 1960s, producers of vacuum tubes continued to exist. They supplied replacement parts for existing sets and made products for the hobby and collector markets. Similarly, producers of vinyl, long-playing records still exist, although these have been rapidly and overwhelmingly overtaken by producers of compact discs and digital downloads.

A recent, but unsuccessful, attempt at entry in the declining newspaper industry illustrates technological substitution pitfalls. Dan Gilmour tried to reinvent journalism by creating Bayosphere. Bayosphere was a start-up that focused on local news. Gilmour's vision was to have armies of local people write their own news stories and blogs to produce coverage that no print newspaper could match. Print news has been in decline for many years and continues to lose advertising to the Web as well as circulation to other media. The Bayosphere venture failed because local newspapers also used the Web for local reporters, Web advertising didn't emerge, and the blog had low participation. The venture lasted only eight months.[52]

Changes in Tastes and Preferences. Changes in tastes and preferences result in demand shifting to alternative industries, but do not cause immediate extinction of the declining industry. The declining consumer industries noted previously reflect changing tastes. For example, the underlying trend today is toward healthier lifestyles. However, millions of Americans each year have a steak for dinner, accompanied by a whiskey and a cigarette after dessert. While the volume of these three products continues to be high, sales are decreasing a little each year.

Rhonda Kallman has entered two declining niches and done so successfully. She is a veteran of the beer wars and helped co-found Boston Beer (Sam Adams). More recently, she founded the New Century Brewing Company, which introduced the Edison brand. Edison is the only patented light beer and is sold at Trader Joe's grocery stores. Kallman also recently launched Moonshot—a beer with caffeine. Note how she found twists on consumer tastes to reinvigorate her products' images.[53]

Changes in Demographics. Changes in demographics are reflected in overall product demand (see Chapter 3). As the baby-boom generation made its way through the population cycle, its members first created a boom in children's clothing and furnishings, followed by a decline in these industries. They then bought automobiles and residential real estate, which mushroomed; now each of these industries is in decline. The boomers are aging, as are their parents, which makes health care the fastest-growing segment of the gross national product (GNP). Guess what will occur when the boomers start to die? Health care will decline, and the mortuary business will boom.

Achieving Success. Under certain conditions, new entrants can establish successful niches in declining industries. The key for the new entrant is to find ways to help the incumbents leave the industry and then purchase their assets at low prices. This is an imposing task, however, because a number of factors increase the height of the exit barriers for firms in declining industries. These factors are:

- the low liquidation value of specialized assets
- the interrelationship of the business in decline with other businesses not in decline
- the potentially negative effects of exiting on financial markets
- the emotional and managerial effects of calling it quits

From the viewpoint of the entrepreneur, an opportunity exists if an industry is still attractive and the entrepreneur has or is able to acquire resources with the attributes of sustainable competitive advantage.

Fragmented Industries

Figure 4.2 shows the life-cycle curve for an industry that has, over time, consolidated. *Consolidation* means that the number of firms decreases, the birth rate of new firms diminishes considerably, and larger firms have advantages of scale and scope. However, not all industries are dominated by large firms with megamarket shares. In other words, not all industries go through the life cycle depicted in Figure 4.2. Industries that do not are called **fragmented industries.** Examples include professional services, retailing, distribution services, wood and metal fabrication, and personal care businesses, such as hairdressers and barbers.

The causes for fragmentation are diverse. Low-entry barriers can cause fragmentation because firms will always be faced with new challengers and therefore be unable to grow. An industry may not be able to generate economies of scale, because being larger brings no cost advantages. In these cases, firms do not get larger, and consolidation never takes place. Indeed, there may be diseconomies of scale; costs go up (on a per-unit basis) as firms grow. High transportation and inventory costs may keep firms small and geographically limited.[54]

The effect of firm size on buyers and sellers also can keep an industry fragmented. If neither buyers nor sellers see advantages in dealing with larger firms, they will avoid such firms and negotiate with smaller, less powerful firms. Sometimes market niches are too small to support larger firms because market needs are so diverse. Any or all of these conditions can keep an industry from the path described in Figure 4.1 and hence keep the firms in the industry small and relatively powerless.

Most of what we understand to be the small business sector of the economy is actually the set of fragmented industries and the ventures within it. Businesses in fragmented industries can be profitable, and they can grow to be relatively large. But by definition, if they are large enough to have a market share that can influence conditions, the industry is no longer fragmented.

Overcoming Fragmentation. New ventures in fragmented industries sometimes have the potential to introduce strategic, technological, or managerial innovations that may help the industry overcome fragmentation. If the new venture enters with technologies that introduce economies of scale, the venture will grow larger. For example, the brewery industry used to be fragmented, with thousands of local brewers. The technological breakthrough that overcame this fragmentation was the refrigerated freight car, which enabled brewers to ship their beer long distances without danger of it spoiling.

Fragmentation may also be overcome by strategies that reconstruct the way firms operate. The sneaker used to be a fragmented product in the sporting goods industry. With few exceptions, it was sold as commodity footwear for kids (Keds, Converse). When it was reconstructed as an "athletic shoe," developed technologically, and promoted as a personal fashion statement, the result was a highly profitable industry dominated by a few very large firms (Nike, Reebok, Adidas).

Another method of reconstructing an industry is to separate the assets responsible for fragmentation from other assets. This is known as *unbundling*. Two classic examples of unbundling are campgrounds and fast food.[55] These industries are characterized by thousands of small owners. Both require tight local control and supervision and must be located near their customers, but significant economies of scale in purchasing and marketing were achieved through franchising. Local control was maintained by the franchisee, and purchasing and marketing economies were obtained by the franchisor. The initial beneficiaries of these economies were McDonald's and KOA.

Investors, and especially venture capitalists, are increasingly targeting fragmented industries as neglected but high-potential opportunities. Why? Because a firm that overcomes fragmentation can become the industry leader, achieve enormous size and profitability, and provide rates of return in the thousands of percent range. The Chicago firm of Golder, Thoma & Cressy is often credited with originating this investment strategy. So far, it has applied its strategy to the nursing home, answering service, and bottled water businesses. Other industries ripe for consolidation are small-niche food processors, small-town newspapers, security alarm companies, and (the ultimate local business) funeral homes.

The strategy is not easy to execute. First, the investor identifies and acquires a company in a fragmented industry, one with no market leader. Then a new management team is recruited to run the business. Together the investors and new managers identify and negotiate to buy a few additional companies in the target industry. The hardest part is next: consolidating all the companies under a common name and set of operating practices. If this strategy works, the payoffs are huge.[56]

Coping with Fragmentation. Quite often the new entrant lacks the resources, means, or imagination to overcome fragmentation. Excellent money can still be made, however, from high-quality implementation, and the firm that learns to cope with fragmentation can thrive. A solid and profitable small business can be built on the following foundations:

- *Regimented professional management.* The introduction of managerial techniques and professionalism into small-business operations can keep the firm profitable even under strong price pressure.
- *Formula facilities or franchising.* High degrees of standardization and efficient, low-cost operations provide protection against eroding margins.
- *Specialized niches.* A business that is highly specialized by product type, customer type, order type, or geographic area can achieve minor economies of scale and add high value for buyers.

Warning! A firm can be so specialized that it may not have enough customers to be viable. Do not plan to open a pen repair shop, a shoelace boutique, or a restaurant based on the concept of toast (although one based on breakfast cereal has apparently been founded).

CRAFTING AND EVALUATING STRATEGY

Amar Bhide, in his important article on how entrepreneurs craft strategy, noted that the most important elements for entrepreneurial success seem to be speed in seizing opportunities and eliminating unpromising ideas, a concentration on important issues, and the use of realistic and spontaneous actions that include changing course if necessary.[57] His recommendations are:

- Screen out losers quickly.   In the crafting of strategy, entrepreneurs frequently must be very fast and agile because speed to market or to access resources can confer an advantage.   This means the entrepreneur has little time for long, drawn-out data collection and analysis.   Therefore, entrepreneurs must use a few basic rules that have worked well for them as individuals in the past.   These rules enable them to be decisive.
- Focus on a few key issues.   These issues will vary depending on the entrepreneur and the opportunity.   If the opportunity is in retail, location will be a "go/no go" issue.   If the opportunity is the manufacture of a new pharmaceutical, regulatory approval and licensing will be the key.   The issues the entrepreneur should consider will all depend on the situation.
- Do not wait until all of the analysis is complete, and all the answers to the questions are known before getting started.   The entrepreneur has to integrate action and analysis. In fact, it is not uncommon for entrepreneurs to do their market research by simply trying to find customers.   If customers are found, these particular customers should be captured first. The information gathered in the action-research stage will be used as data to revise and reconfigure the opportunity. The data may indicate that some or all of the opportunity is not what it appeared to be in the early screening stage. If no customers are found, the entrepreneur should be prepared to change course.

Entrepreneurs who wish to take a more systematic and deliberate approach can break the process up into more discrete parts. Opportunity assessment has five different stages (see Figure 4.3). Each stage focuses on analysis and the actions that must be taken. Analysis rests on the entrepreneur's understanding of the nature of the business that he or she wishes to create. Traditionally, entrepreneurs must ask the question, What is my business? They then attempt to answer the question in terms of a target customer and the target's buying needs, tastes, and preferences. In a world with volatile markets and changing tastes and preferences, keeping up is a dicey proposition. So, in opportunity assessment, entrepreneurs should initially assess their core, stable set of *internal* capabilities rather than volatile external resources.

Stage 1: Identification

The first stage requires entrepreneurs to identify and classify the resources they currently have and can control in their initial efforts to create a new venture. Identification and classification should be structured using the six categories previously described: financial, physical, human, technological, reputational, and organizational assets. A resource is currently controlled if the entrepreneur and the top-management team have immediate and unimpeded access to it, legally and physically. An asset is controllable to the extent that it may be obtained sometime in the future. For a rigorous analysis, a probability distribution can be conducted that indicates the likelihood of obtaining the resource. If it is extremely high or low, this probability can be factored into the next part of the stage 1 assessment.

The second part of stage 1 entails determining the relative strengths and weaknesses of the resource bundle and configuration. The entrepreneur should then examine how to use these resources and explore what business opportunities exist to make the most of them. What criteria should the entrepreneur use for this evaluation? The four attribute criteria: Is the resource under investigation rare, valuable, hard to copy, and nonsubstitutable?

The entrepreneur also needs to ask, to what degree. To the extent that the entrepreneur can answer yes to the first question and quite a bit to the second, he or she has the basis for competitive advantage.

Stage 2: Capabilities

A firm's capabilities are the skills, knowledge, and abilities needed to manage and configure resources.[58] The second stage, then, is similar to the first, except the analysis focuses on capabilities instead of resources. Few resources, as pure inputs, can form the basis for a successful business. Usually these resources must be used in some way—a way defined by the capabilities of the entrepreneur and those of his or her team.[59] Capability makes the resources productive. The firm should have efficient capabilities to coordinate resources and foster cooperation. The hardest part of this analysis is maintaining objectivity. Entrepreneurs are tempted to overestimate their abilities and skills, or dwell on past accomplishments from which they may not be able to generalize.

- *There is no one-to-one relationship between resources and capabilities.* Each firm can create its own relationship to manage its resources. Most important, though, this relationship should result in smooth coordination and cooperation among the team members

FIGURE 4.3   Resource-Based Approach to Entrepreneurial Opportunity Assessment and Analysis

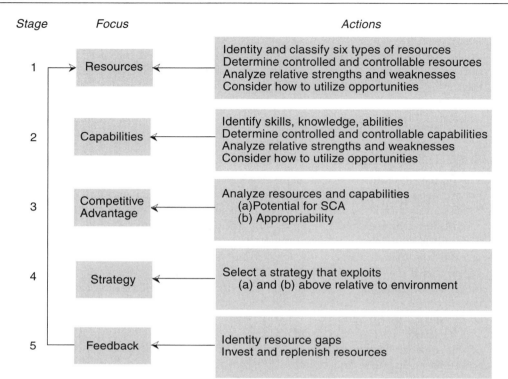

Stage	Focus	Actions
1	Resources	Identity and classify six types of resources Determine controlled and controllable resources Analyze relative strengths and weaknesses Consider how to utilize opportunities
2	Capabilities	Identify skills, knowledge, abilities Determine controlled and controllable capabilities Analyze relative strengths and weaknesses Consider how to utilize opportunities

3	Competitive Advantage	Analyze resources and capabilities
		    (a) Potential for SCA
		    (b) Appropriability

4	Strategy	Select a strategy that exploits (a) and (b) above relative to environment
5	Feedback	Identity resource gaps Invest and replenish resources

who perform the firm's routines. The routines themselves become intangible resources that may have the four attributes.

• *New firms have advantages over incumbents when developing routines and capabilities in industries undergoing great changes.* Older firms will have trouble changing routines to adapt to the environment; new firms can invent routines to fit the new realities. Of course, once the new venture has become established and its routines have been perfected, it is just as open to assault from an even newer challenger, which highlights the trade-off between efficiency and flexibility.

• *Some routines are widely distributed; others reside in the skills and abilities of one person.* For example, Walt Disney World is a complex amalgam of entertainment, art, technology, traffic control, and highly motivated employees. In contrast, the junk bond underwriting at Drexel, Burnham, and Lambert in the 1980s was almost solely a function of Michael Milken's abilities.

Stage 3: Competitive Advantage

Stage 3 focuses on competitive advantage. Here we try to determine whether the competitive advantages(s) identified in stages 1 and 2 may be sustained and if the profits and rents can be protected. Sustainable competitive advantage depends on the firm's ability to move first and create isolating mechanisms. First-mover advantages and isolating mechanisms prevent other firms from copying and crowding the firm's profit. The entrepreneur should ask: Do isolating mechanisms exist for the firm? Which ones should be used to protect our resource advantages?

Any rent that the firm can collect may be eroded. Physical resources may be depleted, depreciated, or replicated, or become obsolete. The probability of appropriation is high, too. The environment will seek to get a share of the rents through taxation (government), increased wage demands (employees), rising input costs (suppliers), or litigation (competitors and lawyers). The new venture's founders and leaders must be sensitive and alert to these pressures. It may serve the new venture well to create hybrid strategies that combine elements of each type of rent and use more than one kind of isolating mechanism.

Stage 4: Strategy

The next stage translates the assessment of competitive advantage into strategy. The firm requires two related strategies: one to protect and manage its resources, the other a product and market strategy. The first strategy has already been discussed in terms of isolating mechanisms and first-mover advantages. The second set of strategies entails dealing with the macroenvironment and the competitive environment described in Chapter 3.

Stage 5: Feedback

In stage 5, the entrepreneur should focus on feedback, that is, evaluating and reassessing the continuous process of new venture creation. Through the first four stages, resource gaps may have appeared and requirements for resources that are neither controlled nor controllable may become apparent. Recycling through the process after having identified the gaps is recommended. Gap-reducing and gap-eliminating strategies can be the focus of the next round. Also, resource bases are inevitably depleted and depreciated. In the next cycle, the entrepreneur must account for these erosions and make plans for investments to maintain resources and replenish stocks and assets.

As we have seen throughout this chapter, no one strategy is best for all new ventures. Because choice is crucial and many paths can lead to success, we need a way to evaluate the strategy after it is chosen but before it is implemented. If we can do this, we can weigh various alternatives against one another and make a better choice without having to incur the consequences of choosing poorly. The following four criteria may be used to evaluate proposals.[60] Each can be viewed as a test; if the strategy passes the tests, it is superior to strategies that fail the tests.

- *Goal consistency test.* Does the strategy help the firm to accomplish its goals? Are the strategy's outcomes predicted to be consistent with those of previous strategies and decisions? Will the strategy enable the firm to maintain its posture?
- *Frame test.* Is the firm working on the right issues? Does the strategy address

resource issues and alignment with the environment? Does the strategy meet the requirements of the industry stage and help acquire and control resources possessing the four attributes of sustainable competitive advantage?

- *Competence test.* Does the firm have the ability to carry out the strategy? Can the strategy be broken down into problems that have solutions? Are these solutions that the firm can work out?
- *Workability test.* Will it work? Is it legal and ethical? Will it produce the desired end? Will the organization be willing to marshal its resources to carry out the strategy?

SUMMARY

In this chapter, we reviewed a combination of theory and practice from both the strategic management and the entrepreneurship literature. Every new venture requires a consistent and workable business model. The business model tells the story of the business, explaining how the business views its products, markets, and technologies. The model also demonstrates how the business intends to make money and how this method is sustainable in the long run.

Entry wedges and momentum factors are the initial entrepreneurial strategies. The major wedges are innovation, parallel types of competition, and franchising. Various forms of sponsorship compose the momentum factors. Resource-based strategies are geared toward rent-seeking behavior. The most prevalent of the five rent-seeking behaviors is the entrepreneurial strategy. The resource-based model also accounts for the rate and direction of a venture's growth strategies. Firms grow in the direction of underutilized resources and toward areas where they have distinctive competencies.

We discussed quality as a strategy in the section on the resource-based framework. The choice of a total quality management strategy does not represent a sustainable competitive advantage for the firm. However, the implementation of such a program can provide advantages, because successful implementation requires superior market knowledge, complex service behavior from employees, and highly developed organizational systems. The best candidates for a successful TQM strategy are firms that already possess these resources.

We then looked at how industry conditions affect entry and strategy for a new venture. Five industry types were discussed: emerging industries, transitional industries, maturing industries, declining industries, and fragmented industries. Although new ventures can be successful in any of these environments, the emerging and fragmented environments provide the easiest entry and are the most typical entrepreneurial choices.

We concluded with a brief overview of the strategy development and evaluation process. Specifically, we identified four criteria for testing the appropriateness of a strategy before embarking on the market test itself. A strategy is appropriate if it is consistent with the goals of the organization, addresses the right issues, can be executed competently, and is workable both legally and ethically.

KEY TERMS

Business-level strategy
Business model
Compatibility
Complementarities
Cooperation
Corporate-level strategy
Creative imitation
Customer contract
Customer uncertainty
Drivers
Efficiency
Enterprise-level strategy
Entrepreneurial rent
Entry wedges
First-mover advantage
Fragmented industries
Franchisee
Franchisor
Functional-level strategy
Geographic transfer
Horizontal integration
Industry life cycle
Information
Intellectual property
Isolating mechanisms
Joint venture
Licensing
Lock-in

Market relinquishment
Monopoly rent
Networking strategy
Novelty
Payments perspective
Positive feedback
Property rights
Quasi-rent
Relational rent
Resource uncertainty
Revenue model
Ricardian rent
Second source
Shakeout
Spin-off
Strategic uncertainty
Strategy
Strategy diamond
Strategy formulation
Strategy implementation
Structural uncertainty
Subfunctional level
Supply shortage
Switching costs
Technological leadership
Underutilized resource
Value pricing
Versioning

DISCUSSION QUESTIONS

1. Why do new ventures need strategies?
2. How do the major entry wedges help create momentum for the new venture?
3. How do the minor wedges supplement the major ones?
4. Evaluate the pros and cons of the minor wedges. Which would be the most or least effective in the long run?
5. Describe the five different kinds of rents. Give examples of how an entrepreneur might attempt to collect these.
6. How will firms employ their resources for growth? Explain the focus effects and synergy effects.
7. Discuss quality as a strategy. Can it be used to achieve sustainable competitive advantage? How?

8. What are the key elements affecting entrepreneurial strategy in the following environments?
   a. Emerging industries
   b. Transitional industries
   c. Maturing industries
   d. Declining industries
   e. Fragmented industries
9. What are the five stages for assessing entrepreneurial opportunities?
10. What are the four tests of strategy? Why is it important to apply the tests before going into business?

EXERCISES

1. Return to the list of companies in Table 4.2. Choose one and answer the following questions:
   a. What unique product/services are being offered?
   b. What VRIN resources does the company appear to have?
   c. What other companies (if any) have been instrumental in the company's success?
   d. How have these companies contributed?
2. Develop a strategy for your new venture.
   a. What entry wedges, major and minor, will you use?
   b. How will you attempt to collect and appropriate rents?
   c. What industry environment are you entering? How will this environment influence your strategy?
   d. Apply the four tests to your strategy. What questions do they raise? How would you answer these questions if they were posed by a banker or venture capitalist?
3. Choose a company from the latest *Inc* 500 list (http://www.inc.com).
   a. Write a paragraph describing the business model of the company.
   b. Use the Strategy Diamond Model to outline what the company is doing, how it is pursuing its strategy, and what its time frame appears to be.
   c. Find another company on the list that is in a similar business and repeat a. and b. above.
   d. Compare the two companies. How are they different? Similar? Which company's strategy seems to be closest to establishing SCA? Justify your answer.

DISCUSSION CASE

Making People Laugh, for Money

In 1998, Evan Spiridellis showed his brother, Gregg, a streaming computer video cartoon produced by the creator of the "Ren and Stimpy" show. "It was silly," he recalls, "but what it made us realize was that there was the potential to get a creative product out there without distribution people getting so involved in ruining the creative process." At the time, Evan was a commercial artist and independent animator, while Gregg was a former investment banker and MBA student at the University of Pennsylvania's Wharton School. But within a matter of months, they were both working out of a garage in Brooklyn to launch a company called JibJab Media, Inc.

While you may not know the name, you may be familiar with JibJab's work. During the 2004 presidential campaign, the brothers produced a cartoon parodying the election with humorous lyrics set to the tune of "This Land Is Your Land." The two-minute spoof attracted more than 70 million hits after it was posted on their Web site (www.jibjab.com). Jay Leno showed the cartoon on the "Tonight" show, which encouraged the brothers to create other political lampoons, including "Good to Be in D.C." and "She'll Be Coming 'Round the Mountain." Their edgy animation has also been featured on the "Today" show, CNN, FOX, and was profiled in both the *New York Times* and the *Los Angeles Times*.

The Spiridellis have not made any money directly from their political cartoons, but their animations have led to other work for JibJab Media. Yahoo commissioned the company to create two humorous shorts. A screening of their work at the 2004 Sundance Film Festival led to a contract to make trailers for some of the films shown there. They are currently working on an animated TV series pilot.

"To use a Wharton term, our 'core competency' is creating the animation," says writer and business manager, Gregg Spiridellis. "But what we would really like to do is be a leader in on-line original content in many areas."

The JibJab site now carries advertising from a major beverage company. Chuckling Spiridellis fans can purchase hats, t-shirts, iPod and desktop downloads, and a DVD with some of JibJab's funniest work from the company Web site. Their political cartoons have also led to a lot of buzz for the company's other projects, which include animation, children's books, and toys for Disney, Scholastic, the History Channel, and other vendors.

JibJab is not the only company tapping into the comic video market. "It is becoming a business instead of a pastime," notes Frank Dellario of ILL Chan Productions, a company that has produced shorts for MTV2 and other commercial vendors. Other online comic video sites include Icebox (www.icebox.com), whose "Queer Duck" animated series was released as a home video by Paramount in 2006, and Mondo Media (www.mondomedia.com), whose "Happy Tree Friends" has aired on MTV, starred in five best-selling DVDs, and adorned merchandise sold in youth-oriented retailer, Hot Topic. Some sites, including JibJab, post humorous videos from amateurs. Fledgling filmmakers often need just a computer, some software, and some volunteer labor to produce a three-minute short for as little as $3,000. Jason Reitman, the son of *Ghostbusters*' director Ivan Reitman, says three short films he posted on the Web with AtomFilms (www.atomfilms.com) helped him raise money for his full-length feature film, *Thank You for Smoking*. Other on-line videographers have ended up with contracts to create commercials for companies like Ford and AT&T.

SOURCE: Adapted from Ronald Grover, "Three Minute Moguls," *Business Week*, January 30, 2006: 91, and Robert Strauss, "Keep on Parody-ing: Gregg Spiridellis," *Wharton Alumni Magazine,* Spring 2005. Retrieved from the Web June 18, 2006.

http://www.wharton.upenn.edu/alum_mag/issues/spring2005/wharton_now_10.html, and www.jibjab.com, www.ice-box.com, and www.mondomedia.com.

Case Questions

1. What business model describes the way JibJab currently does business? If a network selected JibJab's pilot for an animated TV series, how might that model change?
2. What major and minor wedges are in play here?
3. Would you classify the Internet film industry as an emerging industry or a fragmented industry? Why?
4. What kinds of uncertainties do these businesses face? What can they do to reduce those uncertainties?
5. What kind of rent-seeking strategies do you think these businesses can pursue?
6. Many of these Internet film sites appear to be on the brink of generating significant revenue. What advice would you offer them at this time?

CHAPTER 5 The Business Plan

Each plan, like a snowflake, must be different.
—Joseph Mancuso

OUTLINE

LEARNING OBJECTIVES

After reading this chapter, you will understand

- why it is important to write a business plan.
- the elements of a business plan.
- how to write a business plan.
- the kinds of questions people will ask about your business plan.
- how to respond to evaluations of your business plan.

| PERSONAL PROFILE 5 |

Robert Byerly:
Pressed for Success

It wasn't the prices that bothered Robert Byerly about his local dry cleaner. As the principal financial officer at Lomas Financial Corporation, Byerly could afford to have his clothes cleaned at any high-end dry cleaner in the Dallas area. It was the poor service that upset him. When the cleaner ruined a brand new $100 dress shirt, no one even bothered to apologize, so Byerly contacted the Better Business Bureau.

He discovered that many consumer complaints to the bureau involve dry cleaners and that their failure to accept responsibility for shoddy work was what irked customers most. That information and his own experience persuaded him to open his own dry cleaning store and to promise that his business would stand behind everything it cleaned.

First he spent a week at the library doing research. He learned that dry cleaning was a $16 billion industry made up primarily of individual mom-and-pop establishments rather than local or regional chain stores. He found out that cleaners generally relied on discount coupons to build business and that the average dry cleaner brought in $250,000 in annual sales. When he saw evidence that attitudes and government regulations regarding the cleaning solvent percoethylene—perc—were changing, he knew that a business with new equipment would have a technological advantage.

According to one business consultant and author, Byerly's approach to launching his business was unusual: "When people talk about creating or building a business and what they need, they say money or sales," observes Michael Gerber. "They never say more information, but that's what it really takes."

Byerly's research didn't stop at the library. He took clothing to fifteen of the best cleaners in his area, and then hired a marketing firm to assemble a focus group that could evaluate his future competitors' work. Consultant Gerber applauds this step, too. "Too many small-business owners have a technician's mind set rather than a marketing mind set. You have to think like Procter & Gamble. What would they do before launching a new product? They would find out who their customer is and who their competition is."

Because Byerly wanted to create a business that, in his words, "paired five-star service and quality with an establishment that didn't look like a dry cleaner," he also spent $15,000 on focus groups to critique his store's name, appearance, and brochure.

Byerly's planning paid off. His venture, known as Bibbentuckers, looks different from other dry cleaners because it has a slick exterior with snazzy awnings. The service is different, too, because Bibbentuckers' employees pick up and deliver laundry directly to or from customers' cars; serve them coffee, tea, or lemonade while they wait; and will even clean their windshields. The quality of Bibbentuckers' cleaning is different, too: A tiny bar code is attached discreetly to every garment to record the customer's preferences and to allow a computer to track the item through the cleaning process   Each garment is inspected seven times before it is returned to the customer. Byerly's company automatically replaces buttons, repairs pocket holes, and stitches loose hems, and every bit of the Bibbentuckers service is guaranteed.

The first store in Plano, Texas, posted

opening sales indicating that it would gross $1 million in its first year. The store became profitable in just four months, and now has two additional Dallas locations. In keeping with the store's slogan, Byerly's up-front work helped ensure that his new business would be "pressed for success."

SOURCE: Adapted from Ann Zimmerman, "Do the Research," *The Wall Street Journal Online*, May 9, 2005. Retrieved from the Web February 21, 2006. http://online.wsj.com/article_print/SB111524102265424963.html, and www.bibbentuckers.com.

How do we put to use all the analysis and evaluation we did in Chapters 2, 3, and 4? We write a business plan. The development and writing of the plan marks the transition from strategy formulation to implementation of the new venture creation. The entrepreneur or entrepreneurial team members have thus far collected and analyzed information. They have examined their own preferences and goals to understand why they want to go into business. They have evaluated the venture's resource base and determined what is rare, valuable, difficult to duplicate, and nonsubstitutable. They have sifted through mountains of product and market data, analyzing environmental variables, market trends, and the competition. They have performed innumerable mental experiments to visualize what the business will look like, how the products or services will be produced or delivered, and how quality will be continuously monitored and improved.[1]

Now it is time for action. The document produced is the **business plan,** a formal written expression of the entrepreneurial vision, describing the strategy and operations of the proposed venture. The business plan has aliases: Presented to a banker, it may be called a "loan proposal." A venture capital group might call it the "venture plan" or "investment prospectus." It may be offered to potential partners or top managers, suppliers and distributors, lawyers, accountants, and consultants.

However, many firms have no need for a formal written business plan. Some grow out of a hobby or recreational interest and the business is simply an extension of that interest. For instance, a craftsperson or artist who occasionally sells an item does not need a formal business plan to expand sales. Sometimes two or three friends begin a small business—working out of someone's garage to fix appliances or repair cars, for example—and such start-ups do not require business plans. The vast majority of businesses around the world are started for under US$1000, so most **nascent entrepreneurs** do not need written plans. However, the planning process, the effort to envision a desirable future and decide how to make it a reality, is always beneficial, whether or not it results in a written plan.

In some countries, it is possible to start a business and receive financing before putting together a business plan. Strong personal relationships or membership in a community financing group will be sufficient. Friends, family, ethnic ties, and other group affinities help entrepreneurs get started. Increasingly, however, the business-plan model that emerged from the United States is spreading to other regions, especially for businesses that anticipate increasing sales and geographic growth, a steady source of capital, and the possibility of becoming public companies. Most ventures never reach this stage of development and only a tiny fraction of all startups will ever "go public," but the model is widely taught at business schools all over the world. Therefore, if an entrepreneur wants to raise money from outside investors (i.e., people other than friends, family, and fools), he or she should have a business plan.

Patricia Adams, CEO of College Capital, understood this when she went to look for financing. She put together a 15-page plan containing what she thought was the necessary information for investors. She didn't manage to raise the money for her college preparation company till eighteen months later, and by then the business plan filled two three-inch binders. When the economic bubble burst, investors got nervous and wanted more and more information. If, as Adams herself says, this plan is a "little bit of overkill," it makes the point that any business plan must respond to changes in the business environment.[2]

The outside investors are only one of many internal and external audiences for a business plan. The **internal audience** is the executives, managers and employees of the company, and for them the plan is a guide for decision making and for communicating goals, objectives, and preferred methods. The **external audience** is everyone else, including investors, customers, and vendors. It can persuade a landlord to lease a property to the company. It can induce a supplier to offer trade credit right away. The business plan has multiple uses.

Not everyone, even in the United States, agrees that a business plan is needed to start a growth-oriented business that requires outside financing. The founders of scores of famous companies got started without writing business plans: Reebok, Mrs. Fields, Pizza Hut, and Crate & Barrel are noteworthy examples.[3] Best-selling author David Gumpert, an expert on entrepreneurship and investor relations, contends that most business plans are relatively worthless because they are poorly written, poorly thought out, and obsolete by the time the ink is dry.[4] Gumpert prefers a much more organic and incremental process, an "either/or" proposition, but a matter of timing. He recommends that entrepreneurs seeking financing in the new business environment follow this process:

- Get the business going through **bootstrapping.** Bootstrapping consists of methods used to finance a business without resorting to outside debt and equity.[5] (See Chapter 7 for more on this topic.) Then let investors know the venture is up and running. This is the front end of the process.
- Write a synopsis letter briefly setting out the basics.
- Always stay in the financing mode. Entrepreneurs are always looking for financing and must adjust their business and revenue models as needed.
- Show staying power and perseverance. The most frequent responses to entrepreneurial ideas are "It can't be done," "You can't do it," and "It's already been done." Don't let this get in the way, and don't take no for an answer.
- Keep in regular contact with investors.
- Show sales early.
- Prove your business model. Produce a product, sell it for more than it costs to produce, and attract repeat business—that proves the model.
- Finally, complete a business plan. *Now* you have something to write about!

Gumpert's approach emphasizes that "things change" and "stuff happens," so entrepreneurs should not lock in too early to a particular blueprint for action. Also there are many ways entrepreneurs can bootstrap and save money.

This chapter is divided into four sections. The first section suggests that every new venture should have a business plan at some point. The question is *when*? Entrepreneurs who take the bootstrapping approach can wait, but those who are looking at a large-scale project must write their plans earlier. The second section offers a detailed explanation of the components of a business plan. The third section deals with questions an entrepreneur is likely to hear from investors and others. The fourth section offers suggestions for writing and presenting the plan. Entrepreneurs are judged by the way they organize, write, and present their information, so the finished plan must be informative, concise, and complete.

WHY WRITE A BUSINESS PLAN?

When a new venture needs outside financing, it must have a plan. As Gumpert suggests, this may not be necessary at the outset, but eventually it will be.

The Costs of Planning

Entrepreneurs are often characterized as "doers," individuals who like to act and let their deeds speak for themselves, so one cost of a business plan is the entrepreneur's need to sit still long enough to write it. Hiring someone to write the plan is not an acceptable substitute. Outsiders—consultants, accountants, and lawyers—are needed for advice and expertise, but the founder or the initial top managers team should put the plan together.[6] Only the entrepreneurs are sufficiently familiar with all the details, and it is they who will make and take responsibility for the major decisions. Investors expect the founders to be involved in and knowledgeable about all aspects of the proposed enterprise.

Developing and writing the plan takes time, money, and energy, and some entrepreneurial teams believe that these resources are best applied to actually working in the business. In the short term that may be true, but over the long haul the team is the company's most valuable, rarest, and most unique resource and its leaders are the architects of organizational purpose.[7] At some point, then, the best use of the entrepreneurs' time and energy is in creating, refining, and pursuing their vision.

Every business plan must deal with economic uncertainty and the risks facing the firm, so there is a psychological cost in writing a plan that delineates everything that can go wrong. Entrepreneurs are optimists who believe in the power of their own efforts.[8] They believe they will succeed, but a serious business plan exposes the venture's vulnerabilities. To offer full disclosure to a potential investor, partner, or supplier, the plan has to list the risks of the business, one by one.[9] Recognizing these risks and facing an uncertain future can be uncomfortable, and it is one reason some business plans are never written.

A final obstacle to writing a business plan is the fear, real or imagined, of prematurely closing off the new venture's strategic direction. Should a new venture's strategy be focused on a narrow segment of the market? Should the firm be more open to opportunity, pursuing a broad market strategy? If the purpose of a plan is to encourage focus, will it keep the entrepreneurs from remaining flexible? This is the trade-off between planning and reacting.[10]

The Benefits of Planning

The business plan can personally benefit the entrepreneurial team. Founding a new business can be enormously fulfilling and exhilarating, but it is also anxiety-ridden and tense. Usually a great deal of money is at stake, and the consequences of poor decisions can affect many people for a long time. In developing and writing a business plan, the entrepreneurial team reduces these anxieties and tensions by confronting them. They come to grips with potential negative outcomes and the possibility of failure. The knowledge that comes from this experience can reduce the level of worry and anxiety.

Conflicts. On a personal level, entrepreneurs may find themselves in conflict with the demands of the new business. The founder may be motivated by the desire for substantial income, public esteem, a sense of stability, and time for leisure and recreation once the venture is off the ground, but the demands of the organization may get in the way.

First, a new firm requires reinvestment, and the more successful it is, the more money it needs for growth. This interferes with an entrepreneur's desire for substantial personal income: He or she may have to reinvest much of the initial profit. Second, acting as a leader and manager often requires making tough personnel decisions. Individuals hurt by these decisions may not hold the entrepreneur in high regard and maybe even become enemies.

That anticipated period of stability may not materialize. Starting a new venture can be exhausting, and entrepreneurs may feel they deserve to rest on their laurels, but often the business will then be in a position where more risks need to be addressed, additional crucial decisions have to be made, and earlier plans and strategies have to be reformulated. When this happens the firm is in conflict with its creator, and the dreamed-of time for leisure or family or community service must be deferred.

Business plans help entrepreneurs deal with these conflicts by recognizing issues before they become serious problems. By anticipating these conflicting values and writing them into the plan, entrepreneurs can reduce their own emotional strain. When a specific conflict arises, the entrepreneur can refer to the business plan to help resolve it.

When Sheri and Stuart Meland started their business, they did not plan for the problems that success would bring.[11] A lot of people plan carefully for coping with failure, but what if their success exceeds their hopes? In July 2002 while they were graduate students, the Melands started http://madcityhomes.com, offering flat-fee listing services for residential home sellers. They listed 60 homes the first year, then 210, then 433. Their operating costs are very low, but now the Melands are not sure what to do—sell the business and return to graduate school? Stick with this profitable business?

Thomas Kinnear, a professor of entrepreneurial studies, says that in the early stage of business success founders "basically end up having to decide whether they're going to be consumed by their own business. A lot of these people who stay wreck their own business," because they are not the right people to carry it on and they did not plan on such success.[12]

Planning and Performance. The firm also benefits from the planning process. Research shows a positive relationship between planning and performance in new and small firms.[13] That is, firms that plan perform better and are more likely to succeed than firms that do not.[14] There are four reasons why this is so.

1. Comprehensiveness: The business plan has to deal fully with all major issues facing the new venture. This comprehensiveness enables the entrepreneur to see possible sources of trouble and develop contingent strategies for confronting these problems. It forces the entrepreneur to develop and demonstrate industry-related competence.[15]
2. Communication: The business plan communicates the venture's concept and potential to various audiences. A plan that effectively transmits the founder's vision and excitement can attract valuable resources to the new venture.
3. Guidance: The business plan sets goals and milestones for the new venture by laying out the entrepreneurial team's intentions and establishing the values the founders intend to foster and preserve. Over time the plan can be a roadmap guiding managers and employees in their decision making. "When in doubt, consult the plan" can become the firm's motto in the exciting and turbulent months and years to come. Without such guidance, an organization can lose sight of its original purposes and strengths.
4. The Planning Process: Putting together a business plan, consulting it frequently, and periodically reviewing and revising can improve the venture's performance even if some aspects of the plan become obsolete before the ink is dry. The process of collecting information, sharing analysis, developing norms for decision making, enunciating the values of the leaders, reviewing objectives, and linking these with action helps make the company better.

The Internet provides researchers and analysts with valuable sources of business information that were once difficult or expensive to access. Google and Yahoo are the most prominent search engines, but now Wikipedia is developing reliable information on business, including industry statistics and sources. A few of the best sites for new venture creation are listed here:

http://inc.com
http://dir.yahoo.com/BusinessandEconomy/Directories/
http://www.lexisnexis.com/academic/
http://www.berinsteinresearch.com/stats.htm
http://www.census.gov/econ/www/widemenu.html

ELEMENTS OF THE BUSINESS PLAN

We offer one version of a standard business plan template below, but it is not the completion of the template that makes a business plan compelling. There are even pre-packaged templates, and anyone can simply fill out a form. To speak the language of investors and produce a document that will be useful for decision making and planning, however, requires the entrepreneur to understand and communicate four crucial and interdependent elements:

- People: Who are the key figures in the new enterprise?
- Opportunity: What is the business model?

- Context: What does the big picture look like?
- Risk and Reward: What can go right and what can go wrong?

Sahlman explains that these four elements are critical for investors and for internal use. As we saw in Chapters 2, 3 and 4, the dimensions of entrepreneurship include the people, the organization, the big picture, and the industry context.[16]

The business plan follows the general format for documents:

1. The first section tells the audience what the entrepreneur is going to tell them. This prepares them for what is coming.
2. The major middle sections give the audience the information and arguments that are central to the company's purpose.
3. The last section reminds the audience what it has heard and summarizes the presentation.

There are many variations on this, theme,[17] but they all include the same essential elements.

Preliminary Sections
Outline.

- Cover page
- Table of contents
- Executive summary

1. Type of Business
2. Company summary
3. Management
4. Product/service and competition
5. Funds requested, collateral, use of proceeds*
6. Financial history, financial projections*
7. Deal structure, exit*

*Required if the plan is used for financing.

Estimates indicate that, on average, a reader spends less than ten minutes evaluating the plan for a new venture.[18] To induce that reader to go on to the main body of the document and consider the details, the opening sections must be both attractive and informative.

Cover Page. The cover page includes the following information:

- Company name, address, telephone and fax numbers, and e-mail address. The reader is more likely to contact the entrepreneur if it's easy to do so.
- The name and position of the contact person, one of the firm's top executives, who must be fully prepared to answer questions about the plan.
- The date the business was established (e.g., "established 2006") and the date of this version of the business plan (e.g., "February 2007").
- The full name of the organization from which funding (or credit, or a supplier agreement, etc.) is being sought.

- The copy number of the plan (e.g., "copy 2 of 7"). This is a matter of security and exclusivity. For security reasons, the entrepreneur must know how many of the plans are in circulation and who has them. Eventually, all of them should be returned because a business plan contains sensitive and strategic information that must not fall into the hands of unscrupulous competitors. Exclusivity, the second reason for limiting circulation, simply means that it is not good practice to have dozens of copies of the plan circulating in the financial community. Financiers like to consider opportunities that are not concurrently offered to others. If a plan is overcirculated, it acquires a negative reputation as "shopworn."
- The company's logo. Every firm should have a logo, a design, picture, or ideograph that represents the company. The association of a company name with a pictorial design gives the reader (and eventually the customer) two ways to remember the company and its products. A new venture can employ clip art or the latest computer technology to design its own logo using a graphics or drawing program from a personal computer. A large firm with a substantial budget can hire an advertising agency and a commercial artist to design its logo. A venture should also have a tag line, which is a short, descriptive, easy-to-remember, and sometimes humorous phrase that connects to the business and appeals to customers.

Sometimes a logo can be more than just a picture or symbol for the company. In Street Story 5.1 we see a company transformed by its logo and tag line These elements have become the most memorable and distinctive parts of the business.

Table of Contents. The table of contents follows the cover page and adheres to the format of the business plan elements. Each major section is numbered and divided into subsections, using one of two common numbering methods. The Harvard outline method uses Roman numerals for main headings, capital letters for major sections, Arabic numbers for subsections, and the number-letter combination (e.g., 1a) for even smaller subsections. The decimal format numbers each major heading, starting at 1.0, and subsections that follow are numbered 1.10, 1.11, . . . 2.0, 2.10, 2.20, etc. The executive summary and the appendixes are not numbered this way. The executive summary precedes the numbering and, therefore, has no number; the appendix numbers are in Arabic preceded by "A" (A.1, A.2, and so on) to indicate that they are appendixes.

If the plan has a significant number of tables, figures, drawings, and exhibits, a separate table can be prepared listing these with their titles and page numbers. Any consistent and coherent organizing method may be used. However, because the purpose of the table of contents and the table of figures is to make it easier for readers to extract pertinent information, complicated and arcane systems of cataloging should be avoided.

Executive Summary. The **executive summary** is the most important part of the business plan because it is the first section of substance that the reader sees. Most readers, especially investors, never read beyond the summary. They have too many plans to read and too little time. Thus, if the summary is not convincing, the reader goes on to the next plan. It is estimated that only 10 percent of all business plans are read thoroughly, meaning that 90 percent are rejected after the summary.[19]

Although the summary is the first part to be read, it should be the last part written

STREET STORY 5.1

Cracked for Success

First there was a Chihuahua selling Mexican food. Then there was a quacking duck peddling disability insurance, animated frogs marketing beer, and a golden retriever pushing canned beans. Now there's a cracked piece of cement hawking basement repairs.

That piece of cement, Mr. Happy Crack, has transformed a lackluster father-and-son small business into a thriving enterprise with $10 million in annual revenues and more than ten franchises in eight states.

After spending thirty years building homes, Mike Kodner started a company to repair cracks in poured concrete foundations by injecting them with an epoxy resin. He named the company Crack Team USA, which got him a few laughs but not a lot of business.

Kodner's son Mike wanted to promote the business in a way that would go beyond the usual guarantees and promises offered by most residential service companies. While he was driving to work one day, the image of a cartoon character with a big crack in the middle of his cement forehead and a smiling face popped into Kodner's head. Then he came up with the tag line, "A Dry Crack Is a Happy Crack!" Within a few weeks the new logo appeared on the sides of buses all over St. Louis, and Mr. Happy Crack and the Kodners' business were catapulted into the limelight.

Today Kodner sells more than basement repairs. The company gets calls from all over the country for merchandise bearing the Mr. Happy Crack logo. Its Web site (www.mrhappycrack.com) sells t-shirts, underwear, mugs, plush figures, bobbleheads, and even toilet paper emblazoned with the smiling mascot.

Five percent of company sales come from the merchandise. Mr. Happy Crack makes appearances at festivals and major league baseball games, and has even been a guest on the "Tonight" show.

The logo helped the core business, too. John McCarthy of Boston says he looked for a franchise for ten years before he discovered the Crack Team. "We were in hysterics, my father and I, looking at everything and we hadn't even gotten to the financials yet," he says, describing discovering the company on the Internet. McCarthy calls Mr. Happy Crack an "unbelievable promotional tool," and reports that some customers insist he throw in a t-shirt as part of the deal. Not that he's complaining. McCarthy's sales doubled each month during his first six months of business. Bob Kodner says Crack Team franchises generally become profitable within one year, and that a franchisee with one employee and one truck can gross $200,000 to $250,000 in a year.

Mr. Happy Crack has helped make the Crack Team the leader in foundation repair in the United States. The elder Kodner says the company is protecting its mascot by being careful about overexposure, but he jokes that the company may adding a second slogan: We Also Fix Basements.

SOURCE: Adapted from Gwendolyn Bounds, "Owner's Logo Inspiration Transforms Company," *The Wall Street Journal*, October 25, 2005. Retrieved from the Web October 25, 2005.
http://www.online.wsj.com/article_print/SB113019302751378106.html, www.thecrackteam.com, and www.mrhappy-crack.com.

and should be one to three pages in length, with absolutely no padding or puffery. A sample summary for a hypothetical company is presented in Street Story 5.2.

The company name and contact person should appear as they do on the cover page. Suggestions and recommendations for preparing the other sections of the executive summary follow.[20]

- Type of Business: The summary should describe the firm's industry or sector in about ten words. Some investors will not invest in certain industries, so being clear up front saves time for everyone.
- Company Summary: This thumbnail sketch of the firm's history and background emphasizes the positive—briefly. More than half a page (150 words) is *not* a summary. A statement defining the firm's primary product or service should not be complicated by lists of product extensions or auxiliary services. Instead, stress should be placed on the uniqueness of the product or service. If it is not unique, why will it succeed?
- Management: The people running the company matter more than any other factor, but the summary need not include a lot of detail. Listing the top two or three people and emphasizing their industry experience should suffice.
- Product/Service and Competition: Mentioning the competition defines the niche the firm occupies. Again, this description should be no longer than half a page (150 words).
- Funds Requested: This brief statement specifies the exact amount of money needed and the investment vehicle: debt, equity, or some hybrid. If the firm is flexible in this regard, the summary should state both the company's preference and its willingness to consider alternatives. In this case an investor may make a counterproposal and the deal can be restructured.
- Collateral: If the summary offers a debt instrument, it should indicate whether and in what form collateral will be available. The more collateral the company has, the lower the interest rate it will be charged and the less equity it will have to give up.
- Use of Proceeds: The financial section in the main body of the business plan should specify how the money will be used. Overly broad terms like "pay expenses" and "increase working capital" do not inspire confidence, so entries such as "pay salaries" and "build inventory" are preferred.
- Financial History: The firm's financial history should include only the major categories—revenues, net income, assets, liabilities, and net worth—for the last two or three years. Figures presented in the history must coincide exactly with those in the main body of the plan. This section is omitted if the venture is completely new.
- Financial Projections: These projections follow the same format as the financial history, covering two or three years and matching the figures in the main body of the plan.

Street Story 5.2 provides an example of an executive summary for the proposed company Babyyourway.com. The rest of the business plan (abridged) can be found in the Appendix to this chapter.

Major Sections
Outline.
    I. Background and Purpose
        A. History
        B. Current situation
        C. The business model and resource-based elements

STREET STORY 5.2

Business Plan Executive Summary

Babyyourway.com
13310 Grouse Point Trail
Carmel, IN 46033
Ph: (555-555-8666)
www.babyyourway.com
Contact: Matt Sifferlen

Type of Business: Babyyourway.com is a retailer of customized children's merchandise.

Company Summary: Babyyourway.com aims to provide a unique shopping experience that allows customers to quickly and effortlessly purchase personalized keepsakes for the special children in their lives via a user-friendly Web site that truly puts the customer in control of the shopping experience. Babyyourway.com taps into the convergence of two market forces: (a) Increasing popularity of shopping for unique and boutique items via the Internet and (b) The fact that the fastest growth in U.S. population in the next 5 years will be in the 45-64 age group. Parents and grandparents are spending increasing amounts of money on apparel and merchandise for their newborn, infant, and toddler children and grandchildren. As boomers become grandparents at a rapid clip they will continue to use their disposable income to shower their grandkids with gifts. Bibs and other related children's merchandise are fun and inexpensive gifts.

Management: Babyyourway.com is managed by the four primary partners. Each partner brings an extremely valuable set of expertise and experiences that will allow the group to successfully oversee this new venture. The team has a combined 45+ years of experience in consumer and technology product development, brand and product management, marketing, operations management, information systems, and commercial bank-ing. Each member has an MBA from the Indiana University Kelley School of Business, one of the top 20 MBA programs in the nation.

Product and Competition: Boomer spending has already fueled the success of children's apparel retailers like Babies-R-Us, Children's Place, Baby Gap, and Gymboree. However, while all of these retailers have been successful at marketing mainstream, mass-produced, off-the-shelf products provided by their own large suppliers, none of them offers a personalized shopping experience. And while some of them dedicate limited online resources to customized products, these efforts are low-profile and ineffective because low volume transactions are out of favor with corporate behemoths that want to be all things to all people. Unlike our competitors, babyyourway.com embraces customization, offers a service that does not just embroider a baby's name on an item, and markets that as "personalized." Instead, we will offer a unique opportunity for shoppers to truly customize their bibs and other apparel purchases using a variety of online tools to select color scheme, text, materials, and licensed content. This puts customers in control of the purchasing experience and allows them to add the personal touches that today's shoppers value.

Funds Requested: It's anticipated that we will need an initial cash injection of $300,000. We would prefer debt financing, but we are open to other financing alternatives, including offering an equity stake to investors.

Use of Proceeds: We need the proceeds to purchase a DuPont Artistri digital printer, to assist in funding our substantial year-one advertising expenses, and to purchase our initial inventory.

Financial Projections:

Projections	($000) Year 1	Year 2	Year 3	Year 4	Year 5
Revenue	$350,000	$560,000	$896,000	$1,568,000	$2,744,000
Net Income	($298,627)	($144,527)	$131,176	$ 592,379	$1,572,055
Assets	$473,373	$349,847	$549,623	$1,230,202	$2,988,457
Liabilities	$413,414	$340,396	$314,978	$ 309,160	$ 447,181
Net Worth*	$ 59,959	$ 9,451	$234,645	$ 921,042	$2,541,276

*Note: Discretionary owner distributions may be taken beginning in Year 3 depending on company profitability.

Exit: It is our full intention to continue the business as a going concern. However, if we feel that the best way to extend our brand and market reach is by selling ownership to a larger entity, those offers will be considered, particularly if they provide a lucrative package to all shareholders and investors. As evidenced by our financial projections, by end of year 5 we will potentially have a Net Worth of $2,541,276. As an LLC, all owners of equity will be rewarded annually with ownership distributions according to their percent of ownership. If any owner should desire to sell his/her interest in the company, this request would be honored based on standard practices of our legal entity structure at the time of such an occurrence.

SOURCE: Babyyourway.com business plan. See Appendix A for the main body and exhibits of this business plan.

II. **Objectives**
   A. Short term
   B. Long term
III. **Market Analysis**
   A. Overall market
   B. Specific market
   C. Competitive factors
   D. Macroenvironmental influences
IV. **Development and Production**
   A. Production processes
   B. Resource requirements
   C. Quality assurance
V. **Marketing**
   A. Overall concept and orientation
   B. Marketing strategy and resources
   C. Sales forecasts
VI. **Financial Plans**
   A. Financial statements
   B. Financial resources
   C. Financial strategy
VII. **Organization and Management**
   A. Key personnel resources
   B. Human resource management strategy
VIII. **Ownership**
   A. Form of business
   B. Equity positions
   C. Deal structure*
IX. **Critical Risks and Contingencies**

   X.   **Summary and Conclusions**
   XI.   **Scheduling and Milestones**
Appendixes

The main body of the business plan contains the strategic and operating details of the new venture. Some redundancy among the sections is inevitable because the business is an integrated system and is necessarily self-referencing. This is not inherently bad. Some redundancy helps to focus the reader's attention. Where possible, using a reference such as, "See Section III, Market Analysis" is preferable to repeating verbatim a long segment of the market analysis.

Background and Purpose. This introductory section creates a context for understanding the business. Although history is not destiny in business, it is important that readers be able to gauge how far the firm has come and precisely where it is now in the new venture creation process. Suggestions and recommendations for preparing this material follow:

- History: This section, a brief description of the venture and its history, is especially important if the firm is offering a unique product or service. It tells potential investors that this company is a "prime mover."
- Current Situation: This includes a brief description of the product or service, its potential customers, and the technology necessary to make and deliver the product. This **product/market/technology configuration** (P/M/T) is the most concise statement about your business. There is ample opportunity to expand on this later in the plan. If the product or service is so technical that a non-expert might not understand it, create an exhibit or an appendix with a photograph or drawing of the product, list its technical specifications, and present any available test results.
- The Business Model and Resource-Based Elements: This section tells the story of the business: its customers, product, technology, and revenue model. How will it make money? What key resources will contribute to the firm's success? How will these resources be translated into a unique product or service with a competitive advantage? This is the first introduction of the strategy statement.

Objectives. Objectives are desired outcomes, and every new venture has three broad objectives: creation, survival, and profitability. For firms with an operating history, of course, only survival and profitability are pertinent. Objectives are viewed in terms of time frame and measurement. Short-term objectives can be achieved within one year. Long-term objectives generally require three to five years.

The measurement of how well an objective has been achieved can be quantitative or qualitative. **Quantitative measures** are stated as numbers—return on sales, return on equity, employee turnover, etc. They usually concern the degree of the firm's efficiency: how well it has deployed a given set of resources. For example, a quantitative objective involving gross margin shows cost of goods sold and direct labor charges as a percentage of sales. A high gross margin indicates an efficient ratio of cost to revenue, and a low gross margin indicates inefficiency.[21] Quantitative objectives tend to concern operating issues and the short term.

Qualitative measures, on the other hand, resist reduction to numbers. For example, "to be a good corporate citizen" or "to have a reputation for integrity" or "to develop innovative products" are hard to quantify. Qualitative objectives involve the effectiveness of the new venture, the extent to which the firm maintains and expands its position in the competitive environment and in the macroenvironment. Qualitative objectives, therefore, concern with external and environmental issues and are viewed over the long term.

Table 5.1 lists possible objectives, and the three dimensions are shown as continua along the arrows. The objectives toward the top of the list (beginning with sales profitability) represent short-term, quantitative measures of efficiency. The objectives toward the bottom (anchored by social concern/responsibility) represent long-term, qualitative measures of effectiveness. The firm's objectives should be both realistic and challenging and should be consistent with the rest of the narrative and with the plan's financial projections.

Market Analysis. The market analysis section aims to convince the reader or investor that the entrepreneur fully understands the competitive environment and the macroenvironment. It must demonstrate that (1) the addressable market for the product or service is substantial and growing, and (2) the entrepreneur can achieve a defendable competitive position. Suggestions and recommendations for market analysis follow:

- Overall Market: A description of the firm's industry includes its current conditions, and its projections for sales, profits, rates of growth, and other trends. Who are the leading competitors and why have they been successful? Where is the market located and what is its scope—international, regional, national, local? Because investors prefer industries with the potential for large sales volumes and high growth rates, they need to see the big picture.

TABLE 5.1 Specific Objectives

Measurement of Objectives			Time Frame for Objectives
Objective	Efficiency	Quantitative	Short Term
Sales Profitability			
Market share			
Market position			
Productivity			
Product/service quality			
Innovation			
Employee morale			
Training/development			
Social concern/responsibility			
	Effectiveness	Qualitative	Long Term

- Specific Market: In narrowing the focus to the target market, segment, or niche in which the firm will operate, the plan describes current and projected conditions, leading competitors, and customers. How are purchasing decisions made, and by whom? If a market survey has been conducted, its findings can be presented in an appendix. What conclusions can be drawn from it? What are the best case, likely case, and worst case sales projections for the total market segment? List the five largest buyers. What percentage of the firm's sales is projected to come from these customers? What are the trends for your customers' profits and incomes? How will the firm continue to assess its customer base and update information?
- Competitive Factors: This extremely important section describes and explains how each factor covered in Chapter 3 affects the firm's sales and profitability. It analyzes the competitive nature of the firm's industry and the industry's attractiveness; the power of the buyers and the suppliers; the availability of substitute products and services; the height of entry barriers; and the nature of the current rivalry. It must demonstrate how its resource base and strategy address these factors and evaluate the positions of the most important competitors, comparing its strengths and weaknesses to those of the market leaders. Finally it summarizes your firm's competitive position.
- Macroenvironmental Influences: This vital section demonstrates the venture's knowledge and competence by evaluating the impact of the macroenvironmental factors described in Chapter 3. It analyzes the political, economic, technological, sociodemographic, and ecological factors that affect the firm, presenting best, most likely, and worst case scenarios. It concludes with an assessment of the risks that each of these factors poses for the firm's survival and profitability.

Development and Production. This section deals with the most important elements of research, development, and production of the basic product or service.

- Production Processes: This outline of the stages in the development and production of the product or service include brief comments on each stage, detailing how time and money are allocated in the production process or service delivery system. A discussion of the difficulties and risks encountered at each stage can be accompanied by a flowchart illustrating how the core function is accomplished. The possibility of subcontracting each stage should be evaluated and make-or-buy decisions must be explained. What resource-based competencies provide the firm with advantages in the production process?
- Resource Requirements: This is an analysis of each resource employed in the production process. These resources, described in Chapter 2, may be financial, physical, human, technological, reputational, and organizational. Where in the production process does the venture possess valuable, rare, hard-to-copy, and nonsubstitutable resources? What are the cost/volume economics of the production process or service delivery system? What are the current trends in the cost of resource procurement?
- Quality Assurance: Quality dimensions (product, user, process, value) were described in Chapter 1. What is the firm's perspective on quality? How will quality be defined and measured in the production process. Will the new venture employ total quality management techniques and systems?[22]

Market Analysis. This section describes the actual marketing strategy of the firm or new venture. This strategy must be consistent with the objectives stated earlier. The marketing section explains how the firm will exploit its resource base to create a total marketing focus. It also describes how the new venture connects with its customers.

- Overall Concept and Orientation: The description of the venture's concept in the background section can be given a marketing focus by transforming it into a statement of customer orientation. What benefits and positive outcomes will the customer derive from interaction with the firm? Evaluate the resources that the firm or new venture has or can control in creating high levels of customer awareness and satisfaction. This introduction demonstrates a commitment to the marketing effort.
- Marketing Strategy: This brief description of the primary product or service's P/M/T along with that of the major competitors can show how marketing strategy will support the product or service's strengths and exploit competitors' weaknesses. Identifying the target market and using data from market research demonstrates why the company is competing in this particular segment. Why and how does its product appeal to this segment? How does the marketing strategy communicate and activate this appeal? What image does the firm want to adopt? Is this image consistent with the product or service? Why will it appeal to customers? How will the image be communicated? That is, what are the plans for packaging, branding, and labeling the product? What advertising, promotional activities, and campaigns are proposed? This also requires a budget and a breakdown of marketing costs (usually in dollars per 1,000 people reached). Advertising materials (copy, storyboards, and photographs), if available, are included in an appendix.
- Pricing: Here the plan discusses pricing strategy. How do the company's prices compare with the competition's? Is the pricing strategy consistent with the firm's image? Does it create value for customers? What is the profit margin per unit under various pricing schemes? What is the credit policy and is it consistent with purchasing patterns in the industry? What is the warranty policy? What about service after the sale? How will the company create and foster ongoing relationships with buyers and encourage repeat business?
- Distribution: How will the product or service be distributed? Include a description of the geographic scope and the channels of distribution.

Sales Forecasts. The sales forecast is derived from three elements of market analysis: (1) the size of the market in units and dollars, (2) the fraction of that market that the firm can capture through its marketing efforts (market penetration rate), and (3) the pricing strategy.

Sales forecasts are often best presented in an exhibit or chart. They can be shown as units of products (or number of services delivered) as well as in dollars. The entrepreneur multiplies product units by predicted average price (and offers the justification for this price). Using a five-year time frame, the plan presents a best case, most likely case, and worst case scenario. What separates the best, most likely, and worst cases? A graph can illustrate sales trends and growth.

Financial Plans. The sales forecasts conclude the marketing portion of the business plan and begin the financial analysis portion; they represent the "top line." The purpose of the financial analysis section is to illustrate the "bottom line." Bankers and potential investors evaluate this section to see whether enough profits will be generated to make the venture an attractive investment. It also serves as the financial plan for the firm's executives. This section is numbers oriented, and it should give the audience what it wants: rows and columns of figures, carefully labeled and footnoted.

If the firm has an operating history, the financial statements must summarize its past and current performance. For past performance, it calculates ratios that highlight profitability, liquidity, leverage, and activity, then compares these ratios with industry averages collected from trade data.

If the firm is a new venture, it must present the following:

- Projected profit and loss statements (income statements) for 5 years—monthly for the first year, quarterly for the next two years, and annually thereafter.
- Projected cash flow statements and analysis—monthly for the first year and until the firm has positive cash flow, quarterly for the next two years, and annually thereafter.
- Projected balance sheets for the ends of the first 3 to 5 years.

Each statement should be referenced and discussed but should be placed in a financial appendix. If the statements and projections indicate seasonality and cyclicality, the reader must be told what each statement means and what its overall message is.

A break-even analysis for a service business shows how many hours of the service must be sold. For a product business, it indicates how many units of the product must be sold. A table of break-even points should appear in the appendix.

A summary of financial resources begins with start-up costs for the business, a detailed list of all physical assets the firm needs to purchase or lease and a statement of organizational costs (e.g., legal, architectural, engineering, etc.). How much money will the business need? What can be offered as collateral for debt? How will the loan be repaid? Financial statements must, of course, include such repayment. How will the money be used? A use-of-proceeds exhibit is helpful. Investors generally believe that initial proceeds that are expensed—research, development, and training costs—are riskier than money spent on capital equipment, land, and buildings.

Provide details and the references if the firm has established credit it will not initially need. Also provide a list and an aging statement if the firm has receivables. What are the probabilities of collecting these receivables? Include a description of existing debt, a list of delinquent accounts and their amounts, and a statement of any accounts payable and the period of time that these debts have been outstanding.

The firm's **financial strategy** consists of two components. The first comprises the sources and uses of funds. What are the preferred sources of new capital—continuing operations, new debt, or new equity? What combination is appropriate, and what debt/equity ratio and degree of financial leverage is the firm targeting? In terms of use, what are the firm's priorities for the excess cash generated by operations and by additional financing? Is expansion and growth the priority or are dividends? Both managers and investors will be guided by these strategic decisions.

The second component of financial strategy comprises the internal control and monitoring systems. What safeguards are proposed to ensure the security of funds generated by operations and by any additional borrowings or equity offerings? What systems or procedures will monitor and control cash disbursement? What are the firm's internal audit procedures? Who are the firm's external auditors?

Organization and Management. From beginning to end, the business plan is a document with a purpose. In the preliminary sections, it introduces the firm in a general way. In the main body, the firm reviews its objectives, its market, and the strategy for reaching its objectives. The financial portion indicates the funds needed to launch the venture and the predicted size of sales, profits, and growth. The question that recurs to the reader throughout is: "Why should I believe any of this?" The answer lies in the section on organization and management. This section describes the firm's people— the entrepreneurs and top management team—as well as the firm's technical, reputational, and human resources. Before proceeding to the section on ownership, which presents the deal and actually asks for money, the reader wants to know that the people involved are of the highest quality. The saying goes, "Give us a B plan with an A team over an A plan with a B team . . . every time."

Key personnel resources are presented on an organization chart with the names and titles of the key executives. Brief synopses of these individuals' previous experience, education, and related qualifications are included, and complete resumes of top managers and key executives may be placed in an appendix. Readers will want to know whether these people have worked together before and in what capacity.

What are these individuals' contributions to the company? Who will do what, and why was he or she chosen for that role? What contractual relationships exist between the company and its principals, and between the principals? Are there employment contracts, severance packages, or noncompete agreements?

Initial salaries, incentives, bonuses, pensions, and fringe benefits of the top people are also of interest to investors. It is wise to keep initial salaries low to conserve cash and to keep deferred compensation (stock options and the like) high to produce long-term commitment. What key positions remain unfilled? Job descriptions of these positions should include the unique skills, abilities, and experience the firm needs, and plans should be presented for attracting, developing, and retaining key personnel. Without such plans, people problems will inhibit growth.

A list of the firm's board of directors, their ages, their relevant experience, their other corporate affiliations, and their connection with the firm is another component. Providing the names of the legal, accounting, banking, and other pertinent organizations (marketing or advertising agencies, consulting firms, and the like) can also influence investors.

A statement of the firm's basic philosophy concerning human resources and management strategy is also important. Does it favor close or general supervision? Will the workforce be unionized? What is the firm's approach to collective bargaining? What is its position on employee compensation, profit sharing, and employee ownership? What is the rationale for such programs? How will the firm manage and control health-care and insurance costs? What are its strategies for employee and management development and training, for continuing education, and for hiring and promoting from within? What factors dictate criteria for promotion? How will performance be assessed? How many employees does the firm currently have, or how many will be required to start the new venture? What are these employees' responsibilities, positions, and job descriptions? What percentages are skilled and unskilled? A pertinent analysis of the relevant labor markets by type of skill and geographic scope is required.

What equal opportunity employment and other government regulations affect the firm

and its workforce? What strategies are in place to meet legal and regulatory obligations?
Ownership. In this section, the founders describe the legal form of the business, the contractual obligations of the owners to the firm and to each other, and, if the business plan is a proposal for financing, the nature of the deal. Note that only after the reader is familiar with the experience, reputation, and character of the entrepreneurial team is it appropriate to ask for money.

A description of the firm's legal **form of business**—sole proprietorship, partnership, regular corporation, subchapter S corporation—includes a brief explanation of why this is the best fit (see Chapter 8). It discusses any special aspects of the ownership structure, such as subsidiaries, holding companies, or cross-ownership agreements. If the firm is organized as a partnership, it lists the essentials of the partnership agreement and includes the actual agreement as an appendix.

An exhibit can show the amounts of money the founders and executives have invested or will soon be investing in the business. It also shows the **equity positions** that these investments represent. Another exhibit can show any rights to warrants and stock options and indicate their precise nature (exercise price, expiration date). What proportion of equity would be controlled if these were exercised? Are the shares held in beneficial trust? Recent changes in the ownership of the firm should also be noted and explained. What percentage of stock is owned by the employees? (See Chapter 8.)

If these investments are debt, the plan must specify for each the coupon, maturity, and any special covenants in the loan agreement. What is the priority (seniority) of repayment?

A brief outline of the deal structure belongs here. It describes the financing required to start up the business or to fund development or expansion of current activities (see Chapter 8). A three-to-five-year time frame is appropriate. Is the preference for new debt or new equity? What are the potential sources for these funds? For what purposes will the money be used? For equity financing, how much of the company will be offered as stock? A structured deal includes the following information[23]:

1. The number of shares of stock available for the offering, and the percentage of total ownership that this represents
2. The price per share of each unit[24]
3. The revised number of shares and each founder's percentage ownership after the proposed financing is completed
4. The effect of dilution on new investors' shares[25]
5. The potential returns per share to the investor. These need to be consistent with the previously reported financial plans. Avoid projecting something here that has not been presented and validated earlier in the plan.

Critical Risks and Contingencies. In this section the new venture, following the rules of full disclosure, reveals all material and relevant information that a prudent investor needs. The nature of this information is inherently negative, including every reason why someone would not want to invest in the venture. By fully revealing this information, the entrepreneurs perform their legal and moral obligation to be forthcoming and honest about the firm's prospects. Should the investors lose their investment, full disclosure can be a defense against claims of civil or criminal liability. This section typically includes the following categories of information and the potential impact of each on the new venture:

1. Failure to produce the products and services promised
2. Failure to meet production deadlines or sales forecasts
3. Problems with suppliers and distributors
4. Unforeseen industry trends
5. Unforeseen events in the political, economic, social, technological, and ecological environments
6. Failure to survive retaliation by competitors with significantly more resources
7. The problems of unproven and inexperienced management
8. The problems of unproven and undeveloped technology
9. Difficulties in raising additional financing
10. Other issues specific to the firm in question

Concluding Sections

There are a few loose ends and details left to report on in the concluding sections.

Summary and Conclusions. A brief summary of the highlights and key features of the report must include the firm's overall strategic direction, the reasons for believing the firm will succeed, a short description of how the firm will exploit its unique resources to advantage, the firm's sales and profit projections, its capital requirements, and the percentage ownership for the founders and investors.

Because this is a summary, no new information should be reported here. The entrepreneurs may even use the exact words used in earlier sections since repetition will reinforce the message and demonstrate consistency.

Scheduling and Milestones. The business plan outlines a number of actions to be taken in the future, actions discussed in many different sections of the plan. To consolidate the timing of events, the plan should present a schedule in chart form, listing the important milestones to be reached in the near and intermediate term. This helps investors know when the firm will need additional capital infusions and allows them to track the firm's progress. Projected calendar dates for the following events should appear:

1. Seeking legal counsel and accounting services
2. Filing documents necessary to set up the desired legal form of business, and completing licensing requirements
3. Completion of research and development efforts
4. Completion of a working prototype
5. Purchase or lease of production facilities and office and retail space
6. Selection of personnel: management, skilled, semiskilled
7. Ordering supplies, production materials, inventory
8. Beginning production
9. First order, sales, and payments
10. Other critical dates and events

Although it is usually desirable to speed up the timing of a new venture's launch, preparations often take longer than expected, particularly when the firm needs some other organization or set of individuals to act before it can move on to the next scheduled task. Slack should be built into the schedule whenever possible.

Appendixes. This discussion of the elements of the business plan has suggested that certain items, exhibits, and documentation belong in an appendix, so these plans may have a number of appendixes. A partial list of possible appendix sections is shown below.[26]

1. A photograph or a drawing of the product (if appropriate), including title and labels if necessary. If the product or process is highly technical and investors are likely to have the technical section reviewed by a consulting engineer, the entire technical section should be under separate cover.
2. A photograph or drawing of the intended location and physical layout (if appropriate), annotated if necessary
3. Sales and profitability forecasts in chart form
4. Market surveys and documentation of size and nature of market
5. Sample advertisements, brochures, and telemarketing protocols
6. Sample press releases
7. Price lists, catalogues, and mailing lists (just the titles of the lists, not all the contents)
8. All detailed and footnoted financial statements, including income statements, cash flow statements, balance sheets, break-even calculations, and table of start-up costs
9. Fixed-asset acquisition schedule
10. Individual and corporate tax returns
11. Résumés of founders, board members, and key individuals
12. Letters of recommendation or character references
13. Any additional information deemed appropriate

CRITIQUING THE PLAN

Although the entrepreneur has attempted, in writing the business plan, to answer all conceivable questions, readers can still find problems. Investors and other professionals will continue to ask questions and critique the proposal as they read it, and they usually want additional information when they meet the entrepreneur in person. It is impossible to answer all the questions raised by the plan or even to anticipate what they may be. However, readers will apply some general criteria and will usually express four specific major concerns which the entrepreneur will have to address in detail.[27]

General Criteria

The four general criteria that evaluators employ to judge a plan are used both by business professionals and in student business plan competitions. These criteria are:

- Comprehensiveness: The plan must cover all relevant topics and issues. Using a template helps to do this. When one section of a template does not apply, the writer simply includes a page with the topic heading and notes that the section is "Not applicable." This alerts the reader that nothing is missing, and that that topic is not essential to the plan.

- Analysis: The plan needs to go beyond descriptions and use the salient and informative tools of analysis. Resource, industry, competitor and product analyses are typical. Financial projections should include models analyzing percentages, returns, and comparisons with established businesses and industry benchmarks.

- Reasonableness: Assumptions will be questioned by readers. Reasonable assumptions can be compared with benchmarks and facts. They lie within established ranges and experiences. Reasonableness, however is ultmately in the eye of the beholder, and no one would have *reasonably* forecast the success of companies like Google or Youtube. Knowing the audience helps a company determine how to frame its assumptions.

- Writing and presentation: The document needs to be well written, organized, and presented. This is covered in the sections below.

Specific Criteria

Four specific criteria frequently appear in critiques of business plans. These concern the management, the resources, the projections and returns, and the exit or harvest of the venture.

Management. Repeatedly, entrepreneurs and the top management teams are asked, "Who are you?" The reader must find a way to assess the entrepreneur's honesty. The business plan has been read and analyzed, but no written document can answer questions about the character and integrity of the entrepreneur. His or her background will be researched and any inconsistencies must be dealt with. Everyone has inconsistencies of some sort. Even presidential candidates who have lived most of their lives in the public spotlight must deal with this issue.

If there is any doubt about the character of the entrepreneur, the financing will fall through. Entrepreneurs must present their professional histories, answer questions about their motivation, and discuss what they believe they can achieve.

Some entrepreneurs have been preparing for the new venture all their lives, and their previous careers are perfect matches for their intended new businesses. Student entrepreneurs sometimes have the chance to practice defending their management teams and other business plan issues before seasoned entrepreneurs.

Resources. Investors continually review proposals for financing, and one way to spot a business with high potential is by carefully scrutinizing the resource base of the firm. What rare, valuable, hard to copy, and nonsubstitutable resources does the firm have, can it control, or will it produce? Uniqueness is crucial. Also, the firm will need to demonstrate how it can keep the profits and rents generated by its resources. The entrepreneur should be prepared for dozens of "what if" questions describing scenarios in which the resource-based strategy of the firm is attacked or undermined.

Projections and Returns. The firm's top management team will be asked to justify the assumptions underlying the sales forecasts, cost estimates, administrative costs, and net profit figures. Therefore, the data should have a solid foundation in reality. At the same time, projections must be optimistic enough to indicate a solid return for investors. This is a basic conflict in many new ventures, and inconsistencies will be thoroughly examined.

Exit

Investors want to know how and when they will recoup their money. There are many alternative mechanisms for exiting, but the exit will occur in the future after many uncertain and risky activities. The fact that the exit is fraught with peril, however, will not restrain investors from trying to pin down the exact details of the proposed exit. They are naturally concerned about their money, and entrepreneurs should expect them to pose many "what if" scenarios.

The overall evaluation of the plan may rest on the quality of the management team and the current status of the product or service. These areas must be supported in great detail. The evaluator wants to see experienced management in the new business or a closely related business. If this cannot be documented, the entrepreneurs might have to establish an advisory board. Likewise, it is important to establish that the product/service has proven market traction. If the product offers a twist on anything that currently exists, data on comparable products will be helpful. When the product/service is unique to the market, management team experience becomes even more essential. The Rich-Gumpert Evaluation System (Figure 5.1) is a useful tool for checking the ranking an entrepreneur might receive. The most desirable ranking is the 4/4.

FORMAT AND PRESENTATION

The format of the business plan and its physical presentation make the first impression on the reader. Deliberate care and attention are needed to make this impression positive.

Physical Appearance

Ideally the physical appearance of the plan is neither too fancy nor too plain. An extremely ornate binding and cover indicate a disregard for expense and a preoccupation with appearances. Too plain an appearance may suggest a lack of respect for the reader and, ironically, not enough care for appearances. Rich and Gumpert recommend a plastic spiral binding and a pair of cover sheets of a single color.[28] They believe a stapled compilation of photocopied material will not be treated seriously.

The recommended length of the business plan is usually between 40 and 50 pages, plus appendixes. Because the appendixes and supporting documentation can be as long as or longer than the plan itself, it is not unusual to bind these supplements separately.

The pages of the plan should be crisp and clean, with wide margins and easy-to-read type. Graphs and photographs should be of high quality, and all charts and exhibits should be labeled and referenced within the body of the plan.

Street Story 5.3 offers some additional resources for preparing your plan and preparing yourself for writing the plan. Some of these resources will require a financial outlay while others are free.

FIGURE 5.1 Rich/Gumpert Evaluation System

Management status and experience levels ⟶

MORE DESIRABLE

Product service level						
	Level 4 Product/service fully developed. Many satisfied users. Market established.	4/1	4/2	4/3	4/4	↑
	Level 3 Product/service fully developed. Few or no users as yet. Market assumed	3/1	3/2	3/3	3/4	↑
	Level 2 Product/service pilot operable. Not yet developed for production. Market assumed	2/1	2/2	2/3	2/4	↑
	Level 1 A product or service idea but not operable. Market assumed.	1/1	1/2	1/3	1/4	↑
		Level 1 A single would-be entrepreneur	*Level 2* Two founders. Additional slots, personnel not identified	*Level 3* Partly staffed management team. Absent members identified, to join when firm is funded.	*Level 4* Fully staffed, experienced management team.	*MORE DESIRABLE*

SOURCE: David Gumpert and Stanley Rich, from *Business Plans That Win $$$,* 1985. Copyright © by David Gumpert and Stanley Rich. Reprinted by permission of Sterling Lord Literistic, Inc.

Writing and Editing

It is extremely important that the plan be well written and edited. Irrelevant information and self-adulation should be excised, and everything should be presented as concisely as possible.[29]Bad writing will kill a plan, and yet it is not recommended that the writing be jobbed out. It is up to the entrepreneur and the new venture's executives and advisers to write the plan together. A basic guideline for writing a business plan or any kind of business assignment would include:

Getting Help for Your Road Map

"People have great ideas in their head all the time, but it's the people who get it in a business plan who succeed," advises Wes Moss. He should know. Moss is a former contestant on Donald Trump's TV show "The Apprentice" and a self-described entrepreneur advocate.

Fortunately there's a lot of help beyond this textbook for entrepreneurs warming up to write business plans. Those who want additional training or a quick review, for example, can enroll in a face-to-face seminar or an online workshop specifically created for entrepreneurs writing business plans. Some of this training is even free. Resources for finding programs include your local Small Business Development Center, or the Small Business Administration Web site (www.sba.gov). Colleges and universities in your area may also offer specialized programs through their business school or continuing studies office.

The Internet also provides many resources for business plan writers and much of that help is also free. The Small Business Administration's site has basic information along with sample business plans. Washington-based non-profit One Economy uses funding from the eBay Foundation to support a site (www.thebeehive.org) with an interactive program called "Build a Business Plan Tool" which allows nascent entrepreneurs to create a fill-in-the-blank plan up to 40 pages long. They report more than 6,000 people have signed up to use this free program. Dow Jones & Co., the publisher of *The Wall Street Journal*, also sponsors a site for entrepreneurs (www.StartupJournal.com). They have sample plans for a wide variety of businesses—from coffee kiosks to pet photography to high-tech marketing—posted on their site, and also offer a no-cost Web-based tool for creating a mini business plan.

More hands-on help is available from companies that produce computer programs to help develop business plans. Palo Alto Software annually produces a program called Business Plan Pro (www.paloalto.com) for around $100; it uses "wizards" to make plan writing easier. The program can be downloaded from the Web, and is also available in a premier edition with enhanced financials and comparison features. Smart Online (www.onebiz.smartonline.com) offers a similar interactive business plan program as part of a package with accounting, personnel, marketing, and other interface products. They market their bundle of services for a monthly fee of around $50, which allows up to five users to access the site. Smart Online will also evaluate or even write a business plan for a fee ranging from $300 to $3000.

Paying someone else to write a new venture's plan may be the ultimate service (but it is not recommended by most academics and financiers). It's certainly the most expensive; companies such as Masterplanz (www.masterplanz.com) charge up to $15,000 to write a plan. "A lot of people are great technicians, but not great accountants or great writers," says a Masterplanz spokesman.

Entrepreneur Rosalind Resnick has made a business out of helping other entrepreneurs write their plans. The manifesto posted on her Axxess Business Centers, Inc., Web site (www.abcbizhelp.net) proclaims, "People who get things for free generally don't take them as seriously as things they've got to pay for."

SOURCE: Adapted from Jessica Mintz, "First Things First," *The Wall Street Journal*, November 25, 2004. Retrieved from the Web March 4, 2006, http://online.wsj.com/aticle_print/SB110131302046583059.html, www.sba.com, www.thebeehive.org, www.StartupJournal.com, www.paloalto.com, www.onebiz.smartonline.com, www.masterplanz.com, and www.abcbizhelp.net.

Prewriting. The writers should begin by putting their information and thoughts in an outline or another organized form to find out what they know and need to know. At this stage they should also think about the intended audience and arrange the material to suit the purpose of the plan.

Writing and Rewriting/Revising. Ideally every writer should be able to transform an outline into a fully articulated rough draft and then revise that piece for form, coherence, and style. Personal computers have made this process much easier. Clear and concise writing is the goal, but writers can get bogged down in the rewriting and revising part of the process. The best way to prepare for writing under a deadline is to practice writing every day.

Editing. Editing is the final step, and a number of helpful tools are now available, including the computer's spell checker and thesaurus. Some word processing software includes a grammar checker but be careful of words that sound similar or typographical errors. The program might not catch these. If time permits, a colleague or friend of the entrepreneur might read and critique the plan. What matters most is that the plan says what the entrepreneurs want it to say. Despite the numerous published guides for writing business plans and the general agreement on content, entrepreneurs continue to submit poorly written plans.[30] One researcher reviewed 20 business plans submitted to venture capitalists and found that:[31]

- 30 percent failed to include a specific business strategy.
- 40 percent of the teams lacked marketing experience, and the marketing sections of the plan were weakly developed.
- 55 percent failed to discuss technical idea protection.
- 75 percent failed to identify the details of the competition.
- 10 percent had no financial projections at all; another 15 percent omitted balance sheets; and 80 percent failed to provide adequate details of the financial projections.

The more deficiencies in the plan, the lower the odds of gaining support from venture capitalists.

Some entrepreneurs may be tempted to let someone else write the plan or to rely on a computer program or template. Writing a business plan is a chore—-like writing a term paper. But no computer program or professional business plan writer can make lemonade from a lemon of a business idea. The maxim "garbage in, garbage out" applies.[32]

SUMMARY

Every new venture needs a business plan. The advantages of writing a plan far outweigh the costs. The purpose of the plan is to enable the top executives of the established firm or new venture to think about their business in a comprehensive way, to communicate their objectives to individuals who may have a stake in the firm's future, to have a basis for making decisions, and to facilitate the planning process.

The essential elements of the plan are generally recognized. The preliminary sections set the stage for the reader and make the first impression. They should be professional, concise, and informative because readers may put the plan aside if it doesn't catch their interest at the outset. The major sections describe the new venture's strategy, operations, marketing, management, financial plan, and ownership structure. These sections need to be as detailed as possible and internally consistent. The concluding sections deal with details on timing, schedules, and milestones, and provide a summary. The appendixes contain reference material for documentation.

Each plan must be well written and organized, and it must anticipate the many questions readers will have. No plan can answer all such questions, so the entrepreneurs must be familiar with all the details so they can respond to unanswered questions and critiques.

KEY TERMS

Bootstrapping
Business plan
Effectiveness
Efficiency
External audiences
Internal audiences
Logo
Long-term objectives

Nascent entrepreneur
Objectives
Product/market/technology configuration
Qualitative measures
Quantitative measures
Short-term objectives
Tag line

DISCUSSION QUESTIONS

1. Discuss the costs and benefits of writing a business plan.
2. Who should write a business plan? Who should not bother? Who must write a business plan?
3. Why are the preliminary sections so important?
4. What information should be conveyed in the executive summary?
5. Distinguish between short-term and long-term objectives. Between quantitative and qualitative objectives. Between efficiency and effectiveness. Give examples.
6. How is the market analysis section linked to the marketing section?
7. How is the marketing section linked to the financial sections?
8. How are the financial sections linked to the management and organization sections?
9. How are the management and organization sections linked to the deal structure and ownership sections?
10. What questions are likely to be asked by investors reading your business plan? Why are these concerns important to the investor?
11. Discuss the benefits of careful presentation and effective writing style.

EXERCISES

1. Draft an outline of your (or your team's) business plan.
   a. What information do you already possess? Write it in draft form.
   b. What information is still required? Prepare a plan to obtain this information.
2. Prepare as much of the executive summary of your business plan as you can. Be concise but informative. Follow the model given in the chapter.
3. Critique a business plan. Examples can be found in the case section of this book, the appendix to this chapter, or may be provided by your instructor.
   a. How well does the business plan address the key issues?
   b. What changes and improvements would you make to the plan?
   c. How well done is the presentation and writing? How has this influenced your impression?
   d. Would you be interested in investing in this business? Why or why not?

DISCUSSION CASE

Taking Plans to the Next Level

Sometimes the best thing you can do with your business plan is submit it to a business plan competition. Business plan competitions provide entrepreneurs with a check point in plan development and input into an imprecise and iterative process.

A business plan competition helped transform Steve Manning's idea into an actual venture. When he was an undergraduate majoring in Parks and Recreation Administration, Manning interned at a national park where he observed that kudzu vines were destroying many of the indigenous plants. The chemicals or fires traditionally used in vegetation management harmed the surrounding vegetation, and Manning thought there had to be a better way. He wondered whether insects could be used.

When he became a MBA student at the University of Oregon, Manning wrote a plan outlining a business that would be a pioneer in a new environmental industry, low-impact plant control. He placed second in the university's New Venture Championship. Using his $4,000 prize plus an additional $250,000 raised from investors he met during the competition, he hired botanists to work out the logistics of eco-friendly plant control.

After graduation in 1997 Manning and botanist Lee Patrick started a company called Invasive Plant Control, Inc. (www.invasive-plantcontrol.com), now recognized as one of the leaders in the Integrated Pest Management approach to vegetation management. Their customers include Shenandoah National Park, Oak Ridge National Laboratories, Paris Island U.S. Marine Corps base, North Carolina State Parks, and the city of Pittsburgh.

Manning obviously believes in the value of business plan competitions, because he returned to the University of Oregon in 2006 to provide funding in his company's name for the Original Innovation Award at the New Venture Championship.

Not everyone who enters a business plan competition makes the jump to new venture creation quite so easily, but many walk away with something more valuable than prize money. Bobby Price, working with his MBA student wife and his dentist father, won the 1999 Wake Forest Babcock Elevator Competition (team members have to pitch their idea to judges during a two-minute elevator ride) with a plan to manufacture dentures with implanted GPS computer chips. Their prize was a meeting with venture capitalists, but the investors doubted that the product would succeed in the marketplace. They were much more positive about the Prices' other idea, a revolutionary way to make and store denture molds. Altadonics, the company the family created, now distributes new denture mold kits to dentists in North Carolina.

In 2002 entrepreneur Joern Kallmeyer made it to the semifinals of MIT's $50K Entrepreneurship Competition with his plan for a company to manufacture ceramic heat exchangers that would recycle heat produced by engines. His plan didn't win, largely because the judges misunderstood Kallmeyer: He didn't intend to produce the heat exchanger himself, but to license it to other manufacturers. The entrepreneur took the rejection in stride. "This [feedback] was so important because the judges act as a sounding board for how investors might react," he says. Kallmeyer submitted a reworked plan to the UC-Berkley Haas Social Venture Competition and won $25,000. His new plan has helped him raise an additional $1.75 million.

SOURCE: Adapted from Jennifer Merritt, "Big Plans on Campus," *Business Week Small Biz,* Fall 2004: 57; and from Steve Manning, Lindquist Center for Entrepreneurship. Retrieved from the Web June 27, 2006. www.lcb.uoregon.edu/lce/Manning.html, and www.invasiveplantcontrol.com.

Case Questions

1. Identify three business plan competitions to which you could submit your business plan. Why did you select these particular competitions?
2. If you were to submit a plan to a competition, what particular kind of feedback would you be looking for?
3. In addition to feedback for your plan, what else could you learn from participating in a business plan competition or from researching competitions on the Internet?

APPENDIX

Babyyourway.com Business Plan

History and Current Situation

Babyyourway.com uses a parallel competition entry wedge strategy. We are taking an already popular market niche (children's apparel) and placing a more focused emphasis on providing a customized, online approach. Many companies and Web sites offer bibs, but none of them offer a genuinely customized experience, allowing the purchaser to build a truly unique bib. We do not have to spend significant resources educating customers about bibs, onesies, burp cloths, etc., since we are not offering new product lines. Instead we are applying personalized touches to existing products. We will focus our efforts on communicating the value of the products and services we provide on our site, and on making the site award-winning for its ease of use.

The Product. Babyyourway.com will be an online retailer filling a horizontal niche in the online sales of custom baby bibs and apparel. Initial focus will be placed on a limited line of children's apparel products (bibs, onesies, tees, blankets, burp cloths). If we succeed and grow in this market, we will branch out into other customized baby items that our niche customers would appreciate. Some of the critical success factors for delighting our customers and sustaining our profitability will be:

- We will focus on delivering quality products that can be created by our customers via a user-friendly, intuitive, and fun Web site. Customers will be able to hand-pick the materials and content for their bibs and to preview their purchases before completing the sales. Customers can also upload any image(s) that they want printed on the bib.
- We will depend heavily on an aggressive marketing campaign (i.e., making sure the 4 Ps are properly aligned) since we will have to attract our niche customers and prove the value of our products and services immediately since there are little to no switching costs involved.
- We will build a moat around our core business by forming strategic licensing arrangements with schools of all levels, pro sports teams, record labels, and other businesses and institutions to gain nonexclusive rights to popular designs, logos, phrases, etc.

The Market. There are already companies in this niche engaged in the online marketing of customized children's apparel. However, we have learned that these companies fall into one of two categories. They are either:

1. Large players with in-house product lines that do not embrace customization but rather offer only very limited customization options as a complementary service to their core products. Example include Babies-R-Us, Gymboree, and Baby Gap.
2. Online boutique shops that offer more customization options but operate on a very small scale, focusing on local providers that lack the capacity, the sophisticated online presence, and/or the resources to emerge as national providers.

The children's apparel market in general is in the maturing stage. In addition to the niche players mentioned earlier, Wal-mart, Target, Kohl's, and other larger retailers aggressively market children's apparel. However, no major player has emerged from the custom bibs or custom baby apparel competition, and nobody dominates the online marketing of such apparel. We are confident that this business venture would step into an industry (custom baby/children's apparel) that is in the transitional stage of its lifecycle. Shoppers in this niche have sophisticated preferences and tastes along with high levels of disposable income, so there certainly is plenty of potential for growth. Still, it is prudent to assume that this window of opportunity is probably closing and that the industry will undergo a shakeout after which only a few players can emerge as victors.

The Technology. Babyyourway.com will purchase a DuPont Artistri digital printer that employs new inkjet textile technology, making individual customization cost-effective as shown by the following chart. Resolution can be varied to extremely high levels (720dpi) and the printer can be purchased for only $185,000. A single printer will have the capacity to handle projected demand for the first three years and can to handle the demand for the first 5 years with the addition of a second shift. This technology has been on the market for only two to three years, and prices have dropped steadily. This makes Babyyourway.com's entry timing nearly perfect. Unlike many of our competitors, we don't need to make the transition from older silk screen equipment, but we are far enough down the product introduction curve to be poised to take advantage of a new technology with most of the bugs worked out.

2020 vs. Rotary Screen Printing

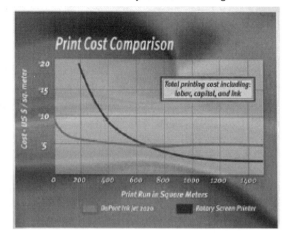

Mission Statement. Our performance and success will be driven by our core purpose and core values as listed below. With these as the compass for our efforts, we are confident that we will continue to find ways to discover and embrace opportunities that will delight our customers, serve our stakeholders, and lead to profitable financial performance.

Babyyourway.com Core Purpose: To increase family bonding through the creation of personalized keepsakes.

Babyyourway.com Core Values:

- To make the creation and selling of customized merchandise fun for us and our customers
- To allow families everywhere to enjoy personalized products
- To treat our employees with the highest respect. They are our most important asset and have an ownership stake in the company.
- To be flexible in meeting our consumers' unique and changing needs and desires
- To strengthen families by giving back to the community and supporting charities for children

Objectives

We will strive for market recognition, market leadership, and customer satisfaction while being oriented to the bottom-line. Short-term plans are to maintain our focus on a limited variety of custom children's apparel items. Once we build some momentum and gain brand recognition in the marketplace, our long-term goals include branching out into other customized baby items like teddy bears and other plush animals. We will also explore contracted manufacture or licensing of other items. Our Web site will continuously evolve to offer additional pages or "stores" offering new product lines, regional preferences, special promotions, etc. We will target our Web advertising efforts on the leading search engines (Yahoo, Google, and MSN) to make our site a top destination or referral for all online children's apparel searches. Other marketing efforts may include purchasing ads in leading parenting magazines (e.g., *Parents*, *Parenting*, and *Child*). Depending on our initial success and profitability, longer term plans may include further testing of our model in shopping malls, first with low-cost kiosks and then with a larger interactive store like the Build-a-Bear shops. Our short-term financial goals include:

1. Sales of $350,000 in Year 1
2. Gross profit of $250,000 in Year 1
3. Customer satisfaction rating > 90 percent after 12 months

Our long-term financial goals include:

1. Sales of $750K by Year 3
2. Sales of $1.5 million by Year 4
3. Ranking in the top three (based on market share) of all online retailers offering custom children's merchandise by Year 3
4. Net worth of $1,000,000 after five years.
5. Customer satisfaction rating > 95 percent by Year 3

Big, Hairy, Audacious Goal (BHAG). We want babyyourway.com to be the Amazon.com of customized baby products! We want to revolutionize how and where customers purchase gifts for their grandkids, kids, nieces, and nephews. Purchasing off the shelf gifts from a standard children's retailer will no longer be the norm. Parents, relatives, and friends will prefer to purchase personalized items from babyyourway.com, which will be the most recognized and dependable company offering unlimited choices for its customers. Receiving a babyyourway.com product will be an eagerly anticipated rite of passage for every new parent. Our trademarked wrapping paper will signal the contents are a personalized gift from the heart. Parents will rush to rip open the wrappings to see the love and care that went into designing the item for their child.

Market Analysis

In the overall market the children's apparel niche is relatively uncompetitive compared to other apparel niches. For decades, there were essentially only two criteria that parents used when purchasing clothing for their kids: price and durability. The cheaper the better, but not so cheap that it couldn't sustain a few romps in the grass and mud. Now there is a third criterion that weighs more heavily when shopping for children: cuteness.

Retailers that are struggling for growth in the adult and teen lines are now starting to embrace the rapidly growing and profitable children's apparel niche. Old Navy and the Gap (with Baby Gap) were among the first apparel retailers to mass-market "cute" and unique clothing specifically for infants and toddlers, and they now dedicate significant floor space and even entire divisions to the sales of children's clothing. Their successes have gotten the attention of other large retailers, and now department stores like Kohl's, Target, and Wal-Mart are dedicating a growing amount of floor space to children's apparel. Other smaller national competitors have emerged (like Gymboree, Children's Place, and Babies-R-Us) to focus exclusively on marketing branded children's apparel. Most large clothing retailers still claim that children's apparel is less than 5 percent of total revenues, but it is one of the few areas experiencing growth so they are not likely to abandon this niche in the foreseeable future.

Specific Market. With our focused approach to personalized keepsakes for children, we are competing against much smaller competitors than the general children's apparel titans mentioned in the previous section. Where those companies aim to mass market homogeneous product lines, we offer a service that allows each customer transaction to end in the purchase of a truly unique item.

In the B2B market, a branding industry blossomed in the '70s, comprising many companies offering branded polo shirts, t-shirts, sweatshirts, uniforms, ball caps, and golf balls primarily for corporate clients. These companies typically take a customer's image or logo and embroider or print it onto items provided by the corporate customer. Companies that have established relationships with large corporate clients have been successful using this approach. Some, like www.branders.com, have leveraged the Internet to offer this type of service more quickly and efficiently than their bricks-and-mortar competitors. These businesses focus on corporate clientele and have essentially ignored the children's apparel market. Their only participation in the children's market is via branded (with a hospital or pharmaceutical company name) caps and other items provided to newborns as they leave the hospital. These B2B companies deal in large volumes of products that are limited in customization and therefore in "cuteness" and uniqueness. Still, their volume-based approach allows them to enjoy favorable economies of scale.

The B2C market, the initial target market for Babyyourway.com, is even more fragmented. Several home-based operations, local in scope, offer customized embroidering of baby items like bibs and blankets. These companies do not have the capacity, the sophisticated online presence, or the resources to emerge as national providers. Babies-R-Us has recently added to its Web site an area titled "Personalized by Babies-R-Us" that offers the embroidering or stitching of a child's name, birth date, etc., on various items. Their approach appears to be to offer as many products as possible but to offer only a limited amount of content and flexibility in the ways that customers can personalize their purchases. We are taking a different approach, allowing as much flexibility as possible in the personalization, but initially offering only a limited variety of physical products. No large competitors were built, as we are, with customization in mind from the ground up.

Competitive Factors

Bargaining Power of Buyers. The lack of similar competition and the low price points of our products are in our favor. We estimate that the overwhelming majority of our products will be priced below $50. Our customers will be price sensitive: Most gift-givers have a predetermined spending threshold for their purchases. We will thus have to allow online sorting and searching of our products by price points since that will be a key criterion for our customers. Our product quality will have to be acceptable, but it will be our service and the "cuteness" of our products that will differentiate us from our competition. We anticipate that more competitors will enter this market, so it will be critical for us to please our customers and provide them with a user-friendly and service oriented environment.

Bargaining Power of Suppliers. Our raw materials, basic children's apparel items, are readily available from numerous suppliers. We will negotiate the lowest possible purchase prices for these items and will actively monitor our suppliers' pricing to ensure that we are minimizing our input costs. We know that our initial low volume of transactions will prevent us from maximizing volume discounts, but once we increase our sales volume we will be able to negotiate better pricing. There are many suppliers of jersey cloth, t-shirts, and bib substrates. These suppliers have been selling to screen printers for years and are well accustomed to their needs, and those needs are very close to ours. With the advent of sophisticated Web search engines such as Froogle.com and Shopping.com, this has become a commodity market and we will need to take prices of such materials as a given.

The Threat of Relevant Substitutes. As noted earlier, there is little competition offering the same combination of customization with children's apparel, but indirect competition is growing as leading retailers try to capture as much of the children's apparel market share as possible. These retailers have a distinct advantage in their physical locations that customers are already visiting. It is likely that once we reach a certain tipping point, these larger companies will move aggressively if they view us as chipping away at their core customer base. Our strategy allows us to build equity while remaining under the radar of most large firms. We anticipate that, by the time they effectively implement a business strategy to embrace customization, we will already own that equity in the minds of the public. Several other auction sites have come along since eBay, many quite good, but none will dislodge eBay as a synonym for online auctions unless the business model radically changes.

The Threat of New Entrants into the Industry. As our market niche grows, we anticipate more competition from the B2B competitors mentioned earlier. These branding companies already understand the production processes needed to deliver customized products, but they currently do not have our B2C marketing know-how or focus. Existing online shops like branding.com could decide to expand into the B2C marketplace in order to diversify their revenue streams.

There are limited barriers to entry due to the low fixed costs involved in procuring our core products and launching an e-commerce site. That is why we plan (see Objectives) to create entry wedges wherever possible by obtaining nonexclusive rights to popular content. We will also create and market our own unique products to further differentiate our offerings and extend our brand presence. Our commitment to continuous innovation and our deep understanding of our customer base will allow us to outmaneuver newer entrants.

The Rivalry among Existing Firms. The battle for the wallet share of brick-and-mortar retail shoppers is growing in intensity as evidenced by the rapid growth of children's apparel stores like Babies-R-Us and Children's Place. Fortunately for us, the quality of the rivalry among national competitors in the online B2C marketplace focusing on customized children's apparel is tame in comparison. This lack of direct competition should help during our introductory months, and it highlights how important it will be for Babyyourway.com to build market awareness and brand recognition quickly in order to gain an immediate market advantage.

Macroenvironmental Influences. We focus here on two trends: online shopping growth and the baby boomer demographic.

The shopping habits of Americans are always evolving. Just 20 years ago, most Americans made the majority of their apparel purchases at conventional department stores. From 1998 to 2003, however, clothing store sales increased 22 percent while sales at conventional department stores fell 10 percent. This decline resulted from the success of shopping malls, catalog sales, and the Internet. Shopping malls are now dominated by chain apparel merchandisers that use their marketing muscle and financial wherewithal to open dozens, if not hundreds, of new stores each year, often only blocks apart. Catalog sales have been very successful for some ventures.

The marketers that have succeeded with clothing sales over the Internet have fallen primarily into one of two groups: (1) those that sell standard items customers are already familiar with, and (2) those that sell specialty items that customers aren't likely to find in local stores. Many companies use the Internet merely as a resource for sharing product specifications and messaging, simply as a way to entice customers into their bricks-and-mortar locations. There is strong and convincing evidence of a continuing trend: Americans are gravitating toward Internet purchasing. Internet retail sales alone increased from about $20 billion in 1999 to $141 billion in 2004. 2004's numbers are a 24 percent increase over 2003's, and according to Forrester Research predictions, online sales will increase another 20 percent in 2005. Even with these gaudy growth numbers, Internet sales as a whole still comprise only 2 percent of retail sales, indicating that there is plenty of room to run in this expanding market. This encouraging market growth was a significant factor in our decision to focus initially on an online delivery of our babyyourway.com model.

In addition to leveraging the rapid growth in the Internet retail landscape, we also believe that Babyyourway.com targets a rapidly growing market, the baby boomers. From 2000 to 2010, the population of the United States will grow 10 percent. The 5 to 19 and 19 to 24 age groups won't grow at all. The strongest growth will be in the large and affluent 45 to 64 age group, which will grow 30 percent. Since parents and grandparents with disposable incomes are our target customers, we are confident that by targeting this demographic we are placing babyyourway.com in the best position to take advantage of growth opportunities in our customer base. On the surface this data may seem discouraging. After all, children are the users of our products and their population growth will be flat, but the success of Babyyourway.com depends on the people whose names appear on the credit cards. Due to a relatively small initial capital investment, only a tiny segment of these markets is needed in order for Babyyourway.com to generate the cash flow necessary to survive and flourish.

Development & Production

Production. Babyyourway.com's production will revolve around the DuPont Artistri digital printer. Digital printing technology, essentially a large inkjet printer with textile capability, is the only way to make individually customized printing economically feasible. The setup costs are very small compared to traditional silkscreen printing. We believe consumers will be delighted with the results since our unique digital printing technology chemically fuses the ink with the fabric molecules for superior feel and durability. This method is far superior to both silkscreening and heat transfer.

The production process begins with the purchase of raw apparel. Initial expenses will be high for obtaining this incoming material inventory. Materials will be received by logistics personnel and racked in the incoming material warehouse. As orders are received from the Web site, the master printer will set up for the next day by uploading patterns into the machine's software. The master printer will always be working on the next day's production. The print tender will load apparel onto the printer's blanket based on the queue generated the day before by the master printer. As each shirt (bib, onesie) is loaded, the order number will be attached to the apparel, somewhat like a department store price tag. At any stage in the process the clothing can be checked against the order in the computer. The tender will also be responsible for offloading the printed apparel, performing periodic online pass/fail quality checks, and bringing any questionable results to the master printer. A logistics employee will take the printed apparel to shipping where it will be packed, addressed, and shipped via FedEx or UPS. Matching the shirt number to the invoice number will also be done at this point. The shipping department will be responsible for completing the order by emailing the tracking number and shipment date to the customer's email address and by closing out record keeping in Babyyourway's computer system. See Appendix B for additional details regarding projected production requirements.

Quality control will be handled by the master printer, who will check a random sample of products for color match, opacity, dot gain, and other measures recommended by the DuPont Company for users of their equipment. Training will be handled by DuPont as part of the Artistri's purchase price. All quality results will be tracked with Quality Windows or equivalent software, thereby allowing trends to be monitored before they become problems. The precise order for the apparel can be referred to in the computer if there are questions. Orders will be traced through the process from raw material to shipment using commercially available production software. As Babyyourway.com grows, additional ISO 9000 principles will be implemented, though certification may not be sought due to expense and the fact that it has little perceived value in the B2C marketplace.

All maintenance will be handled during downtime by the master printer and printer tender per DuPont guidelines. Extensive overhauls will be contracted out to the DuPont Company. Engineering will also be contracted out on a project-by-project basis.

Development. R&D at Babyyourway.com will be focused in three separate areas, and the importance of each will vary over time. These are 1) Process Improvement, 2) Ink Effects, and Raw Materials, and 3) New Technology. Process improvement will focus on optimizing the manufacturing and design process to get the most efficiency out of our resources. This represents the bulk of our efforts during our early years and is focused on making Babyyourway.com profitable as quickly as possible by minimizing costs. The should result in an optimized process and an intimate knowledge of the process and equipment for all manufacturing personnel. The methodologies used will be DOX experimentation, industrial engineering concepts, and process control creation.

In contrast, New Technology efforts will start small and ramp up over the five-year planning horizon. These efforts will be focused on breakthrough results to differentiate Babyyourway.com from the competition and create a sustainable competitive advantage. Efforts here will include working with DuPont to be a test bed for their ideas where possible, working with local university student resources to create new possibilities from our existing equipment, and scanning trade shows and other events looking for the next big thing. This is truly breakthrough work and it will require smart partnerships with experts in the field. Babyyourway.com will not yet have the resources necessary to drive breakthrough results alone. It is fully expected that capacity and the need to innovate will dictate new equipment purchases no later than Year 7. This R&D effort is dedicated to ensuring that we choose and optimize the best possible equipment.

Finally, a constant, relatively low effort will be directed at trying out incremental improvements with the equipment and suppliers we have. This will include testing new inks, such as metallics, trying out new apparel products from suppliers, etc. The primary methodology employed here is the industrial experiment wherein new items are tested under controlled conditions and the results scrupulously measured to determine the impact. This is not breakthrough work. It is a process of trying out various different options that suppliers (apparel manufacturers, ink suppliers, DuPont) have to offer so that we can stay abreast of the current best products and processes in the field.

The chart below summarizes the discussion.

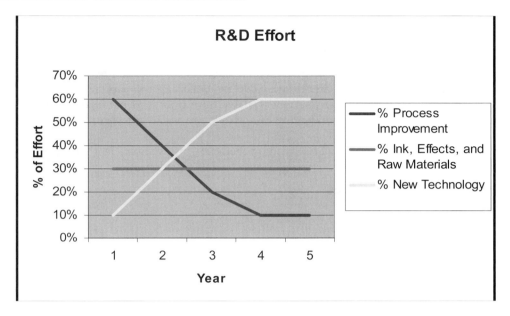

Marketing

Concept and Orientation. Babyyourway.com's Core Purpose is to increase family bonding through the creation of personalized keepsakes. We will do this by making the selling and creation of customized merchandise fun for us and our customers. Customers will log onto our site and be pleasantly surprised by the choices available to create and purchase a truly unique gift for the special children in their lives. While our products will be unique, they will also be affordable since the physical materials (bibs, onesies, and tees) are readily available and inexpensive. What will truly differentiate Babyyourway.com's products is the bottomless inventory of digital images, logos, pictures, etc., that customers can use because of our unique digital printing technology. Our superior offerings and our dedication to service combined with our relentless marketing efforts will make Babyyourway.com the destination of choice for online shoppers who want to purchase a truly special gift for their special little ones.

Market-Driven Approach. As stated in our Core Values, we will be flexible at all times in meeting consumers' unique and changing needs and desires. The principals of this company have vast experience in implementing a market-driven marketing approach. Key to this approach is an "outside-in" angle that relies on input and feedback from customers and abandoned site visitors (those that shop but don't purchase) to continuously improve any and all of our offerings. This market-driven approach applies to all of our internal processes as well, since only by sharpening all skills that touch the customer experience will we truly be capable of delivering the world-class service that will differentiate us from our competitors. We will rely on focus groups, online surveys, and various other market research methods to ensure that the voice of the customer is the guiding force in all that we do. We strongly believe that a market-driven approach will best position us to be operationally nimble and quick to adapt to any changes in our core customer criteria.

Marketing Strategy

Product. Bibs, tees, onesies, and blankets will be our initial product offerings. Our research indicates that these are products that customers would like to customize, and that they are willing to pay for the ability to do so via a user-friendly process that's not too expensive. These products also have the added benefit of being readily available from dozens of national and international suppliers at very reasonable costs and being essentially immune to any erratic price fluctuations.

Pricing. At a basic level, pricing will depend on the following variables that are or are not components of each purchase:

- Product (e.g. bib, tee, onesie)
- Size
- Quantity and number of images

Most items will be available for less than $50, and the average single-item purchase is estimated to be in $30-$40 range. Our COGS will not be significant, and we expect Gross Margins to stabilize around 80 percent. Thus we are not likely to raise prices significantly, at least initially. By keeping our operating expenses aligned with our projected amounts, we will position ourselves to significantly boost our Net Profit Margin without raising prices once our sales volume increases.

We will not offer varying levels of fabric quality; instead we will offer only high quality fabrics. Our research repeatedly shows that customers expect customized purchases to be of above average quality. Using profit maximizing pricing techniques, we will seek to increase prices on popular items in order to extract as much consumer surplus as possible from our customers.

Research also indicates that, although clients want as much variety as possible in their product choices, they want pricing to be straightforward—no trivial a la carte charges that subtly run up the purchase price. We embrace this request and will offer a streamlined pricing schema driven by the above listed variables and outlined in detail on our site.

Place. We will be an online retailer. As such, we will dedicate significant resources to building our virtual store and to all the other processes critical to an efficient e-commerce operation. The creation and ongoing upkeep of our site will be one of the most expensive undertakings of this venture. However, our research clearly shows that customers will instantly abandon any site they find confusing, unprofessional in appearance, or slow in loading pages and content. We want to make sure that we deliver 100 percent satisfaction on each of these criteria. Depending on the degree of our initial success and profitability, longer term plans may include further testing our model in shopping malls, as noted earlier.

Promotion. As an e-tailer, we will utilize the most proven online advertising techniques. One major element of this effort will be the purchase of prominent keyword search results with the major search engines like Yahoo, MSN, and Google. Particularly in the first 12 months, it will be critical that we keep our name in front of our customers so that they are made aware of our site and its offerings. We will also explore the use of other conventional online advertising methods like banner ads on popular parenting sites. Note that the advertising and promotions budget is higher in the first year in order to quickly build our brand awareness and capture as many customers as possible. Our team has significant marketing experience, so we will closely monitor the effectiveness of our marketing spend and quickly reallocate advertising and promotion resources to the most effective areas.

The second component of our advertising and promotion strategy is to collect customer and site visitor information so we can build a customer and prospect database that can be targeted via email for ongoing promotions. We will collect email addresses and distribute targeted messaging to build our brand with customers and may also offer them loyalty savings with emailed coupons.

Packaging. We want our packaging to be unique. As noted in our Big, Hairy, Audacious Goal, we want our customers to see our packaging and quickly connect with the joy associated with our products. Furthermore, we want the first-time parents' recognition of their first babyyourway.com package to be a rite of passage. To generate the buzz and emotion necessary to build this powerful association, we will have to create a truly unique and identifiable package. We believe that the most effective packaging would be mint green boxes with soft yellow polka dots (unisex colors) and with our logo prominently displayed on the lid of each box. These colors can be used for all gifts, and the polka dots are a fun and quickly recognizable pattern. We want parents to notice our packaging from across the room at Christmas, birthdays, baby showers, etc., so that they know right away that their baby is the recipient of a very special and unique gift from babyyourway.com. This packaging will be highly visible on our Web site and in all our advertising.

Competitor Strengths. Many of the brick-and-mortar competitors we've mentioned have established their online presence and appear to be committed for the long haul. These firms have significantly larger marketing budgets than ours, and this will certainly make them very tough competition. The rapid expansion of mass merchants like Wal-Mart and Target has pressured all clothing retailers at the lower end of the market. These mass merchants sell other products besides clothing and are often a one-stop destination for customers. From 1999 to 2003 mass merchants' total sales increased 80 percent while clothing store sales increased only 13 percent. Paramount to the success of the mass merchants is their ability to offer lower prices because they buy in larger quantities and at lower prices than their smaller competitors. This market domination by large retailers is why we are considering pushing into traditional retail channels only after proven success with the Babyyourway.com site.

But although these mass merchants dominate traditional retailing, they have not emerged as dominant e-tailers. More savvy competitors like Amazon.com have done a better job of marketing to online shoppers. The retail landscape is littered with many successful small specialty retailers with smaller budgets that compete very effectively with large retailers by targeting their products at specific customers, by offering products too distinct or specialized for big-box retailers to carry, or by providing a higher level of service. The explosive success of eBay has proven that in the online marketplace there is insatiable demand for unique items from boutique operations with low resources and no brick-and-mortar presence.

Fortunately, our competitors in the online customized children's apparel niche (see the Market Analysis section) do not comprise the typical retail heavyweights like Wal-Mart and Target. Our competition is very fragmented, is typically locally focused, and often focuses on marketing to business and institutional clients rather than to consumers. We believe we can quickly carve out a niche as the preferred national provider of personalized keepsakes. eBay will be a formidable competitor since it has evolved into the preferred destination for all shoppers seeking unique items. However, our research confirms that there is no national provider of customized children's apparel on eBay or other similar auction sites. Virtually none of the companies on eBay offer world-class service, which is one of the pillars of the babyyourway.com approach. Nonetheless, it will take a successful and sustained marketing campaign to steal significant eyeballs away from eBay.

Customer Service. Our customers will expect us, as an online retailer, to offer adequate online support. We intend to make both email support and live chat support available to meet customers' presale questions. Live chat support costs are included under Marketing & Selling expenses on the Income Statement in Appendix A. Post-sale support will include a "satisfaction guaranteed" returns policy. A Frequently Asked Questions (FAQ) page on the Web site will answer the most prevalent pre- and post-sale questions. We do not plan to offer an 800 line for telephone support unless client demand requires it. In that case we would likely consider outsourcing this function.

Distribution. We will ship via either FedEx or UPS. Both offer global coverage and their rates are comparable, so we will choose one after closer evaluation of their services. Customers can choose the timeframe for delivery on the checkout page.

Sales Forecasts. It was difficult to do an apples to apples comparison between our proposed model and the existing competition because ours is a very fragmented niche consisting of several small players that do not provide public information. We have formulated our forecasts based on conversations with other e-tailers and industry suppliers and on market information provided by Forrester Research, RMA, and First Research. We started off estimating conservatively that we could sell approximately 28 items per day in Year 1 at an average transaction of $35. Driven by a significant advertising and promotions budget, we expect sales to increase 60 percent year to year for Years 2 and 3, followed by a tipping point somewhere in Years 4 and 5. At that point we will experience 75 percent year to year sales growth. As outlined in the Market Analysis section, we truly believe that the market for our products is rapidly expanding. This combination of a growing market with repeat business makes us confident that our pro forma projections can be met. See Appendix A for our full detailed projections for Years 1 through 5.

Financial Plans

Source of Funds. Seed funds for Babyyourway.com will be generated exclusively through the founders' equity stakes. However, in order to purchase the necessary production equipment, we will need to raise an additional $300,000 in capital. The preferred method is through debt, allowing the founders to maintain their initial equity stake. However the management team is open to other structures, based on the merits of each offer. Babyyourway.com will be structured as an LLC corporation.

Assumptions.

- The initial Web site will be largely designed and developed internally, thus reducing the upfront requirement for cash.
- The Internet will remain an accepted purchasing channel for consumers.
- As a LLC corporation, the owners will be responsible for paying all potential taxes through their personal tax returns. The corporation will not have tax liability.

For pro forma financials, see attached Appendix **A**.

Exit Strategy. The goal of this company is to grow organically through sustainable efforts with the founders maintaining substantially all the equity. As evidenced by our financial projections, we expect that by end of Year 5 we will have a Net Worth of $2,541,276. Because the company is an LLC, all equity owners will be rewarded annually with ownership distributions according to their percent of ownership. If any owner desires to sell his/her interest in the company, this request will be honored based on standard practices of our legal entity structure at the time of such an occurrence.

Internal Controls and Monitoring. Cash flow will initially be monitored by Matt Sifferlen and Neal Cawi. A secondary quarterly check will also be done as part of our quarterly CPA-compiled financial statements provided by Ernst & Young's Indianapolis location.

Organization and Management

Key Personnel Resources. Babyyourway.com will be managed by the four primary partners. Each partner brings extremely valuable expertise and experience that will allow the collective group to succeed. The following chart indicates each partner's functional areas of ownership.

Neal Cawi	*Brian Erdman*	*Dave Rucker*	*Matt Sifferlen, CEO*
•Product R&D	•Sales	•Operations/	•Finance
•IT and IS	•Marketing	supply chain	•Customer service
	•Consumer research	•Quality control	•Administration (HR)
		•Purchasing	

Neal Cawi brings almost 15 years of IS expertise to babyyourway.com. He has the proven skills necessary to launch a successful start-up company (IS consulting firm). Neal will own Product Research & Development as well as IT/IS.

Brian Erdman brings an engineering background and five years of marketing and branding experience (primarily at P&G) to the management team of babyyourway.com. Brian will head the venture's sales, marketing, and consumer research.

David Rucker, with almost 15 years experience in operations and product development at P&G, will own operations, supply chain, purchasing, and quality control for babyyourway.com.

Matt Sifferlen has more than a 10-year background in financial services and banking. He will own financial management, customer service, and overall administration (including HR) for babyyourway.com. Matt will also serve as CEO.

In addition, it is important to note that several of the partners have experience and backgrounds in areas outside their immediate responsibility for Babyyourway.com. For instance, Matt Sifferlen has worked with Web-based program management in addition to his financial background. Branding and marketing specialist Brian Erdman also has a thorough knowledge of consumer research acquired at P&G as well as an engineering background. Neal Cawi, our IS expert, also has sales experience and has participated in the start-up of a successful new venture. Product supply, development, and quality specialist David Rucker, has had significant exposure to the commercial side of running a business through his interactions with brand managers and sales employees at P&G. All four partners have MBAs from Indiana University's respected Kelley School of Business. This blend of practical strategic and tactical skills will allow them to continually challenge each other in making the best decisions for babyyourway.com.

The résumés of each partner are found in Appendix C of this document (omitted).

Partner Compensation and Incentives. Starting in Year 2 each partner will receive an annual salary of $20K to subsidize normal costs of living. As the company grows, the compensation package will be revisited. The primary incentive for each partner to deliver strong results is his ownership/equity stake in the company's long-term success. Owners will also be eligible to take discretionary distributions from the company once an agreed-upon level of profitability has been achieved.

Board of Directors. Babyyourway.com will not initially integrate a hired board of directors to oversee and consult on the start-up operation. Over time, as the company grows and business complexities increase, the partners will be open to bringing in a board of directors. Note, however, that the partners are open to accepting an initial financing offer. Each potential financing arrangement will be evaluated on its own merits. Details are in the Deal Structure section below.

Human Resources Management Strategy. During the start-up period, Babyyourway.com will be very closely run by the core team. Their combined expertise and experiences coupled with their intent to closely manage the venture for the first couple of years mean that the owners will personally support several functions, including HR management. There will be no initial need to divert significant funding toward HR.

As Babyyourway.com grows, the core management team's ability to own the HR role will be challenged. At this point, the management team will look for an outsourced HR provider to ensure that the company's most important asset, its people, are sufficiently cared for. As the company grows, a formal development and training program will be implemented to make certain that the staff is adequately equipped to drive Babyyourway.com toward success. Early thinking is that this evaluation process will mirror that of many successful larger corporations such as P&G and GE, where all employees are evaluated annually and this evaluation links directly to the company's recognition and reward system. In addition Babyyourway.com will give all employees some stock ownership (specifics TBD) to further create an environment of employee ownership and to align the interests of individual with the interests of the company.

At the start, the management team is very committed to driving the company toward long-term success and is willing to sacrifice short-term personal gain. The LLC structure offers the owners the advantages of a corporation's limited liability and a partnership's taxation. (Note: This is why no federal income taxes are listed on the provided pro forma financials). As the company grows and new employees are brought on board, the company's entity structure and compensation packages will be revisited to attract and retain top-caliber talent without significantly reducing cash flow through high overhead. The current thinking is that an attractive stock option program can tighten salary outlays.

Babyyourway.com will initially allocate a modest amount of funds (TBD annually) to subsidize healthcare costs for the four management partners. As the company grows and new employees are hired, the total benefit package will be revisited to attract and keep top caliber talent without significantly reducing cash flow through high overhead. This will likely look like subsidized health care and a set of "creative" perks aimed at retention, possibly including both culture-driven perks and nontraditional incentive programs. Typical benefits such as vacation time and 401K (or employee ownership) will be introduced as the scale and success of Babyyourway.com allows. The details of these HR programs are TBD based on the needs of Babyyourway.com at the time of implementation.

Babyyourway.com will be an Equal Opportunity Employer.

Ownership

Form of Business. Babyyourway.com is a limited liability company. Each partner is liable only for the amount of his/her personal investment. No other legal liability exists. The actual partnership agreement contains no special conditions or clauses.

Equity Positions. The following table illustrates the owners' equity positions.

Partner	Investment
Neal Cawi	$100,000
Brian Erdman	100,000
David Rucker	100,000
Matthew Sifferlen	100,000
Total Owner's Equity	$400,000

Each partner is contributing an equal share of personal funds to the company's start-up requirements, so each partner retains an equal share in the business. This personal investment is a strong signal of the level of each partner's personal commitment.

Deal Structure. Babyyourway.com will require $300,000 to start up and to grow at the rapid rate necessary to achieve its potential. These funds will initially be needed for the purchase of production equipment (See Production and Development section) and to fund advertising and inventory outlays. The deal structure will ultimately be negotiated with the investor. The Babyyourway.com management team will consider a number of financing structures from potential investors, including those that require an equity stake in venture.

Critical Risks and Contingencies

As with any start-up business, risks must be considered. The following list specifies some key risks associated with investing in babyyourway.com.

- Failure to meet production deadlines or sales forecasts: For any startup, the coordination of raw material inventory purchases, capital equipment acquisition, production startup, and logistics all present challenges, particularly in the area of cash flow. Late deliveries by suppliers or problems with capital equipment can dramatically affect the initial supply chain.
- Failure to produce the products promised: While the DuPont Artistri has been on the mar-

ket for about three years, its primary purpose is the printing of textiles in bulk form, not finished t-shirts and other apparel. We've been assured it can be used for this purpose, but some development and fine-tuning may be required to optimize the process.

- Problems with suppliers: As a new business, Babyyourway.com will have very little leverage with suppliers. Given the commodity nature of the raw materials required, we don't see this as a major concern because there are substitute suppliers.

- Unforeseen industry trends: A breakthrough in digital printing beyond the technology we are exploiting could put Babyyourway.com at a disadvantage and require additional investment. Digital printing is a rapidly expanding industry and development is occurring at a rapid rate. Also if a major e-tailer or brick-and-mortar retailer puts significant effort into customization, Babyyourway.com will face significant competition where none exists today.

- Unforeseen events: Babyyourway.com requires discretionary income to survive. Customization is a luxury, albeit not a very expensive one. Economic downturns will disproportionately affect our company. Nonetheless by positioning our products as gifts for one of life's most important occasions (the birth of a child), we will be better insulated against changing spending habits than products designed primarily for the purchaser. Family members are more likely to splurge on new babies than on themselves.

- Failure to survive retaliation by competitors with significantly more resources: Several online presences pose a risk to Babyyourway.com if they decide to enter the customizable baby products business. Amazon.com is just one of many examples. The resources behind such a company would make it a significant threat. Babyyourway.com would rely on first-mover advantages to mitigate this risk since the existing "e-powers" are not currently in our business.

- Risk of inexperienced management: As with any company, the quality of the management team is critical to success. Babyyourway.com has limited experience in new venture creation, but the experiences of the team combined with available external resources (such as working with DuPont and with local universities on R&D) will mitigate this risk. Also, business incubators, SCORE, and other SBA resources will be exploited to the fullest possible extent.

- Need for additional financing: The company intends to rely on internal cash flow generation to fund its growth, but we realize that as Babyyourway.com continues to grow, additional investor financing may be required. The dynamic nature of the economy and the resulting impact on the venture funding market could (positively or negatively) affect the competition for available investment funds. Sound management coupled with a well thought-out business model should enable Babyyourway.com to succeed in soliciting future developmental funds if necessary.

- Risk of competitive entry: The raw materials needed to introduce the babyyourway.com products are readily available. Babyyourway.com would mitigate this risk by being a first mover and working steadily to develop brand equity. High advertising spending the first year on such existing online sites as Google, distinctive packaging, a user-friendly interface, and a business model designed for low-cost customization, will all work to make Babyyourway.com synonymous with classy, thoughtful baby gifts. Placing products in social settings (baby showers, family reunions, etc.) will maximize word of mouth. By moving quickly, expanding rapidly, and marketing effectively Babyyourway.com will build the most important sustainable competitive advantage in this field—its name and reputation. As Babyyourway expands R&D will ensure that its products remain best in class by keeping ahead of the copycats.

Summary and Conclusions

We truly believe that the time is right for this venture. As outlined in several areas of this report, compelling evidence shows that online shopping and our targeted customer demographic are going to continue growing. We also see increasing consumer interest in unique and personalized gifts. Today there is no single national preferred online provider of customized baby apparel, so the market is very fragmented. Unlike our competitors, Babyyourway.com embraces real customization, not just the embroidering of a baby's name on an item. Instead, we will offer shoppers a unique variety of online tools to define color scheme, text, materials, and licensed content. This puts the customer in control and lets her add the personal touches that today's shoppers value. Some small players today offer such services, but none of them have the vision, focus, and passion of Babyyourway.com for offering customers throughout the country the widest possible variety of customized choices. Babyyourway.com will fill this underserved niche by leveraging the management team's combined 45+ years of practical experience in consumer and technology product development, brand and product management, marketing, operations management, information systems, and commercial banking. After operating in the red the first couple of years during the company's startup period, our projections indicate that babyyourway.com will rapidly emerge as a profitable enterprise and be in a position to significantly reward all stakeholders by year 5.

Scheduling and Milestones

The major milestones are listed below:

- Legal Entity Formation (completed May 2005)
- Legal representation by Baker & Daniels, Indianapolis office (August 2005)
- CPA representation by Ernst & Young, Indianapolis office (August 2005)
- Small Business Banking, Cash Management, and Deposit Relationship with Irwin Union Bank, Carmel location (August 2005)
- Completion of R&D efforts (September 2005)
- Purchase of Production Equipment (October 2005)
- Completion of a Working Prototype (November 2005)
- Building of Web Site (October - December 2005)
- Hiring of Personnel (September - December 2005)
- Ordering Supplies, Materials, Inventory (November 2005 - January 2006)
- Beginning Production—Beta (December 2005)
- Beginning Full Production (January 2006)
- First Shipped Sale (January 2006)

Project Income Statement

	Year 1	Year 2	Year 3	Year 4	Year 5
Sales	350,000	560,000	896,000	1,568,000	2,744,000
Less expenses:					
COGS-Materials	36,960	59,136	94,618	146,101	217,325
COGS-Design & Printing	11,667	18,667	29,867	46,118	68,600
COGS-Distribution (5% of sales)	17,500	28,000	44,800	78,400	137,200
Total COGS	66,127	105,803	169,284	270,618	423,125
Gross Profit	283,873	454,197	726,716	1,297,382	2,320,875
Sales & marketing	75,000	95,000	95,000	125,000	125,000
G&A					
Owners salaries	—	80,000	80,000	100,000	120,000
Salaries	310,000	310,000	310,000	310,000	310,000
Advertising	100,000	35,000	35,000	50,000	50,000
Rent	24,000	24,000	24,000	36,000	36,000
Hardware	3,000	3,000	5,000	5,000	5,000
Software	22,000	22,000	10,000	10,000	10,000
R & D	40,000	15,000	15,000	40,000	60,000
Depreciation (5-yr straight line on printer)	37,000	37,000	37,000	37,000	37,000
Interest	(28,500)	(22,276)	(15,460)	(7,997)	(4,180)
Total sales, marketing & other expenses	582,500	598,724	595,540	705,003	748,820
Net income before tax	(298,627)	(144,527)	131,176	592,379	1,572,055
Income tax expense	—	—	—	—	—
Net Income	(298,627)	(144,527)	131,176	592,379	1,572,055

Projected Cash Flow Statement

	Year 1	Year 2	Year 3	Year 4	Year 5
Net Income	(298,627)	(144,527)	131,176	592,379	1,572,055
Depreciation	37,000	37,000	37,000	37,000	37,000
(Increase) decrease in AR	—	—	—	—	—
(Increase) decrease in inventories	(43,750)	(6,250)	(25,000)	(50,000)	(35,000)
Increase (decrease) in AP	35,000	21,000	68,600	88,200	186,200
Increase (decrease) in salaries payable	—	—	—	—	—
Increase (decrease) in IT payable	—	—	—	—	—
Cash flow from operations	(270,377)	(92,777)	211,776	667,579	1,760,255
Investing					
Acquisition of P,P, & E	(185,000)	—	—	—	—
Cash flow from investing	(185,000)	—	—	—	—
Financing					
Issue of long-term debt *	300,000	—	—	—	—
Increase (decrease) in paid-in capital	400,000	—	—	—	—
Cash flow from financing	700,000	—	—	—	—
Change in cash	244,623	(92,777)	211,776	667,579	1,760,255
Cash, Dec. 31, last year	—	244,623	151,847	363,623	1,031,202
Cash, Dec. 31, current year	244,623	151,847	363,623	1,031,202	2,791,457

* Long term debt project is made up of two loans:
  1. Equipment loan—5 years at 9.5%
  2. General loan—3 years at 9.5%

Projected Balance Sheet

	Year 1	Year 2	Year 3	Year 4	Year 5
Cash	244,623	151,847	363,623	1,031,202	2,791,457
Accounts receivable	—	—	—	—	—
Inventories	43,750	50,000	75,000	125,000	160,000
Total current assets	288,373	201,847	438,623	1,156,202	2,951,457
P,P, & E (net)	185,000	148,000	111,000	74,000	37,000
Total assets	473,373	349,847	549,623	1,230,202	2,988,457
Liabilities and owners' equity					
Accounts payable	35,000	56,000	124,600	212,800	399,000
Current portion LTD	94,018	94,018	94,018	48,181	48,181
Salaries payable	—	—	—	—	—
Income taxes payable	—	—	—	—	—
Total current liabilities	129,018	150,018	218,618	260,981	447,181
Long-term debt	284,396	190,378	96,360	48,179	
Bonds payable	—	—	—	—	—
Total liabilities	413,414	340,396	314,978	309,160	447,181
Paid-in capital	400,000	—	—	—	—
Retained earnings	(340,041)	9,451	234,645	921,042	2,541,276
Total owners' equity	59,959	9,451	234,645	921,042	2,541.276
Total liabilities & owners' equity	473,373	349,847	549,623	1,230,202	2,988,457

'Note: Discretionary owner distributions may be taken beginning in Year 3 depending on company profitability.

Projected Key Ratios

	Year 1	Year 2	Year 3	Year 4	Year 5
Sales Growth	0.0%	60.0%	60.0%	75.0%	75.0%
% of Total Assets					
Accounts receivable	0.0%	0.0%	0.0%	0.0%	0.0%
Inventory	9.2%	14.3%	13.6%	10.2%	5.4%
Total current assets	60.9%	57.7%	79.8%	94.0%	98.8%
Long-term assets	39.1%	42.3%	20.2%	6.0%	1.2%
Total assets	100.0%	100.0%	100.0%	100.0%	100.0%
% of Total Liabilities					
Current liabilities	31.2%	44.1%	69.4%	84.4%	100.0%
Long-term liabilities	68.8%	55.9%	30.6%	15.6%	0.0%
Total liabilities	100.0%	100.0%	100.0%	100.0%	100.0%
% of Sales					
Sales	100.0%	100.0%	100.0%	100.0%	100.0%
Gross margin	81.1%	81.1%	81.1%	82.7%	84.6%
S,G,& A expense	21.4%	17.0%	10.6%	8.0%	4.6%
Advertising expense	28.6%	6.3%	3.9%	3.2%	1.8%
Profit before IT	-85.3%	-25.8%	14.6%	37.8%	57.3%
Main Ratios					
Current	2.24	1.35	2.01	4.43	6.60
Quick	1.90	1.01	1.66	3.95	6.24
Total debt to total assets	0.87	0.97	0.57	0.25	0.15
Total debt to net worth	6.89	36.02	1.34	0.34	0.18
Pretax return on assets	(0.63)	(0.41)	0.24	0.48	0.53
Assets to sales	1.35	0.62	0.61	0.78	1.09
Additional Ratios					
Net profit margin	(0.85)	(0.26)	0.15	0.38	0.57
ROE	(4.98)	(15.29)	0.56	0.64	0.62
Activity Ratios					
AR turnover	—	—	—	—	—
Collection days	—	—	—	—	—
Inventory turnover	8.00	11.20	11.95	12.54	17.15
AP turnover	10.00	10.00	7.19	7.37	6.88
Payment days	36.00	36.00	50.06	48.86	52.35
Total asset turnover	0.74	1.60	1.63	1.27	0.92

BABYYOURWAY.COM PRODUCTION REQUIREMENTS

		Yr 1	Yr 2	Yr 3	Yr 4	Yr 5
A	Sales	350,000	560,000	896,000	1,568,000	2,744,000
B	Avg Price/unit	15	15	15	17	20
C=A/B	Units sold	23,333	37,333	59,733	92,235	137,200
D	sq meters / unit*	0.625	0.625	0.625	0.6875	0.75625
E=C*D	sq meters consumed	14,583	23,333	37,333	63,412	103,758
F	%Uptime	50%	60%	70%	80%	80%
G	Hours per year**	2,000	2,000	2,000	2,000	2,000
H=F*G	Hours available	1,000	1,200	1,400	1,600	1,600
I=E/H	Required capacity (m/hr)	15	19	27	40	65
J=C/H	Required capacity (units/hr)	23	31	43	58	86

* Assumes small t shirts and onesies first three years, increasing product mix years 4&5, includes waste
** Assumes 1 shift, 5 day operation, 2 weeks of holidays

Printing Equipment Options

Machine	Capacity	Resolution	Cost	Payment^
Dream Machine	150 sq m/hr	600 dpi	$600,000	($12,601.12)
DuPont Artistri	30-50 sqm/hr	360-720 dpi	$185,000	($3,885.34)

^ Assumes 5 year, 9.5% loan

	Yr 1	Yr 2	Yr 3	Yr 4	Yr 5
Ink & Op Cost (assume $0.50 / shirt)	$ 11,667	$ 18,667	$ 29,867	$ 46,118	$ 68,600

Printer Staffing

		Yr 1	Yr 2	Yr 3	Yr 4	Yr 5
J	Required capacity (units/hr)	23	31	43	58	86
K	Printer staffing	2	2	2	2	2
L=K*50k	Printer wages and benefits	100,000	100,000	100,000	100,000	100,000

Logistics Staffing

		Yr 1	Yr 2	Yr 3	Yr 4	Yr 5
J	Required capacity (units/hr)	23	31	43	58	86
M	Logistics, packaging, shipping	4	4	4	4	4
N=M*35k	Logistics wages, and benefits	140,000	140,000	140,000	140,000	140,000

(continued on next page)

BABYYOURWAY.COM PRODUCTION REQUIREMENTS (continued)

OPTION A - FAB SHIRTS OURSELVES

		Yr 1	Yr 2	Yr 3	Yr 4	Yr 5
Commercial Sewing equipment						
J	Required capacity (units/hr)	23	31	43	58	86
O	units/hr/machine	2	3	3	4	4
P=J/O	machines needed	12	10	14	14	21
Q	Capital required*	12,000	0	2,000	12,000	7,000

* Assumes $1000/machine, 3 year life

		Yr 1	Yr 2	Yr 3	Yr 4	Yr 5
Staffing						
R	Sewers (machines * 1.1)	13	12	16	16	24
S=R*35k	Sewer wages and benefits	455,000	420,000	560,000	560,000	840,000

		Yr 1	Yr 2	Yr 3	Yr 4	Yr 5
Material						
E	sq meters consumed	14,583	23,333	37,333	63,412	103,758
T	Cost per sq meter*	3.5	3.5	3.5	3	3
U=T*E	Material cost	$ 51,042	$ 81,667	$ 130,667	$ 190,235	$ 311,273

* Includes volume discount year 4 and 5

	Yr 1	Yr 2	Yr 3	Yr 4	Yr 5
TOTAL COST OPTION A (Q+S+U)	$ 518,042	$ 501,667	$ 692,667	$ 762,235	$ 1,158,273

OPTION B - PURCHASE SHIRTS THEN PRINT

		Yr 1	Yr 2	Yr 3	Yr 4	Yr 5
Staffing						
V	Add'l logistics staff for shirts	2	2	2	2	2
W=V*35k	Add'l Logistics wages & benefits	$ 70,000	$ 70,000	$ 70,000	$ 70,000	$ 70,000

		Yr 1	Yr 2	Yr 3	Yr 4	Yr 5
Material						
C=A/B	Units Sold	23,333	37,333	59,733	92,235	137,200
X=C*1.1	Shirts needed (including waste)	25,667	41,067	65,707	101,459	150,920
Y	Cost per shirt	1.44	1.44	1.44	1.44	1.44
Z=X*Y	Material cost	$ 36,960	$ 59,136	$ 94,618	$ 146,101	$ 217,325

	Yr 1	Yr 2	Yr 3	Yr 4	Yr 5
TOTAL COST OPTION B (W+Z)	$ 106,960	$ 129,136	$ 164,618	$ 216,101	$ 287,325

OPTION B PREFERRED

AA=L+N+W Total Salaries	$ 310,000	$ 310,000	$ 310,000	$ 310,000	$ 310,000

6 Marketing the New Venture

"If you can't sell a top-quality product at the world's lowest price, you're going to be out of the game."
—*Jack Welch, former Chief Executive Officer, General Electric, quoted in* Fortune, *January 25, 1993.*

──────────────── OUTLINE ────────────────

──────────────── LEARNING OBJECTIVES ────────────────

After reading this chapter, you will understand

- the importance of marketing in entrepreneurial strategy.
- the basic methods for start-up market research.
- how to formulate a marketing strategy.
- how to apply the core tools of marketing management to the requirements of the new venture.
- the key similarities and differences for marketing Internet-based businesses.
- a variety of sales forecasting methods.

PERSONAL PROFILE 6

Jim Buckmaster:
The Business of Making Less Money

He's the President, Chief Executive Officer and Chief Financial Officer of the seventh most popular English-language site on the Internet. His Web site posts ten million classified ads and has more than four billion estimated page views every month, but most users pay absolutely nothing. The company incorporated as a for-profit organization in 1999 and collected $25 million in fees during 2005. Most analysts believe Craigslist (www.craigslist.com) could easily rake in $500 million a year if Jim Buckmaster wanted it to.

But it's service, not profit that drives the company. To the chagrin of entrepreneurs struggling to make as much money as they can, Buckmaster seems content to profit from only a small segment of the classified ads on Craigslist. He says that unlike other sites, "Our primary mindset is philanthropic—to offer what we see as a public service." Craigslist was founded in 1995 by Craig Newmark, a software engineer who launched it on his home PC as a noncommercial community bulletin board for the San Francisco area. Buckmaster's experience with the site was limited to finding an apartment and selling a futon until the computer programmer listed his résumé on Craigslist and Newmark offered him a job. As the site's lead programmer and Chief Technical Officer, Buckmaster took the venture to a multiserver operation, expanded its community to multiple cities and countries, and added features like a search engine and discussion forums.

Craigslist currently charges for job postings in the San Francisco area, charges slightly less for jobs listed in the New York and Los Angeles areas, and even less for housing listed by brokers in New York City.

"We're much more comfortable charging companies than charging individuals," explains Buckmaster. "Businesses are better equipped to afford a small fee and businesses can pay for fees out of pre-tax dollars where on average users are less able to pay a fee and they have to pay in post-tax dollars."

Buckmaster has an answer for those who criticize Craigslist's disinterest in maximizing revenues: "In the big Internet boom, thousands of companies were set up," he says. "With the exception of us, pretty much all of them were set up with the primary objective being to make a lot of money. Almost all of those businesses went under and never made any money. Even businesses like Amazon still haven't made any money. They are still, over their entire lifetime, net negative. Here we are—we've been in the black since 1999." Because Craigslist has few outside investors (although eBay purchased a minority stake in 2004), it is not under pressure to produce growth at any cost. Its growth has been organic—occurring only when the company and its market were ready.

One thing that keeps Craigslist in the black is its use of no-cost open-source software. The Web site has an unsophisticated appearance, but that doesn't keep it from being effective. Another strength is its low labor cost: Because users do most of the postings and much of the policing of the site, the company employs only 21 people.

Buckmaster notes that today "there are more and more businesses where huge amounts of value can flow to the user for free. I like the idea, just as an end-user, of there being as many businesses like that as possible." Given the success of Craigslist, there are apparently a lot of other end-users—including some willing to pay to reach others getting a free ride—who feel the same way.

SOURCE: Adapted from Brian M. Carney, "Zen and the Art of Classified Advertising," *The Wall Street Journal*, June 17, 2006: A10; "A Talk with Craigslist's Keeper," *Business Week Online*, September 8, 2004. Retrieved from the Web May 7, 2006. http://www.businessweek.com/bwdaily/dnflash/sept2004/nf2004098_1574_db051.htm and www.craigslist.com.

THE MARKETING AND ENTERPRENEURSHIP INTERFACE

THE quotation that opens this chapter illustrates the importance of effective marketing in today's competitive international environment: An entrepreneur must give the customer the most for the least or go out of business. A closer look, however, reveals that this statement can't quite be taken at face value. "A top quality product" may not be easy to define. There is more than one standard for quality; and various top quality products are available at any given time. Determining what represents top quality is often a marketing decision. "The world's lowest price" implies that there is a specific lowest price, but this is not true. A price adheres to a product/market, and just as there are many standards for top quality, there are also many possible prices. The entrepreneur's pricing decision is also a marketing function.

Finally, the quotation says that if you fail, you are out of the game. This is correct—but in business there is more than one game going on at any given time. Not all customers are the same: They have, as we noted, different preferences and standards, they are located in different parts of the world, and they belong to different demographic groups. The entrepreneur's choices of which games to play, therefore, are marketing choices resulting from the venture's marketing strategy. So is the statement of the former General Electric CEO correct? Indeed it is—once the full range of marketing strategies, choices, and functions has been considered.

Marketing contributes to the entrepreneur's success in two ways: (1) It determines the manner in which the firm's resource advantages will be defined and communicated, and (2) it is a major factor in creating a sustainable competitive advantage (SCA). The first role of marketing is fairly straightforward. Organizations—companies—add value to bundles of resources for buyers, and the culmination of this activity is the transaction between buyer and seller and their subsequent relationship. Because marketing activities focus directly on the nature of the transaction—the product, its price, the location and time of transaction, and communications related to the event—marketing activities are crucial to the success of the firm.

The second role of marketing is "as its own resource." Referring back to Table 2.2, marketing capability and skills encompass intellectual and organizational resources. Marketing can be a source of SCA. Effective marketing strategies (or aspects of a total strategy) can be unique, valuable, hard-to-copy, and nonsubstitutable. Aspects of a marketing strategy can exist across resource categories, including technological components, human dimensions, and reputational characteristics, and the effective coordination of these elements requires organizational resources. The development of marketing capability by the new venture is therefore a double imperative. The omission of a marketing plan by an entrepreneurial team is a red flag for investors and concerned stakeholders.

Marketing activities have much in common with entrepreneurial activities, so much so that many entrepreneurs point to their ability to sell as the key to their success.[1] Both are concerned with customer needs, new product and service ideas, monitoring the environment, and communication—and both marketing and entrepreneurship are growth-oriented. Marketing and entrepreneurial activity are linked by common perceptions, goals, and behaviors. Yet many entrepreneurs underestimate the value of marketing and ignore some of its key functions. A study of venture capitalists indicated that effective market analysis could reduce new venture failure rates by 60 percent and that 75 percent of entrepreneurs ignored negative marketing information.[2]

In this chapter we will flesh out the significant marketing decisions and activities that a new venture must perform.[3] We will follow the format in the marketing section of the business plan presented in Chapter 5, beginning with a look at the new venture's overall marketing concept and orientation. Then we will examine the marketing resources controlled by and available to entrepreneurs and their firms. Next we will review the key elements of the new venture's **marketing strategy**, with special emphasis on market research—potentially a source of SCA—and continue with a presentation of the special issues involved in marketing Web-based firms and marketing on the Internet. We will conclude with a description of various methods of sales forecasting. A reliable and valid sales forecast is the critical outcome of the venture's marketing activities and provides the bridge between the entrepreneur's plans and aspirations and the organization's financial potential and performance. In the appendix to this chapter we illustrate the market potential/sales requirement method, a sales forecasting technique that combines demand forecasting and profit planning.

MARKETING CONCEPT AND ORIENTATION

The marketing concept is a managerial prescription (an "ought-to-do") for setting marketing goals and managing exchange transactions. It requires an understanding of potential and actual customer needs and of the costs of meeting those needs. The entrepreneur then devises and implements a total system that integrates marketing with the other business functions. The single most important objective of marketing is customer satisfaction. **Customer satisfaction** is achieved when a firm provides user-based quality and value (the quality/price ratio) to its buyers.

Customer Orientation

The employment of the total marketing concept is fairly well established in most small businesses and new ventures,[4] but there are other orientations to consider: for example, production orientation, sales emphasis, or social orientation.

Production orientation is preoccupied with manufacturing-based or product-based quality and is internally directed. Production-oriented ventures are often founded by engineers, inventors, or high-tech wizards, people fascinated by the gadgets and gizmos they are attempting to bring to market.

Sales orientation is not marketing orientation. Sales-oriented firms make selling their number one priority. Developing long-term relationships with customers, integrating business functions to provide maximum satisfaction, and striving to deliver the product or service at the lowest possible price are not primary concerns. For sales-oriented ventures, moving product out the door is Job #1.

Increasingly, **socially oriented** firms are succeeding. Examples such as Ben and Jerry's[5] ice cream and The Body Shop[6] prove that a social conscience need not be in conflict with business effectiveness. Often these firms' products affirm the customers' own social concerns, and those customers will pay a premium because a certain percentage of their money will go to support social causes espoused by the founding entrepreneurs, or because they believe the products are environmentally sound.

Market Research

A marketing priority requires that customer satisfaction be the company's primary objective, and understanding what will satisfy the customer in any particular business concept requires extensive knowledge of those potential purchasers. Market research is designed to provide that information.

Market research can be defined as "the systematic and objective process of gathering, coding and analyzing data for aid in making marketing decisions."[7] In Chapter 3 we introduced a framework for analyzing customers, competitors, and industry forces, and that data came from market research. Effective market research can help the new venture answer such important questions as:

- **Who is the customer?** The customer profile includes demographic characteristics, values and attitudes, buyer and shopping behavior, and buyer location. Customers may be local, regional, national, or international. Understanding the customer is the basis for market segmentation.
- **Who are the players?** The profiles of existing and potential competitors can indicate the likelihood of retaliation and the probable nature of their reactions.
- **How can the customer be reached?** Distribution networks and channels are responsible for the actual delivery of the product or service. Sometimes the answer to this question falls back on standard industry practices: "ship by common carrier," "retail channels," "in-house sales force." But other times the distribution system *is* the business—as with Avon, Domino's Pizza, and Amway.

Conducting market research, an early step in new venture creation,[8] is a common practice among small businesses. As many as 40 percent of smaller businesses do market research, and the vast majority are satisfied with the results.[9] This research need not be expensive or time-consuming. In fact, answers to the important marketing questions are frequently well within the grasp of the entrepreneur, and most market research can be done by the founders themselves.

Conducting market research is a six-step process.

Step 1 begins with a definition of the purposes and objectives of the study. Deciding at the outset what questions need to be answered will save time and money and will also make the results easier to interpret. In this important preliminary stage, the researcher specifies the nature of the problem, determining what facts, knowledge, and opinions can help the entrepreneurs make a better decision.[10] For example, asking potential customers whether they would buy your product is not as effective as asking if they would buy at specific price points. The more focused the question, the better the chances of generating valid and reliable answers.

Step 2 is the point at which the researcher decides which data sources—primary or secondary—are best suited to the objectives of the study. **Primary data** are generated from scratch by the research team. **Secondary sources** consist of data, information, and studies that have already been completed and published by others. These sources are useful for planning original-data collection activities because they contain in-depth background information on customers and markets, most are easily accessed, and access is generally either free or inexpensive. Virtually unlimited information is available from hundreds of sources. Some published studies are examples of concept, product, and market tests similar to those the new venture might want to conduct. These are frequently available over the Internet and/or in public libraries, and they are always available in the business libraries of major business schools.

One fine example of the use of secondary sources can be demonstrated in the founding of Quantum Health of Columbus, Ohio. In 1999 Kara Trott was working as a corporate lawyer with clients in the healthcare industry. She saw first-hand how economic competition between providers and insurers was causing problems for patients, and she wanted to make a difference. Her ideas met with a good deal of skepticism, but nevertheless she did her research. Using data supplied by her law firm's clients, she tracked the healthcare decisions of almost 3,000 patients, 260 doctors, and 140 other healthcare employees. She found that about 50 percent of patients leave doctors' offices without knowing what to do next. Few received guidance or answers to their questions, so they often chose the wrong type of specialist for their problems. On average, these errors cost an additional $3,500. With this data in hand, Trott quit her job and started Quantum to help patients ask better questions, make better decisions, and save everyone money. The business model? She collects a percentage of the money saved by employers. Last year Quantum managed 52,000 patients (a 100 percent increase year over year), and her revenues rose to $7 million. That initial research was the basis for the business idea, the pitch to companies, and the clincher to financiers.[11]

After secondary sources are consulted and data organized, primary data collection can be conducted if needed. Three common entrepreneurial primary-data projects are the concept test, the product test, and the market test.

Concept testing occurs very early in new venture planning, often before the final venture configuration is complete. The purpose of the concept test is to determine whether customers can envision how the product or service will work and whether they would purchase it. Customers respond to a *description* of the product or service. After reading the description, they are asked whether they understand the product and would be likely to purchase it.

Concept testing can also be used for potential investors, suppliers, or members of the managerial team. Each of these groups is in a position to evaluate the new venture concept, and the entrepreneur can gauge whether the concept is likely to be accepted by these important stakeholders. In addition, feedback from these people at the concept stage enables the entrepreneur to make adjustments and alterations to the concept that can save time, money, and reputation down the road.

Product testing requires having potential customers or investors react to the actual use of a new product or service. Subjects may use the product briefly and even take it home for a more intensive test. Product testing is less abstract than concept testing, so the responses it generates are more reliable. However, some products are so expensive to manufacture, even as prototypes, that product testing is unrealistic.

Market testing is the most complex and expensive approach, but it is also the most realistic and most likely to produce reliable results. In a market test, the product or service is introduced using the full marketing strategy in a limited area that is representative of the broader market. It attempts, in essence, to actually market the product, usually in a limited geographic area. For ventures inherently limited in geographic reach, the market test is the actual beginning of business operations. Small manufacturing operations seeking broad product distribution are candidates for the market test research.

Each of the three types of test has costs and benefits, and proper selection requires a fit between the entrepreneur's needs and resources and the type of product or service under consideration. Table 6.1 summarizes each test and its appropriateness in a variety of situations. An indication of *high appropriateness* means that the test fits the need. *Moderate and low appropriateness* levels indicate that the test might not deliver the necessary information.

Step 3 in market research is the development of the data collection instrument or test. Market research data can come from one or multiple sources. Results are more likely to be valid if various sources are employed. For customer studies, personal and telephone interviews, focus groups, and direct observation might be appropriate. Mail studies and surveys are common data sources. Whichever method is chosen in step 2, a properly designed data-collection instrument is required. This is self-evident for interviews and surveys research, but it is also important for secondary-data sources. These data sources can overwhelm the market researcher because the abundance of data tends to make the researcher believe that all of it is important. Too much data can be as dangerous as too little, and it also translates into extra expense and extra effort in coding and analyzing large data sets. Researchers should know precisely what sort of data they need

Table 6.1 Marketing Research: Appropriateness of Primary Data Collection Methods

New-Venture Characteristic	Concept Test	Product Test	Market Test
Single-product venture	High*	High	High
Multiproduct venture	Moderate to low	Moderate	Low
Importance of pricing strategy	High	High	High
Importance of promotion	Moderate to low	Moderate to high	High
Importance of distribution	Moderate to low	Moderate to high	High
Introduction of innovations— continuous	High	High	High
Introduction of innovations—occasional	Low	Moderate	High

*High appropriateness means a good fit between the test and the characteristic of the venture. Moderate and low appropriateness indicate that caution should be used because the test may not generate the type of information required.

SOURCE: Adapted from G. Hills and R. LaForge, "Marketing and Entrepreneurship: The State of the Art." In D. Sexton and J. Kasarda (eds.), *The State of the Art of Entrepreneurship* (Boston: PWS-Kent, 2006): 164-90.

before consulting secondary sources. There are a number of online survey Web sites, such as http://zoomerang.com and http://surveymonkey.com.

Step 4 is designing the sample. Occasionally a researcher will be able to speak to all of the people or collect data on all of the companies of interest. In this case, a census is performed instead of a sample. But usually the large number of people or companies makes it necessary to focus on a small proportion as representative of the total population—a sample. The key issues in sample design are representation and reliability. A sample need not be large to be representative of the whole population. National polls of voters may include only 1,500 participants to represent 60 million voters, but if the sample is properly chosen these polls are surprisingly accurate. To guarantee statistically pure national samples, the venture probably should employ professional market researchers. For smaller, do-it-yourself efforts, researchers must simply ensure that the people they speak to have the necessary information, and *very* small samples—one, two, and three respondents—are seldom sufficient.

Step 5, data collection, is the actual execution of the study. Data must be collected in an unbiased and uniform manner. The correct design of the instrument and sample help to ensure this, but it is also important to train survey recorders and telephone interviewers, check the data records for errors, and scan responses.

Step 6 encompasses the final stages of a market research project: analysis of the data and interpretation of the results. Often a final report is written, even when the project is relatively small and the goals of the study fairly narrow. This ensures that a record exists for the future and that others in the organization can refer to the study as necessary. One important caveat about market research—it can tell you what *is*, but it frequently cannot tell you what *could be*. Henry Ford once said, "If I had listened to customers, I'd have given them a faster horse."[12]

Market Research on Innovations. Market research on innovative products and services is particularly relevant for entrepreneurs. Considerable work has been done in this area of buyer behavior. The entrepreneur whose objective is to successfully introduce a new product or service has three intermediate goals: (1) to remove impediments to the purchase of the innovation, (2) to increase acceptance of the new product, and (3) to encourage repurchase over time. Impediments always confront an innovation, and they can take many forms. For example, existing channels of distribution may be difficult to breach, making it hard to present the product to the target market.

Next, the innovation entrepreneur must attempt to appeal to a wide audience and to gain broad market acceptance. Initial buyers may have special characteristics that make innovations appealing to them—for example, high levels of education and literacy, high levels of income, an open attitude toward change, sensitivity to external changes, and high social status. Age is negatively correlated with the propensity to adopt innovations. However, the segment of buyers immediately attracted to the innovation is usually too narrow to support production and organization. Marketing can broaden the appeal, and once the product or service is widely used, repurchase can be encouraged.

The marketer who understands the **diffusion process** is in the best position. Diffusion refers to the aggregate market understanding and acceptance of an innovation, whether it is a product, a service, or an idea. The most widely accepted model for the diffusion process has five stages.[13]

- At the **knowledge stage** people become aware of the innovation. Information is disseminated through various media, and this public exposure is reinforced with physical and social stimuli to create awareness of the product. The earliest messages enable the consumer to recognize the innovation and recall its attributes. This is when the entrepreneur must convey important facts and compelling images to the public.
- During the **persuasion stage**, favorable attitudes toward the product are articulated. These more sophisticated messages describe operating and performance characteristics as well as buyer benefits. The risks of purchase are weighed against the risks of non-purchase in the consumer's mind. Marketers compare similar or competing products to the new product and link it to positive images and personalities, creating what is known as the **halo effect.** Because consumers are actively searching and processing information about the product at this stage, advertising and various marketing communications become powerful tools. Now the entrepreneur can demonstrate the relative advantages of the product or service, as well as its compatibility with buyers' values, needs, and behavior.
- At the **decision stage**—the crucial "make or break" time for the entrepreneur—the product or service is ready to be either accepted or rejected. Now, social and economic pressures are brought to bear, leading the customer through a series of smaller decisions that will lead to the purchase of the product. Here the entrepreneur must close the sale.
- At the **implementation stage,** the customer is actually using the product or service. During this trial period, another crucial time, the venture is at risk in two ways. First, it may be misused by the customer. Second, the marketing may have raised unrealistic expectations for its performance, thereby disappointing the purchaser. On the positive side, this is also the time when customers can experience user-friendly aspects of the innovation and directly observe its benefits.
- Finally, at the **confirmation stage,** customers either reverse their decision (no repurchase) or are reinforced to repeat it (repurchase).

Figure 6.1 illustrates the diffusion process.[14]

MARKETING STRATEGY

Marketing strategy is the set of objectives and the configuration of activities that enable the new venture to implement a total marketing concept. In the resource-based approach to sustainable competitive advantage, there are two keys to success. The first is to identify and control rare, valuable, hard to duplicate, and nonsubstitutable resources. This gives the firm its distinctive competence and its competitive edge. The second key is an alloy, consisting of creativity and luck. A recent study reported that among the twenty biggest retail outlets for top American brands, the three primary sources of sustainable advantage were location, service, and luck (serendipitous creativity).[15]

The study indicated that location, the primary aspect of a retailer's distribution strat-

FIGURE 6.1   The Diffusion Process

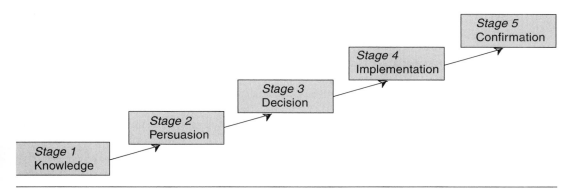

egy, is the key component of its overall marketing strategy. Locations are always evaluated relative to their rents. When rent paid is appreciably lower than the property's value to the retailer, the venture has an enormous initial advantage. Great service is another key component of the marketing strategy. The leading Lexus dealer in the United States washed all of his customers' cars after Hurricane Andrew to rid them of acid created by burning debris. Luck and creativity matter because they are so difficult to duplicate. According to Phillip Kotler, international marketing guru at Northwestern University's Kellogg School of Management, successful outlets are likely to be "more creative. They may depart from some of the standard procedures—and perhaps even the principles in some cases . . . ."[16]

Here we hear echoes of Sam Walton's Rule Number 10: "Break all the rules."

Both the resource-based approach to marketing and the total marketing concept require that the marketing concept focus on the firm's distinctive competencies. Any advantages should be pressed through marketing strategy. So—what is our distinctive competence? We have already explored this topic in Chapters 2 through 5. The next question is: Who values our competence? We considered this subject along with our resource analysis, but we include it in our marketing discussion because it involves selection of target markets and segments. The subsequent questions are: What marketing activities enable us to interact most effectively with our markets? How will the marketing variables—price, promotion, product characteristics, and distribution—be set to increase our market? And finally: Given a set of marketing activities, how much can we expect to sell? We will address this issue below in the section on sales forecasting.

Selection of Markets and Segments

Not all customers are alike. Our analysis of buyer characteristics in Chapter 3 indicated that buyers differ, for example, in price sensitivity, brand loyalty, and requirements for quality. Market segmentation is the identification of distinct heterogeneous buying groups and the development and implementation of a marketing strategy to fit each group. **Market segmentation** enables the venture to discriminate among buyers for its own advantage. For example, if cutting-edge technological innovation is a major strength of the venture, it can focus on buyers who demand high-tech products and services. If efficient operation is the core entrepreneurial competency, the venture can aim for the most price sensitive buyers. It is virtually impossible to be all things to all people, to achieve world-class customer satisfaction across all classes of customers, so effective market segmentation enables the firm to serve some segment of customers exceedingly well.

Bases for Segmentation. Sometimes markets can be segmented along very broad lines: consumer end users versus commercial end users, for example. Commercial end users can be further segmented into manufacturing businesses, distribution organizations, wholesalers, retailers, service organizations, and not-for-profits. These are distinctly different types of buyers, and each is likely to have a distinguishable set of needs. Markets can also be segmented geographically by determining the scope of the venture's operation: global, regional, domestic, or local.

Segmentation methods are widely used by new ventures and small businesses. One study reported that 62 percent of businesses employed some type of market segmentation strategy and that *effective segmentation strategies produced significant differences in return on invested capital*.[17] In other words, not only do segmentation strategies lead to higher customer satisfaction, but this satisfaction translates into profits. Table 6.2 presents a range of segmentation techniques, the percentage of small firms that employ them, and the reported effectiveness of each method.

Marketing Activities

Four major marketing decisions must be made once the target markets are selected. These decisions are not made in isolation but are intertwined with each other and with the venture's distinctive competencies, target market, and macro and competitive environments. These decisions concern pricing, product and service configurations, distribution strategies, and promotional campaigns.[18]

Pricing. A **price** is the exchange value (usually denominated in money) of the venture's goods and services, and price has many aliases: fares, taxes, tuition, fees, tips, interest, and tolls. The pricing decision is probably the most important major marketing activity because it directly affects the value relationship (quality divided by price). A poorly priced product is a misplaced product in relation to the competition, in the perceptions of buyers, and in relation to the firm's other products and sources.

An entrepreneur must make fairly accurate price decisions even before the product is introduced to the market, because the price has a direct impact on the sales forecast. If pricing is wrong, forecasts are wrong, and so are projected cash flow and profits. An incorrect pricing decision can get the entrepreneur a "green light" on launching the business when more accurate forecasting would have generated a "red light" and saved everybody time and money.

Different pricing objectives require different pricing strategies, but the primary objective of pricing is to make a profit. Seven of the most popular pricing strategies are discussed below, and each of them can help the venture achieve its primary objective.[19]

Cost-based pricing is the simplest strategy. After the entrepreneur determines the cost of producing the product or delivering the service, a mark-up is added. This method

TABLE 6.2   Bases for Market Segmentation: Usage and Effectiveness

Basis	Usage[a]	Effectiveness[b]
By geographic areas: such as state, county, census tract	13.6%	3.9
By demographics: such as age, income, gender.	15.5	3.6
By social class: high, middle, low.	4.9	3.8
By lifestyle and opinions: such as hobbies, job type, political view.	4.4	2.7
By personality traits: such as masculinity, femininity, assertiveness.	4.1	2.6
By purchasing decisions: based on when customers get ideas.	2.4	3.7
By purchasing timing: based on when buyers buy.	3.1	4.2
By time of use: based on when customers use products.	6.3	4.3
By benefits sought: based on what customers want.	11.8	4.6
By extent of usage: such as high users, ex-users.	6.9	3.1
By buyer loyalty status: such as very loyal, ready switcher.	5.2	2.7
By buyer readiness: based on degree of awareness and intent.	3.8	3.9
By buyer attitudes: such as enthusiasm, hostility.	5.6	4.1
By marketing attribute: product characteristic, price sensitivity.	8.0	2.5

[a]Indicates primary method. [b]Indicates satisfaction with technique on a scale of 1 to 5. Mean for all dimensions is 3.6. Satisfaction will vary by type of business but this bias was not reported in the data.

SOURCE: Adapted from R. Peterson, "Small Business Usage of Target Marketing," *Journal of Small Business Management,* October 1991: 79-85.

is widely used in the construction industry, by professional partnerships (lawyers, consultants, accountants), and by government contractors. To demonstrate, let's assume that our entrepreneur is starting a one-person consulting firm. She estimates that her variable cost per hour (primarily her hourly wage) is $50. Her fixed costs are estimated at $100,000 per year and she expects to bill 2000 hours for the year.

- Variable cost $50
- Fixed costs $100,000
- Expected unit sales   2,000 hours
- Cost per unit $100/hour

Now suppose our entrepreneur wants to earn a 50 percent markup on sales. The equation looks like this:

Markup price = (Unit cost/1-desired return on sales) = ($100/1-.5) = $200/hour
This is also the equivalent of a 100 percent markup on cost. From this data we can calculate the break-even volume:

Break-even volume = Fixed cost/(Price-variable cost) = \$100,000/(\$200-\$100) = 1000 hours

Target profit pricing bases its calculations on simple break-even analysis. Let's change our example to a product, a small digital MP3 player. Now look at the break-even volume at different prices based on these data assumptions:

Investment	\$1,000,000
Fixed costs per year	\$1,300,000
Variable cost	\$1,000,020

If the entrepreneur wants a 20 percent return on investment, that is \$200,000. Consider the effects of various prices on sales estimates and profits by building a break-even volume and profit table.

At \$28 per unit, the venture will lose \$16,000. Since this price is too low, the entrepreneur moves it up in \$4 increments to find out where the venture becomes profitable and approaches the target of \$200,000. Note that as price rises, unit demand falls. At \$36 per unit, the product reaches its maximum estimated profit of \$180,000. This falls short of the target, but if prices go higher, the demand falls and so does the projected profit. The only way to reach the target is to reduce the amount invested by using capital more efficiently or by reducing our variable costs to allow for more margin per product. Reworking investment levels, cost estimates, demand estimates, and profit targets is often necessary for a new venture.

Skimming the market identifies a price-insensitive segment and charges the highest price the market can bear for short-term profits. It works when:

- No comparable products are available.
- Costs are uncertain.
- The product has an extremely short life cycle.
- A drastic innovation or improvement has been made.
- Competitors are unlikely to enter the market (due to high entry barriers, high promotion costs, expensive R & D costs, or other isolating mechanisms).

TABLE 6.3   Break Even Volume and Target Pricing

1	2	3	4	5	6
Price per unit	Unit demand to break even	Expected unit demand at given price	Total revenue (1 x 3)	Total costs*	Profit (4 − 5)
(\$)28	37,500	35,500	\$ 994,000	\$1,010,000	− \$ 16,000
32	30,000	33,500	1,072,000	970,000	102,000
36	18,750	30,000	1,080,000	900,000	180,000
40	15,000	21,000	840,000	720,000	120,000
44	12,500	11,500	506,000	530,000	− 24,000

*Assumes fixed costs of \$300,000 and variable cost of \$20/unit

After price-insensitive segments have been skimmed, prices are gradually reduced to include more sensitive segments. The primary advantages of this strategy are:

- It provides quick cash for reinvestment in promotion or product development.
- It allows for a market test before starting full-scale production.
- It suggests that the product is of very high quality.

The major disadvantages are:

- It requires the existence of a price-insensitive market segment.
- It can create ill will in the market. Prices are perceived as "too high" and "exploitative" by those who cannot afford the product and who have to wait for the introduction of the lower-cost model. This was true with the early introduction of high-definition television.
- It can attract potent competitors looking for similar high returns.

Exploiting the experience curve gives an advantage to the more experienced manufacturer or service provider who is more knowledgeable and efficient. This entrepreneur may be able to decrease some variable costs, then take advantage of these decreasing costs by "riding down the demand curve." This means that as costs decrease, prices are set to decrease proportionately, effectively increasing volume and expanding the market. Thus, it is possible to maintain margins (price minus variable cost) and increase market share. This strategy is most often employed by established companies launching innovations like new computer chips, in durable-goods industries (where the experience-curve effect is most often noted), and in markets where the product life cycle is long enough to ride down the curve.

The advantages of this strategy are:

- It enables the firm to exploit its low cost position.
- It permits slow changes in price that do not alienate customers.
- It does not require profit objectives to be sacrificed for market share.

Its disadvantages are:

- Some buyers are discouraged by high initial prices.
- Price reductions may anger buyers who bought earlier.
- The experience-curve effect must be a documented reality. If the experience curve cost reductions do not emerge then the pricing strategy will be ineffective.

Meeting the market (competitive) pricing is simply pricing a product or service at the same level as the competition. If this practice is generally accepted by competitors within a segment, competition will not be based on price. Instead, firms will jockey for dominance based on distribution, promotion, and product improvement. These forms of competition expand the market for everyone by making the products more attractive, easier to buy, and better known. This type of pricing is most likely to prevail when competitors face each other in a number of markets and wish to avoid devastating price wars, when costs are reasonably predictable over the entire product life cycle, and when the market is still growing.

The major advantages of this strategy are:

- It requires less analysis and research.
- It treats all buyers, early and late, the same.
- It reassures other firms that there is no threat of a price war.

The disadvantages are:

- It requires the use of other marketing tools to gain differentiation.
- Its recovery on investment is slower.
- It is difficult to overcome errors in initial cost estimates.

Achieving maximum market penetration is a strategy whereby the venture builds market share as quickly as possible by entering with low prices. It stimulates market growth. If this plan is successfully executed, the venture will be entrenched as the market-share leader and positioned for long-term profitability. The low price implies low margins, which will deter some competitors from entering. It is most useful in mass consumer markets when:

- The product has a long life span.
- There is easy market entry.
- Demand is highly price-sensitive.
- There is no "top" of the market to skim.
- There is some experience-curve effect.

The primary advantages of this strategy are:

- It discourages entry of competitors.
- It focuses customers' attention on value.
- It enables maximum penetration and exposure over a short time period.

Penetration pricing has a downside because:

- It assumes a degree of price inelasticity that may not be present.
- It stimulates high volumes that the venture may not be prepared to meet.
- It requires large initial capital investment to meet high volumes.
- It is vulnerable to large losses if errors are made.

Establishing preemptive pricing is a "low ball" strategy designed to keep potential competitors—or force existing competitors—out of the market. Prices are set as close to expected variable costs as possible, and cost savings are passed on to buyers. Because costs often decrease over time, initial prices will be below cost. Preemptive pricing is often employed in consumer markets and is sometimes combined with other product-pricing strategies that can help subsidize this potentially short-term money-losing policy. If this strategy succeeds, its major advantage is that it limits competition. If it fails, however—if competitors match the low prices—losses can be enormous.

In addition to these strategies, numerous other pricing tactics are employed in various situations. Table 6.4 offers a primer on creative pricing

Pricing policies also have legal implications and constraints. The **Sherman Act** prohibits conspiracy in restraint of trade. Such conspiracy includes collusive pricing and price

TABLE 6.4 A Creative Pricing Primer: Approaches and Examples

Approach	Description	Examples
Bundling	Sell complementary products	Contact lens and solution in a single package
Unbundling	Divide products into separate elements	iPod accessories and add-ons
Trial pricing	Introductory sizes and short trial periods	Starter memberships; preview fees
Value-added pricing	Include "free" services to appeal to bargain hunters	Free service contract for durables
Twofers	Buy one, get one free	Pizzas, theater tickets, companion fares
Pay one price	Fixed-cost admissions or club memberships	Amusement park rides, salad bars, all-you-can-eat buffets
Constant promotional price	List price is never charged	Consumer electronics, auto sticker prices
Pricing tied to variable	Set a "price per" schedule	Steak by the ounce in restaurants
Captive pricing	Lock the customer into a system with one inexpensive component, one expensive	Razors and razor blades
Fixed, then variable	A "just to get started" charge, followed by a different rate	Taxi fares, phone calls tied to usage
Price point breaks (psychological)	Price just below psychological threshold	Charge $4.99 instead of $5.00

SOURCE: Adapted from M. Mondello, "Naming Your Price," *Inc.*, July 1992: 80-83.

fixing. Although entrepreneurs are expected to make pricing decisions independently, market research into competitors' prices and signaling through price changes are legal.[20]

The Federal Trade Commission regulates pricing practices and prohibits deceptive pricing. Deceptive pricing occurs when it is difficult or impossible for the buyer to actually understand what the price of a product or service is. Some products, like insurance, are complicated by nature and require simplified explanations of price policy. The **Truth in Lending Act** requires lenders to explain the true price of credit (interest and finance charges) to borrowers.

The **Robinson-Patman Act** and the **Clayton Act** prohibit **discriminatory pricing**. Illegal price discrimination exists when identical products or services are sold, under similar circumstances, at different prices to different customers or to different market segments. What actually constitutes discrimination is the subject of many volumes of legal text, briefs, torts, and statutes. Basically, however, the following tenets of price discrimination are established:

1. Different prices cannot be charged based on buyers' membership in social, ethnic, or religious groups.
2. Socioeconomic factors such as age, income, and gender may not be used as a basis for price discrimination.

3. Sellers can charge different prices in different markets, when the market is defined as the circumstances of location and cost.
4. If the costs of serving a market are variable, then the prices charged in those markets may also vary, as, for example, trade discounts and volume discounts.
5. Lower prices are legal if they are necessary to meet the competition—e.g., discounts for children and senior citizens, and group rates on travel and insurance.

Arbitrary and capricious pricing is bad business and may be against the law. It is bad business because it affects the value relationship in unanticipated ways. Customers who receive products or services with unpredictable value are not likely to be happy or satisfied.

Product and Service Decisions. Product decisions determine the bundle of physical and psychological attributes that form or are associated with the core benefit to be delivered. A **product** can be defined as "anything that can be offered to a market for attention, acquisition, or consumption."[21] In the case of a physical product, entrepreneurs make decisions about style, packaging, colors, sizes, and extras that can be purchased separately. The product decision also includes the desired product image, the likelihood that the product can be branded, and whether warranty and after-sale service will be provided.

The product mix of a new venture may consist of a single product of a single design. However, because many companies are launched with more than one product, we discuss a **product mix** with three attributes. **Product width** means the number of different product lines the company offers. **Product depth** refers to the average number of items offered by the company within each product line. **Product consistency** refers to how closely related the various products are in terms of end use, production and distribution requirements, target markets, or segment appeal.

Service-related decisions parallel product-related decisions with a few important differences. Services usually incorporate some degree of customer involvement and participation. Part of the service design decision involves the extent of this cooperation. For example, in the design and delivery of educational services, the customer's involvement can range from passive listener to active "hands-on" learner. Restaurants can be designed with various levels of involvement, from traditional table service to self-service salad bars to cafeteria-style self-service and table clearing. The three major service-related decisions are:

- **Service Intensity**—the degree of depth and development the customer experiences. Roller-coasters provide an intense experience within a narrow—literally confined to the track—service range. Package delivery services are less intense, but extensive.
- **Service Extensiveness**—the range or scope of the services. The package-delivery service can deliver a wide variety of parcels just about anywhere in the world. The more subservices or variations provided, the more extensive the service.
- **Service Time**—the pervasive decision for service design. When will the service be available and how long will it take? Will services be provided continuously or will interruptions be acceptable and appropriate? How frequently can the service be provided while maintaining server quality and customer interest?

Taken narrowly, product and service decisions include all the variables that make up product quality (see Chapter 1). Because these variables adhere to the object produced or the service delivered *before* user-based quality and value are assessed, good product decisions are necessary but not sufficient to guarantee success. They must be made in the context of all the other marketing decisions.

Product and service concepts fall into two broad categories of products and services: consumer goods and industrial goods. Consumer goods are sold to and used by individuals. Those individuals are usually the end-users (no resale), and the goods are often consumed or employed in the condition in which they were purchased. Consumer goods are categorized into four types: convenience goods, shopping goods, specialty goods, and avoidance products and services.

- **Convenience goods** are well-understood products. They resemble commodities in that there are many substitutes available, there is little price differentiation, and people seldom spend much time investigating these products and doing comparison shopping. Examples are soft drinks and cereals. Final sale margins are typically low. The primary method of competition is branding, and firms will spend millions of dollars to generate and protect a brand image. Given the maturity of this type of product, its general availability, and its well-financed and experienced marketers, there are not many new entries in this type of product. The few entrepreneurs who will succeed in this category will find specialized niches that they can protect or that are too small for larger firms to serve.
- **Shopping goods** are items that customers actively investigate before purchasing. They consult consumer guides, comparison shop, ask their neighbors, and are influenced by promotions. These products are often expensive consumer durables whose characteristics change frequently due to technological improvements. Cars, sporting goods, houses, and computers fall into this category. Shopping goods can be differentiated in many respects and represent an opportunity for the entrepreneur with a unique product or a complex service. Because customers look for information, the ability to communicate the benefits and value of the new product is imperative. Final sale margins are relatively high, which helps to offset lower volumes.
- **Specialty goods** are items that most consumers do not even consider buying, items that appeal to a narrow segment of customers. Luxury products fall into this category. Examples are world-class restaurants, expensive furs, and top-notch international resorts. The buyer seldom comparison shops, preferring to locate a seller with an excellent reputation and to rely on this entrepreneur. Inventory is expensive, margins are very high, and the successful achievement of all of the quality dimensions is the key to success.
- **Avoidance products** are essential services that people purchase only when faced with a crisis or some other negative motivation. Funeral services, life insurance, legal services, and estate planning are examples. Many of these, such as mortuary services, are not aggressively marketed; others, like life insurance, are pushed on customers incessantly. Creative entrepreneurs may find ways to convert these avoidance products into shopping goods. For example, the prepaid funeral is now actively marketed to the growing population of older people.

Industrial or business goods are usually sold to businesses or their intermediaries (wholesalers or distributors) either for resale or for use in the production of another good or service. Examples of industrial goods are raw materials, machines that make products or make other machines (machine tools), and supplies for factories or offices. There are five basic types of industrial product: direct materials; indirect materials; capital assets; contracted services; and maintenance, repair, and operating supplies (MRO).

- **Direct materials** include the raw materials, subassemblies, and components used in manufacturing. For example, in manufacturing MP3 players, direct materials include the electronics that are the guts of the player; the cases to hold the electronics; any coatings applied to the casings; any displays, knobs, or dials attached to the player; and the wires and headphone apparatus.
- **Indirect materials** are the supplies used in the manufacturing process but not physically incorporated into the final product. Office supplies are the most common example. Because these supplies are often difficult to differentiate and are sold at prices very close to cost, they are like commodities. In this case, entry barriers are high and new entry opportunities are limited.
- **Capital assets** are major machinery and equipment purchases, buildings and land, and construction projects for plant and leasehold improvements. These purchases (and subsequently sales) are different from other types of industrial products. Capital assets are usually purchased as a result of budgeting decisions and plans. Because of the large sums of money involved, high-level executives are often the decision makers. Because each side has so much at stake, negotiations between vendor and buyer tend to be complex.
- **Contracted services** include a broad range of activities including consulting, engineering, market research, and accounting. In Chapter 1 we referred to the trend for larger organizations to keep only the core distinctive competence under their direct control and to subcontract other auxiliary services. This "shamrock" organizational form was described as promoting entrepreneurship by creating the need for all sorts of contracted services. There are many niches available in service contracts, and firms that succeed will do so by successfully managing exceedingly complex tasks and relationships.
- **Maintenance, repair, and operating (MRO) products** form a large market composed of the many essential supplies that businesses cannot do without: Light bulbs, janitorial supplies, and toilet paper are examples. The procurement of these items usually falls to a purchasing agent. PAs will expect competitive prices, but most of all they value vendors who can guarantee convenient delivery schedules and who have an established reputation for reliable service.

Business marketing is different from consumer marketing because the buyers are different, and the criteria by which they make decisions are more complex. Table 6.5 summarizes these differences.

Note that many business-buyer characteristics are salient for the application of the Porter model of competitive industry analysis covered in Chapter 3. This emphasizes that the strategies and tactics of business marketing are different from those of typical consumer marketing.

TABLE 6.5   Dimensions of Business (Industrial) Markets

Characteristics of Industry Structure
  Fewer but more powerful buyers
  Geographically concentrated buyers
  Demand derived from consumer demand
  More inelastic demand means less price-sensitive in the short run
  Quantity orders likely to change quickly depending on inventory levels

Organizational Characteristics
  More people involved in the buying decision
  Professional standards and ethics for buying activities

Decisions and Processes
  Complex decisions
  Interdependent with other organization functions
  Formal processes and established rules
  Long-term relationships important
  Supplier development programs for vendors

SOURCE: Adapted from P. Kotler and G. Armstrong, *Principles of Marketing* (Upper Saddle River, NJ: Pearson Prentice-Hall, 2006): 171.

Distribution. Distribution decisions and activities relate to the location of the business and the choice and availability of distribution **channels**. These decisions are strongly affected, if not completely constrained, by the type of venture. Certain businesses—retailers, wholesalers, warehousers, catalogers, telemarketers, franchisers, and online firms—are themselves distributors or channels. This reality limits the choices for entrepreneurs unless they are willing to reconfigure their ventures in some subtle way. If they are, the decision becomes more strategic and less tactical and is therefore not a distribution decision at all.

The major objective of a distribution or location decision is to get the venture's product or service to the target market. When the product or service is defined carefully and the target market is identified, distribution and location decisions should be clear. Effective distribution and channel activities match product to customer and complement these previous decisions.

Consumer distribution channels can employ as many as three intermediaries between producer and consumer. There are occasions, of course, when no intermediaries are used, as in the "factory-direct sales" system. In this case the venture manufactures a product and sells it to the customer right from the factory. Since most manufacturers lack the resources to do this well, they generally employ intermediaries. Figure 6.2 illustrates a consumer distribution chain. Any segment of the chain can be eliminated if industry practice, cost considerations, or venture resources dictate.

A few select entrepreneurs reach their customers through television. Television time is expensive, but the **infomercial** format puts products directly in front of the audience. Infomercials, sometimes referred to as paid programming, are usually thirty-minute tel-

FIGURE 6.2   Distribution Channels for Consumer Goods

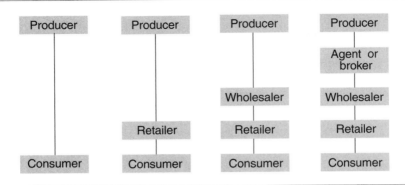

evision programs paid for by the entrepreneur/marketer and aimed at demonstrating the product and marketing it to prospective customers. These shows are designed to provoke a direct and quantifiable response and are often edited and altered to increase response rates.

Entrepreneurs who cannot afford to produce their own infomercials and buy the television time may turn to alternatives like the Home Shopping Network and QVC. Using television to introduce and promote a product offers instant widespread exposure, costs very little, and can result in significant sales. Feedback can be negative if the product does not sell, but at least the feedback is received quickly. Street Story 6.1 deals with some QVC hopefuls and their products.

The Internet also enables the entrepreneur to go directly to consumers. Most entrepreneurs have an affinity for the direct sales approach, and they often try to build large networks of representatives for their products. Street Story 6.2 demonstrates how effective networks work.

Business distribution channels are employed when the producer is selling to another organization, especially one that uses purchasing agents and has a specialized purchasing organization. The possibilities are diagramed in Figure 6.3. As with consumer channels, circumstances determine whether a certain node can be skipped or eliminated.

Institutional and **government markets** have their own special characteristics, channels, and buyer behavior. The institutional market is composed of schools and universities, hospitals, nursing homes, prisons, and other institutions. These entities have different objectives and sponsors and are characterized by low budgets and captive populations. Segmentation strategies work well for these buyers.

Government markets exist at many levels. In the United States, municipal, county, state, and federal bureaucracies purchase billions of dollars in goods and services. Other countries have their own hierarchies. Selling to a government frequently involves a bidding process, though this can be bypassed in special situations (such as urgent need or hard-to-find products). Government sales frequently require extra paperwork and oversight, but the government pays on time, usually does repeat business, and may offer set-aside business opportunities for small businesses and minority-owned organizations.

| STREET STORY 6.1 |

Making Your Product a TV Star

Doug Krentz's wife thought it sounded like a great opportunity. "I don't care if you have to call in sick and fake a broken leg, but you're going to Virginia on Monday," she told him. She wanted him to attend a trade show in Arlington sponsored by QVC, the home-shopping network, for potential vendors. Krentz, an avid mountain biker, had invented a portable pressure jet washer called The Dirtworker. Powered from a car's cigarette lighter, it could be used to clean bikes, sports gear, beach chairs, and other items before loading them into a car.

Over 450 inventors, designers, and manufacturers joined Krentz at the QVC Product Search event (www.qvcproductsearch.com) in January 2005. That forum was one of more than ten sponsored by the retailer at locations around the country that year. Each aspiring supplier had ten minutes to pitch his or her product to a QVC product specialist for a no-cost evaluation, and an opportunity to learn something about marketing.

Every week QVC offers some 250 new products in a TV market that reaches 160 million homes worldwide. The most fortunate entrepreneurs from each forum were chosen to offer their products on air and to receive a $20,000-25,000 initial purchase order from the television retailer.

"We're always looking for new and innovative products to bring to our discerning customers," explains Marilyn Montross, QVC's director of vendor relations. The company (www.qvc.com) has sponsored product searches since 1995. Generally they are on the lookout for products that can be visually demonstrated effectively (like high-tech blenders), that make life easier (like the robot vacuums), or that solve some common problem (like laundry stains). The products must appeal to a broad audience (most QVC viewers are women, but they also buy for men), have unique features, and retail for $15 or more. QVC does not sell firearms, furs, or tobacco products, and will not feature a product that involves any type of sweepstakes or questionnaire.

In 2006 QVC joined forces with Count-Me-In, a non-profit organization, and OPEN, the American Express program for small business, to sponsor the Make Mine a $Million business program. The three sponsors are focusing on women entrepreneurs because statistics show that, while almost 11 million businesses in the United States are owned by women, only 3 percent have annual sales of more than $1 million.

Best-selling products discovered by QVC during the 2005 product search include a choke-free body harness for small dogs, scented soy candles, a heart-shaped silver pendant that is also a bell, and a cookbook written by a 92-year-old author. Doug Krentz's Dirtworker is not on the list, but his product will soon be available on the Internet (www.dirtworker.com).

SOURCE: Adapted from Rachael King, "The Big Pitch," *Business Week SmallBiz,*Spring 2005: 58-64; "QVC Is Calling All Entrepreneurs," *The Business Journal*, April 17, 2006. Retrieved from the Web July 6, 2006, http://www.business-journal.com/archives.20060417QVC Auditions.asp, www.qvc.com, www.qvcproductsearch.com, and www.dirtworker.com.

Promotion. Promotion consists of the methods and techniques that ventures use to communicate with customers and with other stakeholders. The purposes of promotion are to inform and persuade. Included in the promotional mix are advertising, personal selling, sales promotion, publicity, and public relations. Each of these activities has dis-

STREET STORY 6.2

E-Commerce Makes Selling Easy

Sue Wilson, Janet Rickstrew, and Mary Tatum were already avid do-it-yourselfers when they met playing basketball at their local recreation center. But they were also frustrated DIYers because the hand tools they were using were too large for their hands, and the instructional workshops offered by the chain hardware stores were geared toward men. After attending a direct sales party for kitchen tools, the three friends decided to start a company selling tools specifically designed for a woman's smaller hand and marketed through enjoyable and relaxed "tool parties" in people's homes.

The entrepreneurial trio recognized from the start that education was the key to the success of Tomboy Tools, Inc. (www.tomboy-tools.com). "We chose the direct sales industry because it allowed us to combine great tools with educational demos and techniques, which help to empower women to become confident and competent homeowners," says president and CEO Wilson. Women can learn how to repair a leaky faucet, patch drywall, or install ceramic tile at a Tomboy Tools party before purchasing the tools to make those jobs easier. In the tradition of Tupperware and Mary Kay, customers can purchase additional tools at a discount when they host a party to share the Tomboy Tools motto—"Women – Tools – Knowledge — Pass It On"—with their friends.

According to the Direct Selling Association, 55 percent of adult Americans have purchased goods or services from a direct sales representative, primarily during in-home demonstrations or parties. Direct sales totaled $29.73 billion in the United States in 2004, with personal care items like cosmetics and jewelry leading, followed closely by home and family care items such as cookware and appliances. It is not surprising, then, that almost 80 percent of direct sellers in the United States are women.

Direct sales can be "great for entrepreneurs because they don't need a million dollars to get started," notes Amy Robinson, spokeswoman for the DSA. Andrew Shure relies on the Internet to recruit both representatives and customers for his new line of natural lifestyle products for pets (www.shurepets.com). Thanks to the Web, he doesn't have to plead with storeowners for shelf space as he did earlier in his career when he marketed toys to retailers. "In today's environment, it's as easy for people to find us in Nevada as it is in Chicago," Shure says.

Natural health and beauty products entrepreneur Nadine Thompson uses conference calls and emails from home to communicate with her 9,000 sales consultants. Thanks to e-commerce, her Warm Spirit Inc. (www.warmspirit.org) chalked up $6 million in annual sales after just five years of operation. "It's a great way to work a business," says Thompson.

SOURCE: Adapted from Gwendolyn Bounds, "Direct-Sales Operations Gain, with Boost from the Internet," *The Wall Street Journal,* October 26, 2004: B4. Retrieved from the Web. www.dsa.org, www.tomboytools.com, www.shurepets.com, and www.warmspirit.org.

tinctive characteristics, so promotion strategy tends to be complex—complex enough to be a source of SCA.

The design and execution of a promotional strategy depends on the other three major variables: price, product, and distribution. After consideration of these three, the venture designs a promotional strategy that is either a pull system or a push system. A **pull system** draws customers into contact with the firm and its products. For example, when

FIGURE 6.3   Channels of Distribution for Industrial Markets

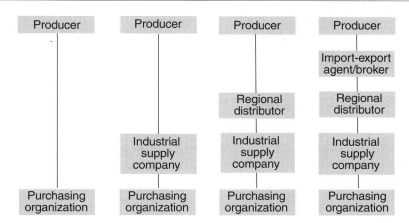

a celebrity endorses a product on television, the advertisement is attempting to pull the viewer into contact with the retailer. A **push system** puts the product in front of the customer, making distribution aggressive and purchase convenient. Coca Cola uses one of the most effective push strategies in the world. Intensive vending penetration and bottler incentives (distribution activity) place most of the world's population within easy reach of a Coke.

Advertising is "any paid form of nonpersonal presentation and promotion of ideas, goods, or services by an identified sponsor." According to Kelsey Group research, small companies spend about $30 billion annually.[22] Ads can be placed on television or radio, in newspapers and magazines, in the Yellow Pages, and so on. Consumers report that when they look for information on local businesses, 61 percent turn to the Yellow Pages first.[23] Infomercials (see Street Story 6.1), outdoor displays, direct mail, and novelties are also forms of advertising. Because of the variety and complexity of forms and messages, it is difficult to generalize about advertising, but the following attributes are notable:

1. Advertising is a public presentation. Its high visibility confers credibility on the product or service. Because it is delivered anonymously to a large group, it implies a certain standardization of the product.
2. An advertising message can be repeated over and over to impress itself on the consciousness and subconsciousness of the buyer. If one brand's advertising is more embedded in the buyer's consciousness (top-of-the-mind recall), that product has a clear advantage, especially for convenience goods and impulse shopping.
3. Advertising can not only inform and persuade but can also associate a product or service with other favorable images in the buyer's mind. Through copy, artwork, sound, and music, advertising can influence the buyer's mood.
4. The impersonality of advertising enables consumers to turn away, switch off, or ignore the venture's messages without cost or obligation.[24]

The major variables in designing an ad campaign are budget, message content, context, choice of media, timing, and means of evaluating effectiveness. New ventures usually operate on limited budgets and target niches that can be defined geographically or by consumer interest. This lends itself to the use of local media or special-interest publications. Yellow Pages and Yellow Book advertising and well designed and targeted direct mail are often very effective.

Personal selling uses oral presentation, supplemented by other media (overhead slides, computer graphics), in formal settings or informal conversations to persuade prospective buyers.[25] The decision to use personal selling has as much to do with management and human resources as with marketing, because a company needs a sales force in order to implement it, though sometimes personal selling is done by manufacturer's reps or by the entrepreneurs themselves.

The decisions involved in a sales force strategy are complex and, like advertising, are contingent on product, distribution, and pricing. The major elements are sales force size, sales force territory, recruitment and selection of salespersons, training, incentive schemes and promotions, and supervision and evaluation. Because of this large number of variables, particularly the social complexity of the relationship between salespeople and their customers, an effective sales force can be a source of SCA. "Selling" is only one of the tasks of salespersons.

The basic design of the sales job depends on the rest of the marketing mix and the characteristics of the market, but the job includes as many as five additional functions:

1. **Prospecting** is the search for additional customers. Sometimes these have been identified by the company. These are known as "leads." At other times the salesperson makes "cold calls," contacting individuals and companies with no previously expressed interest in the product or service. This is a difficult task because the salespeople meet with high levels of rejection, so cold calls can seem like wasted effort. Now a new set of software tools and online services are available to minimize both rejection and inefficiencies. These social network services are more effective than cold calling. According to Anu Shukla of RubiconSoft Inc., "You know who you are calling and who they report to, to make the call more fruitful."[26] Some of these popular sales lead generation tools are:
   - CI Radar (http://www.ciradar.com)
   - Hoover's Inc. (http://www.hoovers.com)
   - iProfile LLC (http://www.iporfile.net)
   - Jigsaw Data Corp. (http://www.jigsaw.com)
   - LinkedIn Ltd. (http://www.linkedin.com)
   - Spoke Software Inc. (http://www.spoke.com)
   - Zoom Information Inc. (http://www.zoominfo.com)

2. **Communicating** information to existing buyers or potential buyers is a basic sales function. The subject of the communication may be price, product characteristics, new product developments, or competing product comparisons.

3. **Servicing** customers includes consulting them about any problems, providing technical or managerial assistance, and helping with financing or delivery schedules.

4. **Information collection** and gathering competitive intelligence are also parts of a

salesperson's job. Salespersons are sources of market research, passing on customer satisfaction information and data on how customers are receiving the competition.

5. **Allocating** scarce products when supply cannot keep up with demand is one of the more difficult tasks of sales.

Personal selling is most appropriate in a relationship that goes beyond mere transaction. In such cases the relationship between salesperson and buyer is based on the seller's recognition, knowledge, and understanding of the buyer's problems and needs, and on the ability to solve those problems and meet those needs. It is one of the most expensive ways to reach customers, but because of the intensity of the salesperson's involvement, it can be the most appropriate and most effective method.

Publicity is "non-personal stimulation of demand for a product, service, or business unit by planting commercially significant news about it in a published medium or obtaining favorable presentation of it on radio, television, or stage that is not paid for by the sponsor." By definition publicity is free, but many firms allocate significant budgets to **public relations**, activities that create a favorable image in the mind of the public. These reputation-building tactics, if successful, can be a source of SCA. For example, many recent start-ups emphasize their "all natural" products and environmentally conscious images. These companies are selling an altruistic image.

There are three distinctive attributes of publicity:

1. **Legitimacy.** Many people believe almost everything they see or read, especially when it comes from a previously credible source such as the local newspaper or television station. Sometimes the media report publicity releases as if they were the product of objective news reporting.
2. **Surprise.** A publicity release can catch buyers when they are not expecting a sales pitch, packaging the information as news, not sales. Buyers who are not receptive to advertisements or sales calls may listen intently to "news."
3. **Attractiveness.** Like advertising, publicity aims to get the buyer's attention. Its context can bring other favorable images to customers' minds.

Because the media are inundated with requests for publicity, it is not always easy for a particular firm to stand out. A well-organized event reported in a well-written press release can help. Good organizational citizenship is also a good source of publicity: Participation in civic events and clubs, professional and trade associations, philanthropic activities, and well-regarded political causes are examples.

Sales promotions are "those marketing activities, other than personal selling, advertising, and publicity, that stimulate customer purchasing and dealer effectiveness." Examples include point-of-purchase displays, trade shows and exhibitions, promotional events, and other nonroutine selling efforts. Sales promotions offer inducements to buyers—reduced prices for items through coupons, volume discounts, or attractive financing terms. By effectively reducing the price, the seller increases the value to the buyer.

Such promotions are also attention-getters. They are often presented in urgent terms—"a once-in-a-lifetime opportunity"—suggesting that quick action is needed. This appeals to the economy-minded, low-income, non-brand-loyal shopper. One of the most important sales promotions for a new venture is the Grand Opening Sale. This represents a one-of-a-kind opportunity for the firm, and can be followed by anniversary sales. For retail and service businesses, media coverage like remote broadcasts are popular. Introductory price discounts can attract customers, and repeat business can be generated by offering coupons or discounts for future dates.

Other sales promotions are event-based. Mother's Day, Father's Day, and Christmas are ideal occasions for promotional campaigns. Some promotions are contests, like the cloying magazine sweepstakes that offer $10,000,000 for returning the direct-mail response cards. These have become so ubiquitous that entrepreneurial opportunities exist for individuals who are particularly creative or experienced in these activities and can come up with fresh angles. Telemarketing firms, contest promoters and organizers, mailing list sellers, and event consultant firms have sprung up to serve these needs.

The frequent and persistent use of sales promotions, however, can have negative effects on a business. For instance, promotional discounts are expected by consumers, who will not purchase unless a discount is offered. Auto manufacturers repeated factory-rebate sales promotions so many times that car shoppers, expecting the promotion, would not buy until the rebate was offered. Faced with slowing sales, manufacturers then offered the rebates, thus reinforcing this wait-and-see behavior. Another risk inherent in sales promotion is the demeaning of the product or service's image. The promotions may be seen to imply that without them, people would not be interested in buying the product. With buyers concerned about brand image and status, frequent and carelessly used promotions raise doubts.

The configuration of the major promotional tools—advertising, personal selling, publicity, and sales promotion—is called the **promotional mix**. The appropriate mix depends on the marketing environment and other marketing dimensions. The entrepreneur should remember that no element of the promotional mix should be neglected.

MARKETING ON THE INTERNET

An Internet strategy is integral to almost every venture's marketing. What form will it take? In Chapter 4 we provided a framework for Internet strategy using the Information Rules. This section presents the Internet as a desirable marketing tool:

- It lowers the cost of communication between people and companies and within networks.
- It lowers the cost of transactions between people and companies and within networks.
- It lowers the cost of searching for information.
- It lowers the cost of monitoring transactions and search processes.

The Internet has expanded traditional **word-of-mouth** promotion into **viral marketing**. Word-of-mouth promotion encouraged people to tell their friends about a product or service. Viral marketing encourages people to link their friends to a Web site or search for a product using one of the ubiquitous search engines. For example, Adi Sideman accidentally stumbled on viral marketing's power when he forwarded a link to some friends and found that people he had never met emailed him back. His business, Oddcast Inc., uses this technique to promote its interactive technology products. In fact, at a recent meeting of the Word-of-Mouth Marketing Association, the message was clear—Don't advertise!—because viral marketing is the only way to go![27]

Marketing on the Internet removes any geographic disadvantages a venture may face. Street Story 6.3 shows how firms can use the Internet to go global, sometimes without even intending to.

The Net is especially revolutionary in information-intensive industries where the costs noted in the list above constitute the greatest percentage of overall cost.[28] For example:

- **Financial services.** Most financial service transactions can be delivered electronically (indeed electronic fund transfers have been in use for years). In many ways, financial services are ideal for the Internet because there is no physical product; however, banks have not yet perfected the process of online bill paying.
- **Entertainment.** Much entertainment can be digitized, which is ideal for the Internet because one customer's consumption of entertainment services does not affect another customer's ability to consume the same services. There may be a limited number of seats in a theater, but a virtually unlimited number of viewers can watch a performance on the Web. Again, no ideal business model has yet been constructed.
- **Health care.** Delivery of actual health-care services requires person-to-person contact, but much of the business end concerns patient information and insurance application and payment. The Internet can handle these, but who benefits? Service providers? Insurers? Patients?
- **Education.** Online learning is a growing business. Many students already use the Internet to apply for admission, register for classes, check grades, and pay tuition and fees. This is clearly beneficial, but observers worry that online classes will depersonalize the educational experience.
- **Government.** Taxes can be filed online now, and constituents can contact their representatives and other officeholders by email, but there are broader possibilities. With the right infrastructure and education, government could deliver a great deal of information about services, laws, taxes, and defense, and citizens could offer feedback and input. To create a really effective network, however, would cost the government billions, and there are other priorities that may take precedence.

The Internet affects some industries only incrementally, generally those industries that involve the creation, transformation, and transportation of an irreducible physical entity. Whether this is an immutable reality remains to be seen. Somewhere out there an e-entrepreneur may be devising ways to adapt such products to the world of Internet business.

- **Retailing.** Elaborate Web sites and graphics received much attention during the original e-tailing revolution, but success was actually determined by back-of-the-house logistics and the ability to "move the boxes around" more efficiently than the competition. Even in a high-tech world, the basics remain important.
- **Manufacturing.** There is no substitute for high-quality manufactured goods. Intranet communications and supply chain management are important areas for electronic commerce, but the key is still the high-quality product, not the Web site.

Global Glitches

On its Web site, BlueTie, Inc., calls itself a "global company," but it wasn't always. The venture (www.bluetie.com) was founded in 1999 as a provider of email and collaboration software to Internet service providers and small businesses, and its target market was limited to subscribers in the United States.

Then in 2001 the company began to attract customers from Canada and Australia. "Because we're Web based, people started signing up from anywhere in the world," says David Koretz, BlueTie founder and CEO. These new customers turned out to be a mixed blessing. For example, BlueTie originally developed its software to display times and dates for the 4 different time zones in the continental United States. Translating that capability to 24 time zones around the globe cost BlueTie, according to Koretz, something "in the six figures". Format was a problem, too. Americans read and write *July 10, 2007* as *7/10/07*, but in other countries that would be read as October 7, 2007. Also, some countries use a 24-hour clock by which U.S. 3:00 p.m. is 1500 hours. At the same time that BlueTie was dealing with these issues, customer support to countries in different time zones became problematic for the 20-person staff.

Less-sophisticated vendors have encountered other problems in going global. Kevin Reichard, a futon store owner in Wisconsin (contact at kevinreichard@earthlink.net), was excited about a $1500 order from Israel before he realized that shipping would cost as much as the merchandise. The manager of the Space Store (www.thespacestore.com) in Texas shipped 30 polo shirts with NASA logos to Romania before discovering that the customer's credit card was a dud. Now Space Store founder Dayna Steele Justiz no longer accepts credit card orders from certain countries—including Russia, Croatia, Bosnia, and Indonesia—and requires additional verification for card purchases from some other countries.

"There are hidden costs in acquiring customers overseas if you haven't done your homework," notes Scott Southall, the managing director of a Virginia small-business consulting firm. Still, many entrepreneurs find that the global marketplace enabled by e-commerce justifies the extra effort and expense.

SOURCE: Adapted from "Internet Turns Firms into Overseas Businesses," *The Wall Street Journal*, December 16, 2003: B4. Retrieved from the Web. www.bluetie.com; and www.thespacestore.com.

- **Travel.** Transactions such as ordering tickets or making reservations are good applications of Internet technology, as are search processes that enable customers to check out hotels, resorts, and conference sites. Eventually, someone has to get on an airplane or into a car (or on a train, boat, or tram). What happens in the real world is the biggest factor in customer satisfaction.
- **Power.** Energy exchange and management are good applications. The Energy Exchange (http://www.enex.com/), for example, provides a complete toolkit marketing energy-related products and services, including financing. At the end of the day, however, the generation of power is a physical process and there is now insufficient generating and transmission capacity—not a problem the Web can solve.

To summarize: The Internet entrepreneur needs to scan and analyze both industries and geographic regions to spot opportunities. Some opportunities depend on local knowledge of language and customs and on a network of contacts. Other opportunities may be constrained by industry and economic forces the entrepreneur cannot change.

The Resource-Based View and the Internet

The resource-based view is a theory of what makes new ventures successful. It states that companies with rare, valuable, hard-to-copy, and nonsubstitutable resources and capabilities will achieve a sustainable competitive advantage. Resources and capabilities may be physical, reputational, organizational, financial, intellectual, and/or technological (**P-R-O-F-I-T**). Let's review these and see how they influence the success or failure of marketing efforts by Web-based businesses, e-commerce, and e-entrepreneurs.

Physical Resources. In Chapter 2 we concluded that physical resources, things you can buy in a market, seldom play a decisive role in the success of an e-business. Nevertheless, a couple of physical elements do seem to matter—logistical capabilities and "bricks and mortar" presence.

Web-based businesses must often be able to gather the components of an order, box them, ship them, and deliver them. The **inbound logistics** of taking orders are usually handled through the Web site. The **outbound logistics** require the correct product to be sent to the correct customer by the promised delivery date. This has sometimes proved problematic for e-entrepreneurs. Many e-tailers, failing to anticipate the problems of outbound logistics, did not invest in the necessary physical resources (warehouse capacity and product-picking and moving equipment) to fill the orders they received. Others tried subcontracting order fulfillment to independent businesses like Fingerhut Business Services, Inc. But fulfillment companies have problems of their own: they operate on narrow margins and face tough competition. An e-tailer has to make a choice: [29]

1. Build a fulfillment capability. On the positive side, this gives the entrepreneur a greater degree of control; full knowledge of the fulfillment system's capacities, timing, and quirks; and a fulfillment agency that handles only the entrepreneur's products. On the negative side, a state-of-the-art warehouse costs around $20 million.
2. Hire someone else to handle fulfillment. On the positive side, this eliminates the need for a huge capital investment and opens the doors for money-saving volume discounts that can be negotiated with companies like Federal Express. On the negative side, during busy merchandising times, the contractor may not be able to handle the order volume, which means that the quality of delivery service is uneven.

The other question is: Should an e-business also have a "bricks and mortar" presence? Many companies began as stores or manufacturing plants and then added a Web-based capability. These companies can relate to suppliers and customers at one or more locations. Businesses that begin on the Web can be at a disadvantage. Such new ventures must decide whether a physical presence is critical to their success—and they have very little information to go on in making that decision.

Reputational Resources. A good reputation is critical to e-commerce success. First, it gives a business positive word-of-mouth and viral marketing reports. Second, it creates trust. This is vital because of the remoteness of much e-commerce. Consider eBay's rating system for buyers and sellers. At each transaction, buyers and sellers rate their satisfaction with the other party, and this rating is made available to other buyers and sellers. Trust and security are the keys, but how important is branding? It is important, but it is not enough to overcome the other things that can go wrong in e-commerce.

Organizational Resources. Customers are looking increasingly for timely responses, informative content, clear displays, and if needed, real people to talk to. It takes coordination, commitment, and leadership to meet these needs. Internal communication capabilities are essential. A *critical organizational capability* is a knack for using and organizing information to create and capture value, exploiting what the Web does best and most cheaply: collect, arrange, manipulate, and send massive amounts of data. Value creation and capture on the Web require low-friction distribution, interconnectivity, and viral marketing—all organizational elements.

Financial resources—cash, credit, and access to capital markets—have not proven critical in e-commerce success or failure. Individuals and institutions may invest billions of dollars, but the amount invested appears unrelated to survival in the marketplace. In fact, it has sometimes seemed that an entrepreneur needed only the idea for an Internet company to generate start-up money. At other times, it seemed that even more money was needed.

For example, while an undergraduate at Yale, Michael Stern and his colleagues raised $1 million in commitments to invest in campus Internet ventures. He was a campus venture capitalist who burned through most of that money with no winners in his portfolio. "I wish we had had more money to put into companies. Ultimately, we would have done really well." Or would he ultimately have lost even more?

"Maybe we were fools to give them the money in the first place. They were bright kids with ideas. We were all suffering from a mania," lamented Ben Karp of Dagim Consulting, who was the Yale students' original backer.[30]

Of course, financial management skills and financial resources endowment are two different things. With financial skills e-entrepreneurs can competently handle endowments and manage the "burn rate." Good financial management can enable a company that is short on cash to survive long enough to turn a profit or find a partner or investor, while poor financial management can destroy any company, no matter how large its cash pool.

Intellectual resources and **intellectual property** are the intangible property, knowledge, and skills of an e-venture. As valuable sources of sustainable competitive advantage, they are well worth defending. The leading online auction site, eBay, aggressively defends what it considers its intellectual property. Smaller auction sites have challenged eBay, but in doing so some have violated the agreement between eBay and its buyers and sellers. Auctiva, for example, links eBay's postings with its own listings, and eBay has gone to court to stop the practice.[31]

Other e-commerce businesses also protect their intellectual property. For example, Amazon.com has patented its "one-click" buying process. Priceline.com has the rights to the "name your own price" business model. There is even a Web site that will help investors use statistical tools to value intellectual property.[32]

One interesting sidelight of the dot-com bubble's deflation is the devaluing of the intellectual property of defunct dot-coms. For example, eToys, which is in bankruptcy, has not been able to sell the proprietary management system it developed to guarantee on-time delivery of over a million Christmas toys. The company spent $80 million on a system that now appears to be worthless. Firms with billion-dollar valuations that spent millions on Super Bowl advertising have been unable to recoup that investment. When Petsmart.com bought Pets.com, it promptly junked the corporate icon sock puppet. The brands, trademarks, and associations of failed dot-coms and other failed businesses are not of much value to their former owners.

Technological resources are valuable in the start-up and running of e-commerce businesses. Indeed, many of these firms rely for their very existence on technological capabilities. Electronic entrepreneurs who promise cutting-edge technology but cannot deliver are doomed. One major technological advantage is a grasp of the effectiveness of the firm's Web presence. This is especially true in terms of Web advertising which is increasingly expensive for start-ups, but also hard to evaluate. Street Story 6.4 describes some new tools for e-entrepreneurs seeking to make their advertising more effective.

To review: The Internet companies' obsession with financing and the amounts that they raised were examples of misplaced energy in the long term. Financial *endowments* are not critical resources, but financial *management* is. Organizational capabilities, intellectual property, and up-to-the-minute technology are also sources of sustainable competitive advantage.

What Have We Learned?

When the Internet bubble burst at the beginning of the twenty-first century, a *Fortune* cover story discussed the lessons learned by e-entrepreneurs in their dot-com business ventures.[33] These are lessons that nascent Internet entrepreneurs can use to avoid the errors of the Web pioneers:

1. *The Internet doesn't change everything.* It is not a disruptive technology, but one that complements existing businesses.
2. *If it doesn't make sense, it doesn't make cents.* Businesses need to make profits. The search for successful business models continues.
3. *Time favors existing businesses.* Many of the early start-ups taught important lessons in what not to do. Dot-com investors paid for everyone's education.
4. *Making money is harder than it looks.* Even B2B, which looked as if it couldn't miss, now has the same gloomy outlook as B2C ventures. It's just not easy.
5. *There is no such thing as "Internet time."* Things can change fast, and the Internet helped us understand that, but too often "Internet time" meant leaping before looking and was used to justify an absence of discipline.
6. *"Branding" is not a strategy.* Historically, most companies have grown organically and developed a brand by producing high-quality products or services over time. Instant branding—skipping the many years of fine service—doesn't work.
7. *Entrepreneurship cannot be systematized.* "The idea that you can institutionalize the creation of entrepreneurial ventures is bunk," according to venture capitalist Bill Unger. True. You must not follow the rules. You must break them.
8. *Investors are not your customers.* The ability to attract investors is different from the

STREET STORY 6.4

Checking the Clicks

When is a loss leader a real loser?

Retailers often promote one product at a special low price in order to lure customers to their stores or Web sites. The merchant decides, in effect, to make less profit on this "loss leader" in exchange for increasing customer traffic and upping the sales of other items.

Online and catalog jewelry retailer Limoges Jewelry (www.limoges.com), however, found that the $19 cubic zirconia ring they had listed on comparison Web sites like Shopzilla.com and Shopping.com was not producing the expected results. Shoppers were clicking on the ring at the comparison sites, costing Limoges 40 to 65 cents per click, but few were actually buying the ring. So the retailer enlisted the services of Mercent Corp. to help spend its marketing dollars more effectively.

Mercent, an e-commerce service and technology provider founded by former employees of Amazon.com, sells software that allows retailers to analyze every item listed on a comparison site, track the number of clicks on that item, and tally the total dollar value and cost of any sales. This information lets e-tailers eliminate items or sites that aren't cost effective. After using the Mercent software for four months, Limoges found that its costs were down 10 percent and its sales for the same period were up 47 percent.

Analysts estimate that marketing costs for Web-based retailers have risen from 6 percent of sales in 2004 to 18 percent of sales in 2005. Vehicles like search ads (the advertising that appears when a shopper types a request into a search engine) appeal to some e-tailers, but many find them expensive and have difficulty measuring their effectiveness. Scott Buck, owner of a new Web site for high-end garden tools and accessories, cancelled his search advertising because of the strain on his advertising budget and the uncertainty of its results; he said it gave him a "Russian roulette mentality." Switching to product placement on comparison-shopping sites increased his sales (www.gardenhardware.com) but the fees ate up half of his proceeds. "You really do need pieces of technology to make [marketing] profitable," Buck observes.

Even experienced Internet advertisers use diagnostic tools to guide their advertising. Companies actually bid to place the small text ads that appear on search engine Web sites, and auction site eBay is one of the highest bidders. The firm now uses a software system called Triton to determine how much they should bid for various search keywords. A specific search term like "Nike Shoe" may be a good buy because fewer e-tailers will bid for that keyword than for the generic term "shoes." Plus, clicks on a specific term are more likely to generate sales. The company reports that the average cost per keyword bid has dropped 74 percent, a significant savings for a company with a portfolio of more than 15 million terms.

SOURCE: Adapted from Mylene Mangalindan, "Ad Vantage," *The Wall Street Journal*, June 19, 2006. Retrieved from the Web June 19, 2006. http://online.wsj.com/article_print/SB115048693396382653.html, www.limoges.com, www.mercent.com, and www.gardenhardware.com.

ability to serve customers and make a profit. If you can't do the latter, the former will disappear.

9. *The Internet* does *change everything (despite #1).* It does not change the old industrial order, but it does change the way that order does business.

10. *The Internet changes your job.* Information is everywhere, and if you can't do your job better because of it, watch out.

11. *The distinction between Internet and non-Internet companies is fading.* Clicks and bricks is a model that works. Every business can use B2B networks to improve purchasing.

12. *The real wealth creation is yet to come.* We were all too eager. These things take time. The dot-com revolution may be dead, but the Internet revolution is just beginning.

Recent Trends

A number of recent trends in Internet marketing need to be considered by e-entrepreneurs. These may or may not turn out to be long-term factors, but they represent the direction that Internet marketing is moving now:

- Securing a recognizable Web domain name is getting harder. Companies have bought unused domain names and are waiting to sell or auction them to entrepreneurs, thus cashing in on their ability to spot a good name or a coming trend.[34]
- Securing a good domain name helps a business, but more and more consumers are becoming very security conscious and may resent any monitoring of their Web use. As a result, they block cookies from being deposited on their computers, which means that the consumer's computer will not recognize that it has previously been to a Web site. This makes it very hard to generate repeat business.[35]
- Popular search terms are becoming increasingly expensive. When a new venture uses a search engine like Google or Yahoo to present itself, it pays for the privilege. Words are like real estate—there is a limited supply. Each time a customer searches by using a key word, the advertising that appears has to be paid for; displaying the ad is no guarantee that the customer will "click through" to the company's Web site.[36]
- Even if customers click through, there is the danger of "click fraud." Because the company is charged by the search engine firm every time a customer clicks through, false clicks are expensive. Cyberthieves have generated "bots" that make fraudulent clicks. These bots are software programs that are difficult to detect and easy to change. Using bogus clicks, dishonest Web-site owners can boost their own revenue and drain a company's ad budget.[37]
- Recommending one product when another is being searched for is a great marketing tool, but this cross-selling can annoy and offend customers. When Walmart.com customers requested the Martin Luther King and Jack Johnson biographies on DVD, they were offered "Planet of the Apes" and "Ace Ventura: Pet Detective." Complaints came flooding in, and Wal-Mart removed its cross-selling recommendation system. The lesson here is to thoroughly test these systems.[38]
- Affiliate programs enable entrepreneurs to piggyback on more popular but related Web sites, but it takes real skill. Myriad sellers are out there attempting the same thing. How does an entrepreneur stand out? An estimated 25,000 affiliates make a living wage, but the vast majority earn almost nothing. Entrepreneurs may want to use an affiliate network (like Peformics or LinkShare) to increase their odds and

monitor success. If an affiliate program is not working, they can replace it with something else.[39]

- Blogs are Web logs and blogging is a national passion. Can bloggers make money at it? Jason Calcacanis founded Weblogs, Inc., a network of blog sites that was purchased by AOL in 2005. He suggests that the primary way to make money is to "curate" blogs by grouping them and then marketing the group. An entrepreneur can, of course, go solo, but the economics are not attractive. Giving ad space to a company like Google AdSense can generate $3-10 per 1000 views. A blogger who generates a heroic 500,000 pages a month can make between $1,500 and $5,000 per month and might want to keep the day job. B2B is more lucrative because revenue per 1000 page views is higher, but massive volume is still the only way to make money.[40]
- TV advertisers have always purchased time on shows based on when they are aired and who the audience is, and now Web sites are following suit. Ads can be bought and sold according to the time they will appear on the site. Prices vary depending on peak viewing hours and viewer demographics. If the entrepreneur sells globally, rates may be lower when the domestic market is sleeping and the international target is awake.[41]

SALES FORECASTING

Sales forecasting is the intersection of marketing research and marketing effort. It is the first step in determining whether a new venture will be profitable. The sales forecast is the logical *last* stage of the marketing plan, and analysis is the *first* stage of financial analysis.

Two broad techniques are used to forecast sales: data-based methods and judgmental methods. Examples of data-based methods are correlation analysis, multiple regression, time-series analysis, and the use of econometric models. Examples of judgmental methods are: sales force estimates, executive consensus, historical analogies, and "intention-to-buy" surveys. Most of these methods are appropriate for large firms in well-established markets. The best predictor of next year's sales is almost always last year's sales, but just knowing this does not help the new venture.

Market Potential/Sales Requirements (MP/SR)

This method[42] combines elements of both judgmental and data-based techniques and provides important insights into the financial consequences of the forecast. This approach uses two different perspectives for the venture—likely sales and needed sales. The market-potential technique is a "top-down" method that looks at the big picture. The sales-requirements technique is a "bottom-up" exercise that starts with the firm's costs and expenses and then determines the sales needed for profitability. These techniques can be conducted simultaneously. Figure 6.4 diagrams the two techniques.

In the figure, market potential appears on the left side. This is the total number of people, demand transactions, or dollar volume in the product/service category. Trade association data, census statistics, and chamber of commerce reports are all good sources of this information.

Next the entrepreneur defines the target or market segment to narrow the total potential. Defining the trade area and venture reach will focus more tightly. In the case of an emergency medical center, for example, how far will people drive to the EMC? Where is the next closest competitor located? Finally, the forecaster estimates market potential in terms of the number of customers, purchase frequency, and expenditure per transaction. A little arithmetic—customers x frequency x expenditure per transaction—will reveal the estimated market potential.

FIGURE 6.4   Market-Potential/Sales-Requirement Approach

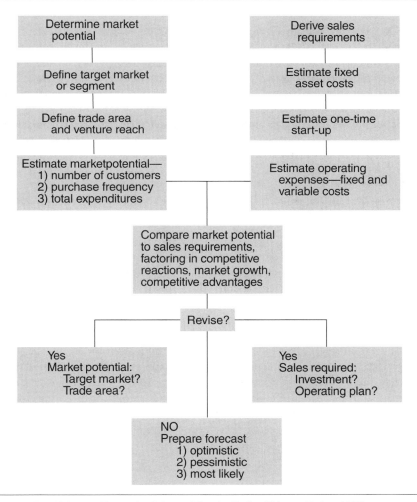

SOURCE: Adapted from K. Marino, *Forecasting Sales and Planning Profits* (Chicago: Probus, 1984).

The right side of Figure 6.4 shows the sales requirements, that is, the estimated volume of sales needed to cover costs and provide a return to the entrepreneur and investors. The entrepreneur estimates the fixed asset (capital) costs of operation and the one-time start-up costs, then forecasts fixed and variable operating expenses. This should include the required return on investment for the financiers. The conclusion of this exercise is a break-even analysis that illustrates sales levels and margin requirements to make the company financially sustainable.

After completing these analyses, the forecaster factors in competitive reactions, market growth, cost increases, and competitive strategies, and compares the market potential with the sales requirements. Dividing the market potential figure by the sales requirement number gives the estimate of market share. What are the possible outcomes?

- If the venture requires a very large percentage of the market, the business model needs to be revised by reviewing the target market and the trading area.
- If the venture cannot break even without capturing a heroic share of the market, revise the operating plan: Can expenses be curtailed? Can margins be raised? Is the company operating at the best scale—should it be bigger to generate economies of scale or smaller to save operating expenses?
- If the market potential is a relatively large factor of the sales requirements, the business is financially feasible, and it is time to prepare forecasts for most likely, optimistic, and pessimistic scenarios.

Other Techniques

Entrepreneurs can use other techniques to forecast sales. In fact, it's a good idea to use multiple methods. Most are beyond the scope of this book, but a few possibilities include:

1. Find benchmarks for similar start-ups in similar circumstances. What are typical estimates for sales per square foot, sales per employee, sales for invested capital?
2. Estimate product/service capacity. At a given scale, how many units can be produced? How many customers served? What percent of capacity is the venture likely to use? Optimistic case? Pessimistic? Levels of capacity utilization can provide a sales forecast.
3. Build the forecast from the ground up. If there are four products and three related services, estimate each separately. How many sales are likely per day? How many customers per hour? What is the yield from sales calls? Internet hits? Aggregate from the specifics and adjust for reality (such as diminishing marginal returns).
4. Prepare multiple forecasts under different scenarios. Consult other industry participants about these forecasts, then adjust them as needed.

SUMMARY

Marketing and entrepreneurship relate in a number of ways, and marketing is critical to the success of any new venture. It is important for a new venture to take a total marketing approach to the customer and design a business system that can ultimately provide a high level of customer satisfaction.

Market research need not be extensive, sophisticated, or expensive, but it must determine what customer satisfaction means for the target market. It also provides other critical information about the target market, information that can help with marketing strategies and activities. These activities—pricing, product/service decisions, promotion, and distribution—form the core of the venture's marketing effort. Because these activities are complex and the relationships between them ambiguous, the marketing strategy, organization, and resources can be a source of sustainable competitive advantage.

The Internet offers a variety of opportunities for a new venture and its marketing activities. Innovative marketing techniques such as affiliate programs and search engines enable a venture to reach previously unapproachable customers, but there are difficulties: weak security and consumer concerns about fraud.

Sales forecasting is the bridge between the venture's marketing decisions and its financial decisions and outcomes. The sales forecast represents the "top line" of the venture's financial picture. Both bottom-up and top-down approaches to sales forecasting should be employed to ascertain the venture's prospects for success or failure.

KEY TERMS

Break-even volume
Channels
Clayton Act
Concept testing
Confirmation stage
Cost-based pricing
Customer satisfaction
Decision stage
Diffusion process
Discriminatory pricing
Distribution
Government market
Halo effect
Implementation stage
Inbound logistics
Infomercial
Institutional market
Knowledge stage
Market research
Market segmentation
Market testing
Marketing strategy
Outbound logistics

Persuasion stage
Price
Primary data
Product
Product consistency
Product depth
Product mix
Product testing
Product width
Production orientation
Promotional mix
Public relations
Pull system
Push system
Robinson-Patman Act
Sales orientation
Secondary sources
Sherman Act
Social entrepreneurship
Target profit pricing
Truth in Lending Act
Viral marketing
Word of mouth

DISCUSSION QUESTIONS

1. In what two ways does marketing contribute to new venture success?
2. Discuss the marketing-entrepreneurship interface. What are the points of similarity, the differences, and the potential pitfalls?
3. What questions can market research help the entrepreneur answer?
4. What are the steps in conducting market research?
5. Compare and contrast concept testing, product testing, and market testing.
6. Describe the diffusion process. How can the entrepreneur use this knowledge to design effective marketing campaigns?
7. What are the bases for market segmentation?
8. What are the pluses and minuses of the following pricing tactics?
   a. Skimming the market
   b. Exploiting the experience curve
   c. Meeting the market
   d. Achieving maximum penetration
   e. Establishing pre-emptive pricing
9. How do product and service configurations influence marketing strategy?
10. What are the key elements of promotional activities?
11. What are the essential characteristics of Internet marketing from the Resource-Based View framework?
12. What lessons have we learned about marketing on the Internet?
13. Describe the MP/SR forecasting method. What are its costs and benefits?

EXERCISES

1. Develop a list of questions regarding the marketing of your product or service as described in your business plan. Prioritize the questions from "required to know" to "would be nice to know." Using the six-step process described in the chapter, conduct market research to answer these questions, starting with your highest priority and working down.
2. Develop the marketing section for your business plan. Discuss customer orientation, marketing strategy, and tactical decisions such as price, product/service offered, distribution, and promotion.
3. Develop an Internet marketing strategy for your proposed business. Do a mock-up of a Web page and links.
4. Develop a sales forecast for your business covering three scenarios: pessimistic, optimistic, and most likely. What level of sales is required to break even? Review your marketing strategy for consistency with your sales forecast.

DISCUSSION CASE

Making a Difference on the Web

It's the kind of store the Internet was supposed to eliminate—a ma-and-pa brick-and-mortar retailer selling low-margin cameras, computers, VCRs, and music equipment.

But 35-year-old J & R Electronics (www.jr.com) has managed to survive the onslaught of the Web by finding ways to transfer the experience customers have when they visit its Manhattan store in person to the experience customers have when they shop online.

For example, J & R posts a picture of its physical store on its home page, and includes different exterior and interior shots of the store on other main pages. It links photos from store-sponsored events, like appearances by athletes or rock stars, to its Web site, and does occasional live Web casts. "We tried to re-create the feel of our brick-and-mortar store," says co-owner, Rachel Friedman about the things the company has done to make virtual shopping more concrete.

While other Internet stores have a toll-free phone number for customer assistance, J & R lists over a dozen of its salespeople by name on its Web site, and provides each salesperson's direct extension, days and hours each is in the store, area of expertise, number of years on staff, along with a brief biography. This practice allows cyber-customers to request advice from a knowledgable salesperson when they make their toll-free call.

Before it started selling on the Web, J & R had an established reputation in the New York metropolitan area, and had been a catalog merchant for some time. But the firm had trouble differentiating itself from all the other Internet electronics retailers. To attract more customers, J & R became one of the first companies to partner with Amazon.com, Inc.

When customers shop for an MP3 player or a computer-printer on www.Amazon.com, J & R is one of the merchants they can select to fulfill their order (the company is identified on Amazon as J & R Music and Computer World Storefront). "The Amazon partnership is a great way for J & R to build brand identity and brand familiarity," observes Donna Hoffman, codirector of the Sloan Center for Internet Retailing at Vanderbilt University. "People think 'If it's on Amazon, it must be good'." Amazon collects and posts customer feedback about J & R, which helps build the store's Web reputation. The company's arrangement with Amazon also allowed J & R to rely on Amazon's Web page and order-processing technology, rather than struggle with its own in-house software when it first started selling on the Web. "Especially for smaller companies, it's better to license technology that's already been tested, and to let someone else put a billion dollars behind it," says Drew Sharma, managing director of an Internet marketing agency called Mindfire Interactive. "If you can stand on the shoulders of giants, then why not?" The electronics company also has deals with other Web sites in which it pays a commission on sales that affiliate sites refer.

J & R still sends out catalogs and does a lot of newspaper advertising in the New York City area, which was its primary marketing target before it began selling on the Internet. Vanderbilt's Donna Hoffman notes that many customers shop both online and offline for a product before making a purchase, and suggests the links between these two methods will be the "next frontier" of Internet growth.

SOURCE: Adapted from Andrew Blackman, "A Strong Net Game," *The Wall Street Journal*, February 25, 2004. Retrieved from the Web February 22, 2006. http://online.wsj.com/article_print?SB109837534277251934.html, www.jr.com and www.amazon.com.

Case Questions

1. What was the primary challenge for J & R's Web-based marketing strategy?
2. How did it meet this challenge?
3. What challenges does J & R face for the future?
4. How is J & R meeting this future challenge? What additional recommendations do you have?

APPENDIX

Case Study: EMC Site Expansion

Dr. Anthony Petrillo founded the Emergency Medical Center as a free-standing emergency center (FEC). The FEC concept, relatively new at the time, is a cross between a physician's office and a hospital emergency room. The typical FEC offers extended hours (8 a.m. to 11 p.m.), has lab and X-ray facilities, and will treat any non-life-threatening trauma or medical problem on a no-appointment basis.

The EMC opened in 1982 and grew rapidly its first year. Then Dr. Petrillo learned that a good location had become available in another section of the same city, so he considered opening a second center. Based on a study of traffic patterns and population density in the area, proximity to area hospitals, and the sales experience gained in EMC #1, sales forecasts for EMC #2 were prepared. After leasehold improvements, equipment costs, and operating expenses were estimated, opening EMC #2 looked like a good idea.

The facility opened with a fanfare of advertising and press releases. Sales immediately exceeded the first month's forecast, but after several months of continued growth, sales (that is, patient visits) leveled off below the break-even point. Forecasted growth did not occur, and cumulative operating losses mounted. Remedial action was taken in the form of intensified advertising. A personal selling program was directed at area businesses whose personnel might need treatment for work-related injuries. Neither effort stimulated the necessary growth. Less than a year after its opening, EMC #2 closed and consolidated its operations with the original—and still successful—EMC #1.

Convinced, in spite of EMC #2's failure, that multiple sites could offer important economic advantages in terms of advertising, purchasing, and management, Dr. Petrillo continued to seek feasible locations for a second EMC facility. Eventually, a real estate developer contacted him about a site being developed in a small town about 22 miles outside the city where EMC #1 was located. The development was situated at the intersection of an interstate and a state highway in a town with one general hospital, a student health service on a university campus, and about 18 private physicians' offices. The developer and several of his financial backers believed that the community's growth warranted additional medical facilities. They were planning to construct single-story building on the site and were willing to finish a 2,000-square-foot section to Dr.

SOURCE: This case was written by Kenneth E. Marino for his book *Forecasting Sales and Planning Profits* (Chicago: Probus 1984). It is reprinted here with the generous permission of its author.

Petrillo's specifications and to give him a three-year lease with renewal options at an annual rental of $7.50/sq. ft.

Dr. Petrillo requested a sales forecast for the venture and agreed, if the forecast was positive, to negotiate with a bank and an equipment leasing firm.

Step 1. Determining Market Potential

The **target market** for ambulatory health care includes the entire population. Everyone is subject to minor injuries such as cuts, sprains, or fractures, and to minor illnesses such as colds and flu. Industry consultants and the National Association of Free-Standing Emergency Centers (NAFEC), the industry trade association, define the target market more narrowly: They view the primary targets for EMC services as families with young children, working women, and individuals with no regular physician. These refinements can be helpful in designing and placing advertising, but it is wise to consider the total population as the target market.

In this small community the proposed site can be reached in 10 to 12 minutes driving time from anywhere within the city limits, so the whole vicinity is in the **trade area**. The site is on the opposite side of town from the general hospital, so almost no one would have to drive past a competitor to reach the EMC.

Market potential can be derived from census studies. The 1980 census reports that the city and its immediate residential areas are home to 27,531 people, 8,924 households. The town has grown substantially in the 1970s—the number of housing units grew 55 percent. This is a plus because people relocating to the area are less likely to have established physician relationships. Based on discussions with city officials and members of the Chamber of Commerce, growth is believed to have continued, though at a slower rate, during the 1980s.

In terms of market potential, NAFEC estimates that the average individual experiences one or two incidents of minor trauma or illness per year. Assumed rates of population growth reveal estimated total market potential (patient visits).

Total patient visits for 1984 are estimated to be between 28,649 and 64,414, but such a broad interval may not be useful. The middle column of Exhibit 6.A.1 represents a more reasonable interval. Based on an average incident rate of 1.5 per person per year, total market potential would be estimated at 43,000 to 48,000 patient visits per year (Exhibit 6.A.2).

Step 2. Deriving Sales Requirements

Fixed asset requirements for the site consist entirely of equipment costs, both medical equipment and standard office furniture and equipment. New construction will eliminate the need for leasehold improvements such as plumbing modifications and remodeling.

Local medical supply and office supply dealers familiar with the used equipment markets in the area are the sources of price estimates in Exhibits 6.A.3 and 6.A.4. Price estimates reflect a mix of new and used equipment. Total fixed asset requirements are estimated at $64,500.

The **nonrecurring start-up expenses** involved in opening an EMC facility are substantial, as noted in Exhibit 6.A.5. The figures were compiled from Dr. Petrillo's experience with EMC #1.

Estimated operating expenses (Exhibit 6.A.6) for an EMC are predominantly fixed, meaning that sales activity has little or no effect on these expenses. Salaries for physicians and nonphysicians (e.g., receptionist, X-ray technician) must be paid regardless of patient visits, as must rent, utilities, and security services.

Monthly expenses for malpractice insurance are billed on a per-patient basis (approximately $0.70/patient). Supply expenses also vary with the volume of patient visits and are, therefore, a

Exhibit 6.A.1: Population Projections Based on Various Growth Rates

	Numbers of People		
	Annual Growth=1% (pessimistic)	Annual Growth=2.5% (likely)	Annual Growth=4% (optimistic)
1980	27531	27531	27531
1981	27806	28219	28632
1982	28084	28925	29778
1983	28365	29648	30969
1984	28649	30389	32207
1985	28935	31149	33496
1986	29225	31928	34835
1987	29517	32726	36229

EXHIBIT 6.A.2: Logan Total Patient Visits Based on Growth and Annual Incident Assumptions

	Total 1984 Patient Visits		
PopulationGrowth	Average Visits Per Person–Year		
	1	1.5	2.0
1.0% (pessimistic)	28,649	42,973	57,298
2.5% (likely)	30,389	45,584	60,778
4.0% (optimistic)	32,207	48,310	64,414

EXHIBIT 6.A.3: Medical Equipment Requirements for Proposed EMC Facility ($51,000)

THLaboratory ($6,000)
TBRefrigerator
Microscope
Blood gas analyzer
Autoclave
Stain tray
Urinometer
Centrifuge
Microcrit reader
Incubator

X-ray ($30,000)
X-ray system
Processor
Float table
Bucky table

General ($15,000)
Trauma stretchers
I.V. stands
EKG
Oxygen
Suction unit
Suture sets
Ambu bag
Wheelchair
Crash cart
Head lamp
Surgical table
Cast cutter
Defibrillator
Woods lamp
Laryngoscope

EXHIBIT 6.A.4: Office Furniture and Equipment Requirements for Proposed EMC Facility ($13,500)

Office Equipment ($3,500)
File cabinets
Typewriter
Calculators
Desktop copier

Miscellaneous Furniture ($4,000)
Break room furniture
Microwave/compact refrigerator
Waiting room furniture
Window treatments/fixtures

Exterior Signs ($6,000)
Free-standing illuminated sign
Building-mounted signs

EXHIBIT 6.A.5: Nonrecurring Start-Up Expenses

Direct mail advertising (pre-opening)	$ 2,300
Legal/accounting	300
Rent/utilities deposits	4,226
Prepaid malpractice insurance	3,100
Housekeeping/security services	500
Initial medical supplies inventory	3,803
Nonphysician salaries (preopening)	1,500
Sundry	2,000
	$17,729

EXHIBIT 6. A.6. Estimated Monthly Operating Expenses for Proposed EMC Facility

Fixed Expenses	
Advertising	$ 2,000
Rent/utilities[a]	1,500

(continued in following column)

(continued from preceding column)

Legal/accounting	200
Manager salary	1,600
Nonphysician salaries	8,050[b]
Physician salaries	10,000
Postage	200
Security/housekeeping	250
Telephone	250
Depreciation[c]	1,075
Sundry	1,225
Total Fixed Expenses	$ 26,350

Variable Expenses	
Malpractice Insurance	$ .70 per patient
Supplies[d]	4.67 per patient
Total Variable Expense	$5.37 per patient

a. $1,250/month rent + $250/month average utility expense
b. Estimated at 115 percent of salaries to cover FUTA, FICA, Workmen's' compensation, and state unemployment.
c. Fixed assets of $64,000—straight line, 5-year life (60 months)
d. Estimated from experience at EMC #1

variable expense. The supply cost per patient has historically averaged $4.67. The total variable cost per patient is then estimated at $5.37.

Deriving sales budgets requires developing a sales budget that can support the business. The break-even sales budget is easily calculated from Exhibit A.6. Estimated monthly fixed operating expenses are $26,350. The average patient charge at the original EMC is $37.00. Assuming the same average charge at the new facility, each patient visit contributes $31.63 ($37 minus $5.37 variable expenses). Therefore, the facility breaks even at 833 patient visits per month ($26,350/$31.63), as seen in Exhibit 6.A.7.

This break-even computation ignores financing costs. Whatever its sources of capital, a venture must earn a rate of return. If Dr. Petrillo personally supplies all the capital, he will need a return on his investment. If the capital is borrowed from a commercial bank or an equipment leasing firm, revenues must cover interest expenses.

The required capital investment includes medical equipment ($51,000—Exhibit 6.A.3), office equipment ($13,500—Exhibit 6.A.4), and nonrecurring start-up expenses ($17,729—Exhibit 6.A.5). In addition, operating expenses in the early months will exceed revenue. To establish a reserve of three months of operating expenses will require approximately $80,000 in additional capital. Total start-up capital is, therefore, estimated at $162,229. At a cost of capital of 18 percent, the facility must generate an additional $29,201 per year ($2,433 per month) to cover its capital costs.

Adding these considerations raises the number of patient visits to 910 a month to break even ($26,350 + $2,333)/$31.63).

Step 3. Judging Likely Market Share

Of the estimated 43,000 to 48,000 annual patient visits in the trade area, EMC must capture 23 to 25 percent to break even and cover its capital costs, and that means substantial market penetration.

EXHIBIT 6.A.7   Break-Even Analysis for EMC Facility at Logan

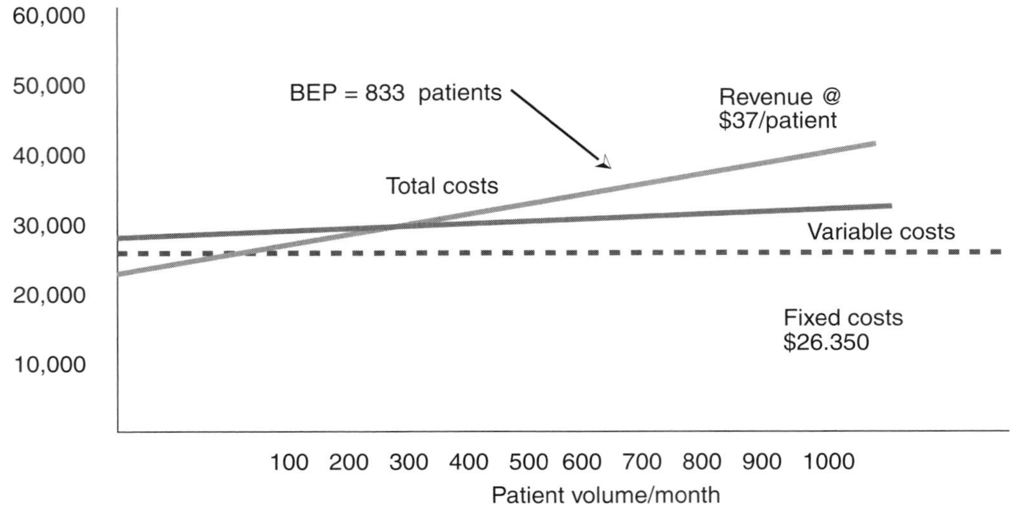

The question facing Dr. Petrillo is: How likely is EMC to achieve such a market share? This is, of course, a complicated question involving both patient reactions and competitive reactions.

The **competitive advantages** of an EMC are convenient service without an appointment and without the usual lengthy wait at a hospital emergency room. Lower overhead costs make EMCs less expensive than hospitals for virtually any procedure. The combination of economy and convenience created a favorable response in the original EMC trade area and in other cities where EMC-type facilities have been opened.

In terms of competition, this trade area is served by a general hospital with an emergency department and eighteen physicians' offices. Several of the physicians are specialists such as obstetricians and are therefore not direct competitors of EMC. Still, 11 of the physicians are either general or family practitioners, so their behavior will affect the EMC sales forecast. Faced with the EMC's entry into the market, how are these competitors likely to react?

In rapidly growing markets, the entry of a new competitor does not usually evoke a strong response. The new entrant's success is less a function of taking market share from existing competitors than of meeting a growing demand. Yet only under the most optimistic growth projections is it conceivable that EMC could prosper by serving only new residents in the community. EMC must attract patients from existing medical facilities. Physicians in private practice with established patient relationships are not likely to be severely injured by the entrance of EMC. However, they generally view advertising and aggressive promotion as inappropriate, so they are likely to "bad-mouth" EMC and raise questions regarding the quality of care it offers. The hospital stands to lose the most and can be expected to react more strongly. Hospitals have recently adopted advertising programs, modified fee schedules for minor emergencies, and changed staffing and triage activities to reduce waiting time in emergency departments. In short, the hospital is in a position to negate the EMC's competitive advantages.

In summary, EMC has very real competitive advantages over traditional medical care providers, but the hospital may react strongly to EMC's entrance into the market. Faced with its own high fixed costs, the hospital will be forced to react if EMC approaches a 25 percent market share. For that reason, Dr. Petrillo believes that the operating plan must be changed in order to lower the break-even market share. Estimated operating expenses—which Dr. Petrillo believes are accurate—cannot be reduced. This focuses attention on the fee structure. By raising the fees on certain routine procedures and lab tests, revenue per patient visit can be raised to $41, which lowers the break-even market share to about 20 percent, an achievable level of penetration.

Step 4. Preparing the Forecasts

Dr. Petrillo and the EMC staff prepared three separate sales forecasts based on different assumptions of growth in the average number of patients treated per day. An optimistic forecast assumed that the EMC would reach the break-even number in 6 months, a pessimistic forecast projected 14 months, and a conservative but likely forecast estimated 10 months.

Exhibit 6.A.8 is the optimistic forecast. Once sales revenue is estimated, projecting the estimated cash flow is a fairly straightforward task. Pessimistic and likely forecasts were also prepared. By adding interest expenses into fixed costs, the same series of forecasts could be developed reflecting the costs of capital performance level as opposed to the break-even performance level. Dr. Petrillo commented:

> The forecasting activity has provided us with a couple of advantages. First, it forced us to look hard at the market, the competition, and our costs structure. It also forced us to modify our fee schedule in light of those conditions. Second, it gave us a rational basis for negotiating a line of credit with our bankers. They can see where the money is to go, how much we will need, and at what rate we will be able to pay the line down. Finally, the forecasts set some standards by which we can evaluate our progress. If we're behind our forecast come month 4 or 5, I know I'll have to get our credit line raised, and intensify our promotion efforts. It also gives my managers some targets to shoot for regarding expenses.

EXHIBIT 6.A.8: Emergency Medical Center Sales and Cash Flow Forecast Optimistic Case: Break Even at Month 6

	Month 1	Month 2	Month 3	Month 4	Month 5	Month 6
Average patients/day	5	10	15	19	23	27
Revenue ($41/pt visit)	$ 6,150	$ 12,300	$ 18,450	$ 23,370	$ 28,290	$ 33,210
Cash received[a]	3,998	9,840	15,683	20,726	25,399	30,074
Cash expenses[b]	26,081	16,886	27,692	28,335	28,980	29,625
Cash gain (loss)	(22,083)	(17,046)	(12,009)	(7,609)	(3,581)	449
Cumulative cash position	(22,083)	(39,129)	(51,138)	(62,328)	(62,328)	(61,878)

	Month 7	Month 8	Month 9	Month 10	Month 11	Month 12
Average patients/day	30	33	35	37	38	39
Revenue ($41/pt visit)	$ 36,900	$ 40,590	$ 43,050	$ 45,510	$ 46,740	$ 47,970
Cash received[a]	33,948	37,453	40,159	42,497	44,034	45,203
Cash expenses[b]	30,108	30,591	30,913	31,236	31,397	31,558
Cash gain (Loss)	3,840	6,862	9,245	11,261	12,637	13,645
Cumulative cash position	(58,038)	(51,176)	(41,931)	(30,670)	(18,033)	(4,388)

a. Estimated as: 65 percent revenue received on 0-31 days, 35 percent revenue received in 31-61 days, 5 percent allowance for bad debts and adjustment.
b. Cash expenses = (Fixed expenses - Depreciation + $6.47 (Patient visits) = 25275 + 5.37 per patient.

7 Foundations of New Venture Finance

Anything for a friend, for a fee.
—Fred Allen, 1940s radio personality

OUTLINE

Determining Financial Needs
    Working Capital and Cash Flow
      Management
    Across the Venture's Life Cycle
Sources of Financing
    Equity-Based Financing
    Debt-Based Financing
New Venture Valuation
    Asset-Based Valuations
    Earnings-Based Valuations
    Discounted Cash Flow Models

Legal and Tax Issues
    Legal Forms of Organization in the
      United States
    Private Placements under U.S.
      Securities Laws
U.S. Bankruptcy Laws
Summary

LEARNING OBJECTIVES

After reading this chapter, you will understand

- how to determine the amount of *capital* a new venture will need.
- the types of *financing* available to the entrepreneur.
- the elements involved in *cash and working capital management.*
- the pros and cons of different forms of financing—*debt versus equity.*
- the major concerns of bankers and how *to approach them for a loan.*
- the methods for *valuing* a new venture.
- the *legal forms of organizing* a business in the United States.
- the special conditions involving *taxes, private placements,* and *bankruptcy.*

PERSONAL PROFILE 7

As Good As It Gets

In 1989 Annie Withey used what she calls guerilla marketing to get boxes of her new natural macaroni and cheese product on supermarket shelves. She and her husband traveled to folk concerts, ski lodges, store parking lots, and "wherever there were crowds, handing it out, and saying, 'If you like this product, tell your stores,'" Withey relates. The strategy worked. Today Annie's Homegrown, Inc., has nationwide distribution of more than 80 natural and organic products, including boxed and canned pasta meals, boxed pasta, graham cookies, cheese crackers, and boxed vegetarian Indian entrees. The company is the second largest brand of macaroni and cheese in the United States.

But Annie's Homegrown (www.annies.com) sees itself as much more than a mac 'n' cheese distributor. These entrepreneurs describe their venture as "a good company with good people that makes good food and does good stuff." That good stuff includes scholarships for college students majoring in environmental studies, donations of their crackers and grahams to organizations that benefit education and the environment, and involvement in other programs promoting organic agriculture, recycling and earth-friendly programs. This company has a social mission in addition to its profit motive.

Today, with over $34 million in annual sales, Annie's Homegrown is long past the point where handing out samples in parking lots is effective. But in 1998 when the company needed money to develop new products and extend its market penetration, particularly into mainstream supermarkets, it got investments from two small natural food companies, Consorzio and Fantastic Foods. Then in 2002 Annie's made a deal for a cash infusion of $20 million from Solera Capital LLC, a $250-million private equity firm run by

women. "We had to look at the financial ramifications, but for a company like Annie's, a cultural connection was critical," Annie's Homegrown CEO John Foraker says about the partnership.

Molly Ashby, CEO of Solera Capital explains, "Solera's investment in Annie's is consistent with our strategy of investing in category-leading brands in markets poised for significant growth. Natural and organic food is one of these markets."

Natural and organic goods are big business today. According to the Organic Trade Association (OTA), organic food sales topped $13.8 billion in 2005, a more than 16 percent increase over the previous year. Many consumers are concerned about the harmful effects of food additives, pesticides, and genetically engineered ingredients in foods, and are willing to pay more for high quality, healthy foods. "We appeal to a consumer who is less price-sensitive and willing to pay more to feel good about what they eat," says CEO Foraker. While organic foods currently represent only 2.5 percent of total food sales, experts predict sales will continue to grow at 20 percent per year, with natural food sales growing at 8–10 percent. Conventional food sales are expected to languish at 1–2 percent.

In 2004 Solera purchased Annie's other investors, Consorzio and Fantastic Foods, and combined them with Annie's Homegrown to create Homegrown Naturals, Inc. Annie Withey now serves as "inspirational president" of that company.

SOURCE: Adapted from Tara Siegel Bernard, "Willing a Place on Grocery Store Shelves," *The Wall Street Journal,* March 29, 2005: B3; "Solera Capital Acquires Majority Interest in Annie's Homegrown, Inc.," from Homegrown Natural Foods, Inc., August 13, 2002. Retrieved from the Web July 21, 2006. http://www.www.csrwire.com/article.cgi/1251.html and www.ota.com.

As the quote that opens this chapter indicates, it is now time to talk about money. New venture financing deals with obtaining the money the entrepreneur will need to start the business, but it is more than that. It is also about creating value and wealth, allocating that value among the investors and founders, and determining financial risk for the business. This chapter and the next will explore and elaborate on these matters.

The quote has particular meaning for the financing of new businesses. It means that the parties to a transaction, especially an investment, should not take unfair advantage of each other; there should be consideration (a fee) for rights and privileges granted. Also, no matter how close it is, the personal relationship of the investors and founders takes a back seat to the overriding priority—the successful launch of the new venture. The quote is also a reminder that money is important, and its importance must never be minimized. People can and will talk about their devotion to the business, their concern for the products and customers, their involvement with the "cause." These may be very real, valid, intrinsic motivations, but dismissing the importance of money and the creation and protection of wealth is naive and dangerous. People are concerned with financial issues, and some people care passionately about money. If the entrepreneur is such a person, he or she is not alone.

Financing is one of the major hurdles for an entrepreneur. A Dun and Bradstreet survey reported that financial trouble (e.g., excessive debt and operating expenses, insufficient working capital) is responsible for 38.4 percent of business failures. Add an additional 7.1 percent for inexperience (including financial inexperience), and it is clear that almost half of all ventures fail because of poor financial management.[1]

We begin the chapter by discussing the nature of financial resources. Next, we turn to the crucial issue of determining how much money the new venture will need at the outset. The initial financing requirement depends largely on the enterprise's cash and working capital management. We summarize these elements.

The chapter continues with a discussion of the sources and types of debt and equity financing and concludes by presenting a number of models for valuing new firms. The valuation process is crucial to both investors and entrepreneurs as a vehicle for determining how the profits of the firm will be allocated. It sets the stage for financial negotiation and deal structures.

A word of caution before beginning our financial analysis: Modern financial theory was developed in an attempt to understand the performance of the stock market, specifically the New York Stock Exchange. Many of the concepts and tools taught as foundations of financial theory are best employed when analyzing companies represented on major stock, bond, commodities, currency, options, and futures exchanges. Because the underlying theory and techniques were not built with entrepreneurs in mind, applying them to new venture financing may not be appropriate. Entrepreneurs and the individuals and firms who invest in new ventures must, therefore, be cautious in applying financial theory developed for stocks and bonds, a theory that may send incorrect signals for firm value and risk.[2]

DETERMINING FINANCIAL NEEDS

We now turn to the financial aspects of starting a new business. Financing alone seldom provides a sustainable competitive advantage, but most ventures need financial resources to get started—even those that are primarily bootstrapped or start without business plans. (To obtain optimal benefit from the material in the rest of this chapter and in Chapter 8, students should be familiar with basic accounting and financial statements. In addition to the many excellent textbooks on the subject, online sites can help jump-start an understanding or refresh rusty skills. See the endnote for references).[3]

The table below shows the top reasons that most businesses fail, based on a sample compiled by consultants who help troubled companies.

The primary reason for failure is too much debt. A firm with debt must make regular interest payments and must be prepared to repay principle either bundled with the interest payments or all at the end. Failure to make the payments is one cause of business bankruptcy. This flaw can be embedded in the business at the outset if a poor financial structure leaves the founder with too much debt relative to equity; it can also arise later when the business has to borrow to cover expenses; or it can occur as a function of inexperienced management or poor planning. Whatever the origin of this problem, the lesson is that poor financial management, poor planning, and inexperienced management all contribute to business failure.

How much money does the entrepreneur need? One of the most important and difficult tasks for start-up entrepreneurs is determining how much money they need. If they raise too little money by underestimating the business's needs, the firm will be **undercapitalized**. Undercapitalized businesses may run out of cash, borrowing capacity, and the ability to raise additional equity just when a new infusion of funds could get it over some hurdle. If that happens, the firm goes out of business. It is often said that for new firms "cash is king," because when an entrepreneur runs out of cash, the king is dead—and the business is often lost.

It may seem impossible to many entrepreneurs, but being **overcapitalized** is a significant danger as well. An overcapitalized firm raises too much money and sends the wrong signals to the stakeholders. For example, thinking that business is better than it actually is, employees may press for wage and benefit increases. Customers may take longer to pay knowing that the new venture has plenty of cash on hand, and suppliers could demand more immediate payment. If the cash is spent on frivolous perquisites or office decor, investors will lose confidence. Also, excess cash earns no or very low returns, which diminishes total return to investors.

TABLE 7.1 Causes of Business Failure

Reasons for Failure	Percentage of Businesses
Too much debt	28%
Inadequate leadership	17
Poor planning	14
Failure to change	11
Inexperienced management	9
Not enough revenue	8
Other	13

SOURCE: *BusinessWeek*, August 25, 2003: 14. Data from Buccino & Associates, Seton Hall University.

Overspending on non-critical areas is especially troublesome because of the signals it sends to employees and vendors. Entrepreneurs sometimes waste money on things they do not need: expensive art for the offices, luxury vehicles for themselves and other executives, first class travel, and retreats at fancy resorts. This says, in effect, "We have plenty of money." Customers will realize that they are paying for all of this through higher prices—-if there are any customers left.

There must be a balance between raising so little money that the firm is unprepared for a down cycle and raising so much that investors, suppliers, customers, and employees are adversely affected. Sometimes entrepreneurs raise too much money by selling or encumbering too much of the business. The wise ones who resist the temptation to continue selling more equity than necessary can sell additional equity sometime down the road when it is both really needed and much more valuable. This **phased financing** is discussed in the next chapter.

Working Capital and Cash Flow Management

The entrepreneur must focus on working capital and cash flow from the beginning of the financing process. Accounting profits do not pay the bills; only positive cash flow keeps a business solvent. It is estimated that over 60 percent of the average entrepreneur's total financing requirements are invested in working capital, 25 percent in accounts receivable alone.[4] Sufficient working capital is vital to the survival of the enterprise, and well-managed working capital and cash flow can significantly increase the profitability of the new venture.

Working Capital Concepts. Working capital has two components. **Permanent working capital** is the amount needed to produce goods and services at the lowest point of demand.[5] Its form may change over the course of the cash flow cycle (for example, from inventory to receivables to cash), but permanent working capital never leaves the business. As the firm grows and sales increase, the amount of permanent working capital increases as well. **Temporary working capital** is the amount needed to meet seasonal or cyclical demand. It is not a permanent part of the firm's financial structure. When these peak periods end, temporary working capital is returned to its source.

A firm with too little permanent working capital runs the risk of losing business. If inventory levels are kept too low, stockouts occur and sales are lost. If the venture's accounts receivable policy is too restrictive, good customers who prefer to pay on credit may turn away. If cash balances are too low, the venture runs the risk of being unable to procure supplies or pay its bills. This diminishes its ability to take advantage of short-term purchasing opportunities and damages its reputation.

An enterprise with too much working capital for a given level of sales is inefficient. Stock and inventory levels will be much higher than necessary to fulfill customer orders. Receivables will represent too large a percentage of sales, and the venture will be providing inexpensive financing for its customers. Cash levels will be more than needed for transactions and precautionary uses. Each dollar invested in working capital must return at least the internal rate of return of the rest of the venture's investment to be "pulling its weight" in the financial structure.

The Cash Flow Cycle. The **cash flow cycle** and its importance to the profitability of the firm are illustrated in Figure 7.1.

The top portion of the figure shows the **production cycle** from material ordering to finished goods inventory. It also shows the cash cycle from payment for raw materials through the collection of receivables. The bottom half of Figure 7.1 illustrates the corresponding sources and uses of cash and the formula for calculating the length of the cash cycle.

Segment 1 represents the time period of accounts payable for raw material. The gap

FIGURE 7.1   The Cash Flow Cycle

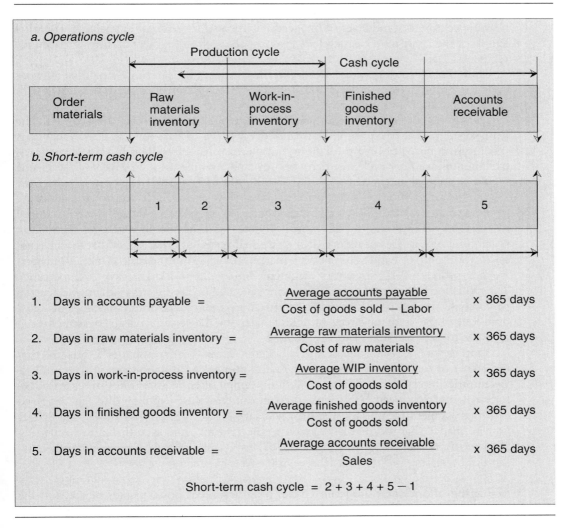

between the time the entrepreneur receives supplies and the time she has to pay for these supplies (account payable) is a source of financing. Here it reflects the time from the receiving of materials until approximately half of them are used. Segment 2 represents the time period in which raw materials remain in inventory. This segment corresponds to the time from their entry into raw materials inventory to the time they enter work-in-process (WIP) inventory. WIP inventory represents the partially completed product that is still being worked on.

Segment 3 represents the time when WIP goods are counted in inventory. They are now finished goods. Segment 4 represents the time goods spend in finished goods inventory, and segment 5 represents the time that goods that have been sold are in receivables.

Figure 7.1 gives the formulas for calculating each of these ratios. The figures used to calculate these ratios are found on the pro forma balance sheet and income statement for the new venture or on the actual financial statements for the existing business. The total length of the short-term cash cycle is given by the sum of segments 2 through 5 minus segment 1.

Figure 7.2 illustrates the significance of these ratios. The top shows a typical cash flow cycle for a sample firm, and the bottom half depicts a "controlled" cash flow cycle with much of the slack and waste removed.[6]

The top half of Figure 7.2 indicates an uncontrolled cash flow cycle of 120 days. The firm, through debt or equity, must finance every dollar of sales for 120 days. What does this mean in terms of firm profitability? If the firm has $5 million in sales before controlling the cash flow cycle, the net working capital required for 120 days of sales value would be approximately $1,643,836 [($5,000,000/365) x 120]. The bottom half of the figure shows a hypothetical "controlled" cash flow cycle. After control measures are introduced and the cash flow cycle is tightened, the required working capital is reduced to $616,438 [($5,000,000/365) x 45]. Where has the difference of over $1 million gone? Typically, it goes to reduce debt or to be invested in other assets that can increase sales. For example, Figure 7.2 shows a marked reduction in the time it takes to process work-in-process (WIP) inventory (segment 3: 40 - 25 = 15, 15/45 = 37.5 percent). The reduction in working capital requirements could be used to retire the debt incurred to purchase the machine that made manufacturing so much more efficient. This illustrates one of the dramatic effects of tightly managing the venture's cash: Investments can be made to pay for themselves very rapidly.

Another way of seeing the dramatic benefits of cash management is to imagine that the owner of this hypothetical company needs to raise $1 million from venture capitalists in order to expand the business. Venture capital often requires rates of return of between 30 and 50 percent. If the entrepreneur can raise the $1 million through improved cash management techniques, the firm will save between $300,000 and $500,000 per year in finance charges (dividends) paid to the venture capitalists. If the firm is netting 10 percent on sales of $5 million ($500,000), the cash control measures are the equivalent of increasing profitability between 60 and 100 percent.

Managing and Controlling the Cycle. Many excellent books detail the steps in the process of managing and controlling the cash flow cycle, so we will only summarize

FIGURE 7.2   Controlling the Cash Flow Cycle

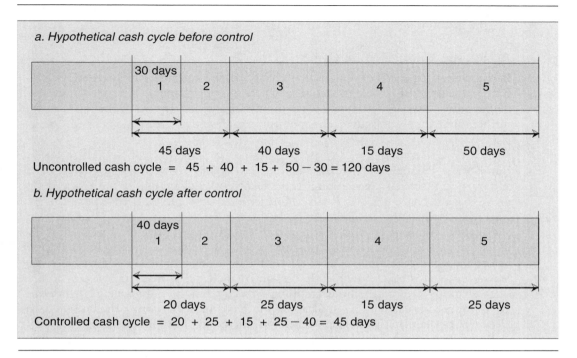

a. Hypothetical cash cycle before control

| | 30 days | | | | |
| | 1 | 2 | 3 | 4 | 5 |

45 days   40 days   15 days   50 days

Uncontrolled cash cycle = 45 + 40 + 15 + 50 − 30 = 120 days

b. Hypothetical cash cycle after control

| | 40 days | | | | |
| | 1 | 2 | 3 | 4 | 5 |

20 days   25 days   15 days   25 days

Controlled cash cycle = 20 + 25 + 15 + 25 − 40 = 45 days

them briefly.[7] As the examples presented indicate, however, this is a subject that requires close attention and tenacious control by top management.

- Accounts payable: The longer the average accounts payable for the firm, the shorter the cash flow cycle. Therefore, entrepreneurs should develop relationships with vendors that enable them to extend payments when needed. Accounts payable are part of the permanent working capital of the venture and should be managed, not reduced.
- Raw materials inventory: This is part of the permanent working capital of the firm, but the entrepreneur must keep it as low as possible. Just-in-time delivery systems, a good management information system, and accurate sales forecasting can help keep raw materials inventory down.
- Work-in-process inventory: The Japanese *kanban* system of tagging and monitoring all work in process will help, as will the introduction of efficient operations, worker training and incentives, and capital investment.
- Finished goods inventory: The managers should seek to develop relationships with buyers that will enable them to deliver as soon as the product is made. If buyers can warehouse the goods, they can take delivery and thereby finance the seller's finished goods inventory. Accurate sales forecasts and management information systems are vital.

- Accounts receivable: The key variables are payment terms, credit limits, and collection programs. Customers should be encouraged to pay their bills on time and, if the discount does not hurt margins, given incentives to pay early.

Across the Venture's Life Cycle

Will the financial needs of the business change as different challenges arise? Of course. Entrepreneurs must be able to recognize where their firm is in its life cycle and to specify the precise uses of these funds. By demonstrating to investors how the financing will further the venture's objectives, entrepreneurs significantly increase their chances of closing the deal.

Early-Stage Financing. There are two categories of early-stage financing: seed capital and start-up financing. **Seed capital** is the relatively small amount of money needed to prove that the concept is viable and to finance feasibility studies. Seed capital usually is used to investigate the possibilities of a business, not to start it. **Start-up capital** actually gets the company organized and operational. It puts in place the basics of product development and the initial marketing effort. Start-up capital is invested in the business before any significant commercial sales; it is the financing required to achieve these sales. Start-up capital is also known as **first-stage financing**. For many businesses, all first-stage financing comes from **bootstrapping**—that is from the entrepreneurs themselves.[8] We introduced bootstrapping in Chapter 5 in the context of writing the business plan. Now we consider it in its financial sense—raising capital from personal sources.

Bootstrapping requires a sure sense of the entrepreneurs' risk/reward preferences. By using only their own money, they can keep more of the rewards of a successful venture, but they also put more of their own assets at risk. These assets frequently include their homes, their bank accounts, and any retirement accounts. Bootstrappers frequently max out their credit cards.

It is a mistake to bootstrap without considering the next stage. Entrepreneurs can get a business started by bootstrapping, but when it starts to grow they need outside capital. The amount provided by bootstrapping is almost always limited by the modest net wealth cap of the entrepreneurs and the team. Recycling these dollars as revenue starts to come in can grow the business only so far. Conserving cash is critical. Investing these recycled dollars in fixed assets actually shrinks the potential size of the business since these funds cannot be used for working capital. Eventually a growing business needs to move to the next stage.

Expansion or Development Financing. There are three sequential categories of financing in the expansion stage. **Second-stage financing** is the initial working capital that supports the first commercial sales. It goes to support receivables, inventory, cash on hand, supplies, and expenses. At this point, the firm may not have a positive cash flow. **Third-stage financing** is used to ramp up volumes to the break-even and positive-cash-flow levels. It is expansion financing. Throughout the third stage, the business is still private, a majority of the equity still in the hands of the founding top management team. **Fourth-stage financing**, sometimes known as **mezzanine financing** (because it is between the cheap balcony seats and the more expensive but desirable orchestra seats), is the bridge between the venture as a private firm and the prospect of a public offering. Mezzanine financing enables successful privately held companies to obtain financing without going public, letting the owners keep control. Mezzanine financing is a blend of traditional debt financing and equity financing, with some benefits of both. It has the no-collateral benefit of equity and the control benefit of debt. But in order to make it profitable for the lender, interest rates are frequently much higher than market, in the 20-30 percent range. Lenders also have the right to convert the debt to equity if there is a default.[9]

Most new ventures remain small, never going beyond first- and second-stage financing, and almost none will qualify for venture capital funds. Yet at the initiation of a venture, at its creation, all is still possible even if the odds are long.

Street Story 7.1 offers additional practical advice on cash management. It may be more an art than a science and it requires attention and creativity.

SOURCES OF FINANCING

The initial financial objective of the entrepreneur is to obtain start-up capital at the lowest possible cost. Cost is measured in two ways. One is the return that will have to be paid to the investor. The other is the transaction costs involved in securing, monitoring, and accounting for the investment. An investor may be satisfied with what appears to be a below-market return on investment, but if the cost of the transaction is significantly high, the entrepreneur may wish to consider an alternative source of financing. The long-term sources of cash for the venture are debt and equity. In most cases, equity financing is more expensive than debt financing: Pure debt has a fixed return over a period of time, but the potential gains for investors in equity financing are unlimited. Figure 7.3 illustrates how these two sources combine to build the liquidity level of the firm.

The types and sources of financing available to the new venture depend primarily on four factors:

1. The stage of business development: The more developed the business, the higher the chances and the better the terms for outside financing.
2. The type of business and its potential for growth and profitability: High-potential firms can attract financing at better terms.
3. The type of asset being financed: The more stable the market for the asset, the easier it is to sell and to recover costs for the lender in case of default.
4. The specific condition of the financial environment within the economy: When the economy is good, lenders and investors are looking to put their cash to work at a profit. When the economy is poor, investors are conservative and reluctant to invest.

The elements of the overall financial environment that should be considered are:

- Interest rates and their term structure: Under the normal rate structure, short-term rates are lower than long-term rates, so the borrower generally prefers a series of short-term loans. When this is reversed, the borrower prefers a long-term, fixed-rate

STREET STORY 7.1

Ten Top Cash Rules

Commercial Credit Co. LLC is the kind of success story every entrepreneur dreams about. Started with just $5,000 in personal savings, the high-tech equipment-leasing company in Irvine, California, posted $11 million in sales after just two years. But even success can produce headaches. Founding partner Jeff Chasin says, "After about a year, we realized that there were all kinds of questions we were too busy running the business to ever answer. Like, what should we do with whatever excess cash we might have, *and* how would we really ever know for certain if we did have any excess cash?"

For all the entrepreneurs struggling with cash management questions, here are ten tried and tested rules.

Rule 1: Never run out of cash. *Inc.* magazine columnist and author of this list Philip Campbell says, "Running out of cash is the definition of failure in business."

Rule 2: Cash is king. The Roman poet Ovid wrote, "How little you know about the age you live in if you think that honey is sweeter than cash in hand."

Rule 3: Know the cash balance right now. As sixteenth-century British philosopher Sir Francis Bacon advised, "Knowledge is power."

Rule 4: Do today's work today. Stephen King, president of financial accounting firm Virtual Growth, points out, "There are often ways for companies to improve their cash position simply by making certain that their billing, collections, and payables systems are operating as efficiently as possible."

Rule 5: Either you do the work or have someone else do it. Donna McGovern, accountant and owner of Ideal Business Solutions, reports that Commercial Credit hired her

as its part-time Chief Financial Officer to make sure they had not "miscalculated their cash needs or owed a client money but had their funds tied up in the wrong kind of investments."

Rule 6: Don't manage from the bank balance. Once again from Sir Francis Bacon: "Money is a good servant but a bad master."

Rule 7: Know what you expect the cash balance to be six months from now. Donna McGovern advises, "Once you understand your cash position, you can often follow a course similar to the one families follow when building up an emergency nest egg: Put small amounts of extra cash in a money-market account" or another investment vehicle where it can earn interest and still be accessible.

Rule 8: Cash flow problems don't "just happen." Did anyone believe former Enron Chairman and CEO Kenneth Lay when he said, "I mean, the company had a lot of strong cash flows when it went into bankruptcy"?

Rule 9: You absolutely, positively *must* have cash flow projections. Not having them is like driving a car with your eyes closed.

Rule 10: Eliminate your cash flow worries so you are free to do what you do best: Take care of customers and make more money. As stock market analyst Robert Prechter, Jr. says, "There's nothing wrong with cash—It gives you time to think."

SOURCE: Adapted from Philip Campbell, "The Ten Absolutely Must-Follow Cash Flow Rules," *Inc.*, September 2004. Retrieved from the Web July 8, 2006. http://www.inc.com/resources/finance/articles/20040901/10rules.html; Jill Andresky Fraser, "The Art of Cash Management," *Inc.*, October 1998. Retrieved from the Web July 8, 2006. http://pf.inc.com/magazine/19981001/1019.html.

FIGURE 7.3   Permanent Sources of Venture Financing

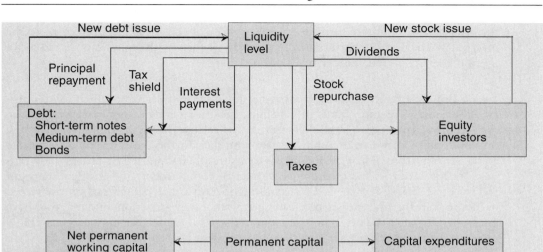

loan. Lenders are most concerned about payback and collateral and try to match the term of the loan with the life of the asset.

- The level and trend in the stock market: A high and rising stock market means people have cash and are willing to accept more risk in investing. A falling market makes investors more conservative.
- The health of various financial institutions, such as savings and loans, commercial banks, and international financial institutions: Institutions under pressure are very conservative and likely to invest only in ventures that are virtually risk free.
- Level of confidence in the economy: High confidence promotes liberal investing.
- Government monetary and fiscal policy: When the government is running large deficits and basically monetizing the debt, there are inflationary consequences. Inflation weakens the currency and benefits borrowers. When the central bank (the Federal Reserve Bank in the United States) targets inflation to counteract government spending, the deflationary effects benefit lenders (the bond market).

The entrepreneur and the top management team need to be sensitive both to threats to the successful financing of the venture (such as low consumer and producer confidence) and to special opportunities such as government finance programs and subsidies.

Equity-Based Financing

The liabilities and equity side of the balance sheet lists the general types of financing. On the balance sheet, they are listed in ascending order of risk—and therefore cost—to the investor. We begin from the bottom of the balance sheet with equity capital and move up to the less risky and cheaper types of financing.

Inside Equity. Financing based on an ownership stake in the new venture is called **equity**. All businesses require equity. Initial equity most frequently comes from the founder, the top management team, and their friends and relatives. Founders traditionally make personal equity investments commensurate with their financial means. They do this for a number of reasons: Their own money is easiest to obtain, putting up money shows future outside investors the entrepreneurs' level of commitment, and it offers the right incentives to business owners. It is almost imperative that people put up their own money to start their businesses because it proves that they are serious and that they have put something at risk. This is the basic source of start-up capital for entrepreneurs. How much of their own money are they prepared to invest in their business?

This is a complicated question. On the one hand, they should be prepared to invest everything so they don't send the wrong message to other investors. If the entrepreneurs hold back, investors might perceive a lack of confidence in the venture's success. On the other hand, it is unreasonable to think that starting a business means that an entrepreneur's financial future will be "all or nothing." Founders should keep a reasonable amount of capital out of the business, safely set aside to protect their families and themselves. The amount held in reserve depends on the situation, but it is reasonable and fair to set aside money for the following:

- Children's education
- Retirement accounts (depending on age)
- Health savings accounts and insurance
- Home equity (depending on the size of the home)
- Amortization of previous personal debts.

In fact, however, it is not unusual for entrepreneurs to put all of their financial assets at risk in starting a new venture.

Their next step is to approach the people they know best and who know and trust them—family, friends, and other "true believers" (sometimes referred to as "fools"). These folks may be relatively unsophisticated investors and are less likely to demand to see a business plan. They may be willing to invest despite the apparent lack of an exit strategy to get their money back, and they frequently require less than market-adjusted risk rates of return. A book on investing strategy would recommend that these investors act more professionally, but they are by definition *not* professionals. This is the most popular source of financing in the United States and probably the most popular in the world.

Take the case of Matthew Oristano, the CEO and major shareholder of People's Choice TV of Shelton, Connecticut. This $25 million wireless-pay-tv company struggled for eight years to secure the financing it needed to make a big impact in the industry. In its early days, family funds financed the future. Matthew offers this tip to other entrepreneurs employing family resources: "When you are dealing with family investors, it should be clearly defined which family members are actively involved in the business and which are involved only financially. To avoid confusion or misunderstandings, everything should be documented the same way any other financial relationship would be."[10]

At the beginning of the business, the risk is highest, and start-up equity carries with it the highest risk of total loss. Therefore, it also carries the highest returns if the business is successful. These initial investments are equity from the point of view of the firm, although the actual sums may have been borrowed. For example, an investor can borrow against the value of his home (and incur or increase the mortgage) to make an equity investment in the new venture. Equity from the owners, the top managers, friends, and relatives is called **inside equity** because it is generally believed that these investors will vote their stock in agreement with the company "insiders."

Outside Equity. Investors who have no personal relationship with the venture are called **outside equity investors**. Outside equity comes from three sources: private investors, venture capital, and public offerings.

Private investors, sometimes called **angels**, are wealthy individuals interested in the high-risk/high-reward opportunities offered by new venture creation. Private investors are, in fact, the largest single source of funds for new firms.[11] Wealthy investors exist in all communities and all cities in the developed world. The best way to reach these people is through personal introduction by acquaintances or associates: lawyers, accountants, consultants, and others in the economic network of a community.

A new development in angel investing is the creation of angel trade groups with names like "Indiana AngelNet" and "Central New York Angels." The groups meet to discuss investment strategy and to hear entrepreneurs make their pitches. Most have Web sites and a few have full-time staffs. There is even a national organization called the Angel Capital Association whose goal is to raise the visibility of angel investing and help investors benchmark practices and adopt innovations.[12]

Wealthy investors will want to see a business plan or offering memorandum. Obtaining expert legal counsel in this process is crucial. Many securities laws, both state and federal, regulate the sale and distribution of stock.[13] Failure to comply with these laws and regulations can enable the investor to sue the entrepreneur for recovery of his or her investment if the company goes broke.

The main advantages of obtaining early financing from wealthy investors is their relative accessibility and the size of the investment pool. Also, these individuals may be in a position to lend their positive reputations to the venture when additional funds are needed.

There are also disadvantages. Many wealthy people made their money in the professions or inherited it. They may lack the business expertise to advise the entrepreneur wisely. Even when wealthy investors are businesspeople, they may have made their money in different types of business or long ago under different conditions.

A second disadvantage is their inability to continue investing in the future—even rich people have limits. The usual range of investments from wealthy individuals is $10,000 to $500,000, with an average investment of about $50,000.[14] This may be enough in the early development stages, but additional money will be needed later if the firm is successful. These additional sums may be out of reach for the angel or the angel may not want to put too much money in a single business.

A third problem concerns the relationship between the angel and the top management team. Private investors tend to be overprotective of their investment. They often call the entrepreneurs or complain when things are not going well. If the business is accessible and local, they may even visit in person, creating headaches for the entrepreneur.[15]

Small business investment companies (SBICs) are privately owned and managed investment companies that combine private equity capital with debt borrowed or guaranteed by the government at favorable rates. They typically will lend the entrepreneurs twice as much as the amount of equity invested. SBICs are regulated by the government. In 2007 there were 385 active licensed SBICs and there is a National Association of Small Business Investment Companies based in Washington, D.C. SBICs cater to businesses with less than $6 million in after-tax earnings and net worths of less than $18 million. Their investments are typically $2-3 million per company and it is difficult to get SBIC financing. "Typically, of all the companies that come to us, we might fund one in 100," says George Kenney, founder of Shepherd Ventures LP, a San Diego SBIC.[16]

Venture capital is outside equity that comes from professionally managed pools of investor money. Instead of wealthy individuals making investments one at a time and on their own, they pool their funds along with those institutional investors and hire professionals to make the investment and related decisions.

The venture capital industry has long been associated with new venture creation and has its own entrepreneurial history.[17] As in any industry the factors that affect profitability are the power of the buyers (investors), the power of the suppliers (entrepreneurs who supply the deals), the threat of substitutes, the height of entry barriers, and rivalry between venture capital firms. Also, macroenvironmental factors create both constraints and opportunities for these firms, just as they do for new ventures. These macro factors depend on the type of industry the venture capitalists specialize in. Because industry-specific knowledge is required for evaluating new venture financing proposals, venture capitalists tend to specialize in certain industries. For example, there are high-tech venture capitalists who look for cutting-edge technological investments, distribution-type venture capitalists who invest in ventures that provide logistical benefits, and restaurant specialists who look to invest in the next Domino's or McDonald's restaurant chain.

Venture capital is **risk capital**: The investors are aware of the high risk that they will receive little or no return on their investment. To compensate for this risk, venture capital looks for deals that can return at least 35 to 50 percent compounded over the life of the investment (typically a five-year planning horizon). To achieve such lofty return, the business opportunity must be extremely attractive with a potential for very strong growth, and the venture capitalist must be able to own a substantial portion of the firm. However, venture capitalists can often bring additional money to the table when needed, and provide advice based on experience and on important industry contacts.

One new venture capital firm has very specific advice and contacts. It is In-Q-Tel, established by the Central Intelligence Agency (CIA) to tap into high-tech firms and security-related ventures. The Federal Bureau of Investigation (FBI) and Defense Intelligence Agency (DIA) participate in In-Q-Tel, and the Army and the National Aeronautical and Space Administration (NASA) plan similar venture capital opportunities. Hundreds of millions of dollars have been invested since 1999 and more since 9/11/2001. "Through In-Q-Tel, the FBI has been able to review new, cutting-edge technologies that have not yet been fully developed for the commercial market," says Jack Israel, the FBI's chief technology officer.[18]

We will return to the subject of venture capital in the next chapter, when we discuss how investors evaluate proposals, structure deals, and negotiate.

Public offerings are the ultimate source of outside equity and wealth creation. When you own 100 percent of a company that earns $500,000 per year, you make a very good living. When you own 50 percent of a company that makes $500,000 per year, is publicly traded, and is valued at 25 times earnings (25 x $500,000 = $12.5 million x .50 = $6.25 million), you are a multimillionaire. Often, in order to go from well-off to rich, the founders of the venture must take their firm public. This type of financing creates significant wealth because it capitalizes earnings at a multiple (the price-earnings ratio). "Going public" is done with the aid of an investment banker through an investment vehicle known as the **initial public offering (IPO)**.

The IPO enables a firm to raise much more equity capital than was previously possible. It also allows the entrepreneur, the top management team, and the earlier investors who still own shares of the firm to sell some shares. This event, often eagerly anticipated by founders and early investors, represents one of the most lucrative financial opportunities in a businessperson's career. The value of the firm increases by an estimated 30 percent at the completion of a public offering.[19] The appendix to Chapter 7 offers a detailed look at the process of going public.

For entrepreneurs and their top managers, going public is the culmination of years of hard work, public recognition of their success, and the delivery of long-delayed financial rewards. On the downside there are disadvantages and real costs to going public, costs that entrepreneurs should weigh against the benefits of going public. The pros and cons are detailed in Street Story 7.2. Street Story 7.3 deals with the important factors that must be considered in deciding whether to go public.

Debt-Based Financing

Debt is borrowed capital. It represents an agreement for repayment under a schedule at an interest rate. Both the repayment schedule and the interest rate may be fixed or variable or have both fixed and variable components. In most cases, debt costs the company less than equity. Interest rates on debt are historically less than rates of return on equity. Why would entrepreneurs ever seek anything but debt? Because debt often requires collateral and its repayment always requires discipline to meet the regular interest and principal payments. Failure to meet those payments puts the company in default and in jeopardy of forced bankruptcy. If the loan is collateralized (i.e., has encumbered a specific physical asset as assurance of repayment of principal), default may cause the loss of that asset. Therefore, entrepreneurs often seek higher-cost equity because share-owners have no legal right to the dividends of the company, and the equity holder is the owner of last

---

STREET STORY 7.2

Going Public: Pros and Cons

Going public may be the entrepreneur's dream, but it has costs as well as benefits. What are the advantages of going public?

For the business:

1. Cash for expansion
2. Cash for acquisitions or mergers
3. Greater accessibility to long-term debt
4. Increased employee benefit plans and stock incentives
5. Increased public awareness of the company.

For entrepreneurs, top managers, and early investors:

1. Cash, enabling the entrepreneurs to diversify their personal portfolios
2. Establishment of an ascertainable value of the company for estate purposes
3. Equity available for executive incentives and compensation
4. Personal satisfaction
5. Liquidity for the entrepreneurs
6. Ability of entrepreneurs to maintain effective control of the company.

What are the disadvantages?

For the business:

1. The need to conform to standard ac-

counting and tax practices and Sarbannes-Oxley restrictions
2. Lack of operating confidentiality
3. Lack of operating flexibility (cannot make quick major changes without proceeding through the governance process)
4. Increased accountability (could also be viewed as an advantage)
5. Demand for dividends from stockholders
6. Initial cost of offering and ongoing regulatory costs
7. Conflict between short-term and long-term goals.

For the entrepreneurs:

1. Need to please and coordinate with more stakeholders
2. Possible loss of control through a takeover
3. Increased visibility for job performance
4. Increased accountability for earnings per share
5. Restrictions on insider trading, conflicts of interest
6. Focus on managing stock price
7. Internal bickering and politics.

SOURCES: R. Saloman, "Second Thoughts on Going Public," *Harvard Business Review* 55 (September–October 1977): 126–131; S. Jones and B. Cohen, *The Emerging Business* (New York: Wiley, 1983).

---

resort. If the company is liquidated or forced into bankruptcy, equity shareholders receive only the residual value of the firm after all other claims are settled.

Some entrepreneurs finance their businesses with equity instead of debt for another reason: They often cannot get loans. Banks and other lending institutions are conservators of their depositors' money and their shareholders' investments. In certain economic climates, they are extremely reluctant to lend money to risky ventures, and they are hardly ever in a position to lend money to start-ups. Thus, the entrepreneur is forced to raise equity capital in the initial stages and to continue raising equity even after the early stages. Because it is difficult for new and small businesses to procure debt financing, various agencies and departments of the government offer special programs to help.

STREET STORY 7.3

IPO: Not an Automatic Yes

Entrepreneur Yuchan Lee says the decision to take his company public involved both logical "left brain" and intuitive "right brain" judgment. Lee's Unica (www.unica.com) marketing management software company had already raised $11.2 million in private equity and been named one of *Inc.* magazine's fastest-growing companies for four years in a row before its IPO in August 2005. Still, Lee weighed a number of factors before taking the big step.

"The left brain portion is straightforward," Lee explains. "The financial market has a fairly clear set of parameters around which companies are qualified to go public from a metrics standpoint: revenue level, revenue growth rate, operating income, EPS, market potential, market position, management team completeness, and so on.

"The more subtle part of this decision is the right brain portion," Lee suggests. "That is a judgment about a level of confidence, from international operation readiness to market momentum."

There are distinct advantages and disadvantages to taking a company public through an IPO, all noted in Street Story 7.2. For the business itself the advantages include cash for the company to expand, cash the company can use for acquisitions or mergers, greater accessibility to long-term debt for the company, increased employee benefits plans and incentives with stock, and increased public awareness of the company. For the company's early investors, including the founding entrepreneurs and top managers, the benefits can include cash when their equity is exchanged for publicly-traded stock, the establishment of an ascertainable value of the company, equity made available for executive incentives and compensation, liquidity for entrepreneurs, financial control of the company, and personal satisfaction.

VentureOne, a research firm owned by Dow Jones & Co., reports that IPOs of U.S. companies dropped 9 percent, from 237 in 2004 to 215 in 2005. The decline in the subset of IPOs backed by venture capitalists was more dramatic: a drop of 39 percent from 67 in 2004 to just 41 in 2005. Venture-backed IPOs also raised 45 percent less in the third quarter of 2005 than during the same period the previous year.

One reason for the downward trend may be new auditing and fiscal reporting requirements, including the 2002 Sarbanes-Oxley law. This legislation requires top managers to certify the accuracy of the company's accounting, information technology, and control systems, and imposes stiff penalties for any violations.

Questions an entrepreneur should ask when considering taking his or her company public through an initial public offering include:

1. Is your company big enough? IPOs today should be able to generate at least $75 to $100 million through stock sales and shareholder selling.
2. Is your company growing fast? Institutional investors are generally looking for strong growth prospects.
3. Do you have an experienced CEO and CFO? Do you have other pieces of sound corporate infrastructure in place?
4. Can your company accurately forecast revenue and earnings? Shareholders who think they've been mislead may initiate lawsuits.
5. Is the market environment right? Are companies similar to yours getting the financing they want?
6. Is your company ready? An IPO generally takes a year from the first organizational meeting, and top management will still

have to guide the company at the same time that they attend to the mechanics of going public.

"It's not easy," reports David Brown, CEO of Website Pros Inc., a company that went public in 2005. "We're in a tough business cycle for IPOs right now."

SOURCE: Adapted from Rebecca Buckman, "Tougher Venture: IPO Obstacles Hinder Start-Ups," *The Wall Street Journal*, January 25, 2006: C1; Bruce R. Evans, "When It's Time to Think About an IPO," *Inc.*, November 1, 2005. Retrieved from the Web July 7, 2006. http://www.inc.com/resources/inc500/2005/articles/20051101/evans.html; R. Saloman, "Second Thoughts on Going Public," *Harvard Business Review* 55, September-October 1977: 126-131; S. Jones and B. Cohen, *The Emerging Business* (New York: Wiley, 1983).

One of the fastest growing and most popular of these is the "micro lenders" program that frequently targets women entrepreneurs and minority-owned firms.

Micro Loan Programs. Businesses owned by women and minorities have had difficulty getting debt financing, partly because of discrimination but also because they start the wrong types of business. Small start-ups in service industries have no collateral, have high failure rates, and present no entry barriers to protect against competition, yet the growth rates of start-ups by women and minorities are high.

To address the gap between the need for debt financing and the availability of credit, the government and the private sector offer micro loans. The U.S. Small Business Administration manages a **micro loan** program to help women and minorities get loans of up to $35,000 at market interest rates. Professor Mohammed Yunus founded the Grameen Bank as a way to help women in India pull themselves up from extreme poverty and increase their independence. This micro loan program has made over 5 million micro loans, and Yunus received the Nobel Peace Prize in 2006.[20]

Positioning for a Loan. The time to establish a relationship with a banker or lender is *before* a loan is needed. Because of their inherent conservatism, banks do not lend money in emergencies (unless they already have some money at risk) or on short notice. Entrepreneurs should call the presidents of the banks they might use and introduce themselves. They can set up a meeting to tell the president about the business, but should not ask for a loan at this meeting. Instead, they should ask who in the loan department might be a good match for the firm's business-financing needs. When they call the person the president recommended, they can tell him or her that the president referred them.

Bankers look for answer to four key questions when evaluating a business proposal. The answers to these questions should be clearly and concisely communicated both in writing and in discussions between the entrepreneur and the lender.

1. What will the money be used for? Are there other sources of financing to help spread the risk?
2. How much money is needed? Asking for too much means paying for unnecessary financing. Asking for too little may mean being unable to keep the business on track.
3. How and when will the money be paid back? Time is money, and the sooner the repayment, the higher the return and lower the risk for the bank.

4. When is the money needed? Is it all going to be used now, or is it possible to draw down a balance over time?

Of primary importance to the lender is the firm's ability to repay the loan. That is the first criterion. In considering the loan application, bankers also look for five things that all begin with the letter C.[21]

- *Character.* The banker's best gauge of whether the entrepreneur will be willing and able to repay the debt is his or her previous borrowing and business experience. To pass the character test, the borrower must be credit-worthy and a person of demonstrated integrity.
- *Capacity.* This is a numbers game. The banker wants to be sure that the business has the capacity (ability) to repay the loan—interest and principal. Evidence of capacity is the cash flow, the coverage ratio (earnings divided by debt service), and any personal guarantees.
- *Capital.* The lender is not interested in financing a business if the loan is its only source of long-term capital. This would mean 100-percent leverage. In case of default, the bank would own the business, and banks are already in a business of their own. They are interested in companies with sufficient equity to indicate that (1) the owners of the firm are putting up their own money in good faith because they believe in the deal, and (2) the debt/equity ratio of the venture is in line with comparable types of businesses.
- *Conditions.* These particulars of the industry, the firm, the general economy, and the current risk position of the bank add complexity to the lending decision. The entrepreneur's business may be in good shape and the entrepreneur of fine character, but if the economy is taking a turn for the worse and the venture's industry (for example, construction) is leading the way, then the banker may deny the application. Banks are always in a position of asking, "What can go wrong here and what happens to our depositors' money when it does?" Bankers are generally risk-averse.
- *Collateral.* If a loan has collateral, the creditor can sell a specific asset to ensure that the principal and accrued interest obligations are met. Collateralized loans generally have a slightly lower interest rate than unsecured loans, but the quality of the collateral is important if the lower rate structure is to apply. Some assets may not be salable at anything approaching the value of the loan, so although these may be required as collateral, they will not lower the rate. For businesses with short operating histories and service businesses with little tangible property, collateral often takes the form of personal guarantees and key-person life insurance.

Searching for a Lender. Entrepreneurs often find themselves in a seller's market when it comes to searching for a loan. Sometimes it may appear that the chances of receiving a business loan are zero, but the entrepreneur can do a few things to improve those chances. First and foremost, the entrepreneur must meet the requirements of the five Cs. Then the management team can begin to shop around as if they were hiring the bank to be their lender.

As in any hiring situation, they should check the bank's references. Other people who do business with the bank will be able to tell them whether it is a friendly institution, willing and able to work with the venture in good times and bad. Some banks have reputations for foreclosing early or for calling in loans when the bank's balance sheet needs cleaning up.

The firm should look for a bank with experience lending in its industry. Banks have different specialties, in a sense, and their loan officers and lending committees have particular knowledge resources. If the lenders have experience in the borrowers' area, they are more likely to understand the details of the loan application. The size of the bank is also a factor. A bank that is too small for the firm will not be able to finance follow-up loans. Banks have regulations about how much they can loan to a single client. A bank that is too big may consider the firm's account trivial compared to the mega-deals it handles. If the business is international and will involve importing, exporting, or carrying on a banking relationship outside the home country, it needs a bank that is experienced in these matters and has correspondent relationships in the host countries.

Personal chemistry is also important in choosing a banker. Entrepreneurs are advised to do business with people they like and people who like them. The bank they choose should have on staff someone who will be their champion, who will present the firm and its prospects in a positive light within the bank itself even when the entrepreneurs are not personally there.

There are additional criteria to consider when looking for a banker:[22]

- Does it see the firm through adversity? A good bank will help during a difficult spell. It will be patient in waiting for repayments and may even extend more credit to meet external obligations like payroll.
- Does it save the firm time? When an entrepreneur has an opportunity that requires fast action, a solid bank can make decisions quickly and extend credit.
- Does it treat the entrepreneur as an individual? When the Reynolds firm, a Lynnwood, Washington, retail-store fixture manufacturer, met with the loan officer at a local bank, he was practically overwhelmed with detailed questions about his business. The company got the loan and the bank got the rest of the company's business. "I decided that if they were smart enough to ask these intricate questions, they must be worth banking with," explains Paul A. Abodeely, Reynolds CEO.
- Does it teach and advise? Frequently banks have long experience in certain types of businesses. A good bank will share this expertise and help train and counsel its clients. Can you call for advice when you need it?
- Does it do something special? By 10 a.m. every morning, there's a report from his local bank sitting on the desk of Jack Greenman, financial officer of the Sterling Healthcare Group, Inc., in Coral Gables, Florida. The report shows all the previous day's deposits and disbursements, including deposits from lockboxes in 19 states that the bank has swept into its central account. The service doesn't cost Sterling Healthcare a dime.
- Does it accept responsibility? Garden-tool maker DeJay Corp. of Palm Beach, Florida, was upset when a bank posting error caused some of its checks to bounce. But they were smiling when the bank not only apologized, but also called every customer and vendor who might have received such a check and explained that it was the bank's mistake.

- Does it let the company borrow against the future? TPL, a technology-equipment manufacturer in Albuquerque, won a big U.S. Army contract and then discovered that their bank wouldn't increase their existing $250,000 line of credit. Another bank 100 miles away heard the TPL story through the grapevine and extended them the half-million dollars they needed, saying, "You're the kind of company we need to encourage in New Mexico."
- Does it find customers for the firm? A bank in Southern California played match-maker for two of its customers, garment manufacturer Flap Happy and the local science museum. When the museum expanded its gift shop, Flap Happy hats were included in the retail mix.

These stories demonstrate that some commercial banks are willing to "go the extra distance" to attract small business customers. Entrepreneurs need to shop around and communicate to find a lender who can be a true partner in their success. However, there are times when bank financing is simply not available. Are there other options for entrepreneurs? Here are two:

- Merchant cash advances: If a company sells primarily to customers using credit cards and is in dire financial straits, it might be eligible for a merchant cash advance. For example, AdvanceMe, Inc., of Kennesaw, Georgia, which specializes in credit-card-receivable financing, will advance small amounts to merchants and receive repayment by garnishing a small percentage of each credit-card sale. Interest rates are high, between 20 and 35 percent, but the money is received quickly and the merchant needs no collateral.[23]
- Micro-mezzanine financing: Sometimes a business is profitable but has no more debt capacity. Venture capital is not available or advisable because of the large equity shares taken by the VCs. Micro-mezzanine financing is unsecured subordinate debt that can help a business fund an acquisition or an expansion, or even buy out another investor. It is called "mezzanine" becausee it lies between bank debt and outside equity financing. One mezzanine investor, Snowbird Capital of Reston, Virginia, lends amounts between $500,000 and $5,000,000. Interest rates are in the range of prime plus 5 percent, maturity is five to seven years, and the investor wants warrants to purchase stock in case the firm goes public.[24] (Warrants are covered in Chapter 8.)

Types of Debt Financing. The two basic types of debt financing are asset-based financing and cash flow financing. **Asset-based financing** is collateralized. The most common form of asset-based financing is trade credit. Trade credit covers the period between product or service delivery to the new venture and the date when payment is due. It is not uncommon to have a 25- to 30-day grace period before payment without penalty is expected. A discount is sometimes offered for early payment.

Asset-based financing is simply borrowing money to finance an asset, short-term—seasonal accounts receivables—or long-term—equipment or property. When a specific asset is identifiable with the borrowing need, asset-based financing is appropriate. Table 7.2 illustrates some types of bankable assets and the typical maximum percentage of debt financing the firm can count on.

TABLE 7.2   Asset-Based Financing and Borrowing Limits

Type	Borrowing Limits
Accounts receivable	For short-term receivables: 70%–80%; for longer-term receivables: 60%–80%[a]
Inventory	Depending on risk of obsolescence: 40%–60%
Equipment	If equipment is of general use: 70%–80%; if highly specialized: 40%–60%
Conditional sales contract	As a percentage of purchase price: 60%–70%
Plant improvement loan	Lower of cost or market appraisal: 60%–80%
Leasehold improvement	Depending on general reusability: 70%–80%
Real estate	Depending on appraisal value: 80%–90%
First mortgage on building	Depending on appraisal value: 80%–90%

[a] This is from a factor, a business that specializes in collecting accounts receivable and overdue debts for firms and lending them money against the total invoice amounts.

For example, a new venture with a positive cash flow conversion cycle (it spends before it receives) could borrow 70 percent of the money needed to finance accounts receivable with the receivables themselves as collateral. Up to 60 percent debt financing is possible for inventory with the inventory as collateral. Note that the more stable, long-term, and tangible resources have higher debt ceilings; the short-term, high-turnover assets have lower ceilings.

Smaller banks have traditionally turned away from asset-based financing because they lacked the ability to evaluate and dispose of collateral. However, these banks are increasingly moving toward developing special expertise in asset-based financing. In 1989, it was estimated that small businesses would borrow over $100 billion with asset-based financing.[25]

Cash flow financing refers to unsecured financing based on the underlying operations of the business and its ability to generate enough cash to cover the debt. Short-term (under one year) unsecured financing is usually used as temporary working capital. A line of credit is an intermediate level of unsecured financing. Long-term unsecured financing takes the form of a note, bond, or debenture. Because the debt is unsecured, banks may take other precautions to protect their asset (the loan). These protections or **covenants** are agreements between lender and borrower concerning the manner in which the funds are disbursed, employed, managed, and accounted. For example, an unsecured loan covenant might require the borrower to maintain a certain minimum balance in an account at the lending institution. In this way, the bank can restrict a portion of its funds from general use, raise the cost of the loan to the borrower, and potentially attach the balance in case of default. Further details on this type of financing and its limits are discussed in the next chapter.

Before we leave the subject of cash flow and debt financing, let's take a look at the unfortunate story of Ruminator Books, which faced severe financial problems and went looking for a solution. Did they find it? The answer is in Street Story 7.4.

STREET STORY 7.4

A Cliffhanger Ending

Ruminator Books was once the largest and best-known independent bookstore in the United States.

David Unowsky started the store in Minneapolis in 1970 with just $12,000. Originally called the Hungry Mind, the store opened in a 1200-square-foot location with only enough space for one narrow aisle between stacks of books. Two years later the store was named the exclusive textbook vendor for Macalester College, and eventually it moved into a 7800-square-foot space owned by the college.

For a while business was good. In addition to the college traffic, customers gravitated from around the Twin Cities to shop at the store, and a popular restaurant opened next door. During the early 1990s sales rose 20 percent each year. The store had 26 employees, most of them salaried, with benefits including health insurance, a retirement plan, paid vacations, and maternity and paternity leaves. Ruminator Books was proud to personally introduce Minneapolis readers to big name national authors like John Updike and Alice Walker and to host readings of their work. Like other independent bookstores, Ruminator began to face increasing competition from national chains and even large *chai* (tea) stores. Ironically, however, the real seed for Ruminator's demise came from what initially sounded like a great opportunity. In 2000 the Open Book opened a center for book lovers in a different Minneapolis neighborhood and Unowsky opened a satellite store there. Other tenants, including the Loft Literary Center and Milkweed Press, did well despite the Center's remote location and the absence of foot traffic. But the new store was a money pit for Ruminator Books. "It was beyond my level of competence," moans owner Unowsky. "I wasn't wired to run two bookstores." Adding to his problems was a new computer system that was supposed to network the two stores but never worked. Unowsky chalked up losses in excess of $500,000 before closing the satellite store in 2003.

His creditors included many book publishers who stopped shipping books, damaging the main store's inventory. His landlord, Macalester College, threatened to take possession of his main store if Unowsky didn't pay the $600,000 he owed them.

For a while it looked as if the bookstore might miraculously overcome its financial problems. Unowsky sold his original Hungry Mind name to an online learning company for a big cash infusion. Many famous authors whose books the store had promoted donated items for a fundraising auction. And one loyal customer, a former corporate financial analyst, offered to personally invest $200,000 and stepped in to help Unowsky in his negotiations with Macalester.

But in July 2004 negotiations broke down, and Unowsky was forced to close the store. Because he had emptied his retirement account, remortgaged his house and taken $100,000 in cash advances from his credit cards to save the store, he had to declare personal bankruptcy too. After a six-month hiatus writing reviews and other articles, Unowsky went to work for Magers & Quinn, a Minneapolis bookstore that specializes in rare and collectible books.

SOURCE: Adapted from Cynthia Crossen, "Mismanagement Closes a Bookstore," *The Wall Street Journal*, September 28, 2004: B4; adapted from Marianne Combs, "Ruminator Bookstore Closing," Minnesota Public Radio, June 29, 2004. Retrieved from the Web July 8, 2006. http://news.minnesota.publicradio.org/features/2004/06/29_combsm_ruminator.

NEW VENTURE VALUATION

What is the new venture worth? How can it be valued? Determining value is a problem that cannot be avoided even though the methods for calculating it are uncertain and risky. When a new business is created by purchasing another business or its assets, a valuation is required to ensure a fair purchase price and to determine taxes.

A valuation is also needed when a new venture is created and the entrepreneurs need equity investors. In this case, the valuation tells investors approximately what their investment might be worth in the future.[26] Investors need this information to calculate their expected return on investment and bargain for a share (proportion of stock) in the venture that will bring this return.[27]

Because of lack of historical data, the valuation of new ventures and small businesses is difficult and uncertain. There is no efficient market to determine value since these ventures do not trade their equity on a stock exchange and thus have no market value in this sense. They have no record of accomplishment either, no indication of potential future earnings. Unproven companies need to raise equity without being able to show investors historical returns.[28]

Nevertheless, valuations must be made. Three basic approaches to valuation include **asset-based valuations**, **earnings-based valuations**, and the use of **discounted cash flow models**.

Asset-Based Valuations

Asset-based valuations reveal the investors' maximum exposure. The purpose of these valuations is to determine how much the venture would be worth if it were forced to cease operation and be sold for its tangible and intangible parts. Asset-based valuations can also be used to determine the cost of assets. There are four types of asset-based valuations: **book value, liquidation value, adjusted book value,** and **replacement value**.

Book Value. The book value of an asset is the historical cost of the asset less accumulated depreciation. An asset originally purchased for $10,000 and depreciated on a straight-line basis for half its useful life has a book value of $5,000. A fully depreciated asset has a book value of zero even though it may still be worth something. Because accelerated depreciation schedules and techniques are employed primarily as tax shields, during the early life of an asset its book value may understate its economic value. Frequently, the book value of an asset is simply an artifact of accounting practice and bears little relationship to its actual economic value.

Adjusted Book Value. Sometimes an asset's book value and its actual economic value are so at variance that book value must be adjusted to give a better picture of what the asset is worth. This adjusted book value can be higher or lower, depending on the circumstances. Upward adjustments are often made to account for land values. Adjusted book valuations increase the value of real estate, which often rises over time, but—because of accounting rules—is always left on the books at historical cost. Many businesses are undervalued on the books because the land they own and control is worth many times the value of the business itself. Examples of this phenomenon include land-based businesses such as hotels, parking lots, and golf courses.

Land value can be adjusted downward if, for example, a parcel of property has major environmental problems and incurs cleanup costs. Sometimes neighborhoods and areas deteriorate for a variety of reasons, and once-valuable property is worth less than its historical cost.

Inventory valuations are sometimes adjusted downward because the parts, supplies, or stock have become obsolete. A computer store retailer with a stock of machines produced by out-of-business manufacturers might have to write down the value of the inventory. A clothing retailer who over-ordered and has a large stock of last year's fashions is in a similar position. On the other hand, if held long enough, obsolete inventory and out-of-fashion stock can be a source of *increased* value. Eventually, this merchandise becomes rare, and long-held worthless goods can become a source of revenue.

Replacement Value Replacement value is the amount it would cost to duplicate the firm's current physical asset base at today's prices. When valuation is used for buying or selling a business, the replacement value of the assets can be a point of reference in negotiations between buyer and seller. Because inflation is the historical trend in developed Western economies, the replacement cost of an asset is frequently higher than the original cost. But not always: Because of technological and productive improvements, the replacement cost of computers and computing power is an example of a downward trend in replacement costs.

Liquidation Value. This is the value of the assets if they must be sold under pressure. Sometimes firms face extreme cash shortages and must liquidate assets to raise cash to pay their creditors. At other times, courts order liquidation under bankruptcy proceedings. When buyers know that a venture is being forced to raise cash by liquidating, they can negotiate to pay below-market prices. Often liquidation is done at auction, and the prices paid might be only 10 to 20 percent of the market value of the assets. The liquidation value of assets represents their absolute floor value. From the investor's point of view, the difference between the value of the investment and the liquidation value of the assets (after priority claims are met) represents the maximum risk or exposure for the investment.[29]

Earnings-Based Valuations

Earnings valuations entail multiplying the earnings of the venture by a price-earnings ratio or dividing the earnings by some capitalization factor (mathematically equivalent techniques). There are two inherent problems: The evaluator must determine which earnings to use for the calculation and which factor is most appropriate for capitalization. The resolution of these issues is not trivial. Differences in valuation provide arbitrage opportunities that can be practically riskless and very lucrative.[30]

Which Earnings? Three possible earnings figures can be used to calculate an earnings valuation.

Historical earnings are the record of past performance. This is no guarantee of future achievement, but it is sometimes an indication. In cases of valuation for the purpose of buying or selling a business, sellers rely on past performance for their valuation; after all, their management was responsible for that performance. But in most cases the sellers will no longer be part of management, so the context for the historical performance no longer exists. In such cases, historical earnings should not be used to predict future performance.

Future earnings and the historical resource bases are a middle-of-the-road approach to calculating value. They correctly identify for the future the important earnings stream out of which dividends will be paid. Also, the firm's future earning capacity determines market value. However, the use of the historical resource base assumes that the relationship between the firm's capabilities and its environment will remain unchanged. This calculation represents the value to a current owner who anticipates no major changes in the assets of the firm, its strategy, or its competitive or macro situation. In a buy-sell situation, the buyer should not rely on this estimate because of the high probability that the underlying resource base will be modified under new ownership.

The present and future resource bases make up the most appropriate measure of earnings in both buy-sell and new venture valuations. Future earnings are the basis for future returns which flow directly from whatever new resources and capabilities the firm's founders and top managers developed. Valuation is a forward-looking process, and its calculation requires estimates of future performance.

In addition to the problem of determining which earnings to include and under what circumstances to include them, valuation must grapple with the problem of comparable earnings. Earnings can be stated and calculated in a number of ways: earnings before interest, depreciation, taxes and amortization (EBIDTA), earnings after taxes (EAT), and earnings before and after extraordinary items. Extraordinary items should be omitted from earnings calculations because they represent non-normal operating situations and one-of-a-kind events. Valuations focus on an ongoing business, not on special situations.

Both EBIDTA and EAT are earnings legitimately used in the valuation process. The advantage of EBIDTA is that it measures the earning power and value of the business fundamentals and underlying resources *before the effects of financing and legal (tax) organization*. From the viewpoint of a new venture in search of financing or in a buy-sell situation, EBIDTA is preferred because financial and legal structures may be altered according to the tax preferences of the owners. However, EAT is also a reasonable and workable figure to examine. The important consideration is consistency in valuation methods. The entrepreneur should not employ EAT for one scenario and EBIDTA for another.

Which Capitalization Factor? Determining the capitalization factor is also an exercise in both estimation and judgment. The **capitalization factor** or **price-earnings (P-E) ratio** is the multiple that represents the consensus among investors concerning the growth and reliability of the firm's earnings over time. The P-E ratio is the price an investor is willing to pay to buy a claim on $1 worth of current earnings. Higher P-E ratios mean that investors believe earnings will be much higher in the future; lower P-E ratios indicate that investors do not believe earnings will increase very much.[31]

For example, large, stable, slow-growth businesses are often capitalized at five to ten times earnings. Firms expected to grow as much as or slightly better than the overall economy might have price-earnings ratios in the teens or low twenties. Small firms with high-growth potential often come to market at IPO at multiples of 30, 40, and 50 times earnings. Their earnings are valued at higher ratios because certain investors look for the high-risk/high-reward stock that could be the next Google, Microsoft, Cisco Systems, or Genentech.

No method of determining the correct price-earnings ratio for any specific new venture valuation is exact. The best process generates a range of potential values and evaluates outcomes within the range. There are a number of reference points to check in determining the P-E ratio:

1. Look for similar or comparable firms that have recently been valued and employ that capitalization rate as a base. Unfortunately, there are few "pure plays" available for comparison.[32] Sometimes private valuations are made by buyers or sellers, but these are not public information and may be difficult to access.
2. Estimate the range of the stock market's overall P-E ratio for the period under evaluation. If a bull market is expected, P-E ratios will be above the historical average. In this case, adjust the new venture ratio upward. In a bear market, ratios are down, and the new venture rate should reflect this.
3. What are the industry's prospects? Industries under heavy regulation or competitive pressures are valued lower than those considered "sunrise" industries—that is, industries just beginning to develop under government protection and with little competition.

The earnings methods are commonly used because they are relatively efficient (you need only two reliable numbers) and make for easy comparisons. They are volatile because any change in future earnings estimates produces a valuation change multiplied by what may be a very large number. In addition, from an accounting viewpoint, earnings are designed to minimize tax liability. They seldom represent the amount of cash actually available for returns to investors and owners. To examine these, we need a cash flow model of firm value.

Discounted Cash Flow Models

The value of a firm can also be estimated using **discounted cash flow (DCF) models**. DCF models were originally developed to estimate returns on specific projects over limited time horizons in the context of capital budgeting. They were then expanded for use in valuing publicly held firms traded on major stock exchanges. The application of DCF models to entrepreneurial opportunities is relatively new and must be applied with some caution.

Advantages of DCF Valuation. If used appropriately the DCF model of valuation can provide estimates far superior to those based on assets or earnings. One advantage is that the DCF model's valuation is based on the cash-generating capacity of the firm, not on its accounting earnings. For new ventures, cash is king, and when they are out of cash, they are out of business. An earnings model may depict the business as healthy even when it cannot pay its bills or open its doors to customers. A cash-based model is more sensitive.

Another advantage of the cash model is that it includes cash flow that can be appropriated by the founder/owner and the top management team. Cash payments to the entrepreneurs—e.g., contributions to Keogh plans and other retirement schemes, returns from debt repayments, interest payments, salaries, tax shields and advantages, dividends, and cash replacement perquisites like automobile insurance—can all be included in calculating the value of the firm to its owners. When a firm is owned by hundreds of thousands of small shareholders, these items are irrelevant. (Indeed, they decrease the firm's value to stockholders.) For a closely held firm, however, they are quite relevant.

Disadvantages of DCF Valuation. One of the most important disadvantages of the DCF model is that it was originally used for capital budgeting to provide a reliable ordering of alternatives. Entrepreneurs are not usually evaluating a range of options They are focused on this one venture so the benefit of reliable ordering is lost. If the other essential numeric inputs into the DCF calculation are also unreliable, the valuation will be a prime example of "garbage in, garbage out."

A second problem arises from estimating the numerical inputs into the DCF equation. Three major inputs include an estimate of the period of the cash flow (usually annual), the estimate of the weighted cost of capital (discount rate), and the estimate of the terminal (or horizon) value of the firm. If these calculations are off, the valuation will be wide of the mark.

Discounted Cash Flow Example. To calculate the value of the firm with the DCF model, the following equation is used:

$$V = C_0 + C_1/(1 + k) + C_2/(1 + k)^2 + C_3/(1 + k)^3 + C_n/(1 + k)^n = ? \, C_t/(1 + k)^t$$

Where:

V is the value of the firm.
C is the cash flow in each period t.
k is the firm's cost of capital.

For example, suppose the entrepreneur projected that a business could be started for $1 million and generate the cash flows listed in the following table. If an entrepreneur has a weighted cost of capital of 15 percent and the firm's capitalization rate is .20, its terminal value, or TV, then is $1,000,000/.20 = $5,000,000, and the value of the venture is $3,557,720.

Cash Flows in $000

Yr. 0	Yr. 1	Yr. 2	Yr. 3	Yr. 4	Yr. 5	TV 5
1,000	200	400	800	1,000	1,000	5,000

Method: discount these flows by $(1 + k)^n$

The internal rate of return on this stream of cash flows is 68.15 percent. This is calculated by setting the initial investment ($1,000) equal to the 5-year stream plus the terminal value and solving for k. As long as the entrepreneur can finance this project at rates less than 68.15 percent, value is being created and appropriated by the firm. At rates above 68.15 percent, the value is appropriated solely by the investor.

This brief example illustrates how an entrepreneur might use the DCF model to value the firm from his or her point of view, but it is also important to consider how an investor would value a new venture. One common method investors use is the **residual pricing method**, so called because it is used to determine how much of the firm must be sold to the investor in order to raise startup funds, with the "residual" left for the entrepreneurs.

From the investor's point of view, the pretax annual cash flows generated for Years 1 through 5 are not important, because they will not generally be available to the investor. These will be paid out as perquisites to the entrepreneur and reinvested in the firm to keep it growing. The investor is interested in the after-tax profits at a point (say Year 5). If the pretax cash flow is estimated at $1,000,000 and the after-tax profits are $500,000, this means that, at a multiple (P-E ratio) of 10 times earnings, the firm is valued at $5,000,000 at the end of Year 5.

Instead of using a weighted-cost-of-capital figure—15 percent, for example—the investor would use a **required-rate-of-return** figure because the investor needs to see whether the firm will be able to cover all the risk exposure, expenses, and cost of no- and low-return investments the investor has made. The investor's required rate of return is invariably higher than the entrepreneur's weighted cost of capital because the entrepreneur will also use low-cost debt when possible.

If the entrepreneur wants to raise $500,000 from the investor for an equity share in the business, how much equity (i.e., what percentage ownership of the business) should the entrepreneur offer in exchange?

To achieve a 40-percent return on investment, the investor would need to have $2,689,120 worth of stock at the end of Year 5 (calculated by taking the $500,000 initial figure and compounding it at 40 percent for 5 years $(1.4)^5$). The future-value factor of this term is 5.378. If the investor's stock must be worth $2,689,120 in five years and the total value of the stock will be $5,000,000 in 5 years, then the investor must own 53.78 percent of the company ($2,689,120/$5,000,000).[33]

To calculate the amount of equity ownership the investor will require, the entrepreneur needs to know:

- The investor's required rate of return
- The amount of the investment
- The number of years the investment is to be held
- The after-tax profits for the horizon year
- The expected price-earnings multiple

As we will see in the next chapter, the investor may or may not actually require a 53.78-percent stake in the new firm. Elements such as potential dilution and management control need to be factored into a negotiation. No formula can fully express the complexity of a negotiation process or alleviate the desire of all parties to achieve the highest return for the lowest risk.

LEGAL AND TAX ISSUES

Experienced legal assistance and advice are critical to financing a new venture and resolving the legal and tax issues confronting it. Failing to obtain a good lawyer and accountant is disastrous, so it's well worth the trouble of finding such help. Legal and tax assistance is needed for:

- The formation of business entities
- Setting up books and records for tax purposes
- Negotiating leases and financing
- Writing contracts with partners and employees
- Advice about insurance needs and requirements
- All litigation
- Regulation and compliance
- Patents, trademarks, and copyright protections

Not all attorneys are competent in all the areas listed, but competent legal counsel knows its limitations and can bring in experts as required. As in many other aspects of business, there is no substitute for experience.

The best way to find competent legal service is by word of mouth. Entrepreneurs should then follow up any recommendations by checking with legal referral services and personally interviewing lawyers to decide whether they have a good rapport with a particular attorney and whether this lawyer understands the entrepreneurs' business needs. Good legal counsel is not cheap. Rates can run from $90 to $350 per hour. Some lawyers who specialize in getting new ventures up and running are willing to take equity in lieu of cash as payment for services.

There is an old saying that "a person who acts as his own lawyer has a fool for a client," but some entrepreneurs insist on self-representation. They must then become conversant with the content and process of the law. A course in contracts and real estate law is recommended.

Legal Forms of Organization in the United States

In the United States there are five major types of organization: sole proprietorships, partnerships, corporations, S corporations, and limited liability companies (LLC). Each has its own characteristics in terms of legal identity and continuity, liability, taxation, and financing regulations. The permits and licenses required for operation vary by form of organization.

Sole Proprietorship. The easiest organizations to form are **sole proprietorships.** They make up the majority of small businesses and self-employed persons. The company is simply an extension of the owner. For tax purposes, the sole proprietor completes an income statement (Schedule C), the sole proprietorship is taxed at the individual's rate, and earnings are subject to self-employment tax. A proprietorship ceases to exist when the owner dies, retires, or goes out of business. It cannot be transferred to another person as a going concern. The owner is personally liable for all legal and financial business activities.

Partnership. A **partnership** is defined as a voluntary association of two or more persons to act as co-owners of a business for profit. All partnerships should be regulated with partnership agreements conforming to the Uniform Partnership Act. This agreement should cover such issues as:

- The contribution and participation requirements of each partner
- The allocation of profits and losses
- Responsibilities and duties
- Salaries and compensation contracts
- Consequences of withdrawal, retirements, or deaths
- The manner and means by which the partnership will be dissolved

Partnerships are not considered separate entities for tax purposes. The partners are taxed at only one level, that of the partner. Earnings flow proportionately to each individual, and the tax treatment is then similar to that of the sole proprietor. A partnership ceases to exist on the death, retirement, or insanity of any of the partners, unless a provision for continuation has been made in the partnership agreement.

There are two types of partnerships. A **general partnership** has only general partners and conforms to the description and limitations just listed. A **limited partnership** has both general and limited partners. The general partners assume responsibility for management and have unlimited liability for business activity. They must have at least a 1 percent interest in the profits and losses of the firm. The limited partners have no voice in management and are limited in liability up to their capital contribution and any specified additional debts. A limited partnership can have no more than 35 owners.

The family limited partnership is a special case. These legal structures are set up to provide for continuation of a family firm when the founder retires or dies. Estate taxes on family firms frequently create a cash crisis for the survivors. Sometimes they have to sell the venture in order to pay the taxes. Careful succession planning can mitigate this problem, and the family limited partnership can play a role. Founders and family members must be careful not to run afoul of the Internal Revenue Service when using these partnerships. The IRS has stepped up scrutiny and audits since it discovered that many such partnerships are used primarily to evade taxes rather than to secure succession.[34]
One of the often unanticipated problems of partnerships is that partners are agents for each other. The actions of one partner can cause unlimited personal liability for all the others. This is referred to as *joint and several liabilities.*

C Corporation. A corporation (also called a regular **C corporation** for the section of the law that describes it) is a separate legal person under the laws of the state within which it is incorporated. Its life continues even after the founders or managers die or retire. The central authority resides with the board of directors, and ownership resides with the stockholders. Shares may be bought and sold freely. No investor is liable beyond his or her proportionate capital contributions except for "insiders" in cases of securities fraud or violations of the tax code.

A corporation is taxed as a separate entity according to the corporate tax code and rates. Dividends declared by the corporation are "after-tax" from the firm's point of view, and are then taxed again at the shareholder level. This is known as the "double taxation" problem. To get around this, entrepreneurs often resort to tactics regulated by the Internal Revenue Service under the Federal Tax Code. These tactics usually revolve around issues of salary and interest expense.

Interest expense is deductible from a corporation's pretax profits and, therefore, reduces its tax liability. This may tempt an entrepreneur to lend the new venture money for start-up and expansion capital instead of taking an equity position. This practice is legitimate—up to a point. Under section 385 of the Federal Tax Code, a thinly capitalized company (one with a debt/equity ratio over 10:1) can have its debt reclassified as equity. Also, if the debt does not look like debt because, for example, it has conditional payment schedules instead of fixed coupon rates, it may be reclassified as equity. This means that what were tax-deductible interest payments are now double-taxed dividends.

The losses of regular corporations accumulate and can be used as tax shields in future years. The losses of proprietorships and partnerships are passed along to the principals in the year they are incurred. One exception to this involves "section 1244 stock." If this type of stock is selected in the firm's initial legal and tax organization, the owners of the firm can deduct their losses from their regular income if the business goes bankrupt. If they selected a regular corporation, their losses are treated as capital losses at tax time.

S Corporation. An **S corporation** is a special vehicle for new small businesses that enables them to avoid the double taxation of regular corporations. To qualify for S corporation status, the firm must:

- Offer only one class of stock (although differences in voting rights are allowable)
- Be wholly owned by U.S. citizens and derive no more than 80 percent of its income from non–U.S. sources
- Have 35 or fewer stockholders, all of whom agree to the S corporation status
- Obtain no more than 25 percent of its revenue through passive (investment) sources

Although S corporations are incorporated under state law, for federal tax purposes they resemble partnerships. Usually, stockholders receive the profits or losses of the firm proportionally. This percentage is deemed a dividend. The monies paid to shareholders are considered self-employment income but are *not* subject to self-employment tax.

Limited Liability Company (LLC). The **limited liability company** is a relatively new type of business organization that shares characteristics with both corporations and partnerships. Like a corporation, an LLC is legally a separate entity that provides liability protection for its owners. However, when it comes to taxes, LLCs are treated like partnerships: The LLC does not pay taxes itself and all profits and losses flow through directly to LLC owners and are reported on their tax returns.

Although a corporation is characterized by four basic characteristics (limited liability, continuity of life, centralized management, and free transferability of interests), an LLC maintains its tax status by selecting only two of these traits when it drafts its operating agreement. In other words, if an LLC decides that it will accept limited liability and be organized under a centralized board of directors, it cannot legally continue as an entity after its owners die, and it cannot freely sell and trade its shares. An LLC receives some of the benefits of a partnership and some of the advantages of a corporation, but not all of them. Many firms, therefore, prefer to organize as partnerships or corporations.

LLC owners are called "members" and may be individuals, corporations, trusts, pension plans, other LLCs, or almost any other entity. The company must file articles of organization with the secretary of state in the state where it operates and, in most states, is also required to file some sort of annual report. Still, an LLC spends less time than most corporations producing legal and tax reports. Table 7.3 compares the different forms of legal organization on a number of important dimensions.

Private Placements under U.S. Securities Laws

Whenever an investor supplies money or some item of value expecting that it will be used to generate a profit or return from the efforts of others, a security is created. All national governments regulate the issuance and redemption of securities, as do all U.S. states. In the United States, the regulatory agency that oversees this function is the Securities and Exchange Commission (SEC). Because compliance with SEC regulations is expensive and time-consuming, small firms and new firms find it burdensome to comply. In response to their concerns, regulations have been put in place providing "safe harbors" for small and new businesses. These safe harbors enable smaller firms to issue securities (with constraints and limits) without conforming to the high level of regulation

TABLE 7.3 Legal Forms of Organization Compared

Characteristic	Sole Proprietor- ship	General Partnership	Limited Partnership	C Corp	LLC	S Corp
Limited liability for ALL owners	No	No	No	Yes	Yes	Yes
Owners can participate in management w/o losing liability protection	n/a	n/a	Partially	Yes	Yes	Yes
Number of owners	1	1 or more	1–35	2 or more	2 or more*	1–75
Easy to form w/o maintaining extensive record keeping	Yes	Yes	No	No	No	Yes
Restrictions on ownership	No	No	Yes	No	No	Yes
Double tax	No	No	No	Yes	No	No
Able to deduct business loss on individual return	Yes	No	Yes	No	Yes	Yes

* Except the District of Columbia and Massachusetts

SOURCE: Adapted from "Entity Comparison Chart." Retrieved from the Web July 14, 2006. http://www.llcweb.com/ Entity%20Comparison.htm. Used with permission of Steven E. Davidson, The Limited Liability Company Web site, http:// www.llcweb.com.

that applies to large public offerings (see Chapter 7 on the IPO). These are called **private placements**. The specific regulations should be consulted directly for complete details. Experienced legal counsel should always be retained when interpreting these rules. Minor rule infractions and small deviations from the regulations can cause the firm selling unregistered securities to lose its safe harbor and be left without any protections. These private financing regulations (found in regulations D and A of the SEC rules) include:

- Rule 504: Rule 504 is most useful when a venture is raising small amounts from many investors. A venture can raise up to $1 million during any 12-month period and up to $500,000 free from state registration as well. There is no limit on the number or nature of the investors, no advertising is permitted, and there are qualified limits on resale of these securities. Issuers cannot be investment companies.
- Rule 505: Rule 505 permits sale of up to $5 million to no more than 35 investors and an unlimited number of "accredited" investors. No general solicitation or advertising is permitted, and there are limits on resale. Issuers cannot be investment companies. Disclosure is required to unsophisticated investors but not to "accredited" investors.
- Rule 506: Rule 506 permits the sale to an unlimited amount of investors and an unlimited number of qualified "accredited" investors. No solicitation or advertising is permitted. There is no limit on the nature of the issuer. Unsophisticated investors may be represented by purchasing representatives who can evaluate the prospectus. There must be 35 or fewer investors.
- Rule 147 (intrastate offering): Rule 147 applies to issues that meet the 80 percent rule for assets, income, and use of proceeds. Investors must be residents of the same state. There are no limits on the nature of the issuer, the number of purchasers, or the amount of the issue. There is a nine-month holding period before resale.
- Regulation A: Securities sold under this regulation must be less than $1.5 million in any 12-month period and can be sold only to "accredited" investors. Advertising is restricted, but there are no limits on the nature of the issuer or the number of investors. There are no limits on resale, but an offering circular must be filed and distributed. A "mini-registration" filing in the SEC regional office is required.
- Rule 144: If shares are sold and not covered by regulation A, there are problems with resale because the securities are not registered. This problem can be avoided if they are sold under Rule 144, which requires a holding period and a filing registration before the shares can be resold.
- Intrastate Offering Exemption: Section 3(a)(11) of the Securities Act is generally known as the "intrastate offering exemption." It facilitates the financing of local business operations. To qualify for the intrastate offering exemption, a company must:
  a. Be incorporated in the state where it is offering the securities
  b. Carry out a significant amount of its business in that state
  c. Make offers and sales only to residents of that state.

There is no fixed limit on the size of the offering or the number of purchasers. The company must determine the residence of each purchaser. If any securities are offered or sold to even one out-of-state person, the exemption may be lost. Without the exemption, the company might be in violation of the Securities Act registration requirements. If, within a short period of time after the company's offering is complete (the usual test is nine months), a purchaser *resells* any of the securities to a person residing outside the state, the entire transaction—including the original sale—might violate the Securities Act. Since secondary markets for these securities rarely develop, companies often sell securities in these offerings at a discount.[35]

These regulations refer to **accredited investors**, a very specific legal term.[36] Generally, accredited investors are investment companies, wealthy individuals, and the officers of the issuer of the securities. The language of the regulation indicates the importance of having experienced legal counsel guide the process of issuing and selling private security offerings. More detail can be found at http://www.sec.gov/info/small-bus/qasbsec.htm.

In addition, all the exemptions listed are subject to **integration principles**. This means that the securities must conform to a single plan of financing, be used for the same general corporate purpose, be paid for with the same consideration, and be the same class of securities. They should also be offered or sold at or about the same time. Under Rule 147 or regulation D, any offering made six months prior or six months after will be integrated into the exempt offering. Violation of any of these principles violates the regulation, and the entire offering is considered nonexempt and in violation of the securities laws.

Last, in addition to compliance with all laws requiring securities registration, entrepreneurs must provide potential investors with full and complete disclosure about the security, the use of funds, and any other consideration affecting the decision to invest. Both federal and state laws prohibit making any untrue statement of a material fact or omitting any material fact. A "material fact" is one that a reasonable investor would consider significant in making an investment decision.

An investor who can show that the issuer misstated or omitted a material fact in connection with the sale of securities is entitled to recover the amount paid either from the firm or from the individual directors and officers of the venture. Liability may also be imposed on the entrepreneur as the "controlling person" of the actual issuer. Legal actions on such matters must begin within one year of the discovery of the misstatement and no later than three years after the sale of the security.

Cases such as these are complex and expensive. The court has the benefit of hindsight, which can lead to second-guessing the original issuer. The outcomes frequently depend on who can prove what a "fact" was at the time of the issue. A carefully prepared offering document can be invaluable in legal proceedings.[37]

U.S. Bankruptcy Laws

A discussion of the risky nature of entrepreneurial activity must confront the ultimate negative consequences of risky behavior—bankruptcy. Bankruptcy is an option for dealing with financial troubles, primarily an impossible debt burden. The declaration of bankruptcy by a firm is an attempt to wipe the slate clean, equitably pay off creditors, and start again. Because of the potential rejuvenating effect of bankruptcy and the forgiveness of a portion of debts, a person or a corporation can declare bankruptcy only once every six years.

The specter of bankruptcy is always with the entrepreneur and the firm's financiers. It accounts in part for the high rates of return required by equity investors. Equity investors understand that in a bankruptcy they will likely gain nothing and may even lose all their capital investment, so they need high returns from the winners. Our discussions of the resources that provide sustainable competitive advantage for the venture have implicitly included the prospect of bankruptcy. Ventures created with resources that are rare, valuable, imperfectly imitable, and nonsubstitutable are more resistant to environmental threats, competitive attacks, and internal implementation errors than firms without these resources, and thus more resistant to bankruptcy.

Warning Signs/Predictive Models. Bankruptcy seldom sneaks up on a firm. There are usually warning signs that appear as early as 12 to 18 months before the crisis actually occurs. Financial problems, specifically inability to make interest and principal payments, are the usual precipitating events. However, any time the business's liabilities exceed its assets, it may file a bankruptcy petition. Because of the accounting rule that requires acknowledging liabilities as soon as they are known, firms with cash to pay their debts may find themselves with negative net worth. This can happen when a firm must recognize future liabilities for employee health costs or pensions, but the signals are usually evident earlier and the longer-term cause is poor management. The early signs include unhappy customers, a faulty production or service delivery process, bad relations with investors or banks, employee unrest and work stoppages, and, ultimately, poor financial management.

There are telltale signs of impending crisis. For example, when a firm changes management, advisers, and especially accountants and auditors, it suggests that problems are mounting. These changes often result in late filing of financial statements. Other indicators are:

- Qualified and uncertified accountants' opinions
- Refusal to provide access to key executives
- Sudden search for an alliance partner
- New interest in a merger or acquisition without strategic reasons
- Writing off assets
- Restrictions on credit terms and availability

Because creditors can either save their investments or attempt to save the firm if they are aware of the crisis early enough, research has been conducted to provide an early warning system for bankruptcy. The most famous of these predictive models uses information commonly available in financial documents.[38] There are two models, one for private companies and the other for public firms. The models, equations that calculate Z-scores from a discriminate analysis of the data, are shown in Table 7.4.

By plugging in the venture's actual financial ratios, multiplying these ratios by their weights (coefficients), and calculating the total, an analyst can determine whether the

TABLE 7.4   Predictive Model of Bankruptcy

Model 1: The Public Firm

Z-score = 0.012 (WC/TA) + 0.014 (RE/TA) + 0.033 (EBIT) + 0.006 (MVE/TL) + 0.999 (sales/TA)

If the Z-score is less than 1.81, the firm is in danger of bankruptcy.
If the Z-score is greater than 2.99, the firm is considered safe.
Values between 1.81 and 2.99 are considered cautionary.

Model 2: The Private Firm

Z-score = 0.717 (WC/TA) + 0.847 (RE/TA) + 3.107 (EBIT/T) + 0.998 (sales/TA)

If the Z-score is less than 1.23, the firm is in danger of bankruptcy.
If the Z-score is greater than 2.90, the firm is considered safe.
Values between 1.23 and 2.90 are considered cautionary.

WC = Working capital
RE = Retained earnings
EBIT = Earnings before interest and taxes
MVE = Market value of the equity
Sales = Sales
NW = Net worth
TA = Total assets
TL = Total liabilities

SOURCE: E. Altman, R. Haldeman, and P. Narayanan, "ZETA-Analysis: A New Model to Identify Bankruptcy Risk," *Journal of Banking and Finance,* June 1977: 29–54.

firm is in danger of bankruptcy or is in the safe range. Ventures with Z-scores in the intermediate range need watching.

The Bankruptcy Reform Act of 1978. The Bankruptcy Reform Act of 1978 codifies three specific types of voluntary bankruptcy. These are known by their chapter designations: Chapter 7, Chapter 11, and Chapter 13. Each of these details a separate manner by which the firm and its creditors can seek protection. A venture can be forced into bankruptcy (involuntary) by its creditors under the following conditions:

- When three or more creditors have aggregate claims that total $5,000 more than the value of their collateral
- When there is one or more such creditors and the total number of creditors and claimholders is fewer than 12
- When any general partner in a limited partnership begins legal proceedings

Failure to pay on time is a sufficient criterion for a filing of involuntary bankruptcy, even if the firm has the ability to pay. One way to avoid involuntary bankruptcy is to make sure that no three creditors are owed more than $5,000 in the aggregate and that the firm has more than 12 claim holders.

A **Chapter 7 bankruptcy** provides for the voluntary or involuntary liquidation of the firm. The process requires an accounting of all of the assets of the debtor, identification of all creditors and claimholders, appointment of a trustee to supervise the process, and a meeting of the creditors' committee to work out a plan of liquidation and distribution. The Bankruptcy Reform Act of 2000 added a means test to determine whether a person was eligible to file under Chapter 7.

A **Chapter 11 bankruptcy** is filed for the purpose of reorganizing the firm's debts so it can continue to operate. The goal is to keep the business running and eventually emerge from Chapter 11 as a healthier, albeit smaller, company. Creditors and claimholders may prefer this form of bankruptcy if they believe they are likely to receive more of their money than they would under Chapter 7.

Chapter 11 proceedings are often entered into voluntarily by the owners of the business because once they file, all payments of debts and obligations are stopped until a settlement can be worked out. The process calls for the appointment of a trustee, the formation of a committee of general unsecured creditors, and meetings between the committee and the owners to work out a plan for reorganization. The debtor has 120 days to file the reorganization plan and 60 more days to obtain acceptance by the committee. The plan shows how the different classes of creditors will be treated and how the business will operate until all the classes have had their reorganized claims satisfied. The court must approve the final plan. If it does, the debtor is freed from the old debts and obligated to the new debts as described in the plan.

However, many times firms do not emerge from Chapter 11 and are forced to liquidate under Chapter 7. Evidence suggests that, instead of forestalling liquidation and protecting the venture, Chapter 11 hastens its end. The chances of a small firm emerging from Chapter 11 are estimated at between 10 and 30 percent. The primary reasons for this are:

- The high costs of the legal proceedings to discharge the debts
- The diversion of management's attention—attention that may already be insufficient—to legal proceedings instead of business management
- Weakened bargaining power when creditors come face-to-face
- Market disruption affecting customers and suppliers because of the negative publicity attached to a bankruptcy filing

Sometimes it is wise for the owner to try personal persuasion and negotiation before taking the risky step of filing Chapter 11.

A **Chapter 13 bankruptcy** covers individuals, primarily sole proprietorships, with regular incomes of less than $100,000 and secured debts of less than $350,000. Its purpose is to discharge the debts and protect the person from harassment by creditors. The plan can call for an extension of credit to be paid in full over time or for a reduction in outstanding debt with a three-year payment schedule. The Bankruptcy Reform Act of 2000 requires debtors who file under Chapter 13 to repay either $15,000 or a quarter of their debts over five years.

Options and Bargaining Power. Although debtors and owners in bankruptcy feel stigmatized and powerless, they often have a great deal of latitude and bargaining power because the courts protect them from the full payment of debts. Creditors are usually loath to see anything less than full payment so they often cooperate with the owners to avoid bankruptcy proceedings. The power of the owners derives from the conflicts of interest among the creditors. Because creditors are paid off according to the class to which they belong, their interests differ. Lower- priority creditors are more hesitant to put the firm in bankruptcy because they will receive less. *Therefore, these lower-priority, or unsecured, creditors may even be a source of additional credit to prevent an involuntary bankruptcy!* It is often possible for the debtor to arrange postponement of payments, extended payment schedules, moratoriums on interest and principal payments, renegotiated leases, and forgiveness of accrued interest under these circumstances. Of course, creditors do not have to be so understanding and can move legally against the firm. Good financial and personal relationships are extra insurance for a troubled business.

Some of this has now been codified into law. Recent passage of the Bankruptcy Prevention and Consumer Protection Act in April 2005 has resulted in major reforms in bankruptcy law, outlining revised guidelines governing the dismissal or conversion of Chapter 7 liquidations to Chapter 11 or 13 proceedings.[39]

SUMMARY

Entrepreneurial finance builds on traditional financial theory yet goes beyond it in certain ways, recognizing that the entrepreneurial problem is unique and multifaceted. Financial resources are required, and although they are seldom a source of competitive advantage, they are a formidable hurdle for the entrepreneur.

The entrepreneur must be able to accurately determine the venture's financial needs, not only at the beginning, but throughout the venture's lifecycle. Determining start-up costs, predicting cash flows, managing working capital, identifying sources of financing, and accessing this money are key activities. Equity must be raised both inside and outside the firm; debt, both asset-based and cash flow-based, will lower the overall cost of capital for the new venture.

In the process of raising the money, the entrepreneur will have to confront and solve the valuation question. Three types of valuations are possible: asset-based valuations, earnings-based valuations, and discounted cash flow models. All have their strengths and weaknesses. The use of a specific technique depends on the purpose of the valuation.

Last, the chapter covered some basic legal issues regarding new venture financing and start-up. The choice of organizational form affects business and personal liability, cash flow, and tax assessments. Careful consideration of securities laws can enable entrepreneurs and investors to avoid some of the more burdensome regulations. Bankruptcy, although always a negative from someone's point of view, can also be a bargaining tool for a new venture that needs a little more time and patience from its creditors. Expert legal advice is a must for all these issues.

In the next chapter, we will examine more comprehensive and complex models of valuation and discuss the elements and structure of new venture financial deals.

KEY TERMS

Accredited investor
Adjusted book value
Angels
Asset-based financing
Asset-based valuations
Book value
Bootstrapping
Capitalization factor
Cash flow cycle
Cash flow financing
C Corporation
Chapter 7 bankruptcy
Chapter 11 bankruptcy
Chapter 13 bankruptcy
Covenants
Debt-based financing
Discounted cash flow (DCF)
Early-stage financing
Earnings-based valuations
Equity
Expansion or development financing
First-stage financing
Fourth-stage financing
Future earnings
General partnership
Inside equity
Historical earnings
Initial public offering (IPO)
Integration principles

Limited liability company (LLC)
Limited partnership
Liquidation value
Mezzanine financing
Micro loan
Outside equity
Outside equity investors
Overcapitalized
Partnership
Permanent working capital
Phased financing
Price-earnings (P-E) radio
Private placement
Production cycle
Replacement value
Required rate of return
Residual pricing method
Risk capital
S Corporation
Second-stage financing
Seed capital
Small business investment companies (SBICs)
Sole proprietorship
Start-up capital
Temporary working capital
Third-stage financing
Undercapitalized
Venture capital

DISCUSSION QUESTIONS

1. Why are financial resources not a source of competitive advantage even though they are a continuing hurdle for the new venture? (See Chapter 2 for review.)
2. Why is undercapitalization dangerous for a new venture? How can overcapitalization pose a problem?
3. What are the elements of the cash flow cycle?
4. How can managing and controlling the cash flow cycle save money?
5. How do the financing needs of the enterprise change over time?
6. What variables affect the choice of financing sources for the entrepreneur?
7. What are the pros and cons of raising startup capital from private investors?
8. What are the pros and cons of going public?

9. What steps should the entrepreneur take to position the new venture for a loan?
10. Discuss the models and methods of new venture valuation. What are the pros and cons of each method?
11. Discuss the pros and cons of the various legal forms of organization.
12. How does U.S. securities law aid in promoting entrepreneurship through private placements?

EXERCISES
---

1. Calculate the startup capital needed to finance the new venture described in your business plan.
2. Analyze the cash flow cycle from your business plan pro forma statements.
3. Develop a plan to control your firm's cash flow cycle. Recalculate question 1. How much money did you save?
4. Calculate the prospective value of your new venture at the end of five years by adjusted book value or replacement value, by using the appropriate earnings method, and by using the discounted cash flow method.
5. Match your financing needs to the appropriate sources of capital.
6. Using the residual pricing method, how much equity would you have to sell in order to raise money from a venture capitalist?
7. Choose a legal form of organization for your proposed venture. Justify your choice.

DISCUSSION CASE

Rooting for and Investing in the Home Team

Most people associate celebrity Pat Sajak with the turning letters on the "Wheel of Fortune" TV game show. When Sajak was recruited to throw out the first ball at the May 2005 opening game of the Golden Baseball League in Arizona, it was not just because he's a fan or because he's a celebrity, but also because he's a league investor. "Although I made a good living, it's not like I can buy the L.A. Dodgers anytime soon, so this seemed a nice way to get involved," says Sajak.

The Golden League (www.goldenleague.com), one of five independent baseball leagues currently in existence, was born in an entrepreneurship class at Stanford University. After the Western Baseball League folded in 2002, business graduate students David Kaval and Amit Pavel decided to launch a new West Coast-based minor league.

The key difference between Golden League and other baseball leagues is its centralized ownership. "We saw that that was a superior business model and that we could grow to 20 to 30 teams with that model," says Kaval. Because the league's teams all have the same owner there are no bidding wars for players. Less than ten percent of each team's $1 million operating budget is spent on talent. There's an annual salary cap of $88,000 for the entire three-month, 80-

game season for each player, many of them young men hoping to work up to the major leagues. Economies of scale are another benefit. For example, the league bulk purchases balls for all their teams for just $3 instead of the usual $4. Unlike the major leagues, the Golden League actively recruits advertising sponsors, and every player wears a shoulder patch promoting AlphaFlexOmega5 fish oil.

Centralized ownership permits the league to use profits from the more successful teams to offset losses of the other teams, or to use those funds for league expansion. Describing the minor league baseball experience as an "alternative entertainment platform," the league currently targets for expansion communities far from large cities. Attendance is good because there are fewer competing events.

It took Kaval and Pavel over a year to raise the $5 million they needed to get started. Their target investors were successful entrepreneurs from California's Silicon Valley. Kevin Outcalt, a former Cisco Systems executive, invested $1 million and became the league's first commissioner. Jim Peters, a former President of Staples, Inc., and former President and COO of Ross Stores, invested $1.5 million and became the league's chief operating officer. Investors in the communities where the teams are based tend to be local business leaders who want to realize childhood dreams of being sports moguls.

The league started out with eight teams in 2005 but slipped to six in 2006 thanks to poor attendance. There are four teams in California, and one each in Arizona and Nevada. The league hopes to establish a team in northern Mexico to attract the large Latino population in the Western states, but has so far been unable to make a deal for a suitable Mexican stadium. A Utah team was added in 2007. While they still have a long way to go before meeting their target figures, Kaval says that attendance is up from an average of 1350 per game in 2005 to 1500 per game in 2006. "Year One was about survival. The second year has been about streamlining cost," says Commissioner Outcalt. "Year Three will be when we really pay attention to driving profits."

While some of the millionaire investors say they fully expect a healthy financial return on their investment, others have a more relaxed attitude. "I know some people expect this thing to be a home run," says investor Pat Sajak. "But me, I'd settle for a ground-rule double."

SOURCE: Adapted from Gary Rivlin, "Root, Root, Root for the Start-Up," *New York Times*, July 9, 2006. Retrieved from the Web July 8, 2006. http://www.nytimes.com/2006/07/09/business/your-money/09golden.html?adxnnl=1&adnn and www.golden-baseball.com.

Case Questions

1. Describe the nature of the initial financing of the Golden Baseball League (GBL).
2. How is investment in the GBL similar to and different from financing in technology ventures?
3. Describe and evaluate the GBL's business model. Do you think it can work? Why or why not?
4. What additional recommendations would you make to the owners of the GBL?

APPENDIX

The Initial Public Offering (IPO) Process

A public offering in the United States takes six to nine months to plan and execute. Administrative costs, printing, and legal fees may run from $500,000 to $1,000,000. The underwriters typically receive fees of 7.5 percent of the total proceeds as well as options to purchase additional stock at reduced prices.

The underwriter(s) are the investment bankers and brokerage houses that sell the stock to the public, generally through their retail distribution network. There are three types of selling efforts: best effort, best effort (all or none), and firm commitment. In the simple best-effort case, the underwriter agrees to sell as much as possible of the stock that is authorized, and the public issue goes into effect even if not all the authorized stock is sold. The best-effort scenario occurs when the company is relatively small, the investment banker is regional, and the company's prospects are somewhat in doubt.

The best-effort (all or nothing) scenario requires the investment banker to sell all of the authorized issue or cancel the offering. This means that the company will not go public unless it can sell all its stock and raise all the money it needs for financing its future. The advantage here is that the firm will not become public and undercapitalized. The disadvantage is that fees and costs associated with this strategy are not recovered if the offering is canceled.

The firm-commitment selling effort is the safest and most prestigious for the new venture's IPO. The underwriters guarantee that the entire issue will be sold by buying most of it themselves and reselling it to their customers. This is done for companies with the most solid backgrounds, products, and management. The underwriters share some of the risk of the offering by purchasing shares for their own accounts.

The process of going public begins long before the shares are actually sold. The preliminary stages require the venture to meet the criteria of a public firm: a demonstrated record of growth in sales and earnings, a record of raising capital from other outside investors, a product that is visible in the market and of interest to investors, audited financial statements, clear title to the technology, an estimable board of directors, and a management team sufficiently seasoned to simultaneously run the company and manage the IPO process.[1]

If these criteria are met and the venture's managers have determined that the next step is a public offering, the process can formally begin. At this point, management will solicit proposals from underwriters for the IPO. Underwriters will respond with their philosophy, strategy, and tactics—as well as with the estimated costs of their services. Management must then select among the proposals and may suggest joint and cooperative efforts if that seems reasonable. Once the underwriter is hired, the offering begins.

1. **Organization Conference:** This is the first meeting that brings together the three major parties to the IPO process: management, the underwriter, and the independent accounting firm that will prepare the financial statements. All parties bring their lawyers. They discuss the timing of the IPO, the nature of the offering in terms of amounts to be raised, the selling strategy, and the allocation of tasks. The lawyers inform all parties, but especially management, of the current legal constraints on trading and disclosure.

2. **Initial Registration Statement:** Three major elements comprise the paperwork required by the regulating authorities (the SEC). The first, the registration statement, contains so much detail that a significant number of appendixes are usually attached.

The second component, the **prospectus**, is used to sell the new company stock. In some respects it conforms to regulatory standards, but in other respects it is very much like the business plan. It describes the business, its product/market/technology configuration, along with the competition and operations, and it includes full audited financial statements. It is governed by the rule of full disclosure and must reveal all information known to the company that might materially affect the decision of an investor. From a practical standpoint, then, the company must reveal all risks, all conflicts of interest (real and potential), and all transactions conducted by the top managers that might be construed as self-interest. This provides the firm some legal protection against claims of fraud.

The third component is supplemental data, essentially a huge appendix containing such items as copies of leases, employment contracts of the top managers, sales and distribution contracts, and loan agreements. These can run to several hundred pages.

3. **SEC Review and Comment:** The package is sent to the SEC for review and comment. In its review, the SEC staff looks for internal consistency of business plans and use of proceeds. It reviews the description of the issuer's unique risks, looking for more than simple boilerplate disclaimers.[2] The SEC is interested in areas in which the investor might be misled—for example, overly optimistic descriptions of new-product development, overstatement of the actual size of the firm, exaggerated reports of signed contracts for work in hand, and understatement of projected expenses for the use of proceeds. The SEC does not comment on whether the business will succeed; instead it seeks to protect investors against malfeasance and fraud.

4. **Preparation of the Revised Statement:** No IPO review is approved on the first submission. An SEC review letter will request revisions and resubmission. Amendments are added to the application statement, deficiencies are corrected, and language is modified.

5. **Preliminary Prospectus:** Once the approval letter is issued, the preliminary prospectus, which has been in preparation during this period, can be published and then circulated. This prospectus is sometimes called a red herring because the cover page has a red border and because of the speculative nature of IPOs in general. Neither number of shares to be issued nor price per share is included in this document. The purpose of the preliminary prospectus is to give the new issue visibility within the investment community. Now the underwriting group or syndicate—a group of investment houses that will sell the issue and spread the risk—can be organized by the lead underwriter.

6. **Due Diligence:** The underwriter performs due diligence to ensure that the stock is a legitimate investment. If the underwriter were to sell stock without completing a full investigation, it might also be liable for fraud and damages (both from investors who lost money and from other brokers who lost money and reputation). Independent accountants review the company's financial picture, policies, and prospects and issue a letter to the underwriters detailing what they find. All the lawyers also write letters to each other describing the company's legal situation (current lawsuits as well as potential liability). All this investigative diligence is designed to weed out legal problems before they occur and to protect the underwriters, lawyers, and accountants from liability if they are deceived by the top managers.

7. **Pricing the Issue:** As the company gets closer to declaring the date of the offering, negotiations begin to determine the price of the issue. Many factors are involved: the current state of the stock market, the earnings of the company, the total dollars the company is attempting to raise, the prices and performance record of other recent IPOs, and so on. There is a natural conflict of interest between the underwriters and the current owners of the company. First, the underwriter typically receives 20 percent of the gross spread. The rest of the syndicate selling the issue receives a concession for actually selling the shares.[3] The underwriters have the most to gain if the issue is slightly underpriced: If the new issue comes to market at a discount, the underwriters' customers will be happy because the price will soon rise to its market level. Also, the underwriters can make additional profit, because they often take an option (called the shoe) on as much as 10 percent of the issue. The current owners, on the other hand, want the issue to come to market at a premium. If the issue is slightly overpriced, they will receive more money for the shares they personally sell, and the company will receive more money for the shares that are offered. As the time of the offering nears, the underwriter generally assumes control.[4]

8. **Market Timing and Closing:** The last step is the actual closing of the deal. Once the date of offering is set, the underwriters and managers closely monitor the stock market to be ready for the date of issue. If the market starts to fall precipitously, the offering can be canceled up to the last minute. If the market is steady or rising, the final price is set the night before the offering, and a financial printer works all night to produce the prospectus for the IPO with the price on the front page.

APPENDIX NOTES

1. L. Orlanski, "Positioning for the Public Offering," *Bio/technology* 3, 1985: 882–885; S. Jones and B. Cohen, *The Emerging Business* (New York: John Wiley, 1983).

2. L. Orlanski, "SEC Comments on the Offering Prospectus," *Review of Securities Regulation* 17, no. 11, 1984: 887–896.

3. There is a good deal of evidence that new issues, on average, come to market underpriced. Quality new issues then rise quickly and the underwriters and those favored customers who've been given the option of making early purchases then sell and make a quick profit. Within 6 to 18 months the shares are earning "normal" returns and no excess profits remain for investors. Low-quality new issues decline even more quickly.

4. K. Ellis, R. Michaely, and M. O'Hara, "A Guide to the Initial Public Offering Process," 1999. Retrieved from the Web February 27, 2007. http://forum.johnson.cornell.edu/faculty/ michaely/Guide.pdf

CHAPTER 8

Securing Investors and Structuring the Deal

Things may come to those who wait, but only the things left by those who hustle.
—*Abraham Lincoln*

──────────── OUTLINE ────────────

──────────── LEARNING OBJECTIVES ────────────

After reading this chapter, you will understand

- what constitutes a *good investor,* and a *good investment.*
- the nature of the *investment process.*
- the *financial factors* involved in making a deal.
- how entrepreneurs can *create value* with a well-structured deal.
- the fundamentals of negotiating strategy and tactics.

PERSONAL PROFILE 8

Connecting Different Worlds

Erel Margalit has been at the forefront of the high-tech revolution in Israel, but his background is in philosophy, not engineering or computer science. He sees himself as a visionary who is good at making deals. "I love to connect between different people and between different disciplines," Margalit says. "So I established my venture capital fund, JVP [Jerusalem Venture Partners], which was the second such fund in Israel." He was just 32 when he founded the fund in 1993; today JVP manages more than $680 million in investment funds.

Margalit was the first Israeli included on *Forbes* magazine's Midas List, an annual ranking of individuals who deploy capital to create wealth for investors. In 2006 he was #88 on the list. At JVP (www.jvpvc.com) Margalit has supervised more than 14 successful deals. One of those was the sale of an optical networking systems company with a research facility located in Tel Aviv to Lucent Technology for 78 million shares of Lucent stock in May 2000. The sale of Chromatis Networks was heralded as the most impressive high-tech harvest in Israel before it turned into one of the most visible failures. While Margalit bickered with Israeli tax authorities over how investors in Israeli funds should be taxed, he postponed distribution of the Lucent stock and the price dropped from US $58.125 to less than $1 per share. JVP's investors saw their Chromatis holdings fall by almost 80 percent. Margalit insists it was still a good deal, noting that in the end "our investors multiplied their money by a factor of 60 or 70."

Margalit says that, because Israel is a society of immigrants, many individuals are anxious to prove themselves. "Every Israeli thinks that the difference between him and Bill Gates is just a bit of time," he says. High-

tech firms have produced approximately 40 percent of Israel's growth in the past ten years and make up about 55 percent of Israel's exports. This explosion has been fueled by the mass immigration of engineers and scientists from the former Soviet Union, by national grants to scientists and military research projects, and by the growth of the foreign semiconductor industry. Today Israel has more companies with stock traded on the U.S. NASDAQ exchange than any other Middle Eastern or European country.

In the early 1990s Margalit served as the Director of Business Development for the City of Jerusalem, a job he says he got through a combination of personality and connections. In that position he helped bring more than 70 technology firms to Jerusalem, including Intel, Digital, and IBM. That was his first experience connecting "the world of capital to the world of great inventors." Margalit's current venture capital focus is media technologies, particularly projects that bring engineers and artists together to merge animation with gaming. He was also recently nominated to be chairman of the Israel Broadcasting Company.

Margalit's connection to Jerusalem is still strong, and many expect him to run for mayor one day. If he does, he will use his deal-making skills not only to bring new business to the city, but also to build cooperation between Jerusalem's Arabs and Jews. "I don't know if it will take five or seven or ten years, but there will be an agreement—and then Jerusalem will become a gateway to the Arab world. The 200,000 Arabs who live in Jerusalem will enjoy the advantages inherent in the fact that they belong to the region and have access to the region. They will be the catalyst of a process of economic change throughout the Arab world—instead of being caught between worlds, they will become a bridge between those worlds."

"I am not an optimist," declares Margalit. "I am an entrepreneur."

SOURCE: Adapted from "The Business of Persuasion, *The Economist,* July 8, 2006: 60; Ari Shavit, "JVP in the News," *Haaretz*, June 17, 2006. Retrieved from the Web August 2, 2006. http://www.jvpvc.com/news/20060617-64618.html, www.forbes.com and www.jvpvc.com.

How does the entrepreneur obtain the money to launch the new venture? The chapter's opening quote implies that securing investors is an active process. If the era ever existed when investors beat a path to the door of the entrepreneur with a better mousetrap, it is gone. The entrepreneur cannot be passive and assume that financing will follow automatically from a well-designed business plan. Ventures in pursuit of financing greatly outnumber the investors and the money needed to launch them. The best deal will result from an aggressive, confident, and realistic approach.

What is a deal? It is usually much more complicated than a simple "Give me money, and sometime in the future, I will return it with gain." A **deal** consists of the structure and terms of a transaction between two or more parties.[1] For the entrepreneur, this definition has important implications. The first is that a deal *has a structure*. The structure indicates sets of preferences for risk and reward. These preferences depend on the personal characteristics of the bargainers, the current financial situation of the industries involved, and any pertinent customs and traditions. The second implication is that terms must be negotiated—terms such as the rights and duties of the parties to the deal, the timing of certain activities of the financiers and the entrepreneurs, and the constraints and covenants that establish the rules the parties will follow. These are usually put in writing so that the investors are assured, insured, and reassured that their money is secure.

The final implication of the definition is that there may be more than two parties to the deal. It is unusual (and generally not preferred) for an entrepreneur to obtain all the financing from a single source. This may mean having debt from one source and equity from another. In fact, there are often layers of debt with different risk/ return characteristics, as well as distinct layers of equity. A deal is always a team effort, and many positions are available for the players.

The entrepreneur's key task is to create value. This means making the whole greater than the sum of its parts by using the marketing concept of segmentation to raise financial backing. In essence, the entrepreneur is selling equity in the firm, ensuring cash flow, and guaranteeing return and repayment. Just as products and services have different characteristics that appeal to different people, financial instruments in a new venture financial deal also are differentiated, creating opportunities for market segmentation.

To be successful, the entrepreneur must demonstrate understanding and insight in three areas.[2] First, the entrepreneur and the top management team must understand their business. Without a clear understanding of the business and its environment, they will never be able to reach a consensus with the investors on the fundamentals, let alone the financing. Entrepreneurs must know their business well enough to understand the absolute amount of money they need and when they will need it. They must understand the risks involved and the cause-and-effect factors so that they can explain and defend their actions to potential investors. They need to understand the nature of the returns the business can offer—the sources of these returns, their magnitude, and their timing. Next, entrepreneurs must understand financiers and the context in which they make their decisions. Investors are interested not only in the amount of money they may make but also in the risk of their investment, the timing of the returns, the controls to protect their money, and the mechanisms needed to (1) reinvest if necessary, (2) abandon if prudent, and (3) harvest when appropriate.

Perhaps most important, entrepreneurs need to understand themselves. What are their preferences for ownership, control, wealth, and risk? Without self-knowledge, entrepreneurs may make deals that will not have long-term positive benefits and that can even sow the seeds for a lifetime of discontent and bitterness.

This chapter explores the issues surrounding structuring deals and financing new ventures. We review the process by which entrepreneurs approach investors and examine the criteria investors use to make decisions. Then we build two models to illustrate the issues of deal structure. A simple discounted cash flow example was presented in Chapter 7, and an understanding of this basic model is necessary to understanding the more elaborate models presented in this chapter. The chapter continues with a discussion of the negotiation process. Experience and common sense provide many of the guidelines for the "dos and don'ts" of deal negotiation. Last, we introduce some of the basic concepts in the area of negotiation. Negotiation skills are important for the nascent and practicing entrepreneur, and skilled negotiators give their firms an advantage in resource acquisition and deployment.

APPROACHING INVESTORS

What should entrepreneurs know, in addition to the particulars of their business, when they meet with investors? A knowledge of investing patterns and traditions is vital. The entrepreneur-investor relationship has been modeled as a classic "prisoner's dilemma." There are high rewards for mutual cooperation and big losses for mutual deception. But neither party wants to be played for a sucker and there are short-term rewards for cheating the other party. In the long run, the best strategy is cooperation among all the parties to the deal.[3] A process that promotes social interaction among the participants will produce trust, feedback, and timely information. The goal is a relationship based on fairness and procedural justice.[4]

This concern for investor relations helps to mitigate some of the initial skepticism because at the most basic level, obtaining financing is a selling job. The entrepreneur is selling a part ownership of the new venture (equity), a percentage of the anticipated cash flow (debt), or both. Every selling job requires knowledge of the customers, their purchasing habits, their sensitivity to price, and the substitutes and alternatives available to them. In Chapter 3 we discussed selling products. A review of the concepts of "buyer power" can be applied to financiers and will provide some of the insight needed to plan an effective strategy.

The Ideal Investor

Every entrepreneur has his or her vision of a dream investor, but the ideal seldom exists in real life. What are the characteristics of the ideal investor? The ideal investor:

1. *Is actually considering making an investment.* Investors who are not liquid or have no desire to invest are unapproachable—no matter how rich they are.
2. *Has the right amount of money to invest.* An investor with too little money cannot buy into the deal. An investor with too much money may view this deal as trivial.
3. *Is interested in the business.* Investors should share some of the founders' enthusiasm and optimism about the business's prospects.
4. *Has knowledge that can help the new venture.* Counseling from an investor with experience, expertise, or network resources is ideal. The investor may be savvy about the business or industry, may be knowledgeable about the geographic area where the business will operate, and may know other individuals interested in investing.
5. *Is reputable and ethical.* The investor's reputation is part of the new venture's reputational capital. Ethical standards are important because investors could take advantage of inside information or manipulate their investment to the entrepreneur's disadvantage in a potential conflict of interest.
6. *Has a good rapport with the top managers and founders.* The ability to communicate freely, to get along and see the situation from the founder's point of view can go a long way to easing strain between management and investors.
7. *Has experience in this type of investing.* Because of the wide swings in performance and emotions that are part of the entrepreneurial process, investors who know what to expect and can hang on for the duration are most desirable.[5]

Investors with all these characteristics are rare, valuable, hard to duplicate, and nonsubstitutable human resources that can provide sustainable advantage for the firm.

The ideal investor may be found in any of three primary investor groups:

1. Friendly investors—family, friends, business associates, potential customers or suppliers, prospective employees, and managers. These informal investors are the primary source of financing for most business start-ups. According to the Kauffman Foundation, 44.6 percent of friendly investors are close family members and 27.7 percent are friends or neighbors.[6]
2. Small outside investors—wealthy individuals (e.g., doctors, lawyers, businesspersons) and angels.
3. Formal or professional investors in the venture capital industry.

Hal Bringman is an example of a friendly investor, but he isn't a cash investor. He and his partner are very successful public relations executives. Their firm takes equity in exchange for services that are too expensive for the entrepreneur to afford. When Fabrice Grinda asked them to handle public relations for his new start-up, Zingy, they decided to take a chance on becoming equity owners. Why? Zingy (a provider of downloadable ringtones) had enormous potential in a very hot market. And did the exchange pay off? When Grinda sold Zingy to a Japanese company for $80 million, they were "making a lot more money than if they had taken fees," Mr. Grinda reported.[7]

In another example, professional investors were a source of outside funds and expertise for Software Artistry, Inc., a fledgling developer of artificial-intelligence software packages. The Indianapolis venture capital firm CID Equity Partners invested a total of

$2.2 million in nine separate deals with Software Artistry over a period of five years. More important, CID encouraged the company to concentrate its efforts into developing Expert Advisor, a program that centralizes information from a business's internal experts at a central help desk. This unique and successful software has enabled entities like Sony Electronics, General Mills, and the U.S. Senate to reduce the number of employees handling customer inquiries, cut phone time, and slash the number of transferred calls within the organization. CID also recruited a new CEO for Software Artistry before the company went public. During the initial public offering, CID sold enough of its Software Artistry shares to recoup its cash investment, but retained shares that still gave them a $40 million interest in the venture.[8]

Not all investments have happy endings for the founding entrepreneur and the new venture. Street Story 8.1 is a cautionary tale of investor involvement in the company.

The Ideal Entrepreneur

Investors also have their "dream" investment. It poses little risk, produces a big payoff, and takes place overnight. More realistic investment opportunities require careful study and evaluation. The five most important investment criteria are:[9]

1. *Market attractiveness* includes four major elements: size of market, growth rate of market, access to market, and need for the product. All enable a firm to build volume while sustaining selling margins.

2. *Product differentiation* involves aspects such as uniqueness and patentability. These make the product hard to copy and are bases of sustainable competitive advantage, resulting in higher profit margins. Value added through the employment of technical skills is another aspect and is part of the human and technical resource base of the venture.

3. *Management capabilities,* the skill levels and implementation abilities of management, are also key components. The development of organizational resources requires management capabilities, and the employment of such inert resources as financial and physical assets is enhanced by management and organization.[10]

4. *Environmental threats* matter because research indicates that investors do not separate the industry environment from the macroenvironment, as we did in Chapter 3. The major safeguards that investors look for are protection from competitive entry, resistance to economic cycles (economics), protection from obsolescence (technology), and protection from downside risk.

5. *Cash-out potential* is reportedly the least important factor among all the evaluation criteria, not because money is not important, but because profitability and wealth are the result of all the other factors falling into place. Nevertheless, investors are interested in the potential for merger with another firm and other opportunities for exit. These factors are summarized in Figure 8.1.

Jack Gill of Vanguard Ventures (http://www.vanguardventures.com/team/jg.html) looks for a driven management team, a better solution (where is the pain? will this product/service ease it?), and a unique product. But he cautions against the **BFC proposal** in which the entrepreneur is offering "**B**etter, **F**aster, **C**heaper." While the product might be BFC in the short term, Gill urges investors to investigate whether a new generation

| STREET STORY 8.1 |

Toppling the Top Dog

In 1997 David Handawi had the skills needed to create a security software company: He had a Ph.D. in Operations Research from the University of California at Berkeley, and he had already held several executive positions in software development companies. Handawi had entrepreneurial vision too. He could see a need in the marketplace for software that could make enterprise desktops, laptops, and servers run more securely and efficiently.

When the company he founded began to grow, Handawi did not appear to have the necessary management skills to serve as CEO—even though he had previously been CEO of a telecommunication software company. After a group of outsiders invested $8 million in BigFix, Inc., in 2002, they hired an experienced start-up executive to assist Handawi. When sales still fell short of expectations, they replaced Handawi as CEO with that new hire.

"The last thing somebody wants to do is confront somebody and say, 'You're doing a bad job,'" says Pascal Levensohn, founder of a venture capital firm called Levensohn Venture Partners. But according to Levensohn, almost two-thirds of venture-backed start-ups replace their founding CEOs. Signs that a CEO is in trouble include ignoring input from board members, shirking responsibility when problems arise, and/or making desperate deals. Some floundering CEOs simply start spending more time outside the office, getting involved in political campaigns or charitable projects instead of dealing with issues inside the company.

Despite the awkwardness of confrontation, some investors get burned because of their reluctance to speak up. Levensohn says his firm lost its $1.5-million investment when SingleSourceIT, an Internet start-up company, failed five years ago. Yogen Dalal, a managing director of fellow investor MayField Fund, says, "The CEO change should have been made sooner." Even Randy Wilcox, founder and CEO of SingleSourceIT, admits that allowing him to continue as CEO "in retrospect, was a mistake."

Some start-up founders, of course, have been very successful CEOs: Bill Gates and Michael Dell are two legendary examples. Replacing a CEO isn't always a magic solution. Apple Computer, Inc., floundered after removing cofounder Steve Jobs as CEO in 1985, but has soared since he resumed the position in 1997.

Keith Benjamin, a BigFix board member who was involved in replacing Handawi as CEO, calls the transition "a great example of how to do it the right way." Still, he notes that the founder "was not happy about it." Handawi gave up his office and worked from home for some time after his ouster. But when BigFix refocused its marketing strategy, the company found a new role for Handawi. His technical skills enabled him to deal knowledgeably with the tech buyers at big companies, and the company's software-contract bookings grew more than 75 percent as a result of his involvement. Today BigFix (www.bigfix.com) provides comprehensive and innovative security software to over 350 companies, government agencies, and public sector institutions, and its security software—including products developed and patented by Handawi—has won numerous industry awards.

SOURCE: Adapted from Rebecca Buckman, "When Founders Flounder," *The Wall Street Journal*, January 23, 2006. Retrieved from the Web January 23, 2006. http://online.wsj.com/article_print/SB113797392552153168.html and www.bigfix.com.

FIGURE 8.1   Venture Capital Investment Decision Process

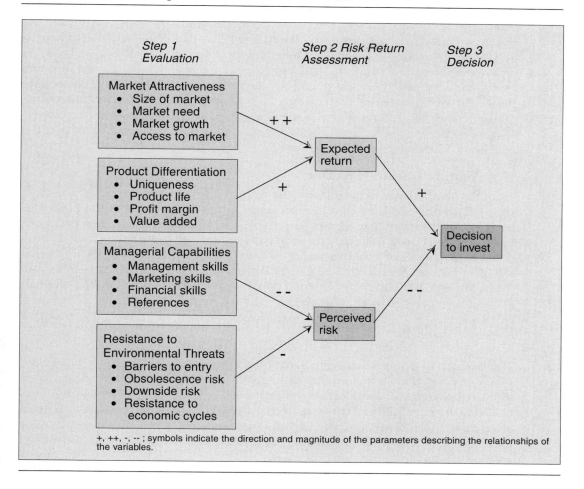

+, ++, -, -- ; symbols indicate the direction and magnitude of the parameters describing the relationships of the variables.

of product will make the BFC irrelevant, or whether someone else is around the corner with ever more BFC.[11]

An investor looks for the fatal flaw in an entrepreneur's plan, perhaps an inconsistency that negates all other positives. The investor attempts to view the new venture proposal as a business system and a set of interconnected parts. Parts that do not fit together are a red flag for investors—perhaps even a deal breaker, a "can't be negotiated demand" that catches the investor's eye and causes him or her to reject the proposal.[12]

Timmons sums up investor criteria in three broad strokes.[13] He says that the investment must be forgiving, rewarding, and enduring. A *forgiving* opportunity has some allowance for variation. In other words, everything does not have to go perfectly for the venture to succeed. Because events seldom turn out perfectly, this is important. If the venture must be launched with the precision and perfection of a NASA space shuttle, investors will steer clear. A *rewarding* opportunity makes money. Returns do not have to be 100 percent compounded annually to be considered rewarding (although it helps). If early projections show returns in the 10 to 15 percent range, though, and the investors know that early projections are optimistic, then the project is not rewarding enough. Finally, the investment should be enduring. An *enduring* venture has a semblance of sustainable competitive advantage and is able to resist economic and competitive pressures. It must endure long enough to provide a clear exit for early investors as they pass the reward and risk to the next level.

New Venture Investor Processes

From the point of view of the investor, the rational investment process is a seven-phase cycle.[14] Each phase is designed to maximize the potential gain (or minimize the potential loss) for the investor at the lowest possible cost in terms of time spent evaluating proposals. Investors usually view the world as teeming with more proposals and entrepreneurs than they can afford to finance or even to review. This is especially true at the top of an investment cycle, like the one for Internet companies that lasted from the late 1990s through 2000. At the trough of a cycle (like the period from mid-2000 through 2001), there appear to be few entrepreneurs and too much money available.[15] Investors' emphasis, then, is on bringing in the most likely proposals and eliminating those that waste time and human resources.

The Search. Investors scan and monitor their environment just as entrepreneurs do. When investors find an opportunity that appeals to them, they make the first contact through a reference or introduction from a mutual acquaintance or business associate. Cold calls are rare. Entrepreneurs should emulate this behavior, but there are directories of venture capitalists for entrepreneurs who cannot arrange a personal introduction or reference.[16] Only a few investors should be contacted at a time. One-at-a-time contacts are too slow and deliberate, but a shotgun approach should also be avoided. The investment community is small and word of a new proposal travels quickly.

One way to expedite the search is to bring investors and entrepreneurs together at a meeting. This is what Demo does. Demo is a Phoenix, Arizona, based event at which selected inventors and entrepreneurs present their ideas to a group of rapacious investors. It resembles speed dating and it is very efficient if somewhat strange. Says Guy Kawasaki, a noted venture capitalist and author, "It is a great event, especially if you understand the dance that is going on: entrepreneurs acting like they don't need capital, and venture capitalists acting like they don't need entrepreneurs." He concludes that the behavior at Demo is like "acting prudish in a brothel."[17]

The Screen. Once in the hands of the investor, the business plan is screened for further interest. In a large investment company, initial screening might be handled by junior staff using the criteria for investor screening discussed above. As the plan passes various tests, it may be moved along to more senior people for serious review and eventually lead to a presentation by the entrepreneur to an investor committee. This enables personal factors and chemistry to enter the equation. The question-and-answer session that follows (or interrupts) the presentation will demonstrate the entrepreneur's mental agility. If the meeting goes well, the evaluation phase begins.

Sometimes the screen takes place without the entrepreneur even being aware of it. A relatively new phenomenon called pre-emptive financing has emerged. **Pre-emptive financing** occurs when the investor approaches the entrepreneur before the entrepreneur needs or asks for money. The initiative comes out of the blue because the investor is trying to buy equity in a company with big potential and avoid the higher price and bidding war that might ensue later on. The entrepreneur has a great deal of power in this situation. Companies targeted for pre-emptive financing are online companies with solid business models, and young companies in wireless communications, computer games, and consumer internet services.[18]

The Evaluation. In this phase, the plan is dissected and evaluated from every conceivable angle as investors perform **due diligence**. Because professional investors use money that is not their own, they are legally obligated to protect their customers' finances by thoroughly investigating the potential of the proposed business. Legal opinions and certified accounting expertise are required. The process of due diligence has precisely the same intent as it does in the initial public offering described in Chapter 7. It is a costly and time-consuming process lasting six to eight weeks.

The evaluation process is more an art than a science. In some cases there is a generation gap between entrepreneurs and investor-evaluators. Young entrepreneurs are proposing businesses like mobile phone services to investors who are not their target customers. David Cowen, a 40-year-old father of three, manages Bessemer Venture Partners of Menlo Park, California. On any given day he might discuss their ventures with people half his age dressed in tee shirts and flip-flops. He has had to learn to download, to blog, and to drink beer with the students at Stanford. He has had to shed his buttoned-down image to acclimate to the next generation of entrepreneurs.[19]

The Decision. After the due diligence phase is completed, investors make their decision. If the decision is "no," entrepreneurs should press for their reasons. They need this feedback before beginning the long and frustrating process again. Common reasons for rejection include:

- *Technological myopia.* **Technological myopia** is the fatal flaw that causes entrepreneurs to become so caught up in the excitement of their technology, processes, or product that they neglect to analyze the market or develop a marketing system.
- *Failure to make full disclosure* is a most serious error. If entrepreneurs fail to divulge pertinent facts that are later discovered, the reputation of the team is damaged and it becomes less trustworthy in the investors' eyes.
- *Unrealistic assumptions* can take the form of exaggerated claims about the product or the market that are then used to produce overly optimistic and improbable forecasts.

- *Management* is crucial to investors. They must have faith in the capabilities of the founder and the management team. As noted earlier, investors often prefer a B proposal with an A team to an A proposal with a B team.

If the proposal is rejected and the entrepreneur receives feedback, he or she ought to respectfully consider that input and attempt to adjust to investor requirements. If the proposal is accepted, the negotiation phase begins and the actual details of the deal can be hammered out.

The Negotiations. The objective of the negotiation phase is to come to an agreement concerning the rights, duties, contingencies, and constraints that will bind the parties to the deal. The first stage of agreement is a short document called the **term sheet**. It outlines the general areas of the investment and the relationship between the parties. A sample term sheet appears in Appendix 8A. This information will later be codified in a formal contract known as the **investment agreement**. An outline of a typical investment agreement appears in Appendix 8B.

An entrepreneur whose venture possesses many of the four attributes of sustainable competitive advantage has negotiating power. However, if the business is already using up cash faster than it generates sales, the power may reside with the investors. The investors and the entrepreneurs must agree on three crucial issues: the deal structure, protection of the investment, and the exit.[20]

The Deal Structure. The two issues to be resolved here are:

1. How is the venture to be valued?
2. What investment instruments will be employed?

We discussed valuation issues in Chapter 7. The entrepreneur wants to justify the highest valuation possible, one that will require him or her to sell less equity and relinquish less ownership. For example, if the entrepreneur can reasonably negotiate a value of $2 million for the business and a $1-million investment is required, the post-investment value of the firm is $3 million. The $1-million investment represents 33.3 percent of the post-investment ownership. If the original valuation had been only $1 million, the post-investment equity ownership position of the investor would have been 50 percent.

The investment instruments are also negotiable. Investors prefer capital structures that maximize their return and minimize their risk. They try to negotiate deals in which their investment is preferred stock or some form of senior debt (with collateral, interest payments, and guaranteed return of principal) *unless* the business is already a success, in which case they want their debt to be convertible into equity! Once the debt is converted, investors can share proportionally in any profits. The entrepreneur, on the other hand, prefers a capital structure of common equity—simple, clean, and requiring no cash payout unless and until the company can afford it.

Many other provisions and covenants can be included in the deal structure. Definitions, descriptions, and examples of these negotiable terms are provided in Appendix 8C.

The Harvest. For many investors, the major returns are realized at the end of the investment's life when the investor cashes out and **harvests** the profits. The details of the harvesting process can be negotiated and spelled out in the investment agreement. **Registration rights** enable the investor to register stock, at company expense, for sale to someone else. Because of restrictive regulation on the sale of private placement investments, investors are required to register their shares (an expensive and time-consuming process) before they may resell them. The two most common registration rights are piggyback rights and demand rights. **Piggyback rights** allow investors to sell shares on any registration statement that the company makes with the Securities and Exchange Commission for sale of shares to the public. **Demand rights** require the company to register the investor's shares for sale (at company expense) on demand— whenever the investor wants. Demand rights are more onerous for entrepreneurs because they can force the company to go public before it wants to. A demand registration exposes the venture to the high costs and external pressures of public ownership (see Chapter 7).

Other forms of investor exit may be negotiated. The entrepreneurs can negotiate a "put" contract, in which they agree to repurchase the investors' shares at a certain date for a certain price. If the put contract has a scale of dates and payment amounts, it can be considered a warrant held by the investors. Other options include exit scenarios in case of merger or liquidation. Entrepreneurs must be careful not to get trapped in a situation in which an investor can call for the liquidation of the business or an immediate cash payout when a merger/acquisition occurs.

The investment agreement cannot anticipate all contingencies. Therefore, both sides need to negotiate the process by which their rights under the contract can be modified. For instance, such modification may require a two-thirds vote of the board.

Negotiations between investor and entrepreneur are paradoxical. While they are going on, the two parties are in conflict since one's gain is often the other's loss. Investors should be expected to do everything possible to secure the investment and increase the potential for return. The wise entrepreneur should negotiate hard for economic rights and provisions favorable to keeping control of the company.

Once the agreement has been reached, the two parties are partners and their gains are mutual and shared.[21] After the investment is made and the proceeds are out into the venture, the relationship between investor and entrepreneur is more like a marriage and less like a haggle over the price of beans. It would be extremely shortsighted for any party to the investment to pollute the atmosphere of the courtship and have that carry over into the marriage.

STRUCTURING THE DEAL

There is no perfect deal.[22] Everyone in a deal negotiation has to make tradeoffs that, in the end, make it suboptimal for someone. At its most basic level, a **deal structure** organizes a set of cash inflows and outflows. It describes what monies are coming into the business as investment and what monies are going out of the business as payments in the form of dividends, interest, and return of principal. At another level, the deal structure indicates levels of risk and reward and addresses the questions of who gets what and when. By breaking the outflows down by type according to risk level, the entrepreneur segments the investor market and sells the investors the level of reward and risk that best matches that investor's profile.

Segmenting the Investor Market

A simplified deal structure is presented in Figure 8.2.[23] To understand the figure, imagine that the cash flows shown represent an investment and subsequent returns in a biotech company that does genetic engineering. The entrepreneurs have calculated that they need $2 million to found the venture at year 0. Figure 8.2 shows their final estimate of cash flows for the project for each year through Year 5.

The **internal rate of return** (IRR) on the cash flows in Figure 8.2 is 59.46 percent. The IRR is calculated by solving for the discount factor that makes the cash outflow exactly equal to the cash inflow. An IRR of 59.45 percent can be deemed sufficient to proceed with the analysis. The five-year projection is also sufficient and typical. However, the example shows only the aggregated bottom-line numbers on the deal. Segmenting the investor market means breaking these numbers down into their original component parts to show the risk/reward attributes of each part of the cash flow.

Table 8.1 does this and indicates that for a $2 million investment, the project generates cash flows from three sources:

1. Tax incentives are positive in the first three years but become negative (tax payments) in Years 4 and 5.
2. Free cash flow (CF) from operations is positive throughout the five-year horizon, rising from $200,000 in Year 1 to $1.2 million in Year 5.
3. The projected terminal value of the business is also a factor. In this example, it is predicted to be $10,000,000. This is derived (hypothetically) by taking the free cash flow for Year 5, subtracting the Year 5 tax liability ($1,200 - $200), and applying a price-earnings multiple of 10 to the result (10 x $1,000,000 = $10,000,000). Note that the Total CF figure is the same as the one used in Figure 8.2.

We can also calculate the net present value of each of the sources of cash flow by discounting the cash flows on any given line of Figure 8.2 by the internal rate of return on

FIGURE 8.2   Biotech Cash Flows Example ($thousands)

	Year					
	0	1	2	3	4	5
Cash Flows	(2,000)	600	600	800	800	11,000

To calculate the IRR of this stream of cash flows, solve for k.

$$IRR = (2,000) = \frac{600}{(1+k)} + \frac{600}{(1+k)^2} + \frac{800}{(1+k)^3} + \frac{800}{(1+k)^4} + \frac{11,000}{(1+k)^5}$$

This equation can be solved with financing programs or spreadsheets like Excel.

TABLE 8.1   Segmented Cash Flow Structure ($thousands)

Source of Flow	Year 0	Year 1	Year 2	Year 3	Year 4	Year 5
Investment	($2,000)					
Tax incentive		$400	$400	$100	($200)	($200)
Free CF		200	200	700	1,000	1,200
Terminal value						10,000
Total CF	($2,000)	$600	$600	$800	$800	$11,000

SOURCE: Adapted from J. Timmons, *New Venture Creation* (Homewood, IL: Irwin, 1994): 774–77.

the whole project (about 59.5 percent). The net present value (NPV) of the investment component is -$2,000,000 in Year 0. The other NPVs are calculated as follows ($000):

$$\text{NPV (tax)} = \frac{\$400}{(1 + .595)^1} + \frac{\$400}{(1 + .595)^2} + \frac{\$100}{(1 + .595)^3} + \frac{-\$200}{(1 + .595)^4} + \frac{-\$200}{(1 + .595)^5}$$

$$\text{NPV (CF)} = \frac{\$200}{(1 + .595)^1} + \frac{\$200}{(1 + .595)^2} + \frac{\$700}{(1 + .595)^3} + \frac{\$1,000}{(1 + .595)^4} + \frac{\$1,200}{(1 + .595)^5}$$

$$\text{NPV (TV)} = \frac{\$10,000}{(1 + .595)^5}$$

The results are:
NPV (Tax) = $383,383—19.1 percent of the returns
NPV (CF) = $647,272—32.4 percent of the returns
NPV (TV) = $968,716—which is 48.5 percent of the returns
Total = $2,000,000 (rounded off)

The example shows that most of the returns from this deal come from the terminal value of the company. This is the riskiest figure in the example because it requires that a great many things turn out right five years down the road. Deals like this are appropriate for venture capital firm investments.

Other Investor Segments. But the entrepreneur would not want to go directly to a venture capitalist for financing. First, the entrepreneur should look for an angel. If that approach fails, the next target is a bank willing to lend money. Finally, the cash flows can be "sold" to less risk-averse investors who will accept lower returns than the venture capitalists. Table 8.2 suggests how these other flows might be partitioned.

The goal, in Figure 8.2, is to raise $2 million. The investment's tax benefits might appeal to a wealthy investor looking for a tax write-off. People in high marginal tax brackets can often protect their incomes or cash flows by investing in businesses that may have high early losses. Entrepreneurs might well be able to convince a wealthy individual with a required rate of return of 20 percent that the tax benefit cash flow projection is accurate and reliable.

TABLE 8.2   Partitioned Cash Flow Structure by Investor ($000)

Source of Investment	Year 0	Year 1	Year 2	Year 3	Year 4	Year 5
Total CF	-$2,000	$600	$600	$800	$ 800	$11,000
>Wealthy investor		400	100	100	-200	-200
>Lending						
institution		100	100	100	100	1,100
=Remaining CF	-$2,000	$100	$100	$600	$ 900	$10,100

How much would the wealthy investor be willing to pay for this cash stream? That can be determined by discounting the tax cash flow by the investor's required rate of return. In this case, we arrive at a present value of $492,155. The investor must see this investment of $492,155 as equivalent to the cash flows from the tax benefits. After a modest amount of convincing, the entrepreneurs hope to receive a commitment from the investor, so they may point out that the tax benefits could be even larger if the firm loses more money in its early years.

With some money now in hand, the entrepreneurs are ready to approach a lending institution such as a commercial bank. Banks are not interested in tax benefits; few of them make enough money to pay very much in taxes anyway. They are interested in the firm's ability to generate cash for interest payments and the repayment of principal. Although the free cash flows of the firm are relatively risky, some portion of them should be considered safe by conservative lending officers. For our example, assume that $100,000 (see Table 8.2) is considered fairly safe in any given year. If the entrepreneurs can find a bank inclined to accept an interest payment of $100,000 each year and a repayment of principal in Year 5 with an interest rate of 10 percent, they can borrow $1 million.[24] Added to the $492,000 from the wealthy investor, the entrepreneurs need only $508,000 to complete the deal.

Selling Equity. There are few alternative sources for the remaining $508,000, so the entrepreneurs are forced to sell equity in their business to a venture capital firm. Venture capitalists are interested in the riskiest portion of the deal, the terminal value. In exchange for this risk, they demand the highest returns (upwards of 50 percent). The management team can use the residual pricing method (see Chapter 7) to determine just how much equity must be sold to raise $508,000 at a required rate of return. To calculate this, they determine the remaining cash flows not previously committed to the wealthy individual or bank (see Table 8.3), then discount it by the venture capitalist's 50 percent required rate of return. This gives a residual value of $1,796,707. The amount of the proposed venture capital investment is $508,000, 28.3 percent of $1,796,707. So the entrepreneurs offer the venture capitalists 28.3 percent of the common equity in their business for $508,000. If the venture capitalists accept the offer, the entrepreneurs have completed their $2-million financing and have kept 71.7 percent of the firm for themselves. In fact, the entrepreneurs are creating value for themselves any time they raise money at less than the total internal rate of return (IRR) for the project (59.5 percent).

Risk Sharing

The previous example is intentionally simplified to show that investors have different risk/reward preferences and that entrepreneurs who can identify these needs have an advantage in securing financing.[25] If the entrepreneurs in the example had gone directly to the venture capitalists, they would have had to part with 79.9 percent of the equity to secure the entire $2 million.[26]

The example assumed that the venture capitalists would take common stock and provide their entire investment up front, at the beginning of the initial period. These assumptions are relaxed in the example that follows.

Risk Sharing: Some Examples. Table 8.3 presents a simplified set of cash flows for a deal.[27] In an all-equity deal with a 40-percent required rate of return for the venture capitalist, the NPV of the set of flows is $1,204. (Readers should calculate this for themselves). The venture capitalist will demand 83 percent of the equity ($1,000/$1,204) for this investment, leaving 17 percent for the entrepreneurs. The net present value for the investors is $0, since 83 percent of this set of cash flows exactly equals the investment of $1,000, and the NPV for the entrepreneurs is $204.

However, the real world is not quite so neat. In a more typical scenario, both future cash flows and the appropriate discount rate are undetermined, and the parties to the deal will disagree about the amount and timing of the cash flows and the appropriate discount rate. The investors and entrepreneurs will disagree about interpretation of laws, regulations, and the tax treatment of certain events. There will be conflicts of interest between the investors and founders, each group seeking to protect its interests at the expense of the other.

If just one assumption is relaxed—if a definite $500-per-year cash flow becomes an *expected* $500 per year cash flow—the actual amount will be known only over time. How does this change the rewards and risks of the deal? The top portion of Table 8.4 shows the effects of this change on a common stock deal of proportional sharing.

Given an equal probability that the returns will be $450 or $550 (with the expected value still at $500), the investor will receive $373 (.83 x $450) in a bad year and $456 (.83 x $550) in a good year. The expected annual return is the average of the two ($415). The standard deviation (a measure of risk) of the PV to the investor is 83 percent of the total deal's NPV standard deviation of $102, or $85. The investor in this sce-

TABLE 8.3   A Series of Cash Flows

	Period 0	1	2	3	4	5
Investment	($1,000)					
Cash flow		$500	$500	$500	$500	$ 500
Terminal value						1,000
Net cash flow	($1,000)	$500	$500	$500	$500	$1,500

SOURCE: From "Aspects of Financial Contracting," *Journal of Applied Corporate Finance,* 1988: 25–36. Reprinted by permission of Stern Stewart Co., New York, NY.

nario receives 83 percent of the rewards and assumes 83 percent of the risk. However, the venture capitalist will desire a different deal structure and, owing to the Golden Rule (whoever has the gold makes the rule), will be able to bargain for it. The investor will negotiate for preferred stock with a fixed dividend and some liquidation preference. The sophisticated investor will probably want the preferred stock to be cumulative as well, meaning that any missed dividend payments accumulate and must be paid before any dividends on common stock are declared. The bottom half of Table 8.4 shows how preferred stock changes the risk/reward ratio in favor of the investors.

In this scenario, the investors receive their expected $415 cash flow dividend regardless of whether the actual cash flow is $450 or $550. In the bad year, the investors receive 93 percent of the cash flow; in the good year, 73 percent. All the risk of a bad year (and extra reward for the good year) is borne by the entrepreneurs. The standard deviation of the investors' returns is zero because there is no variation. Because they hold preferred stock instead of common stock, the investors bear no risk—except, of course, the risk of bankruptcy, which accounts for the 40 percent discount rate.

Investors want preferred stock for two reasons in addition to their desire to minimize risk. First, by enabling the entrepreneurs to achieve maximal gain in the good years, the investors provide incentives for the entrepreneurs to work both hard and smart. Second, the entrepreneurs will not present rosier forecasts than they themselves believe in. Why? Because they know they will not achieve the cash flows necessary for them to realize any of the profits of the business. In essence, they will be working for the investors without hope of personal gain. This process is known as "smoking them out."

TABLE 8.4 Sharing the Risk

Common Stock (Proportional Sharing)	Venture Capitalist	Entrepreneur	Total
Share of total stock	83%	17%	100%
Annual cash received: bad scenario	$ 373 (83%)	$77 (17%)	$450
Annual cash received: good scenario	456 (83%)	94 (17%)	550
Expected annual cash received	415 (83%)	85 (17%)	500
PV of cash received (incl. TV)	1,000 (83%)	204 (17%)	1,204
Net PV (incl. investment)	0	204	204
Standard deviation of PV (and of NPV)	85 (83%)	18 17	102
Preferred Stock	Venture Capitalist	Entrepreneur	Total
Share of total stock	83%	17%	100%
Annual cash received: bad scenario	$ 415 (93%)	$35 (7)%	$450
Annual cash received: good scenario	415 (73%)	135 (27%)	550
Expected annual cash received	415 (83%)	85 (17%)	500
PV of cash received (incl. TV)	1,000 (83%	204 (17%)	1,204
Net PV (incl. investment)	0	204	204
Standard deviation of PV (and of NPV)	0 (0%)	102 (100%)	102

SOURCE: From "Aspects of Financial Contracting," *Journal of Applied Corporate Finance,* 1988: 25–36. Reprinted by permission of Stern Stewart Co., New York, NY.

Staged Financing

Few deals require all the money up front. Most new venture development occurs in stages, so most deals allow for **staged** (**phased**) **financing.** Let's say that the entrepreneurs need $20 million and are willing to sell 75 percent of the firm for this capital investment. Table 8.5 shows one possible way to stage, or phase, the financing. Often, first-stage financing is used for market studies, development of prototypes, and early organizational costs. The amounts are relatively small and are used to prove the venture viable. In this scenario, $1 million goes to pay for these development and start-up costs and buys 50 percent of the venture. The implied valuation, therefore, is $2 million.

As the venture succeeds in its initial efforts, it becomes more valuable. At the second stage, money may be needed to purchase plant and equipment for a small manufacturing facility that will enable the firm to test engineering concepts and design and to produce for a test market. Four million dollars is needed at this stage. The $4 million buys 33.3 percent of the firm. Because the investors already own 50 percent, they end up owning 66.7 percent at the end of this round. Now the company is more valuable: Its implied valuation is now $12 million ($4 million x 3).

If the venture is on track and succeeding as planned, third-stage financing will be needed for a full production ramp-up. If this requires $15 million, investors can be brought up to the originally determined 75 percent ownership by purchasing another 25 percent of the company. The post-investment valuation of the firm is now $60 million. At each stage, the investor is purchasing a smaller piece of the firm at a higher price. Why is the investor willing to do this? As the entrepreneurs meet their goals and milestones, risk is reduced. The continued success makes the venture more valuable and less risky.

The Option to Abandon

Not all staged-financing deals proceed as smoothly as the one depicted in Table 8.5. If things go wrong and the deal turns sour, investors will not want to put additional money in, especially at the $4-million and $15-million levels. That is, they want the **option to abandon.** The example in Tables 8.3 and 8.4 shows what happens in staged financing if

TABLE 8.5   Phased Investment Scheme

Round of Financing	Amount Invested This Round	Percent Received This Round	VC's Share	Founder's Share	Implied Valuation (post money)
First round	$ 1,000,000	50.0%	50.0%	50.0%	$ 2,000,000
Second round	4,000,000	33.3	66.7	33.3	12,000,000
Third round	15,000,000	25.0	75.0	25.0	60,000,000

Formula for the second round: 50% + (33.3%) (1.50) = 66.7%
Formula for the third round: 66.7% + (25%) (166.7) = 75.0%

SOURCE: From "Aspects of Financial Contracting," *Journal of Applied Corporate Finance,* 1988: 25–36. Reprinted by permission of Stern Stewart Co., New York, NY.

the entrepreneurs predict small variance in the expected cash flow of their venture. What happens if the variance is increased? If the variance of outcomes is increased to $50 cash flow in a bad year and $950 in a good year (the expected value is still $500), we increase the importance of reevaluating the investment decision. In Table 8.4, with the spread between $450 and $550, the investor is going to get paid in either case. With the wider spread, however, the investor does not get paid at all in a bad year.

If the venture needs $500 in two stages, the investor must compare two options. Venture capitalists may follow the rule that suggests that they have no choice but to invest in the second round, even if the cash flow is only $50. Another rule, however, says investors may choose *not* to invest in the second round and thereby abandon the project. If the investor abandons the project, he or she forfeits any claim to an annual cash flow and receives a reduced share of the terminal value, $750. Table 8.6 illustrates the possibilities of these cash flow scenarios and rules.

The top portion of Table 8.6 shows a situation in which the investor is required to invest in both years. Because the discount rate is still 40 percent and the expected value of the annual cash flows have not changed from the original example in Table 8.4, the PV of the venture is still $1,204. But because $500 of the investment is delayed one period, the NPV for the entire project rises to $346 from $204.

The bottom portion of Table 8.6 is more complex and requires calculating the average of expected values of a good year and a bad year when the investor may abandon the project after the first period. The good scenario shows a periodic cash flow of $950 and an NPV of $1,262. The bad scenario shows an initial investment of $500, no cash flow, and a terminal value of $750. The NPV of this is ($361). The average of a positive $1,262 and a negative $361 is $451. So, the value of the difference between the expected NPV of the situation at the top of table and the expected NPV of the situation at the bottom is $105 ($451 minus $346). Therefore, the investor can gain up to $105 in expected value by choosing the option to abandon. If the option is granted for free, the investor gains the full $105. Clearly, investors would be willing to pay up to $105 at the outset for the right to abandon. By changing the structure of the deal, the entrepreneur has created value and can sell that value to the investor in the form of an option.

Of course, this is a simplified example. Calculating such options is generally more complicated because there are more than two possible cash flows ($50 and $950) and more than two possible investing stages. But it illustrates the principle that *the deal structure can create value*.

Other option types exist as well. For example, the option to revalue the project determines at what price new capital will come into the deal. A fixed-price option for future financing is one possibility: If the value of the firm is above the exercise price, the investor will invest. If the value is below the exercise price, the investor will allow the option to expire or sell it to another investor who has a different risk/reward profile and preference.

Warrants

A **warrant** is the right to purchase equity and is usually attached to another financial instrument, such as a bond or debenture. Ordinarily, debt holders' returns are limited to interest and principal. The purpose of a warrant is to enable debt holders to add to their

TABLE 8.6   The Option to Abandon the Project

	0	1	2	3	4	5	PV@ 40%
Rule I: VC Invest in Both Years							
Good scenario		$950	$950	$950	$950	$ 950	$1,933
Bad scenario		50	50	50	50	50	102
Expected annual cash		500	500	500	500	500	1,018
Terminal value						1,000	186
Expected cash inflow		500	500	500	500	1,500	1,204
Investment	($500)	(500)					(857)
Expected net cash	($500)	$ 0	$500	$500	$500	$1,500	$ 346

	0	1	2	3	4	5	PV@ 40%
Rule II: VC Has Option to Abandon in Year 1							
Good scenario							
Annual cash flow		$950	$950	$950	$950	$ 950	$1,933
Terminal value						1,000	186
Investment	($500)	(500)					(857)
Net cash flow	(500)	450	950	950	950	1,950	1,262
Bad scenario							
Annual cash flow		0	0	0	0	0	0
Terminal value						750	139
Investment	(500)						500
Net cash flow	(500)	0	0	0	0	750	(361)
Expected (or average) value of scenarios							
Expected net cash	($500)	$225	$475	$475	$475	$1,225	$ 451

Expected value of option to abandon (Rule I minus Rule II): $105

SOURCE: From "Aspects of Financial Contracting," *Journal of Applied Corporate Finance*, 1988: 25–36. Reprinted by permission of Stern Stewart Co., New York, NY.

total return in case the venture turns out to be very profitable. In this case, the warrant is sometimes called an equity kicker: It represents equity that is off the balance sheet if the warrant is exercised,.

A callable warrant enables entrepreneurs to pay off creditors, thereby retiring the debt and recovering the equity according to a fixed schedule. The price of the warrant can be calculated for each period outstanding. Table 8.7 provides an example of the calculation of the price of a callable warrant.[28]

If the investor has a subordinated debenture with a face value of $1 million, a coupon of 10 percent, and a warrant that guarantees a total return of 15 percent, calculating the call price (or value) of the warrant requires two preliminary steps. First, the analyst must determine the present value and cumulative present values of the interest payments. In Table 8.7 the third column shows the present value of the cash flow from the interest payments, discounted at 15 percent. Next, the analyst must calculate the future payment that makes the entire cumulative present value equal to zero at the guaranteed (in this

TABLE 8.7 Calculating the Value of a Warrant*

	Cash Flow Interest	Present Value	Cumulative Present Value	
Value of Period n	Payments	15%	Value to Date	the Warrant
0	-$1,000	-$1,000	-$1,000	$333
1	100	87	-913	-$663
2	100	77	-836	
3	100	66	-770	
4	100	57	-713	
5	100	50		

*Assume: $1,000,000 subordinated debenture with a 10% coupon and warrants attached guarantee debt holder total return of 15%
1. Calculate the future payment in period *n* that will provide for a positive present value equal to the cumulative negative present value to date. This makes the entire present value equal to zero at the guaranteed 15% rate.

For period 5: $663 = \dfrac{X}{(1.15)^5}$ = $1,333

2. The warrant price is the difference between this value ($1,333) and the return of principal ($1,000) = $333.
3. This calculation can be made for any year, thus producing a schedule of warrant prices or values.

case 15 percent) rate. The fourth column in the table shows the cumulative present value.

The actual calculation of the warrant's value, however, requires two additional steps, also described in Table 8.7. The first step calculates the total future payment, discounted (for *n* periods, in this case 5) at the required rate of return (15 percent in this case) that brings the cumulative present value (column 4: $663) to zero. In this example, the amount is $1,333. The warrant price is the difference between this amount and the return of principal ($1,000), in this case $333.

Pitfalls and Problems to Avoid

There is only 100 percent of anything. This is true of the equity in a new venture and the cash flow from a start-up. Attempts to sell more than 100 percent of the equity and cash flow will bring the entrepreneur to grief (and prison). So each time the entrepreneur raises money, the future is somewhat constrained by the acts of the past. Each deal limits future options. In addition, each deal comes with covenants and legal restrictions that further bind the entrepreneur in a net of obligations. Unless the business is self-financing from the start, these constraints are inevitable, and the entrepreneur should focus on the controllable factors, not the uncontrollable ones.

First, the entrepreneur should avoid choosing investors and especially investment houses solely for their size or prestige. The choice should be made based on the needs of the business, not the egos of the founders. Conflicts of interest between financiers, investment houses, and entrepreneurs are inevitable. These should be resolved in favor of whatever is best for the business. Bad advice abounds in these situations. Some of it arises from ignorance, but much from self-interest. Although the entrepreneur is probably new to this game, the lawyers, brokers, and investors are not. Caution is advised. The value-added venture capitalist will often help the venture with advice, networking, and management. Street Story 8.2 offers some examples.

The entrepreneur also needs to guard against his or her own greed. If he or she offers to give up too little—too little equity, too little control, too little authority—investors will walk away. However, the entrepreneur must also guard against the appearance of giving up too much. This appears as either naiveté or lack of commitment to the new venture.

Last, the entrepreneur should prepare for the reality that the need for future financing is always a possibility. The initial and early deals should not foreclose on this need. Incentives for the current investors to invest more should be built into each contract. Incentives for others to invest and not be crowded out or preempted by the initial investors should also remain. Everyone involved in the deal should have some latitude in making decisions and the ability to exit after a reasonable time with their integrity intact (and maybe some money, too). Managing investor relations therefore is a critical task.

Consider the problems facing Joe Strazza, founder of New York based WinMill Software. When he started the company, he sold some equity for initial financing. He raised another $3 million over the next few years, mostly by selling over 100 limited partnerships to family, friends, and fools. This reduced his ownership from 40 percent to 20 percent. When the business was soaring, investors were pleased to receive dividends. If the company were sold, they would reap the capital gains. But when tech tanked in 2000, the investors turned into critics. There were no dividends and they couldn't sell their stock. The board refused permission for buybacks because the company did not have the cash. Investors wanted to become involved in company decision making, and at least one investor gave Mr. Strazza a forty-five minute screaming piece of his mind over the phone. Strazza concludes, "People say they believe in you and like you. But when you're down, you learn it was all about the money. That's a tough lesson to learn as an entrepreneur. You feel like you're losing your friends."[29]

NEGOTIATION SKILLS

Negotiations in many different forms are all around us.[30] Labor organizations negotiate with management, defendants negotiate with prosecutors, and countries negotiate their national interests on the world stage. In business, suppliers negotiate with customers, creditors with debtors, landlords with tenants, management leaders with their subordinates, and entrepreneurs negotiate with sources of financial resources.

A **business negotiation** can be defined as a process in which two or more parties exchange goods and services and attempt to agree upon an exchange rate for them.[31] The process usually includes more than the negotiator and opponent, because constituents of both the negotiator and opponent are often represented too. In other words, in negotiations entrepreneurs represent not only themselves but also the firm and its managers, employees, and stakeholders. The opponent in the negotiations is also likely to have constituents with an economic interest in the outcome of the negotiation. In addition, it is

---

STREET STORY 8.2

Much More Than $$$

Jim Fowler says the venture capital firms that invested in previous start-up companies at which he was an executive were never very involved in day-to-day management. In contrast, he says that investor El Dorado Ventures is "incredibly involved" in Jigsaw Data Corporation, the Internet start-up Fowler founded to permit salespeople to trade business contacts online.

Fowler reports that he speaks several times a week with someone from the venture capital firm that put $2.5 million in Jigsaw, and that there's an almost constant exchange of emails on operational matters, analyst reports, and business referrals. Fowler understands the reasons behind the increased contact: Venture capitalists "have to justify their investments," he observes, and so "they spend a lot more time on them."

"During the bubble, everyone spent time on technology, and they totally ignored the other aspects of business," explains Phil Soran, CEO of Compellent Technologies, a computer storage start-up. Compellent has been working on issues like career development and executive succession with its own venture capitalist investors. "If you don't have good management, it's going to bite you," says Soran.

El Dorado has hosted management-training sessions to benefit the start-ups they're funding, including Jigsaw Data. The VC firm hired Dell Larcen, a professional management consultant, to offer specific advice on finding, interviewing, and hiring top candidates for key management jobs. Fowler used what he learned in those sessions to successfully recruit a new vice president for engineering. "Without a doubt, we would have gone through a less rigorous process" without that training, he reports.

The consultant that El Dorado hired says she is getting more calls from venture capitalists to provide this kind of help for start-up companies. "The pressure [on investors] to get results now is much greater," she says.

El Dorado has already seen its handholding approach pay off with other ventures. "The most important thing to an entrepreneur isn't getting the money, it's getting a partner you can work with who will do the heavy lifting," says Jim Steeb, former Senior Vice President of Access Health. In 1988 Access Health was a small company providing over-the-phone medical advice from nurses as part of a hospital marketing program. With seed funding and management support from El Dorado, it has catapulted to $100 million in annual revenues by switching its market focus and now provides that service to insurance companies. McKesson/HBOC acquired the start-up for $1 billion in 1998. Repeat business indicates the VC's management touch is appreciated; Steeb is one of a group of "returning entrepreneurs" who have gone back to make deals with El Dorado to invest in their second or third new technology start-up.

SOURCE: Adapted from Rebecca Buckman, "Baby Sitting for Start-Ups," *The Wall Street Journal*, March 13, 2006; B1. Retrieved from the Web. www.eldorado.com.

not uncommon for a third party to be involved in the negotiation. The third party is generally some sort of specialist in resolving impasses and disputes and helping negotiators come to terms. Figure 8.3 illustrates the possible elements present in any negotiation.

FIGURE 8.3   The Parties to a Possible Negotiation

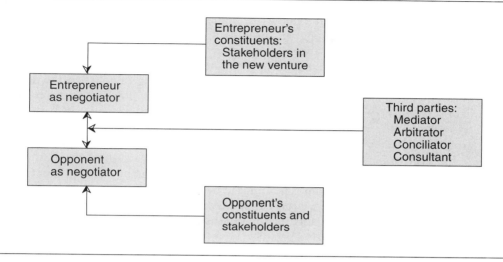

Basics of Negotiation

Every negotiation is about two things: the tangible aspects of the negotiation and the intangibles. The **tangibles** concern the terms of the agreement. Prices, products, services, and delivery schedules are all tangibles, as are financial terms, covenants, guarantees, and representations. In a labor negotiation the tangibles are wages, hours, benefits, and working conditions.

More than the tangibles are at stake in most negotiations, however. Negotiators are also concerned with **intangibles** like the perception of winning and losing. As illustrated in Figure 8.3, the constituencies on each side of the negotiation want the negotiator to get the best terms for its side—to *win*. Yet experienced negotiators realize that concessions, compromise, and good-faith bargaining are the elements that lead to success. From the viewpoint of the constituents, this awareness may look like weakness and potential loss. Negotiators are concerned about saving face as well as about the terms of the agreement.

Another intangible is the reputation of the negotiator. Negotiations are ubiquitous in business, and entrepreneurs are always thinking ahead to the next negotiation. They don't want to be seen as too soft or too demanding. The next negotiation may be more important than the current one. So sometimes negotiators are eying the future and seeking a reputation as "tough" or "conciliatory" or "fair-minded."

Understanding negotiations means recognizing what type of negotiation is being conducted. There are two fundamental types: distributive and integrative. **Distributive negotiations** occur when the object is a fixed amount of a benefit. Because the total is fixed, one party loses whatever the other party gets. It is a zero-sum game. For example, negotiating the price of an automobile with a dealer is usually an instance of distributive bargaining. The more the buyer pays, the less he or she can spend on other things.

The less the buyer pays, the lower the dealer's profit. The goal of the negotiation is to find the line between the dealer's resistance point (the lowest price he will accept for the car) and the buyer's resistance point (the highest price she will pay).

In a distributive bargaining situation, each party's goal is to arrive at a settlement point as close as possible to the opponent's resistance point. Splitting the difference is often the quickest solution, so a seller must understand exactly what his or her own resistance point is and make a realistic, but high, opening offer. Then the negotiator must seek information to establish the opponent's resistance point. When more than one item is up for negotiations, there is a **bargaining mix**. If the negotiators have different priorities for the tangibles and intangibles in the bargaining mix, they can concede ground on the less important items and hold firm on the more important ones.

Integrative bargaining occurs when the outcome is a variable sum. Each side can obtain a better result by cooperating with the opponent than by trying to beat the opponent. It is a variable-sum game and can lead to a win-win situation.

In integrative bargaining, negotiators are concerned not only with their own outcomes but also with the results for the other side. There are certain preconditions for integrative bargaining:

- Each side must understand the needs—both tangible and intangible—of the other side. There must be a free flow of information between the two (or more) sides so that each can continuously readjust its resistance points to achieve the optimum outcome.
- There must be true commonalities of purpose between the two sides. For example, in a labor negotiation, both management and labor want to keep the company from going bankrupt. In a venture capital negotiation, both sides want sufficient capital to launch the business and sufficient operating cash flow to keep it going and growing.
- There must be a willingness to search for solutions. Sometimes the first three conditions are met but one party to the negotiation is more interested in establishing a reputation or proving to be tough and is therefore unwilling to look for integrative solutions.

Regardless of whether the negotiation situation is distributive or integrative, it is recommended that the negotiator evaluate the relevant factors and do some planning before the face-to-face discussions begin. All negotiators should come to the bargaining table prepared, which means understanding the nature of the relationship between themselves and their opponents and knowing their goals for the negotiation. Thought must be given to the issues and to the strengths and weaknesses of the opposition as well as to their own strengths and weaknesses. Last, negotiators should prepare a strategy that can enable the bargainers to focus on the central issues and also be sufficiently flexible to deal with change. The central points for planning are presented in Table 8.8.

Negotiation Tactics

Negotiation is one of the most researched topics in social science. Researchers know quite a bit about how conflict develops and about the techniques and methods used to resolve it. A recent comprehensive review of the literature on negotiations divides this knowledge into five categories: (1) negotiator characteristics, (2) negotiator-opponent

TABLE 8.8   Guide for Prenegotiation Planning

I. The nature of the relationship:
  1. Is this a distributive or integrative bargaining situation?
  2. What has been the past negotiating experience with this opponent?
  3. What future relationship do I wish to have?

II. The goals of the negotiation:
  1. What are my tangible goals in this negotiation?
  2. What are my intangible goals?
  3. What are my priorities for the tangible and intangible goals?
  4. What do I know about my opponent's tangible and intangible goals and priorities?

III. The issues:
  1. What is the best deal I can make in this negotiation, given all the information I have about the situation and the opponents?
  2. What terms and conditions represent a "fair deal"?
  3. What are my minimum resistance points?
  4. How would my opponent answer these same questions? Do I have enough information to answer this question? How can I get this information?

IV. Analysis of the opposition:
  1. What are my opponent's negotiating characteristics, style, and reputation?
  2. What are my opponent's constituents likely to perceive as winning or losing?

V. Strengths and weaknesses:
  1. What are my strengths and weaknesses?
  2. What are my opponent's strengths and weaknesses?
  3. Is my opponent aware of my strengths and weaknesses?
  4. Is my opponent aware of his or her own strengths and weaknesses?

VI. The negotiating process:
  1. What is my strategy?
  2. What climate for the negotiations should I set?
  3. How can I get my opponent to follow a similar pattern?
  4. What procedural rules should we follow?
     a. Timing
     b. Locations
     c. Agenda

SOURCE: Adapted from R. Lewicki and J. Litterer, *Negotiations* (Homewood, IL: Irwin, 1985): 72-73.

interactions, (3) the effect of constituents, (4) the role of third parties, and (5) situational and environmental factors.[32] A sixth factor should be added: timing.

Negotiator Characteristics. Hundreds of studies have been conducted on the characteristics of negotiators and how those characteristics influence the process and outcomes of negotiations. Despite a great deal of interest in this aspect, there is little credible evidence that personality characteristics have a major impact. Occasionally a single study reveals, for example, that an internal-locus-of-control individual is more likely to yield a concession or that a high risk taker is a more competitive bargainer. But overall these studies are inconclusive and little current research is being done on negotiator characteristics. Only one individual characteristic plays a significant role—experience. Experienced negotiators fare better than inexperienced ones.

Negotiator-Opponent Interactions. The area of negotiator-opponent interaction has been more fruitful for researchers. Addressing the question "How should I bargain with my opponent?" they have tested three models of negotiator behavior: exchange theory, behavior modification, and game theory. Exchange theory predicts that norms of reciprocity emerge over the course of a negotiation. In other words, the behavior of one negotiator is reciprocated by similar behavior from the opponent. Behavior modification theory predicts that behavior that is rewarded is repeated and behavior that is punished becomes extinct. This model suggests that a negotiator can shape his opponent's behavior through rewards and punishments. According to game theory, negotiators attempt to figure out the nature of the game—Is it fixed or variable sum?—and then determine the payoffs for each behavior. Using this information, they can either cooperate to achieve the highest joint payoff or defect and try to maximize their own outcome at the opponent's expense.

The evidence seems to indicate that reciprocity is important in negotiation. Negotiators who make high demands and low concessions are most often met by opponents who do the same. Research shows that verbal threats are harmful unless they are delivered subtly and are seen as legitimate. Verbal persuasion, however, is very useful and is often reciprocated, especially when begun as a cooperative behavior,

The use of power is situational, but under the right circumstances it is useful if it is noncoercive. The full use of power in negotiation is problematic. Because of bounded rationality, the user seldom has full information, complete knowledge of cause and effect, or perfect foresight. Therefore the unbridled use of power is likely to have serious negative and unintended consequences.[33]

Last, the evidence shows that precedents are powerful molders of negotiation outcomes, especially if the precedents are seen as fair and reasonable. Therefore, it is difficult to negotiate a unique and creative solution to a problem if there are already known and accepted solutions to it.

Researchers at the Harvard Negotiation Project have made an important contribution to studies of negotiations and have published normative guidelines for negotiating agreements without giving in to the opponent. These guidelines are based on the concept of the **principled negotiation** and the **best alternative to a negotiated agreement** (BATNA).[34] A principled negotiation is neither hard-sell distributive and position-oriented nor soft-sell compromise and concessionary.

Principled negotiations offer four elemental guidelines for negotiators. First, negotiators must always separate the people from the problem. They need to find ways to prevent a (perceived) negative personal style from interfering with the dialogue and communication process. Second, negotiators must focus on interests, not positions. In position bargaining, each party stakes out claims for what it will or will not do. In interest-oriented bargaining, negotiators communicate what is in their best interests and look for ways to address those interests in a productive manner. Third, the parties should generate many options for settlement, as many as possible directed at mutual gain. And fourth, the parties should develop objective criteria and standards by which the result will be measured.

This last point is especially important because it avoids the problems caused by the naked use of power and will. It is imperative that these standards be agreed upon to prevent one side from demanding a concession for arbitrary and capricious reasons. Among the many types of objective standards that can be employed, depending on the situation, are market value, precedent, scientific judgment, professional standards, efficiency, costs, court decisions, moral standards, norms of equity, norms of equality, norms of reciprocity, and tradition.

The second major contribution from the Harvard project is the concept of BATNA. In most distributive bargaining and in some integrative cases, negotiators develop a resistance point, a bottom line which they decide beforehand that they will not cede. If pushed beyond this point for concessions, negotiations must be terminated.

But is this really rational? What if a negotiator wants to buy a business for $500,000 and after protracted negotiation the seller will go no lower than $510,000? Is walking away the rational thing to do? Consider John and Jane Doe, who are selling their house because they are taking new jobs in another city in a month. They want to get $160,000 but the best offer they've received is for $150,000, $10,000 below their bottom line. Is rejecting that offer a good choice?

The Harvard project offers a rational criterion for determining whether to remain at the bargaining table: Instead of setting a bottom line, the negotiators ought to understand what their alternatives are. By knowing their BATNA, the negotiators can protect themselves both from accepting terms that are too unfavorable and from rejecting terms that might serve their best interest.

In the case of buying a business, if there are no alternative businesses on the market that satisfy the buyer's criteria, the BATNA is to resume the search—but herein lies the fallacy of thinking in the aggregate. In the aggregate, there are lots of other businesses out there. But when it comes time to buy, the purchaser negotiates for only one at a time. Each time the difference between the buyer's and the seller's price may come down to $10,000 or even more, so the rational thing to do is pay the price and buy the business. Likewise, in the case of the house, if the BATNA to selling the house is to own two houses, make two mortgage payments, and worry about the security of a property far from home, the rational thing to do is sell the house for $10,000 less than the sellers hoped for.

These examples lead to three crucial conclusions that apply to all negotiations: (1) good negotiators know what their BATNA is; (2) developing an attractive BATNA is a powerful negotiating tool; and (3) knowing the opponent's BATNA helps determine what concessions he or she will make.

Constituent Effects. Figure 8.3 showed that negotiators often represent others as well as themselves. Accountability brings out the competitiveness in negotiators. When constituents are in close proximity or can directly view the negotiation, the result is tougher bargaining, less cooperation, and fewer concessions. This is why negotiators prefer media blackouts: It is difficult to reach a compromise or a win-win result in public.

Role of Third Parties. There are four categories of third parties: (1) mediators—neutral third parties; (2) arbitrators—persons with the authority to determine the outcome; (3) conciliators—parties trusted by the bargainers to make useful suggestions to both sides; and (4) consultants—persons skilled in problem solving and conflict resolution techniques. Research indicates that when the goal of the negotiating parties is to reach a mutually acceptable, long-lasting agreement, third-party facilitators are effective. In other words, if the parties are truly interested in reaching a settlement, they all work toward an agreement.

Sometimes the negotiators have no choice but to use third parties. The labor laws of the United States sometimes demand the use of mediation or binding arbitration. The parties to a negotiation can agree to use certain types of third-party intervention before a disagreement arises. For example, in major league baseball, the owners and the players use binding last-offer arbitration to determine salaries for special classes of players.[35]

Situational and Environmental Factors. The immediate environment in which the negotiations take place can alter the outcome. Pleasant surroundings promote cooperation. There are home-field advantages, just as in sports contests. The party that is at home among familiar surroundings is more relaxed and comfortable. This is a major advantage if the opponent is uncomfortable, rushed, tired from travel, and maybe even suffering jet lag.

The agenda makes a difference too. When there is more than one issue to deal with, more cooperative negotiation is possible. When the entire package is negotiated at one time, there is a greater possibility of compromise than when items are negotiated sequentially.

The remote environment of the negotiation also has an impact. The legal structure of a country can determine whether some negotiations are mandatory or illegal. Social norms affect negotiations: In the West a norm of efficiency makes negotiators task-oriented and likely to rely on rational arguments to influence their opponents. Many countries outside the West do not share these norms. In Eastern cultures, for example, there is much more emphasis on establishing personal relationships. Negotiations in similar cultures adopt shared norms; cross-cultural negotiations can be troublesome. For example, in one study of North American, Russian, and Arab negotiators, it was found that:

- North Americans relied on logic and persuasion. They reciprocated with fact exchange. They made small concessions early and then reciprocated opponents' concessions later. Deadlines were important.
- Arabs tried to persuade by emotion. They allowed their subjective feelings to counter opponents' facts. They made numerous concessions and always reciprocated opponents' concessions. Deadlines were not important.
- Russians were idealistic, trying to persuade by reference to principle. They did not employ concessions as a tactic; in fact, they saw them as signs of weakness. They never reciprocated. They ignored deadlines.[36]

Other studies confirm that each national culture and subculture has its own styles, preferences, and tactics. The Chinese use time very shrewdly, speeding up negotiations when they know that a Westerner must return home soon and slowing them down when that is to their advantage.[37] Cross-cultural negotiations therefore tend to be more competitive and stressful.

The general munificence of an environment also has an effect. In non-munificent environments, the mode of bargaining is likely to be distributive. In munificent environments, it may be possible for all parties to meet their needs, and an integrative mode may prevail. In an ironic twist, however, labor relations may become contentious when unions see signs of a company's profits in its munificent environment. Labor leaders, then, are more likely to engage in distributive bargaining to get what they perceive as their fair share.

Timing. When the parties to a negotiation realize that time is getting short, they are more likely to compromise. Bargaining is often characterized by eleventh-hour dramatics. People worn down by long bargaining sessions are reluctant to start over and unwilling to leave empty-handed. Most people are not professional negotiators and have other things to do.

Evidence shows that time pressure precludes negotiating tactics like stalling and bluffing, and it makes people more realistic. The demands of each side get softer as the deadline nears. Pressure to settle mounts, and concessions are less likely to be seen as signs of weakness, thus saving the negotiator's face with his or her constituents.

Tactically, time can be used to advantage by the shrewd negotiator.

- The shrewd negotiator waits for the deadline to make concessions.
- When a deadline puts the shrewd negotiator under too much pressure, he attempts to renegotiate the deadline.
- If no deadline exists, the shrewd negotiator creates one for a reluctant opponent.
- The shrewd negotiator creates positive incentives for quick settlement if a deadline is nearing.
- The shrewd negotiator avoids being trapped by a deadline and making costly concessions. She knows her resistance points (her BATNA) and offers to extend the deadline if possible.[38]

SUMMARY

This chapter elaborated and expanded the ideas in Chapter 7. The entrepreneur must understand the criteria that investors use to evaluate their decision to invest in the new venture. Because different investors apply different criteria, the entrepreneur can segment the financing market and sell investment vehicles that match the risk/reward preferences of the market.

Investors will use a seven-stage process in the investment cycle. They will search, screen, and evaluate proposals. After evaluation, they will make the decision, negotiate the details, structure the deal, and finally harvest the investment. The elements of the deal structure (risks, rewards, and timing) provide important positive incentives for both the investor and entrepreneur to make the new venture work. The types of investments offered, the manner in which they spread risk and reward, and the use of phased financing and options all combine to make the deal structure one of the more interesting, and potentially lucrative, aspects of entrepreneurship.

Last, we introduced the basic concepts of negotiations. Negotiating skill and capability are an advantage for the entrepreneur. They enable the new venture to obtain resources at below market prices and sell products and services above market prices. The entrepreneur is always negotiating with both the environment and the stakeholders of the new venture.

KEY TERMS

Bargaining mix
Best Alternative to a Negotiated Agreement (BATNA)
BFC proposal
Business negotiation
Deal
Deal structure
Demand rights
Distributive negotiations
Due diligence
Harvest
Intangibles
Integrative bargaining

Internal rate of return
Investment agreement
Option to abandon
Piggyback rights
Principled negotiation
Pre-emptive financing
Registration rights
Staged (phased) financing
Tangibles
Technological myopia
Term sheet
Warrant

DISCUSSION QUESTIONS

1. What are the components of a deal?
2. What three things must the entrepreneur understand in order to successfully complete the financing process?
3. What are the characteristics of the ideal investor?
4. What are the characteristics of the ideal entrepreneur and new venture?
5. Describe the investor process. What are the barriers and major pitfalls for the entrepreneur?
6. Why is the negotiation over the harvest so important?
7. How do risk preferences and risk sharing enter into the deal structure and the negotiation?
8. How do options and warrants add value to the deal?
9. Who are the constituents to a negotiation for financing the new venture? What roles do they play and what tactics might they use to increase their outcomes?
10. Is it *fair* that negotiating skill is so important in determining the outcomes for the new venture? Should the new venture succeed or fail based on its merits alone?

EXERCISES

1. Calculate the cash flows for your proposed venture if you have not already done so.
2. Partition these flows and segment your investor market.
3. Calculate the amounts you need to raise from each source.
4. Calculate the returns for each investor.
5. Develop a risk-sharing financing proposal. Include an option to reinvest.
6. Revise your financing plan to incorporate staged financing at the appropriate times.
7. Add a warrant for your debt investors to raise their return. Calculate the price of the warrant in a five-year schedule.
8. Prepare a brief financial plan for your new venture. What are your financial requirements? How might you negotiate with a banker? An angel? A venture capitalist?

Innovation and Learning

L. John Doerr has helped launch dozens of successful ventures, including Google, Netscape, and Amazon.com, as a partner in the venture capital firm of Kleiner Perkins Caufield and Byers. But six years ago Doerr became involved in a venture capital fund that doesn't expect to earn a penny in profits. The New Schools Venture Fund is instead focused on getting a return in innovative solutions to the problems facing public education.

The New Schools Venture Fund's (http://www.newschools.org) investments include a high-tech high school in San Diego (www.hightechhigh.org); a Web site for parents with advice about helping their children in school and information for evaluating their local schools (www.greatschools.net); and a nonprofit charter school cluster of fifteen K–12 schools (www.aspirepublicschools.org) working to raise the academic performance of California's diverse student population. More than half of the 4,000 children enrolled in Aspire Public Schools are economically disadvantaged; 67 percent are Hispanic or African-American, and 39 percent are English Language Learners. The projects are all dedicated to helping students:

- develop scientific, technological, and literary skills
- learn to work collaboratively in diverse teams
- learn to communicate via new kinds of media
- prepare to participate in American democracy as informed and involved citizens

The New Schools Venture Fund raised its first $80 million from contributions from individuals like Mr. Doerr and from foundations like the Bill and Melinda Gates Foundation, which contributed $22 million. The fund is now trying to raise an additional $125 million by appealing to donors who want to have an impact on public education and who value the fund's expertise in identifying worthwhile projects. Several of Doerr's partners in Kleiner Perkins Caufield and Byers are among the major donors to date, and principals from four VC funds serve on the New Schools Venture Fund's Board of Directors.

Investing in education entrepreneurs is a new frontier for wealthy investors who have lost interest in traditional start-ups. Doerr describes the New Schools Venture Fund as a fresh kind of philanthropy "held accountable by the rigors of venture capital financing." The Fund's Web site says it is the only venture philanthropy fund dedicated to K-12 public education reform.

Doerr claims investing in education is more difficult than backing high-tech ventures. "The education entrepreneurs have it harder. They must overcome massive institutional resistance," he says. So far the California Teachers Association has been skeptical of the charter schools movement, possibly because the schools are not union employers. "And if the high-tech entrepreneurs succeed, they get rich," continues Doerr. "The educators' rewards will be more important in life, but they're not going to get rich."

The educational ventures the New Schools Venture Fund supports are expected to become self-supporting with tax dollars from local, state, and federal sources fairly quickly. "Education is not the filling of a pail but the lighting of a fire,'" observes Ted Mitchell, the Fund's CEO. "We provide the fuel for that fire."

SOURCES: J. Flanigan, "Venture Capitalists Are Investing in Educational Reform," *New York Times Online*. Retrieved from the Web, February 16, 2006. www.nytimes.com.

Case Questions

1. How are venture capital practices being applied to educational reform?
2. What are the pros and cons of using VC methods here?
3. If you were the charter school entrepreneurs, how would you negotiate the investment? What terms would you seek?
4. If you were the investors, how would you negotiate the investment? What terms would you seek?
5. At the end of the day, will this process of educational reform work? Why or why not?

APPENDIX A

Sample Series A Preferred Stock Term Sheet

This Term Sheet is for discussion purposes and summarizes certain proposed provisions of the Company's Series A Preferred Stock. It does not purport to be complete and is subject to, and qualified in its entirety by, the provisions of (i) the Company's Articles of Incorporation, and (ii) the Series A Preferred Stock Subscription Agreement to be dated as of the Closing Date between the Company and each prospective investor (an "Investor"), where such rights will be set forth in full, and the provisions of applicable law.

Principal Terms

Preferred Stock Terms

Financing Size: $_____
Pre-Money Valuation: $_____ (before investment)
Securities: Series A Preferred Stock ("Series A Preferred")
Price Per Share: $_____ ("Original Purchase Price")

Pro Forma Capitalization

Pre-Offering   Post-Offering
Common Stock
Preferred Stock
Options Authorized
            TOTAL

Closing Date: As soon as suitable subscriptions for shares of Series A Preferred totaling [$500,000] (the "Minimum Amount") are received and accepted by the Company (the "Closing Date").

Rights, Preferences, Privileges and Restrictions of Series A Preferred

Liquidation Preference: In the event of any liquidation, dissolution or winding up of the Company, the holders of Series A Preferred will be entitled to receive, prior and in preference to any distribution of any assets or surplus funds to the holders of Common Stock, liquidation amounts equal to the sum of (i) the Original Purchase Price ($____ per share), plus (ii) all declared but unpaid dividends (the "Senior Preferential Amount"). After payment of the Senior Preferential Amount, liquidation proceeds will be shared pro-rata by the holders of the Common Stock and the Series A Preferred on an as-converted basis.

In the event of a merger, reorganization, acquisition or sale of all or substantially all of the assets of the Company in which the holders of the Company's capital stock hold less than 51% of the voting power of the surviving entity, such holders shall be entitled to receive cash, assets or other property distributable in the same manner as is applicable in the context of a liquidation; provided, however, that if the sale proceeds exceed [$15 million], and if the conversion of the Series A Preferred to Common Stock would entitle the holders thereof to receive an amount in excess of the Original Purchase Price per share (as proportionately adjusted for any stock splits, etc.), then the Series A Preferred will be automatically converted to Common Stock.

Voluntary Conversion: The holders of the Series A Preferred will have the right to convert Series A Preferred at the option of the holder, at any time, into shares of Common Stock. The total number of shares of Common Stock into which the Series A Preferred may be converted initially will be determined by dividing the Original Purchase Price by the Conversion Price. The initial Series A Preferred Conversion Price will be the Original Purchase Price. The Conversion Price will be subject to adjustment as discussed below.

Automatic Conversion: The Series A Preferred will be converted automatically into Common Stock, at its then applicable Conversion Price, (i) upon the closing of an underwritten public offering of shares of the Common Stock of the Company in an offering of not less than $20,000,000 (prior to underwriting commissions and expenses), (ii) upon the closing of a Sale of the Company that is not deemed a dissolution under the liquidation preference provisions above, or (iii) in the event that the holders of a majority of the Series A Preferred consent to the conversion into Common Stock.

Anti-Dilution Protection: The Conversion Price will be subject to proportional adjustment for stock splits, stock dividends, recapitalizations and the like. The Series A Preferred also will be subject to adjustment to prevent dilution in the event that the Company issues additional equity securities (or warrants or rights to purchase Common Stock or securities convertible into Common Stock) at a purchase price less than the applicable Conversion Price. Such adjustment will be on a standard, broad-based weighted average basis. The Conversion Price will not be adjusted for issuances of equity securities upon the exercise or conversion of presently outstanding securities, or on the future issuance of stock options to employees, as approved by the Company's Board of Directors and certain other strategic issuances.

Voting Rights: The holder of shares of Series A Preferred will have a right to that number of votes equal to the number of shares of Common Stock issuable upon conversion of the Series A Preferred.

Dividends: No cash dividends may be declared on the Common Stock unless or until a like dividend in an amount equal to or greater than the dividend has been declared on the Series A Preferred (dividends shall be compared on a Common Stock equivalent basis).

Restrictions and Limitations: Except as expressly provided in the Subscription Agreement or as required by law, so long as at least a majority of the original number of shares of Series A Preferred issued remain outstanding, the Company shall not, without the approval of at least a two thirds (2/3rds) majority of the then outstanding shares of Series A Preferred, voting separately as a class, (i) amend, alter or repeal any provision of the Articles of Incorporation or Bylaws of the Company or any other action that changes the voting powers, preferences, or other special rights or privileges, or restrictions of the Series A Preferred (for purposes of clarity, the filing of a designation creating Senior Stock or Parity Stock shall not be deemed to affect the preferences or other special rights or privileges of the Series A Preferred); (ii) increase or decrease the authorized number of shares of Series A Preferred; (iii) voluntarily dissolve or liquidate the Company; or (iv) enter into an agreement resulting in a transfer of more than 50% of the outstanding ownership of the Company.

Registration Rights: Demand Registration: Holders of at least a majority of the shares of Series A Preferred shall be entitled to one demand registration (commencing six months after the Company's initial public offering (the "IPO) and any time while the Company's stock is publicly traded).

Piggy-Back Registration: The holders of Series A Preferred will be entitled to "piggy-back" registration rights with respect to offerings registered by the Company (excluding the IPO), subject to the right of the Company and its underwriters, in view of market conditions, to reduce the number of shares of such holders proposed to be registered.

Registration Expenses: The registration expenses (exclusive of underwriting discounts and commissions) of all registrations will be borne by the Company.

Other Registration Provisions: Other provisions are contained in the Series A Preferred Stock Subscription Agreement with respect to registration rights, including cross indemnification, the agreement by the holders of the Series A Preferred, if requested by the underwriters in a public offering, not to sell any Common Stock that they hold for a period of 180 days (or such other number of days as the underwriters may require) following the effective date of any Company registration statement (subject to certain exceptions), underwriting arrangements and the like.

Notice of Certain Events

Significant Transactions: The Company shall notify the holders of shares of Series A Preferred in the event of (i) certain takings by the Company of a record of the holders of any class of securities for the purpose of determining the holders thereof who are entitled to receive any dividend or other distribution, or any subscription or acquisition rights, (ii) any capital reorganization, reclassification or recapitalization of the capital stock of the Company, any merger of the Company, or any transfer of all or substantially all of the assets of the Company to any other company, or any other entity or person, or (iii) any voluntary or involuntary dissolution, liquidation or winding up of the Company.

Reporting: So long as an investor continues to hold one percent (1%) of the Series A Preferred or Common Stock issued upon conversion of the Series A Preferred, the Company will deliver to the Investor annual financial statements and any other reports or correspondence provided to all of the holders of Common Stock.

Right to Maintain Proportionate Ownership: Each Investor shall have a right of participation to purchase a share of any new securities offered by the Company (other than securities issued to employees, directors, consultants, independent contractors or strategic partners, or pursuant to acquisitions, equipment leases or secured debt financings) equal to the proportion which the number of shares of Series A Preferred held by such holder (on an as-converted basis) bears to the Company's fully-diluted capitalization. For purposes of this Term Sheet, the term "fully diluted capitalization" means the (i) number of shares of capital stock of the Company issued and outstanding, determined on an as-converted basis, (ii) the number of shares issuable upon exercise of outstanding warrants, and (iii) the number of shares reserved for issuance pursuant to the Company's option plans.

<u>Board Rights:</u> So long as the Series A Preferred Investors collectively hold at least _____ shares of Series A Preferred, a representative of such group, selected by the Series A Preferred Investors, shall be entitled to be elected to the Company's Board of Directors.

<u>Expenses:</u> The Company shall pay reasonable fees and expenses of one legal counsel to the Investors.

SOURCE: Retrieved from the Web. http://www.allianceofangels.com/startups/term_sheet.doc.

APPENDIX B

Investment Agreement Outline

Following are the general contents of an investment agreement. The major sections are typical. Details can be added or deleted depending on practice, tradition, and the negotiating skills of the participants.

I. *Description of the Investment*
This section identifies the parties, defines the basic terms, and includes descriptions of the amount of the investment, the securities issues, any guarantees, collateral, and subordinations. When the agreement includes warrants and options, the schedules and timing of exercise are included here. Registration rights, transferability provisions, and dilution effects are all essential parts of the investment and are described in this section.

II. *Conditions of Closing*
The closing of the deal is the actual transfer and execution of documents and funds. Typically, documents need to be submitted to close the deal. These are corporate documents and articles of incorporation, audited financial statements, contracts with related parties that could be construed to represent conflicts of interest, and such important business documents as leases, supplier agreements, and employment contracts.

III. *Representations and Warranties by the Venture*
This section describes in full legal disclosure terms the material facts of the new venture's condition. These typically include:

- That the business is duly incorporated
- That the officers' decisions legally bind the company
- That the offering is exempt from SEC registration (if indeed it is)
- That all material facts have been disclosed

IV. *Representations and Warranties of the Investors*
These are legally binding statements by the investors that they are indeed who they say they are and:

- That they are organized and in good standing
- That the investors' decisions legally bind their corporation or organization
- That they will perform all of their obligations if all conditions are met. This generally means that they will come up with the money if conditions are met.

V. *Affirmative Covenants*
These are all the things the entrepreneurs agree to do under the terms of the investment agreement and in the operation of their business. Typical covenants are:

- Pay taxes, file reports, obey regulations
- Pay principal and interest on debts
- Maintain corporate existence
- Keep books, have statements audited, allow investors access
- Maintain insurance
- Maintain minimum net worth, working capital, and asset levels
- Hold directors' meetings

VI. *Negative Covenants*
These are all the things that the entrepreneurs agree *not* to do in the course of operating their business. Negative covenants may be abrogated with investor approval. Typical covenants are:

- Not to merge with, consolidate with, or acquire another business
- Not to change the corporate charter or bylaws
- Not to sell additional stock unless specified in the agreement
- Not to pay dividends unless specified
- Not to violate any of the affirmative covenants
- Not to liquidate the business or declare bankruptcy

VII. *Conditions of Default*
This section spells out the circumstances under which entrepreneurs are considered to have violated the agreement. These include:

- Failure to comply with affirmative or negative covenants
- Misrepresentations of fact
- Insolvency or reorganization
- Failure to pay interest and principal

VIII. *Remedies*
The specific remedies available to the investors if violation should occur include:

- Forfeiture to the investor of voting control
- Forfeiture of stock held in escrow for this purpose
- The right of the investor to sell his stock back to the company at a predetermined price
- Demand for payment of principal and interest
- The payment of legal costs to ensure compliance

IX. *Other Conditions*
Anything not covered elsewhere.

SOURCE: Adapted from J. Timmons, *New Venture Creation* (Homewood, IL: Irwin, 1994): 774–777.

APPENDIX C

Negotiable Terms to a Financial Agreement

Covenants and Provisions Protecting the Investment [1]

Investors have a legitimate interest in protecting their investment. They do this by seeking certain rights in the financial contract, including cash flow rights, board rights, voting rights, liquidation preferences, and control rights.[2] They seek to do this in various ways.

Antidilution provisions protect investors from having the investment's value diminish if the entrepreneur is forced to seek additional financing. It does not mean that the investors will never suffer shrinkage of their ownership percentage. As long as any new stock is sold at a price equal to or higher than the original investor's conversion price, the original investor does not suffer dilution. If the new stock is sold below the conversion price, the original investor loses economic value—unless an antidilution provision or "ratchet" is included.

There are two types of ratchets: full and weighted. A full ratchet is onerous for the entrepreneur because it requires that the original investor be able to convert all shares at the lower price. In our example, the investor purchased 33.3 percent of the company for $1 million. If shares were issued at $1 each, the investor would own one million shares. Suppose a full ratchet is in effect and the company needs additional financing. Subsequently, it sells shares at 50 cents per share. The conversion rate for the original investor will drop to 50 cents. The 1 million shares become 2 million shares. If 250,000 50-cent shares have been sold, the total value of the shares outstanding is now $4.125 million (the entrepreneur's $2 million, the original investor's $2 million, and the new investor's $125,000). But the original investor's percentage of ownership has risen to 48 percent (2 million shares divided by 4.125 million shares). Over time and in case of financial crises, full ratchets severely reduce the value of the firm to its founders and their share of ownership.

The weighted ratchet is fairer to the entrepreneurs. The conversion price is adjusted down by the weighted average price per share outstanding. The formula is:

$$X = (A \times B) + C/(A + D)$$

where
  X = new conversion price
  A = outstanding shares prior to the sale
  B = current conversion price
  C = amount received on sale of new stock
  D = number of new shares sold
To illustrate from our example, if:
  A = 3,000,000 shares
  B = $1.00
  C = $125,000
  D = 250,000
then the new conversion price for the original investors is $0.9615, not the fully ratcheted $0.50:

$$\frac{(3,000,000 \cdot \$1 \ 00) + \$125 \ 000}{3,000,000 + 250 \ 000} = 0 \ 9615$$

This becomes a critical area of negotiation for the entrepreneur, especially when cheap shares of common stock are offered to officers, directors, employees, and consultants, as is common in start-up situations. A provision should be negotiated that these sales do not trigger the antidilution provisions.

Performance and forfeiture provisions call for the entrepreneurs to forfeit a portion (or all) of their stock if the company does not achieve a specified level of performance. It protects the investor from paying too much for the company in the event the entrepreneur's original projections were too rosy. If the entrepreneur fails to meet the rosy projections, the entrepreneur pays the price of reduced ownership in the company. Also, the forfeited stock can be resold to new executives brought in to improve the firm's performance. This provision motivates the entrepreneur and protects the investor.

In a start-up, a significant portion of the founder's equity may be at risk due to the performance/forfeiture provision. As the company achieves its early goals, the entrepreneur should negotiate less severe penalties and can legitimately negotiate removal of this clause because the firm's performance has shown that the initial valuation was reasonable. If the investors are reluctant to give in on this, the entrepreneur should insist on bonus clauses for beating the projections. In short, for each downside risk, the entrepreneur should negotiate for an upside reward.

Employment contracts motivate and discipline the top management team. They often protect investors from competing with the founders of the company if the founders are forced to leave. All terms of the founders' and top executives' employment contracts (salary, bonuses, fringe benefits, stock options, stock buyback provisions, non-competition clauses, conditions of termination, and severance compensation) are negotiable. Investors want an employment contract that protects their investment in the venture. Especially if investors are buying a controlling interest in the company, the founder will want to negotiate a multiyear deal. The drawback to multiyear contracts is that if the entrepreneur wishes to leave early to do other things, investors can sue for breach of contract and/or prevent the entrepreneur from engaging in a competing business.

Control issues are negotiable and are not dependent solely on the proportion of stock the investors have purchased. All minority stockholders have rights. A nationally recognized accounting firm will be hired to audit the financial statements, and important managerial positions may be filled with people recommended by the investors. All important business transactions (mergers, acquisitions, asset liquidations, and additional stock sales) will require consultation and consent. The entrepreneur who accepts a minority interest after the investment should negotiate for all the rights and options that an investor would.

Shareholder agreements are favored by investors to protect their stake in the company. Shareholder agreements can bind the company when it offers new shares, forcing the firm to offer the original investors rights of first refusal on the new shares. Sometimes agreements call for the management to support the investors' choices when electing board members. Although these agreements are usually made at the insistence of the investor, entrepreneurs can ask for equal power as they negotiate for their stake in the new venture.

Disclosure is the process by which entrepreneurs provide investors with the full and complete details of the information and relationships under which the investor makes his or her decision. The investor requires audited financial statements, tax returns, and assurance that the company is in compliance with all laws and regulations.

Investors are especially concerned about contingent liabilities. Contingent liabilities arise when the company has future liability based on some prior event or action. For example, when a firm produces a product, it has contingent liability if the product is ultimately dangerous, mislabeled, or harmful—even if the company had no reason to expect such a problem at the time of production. Because of the changing nature of U.S. environmental laws, contingent liability often resides in past decisions concerning waste management, disposal of hazardous materials, or use of building materials that prove dangerous or poisonous.

The entrepreneur should attempt to negotiate a cushion to protect the founders and the new venture in case of an omission during the disclosure process. For example, if an omission is honestly made and results in company costs under a certain dollar amount, entrepreneurs will not be considered in breach of disclosure representations. This is also known as a "hold harmless" clause. The representations that the entrepreneurs make should be time-limited.

APPENDIX NOTES

1. See H. Hoffman and J. Blakey for additional details. "You Can Negotiate with Venture Capitalists," *Harvard Business Review*, March-April, 1987.
2. S. Kaplan and P. Strmberg, "Financial Contracting Theory Meets the Real World: An Empirical Analysis of Venture Capital Contracts," *The Review of Economic Studies* 70, no. 2, April 2003: 281-315.

CHAPTER 9 Creating the Organization

Good fences make good neighbors.
—Robert Frost

OUTLINE

LEARNING OBJECTIVES

After reading this chapter, you will understand

- some issues involved in creating and maintaining a *top management team (TMT)*.
- the composition and responsibilities of a *board of directors*.
- the concept of a *virtual organization*.
- the importance of networks and alliances.
- the principles of *Built to Last* ventures.
- how different strategies create different *organizational structures*.
- some *ethical issues* facing entrepreneurs.
- the *balanced scorecard* approach to venture performance.
- some successful strategies from the *entrepreneurial workplace*.

PERSONAL PROFILE 9

Calculating Entertainment

While the term angel usually refers to an investor, some ventures also benefit from the magic touch of a guardian spirit who contributes management expertise instead of capital.

Gretchen Shugart has been that kind of angel for TheatreMania.com (www.theatremania.com). The graduate of New York University's Stern School of Business worked as a banker for Chase, Manufacturers Hanover and the Bank of Montreal before starting her own banking advisory firm for media and Internet companies in 1999. One of her clients was TheatreMania. When the start-up ran into funding problems in 2001, TheatreMania's cofounder and president Darren Sussman recruited Shugart as CEO.

Sussman had played in rock bands and sold lingerie overruns at street fairs before he took a job in the late 1990s marketing tickets online for an off-Broadway dinner theatre show called "Tony 'n Tina's Wedding." Marketing the show on the Internet was such a success that he and producer Joe Corcoran decided to launch TheatreMania.com in 1999. The site sells tickets for Broadway, Off-Broadway, and Off-Off-Broadway shows, in addition to tickets to theatre performances in 40 U.S. cities, Canada, and London. But TheatreMania doesn't just sell tickets. It also posts theatre news, reviews, interviews, and other content, and offers online marketing programs—including box office, telephone, and online ticketing services—to performing arts organizations.

While consumer response to TheatreMania was positive from the beginning, the company ran rapidly through its initial seed money. "I think a lot of entrepreneurs and small business owners don't have a firm grasp on the financial side of the business and the way numbers relate," says Shugart. "Entrepreneurs aren't always the best people to run the business once it really begins growing."

Even before she became TheatreMania's full-time CEO, Shugart had contacted the start-up's creditors to restructure their debt. She and Sussman also decided to make paying their freelance writers on time a priority and to postpone any expansion until they were sure they could afford it. Shugart says the company was "on the brink of the dot-com bubble burst and it was really a matter of fleshing out the business plan and looking for more money." Once the venture was on firmer financial ground, "We were able to get some of the original investors and a handful of new investors to step in."

Today TheatreMania has over 1.2 million visitors a month, and 525,000 registered members. They had $6 million in revenues for the fiscal year ending June 2005, and anticipate $10 million for the year ending June 2006. The company is now debt-free and profitable, and Shugart and Sussman are building the business by reinvesting the profits in marketing and development.

Shugart's business skills continue to play a big role in the company's success. "It all has to do with striking a balance between growing too fast and growing too slow," she says. "We think that service has been a main factor behind our success to date. So that means making sure we have enough call center agents on staff at any given time. It also means having good client support when somebody is having a technology problem." Teamwork is undoubtedly another factor contributing to TheatreMania's growth. "I think he's an optimist and I'm a realist," says Shugart about Sussman. "He thinks I'm a pessimist and he's a realist. Whatever we are, it seems to work well for us."

SOURCE: Adapted from Paulette Thomas, "Combining Dreams and the Down to Earth," *The Wall Street Journal*, September 20, 2005. Retrieved from the Web September 20, 2005.
http://online.wsj.com/article_print/0,,SB112716981854545452,00.html; Robert S. Levin, "The Show Must Go Online," *The New York Enterprise Report*, March 7, 2006. Retrieved from the Web August 12, 2006.
http://www.nyreport.com/index.cfm?fuseaction=Feature.showFeature&FeatureID=317 and www.TheatreMania.com.

W HEN the entrepreneur creates the organization for the new venture, he or she is building fences. These early organizational decisions have a lasting impact on the venture and become part of the company's DNA. As the opening quote indicates, setting and determining boundaries—what is "in" versus what is "out"—affects not only the venture itself but also its neighbors: suppliers, customers, competitors, and stakeholders. The "in" functions are those the organization does through its own people. "Out" functions are performed by other firms, businesses that provide goods and services at the market price.

"Good fences" are boundaries that make sense for the venture's strategies, its transactions with its neighbors, and the resources that provide its sustainable competitive advantage (SCA). When good fences are built, relationships with other organizations—with neighbors—will also be good: that is, profitable and sustainable for both vendors and customers. In setting boundaries the entrepreneur makes choices: what to make versus what to buy; what to own versus what to obtain from other firms; how to grow; and what constitutes sensible growth. All these decisions are part of the process of creating an organization and setting its boundaries. For example, consider a hypothetical new Internet venture. Should it develop its own software or license software from a reputable source? Should it compete with a large established rival (like a Google or Yahoo), or try to develop a partnership with these larger firms? Should it grow through the acquisition of other small start-ups, or through the organic growth in its own customer base?

Usually, before these boundaries are set and these difficult issues addressed, entrepreneurs look for help. They have the difficult task of almost simultaneously launching the new venture and making the transition to professional management. Among their many tasks is assembling a top management team. Members of the team will help the entrepreneur determine organizational boundaries in two ways. First, they provide advice and add their own input. Second, depending on their unique individual or collective skills and experiences, they serve as human resources with the four attributes of SCA: rare, valuable, hard to copy, and nonsubstitutable. These people can help determine the best places to draw the lines around the organization.

From the viewpoint of the founding entrepreneur, this team is assembled by examining the characteristics of top managers and by understanding the process and dynamics of how teams are formed and maintained. Because research shows that some teams produce at higher levels than others, it is helpful to look at high-performing teams.

Next it is important to study the basics and principles of what are called "visionary companies." Such firms were started by ingenious entrepreneurs who figured out how to endow their companies with the kind of organizational culture and leadership that would stand the test of time. They made the successful transition from entrepreneurial to professional management without compromising on either style. This section of the chapter distills the major findings originally presented by Collins and Porras in their best-selling book, *Built to Last*.[1]

Several factors affect the boundaries of entrepreneurial organizations, including an unusual but highly effective form called the "virtual organization." From this follows a discussion of organizational design and structure. Given a set of boundaries and activities, each organization must decide how to delegate authority and responsibility and how to make use of the productive power of specialization. These are the key elements of organizational structure.

One system for managing organizational performance, based on the work of Kaplan and Norton, is the **balanced scorecard**.[2] The balanced scorecard is typically thought of as a tool of professional management and mature organizations, but the balanced scorecard approach to creating an organization assures that the firm will not lack any key components of performance and that the different elements of the organization will work in an integrated fashion.

The chapter concludes with a discussion of the major issues in creating and maintaining an entrepreneurial workplace. The ethical climate and culture should be consistent with high standards and with the aggressive nature of the business. Entrepreneurs want the people who work for them to be as motivated, innovative, and productive as they are. Examples of how entrepreneurs create an exciting environment for their workers are presented at the end of the chapter.

THE TOP MANAGEMENT TEAM

There is little doubt that the top management team (TMT) is a key component in the success or failure of the new venture.[3] The team is crucial to attracting investors, for investors look for experience and integrity in management.[4] The team is also a key element in new venture growth.[5] Without a team to plan, manage, and control the activities of the growing firm, growth will be limited to what the founder can personally supervise and manage.[6]

The general manager of any enterprise—here, the entrepreneur—has three leadership roles to play: organizational leader, architect of the organizational purpose, and personal leader. When the entrepreneur is putting the TMT together, all these roles are in action at once. Because the characteristics of the team help determine the venture's performance, creating and maintaining the TMT is one of the major responsibilities of the founding entrepreneur.[7] As the **organizational leader**, the entrepreneur selects the members of the TMT and works to blend their skills and expertise to ensure high productivity. As the **architect of organizational purpose**, the entrepreneur is an analyst and strategist, helping the TMT determine the business's goals, objectives, and directions. Finally, as the **personal leader** the entrepreneur serves as a model for behavior in the organization.[8] This is the individual to whom people look for leadership in deciding what is right and wrong for the organization. The entrepreneurial leader creates the climate and the culture of the workplace and models the ethical standards of the venture for all to see. The roles of the entrepreneur are summarized in Figure 9.1.

Creating the Top Management Team

A **team** can be defined as "a small number of people with complementary skills who are committed to a common purpose, set of performance goals, and approach for which they hold themselves mutually accountable." How many is "a small number"? Some experts put it anywhere between 2 and 25.[9] However, teams with more than 12 to 15 members must generally form subgroups to facilitate communication and decision making. Subgroups tend to form hierarchies. The pace of group activity slows down, time is lost, and the logistics of meeting face-to-face becomes a problem.[10]

It is useful at this point to distinguish between a team and a working group. A **working group** is a collection of individuals whose jobs are related but not interdependent.

FIGURE 9.1 **Roles of the Entrepreneur as General Manager**

SOURCE: Adapted from K. Andrews, *The Concept of Corporate Strategy* (Upper Saddle River, NJ: Prentice-Hall, 1986).

The members are individually, as opposed to collectively, accountable. They do not really work together; they simply work for the same organization at about the same level in the hierarchy.

In contrast, a team is connected by the joint products of its work. Members of a team produce things together and are jointly accountable for their combined work. In the case of the TMT of a new venture, their joint output consists of the enterprise's managerial systems and processes. Team members value listening and constructive feedback, and they encourage each other in a supportive spirit. The whole of a team is greater than the sum of its parts. Why? Because the venture benefits both from the individual efforts and from the relationships. In fact, these relationships often transcend and overshadow individual contributions. People working on effective teams are sparked, motivated, and inspired by their interactions with the other team members.

The process of TMT formation should begin with an evaluation of the talents, experience, and personal characteristics required in the new venture's operating environment. This evaluation gives the entrepreneur a map of the ideal team. This map helps guide the process of putting the TMT together and of answering the three fundamental TMT recruitment questions: From what sources will TMT members be recruited? What criteria for selection will be used? What inducements will be offered to potential members?[11]

Sources of TMT Members. TMT members are recruited both from people whom the entrepreneur already knows and from "unfamiliars." **Familiars** include family, friends, and current and former business associates. The advantages of choosing familiars are the established trustworthy personal relationships, the entrepreneur's knowledge of each person's capabilities, and the fact that the entrepreneur may already have an established working relationship with them. This prior knowledge and experience can speed up team formation and decision making in the early stages of new venture creation.

Recruiting familiars, however, also has potential disadvantages that arise from the same sources as the positive factors. Familiars may come with the psychological baggage of prior relationships in which the parties' status and circumstances were different. Also, a familiar may have much the same background, work experience, education, and world view as the founder. If they duplicate the entrepreneur's own personal profile, familiars will not bring complementary skills to the team.

There have been some classic cases of problems and crises over TMT participation in family businesses. Herbert Haft, founder and chairman of the Dart Group, fired his wife and son after a personal argument. Ted Turner fired his son Robert from Time Warner's Turner Broadcasting System by telling him during dinner, "You're toast." Family-business expert Wayne Dyer suggests that one way to avert such disasters is to establish a panel that will pre-decide criteria for judging family members' job performance. Such a panel can determine whether a family member is performing poorly and should be fired or placed in a different job.[12]

Unfamiliars are people not known to the entrepreneur at the start of the new venture. They are individuals with the potential for top management who may have had previous start-up experience. Entrepreneurs can find such people through personal connections, business associates, or traditional personnel recruitment techniques: employment agencies, executive search agencies (headhunters), and classified advertising. Unfamiliars are a potential source of diversity for the TMT. They bring in new views, skills, and experiences to complement the entrepreneur's. Their most important potential negative factor is the lack of a prior working relationship with the founder.

Criteria for Selection. If the TMT is to be highly effective and to contribute substantially to enterprise performance, it should be composed of individuals with either of two primary characteristics: These people should either personally possess resources that are rare, valuable, hard to duplicate, and not easily substituted, or they should be able to help the firm acquire and employ other strategic resources with these qualities.

Good personal chemistry between the TMT candidate and the entrepreneur can be a factor in selection. It may be reassuring for the entrepreneurs to feel such a mutual affinity, putting them at ease and creating a comfortable working situation that nurture's the founders' talents and creativity.

One criterion to consider is executive intelligence. Executive intelligence is a combination of emotional intelligence, problem-solving ability, prioritizing skills, and the ability to monitor oneself and learn from mistakes. These qualities are difficult to measure in a traditional job interview. A case interview using hypothetical business problems is more useful.[13]

Members of the top management team are frequently chosen for direct instrumental reasons. Entrepreneurs look for people who in some manner—perhaps through technical knowledge or functional expertise—complement existing human resources and add to the resource base. Other criteria include age, education, and tenure. For example, it has been found that TMTs composed of younger, better educated, and more functionally diverse individuals are more likely to promote innovations and changes in the firm's strategy.[14] On the other hand, TMTs made up of older, longer-tenured people—people accorded high levels of discretion by the CEO—tend to follow strategies that stick to the well-known path and achieve performance levels close to industry averages.[15]

As the company grows, the needs of the venture change and so do the requirements for the TMT. Sometimes a TMT consists of only two people, though this is more common at the launching of the new venture. Street Story 9.1 provides some examples and insight into the recruitment of a second entrepreneur.

Money is frequently a reason for recruiting TMT members. The entrepreneur in search of financial partners usually allows these partners to sit on the board of directors or work on the TMT. Connections (business, social, and technological) are also good bases for choosing members of the TMT. These people help the new venture acquire or gain access to new resources that would otherwise be out of reach for the emerging business.[16]

Cultural Diversity. A final set of criteria address the potential need for demographic and **cultural diversity**. Because background and environment are major influences on individual perceptions and orientations, people from different demographic and cultural groups have different viewpoints. These differences, when expressed and processed by an effective group, can form the basis for a wider understanding of the firm's own environment. Each separate contribution adds to the firm's knowledge of its customers, employees, markets, and competitors, and to its awareness of factors in the remote environment. It has even been suggested that TMTs should be composed to match the conditions of environmental complexity and change. Recent research has suggested that homogeneous TMTs tend to perform better in stable environments and heterogeneous TMTs perform better in rapidly changing environments.[17] Therefore, because entrepreneurs most often operate in rapidly changing environments, a heterogeneous team should be most effective.

However, achieving the benefits of diversity is not easy. Some cultural groups, like the Japanese, fret about having to work with people of different cultures. They often attribute their success to their cultural and racial uniformity. American managers, on the other hand, have more experience in diverse situations. Recent integration of European markets has made Europeans more sensitive to the power of diversity. European firms are now looking for people who are Euro-managers, able to work well within any of the different cultures and ethnic communities in the European Union (EU).[18]

A recent study shows how diversity works.[19] Groups of students were formed to do case analyses in a Principles of Management course, four case studies over the semester. About half the groups were composed of white males and the other half were racially diverse (gender, ethnicity, national origin). The homogeneous groups performed better at first, but the diverse groups had just about caught up by the end of the semester. The diverse groups took longer to figure out how to work effectively with each other, but their rate of improvement was higher and "by the end of the experiment, the diverse teams were clearly more creative than the homogeneous ones, examining perspectives and probing more alternatives in solving the final case study."[20] The study's senior author said that he believes that if the experiment had lasted longer, the diverse groups would have passed the others in overall performance.[21] In the real world of new venture creation, TMTs are expected to last significantly longer than one semester. Therefore, the long-term benefits of a diverse TMT can be achieved.

A Question of Balance

Orbital Data thought it had found the right person for the job. During his tenure as Chief Operating Officer and Executive Vice President of Inktomi, Richard Pierce had helped that company's annual revenues grow to over $200 million and had made it the leading vendor in its technology niche. But Orbital Data founder Paul Sutter and his venture-capital investors wanted to be certain Pierce was the right person to join their software venture's TMT. So they hired Pierce on a 30-day, no-strings-attached basis in January 2004 to see if the fit was right. Both Pierce and Orbital Data later decided to extend the trial to 120 days, allowing Sutter to become thoroughly acquainted with his potential hire. "We spent many a weekend, four or five hours at a time, getting to know each other," Sutter recalls. The trial period turned out to be a good investment; Pierce formally joined the company as Chief Technology Officer that year, and now serves as Orbital Data's CEO and Chairman of the Board.

While trial employment periods are relatively rare, it is not unusual for an entrepreneur to offer the number-two slot to someone he or she has met and liked. Brad Elliott, owner of Elliott Building Group, was impressed by real estate broker John DiPasquale, Jr., when they met to discuss a piece of land. "I saw that he had a lot of deal making energy, which is what you need in this business," Elliott says. He offered DiPasquale a job as head of marketing and land acquisition for his home construction business and later promoted him to CEO. Revenues are up $5 million since DiPasquale joined the company. "I wanted him to help drive me and take the business to the next level," says Elliott. "We balance each other like an old couple."

Personnel experts suggest that entrepre-

neurs do a thoughtful assessment of their company's needs and an honest appraisal of their own strengths and weaknesses before starting to search for a new TMT member. "Then they can figure out what they want in this other person," explains Carl Robinson, a management psychologist at Seattle's Advanced Leadership Consulting. "Nine times out of ten, an entrepreneur wants to bring on board an operations person who knows how to execute and create efficiencies to optimize the organization." Searching without a clear picture of what the company needs isn't effective. "Creating a job just to strengthen your executive team isn't a good enough reason," says Steve Katz, an executive coach from Potomac, Maryland. "That person should bring some ability or knowledge to grow the company."

A good match isn't always obvious. Carolyn Gable, owner of the New Age Transportation trucking company, had a hunch the young woman she hired to be her children's nanny could also be an asset for her company. So Gable made Jenny Talley her office assistant, placing the inexperienced woman in charge of accounting, dispatching, and other duties for the $18 million, 48-employee company. Talley proved adept at learning on the job, and twelve years later she holds the company's number-two slot, vice president for operations, and was recently voted Leader of the Year by the other employees.

In contrast, Frank Bell, CEO of software company Intellinet, had high hopes when he hired Harvard MBA Travis Lewis to be his Chief Operating Officer. Bell now admits the two of them didn't meet often enough, and Lewis's job wasn't clearly defined. Company sales foundered instead of growing, and Lewis left after five years.

Whether it's based on instinct or experience, some commonality between the top two leaders in a firm is essential. "They need to share some of the same style so they can communicate effectively," observes Steve Katz.

SOURCE: Adapted from Dale Buss, "Dynamic Duos," *Business Week Online,* Winter 2005. Retrieved from the Web March 4, 2006. http://www.businessweek.com/print/magazine/content/05_49/b3962401.htm?chan=gl and www.orbitaldata.com.

Inducements. The final factor in team composition is the range of inducements offered to potential members. These take the form of both material and nonmaterial rewards. **Material rewards** include equity (stock in the company), salary, perquisites, and benefits. It is vital that most of these rewards be contingent on performance, even in the early stages of the new venture when performance and profits may still be in the future. Moreover, the entrepreneur should consider the total rewards offered to the potential TMT member over the life of the opportunity. This will obviate giving too much too soon and will solidify the team member's long-term commitment.[22]

Nonmaterial rewards can be equally important. A person may relish learning about the new venture creation process. People who someday will be entrepreneurs themselves may agree to participate in a start-up business as preparation for their own endeavors. Being a TMT member is also a sign of upward mobility, distinction, prestige, and power—an additional inducement for many.

In the final analysis, the TMT will probably consist of both familiars and unfamiliars. Some will be recruited for the team because they are strategic resources. For example, in the biotech industry where genome research is so highly specialized, companies are competing to recruit biotech personnel for their TMTs. "All of the top-level scientists have probably been locked up [by companies]," reports Stanford University Nobel laureate Paul Berg.[23] The scientists themselves are the key resources in such companies. Firms cannot enter unless they have acquired this scientific expertise.

People can also be added to the TMT in a "just in time" fashion, as needed.[24] In the early stages of a start-up—when there is the most uncertainty and the entrepreneur wants the support of trusted people—familiars are probably the best choice. Later, team members can be recruited specifically for their money, connections, skills, and experience as those resources are required.

Maintaining Top Management Teams

The recruitment of the top management team is only the beginning. As the transition to professional management continues, team members must learn to work together and this takes time, especially if the group is composed of individuals from diverse backgrounds and cultures. A great deal of research has been conducted to determine the properties of highly effective work groups.[25] This section offers an overview of the properties as they relate to new venture TMTs.

Goals. It is essential that the goals of the TMT be the goals of the new venture. Research shows that agreement within a TMT on what the goals of the firm should be is positively related to firm performance.[26] However, over time the TMT will develop its own goals and objectives, subject to the overriding vision of the entrepreneur. These subgoals are essential if the team is to create its own identity and sense of mission. The accomplishment of these subgoals will be the joint work product of the team. Sometimes these goals are quite distinct, such as the development and implementation of a management accounting system. Other goals might be fuzzy, such as becoming a leader in innovation. Fuzzy goals are acceptable because they provide increased discretion and flexibility for the team.[27]

Norms and Values. Norms are the team's shared standards for behavior, and values are its desired outcomes. The most important of these norms and values are:

- *Cohesion:* the understanding that when the team gains, each individual member gains
- *Teamwork:* the acknowledgment that collective activities and accomplishments can surpass what any individual can achieve on his or her own
- *Fairness:* the realization that rewards and recognition are based on the contributions of individuals to the team's efforts and its success. This implies an "equal inequality" because the rule is applied equally but the outcomes may be unequal. For example, members of the founding team might have stock options while later employees do not. All benefit when the company does well, but not equally.
- *Integrity:* the adherence to honesty and the highest standards of ethical behavior within the framework of the top manager's fiduciary relationship with the enterprise's owners and investors
- *Tolerance for risk:* the willingness to be innovative and to accept ambiguous situations
- *Tolerance for failure:* the willingness to accept that innovation and ambiguity sometimes end in failure
- *Long-term commitment:* the obligation to promote the interests of the organization, its customers, employees, investors, and other stakeholders
- *Commitment to value creation:* the recognition that personal wealth will arise from the value of the new venture as an ongoing, growing, and profitable entity

Roles. In every group, certain people play certain roles. Sometimes people play multiple roles, changing as the situation warrants. **Contributors** are task-oriented initiators, usually individuals with special knowledge or expertise in the area to which they are contributing. **Collaborators** are joiners who align themselves with those making the contribution of the moment. The presence of these allies increases the likelihood that the contributor's initiative will be accepted. **Communicators** define the particular task, pass information from contributors to other members of the group, and restate positions held by potentially conflicting members. **Challengers** play the devil's advocate. They offer constructive criticism and attempt to portray the downside of the contributor's recommendations. Their role is to ensure that no course of action is taken, no decision made, without considering what can go wrong or whether alternative courses might be more effective.[28] Over the course of a single meeting or day and certainly over the life of the group, any TMT member can successfully play all of these roles.

Communications. Highly developed interpersonal and communication skills are essential to the success of the TMT. Communications have three types of content: task, process, and self-serving. **Task-oriented communication** directly addresses the subject under discussion. Its purpose is to provide substantive information to help the group make a decision. **Process-oriented communication** is concerned with how the group operates and how people behave. It is reflective and attempts to make the group members aware of what is happening in the discussion. Both task and process communications are necessary for effective decision making. **Self-serving communication** contributes neither to task nor to process. It tries instead to put the speaker at the center of the discussion. The content of self-serving communication varies, but it frequently attempts to take credit, assess blame, or accuse another team member of violating the group's norms for behavior.

Effective communicators concentrate on task and process communication and minimize self-serving communications.

Leadership. The founding entrepreneur is both a member of the team and the team leader. In effective teams, however, leadership is often shared, depending on the problem at hand. If a particular individual possesses superior knowledge, experience, skill, or insight, that person takes the temporary leadership of the group.

Benefits and Pitfalls of TMTs

Creating a top management team for a new venture offers the benefits of team decision making—[29] breadth of knowledge, diversity, acceptance of decisions, and legitimacy.[30] The team approach to top management balances skills and attracts vital human resources to the emerging organization. It is also a test of the venture's viability: If no one will join the team, there is serious room for doubt about the venture's potential for market acceptance. A well-developed team will minimize the disruption caused by the loss of any single member, saving the time and energy needed for later recruitment. Such a team also demonstrates to external stakeholders that the founder is a "people person" willing to share authority and responsibility.[31]

However, the team approach to top management is not without potential problems and pitfalls. One researcher notes several possible difficulties. For example,

- TMT members may lack start-up experience.
- They may be recruited too quickly, without careful attention to their long-term commitment.
- The team may be too democratic. Members may feel that they should all vote on everything instead of deferring to the person with the most expertise.
- In an effort to recruit, the entrepreneur may exaggerate the level of decision-making discretion the team will have. The realization of such exaggeration is bound to disappoint and de-motivate team members when they learn that the new venture is wholly controlled by the founder and majority stockholders.
- The TMT may make decisions too rapidly in the mistaken belief that everything must be settled on Day One.[32i]

There are also the problems that can afflict any team—such as inefficiencies of time, **groupthink**, **groupshift**, and poor interpersonal skills.[33] Good group processes take time. People need a chance to discuss, communicate, revise their views, and develop new options. Sometimes time is of the essence, and the entrepreneur cannot wait for group discussion and consensus. Under these circumstances, the team must act quickly and forgo the process it has carefully nurtured.

Groupthink prevents the team from critically evaluating and appraising ideas and views. It hinders the performance of groups by putting conformity ahead of effectiveness. The principal symptoms are rejection of evidence that contradicts assumptions, direct pressure on doubters and nonconformists to drop their objections, self-editing by group members reluctant to present opposing points of view, and the illusion of unanimity. The best ways to avoid groupthink are (1) to have the leader remain impartial until the end of the discussion, and (2) to develop norms that allow all members to express dissent without retribution.[34]

Groupshift is the phenomenon in which the collective decision of a team is either more or less risky than the disaggregated decisions of the team members. Sometimes people take larger or smaller chances in a group than they would on their own.[35] To make their point, people tend to exaggerate their initial positions in group discussions, and these exaggerated positions may become the ones adopted by the group. Moreover, when teams make decisions, the team is accountable, which sometimes translates into "No one is accountable." This sense of diffused responsibility causes members to be less careful about what they approve.

Group effectiveness can also be ruined by the domination of a single member or subgroup of members. If the discussions are so dominated, the advantages of diversity and breadth of knowledge are lost, and people are de-motivated because they cannot contribute. Worst of all, sometimes the person dominating the discussion is neither highly skilled nor knowledgeable. When the mediocre control events, mediocre outcomes can be expected.

The Board of Directors

The top management team may be augmented by a board of directors. In fact, although the board and TMT members may overlap, the board is *not* the top management team and should not attempt to micromanage the venture.[36]

There are two types of boards: an advisory board and a fiduciary board. The primary task of the **advisory board** is to provide advice and contacts. It is usually composed of experienced professionals with critical skills important to the success of the business. For example, if the business is primarily a retail establishment, merchandising, purchasing, and marketing experience are important resources. People who have good contacts and are open-minded, innovative, and good team players are prime candidates for an advisory board.[37] A **fiduciary board** is the legally constituted group whose primary responsibility is to represent the new venture's stockholders. It is usually made up of insiders (the managing founder and senior TMT members) and outsiders (investors and their representatives, community members, and other businesspersons). In firms that are still very closely held—that is, whose founders have not yet gone to the professional investment community for expansion funds—insiders tend to dominate. When venture capital has been used to support growth, venture capitalists often dominate the board.[38]

Members of the board, as trustees of the shareholders' interests, constitute the broad policy-setting body of the company. They advise and mentor the founders and the TMT in the execution of their strategy. Specifically, the board exercises its power in seven areas:

1. *Shareholder Interests.* In representing shareholders, the board is accountable for the new venture's performance. It must approve the audited financial statements and all reports to the shareholders. The board must approve any changes in the venture's bylaws and get shareholder approval as well. The board is also responsible for all proposals made to shareholders and approves the annual report prepared by top management.

2. *Financial Management and Control.* The board sets and declares all dividends. It sets all policies regarding the issue, transfer, and registration of company securities. It approves any financing programs: The TMT cannot seek financing that changes the status of current shareholders without board approval. The board, along with the shareholders, also approves the selection of the outside auditors recommended by top management.

3. *Long-Range Plans.* The board advises top management on its long-term strategy. It does not devise strategies, but it can mold the venture's future using the recommendations of the top managers. The board establishes broad policies regarding the direction and means of growth. It must approve all acquisitions and mergers, subject to further approval by the shareholders.

4. *Organizational Issues* The board elects its chairperson, the firm's president, and (based usually on the president's recommendations) the other officers and top managers of the company. It writes and approves the chairperson's and president's job descriptions. It establishes their compensation levels, stock options, and bonuses, and it subsequently reviews their performance. From recommendations of the president, the board also approves the appointment, termination, promotion, and compensation of the other managers who report directly to the president.

5. *Operational Controls.* The board approves the annual operating and capital budgets. It reviews forecasts and makes inquiries about variances from forecasted amounts. It can request information and special reports from top management, which it may then use to carry out its other fiduciary duties. If performance falters, the board may recommend a reorganization, restructuring, or even voluntary bankruptcy to protect the shareholders.

6. *Employee Relations.* The board approves the firm's compensation policies, pensions, retirement plans, and employee benefit options. It also reviews the behavior of employees and top managers to ensure that they act in accordance with the highest ethical, professional, and legal standards.

7. *Board Internal Operations.* The board is responsible for its own internal operations. Based on the recommendation of the CEO and president, the board members approve their own compensation and expense accounts. They appoint subcommit-

tees to study special issues, such as the protection of minority shareholder rights. They must attend board meetings at the request of the chairperson.

Compliance with Sarbannes-Oxley Section 404. The **Sarbanes-Oxley (SOX)** law was enacted in 2003 in the wake of serious breaches of fiduciary responsibilities and of criminal activities by a few major corporations (e.g., Enron, WorldCom). Section 404 of the act describes the types of internal controls and auditing processes and responsibilities of firms and their boards. Although the congressional intent was to stop abuses by large corporations, the Securities and Exchange Commission has not exempted smaller businesses from the law. Businesses covered by these regulations will incur higher costs of compliance, especially in the first year. If a venture has outside investors and is regulated by the SEC, it must comply.[39]

Guidelines for Successful Boards

Information and research about top management teams and group processes can provide guidelines for successfully selecting and employing advisory and fiduciary boards. These key factors should be part of the creation of the new venture's board of directors:

- Keep the board to a manageable size, 12 to 15 members at most.
- Board members should represent different capabilities and resource bases. For example, the board should have a balance of people with financial backgrounds, operational and industry experience, and local community knowledge.
- Because the board's primary responsibility is to the shareholders, both majority and minority shareholders should be directly represented.
- People with good communications skills and the ability to voice an independent opinion are needed. If everyone agrees about everything all the time, there is not enough diversity on the board.

BUILDING AN ENDURING ORGANIZATION

The founder may not realize it when the venture is launched, but many of the earliest decisions can influence the firm for its entire history. These decisions become the DNA of the company. The **culture** of the organization is imprinted early, and the founder makes the largest impact on that culture. If the organization is going to survive a long time and become a visionary type of company, these initial conditions and decisions should be carefully considered.

Visionary companies are different. James Collins and Jerry Porras reported in a large-scale study the dimensions upon which these differences were based. They reported their results in the now famous best-selling book, *Built to Last*.[40] Collins and Porras seek to identify the characteristics of these remarkable companies as well as the underlying causes of venture differences. For example, what factors explain how Motorola successfully moved from a humble battery repair business into car radios, televisions, semiconductors, integrated circuits, and cellular communications? Zenith started at the same time with similar resources but never became a major player in anything but TVs. How did

Hewlett-Packard remain healthy and vibrant after Bill Hewlett and Dave Packard stepped aside? Texas Instruments—once a high-flying darling of Wall Street—nearly self-destructed after Pat Haggarty moved on. What explains how the Walt Disney Company became an American icon, surviving and prospering through hostile takeover attempts, while Columbia Pictures lost ground and eventually sold out to a Japanese company?

In their research, Collins and Porras found that the visionary companies they identified:

- Are premier institutions in their respective industries
- Are widely admired by knowledgeable businesspeople
- Make an indelible imprint on the world in which we live
- Have multiple generations of chief executives
- Have been through multiple product (or service) life cycles
- Were founded before 1950

This distinguished list includes such icons as Sony, Merck, American Express, 3M, Boeing, General Electric, Ford, and IBM. The *Built to Last* researchers also reviewed the historical record to correct the misunderstandings and misinformation about great companies that had become conventional wisdom. They compiled a list of myths that guided management practice for decades. These are presented in Street Story 9.2.

Collins and Porras sought to understand why these companies were more enduring, more visionary, better organized, and better managed than their counterparts. Their answer is easy to state but harder to do:

> *The continual stream of great products and services from highly successful companies stems from them being outstanding organizations . . . not the other way around.*

In other words, it is the organization—its processes, systems, routines, leadership, and culture—that makes the difference. No amount of great science or product development can overcome a poorly designed and administered organization. Management capability and skill are paramount.

The Venture's Vision

How can you tell the difference between a vision and a vision statement? A *vision* is lived through the everyday experience of the people who work in and with the organization. A *vision statement* is writen words. It makes sense that an organization's development starts with the founder's or founding TMT's vision. The vision determines two essential elements—what core to preserve and what future to strive for. The core is the reason the organization exists and the values and beliefs that it embodies. It is necessary to **preserve the core** or the organization will lose its essential character and become a "nothing special" company. Still, no company can survive for long by simply sticking to its founding principles: It must change and adapt, so the vision must include a commitment to change and progress. The vision must guide the venture's participants to keep the products and services fresh and worthwhile, but must not deviate from the founding principles.

The ideal vision preserves the core and stimulates progress.

Therefore, the vision must have two components. The first is the **core ideology**. The core ideology defines the enduring character of an organization, giving it a consistent

Myths and Misinformation

That management capability is the most important ingredient in the visionary company mix is not an obvious conclusion, and Collins and Porras identify many myths that entrepreneurs and managers believe. For example:

- *It takes a great idea to start a company.* No idea by itself is going to get the work done. A product that downloads the content of a newspaper and reads it to you while you drive to work is a definite winner, but until someone actually starts a company to produce, market, and distribute the product, it is just an idea.
- *Visionary companies require great and charismatic visionary leaders.* There are not enough of these people to go around. And when they are available their egos sometimes get in the way of successful management.
- *The most successful companies exist first and foremost to maximize profits.* If the firm exists only for money, it will be satisfied when it becomes profitable. Visionary companies are never satisfied.
- *The only constant in a visionary company is change.* The core must be preserved, or the venture loses its identity and reason for existing.
- *Visionary companies are great places to work, for everyone.* Not everyone fits in. People who accept the challenge and vision adapt to the culture. Those who don't must leave.

- *Highly successful companies make their best moves by brilliant and complex strategic planning.* If this was possible, everyone would do it.
- *Visionary companies share a common subset of "correct" core values.* There is no one set of "correct" values. What counts are commitment and action.
- *Blue-chip companies play it safe.* If they do, they die.
- *The most successful companies focus primarily on beating the competition.* Competition is important, but not as important as focusing on core values and exploiting unique resources and capabilities. Otherwise, the company becomes a "me-too" organization.
- *Companies should hire outside CEOs to stimulate fundamental change.* Companies should do this only if the outsider also understands how to preserve the essentials of the business.
- *You can't have your cake and eat it, too— i.e., a company can't have homegrown managers and fundamental change.* You have to have both.
- *Companies become visionary primarily through "vision statements."* Great companies deliver great products, not great vision statements.

SOURCE: J. Collins and J. Porras, *Built to Last* (New York: Harper Business, 1997).

identity that transcends product or market life cycles, technological breakthroughs, management fads, and individual leaders. This core ideology is made up of two parts: the core values and the core purpose. **Core values** are a small set of general guiding principles. They should not be confused with specific cultural or operating practices and should not be compromised for financial gain or short-term expediency. **Core purpose** is the organization's most fundamental reason for existence. It goes beyond just making money: It should be a perpetual guiding star on the horizon and should not be confused with specific goals or business strategies. This is all better understood with an example. The list below shows the core values (numbers 1-4) and core purpose (number 5) of the Disney Company:

1. Fanatical attention to consistency/detail
2. Fanatical control and preservation of Disney's "magic" image
3. Continuous progress via creativity, dreams, and imagination
4. No cynicism allowed
5. "To bring happiness to millions" and to celebrate, nurture, and promulgate "wholesome American values"

Another example is from the Sony Corporation. Numbers 1–3 are the core values, and number 4 is the core purpose:

1. Being a pioneer—not following others, but doing the impossible.
2. Respecting and encouraging each individual's ability and creativity.
3. Elevating the Japanese culture and national status.
4. "To experience the sheer joy that comes from the advancement, application, and in- novation of technology that benefits the general public."

The second aspect of the vision is the venture's **envisioned future**. An envisioned fu- ture can be defined by what an organization aspires "to become, to achieve, and to cre- ate." An organization must experience significant change and progress to attain its envi- sioned future. This includes a 10- to 30-year "big hairy audacious goal," or **BHAG**, and a vivid description of what it will be like when the organization achieves the BHAG.

A BHAG (pronounced "bee-hag") engages people. It reaches out and grabs them in the gut. It is tangible, energizing, highly focused. People "get it" right away, so it takes little or no explanation. It is a huge and daunting challenge. A BHAG always:

• Is clear and compelling
• Serves as a unifying focal point of effort, and acts as a catalyst for team spirit
• Engages people
• Has a clear finish line
• Is tangible, energizing, and highly focused

For example, in 1990 Sam Walton set the goal for Wal-Mart to achieve sales of $125 billion by 2000. At the time the largest retailer in the world had sales of $30 billion. This sales target was incredibly audacious, but it was also easy to measure and focused the entire organization on a single future. How did they do? For fiscal year ending January 31, 2000, Wal-Mart reported net sales of $165,013,000,000, 32 percent better than their ten-year BHAG goal and a 20 percent increase over the previous fiscal year. During this time Sam Walton died, but the organization he created endured. Wal-Mart is built to last.

A venture's BHAG should be so bold and exciting that it will stimulate progress even if the organization's leaders disappear before it is achieved. It must be consistent with the company's core ideology and is ideally set 10 to 30 years in the future. It is a goal, not a statement, and should be clear and compelling—no explanation needed. Finally, a BHAG needs to reach outside the comfort zone. It may be ridiculed by outsiders who do not know the firm, but to insiders it is motivating, challenging, and inspirational.

The founder's next step is to write a vivid description of what the company will be like when it achieves its BHAG. This should be specific. For example, Ford Motor Company founder Henry Ford was quoted as saying, "I will build a motor car . . . so low in price that no man making a good salary will be unable to own one . . . the horse will have disappeared from our highways." The future he envisioned came to pass.

Recommendations for Entrepreneurs and Founders

Collins and Porras have some final recommendations based on their "preserve the core, stimulate progress" findings:

- Develop cult-like cultures (preserve the core): Make the company a great place to work *only* for those who buy into the core ideology; reject those who do not.
- Homegrown management (preserve the core): Promote from within, and make sure senior managers are steeped in the core ideology of the company.
- Big Hairy Audacious Goals (stimulate progress): Make a commitment to challenging and audacious goals and projects.
- Try a lot of stuff and keep what works (stimulate progress): High levels of action and experimentation—often unplanned and undirected—produce new and unexpected paths of progress.
- Good enough never is (stimulate progress): Institute a continual process of relentless self-improvement with the aim of doing better and better far into the future.

THE ORGANIZATION'S BOUNDARIES

The previous discussion concerning the creation and maintenance of a top management team assumed that there was sufficient justification for building an organization. That is, the entrepreneur needed help, and the best way to secure this help was to form a TMT. But is it possible to be an entrepreneur without a TMT and, implicitly, without building an organization? A founder could conceivably rely solely on outside contracting and a network of independent suppliers and distributors to produce, deliver, and market the product or service. To understand the choice entrepreneurs face when determining whether to remain on their own or build an organization, we need to understand the forces that determine the organization's boundaries and to consider relationships beyond those boundaries—e.g., in its networks and alliances.

The Virtual Organization

In Chapter 2 entrepreneurship was defined as "the creation of an innovative economic organization (or network) for the purpose of gain or growth under conditions of risk and uncertainty." It was, therefore, possible for an entrepreneur to develop a **virtual organization**. The virtual organization could be the model for global business organization in the years ahead. It consists of a network of independent companies—suppliers, customers, and even rivals—linked by common goals and information technology to share skills, costs, and access to one another's markets. This new, evolving corporate model is fluid and flexible, a group of collaborators quickly united to exploit a specific opportunity.

For example, Kingston Technology Corporation of Fountain Valley, California, is a virtual corporation that has grown to over $500 million in sales. It is a world leader in computer upgrades, and it operates within a network of related firms that lead complementary corporate lives. This is not simply subcontracting. These companies share know-how, markets, and capital. Here's a typical example:

On a recent Tuesday, a Los Angeles branch of ComputerLand received a call from Bank of America. It wanted 100 IBM PCs pronto. The problem: These PCs needed lots of extra memory and other upgrades, the better to run Windows, Microsoft's ubiquitous operating system, and link into the bank's computer network. ComputerLand called Kingston, which snapped into action. Within hours it had designed a sophisticated upgrade system—its particular specialty—and relayed specs to a key partner, Express Manufacturing. Express, which specializes in assembling electronic parts, cleared its manufacturing lines, filled Kingston's order, and sent the finished systems back that very afternoon. By evening Kingston had tested all the components and returned them via FedEx to ComputerLand. By the weekend Bank of America's computers were up and running. "You've heard of just-in-time inventory?" asks VP David Sun, referring to Japan's vaunted principle of cost-effective management. "This is just-in-time manufacturing."[41]

In the concept's purest form, each company that links with others to create a virtual corporation contributes only what it regards as its core competencies. Each firm is organized around its specific rare, valuable, hard-to-copy, and nonsubstitutable resources. All other resources are provided by other firms that also possess the four attributes of sustainable competitive advantage. These advantages, however, remain protected within the other firms.

Technology plays a central role in the development of virtual corporations. Entrepreneurs in different companies can work together concurrently rather than sequentially on computer networks in real time.[42] To participate in a virtual corporation, an enterprise must focus on the things it does best and forge alliances with other companies, each bringing its own special capability. Such an organization would be a world class competitor, with the speed, power, and leading-edge technology to take advantage of market opportunities.[43]

The Incubator Organization

A **business incubator** is an organization that provides resources for new start-ups. It can be a physical incubator locating all the start-ups in the same building and providing shared space as well as shared resources like office equipment and administrative support. A virtual incubator, in contrast, can be geographically disbursed, sharing value-added investors, leadership, and specialized expertise. Street Story 9.3 tells the story of one of the most famous incubators—Idealab—and the entrepreneur who founded it, Bill Gross.

NETWORKING AND ALLIANCES

Today's entrepreneurs are deeply embedded in networks, partnerships, alliances, and collectives.[44] **Networking**, the process of enlarging the entrepreneur's circle of trust, is a negotiation process.[45] How entrepreneurs access networks and how those networks help them succeed are the subjects of this section.

Benefits and Motivations for Networking

Entrepreneurs usually have a wide range of friends, acquaintances, and business associates, and they can use these **informal network** relationships to obtain resources and opportunities for their firms. These networks provide them with information about their environment and enable them to build reputation and credibility for themselves and their firms. Networks of people (and of other firms) are socially complex, casually ambiguous, and usually idiosyncratic. They depend on that particular entrepreneur. The networks themselves can be sources of sustainable competitive advantage, and they can also be a means of procuring *other* sources of sustainable competitive advantage.

Entrepreneurs employ various forms of networking. Chapter 8 pointed out the pros and cons of taking in a partner, and Chapter 9 has already illustrated the benefits of virtual organizations. Chapter 4 discussed joint ventures in terms of momentum factors and entrepreneurial strategy, and Chapter 7 dealt with the importance of networks in finding sources of financing. The modern well-connected entrepreneur has distinct advantages over the rugged individual of previous generations.

There are four basic motivations for **formal network** participation or joint-venture formation.[46]

1. Joint ventures increase the internal capabilities of the venture and protect its resources.
2. Joint ventures have competitive uses that strengthen the current strategic position.
3. Joint ventures have long-term strategic advantages that augment the venture's future resource flexibility.
4. Joint ventures further the social concerns and promote the values of entrepreneurs.[47]

Internal Motivations. Internal uses of alliances are motivated by various cost and risk-sharing arrangements that can reduce uncertainty for the venture. For example, sharing the outputs of minimum-efficient-scale plants avoids wasteful duplication of resources, utilizes byproducts and processes, and may even allow the partners to share brands and distribution channels. Joint ventures can also be used to obtain intelligence and to open a window on new technologies and customers. These relationships can help a firm imitate innovative managerial practices, superior management systems, and improved communications patterns.

When the Japanese industrial giant Matsushita came to Silicon Valley in the late 1990s to learn from the many start-ups there, it was looking for alliances. The company invested $50 million in an incubator and a venture capital fund and drew in nine new high-tech American businesses. All these companies are potential suppliers or partners

---

Hatching Success Stories

Bill Gross started out as a serial entrepreneur. In high school he founded a firm that sold kits to make solar energy products. While he was a student at the California Institute of Technology, he developed a loudspeaker that he and his brother patented and sold as GNP (yes, for Gross National Product) Loudspeakers. After graduation Gross and his brother started another company to market a software add-on for the Lotus 1-2-3 spreadsheet. That company chalked up $1 million in sales and was eventually sold to Lotus for $10 million.

Then in 1996 Gross traded consecutive projects for simultaneous ventures when he founded Idealab. The company was the first tech incubator, an enterprise dedicated to bringing what Gross calls "products and services [which] change the way people think, live and work," to market. Working with capital contributed by 400 shareholders, including Compaq co-founder Ben Rosen and actor Michael Douglas, Idealab funded ideas with up to $250,000 in seed money. The incubator set up a subsidiary for each venture, hired a staff, and solicited additional funding from outside investors. The new businesses operated from Idealab's office, utilizing the incubator's human resources, financial, and public relations services.

At one point in the late 1990s Idealab was supporting as many as 50 fledgling dot-com companies. Some of those new ventures were resounding successes: eToys was one of the pioneers of e-commerce, CitySearch was the first to promote online community directories, and GoTo.com introduced the concept of paid Internet search. GoTo.com, which became Overture Services, was ultimately sold to Google for $1.6 billion.

But in 2001 Idealab ran into problems when the dot-com bubble burst. The incubator lost $800 million dollars and had to close offices and lay off more than half its employees. Some disgruntled backers sued to reclaim their investment. Gross, shaken by the experience, said, "We had to completely reevaluate what we were going to be, what we were going to stand for, what kind of companies we wanted to make." Idealab board member Howard Morgan adds, "For all of us, especially Bill, it was a managerial growing up."

Today Idealab is launching new ventures at a slower and more careful pace, concentrating on just 16 companies with a diverse range of products, including software, hardware, and Web businesses. But the companies are just as innovative as before. In fact, Gross says Idealab is concentrating on "big, impactful [sic], change-the-world companies." These include Energy Innovations, which created a solar collector that harnesses 25 times the power of a traditional solar panel at one-quarter of the cost, and Evolution Robotics, which developed vision-recognition software than can automatically scan grocery carts at supermarkets. Other companies are crafting two-person hybrid cars with revolutionary Stirling engines, developing cell phones that don't need towers, and creating a new kind of Internet search engine. Idealab's most successful start-up is currently Internet Brands, formerly CarsDirect, a company that sells cars and mortgages on the Web. Internet Brands is generating $300 million in annual sales, and four of Idealab's other ventures are also profitable.

Gross is committed to taking care of his investors this time. "I want Idealab to be a way better investment for them than had they invested in the stock markets," he says.

SOURCE: Adapted from Nadira A. Hira, "Idealab Reloaded," *Fortune*, September 5, 2005: 143; www.idea lab.com.

for Matsushita's number one brand, Panasonic. They hope to learn from these companies and to expand their innovation network.[48]

External Motivations. External motivations for alliances usually involve the desire to improve current strategic positions. A set of firms is more likely than a single firm to influence the structure of an industry's evolution. Sometimes a joint venture can preempt possible new entrants, giving the partnership a first-mover advantage that is unlikely to be challenged. This first-mover advantage can extend to accessing the most desirable customers, expanding capacity to serve the entire market niche, and acquiring resources on advantageous terms before they become fully valued. Also, it is quite common to take on a foreign partner when entering that partner's domestic market.

Strategic Motivations. The third motivation concerns the future position and resources of the venture. Joint ventures can be undertaken for creative reasons, to exploit synergies, to develop new technologies, or to extend old technologies to new problems. Joint ventures can be mechanisms that give the firm a toehold in a market that is not completely ready for the product or service. For example, many entrepreneurs are currently engaged in joint ventures in China, India, and Russia, ventures with no current payoff possibilities. But the entrepreneurs recognize that in the longer term, the relationships created and the knowledge developed in these alliances will serve them well.

Social Motivations. Entrepreneurs also engage in networking to promote their own values and social agenda. One example of this is the Social Venture Network (SVN).Its primary goal is simple: The members get to meet other entrepreneurs who are committed to social change through business. This loose collection of entrepreneurs, social activists, corporate executives, and philanthropists has attracted some high-visibility entrepreneurs: Mitch Kapor of Lotus Development Corp.; Joe LaBonte, president of Reebok International Co.; Mel Ziegler, founder of Banana Republic and Republic of Tea; Anita Roddick, founder of The Body Shop International Inc.; and, of course, Ben Cohen, cofounder of Ben & Jerry's Homemade Inc. (SVN is on line at www.svn.org). The Chapter 8 end-of-chapter case concerned a network developing around the social cause of educational improvement. The network brings individuals of common purpose together—but not just any individuals.

Types of Networks

Personal Networks. The **personal network** is an informal network made up of all the entrepreneur's direct, face-to-face-contacts.[49] These include friends, family, close business associates, former teachers and professors, among others. The ongoing relationships in a personal network are based on three benefits: trust, predictability, and voice.[50] Trust enables the entrepreneur to forgo all of the activities and legal formalities that guard against opportunism. Predictability reduces uncertainty. People within the personal network behave the same way time and time again.

The third benefit of the personal network is **voice**—the permission to argue, negotiate, complain, and discuss any problem within the network and still maintain good relations. This permission, or norm, can be contrasted with the norm of **exit**. In relationships characterized by less trust, once reciprocity is broken, displeasure is communicated, or a verbal argument takes place, the parties are disinclined to do business anymore, and they exit the network.[51]

Personal networks have **strong ties,**[52] formed because the relationship has a long history, is based on a family connection, or arises from a common culture, common values, or common associations. Strong ties are especially important in the early stages of business formation, particularly in financing and securing the initial resources for new venture creations.[53]

Extended Networks. The **extended network**[54] consists of formal, firm-to-firm relationships. The entrepreneur develops these by means of boundary-spanning activities with other owners and managers of enterprises, customers and vendors, and other constituents in the operating environment. These are the normal cross-organizational activities required for the operation of an "open system."[55] Extended networks become more important as the firm moves beyond the initial founding stage.

Extended networks contain more diversity than personal networks and, consequently, more information. The relationships are more instrumental and based less on trust, more uncertain and less predictable. The customer of a customer may be included, as well as the supplier of a supplier. There may be many indirect associations in an extended network, so these are **weak ties.**

But there is "strength in weak ties."[56] Weak ties make a network much larger by encompassing more diverse information, people, resources, and channels. Whereas strong ties produce trust but redundancy, weak ties provide unique information about opportunities, locations, potential markets for goods and services, potential investors, and the like. In addition, the extended network adds to the credibility and legitimacy of the firm and expands its reputational capital.

Outside directors involved in the enterprise are good examples of the benefits of weak ties. These outside directors are an invaluable check on the entrepreneur's decisions and possible mistakes, because such directors complement the entrepreneur's information base and offer an objective outside viewpoint. This fresh perspective can change the course of the venture's strategy. For example, Kurtz Bros. Inc, a family-run landscape materials business in Cuyahoga Falls, Ohio, decided to diversify a few years ago. It was ready to move into industrial materials, and initially its management forgot to consult the firm's three outside directors. When these directors heard of the plan, "They were pretty tough on us," concedes Lisa Kurtz, company president. "They told us we were fracturing our organization, and that we should stick to our knitting." The outsiders' views made a deep impression: The family owners quickly reconsidered their decision and liquidated the new unit.[57]

One technological example of the extended network is the proliferation of blogs and electronic bulletin boards designed and used by entrepreneurs to share and receive information. Take the case of Bill Vick, owner of a Dallas-based executive recruiting firm. When he needed new ideas for getting clients and building his visibility and reputation, he put out a call for ideas on a bulletin board used by thousands of entrepreneurs. He received many suggestions, including one that proved to be a bonanza: Vick started mailing boxes of Vick's Cough Drops to sales executives with a postcard saying that his firm could "cure sick sales." A few days later at an industry conference, Vick was shaking hands and handing out more cough drops. "That one idea must have gotten me $25,000 worth of business," he says.[58]

Networking takes a considerable amount of the entrepreneurs' time and money.[59] If the networking does not improve firm performance, it can prove detrimental to the enterprise and frustrating to the entrepreneur. Entrepreneurs should have both strong-tie personal relationships and weak-tie extended relationships. The ideal situation is a network of strong-tie extended relationships which give entrepreneurs the speed and flexibility of strong ties with the informational and resource advantages of an extended network.

Alliance Behaviors. Entrepreneurs engage in four basic types of alliances: (1) confederations, (2) conjugate alliances, (3) agglomerations, and (4) organic networks. These types are distinguished by two characteristics: (1) whether the relationship is direct or indirect (entrepreneur's business to alliance partner) and (2) whether the relationship is with competing or non-competing firms.[60]

Direct contact with competitors is called a **confederate alliance**, or simply a confederation. In concentrated industries where a few firms have most of the market, confederate alliances are usually created in an attempt to avoid competition through techniques such as point pricing, uniform price lists, standard costing, and product standardization.[61] Because these alliances resemble cartels, firms may find themselves in violation of U.S. anti-trust law.

But smaller firms in fragmented industries—particularly new ventures in emerging industries—have many opportunities for cooperation through alliances that are not illegally collusive. For example, firms can share transportation costs by combining orders to make a full-truckload shipment. Or they can engage in bilateral hiring practices. By hiring each other's workers on a regular basis, the firms can share expertise, information, and intelligence about the market, and can upgrade each other's operational procedures by imitating the best of what the other has to offer. For example, in the very fragmented online business education market, the University of Phoenix Online hires instructors from many academic sources. Each instructor contributes information and techniques to the Phoenix curriculum while also learning online techniques from Phoenix. The instructors can bring these techniques back to their own classrooms at their home universities. Both institutions and the instructors are better off for the exchange.

Entrepreneurs must use good judgment in entering into confederate relationships. An unscrupulous competitor can take advantage of the trust inherent in such relationships. Former rivals may collude to raise profits by restraining production, raising prices, and holding back threatening new technologies. The lack of free-for-all competition can lead to complacency that stifles creativity and new ideas.[62]

Direct contact with non-competing firms is called a **conjugate alliance**. Examples include long-term purchasing contracts with suppliers and customers and joint research and development projects. Companies that keep their separate identities and engage in conjugate relationships are mimicking the vertical integration strategies of larger firms to obtain certain benefits without incurring the inherent risks. For instance, a joint R&D effort can enable a manufacturer to test the operating characteristics of a supplier's materials (for a fee) and report back to the supplier how the material holds up under various real world operating conditions (an advantage for the supplier). Like the confederate form, the conjugate form is a task-oriented, tightly coupled, and voluntary relationship in a weak-tie network.

By working together, conjugate networks can do things they could not accomplish alone. For example, in Indiana a network called the FlexCell Group connects makers of metalworking patterns and tools with mechanical engineers, producers of plastic injection molding, a prototype machine shop, and a contract machine shop. All the members are independent companies with annual sales of less than $10 million each. The result is a vertically integrated, virtual single-source supplier. Tom Brummett, owner of the Columbus, Indiana, firm that supplies the network with marketing and management services, says that FlexCell "can offer its existing customer base more capabilities and quicker turnaround time, usually with more cost effectiveness. This is a way for small and medium-size companies to leverage their resources to compete in a global economy." Recently, FlexCell beat out two large multinational corporations from Europe and South America in its bid to produce engine components for a U.S. customer.[63]

An **agglomerate network**, or agglomeration, is a set of indirect relationships between competing firms. It provides the firms with information about the capabilities and competencies that are regarded as necessary but not sufficient for success. Control of the network is maintained by dues and membership rules. Trade associations, for example, are agglomerate networks. They usually exist in highly fragmented and geographically dispersed environments populated by very small, homogeneous ventures, such as retailing and small farms. These networks are loosely coupled, voluntary, and have a low-task structure: No single member of the agglomeration can influence another member to do anything.

An **organic network** is an indirect relationship (indirect in terms of the business, not the individual entrepreneur who represents the firm) between non-competing organizations. These relationships are not task-oriented and may consist of strong-tie linkages, such as friendships and close business connections, or weak-tie links such as chamber of commerce or professional association membership.

The four types of networks are defined by the way they integrate the two dimensions—compete/cooperate and direct/indirect—to produce the two-by-two matrix shown in Table 9.1.

Partner Selection Criteria

Choosing a partner for a joint venture, for an alliance, or even for one of the shorter-term relationships just discussed is crucial for the entrepreneur.[64] A poor choice can doom not only the joint venture but the entire enterprise. Three primary criteria must be met:

1. The potential partner must have a strong commitment to the joint venture.
2. The top managements of the firms must be compatible.
3. The people involved must have had previous positive experience in the trenches.

The first criterion must be met if the firms are to have a mutual sense of responsibility and project ownership. If one side believes the venture is unimportant, it will allot it

TABLE 9.1   A Typology of Alliances

	Direct Contact	Indirect Contact
Competing Organizations	Confederate Alliance	Agglomerate Network
Noncompeting Organizations	Conjugate Alliance	Organic Network

SOURCE: Adapted from G. Astley and C. Fombrun, "Collective Strategies: Social Ecology of Organizational Environments," *Academy of Management Review* 8, 1983: 576-587.

less time and resources and be tempted to behave opportunistically. It may let the other side do all the work and take all the risks while it enjoys the benefits of cooperation.

The second criterion must be met in order to join the two enterprises' cultures and develop a strong sense of trust. The top managements of the two firms must not only be able to work together but also to model cooperative behavior for their subordinates. When subordinates see top managers cooperating and sharing resources and information, they are likely to follow suit. Commitment at the top is essential.

The third criterion asks the partners to build on past experiences. If they have worked together successfully in the past, that history and momentum can work again. There is certainly no guarantee, but the probability of a successful alliance is increased.

After these three criteria are met, the other criteria for partner selection are typically contingent on the goals and nature of the joint venture: product orientation, service delivery, technology sharing, or the like. Partnership is an attractive option when the potential partner has complementary skills with little duplication and when the relationship creates a mutual dependence that makes cooperation in everyone's self-interest. Good communications, similar cultures and values, compatible operating policies, and compatible goals all make potential partners attractive. A partner with a strong reputation is valuable because it can enhance the other firm's legitimacy.[65]

Processes of Reciprocity

How do entrepreneurs position themselves and their firms to enter into these alliances, networks, and cooperative partnerships? Why do people allow entrepreneurs to do this? From the business viewpoint, the primary reason is that the entrepreneurial firm has something to offer the partner—a skill, a process, a technology, a system for administration, access to a customer, or a desirable location.

But it is the entrepreneur who, on a personal level, initiates the contact and maintains the relationships that may turn into contracts and formal arrangements. People allow entrepreneurs to approach them with these cooperative and collective strategies for four reasons:

1. *Friendship.* The entrepreneur has developed a nurturing and caring relationship with the people at the target organization.
2. *Liking.* There is pleasure and comfort in reciprocity and in finding someone with a mutual affinity.
3. *Gratitude.* The entrepreneur has put a member of the target's firm in his or her debt

through a personal or professional favor, and the discharge of that debt (reciprocity) is the mechanism for the cooperation.

4. *Obligation.* The target firm must repay some formal obligation to the entrepreneur.[66]

In each of these cases, the entrepreneur has established a positive environment for cooperation by "being nice" and by doing it first. What kinds of things can entrepreneurs do to encourage cooperative behavior?

1. Share information with the target firm.
2. Help the target firm solve a problem and/or accept help from the target firm.
3. Give and receive favors, both business and personal.
4. Create opportunities for others to receive recognition and achievement.
5. Build and use networks, and allow others access to them. The entrepreneur's strong ties can be another's weak ties.
6. Ask others to make their networks available and piggyback on the reputation and credibility of the partner.

TRADITIONAL ORGANIZATIONAL STRUCTURE

Virtual organizations can and do exist, but for how long? Kingston Technology may be long-lived because its design capabilities are its source of sustainable competitive advantage. In the case of Walden Paddlers, a Massachusetts maker of kayaks, the alliances are built on trust, a much shakier foundation in a low-trust society such as the United States.[67] Walden's dealer and supplier networks were constructed in an informal, personal way based on an appreciation of the kayaking experience. The traditional view of organizational boundaries is based on the strategy-structure hypothesis:[68] **structure follows strategy**. This means that the boundaries of the organization are adjusted periodically to meet the requirements of the firm's strategy. This process is a component of the transition from entrepreneurial management to professional management.

Stage One: Simple Structure

An historical analysis of firm behavior provides the template for this hypothesis.[69] In the earliest stages of firm creation, an organization's boundaries begin and end with the entrepreneur and a few close associates. The strategy pursued by the top management team of such a new business is directed to increasing sales volume. This is the first stage of the organizational structure life cycle.

Stage Two: Departmentalization

As the firm grows larger, entrepreneurs find themselves engaged in more and more administration (e.g., allocating resources to specific functions) and fewer and fewer entrepreneurial tasks. This is detrimental to firm performance. When the volume of the business grows so large that the entrepreneurs themselves can no longer make all the executive decisions, they hire managers: production managers, marketing managers, sales managers, engineering and design managers, and personnel managers. These managers supervise the activities of their various departments, which surround the main core of the business. **Departmentalization** is the second stage of organizational structure.

Stage Three: Divisional Structure

The volume of a business can grow only so large in a single location. Constraints such as plant capacity, transportation costs, logistical issues, and the limits of the market itself mean that if a firm continues to grow, it must expand to other locations. The next strategy, then, concerns geographic expansion. Initially, firms attempt to manage both old and new sites from the original location. As the number of sites increases and the branches and outlets proliferate, however, this becomes impossible. Thus, the structure of the firm must change to meet the demands of the new strategy. The new structure calls for grouping the units within particular regions into geographic divisions. This new structure adds another layer to the functionally differentiated department structure. Both departments and regions report to the firm's headquarters, creating the third stage of structural development: the **divisional structure**.

Stage Four: Multidivisional Structure

Future growth in a single product, like growth in a single location, is a limiting strategy because of satiated demand for the product and missed opportunities from related products and markets. As firms continue to grow, they change to a strategy of related diversification and vertical integration. For example, General Motors integrates with Fisher Body; Jersey Standard expands its refining and marketing; DuPont develops new product groups based on its chemical research and development; Sears moves into the insurance business by merging with Allstate Insurance. This diversification puts new demands on the old divisional structure. Stress and strain are created, inefficiencies arise, and finally a new structure is developed—the **multidivisional structure**, the fourth stage of development. Like the divisional structure, it groups similar products and activities together so employees can achieve maximum productivity.

Stage Five: The Conglomerate

The fifth and final structure is created when the strategy changes from related to unrelated diversification. When firms enter businesses completely unlike any in which they have previously engaged, the old structure begins to break down. Executives in the older divisions do not understand the new businesses and do not share the perspectives of the newer managers. There is no reason to group these unrelated divisions together because they do not share markets, products, or technologies. In fact, it is better to keep them separate so that the performance of each can be measured independently. From this change in strategy comes the **conglomerate**, also known as the **holding company**.

In summary, the "structure follows strategy" hypothesis says that an organization's boundaries arise from the pursuit of different strategies. The boundaries are fixed for periods of time, but as the changes in strategy put stress on the organization's structure, a new structure arises. Each time a new structure comes into being, the enterprise's boundaries expand, as do the activities within those boundaries.

ENTREPRENEURIAL PERFORMANCE: THE BALANCED SCORECARD

The great entrepreneurial organizations perform at very high levels. The question is "levels of what?" Will it be levels of product innovation? Financial performance? Customer service? Internal efficiency? The answer is that great entrepreneurial organizations operate at a high level on *all* of these dimensions. They do so in a balanced way, not emphasizing one over the other, because all of these dimensions work together to produce a successful system. In the early days of a venture, the primary objectives are survival, profitability, and growth. As a firm makes the transition to professional management, it needs to become more sophisticated about measuring performance.

The **balanced scorecard (BSC)** is a systematic management process that generates objectives, activities, and measurements for organizational performance.[70] It is a set of measures that gives managers a fast but comprehensive view of their business. A good balanced scorecard has 15 to 20 different measures derived from the four basic dimensions of entrepreneurial performance:

- Financial dimension (How do we look to our investors?)
- Customer dimension (How do we look to our customers?)
- Internal operating dimension (What do we excel at?)
- Innovation and learning dimension (Can we continue to improve and create value?)

Using these four dimensions to develop a set of criteria, entrepreneurs and the TMT can translate the venture's mission and strategy into a set of comprehensive operating and performance measures. All of the dimensions are linked, as illustrated in Figure 9.2.

Because the entrepreneurial venture's existence is characterized by change and growth, these measures can be fine-tuned to reflect changing circumstances. When the environment of the venture changes rapidly, old criteria can be discarded and new measures can be implemented.

This system helps the entrepreneur balance:

- *The long term versus the short term.* Some of the criteria will capture a three-to-six-month period of activity. Others will attempt to drive the organization to longer-term goals, three to five years out.
- *Lagging indicators versus leading indicators.* Some criteria measure what has happened in the past, like financial performance or manufacturing productivity. These are lagging indicators. Leading indicators relate to the future: Capital investment, training, new hires, and research intensity capture the venture's current activities in anticipation of a future payoff.
- *External performance expectations versus internal performance expectations.* Some measures deal with how the company is managing its relations with the external environment—e.g., customer or vendor relations. Other measures deal with internal operations—e.g., manufacturing efficiency and employee skill acquisition.
- *Financial versus nonfinancial performance.* The balance between these two is critical. Too much emphasis on financial results can choke growth as the entrepreneur seeks to maximize short-run opportunities. Too much emphasis on non-

FIGURE 9.2 Financial and Operational Measures

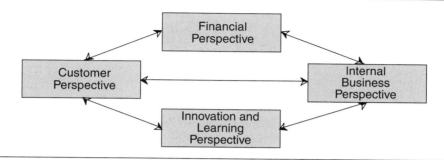

financial measures (such as "eyeballs" captured in Internet scenarios) risks running out of money and willing investors.

- *Driver measures of future performance versus financial measures of past performance.* Drivers are critically important because they indicate that a company is building the capabilities and acquiring the intangible assets it needs for future growth.

There are many good reasons to use the BSC approach. Frequently, entrepreneurs become obsessed with financial performance, but that alone does not indicate how the company is developing for the future. Financial performance is a lagging indicator that measures the past; the entrepreneur should be focused on the future. It requires a balance of financial and other measures to give a complete picture of how the firm is doing. In addition, the process of implementing the BSC makes people aware of the relationships among the four dimensions. All three of the nonfinancial measures must be linked to the financial ones. A good balanced scorecard clearly shows the cause-and-effect relationships in the measures chosen. However, the main lesson for entrepreneurs and their TMTs is: *What you measure is what you get!!!*

The Customer Dimension

Customers' concerns generally fall into four areas: time, quality, performance and service, and cost. Customer dimension goals might include:

- *Time*—reduced delivery time
- *Quality*—reduced defects or warranty claims
- *Performance and service*—increased value perception
- *Cost*—reduced price or costs (e.g., delivery)

More specific measures of customers' goals might focus on:

- Time: on-time delivery as defined by the customer
- Quality: percentage of sales from new and existing products
- Performance and service: market share, customer satisfaction rankings
- Cost: year-to-year cost reductions

It is up to the entrepreneur and the TMT to define the customer dimension goals and choose the measures for meeting them. Each goal is linked in some way to the financial measures and the other goals.

The Internal Business Dimension

This dimension answers the question "What must we excel at?" and is directly related to the venture's resources and capabilities. The internal business dimension can be represented as a three-part value chain:

1. Innovation process—developing new technology and implementing it. One specific example might be developing a new product and introducing it against the competition.
2. Operations process—developing manufacturing and delivery excellence. Examples of specific measures are reduced cycle time, reduced unit costs, and increased yield.
3. Post-sale service process—improving the service program. Examples of specific measures are reduced warranty costs and increased customer retention rates.

The Innovation and Learning Dimension

This internal dimension focuses more specifically on the people in the organization. Its goals can be divided into three subcomponents:

1. *Employee capabilities.* A goal here might be the continued improvement of the technological capabilities of the employees and managers. A specific measure might concern the time it takes to develop the next generation of technological product or service improvement. This goal clearly shows the need for investment in employee training and development as well as the capital investment needed to sustain testing and quality.
2. *Information systems capabilities.* A goal in this area might the development of an expert system of the firm's manufacturing or throughput processes. A specific measure would be the time it takes to develop and test the expert system.
3. *Motivation, empowerment, and alignment.* Examples of goals in this area include increasing employee focus on products and product information, or a reduction in time to market of a new item. The first goal can be measured by the number of products that represent 80 percent of revenue; the latter can be measured by setting a benchmark for the firm's time to market versus the competition's.

Goals and measures are also directly linked to the other areas as well as to financial performance. Balancing the needs of the organization requires attention to these people issues because people and their behaviors are instrumental in achieving the other objectives.

The Financial Performance Dimension

The financial objective of every venture is to provide superior returns to investors. There are three primary ways to do this:

1. Through revenue growth and maximizing the mix of revenue streams. Some goals that can be set to achieve this include:

- Designing and developing new products
- Creating new applications for old products and services
- Finding new customers and markets
- Optimizing the product and service mix
- Developing new relationships and strategic partners
- Executing a new pricing strategy

2. Through cost reductions and productivity improvements such as:

- Increasing productivity
- Reducing unit costs
- Improving distribution channel mix
- Reducing operating expenses and overhead

3. Through superior asset utilization and investment strategies. These can be summarized as:

- Improving the cash-to-cash cycle
- Increasing asset utilization rates

Typically, the specific measures of financial performance revolve around returns on invested capital, returns on equity, and returns on assets. Other important measures are gross and operating margins, market shares, and growth in sales.

As entrepreneurs construct their scorecards, they must remember that a good balanced scorecard has a limited number of measures so that managers are forced to focus, not try to achieve everything at once. Four or five measures in each of the four dimensions are sufficient. A good scorecard brings all the dimensions together in an integrated way and shows how activity on one dimension leads to activity and better performance on another. By showing cause and effect in this way, it guards against sub-optimization and enables all the managers to see what the others are doing.

The benefits of using the balanced scorecard have been shown in many established companies over the years, and the same lessons apply for new ventures. An organization's performance must be integrated and balanced, but there are also other advantages to using the balanced scorecard approach: The scorecard is not only a measuring tool, but also a system of managing. Many companies have used the BSC to:

1. *Clarify* and gain consensus about strategy.
2. *Communicate* strategy throughout the organization.
3. *Align goals* (departmental and personal) to strategy.
4. *Link* strategic objectives to long-term targets and annual budgets.
5. *Identify* and align strategic initiatives.
6. *Perform reviews* (both periodic and systematic).
7. *Obtain feedback* to learn about and improve strategy.

THE ENTREPRENEURIAL WORKPLACE

The new venture is not just a vehicle for the entrepreneur and the top management team to realize their dreams and ambitions; it is also the place where people work. The challenge of the entrepreneurial workplace is to enable employees to share the founders' excitement, motivation, commitment, and satisfaction. Otherwise, they will fail to carry out their tasks and responsibilities energetically and effectively. Part of the entrepreneur's responsibility is to create an organization where the culture, the ethics, and the human resource management system are consistent with the goals and ambitions of the enterprise.

The Entrepreneurial Culture

The **culture** of the organization is reflected in its philosophies, rules, norms, and values. It defines "how we do things around here" for both employees and customers. A strong entrepreneurial culture mirrors the entrepreneurial values of the founders. Entrepreneurs often start their businesses because they want to do things "their own way," and creating an entrepreneurial culture is their opportunity to allow others to do it "their own way." Therefore, it is imperative that the entrepreneurs communicate what they believe is important. This communication can be one-on-one, or it can be shared in meetings, employee newsletters, or other written formats. Often the culture is communicated in rituals, rites, and the folklore of the company.[71] Entrepreneurial companies can do things their own way. For example:

> Amy Miller, president of Amy's Icecreams Inc., of Austin, Texas, is a self-described "hyperactive," so she wants her stores to be hyperactive too. She encourages her employees to toss ice cream from scoop to bowl, and she allows and encourages employees to dance on the freezer tops. To recruit people as uninhibited as herself, she gives potential applicants a paper bag and asks them to do something creative with it.[72]
>
> At Tweezerman Corp. in Port Washington, New York, the slogan is "We aim to tweeze" and the goal is 24-hour service. Working for the tweezer and body-care products company can be frenetic and tense. Because the owner, Dal La Magna, does not employ secretaries, all the employees are constantly in a mad rush to answer phones, letters, and customer demands. The pace creates tensions and fights, so the company has "Fight Day" once a month when all the stored-up steam can be let off. Postponing the arguments gives most people a chance to cool off and get down to work. Also, the company sets space aside for employees to meditate when the atmosphere gets too wacky.[73]
>
> Frank Meeks has 45 Dominos Pizza units in his Washington, D.C., franchise area. Every week he and his managers do a no-nonsense 10-kilometer run before their meeting. "The company believes in integrating health and fitness," Meeks says. Recruits are told about the requirement before they are hired, and the only excuse not to run is a deathbed plea. Meeks does not want any lazy people on the team. The competitive atmosphere makes the meetings more like pep rallies than sales reports.[74]

The entrepreneurial culture is clearly different from the culture of traditional large organizations. It is future-oriented and emphasizes new ideas, creativity, risk-taking, and opportunity identification. People feel empowered to manage their own jobs and time. Everyone contributes to the firm's success, and the common worker is a hero. Communication is frequently horizontal and bottom up—while the worker serves the customer, the manager serves the worker. Table 9.2 compares the organizational culture of the traditional firm with that of the entrepreneurial organization.

Entrepreneurial Ethics

An important part of a new venture's culture is its ethical climate. The ethics of the organization are never clear enough and are frequently ambiguous and shifting. Stereotypically, entrepreneurs are seen as having low ethical standards. The great robber barons of the American industrial revolution—the Rockefellers, Fords, Mellons, and Carnegies—were all seen in their time as ruthless and unethical. In today's Chinese economic revolution, the use of public office for private gain, the lack of a rule of law, and the endemic use of bribery contribute to the belief that the entrepreneur is an unethical, selfish economic animal. In fact, entrepreneurs and small business owners are neither more nor less ethical than other people, but they have different tolerances for different types of unethical behavior. Table 9.3 reports the results of a large study of the ethical differences between managers of small and large businesses.

Entrepreneurs repeatedly face ethical dilemmas, all involving the meaning of honesty. At times the entrepreneur may feel that to be "completely honest" does a disservice to the new venture and his or her efforts to create it. Yet to be less than completely honest puts the credibility and reputation of both the entrepreneur and the new venture in question. These are the dilemmas of the promoter, the innovator, and the transactor.

Promoter Dilemma. When entrepreneurs are in the early stages of promoting their businesses to financial supporters, customers, potential partners, and employees, a cer-

---

TABLE 9.2 Organizational Culture: A Comparison

Dimension	Traditional Organization	Entrepreneurial Organization
Strategy	Status quo, conservative	Evolving, futuristic
Productivity	Short-term focus, profitability	Short-long term, multiple criteria
Risk	Averse, punished	Emphasized and rewarded
Opportunity	Absent	Integral
Leadership	Top-down, autocratic	Culture of empowerment
Power	Hoarded	Given away
Failure	Costly	OK; teaches a lesson
Decision making	Centralized	Decentralized
Communication	By the book, chain of command	Flexible, facilitates innovation
Structure	Hierarchical	Organic
Creativity	Tolerated	Prized and worshiped
Efficiency	Valued: accountants are heroes	Valued if it helps realize overall goals

SOURCE: Adapted from J. Cornwall and B. Perlman, *Organizational Entrepreneurship* (Homewood, IL: Irwin, 1990).

TABLE 9.3   Ethical Issues: Comparison between Managers of Small and Large Firms

Small Firm Manager More Tolerant of	Large Firm Manager More Tolerant of
1. Padded expense accounts	1. Faulty investment advice
2. Tax evasion	2. Favoritism in promotion
3. Collusion in bidding	3. Living with a dangerous design flaw
4. Insider trading	4. Misleading financial reporting
5. Discrimination against women	5. Misleading advertising
6. Copying computer software	

SOURCE: J. Longnecker, J. McKinney, and C. Moore, "Do Smaller Firms Have Higher Ethics?" *Business and Society Review,* Fall 1989: 19–21.

tain euphoria prevails. The entrepreneurs are in a very positive state of mind and want to show the new venture in the best possible light. They give positive impressions about the new venture even though they recognize the dangers, risks, potential pitfalls, and barriers to success. They must weigh the costs of revealing all this negative information against the benefits of being completely honest—the **promoter dilemma**. It is not clear at what point in the process and to what degree promoters are obligated to communicate their darkest fears about the new venture.

Innovator Dilemma. The creation of new businesses often means the creation of new technologies, products, and combinations. The entrepreneur frequently has to decide whether to go ahead and expedite production and distribution or to engage in a long process of product testing for safety. Even if there is no reason to believe the product is unsafe, there is always the risk of the Frankenstein effect: If the unwitting entrepreneur creates a monster, a product that does—or is perceived to do—harm, the new venture will never recover. If the entrepreneur waits until the risk and uncertainty are eliminated, someone else may be first to market—the **innovator dilemma**.

Relationship Dilemma. Over the course of creating a new venture, the entrepreneur becomes a member of a number of different networks—groups of individuals and firms—and conflicts of interest frequently arise because the ethical demands of membership in one group conflict with those of another. For example, the scientist/entrepreneur belongs to academic societies that insist that studies be peer-reviewed and published in professional journals to ensure scientific validity. But this may require revealing important proprietary information that is a source of SCA for the new enterprise—the **relationship dilemma**.

A different type of relationship dilemma arises from some of the entrepreneur's transactions. One example involves investor relationships: If one investor's commitment depends heavily on that of another investor, the entrepreneur may attempt to "ham and egg" it. That means telling the first investor that the second has made a commitment, and telling the second investor that the first investor has done so. From the point of view of the new venture, complete honesty might mean getting no investor commitment. On the other hand, this maneuver means the entrepreneur-investor relationship is less than completely honest.

Entrepreneurs face additional tests of their ethical character. The "finders keepers" problem occurs when value is created through the collective efforts of many firms and individuals, but the entrepreneur can appropriate all of the gain for the new venture. Should the entrepreneur take all the gains, or should they be distributed among all the deserving parties? For example, many people are credited with coinventing such complex products as the Internet, television, or lasers. In the case of the Internet, inventors/entrepreneurs share the credit, while in the case of the laser, contentious lawsuits were fought over decades for money and recognition.[75]

Sometimes the goals of the firm and of the entrepreneur diverge. If the entrepreneur wants to live in high style and spend more than the business can afford, who is to say no? There is often no control over the entrepreneur in this situation.

Finally, entrepreneurs occasionally have to decide whether to engage in unsavory business practices, such as paying bribes, or to forgo business opportunities. In some industries and cultures, such practices are commonplace. Refusing to pay the bribe simply means that someone else will pay it and will get the contract or sale. Should the entrepreneur go along or refuse to deal?

These are difficult issues, and their resolution depends on the criterion used by the decision maker. A **utilitarian rule** resolves the issue by asking, "Which choice produces the most good for the most people?" An **absolute rule** decides the dilemma by consistently applying a moral or religious code—which almost invariably forbids lying, cheating, stealing, and taking advantage of less powerful people. A **relativist approach** to making these decisions looks at what others are doing in the same situation and goes along with the crowd. To further complicate the ethics issues, it is not unusual to find an entrepreneur using all three criteria at one time or another, depending on the situation.

One set of simple decision-making rules and practical advice has been offered by Norman R. Augustine, former CEO and chairman of Lockheed Martin: "If you can answer "yes" to all four questions, then whatever you do is probably ethical," says Augustine.[76]

1. Is it legal?
2. If someone did this to you, would you think it was fair?
3. Would you be content if this appeared on the front page of your hometown newspaper?
4. Would you like your mother to see you do this?

MOST SUCCESSFUL HUMAN RESOURCE PRACTICES

There are few rules for successful human resource practices because each company is different and human resource management is complex. Although standard practices and guidelines are easy to come by, they offer little insight into how to make the venture's human resource management a source of sustainable competitive advantage.[77]

Each business needs to identify its own managerial strengths and develop a system around them. That is what the companies described below have done, and it has earned them a reputation as some of the best entrepreneurial companies in the United States to work for.[78] These practices can be used as benchmarks by others, but the real challenge is to customize them to the special context of each enterprise.

Best Compensation Practices

The level of pay alone does not motivate workers, but it is an essential component. Pay fairness is equally important, and so is a transparent process that enables people to see how pay is determined. Rewards must relate directly to what the company wants its people to accomplish. It is fallacy to hope that people will do A when their rewards come from B.

- A photo-image printing firm empowers employees to determine what skills are needed to do the job and then rewards them for proficiency and for their ability to teach others. They grade themselves.
- A communications equipment maker sets compensation for each employee at the level of customer satisfaction. An annual customer survey and a measure of product service and reliability are used.
- A software services consultant offers customized pay packages with cafeteria-style benefits. A menu of annual salary, hourly salary, or a blend can foster mutual risk sharing between employer and employee.
- A midwestern manufacturer instituted a **gain-sharing** program that rewards employees with a percentage of the savings or profits from their suggestions and innovations. It also encourages ideas with a *Gainsharing News* newsletter.

Best Training Practices

Training is an investment in human resources, and exceptional training can be a source of SCA for the enterprise. Skill-intensive training improves the current level of employee productivity. Training can anticipate changes in the nature of work so that when job requirements change, there is no decline in productivity. Management training serves three purposes: It enables workers to better understand their managers' roles, it helps employees manage themselves, and it prepares people for promotion to management ranks.

- A computer systems installer enables employees to mentor each other. An expert employee spreads both skill and management knowledge to peers.
- An airplane furniture maker focuses training on "learning to learn." Saturday sessions of exercises and role-playing allow people to break down barriers to communication and improve teamwork.
- Coffee megastar Starbucks ties training to business strategy by formally building employees' identification with the company. Classes stress everything from basic product knowledge to interpersonal relationships.

Best Job Autonomy

Employees with the authority and responsibility to do their jobs often display stronger motivation, better work quality, higher job satisfaction, and lower turnover. Job autonomy is a key component in making a company a great place to work. Not all employees can handle the freedom, but allowing autonomy is the best way to manage those who can.

- An instrument manufacturer urges employees to "make it happen," to solve problems, to motivate themselves. The company sets loose boundaries so everyone feels responsible for everything.
- A phone service reseller hires rigorously, trains intensively, and then turns people loose to perform. Little supervision is needed for most people. Progress is reviewed monthly or weekly.
- An automobile dealer empowers salespeople to cut deals on their own and urges service department teams to boost customer satisfaction. The dealer actively solicits and implements employee ideas.

Best Career Advancement

Employee advancement does not always mean promotion up the ladder in the bureaucracy. Indeed, with increasing emphasis on flatter organizations, many businesses would be better off without much bureaucracy. In that case, how are employees to advance and to view their jobs' career opportunities?

- A temporary placement agency grows its own managers and hires from within. It hires for one or two levels up from the position available so that the employee can grow into the job as the company's demand for managers grows.
- A linen distributor maps out career tracks up to 15 years in advance with the expectation that the new hire will retire with the company.
- A small agricultural business clearly communicates career growth opportunities to all employees and promotes competent learners.
- A health policy consultant enables staff members to market their own ideas by developing personal interests that can create new businesses. It promotes lateral job moves if these are beneficial to all.

Best Quality of Life

Increasingly people are merging work with family life. Outside concerns about things such as child care, working spouses, and parental leave all influence job performance. People are concerned about their total quality of life, not just the on-the-job part. The best companies to work for recognize this and make it possible to realistically combine personal values and job requirements.

- A plumbing products manufacturer provides on-site school and child care before and after office hours, financial support for adoptions, and benefits to part-time employees.
- A magazine publisher gives extended family leave at two-thirds pay plus six months' unpaid leave. It allows flexible scheduling and offers dependent-care assistance.

- A research lab established on-site adult day care and child care, an employee fitness center, and an emergency counseling program.
- A commercial packaging maker made on-site laundry facilities available, offered English and high school equivalency classes, provided door-to-door transport, and opened a children's clothing swap center.

One of the most creative sets of human resource practices can be found in the company MySQL. It has employees in over 25 countries—and no home office. So how does it work? Street Story 9.4 helps explain this remarkable company.

These small businesses and new firms have been creative and enterprising in developing human resource systems that integrate the needs of the business and the workers. When the venture's human resources are working at full capacity, they are saving the company money, adding value for customers, adapting to the changing marketplace, taking responsibility, and managing themselves. The entrepreneur must consider the creation and development of the organization as an opportunity to achieve a sustainable competitive advantage.

SUMMARY

This chapter has provided an overview of the theoretical and practical aspects of creating an organization. One top priority for most entrepreneurs is the recruitment, selection, and organization of a top management team. The team serves as the basis of sustainable competitive advantage by virtue of the uniqueness of its members and also as the protector of the venture's resources.

The TMT and the founder are responsible for ensuring that the organization has the potential for long-term success. This requires preserving the core values of the business, while at the same time making sure that there are mechanisms in the organization to stimulate progress and innovation.

Although some ventures can survive as virtual organizations by using the market and alliances as support, most ventures create organizations that are hierarchical and that divide authority and responsibility among their members. As the firm's strategy changes and its industry develops, the entrepreneur must reappraise earlier choices about what to do internally and what to leave to the market.

The performance of the new venture should be measured on four different dimensions: financial, customer relations, internal business process, and growth and development. A balanced approach to performance helps the new venture develop the skills, capabilities, and resources necessary for survival and growth.

The entrepreneur and the TMT are responsible for the business's culture and ethical climate. Creating an exciting and motivating environment for employees is a challenge that must be met. The entrepreneur should employ innovative methods of compensation, training, promotion and advancement, job autonomy, and total quality of life. Attention paid to human resources has long-term benefits for the firm and is a continuing source of advantage.

Working in a Virtual Office

The company's director of support greets each of his staff members every morning by name. "It sends a message that each individual is important to me," explains Thomas Basil. Managers at many companies do the same, but Basil's greeting is a little different: He says hello from an office in the basement of his Baltimore home, using an Internet Relay chat (IRC) to greet employees scattered around the globe.

MySQL AB is a Swedish company that develops and markets high-performance database servers and software (the initials "SQL" stand for structured query language, the language used to make the commands by which data is extracted, sorted, updated, deleted and inserted in a database). With more than ten million installations MySQL is the most popular open source database in the world. Its wide range of customers includes NASA, Amazon, the U.S, Census Bureau, Google, Dow Jones, and the Associated Press.

Seventy percent of MySQL's 320 employees work from home. Most of them are software developers and engineers, workers who don't need a centralized location or a fixed schedule to provide technical support to the company's customers. Many employees were hired over the Internet without meeting or even speaking to another MySQL employee. "We have people with lots of tattoos," says Michael "Monty" Widenius, company cofounder and chief technical officer. "Some of them I would not like to be with in the office every day." Some employees were formerly unpaid users recruited after they developed a new application or an improvement to MySQL software on their own.

Employee productivity is measured by output. "We are strictly a management-by-objective company," says marketing manager Erik Granström. "If you don't produce what you say, you will only get so many chances." In addition to the IRC, employees use a company-developed software product called Worklog to check off tasks as they complete them. While most work in physical isolation, supervisors and co-workers alike are very aware of who is signing in to the IRC or leaving other cyber footprints. "I have a very low opinion of human nature, which is that people are both greedy and lazy," says Widenius, who has put a lot of thought into how to manage people in cyberspace. "Of course you have noble people, but they are a small fraction."

The company is sometimes challenged to duplicate the social or bonding events available to employees in a traditional office. Last December Basil hosted a virtual holiday party for his staff, playing the role of cyber Santa while distributing virtual gifts and drinks to staffers as far away as Russia. "When a company is as spread out as this one you have to think of virtual ways to imitate the dynamics of what goes on in a more familiar employment situation," he says.

SOURCE: Adapted from John Hyatt, "MySQL: Workers in 25 Countries with no HQ," *CNNMoney.com*, June 1, 2006. Retrieved from the Web June 7, 2006. http://cnn-money.printthis.clickability.com/pt/cpt?action=cpt&title=FORTUNE%3A+Banish and www.mysql.com.

KEY TERMS

Absolute rule
Advisory board
Agglomerate network
Architect of organizational purpose
Balanced scorecard (BSC)
BHAG
Business incubator
Challengers
Collaborators
Communicators
Confederate alliance
Conglomerate
Conjugate alliance
Contributors
Core ideology
Core purpose
Core values
Cultural diversity
Culture
Departmentalization
Divisional structure
Envisioned future
Exit
Extended network
Familiars
Fiduciary board
Formal network
Gain-sharing
Groupshift
Groupthink

Holding company
Informal network
Innovator dilemma
Material rewards
Multidivisional structure
Networking
Nonmaterial rewards
Organic network
Organizational leader
Personal leader
Personal network
Preserve the core
Process-oriented
    communication
Promoter dilemma
Relationship dilemma
Relativist approach
Sarbanes-Oxley (SOX)
Self-serving communication
Strong ties
Structure follows strategy
Task-oriented communication
Team
Unfamiliars
Utilitarian rule
Virtual organization
Voice
Weak ties
Working group

DISCUSSION QUESTIONS

1. What are the three leadership roles of the entrepreneur? Give examples of each.
2. How is a team different from a working group? Give examples.
3. Where do the venture's TMT members come from? What are the pros and cons of recruiting familiars versus unfamiliars?
4. What are the arguments for and against a culturally diverse TMT?
5. What types of efforts must be made to maintain a TMT as a high-performing group?
6. What is the role of the board of directors? How can the board and the entrepreneur cooperate to make the venture a success?
7. What is a virtual organization? How can it exist and survive? When is a virtual organization an effective way of organizing the new venture?
8. Why are networking and alliances important for the entrepreneur?

9. What is meant by the "strength of weak ties"?
10. Describe the changes in organizational structure that a firm might go through as it grows.
11. How do entrepreneurial organizations create and maintain culture?
12. What are some of the major ethical issues for the entrepreneur? Give examples. How should these be resolved?
13. How can the management of human resources reinforce the culture, the ethics, and the values of the entrepreneur? Give examples.

EXERCISES

1. Construct an "ideal" TMT for a new venture or for your business plan project.
2. Role-playing exercise: Recruit a potential TMT member away from a large corporation by persuading this person to join your team.
3. Decide which activities your business plan project or venture should do for itself and which it should leave to the market.
4. Create an organization chart for your business plan project. What are the duties, responsibilities, and reporting relationships of the people represented in the chart?
5. What are the entrepreneurial values you wish to create and sustain in your business plan project organization? How will you do this?
6. Create a balanced scorecard for your new venture. What are your goals and what specific measures could you choose?

NETWORKING EXERCISES

1. Identify a trade or professional organization that serves the type of business that you are dealing with in your business plan. Call or write this association and request materials. What does this organization do for its members? How can members get the most out of belonging to this group?
2. Attend a meeting of a professional organization or group. What types of activities go on? What kinds of behavior can you observe? Interview attendees. What reasons do they give for attending these meetings? What benefits have they experienced?
3. Join a student club or group (if you do not already belong to one). Go to meetings and participate in a few activities. Make new friends. What kinds of things did you do to become friends with these people? What is the extent of the relationship? If you were going into business, how could these new friends help?

Buzz, Have You Heard

The event was a lavish mock wedding, featuring food from a top Beverly Hills caterer. The groom, played by California beverage distributor Tony Haralambos, wore a top hat when he marched into his company's conference room. His sales reps chuckled when they spotted the white-veiled "bride," because that role was played by the charismatic founder of Glacéau enriched water products, J. Darius Bikoff.

Haralambos was on the verge of dropping Glacéau products from his inventory when Bikoff began actively courting him. He flew Haralambos to New York and put him up at the swank Four Seasons hotel. Then Bikoff took him on a tour of New York City area beverage distributors to demonstrate how Glacéau products were selling there. "In my head, I'm comparing my market and their market and picturing what I could be doing," says Haralambos. "The dollar signs started becoming visible." When Bikoff proposed terminating his relationships with all other distributors in Haralambos's area and devoting all Glacéau's business to him, the marriage was sealed. The mock wedding was Bikoff's way of kicking off a strategy he hoped would win the California market.

Bikoff was trying to lose 30 pounds when he came up with the idea of enriched water products. Reasoning that processing removed much of the nutritional value from the foods he was eating, Bikoff decided to experiment with adding vitamin C and other minerals to bottled water. "If I put these back in, I figured I'd feel better and have more energy," he says. Bikoff hired a food scientist, a flavorist, a microbiologist, and a dietician to get the potions right.

Apparently it worked. Much of Bikoff's energy today is put into the flashy but effective marketing techniques known as "buzzmarketing." His company has a fleet of vans called Glacéau Tasting Vehicles, or GTVs, that tour the country. At some locations the public is invited to play Spin the Bottle to win a free bottle of one of the company's three product lines. At other locations the company sets up hydrology booths where servers explain the benefits of Glacéau products, attracting tasters with humorous signs. "The goal with products is to give people a great story to tell, so they can tell two friends, and they tell two friends, and so on," says Mark Hughes, author of a book on buzzmarketing.

One of the keys to generating buzzmarketing is being different. That's why Bikoff insists his products should be displayed with bottled water, not sports drinks or soft drinks, and he designs his jewel-colored bottles and hip packaging to make his products look very different from other bottled waters. Even the Glacéau name and the drink names—vitaminwater, fruitwater, and smartwater—set the products apart. It also doesn't hurt that the grape-flavored vitamin water was co-created and endorsed by rap star 50 Cent.

Glacéau faces tough competition. "Coke, Pepsi and Cadbury (owner of 7 Up, Dr Pepper, and others) with their bottling networks can get into almost every venue in the country," says John Sicher, editor and publisher of *Beverage Digest*. Even such logical placements for Glacéau products as the Whole Foods grocery chain are uphill battles. "We've only got a limited amount of shelf space," says Penny Abbenante, Whole Foods' national grocery buyer. "There's got to be a unique slant to their product."

Bikoff has managed to develop his brand into $350 million in sales thanks to both a unique product and a unique marketing approach. Three years after the mock wedding, Haralambos Beverage Company was selling over a million cases of vitaminwater, constituting 20 percent of its revenue and 10 percent of its total volume. They expect vitaminwater to be their number one product in the future, even though new competitors are knocking on their door. Tony Haralambos says he doesn't expect to be stocking any of those competing products. "I have such a great relationship with Glacéau, why would I want to mess it up?"

Note: On May 26, 2007, Coke announced it was buying Glacéau for $4.2 billion.

Adapted from G. Bounds, "Move Over, Coke," *The Wall Street Journal, Special Report Small Business*, January 30, 2006: R1.

Case Questions

1. How does Bikoff generate allegiance to his product?
2. Is Bikoff a "time teller" or a "clock builder?"
3. What is 'buzzmarketing'? How does Bikoff use it to extend the boundaries of the organization?
4. Gary Hemphill, the managing director of Beverage Marketing Corp., says about Glacéau,"They can't compete on price, so it's crucial that they develop a different proposition and build demand from there." Write out Glacéau/Bikoff's value proposition.
5. Write Out Glacéau/Bikoff's value proposition.

10 Intrapreneurship and Corporate Venturing

I propose a simple rule: No one ever made it into the business hall of fame on a record of line extensions.
—*Tom Peters*[1]

OUTLINE

Intrapreneurship
    The Need for Intrapreneurship
    Comparison with Entrepreneurship
Advantages of and Barriers to
    Intrapreneurship
Intrapreneurial Advantages and Resources
    Innovator Dilemmas and
    Organization Barriers
The Processes of Intrapreneurship
    A Five-Stage Process Model
    The IDEO Method

Intrapreneurial Strategies
    Technological Innovation
    Blue Ocean Strategies
Guidelines for Success
    Innovator Solutions
    Freedom Factors
    Rules from Intrapreneurs
Summary
Appendix: The Franchising Alternative

LEARNING OBJECTIVES

After reading this chapter, you will understand

- what intrapreneurship is and why all corporations need it.
- the differences between intrapreneurship and entrepreneurship.
- the processes of corporate idea generation and intrapreneurship.
- the obstacles and barriers to intrapreneurship.
- how to generate and identify intrapreneurial opportunities and strategies.
- the guidelines and recommendations for intrapreneurial success.

Success by Design

His students have helped create a disposable insulin injector, a system to prevent vials of blood drawn from one patient from being mislabeled with the name of another patient, and a baby stroller that can be steered with one hand. "Design thinking," explains Patrick Whitney, "can offer greater, deeper, and faster insight into users' lives to help businesses know what to make in the first place."

Whitney is the director of the Illinois Institute of Technology's Institute of Design (ID), the largest graduate school of design in the United States. Once an aspiring artist, Whitney joined the faculty at the ID twenty years ago when he became intrigued with the way design can enhance everyday lives.

"Designers understand patterns of daily life, look at things in a systematic way, and create innovations that make sense to companies and that can be sustained both environmentally and from the business point of view," explains Whitney. He says the key lies in observation. "Sometimes when you look at things carefully, you recognize that things are different from what they seem."

Whitney's students at the ID study the physical, cognitive, social, and cultural factors involved in peoples' interactions with products, systems, organizations, and messages. In their quest to develop "human-centered design," students examine users' physical capabilities and cognitive functions, along with cultural backgrounds and social situations at the time when they use the product or service. Methods of study include observation, videotaping, and even distributing inexpensive disposable cameras to both students and subjects so they can accurately record behaviors and environments.

Graduates of the ID have found employment at innovation-focused companies such as IDEO, Google, Microsoft, and Yahoo!, under job titles like Design Strategist and Manager of User Interaction Design. The robust job market for ID grads is hardly surprising because, as alumna Kathleen Brandenburg points out, "It's difficult to pick up any business publication today without reading an article about the power of design as a strategic advantage and/or as a means to innovation."

While earning her master's degree in Design at the ID, Brandenburg worked with Motorola's Research and Engineering Group and also with the Doblin Group, consultants who specialize in applying innovative design. After graduating in 1998 she co-founded IA Collaborative, a firm that works on product planning, graphic and interface design, and branding for clients such as 3Com, Accenture, and the Chicago Symphony Orchestra. A project her firm recently completed for Nike illustrates the way design can interact with business. When the sports gear manufacturer needed a new product manual, Brandenburg's company implemented a "design process [which] led to a new user-centered poster and diagram format, which not only made the product far easier to use, but ultimately saved millions of dollars in paper cost, not to mention translation, and distribution costs."

Bridging this kind of "innovation gap" with a groundbreaking product design is exactly what Patrick Whitney has been teaching for twenty years. He and his students don't simply create things that are more pleasing to look at; Whitney insists that business-oriented designers like him and his ID students "help markets create more values."

SOURCE: Adapted from Robert Berner, "Design Visionary: Patrick Whitney Is Out to Bridge the Chasm Between the Cultures of Business and Design," *Business Week*, June 2006: 12; www.id.iit.edu and www.bcainc.org/programs.html.

I N all sectors of today's global economy, large corporations are developing new products and services and creating innovative technologies and systems. When these creations are closely related to existing products or services, they take the form of line extensions, brand extensions, and related-product development. This is *not* what we mean by intrapreneurship in the corporate setting. Brand proliferation and "line extensions can make a lot of money, but Honey Nut Cheerios and Diet Cherry Coke are probably not the path to world economic leadership."[1] As the introductory quote indicates, it is the innovative and novel corporate initiatives that make and break reputations—of companies and of the corporate executives and managers who implement the innovations. The types of innovations discussed in this chapter are discontinuities. They represent a break from the past. The break can take many forms, from technological leapfrogging to products targeted at nonconsumers. These products and services are aimed at doing things differently, not simply better.

Henry Ford once said, "If I'd asked the customers what they really wanted, they'd have said a faster horse." These are words of wisdom. Ford is saying that current customers want better versions of what they are already buying, but supplying that demand is not going to produce breakthrough innovations and open new markets. Current customers are seldom the source of ideas for new businesses. Their focus is on the current business, which suggests that one of business's most relied-upon sources of market research—asking customers—has little value for corporate venturing.

Intrapreneurship can be defined as the development, within a large corporation, of internal markets and relatively small autonomous or semiautonomous business units that produce products, services, or technologies by employing the firm's resources in a unique way.[2] If technological innovations are natural extensions of contemporary scientific development and if they are used to solve old problems more effectively or efficiently, this is *not* intrapreneurship. Innovations and incremental changes are important to corporate success, but they are not part of the intrapreneurship phenomenon.[3] In fact, as shown below in regard to the dilemmas facing corporate intrapreneurs, incremental changes and small innovations are enemies of major intrapreneurial developments.

This chapter will cover only the basics of intrapreneurship. The topic is very broad and more in-depth treatments are available,[4] so this chapter will begin by defining the phenomenon and explaining both why corporations need to be intrapreneurial and how corporate venturing is both similar to and different from independent entrepreneurship. It then examines some basic processes of intrapreneurship with special emphasis on idea generation and presents some concepts introduced in Christensen's *Innovator's Dilemma* (1999) to demonstrate why corporate executives find it so difficult to initiate internal corporate ventures. Discussion of other barriers to intrapreneurship is followed by a section on intrapreneurial strategies based on Kim and Mauborgne's *Blue Ocean Strategy* (2005). The chapter concludes with a set of guidelines for success—actually multiple sets of guidelines since there is no single consensus on how to make corporate venturing work.

INTRAPRENEURSHIP

Intrapreneurship produces something new for the corporation and represents, in its fullest manifestations, a complete break with the past. Intrapreneurship gives the managers of a corporation the freedom to take initiative and try new ideas. It is entrepreneurship within an existing business. It goes by a number of different names, depending upon which academic is speaking or about which company. We will use the terms **corporate entrepreneurship**, **corporate venturing**, and **internal corporate ventures (ICV)** interchangeably with intrapreneurship.

The Need for Intrapreneurship

Why do existing businesses allow this internal entrepreneurship and encourage intrapreneurial efforts?[5] Christenson, in the *Innovator's Dilemma*[6] persuasively argues that the reason for intrapreneurship is the heavy pressure on top corporate managers to generate continued growth. As a successful corporation fills in its niches and its products mature, the growth of the company inevitably slows. Investors are not happy about slowing growth, even in a profitable and stable company, because corporate market values depend most heavily on the prospects for future earnings. But with saturated markets and mature products room for growth is limited. So executives must decide to do something new—but what? That question will be addressed later.

While the growth motive may be dominant in today's market environment, it is not the only motive for corporate venturing. Intrapreneuring also is motivated by the general recognition that the macroenvironment and the marketplace change much faster than a corporate bureaucracy can. Intrapreneurship provides large corporations the opportunity to adapt to the increasingly dynamic, hostile, and heterogeneous environment businesses face today.[7] Consider Johnson & Johnson. This company originally made its mark with consumer products like baby oil, powder, and aspirin. These are now mature products so J&J must look elsewhere for growth in order to continue to please Wall Street, earn its typical 15 percent return on equity, and maintain its annual sales growth of 8-10 percent.

To accomplish these goals J&J has done two things. First, it has tried to reinvent the way it invents and innovates by creating some autonomous units and encouraging its managers to brainstorm. For example, in 2006 the managers of a small J&J unit, Ethicon Endo-Surgery, began to design a new and better surgical clip. A team of engineers and scientists scoured the nation and the globe for every type of clip they could find and brought them back to a large research and development office outside Cincinnati. Free of corporate control and oversight, the team set out to design a new clip.[8]

But J&J did not stop there. It went on a corporate buying spree to grow its increasingly important medical devices business. In 2006 it made a failed attempt to purchase Guidant Corporation, the most important manufacturer of surgical stents. Wall Street punished this failure by driving the stock price down. Top management responded by using the corporation's $16 billion war chest to make acquisitions, because internal venturing cannot keep up the growth needed to placate "the Street."[9]

Corporate entrepreneurship also enables the corporation to diversify from its core business through internal processes. Many companies are averse to trying new technologies and products that were "not invented here." Diversification by acquisition (like J&J) and merger is often risky, with the corporation overpaying for an acquisition (known as Winner's Curse) or merging with a partner that does not share its goals and values. Internal development is often preferable because it allows the corporation to manage the process and control its costs.

Intrapreneurship gives the corporation the ability and opportunity to conduct market experiments. These experiments are comparable to the evolutionary biological process of natural selection. Each intrapreneurial venture is a form of mutation of current corporate resources. These mutations provide diversity. If the corporate and economic environment is receptive to the mutation, it is "selected" and may grow into a large and profitable division or company. Other corporations may imitate the success, and a whole new category of businesses may emerge. Just as entrepreneurship can create entire new industries, so can intrapreneurship.

One safe way to conduct these experiments is through corporate investment in entrepreneurial companies. Intel, the world's leader in innovative microprocessors and chip development, has set up a China Technology Fund with an initial capitalization of $200 million. As of mid-2006 it has made 12 investments in Chinese technology start-ups. The last four investments are in a semi-conductor company, two software development ventures, and a company that focuses on marketing on Chinese university campuses. Intel also invests heavily in India, pursuing similar goals. China currently has an advantage because its government encourages technology and provides infrastructure, "…whereas in India," according to Intel Capital president Arvind Solhani, "the government's involvement is more limited."[10]

Intrapreneurship can also be valuable to established corporations by serving as a training ground for new managers. Corporations can develop future leaders by monitoring the progress of these intrapreneurs. Managers who succeed in the new venture have much to offer the "mother" firm.

Also, intrapreneurial activities open new channels of distribution and media communications, especially since the emergence of the Internet. Established firms use the Internet to sell directly to customers, to form cooperatives with other firms for selling and purchasing, and to develop consumer data and knowledge bases. PepsiCo, for example, has used the Web to find a new generation of customers. Its Web site, http://www.pepsistuff.com, enabled consumers to collect points for prizes on bottle caps. This short campaign netted Pepsi three million logged and registered users, giving the company a database that would have cost millions and taken months to build. Sales volume rose 5 percent during the promotion, and the cost was about one-fifth of a mail-in project.[11]

Another example of this, with a social network twist, is Edmonds.com's launch of CarSpace.com. Edmonds.com is a leader in online car sales and research. CarSpace.com is a place for people obsessed with cars who want to talk about them with folks who share their interest. CarSpace will be part of MySpace.com, a leader in social networking. Edmunds hopes that by consolidating many of the fragmented auto-interest Web sites, it can generate more activity for its core business. CarSpace might even surpass the company's primary site if it gets the right buzz. "Self-generated content creation and networking are now clearly one of the biggest media growth stories," says Curt Hecht, chief digital officer at GM Planworks, General Motors' media agency.[12]

Finally, established corporations use intrapreneuring to augment their bottom lines, primarily through direct investment in entrepreneurial companies. Intel certainly hopes that its China Technology fund makes money for the stockholders.

U.S. companies are noted for their sustained ability to be intrapreneurial. Among these are Procter & Gamble, Johnson & Johnson, and the 3M Company of Minneapolis, Minnesota.[13] 3M has created over 100 new businesses or major product lines in its history. Four out of five of these have succeeded. At 3M any young engineer can pitch a new business or product idea to top management and be appointed head of the project if it is approved. The project or new venture is then set up as a separate business. The innovative product is assigned a project manager (it could be the originator of the idea, but not necessessarily), who remains in charge of the venture until it is successful or abandoned. The project manager can mobilize all the skills and resources necessary for the product's development. Incentives for the new business team are aligned with the project's success—members of the team are rewarded and promoted as the business grows.

But U.S. firms are no longer alone in having distinctive intrapreneurial competence. Table 10.1 lists the world's most innovative companies for 2006. It is based on a Boston Consulting Group (BCG) survey and analysis of over 1000 senior executives in 63 companies. Note that, although not every innovator company achieves above-average returns and growth, as a group the companies greatly exceed the average of the less innovative companies. "Innovation is allowing companies to grow faster [and] have a richer product mix," concludes James P. Andrews, who heads the BCG innovation unit.[14]

Comparison with Entrepreneurship

For the most part, entrepreneurship and intrapreneurship are very similar. In both cases the resource-based view provides the underlying theoretical basis. For the entrepreneur, the resources and capabilities required for success come from personal and market sources. This is true for corporations as well, but most corporations have resource bases vastly larger than those of most entrepreneurs. The entrepreneur must consider both the macro and micro environments for analysis; the corporate intrapreneur must also consider the environment of the corporation itself. Corporate culture, practice and processes are the immediate concern for the intrapreneur.

There are differences. The internal market for ideas, the resource evaluation process, and the individuals who champion intrapreneurship are different from external markets and processes.[15] Both intrapreneurs and entrepreneurs seek autonomy and freedom and have fairly long-term perspectives. Intrapreneurs, however, must be much more sensitive to the corporate hierarchy and way of doing things. This means that intrapreneurs still respond to traditional corporate rewards and must be politically astute. Although intrapreneurs deal with a bureaucracy and a corporate culture, they also have a support system to help with their projects. Intrapreneurs must gather approval; entrepreneurs must gather nerve.[16]

Both intrapreneurs and entrepreneurs disdain status symbols in the short term, preferring to get the venture off the ground. Entrepreneurs can maintain more independence in decision making, but they pay a higher price by putting financial resources at risk. Both corporate intrapreneurs and independent entrepreneurs are likely to have technical backgrounds. Independents have to rely on their own market research, but intrapreneurs have to sell their ideas to their own organizations before worrying about the outside market.[17]

TABLE 10.1 Corporate Leaders in Intrapreneurship and Innovation

2006 Rank	Company	Innovative Processes	Bottom Line Growth	Return on Equity
1	Apple	* +	7.1%	24.6%
2	Google	* +	N/A	N/A
3	3M	*	3.4	11.2
4	Toyota	^ *	10.7	11.8
5	Microsoft	* +	2.0	18.5
6	General Electric	^ *	5.7	13.4
7	Procter & Gamble	^ *	4.4	12.6
8	Nokia	^ * +	0.0	34.6
9	Starbucks	* +	2.2	27.6
10	IBM	^ * +	−0.7	14.4
11	Virgin	+	Private	Private
12	Samsung	^ *	−4.5	22.7
13	Sony	*	−11.0	5.1
14	Dell	^ +	2.0	39.4
15	IDEO	^ *	Private	Private
16	BMW	^ *	9.1	14.2
17	Intel	* +	−0.3	13.8
18	eBay	+	13.0	N/A
19	IKEA	^ * +	Private	Private
20	Wal-Mart	^	1.9	16.2
21	Amazon	^ *	25.0	N/A
22	Target	* +	7.4	25.2
23	Honda	*	8.0	12.9
24	Research in Motion	*	57.0	N/A
25	Southwest Airlines	^ +	−0.1	13.9
	Most innovative companies		3.4	14.3
	S&P 1200 global stock index		0.4	11.1

Legend: ^ Process innovation; * Product innovation; + Business model innovation; N/A Insufficient data.

SOURCE: "World's Most Innovative Companies," *Business Week*, April 24, 2006: 64-65. Data is from the Boston Consulting Group survey, S&P Compustat database, and company reports.

Entrepreneurs must search markets to acquire resources for new ventures, while intrapreneurs typically look inside the organization for resources that are not currently being used or employed efficiently. The intrapreneur can pry these resources (which probably closely resemble the corporation's core resources) loose from some current business operation. In other words, the machines and physical plant the corporation is not using are probably much like the resources that are actually being employed. For example, Hewlitt-Packard's famous skunk works operations were based on using current "borrowed" assets for future projects. The same can be said for human, technical, and organizational resources. The trick, therefore, is for the intrapreneur to employ these resources in a way sufficiently different from their traditional use.

Another basic difference between intrapreneurs and entrepreneurs involves the separation of ownership and control[18]—the agency problem. Entrepreneurs own and control their businesses, so ownership and control are unified and there are no inconsistencies. In a large corporation, however, the shareholders are the principals (owners) and the managers are the agents (controllers). A manager who wants to undertake an intrapreneurial venture must be able to act as a principal and have the same incentives. The owners of the corporation tend to discourage this because they are unwilling to trust managers and give them these types of incentives. Frequently, this means that intrapreneurs are forced to leave the company. This resolves the agency problem, but it often leaves the corporation worse off because the managers leave with resources that are valuable, rare, hard to copy, and nonsubstitutable. Most often these resources are technical information, expertise, and the managers themselves (the human resource). The corporation is deprived of the intrapreneurship it needs to succeed.

ADVANTAGES OF AND BARRIERS TO INTRAPRENEURSHIP

Large companies have certain advantages in creating and exploiting intrapreneurial ideas. Some of these advantages relate directly to the intrapreneurs, who are sometimes more secure operating from within a large organization. They already have a job, a steady income with benefits, and a social network within the firm made up of friends, colleagues, and knowledgeable individuals who can provide encouragement, resources, and technical aid.

Intrapreneurial Advantages and Resources

The financial resources for the internal corporate venture come from the corporation. Although no corporation has unlimited financial resources, most have resources well beyond the capabilities of private individuals and their friends and relatives. This source of financing lowers the personal financial risk for intrapreneurs. Of course, there is an element of career risk if the intrapreneur is unable to make the new venture a success. However, a supportive environment for intrapreneurship is more forgiving of failure than the external environment facing independent entrepreneurs.

Moreover, the corporation has all or most of the necessary resource base of the new venture. It already has a set of organizational systems—marketing, engineering, personnel, legal, and accounting—with many of the attributes that support its sustainable competitive advantage. Finally, most large corporations have a visibility and a reputation that can be extended to the new venture. These can provide early credibility and legitimacy for the intrapreneurial effort and act as strategic momentum factors.

Innovator Dilemmas and Organization Barriers

There are also barriers to corporate venturing and impediments to successful execution.[19] The major barrier is the corporate bureaucracy. Large corporations have many levels of management, and often all levels must approve the use of company resources for the intrapreneurial venture. Rules, procedures, and processes slow down decision making at the very time it should be expedited. A recent study shows that one way to structure an intrapreneurial effort for success is through a "loosely coupled system." The internal venture requires independence and limited contact with the corporate host.[20]

Sometimes the new venture threatens another of the company's products, and the incumbent product managers put up resistance. There are also opposing requests for corporate resources, and resources devoted to the new venture are diverted from established products and markets. Often people do not wish to change their orientations, goals, and behaviors to do the things necessary to implement change. The paradox here is that the very security the large corporation provides for risk taking discourages people from taking any risks.

There are structural impediments as well. Internal capital markets do not include the venture capitalists who are so important to the success of new ventures. These investors have the technical expertise, contacts, and experience initiating new ventures that most corporate executives lack. Without venture capitalists, the investment process becomes a capital-budgeting exercise that may fail to capture all the subtleties of entrepreneurship. Corporations will often manage resources for efficiency and return on investment rather than for long-term advantages.[21]

In the same vein, intrapreneurs do not own the ICV. The incentives and risks are, therefore, different from those of independent entrepreneurship. Uniformly compensating everyone involved—a bureaucratic procedure—removes an important motivating force for the ICV. The result is that the corporation either abandons projects prematurely or escalates commitment to projects with little chance of success.[22]

Some people doubt whether true entrepreneurship can exist inside a corporation.[23] Many companies that began as entrepreneurial ventures lose their fervor and excitement as they become investment-grade corporations. It is difficult to offer the rewards of intrapreneurship without incurring the resentment of other employees and managers. Shifting the major reward mechanism from status and rank to contribution to earnings is a challenge for corporations.[24] Some companies succeed for a while in motivating their brightest people to start ICVs, but because most of the rewards accrue to the corporation, these people are almost always destined to leave and start their own businesses.

An insightful understanding of the problems faced by corporations trying to innovate and venture has been postulated by Christensen (1997). His book *The Innovator's Dilemma* explains the problems of corporate venturing. The research is far-reaching, from the evolution of the hard-disk industry through motorcycles and variety store retailing.

Corporate innovation takes two forms. **Sustaining innovation** is the incremental process and product innovation that helps existing products grow and maintain their market position. **Disruptive innovation** is change that destroys current market positions and technological competence by changing the way customers behave and relate to the product. Corporations' core competences have made them successful. This is what they do. And they have core rigidities—this is what they *don't* do. The core rigidities prevent firms from easily adopting disruptive innovations and forming new corporate ventures. Christensen, like Henry Ford, finds that asking customers about disruptive innovation and revolutionary alternatives is futile. They want faster horses.

Why? They depend on current customers and investors for their success, and disruptive change can upset that balance. The markets for the disruptive new technology or products are generally very small at first. Why hurt the big successful product in order to initiate a product in a small and unproven market? Large firms have well established protocols and processes for market analysis, but it is hard to analyze a new market. Disruptive innovation often competes against nonconsumption—customers who do not yet exist. New markets seldom come out of this analysis well. Lastly, disruptive change frequently enables customers to purchase and consume the new product/service at a lower cost than the existing product/service. From the viewpoint of the firm, innovation is a threat to their already successful market.

Christensen's core recommendation to businesses facing disruptive technology is essentially to divide and conquer: to set up or acquire an independent division organized either as an autonomous unit or as an independent company with stock owned primarily by the parent company. He cites Johnson and Johnson as a good example: Its umbrella of 160 units includes three—disposable contact lenses, endoscopic surgery, and diabetes blood glucose monitors—that were stand-alone divisions for disruptive products that became billion-dollar success stories. He also advises firms not to commit to being either a technology leader or follower. Disruptive innovations have first-mover advantages that sustaining innovations often lack. But his strongest recommendation is simply to be aware that disruptive technology is counterintuitive to existing programs, and that disruptive products rarely make sense in the period when investing in them is critical.[25]

THE PROCESS OF INTRAPRENEURSHIP

The most important part of the process for a corporation is the realization that intrapreneurship is not optional! For the many reasons delineated above, corporations *must* continue to innovate and venture. The real question concerns the locus of that innovation. Where is the emphasis placed? This section reviews the general corporate processes.

A Five-Stage Process Model

There are five recognizable stages in the process of intrapreneurship or corporate venturing.[26]

Problem Definition. Stage 1 is problem definition. Problems—or opportunities—may come from sources within the company or industry. The key to recognizing intrapreneurial opportunities is to be sensitive to change and open to surprise. One source of ideas is the unexpected occurrence: unexpected successes or unexpected failures.[27] If customers demand a product or service into which the corporation did not put much effort or thought, this success can be the source of an entirely new business once enough resources are invested. Similarly, if a product is a failure, understanding why and determining what the customer really wants can also launch an intrapreneurial venture. For example, 3M developed an adhesive that no industrial user seemed to want and was ready to abandon the product. The engineer who led the project took the samples home and let his family use them. After discovering that his teenaged daughters used the tape to hold their curls overnight, he recognized that there might be household and personal uses for the adhesive—Scotch tape.[28]

Incongruities—things that stick out as inconsistent—can also be the source of ideas.[29] That is, disparities between the assumption of an industry or business and economic realities give rise to ideas for intrapreneurial opportunity. Questioning the conventional wisdom ("everybody knows") or the perceived practice ("it's the way things are done") can point up these incongruities. When what "everybody knows" is no longer known and accepted by everyone and when "the way things are done" doesn't work any more, resources can be redeployed to exploit an opportunity.

Because there is now a general recognition that corporate venturing is required for sustainable competitive advantage, companies don't want to wait for serendipity and chance to step in. They want a more systematic approach. For example, toy company FAO Schwartz has try-outs for toy inventors to tap the creative ideas of everyday people. Once a year it hosts people who pitch their ideas in five-minute presentations. In 2006 FAO CEO Ed Schmults and his chief merchandising officer David Niggli saw 22 inventors demonstrate 50 ideas. While this is not strictly corporate venturing, the process does enable a company to mine outside sources of creativity. "I don't see a lot of creativity, a lot of new designs from many toy companies. As a company whose lifeblood is introducing unique products, I think this is a fabulous way to get that quirky, special item," says Schmults.[30]

One ingenious system for generating and affirming venture ideas has been employed by Rite-Solutions. This software company builds sophisticated and classified command-and-control systems for the Navy. It has created an internal "stock market" for ideas. Anyone in the company can propose a venture idea, and the proposals become stocks on a fantasy stock exchange. Each idea receives a ticker symbol, has discussion lists, and e-mail alerts. Prices change as employees (engineers, computer scientists, managers and executives—basically everyone) buy and sell the ideas. This process employs the "wisdom of groups" to gain a consensus about which proposals to pursue.[31]

"At most companies, especially technology companies, the most brilliant insights tend to come from people other than senior management. So we created a marketplace to harvest collective genius."[32]

IBM is on the list in Table 10.1 and it also has a special way to identify future paths and opportunities: the online jam explained in Street Story 10.1.

Coalition Building. Stage 2 requires coalition building. The intrapreneur must develop relationships within the corporate bureaucracy, relationships that will support the innovative project in its early development. This parallels the entrepreneur's search for legitimate partners and supporters. For an idea to attract support, it must in some way "fit" the company and be congruent with company goals. This is a paradox of sorts: If an idea is *too* congruent, it will not be innovative; but in order to sell the idea, the intrapreneurs need to make their case to the company. In addition to personal persuasion, the best

STREET STORY 10.1

A Question of Balance

"We're blessed with more than 300,000 of the most innovative employees in the world," notes Nick Donofrio, senior vice president for technology and innovation at IBM, "but it hasn't always been clear how they could share their ideas."

To facilitate that exchange of intrapreneurial ideas, the largest information technology company in the world sponsored what it calls the Innovation Jam. Billed as an online brainstorm, this 2006 event was a two-session event at which 100,000 IBM employees, customers, business partners, and others from 160 countries were invited to post and respond to innovative suggestions over the Internet. The first 72-hour session in July 2006 was devoted to generating ideas; the second session in September was designed to identify which of July's ideas had the most potential. IBM committed up to $100 million in funding for the best ideas to emerge from this process.

According to a 2006 Global CEO Study conducted by IBM, more than 75 percent of current CEOs rely on clients and business partners to help generate innovative ideas, while fewer than 15 percent expect those ideas to come from inside their own organizations. "More and more businesses are realizing the importance of looking at the innovation of the leading users of their products and services as strong indicators of where their markets are heading," says Irving Wladawsky-Berger, IBM's vice president for technical strategy and innovation. "Collaborative innovation in general, both inside and outside IBM, is a major objective of our Innovation That Matters initiative."

IBM has borrowed from the jazz tradition to promote the exchange of ideas before. In 2001 they hosted an online jam session to develop new business opportunities. In 2002 the topic was good management practices, and in 2003 the subject was IBM values. But the 2006 jam session was the company's largest and the first in which people outside the company were included. It was, in the words of IBM CRO Samuel J. Palmisano, an opportunity in which "a technology company takes its most valued secrets, opens them up to the world and says, "O.K. world, you tell us" what can be done with them.

The 2006 Innovation Jam focused on four topics: Going Places: the transportation of people and goods; Finance and Commerce: secure and innovative ways to make or invest money, purchase items, and finance new construction; Staying Healthy: health care and healthy living strategies, along with their rising costs; and A Better Planet: environmental issues, specifically energy and water. Participants were asked to consider these four topics in the light of six emerging technologies: embedded intelligence (microchips inserted in products for communication and triggering), existing insight, global collaboration of both individuals and companies, practical supercomputing, and intelligent IT systems.

IBM hopes this ground-breaking Innovation Jam will lead to the creation of innovative products and services, along with processes—billing, paying, market research, etc. and business models that are innovative themselves. To get those results the company is even willing to risk a competitor or the media hacking into the online exchange. "Without risk, there is no innovation," notes Ed Bevin, one of the chief IBM architects of the project.

SOURCE: Adapted from Jessi Hempel, "Big Blue Brainstorm," *Business Week*, August 7, 2006 : 70; Irving Wladawsky-Berger, "Some Personal Reflections on the Changing Nature of Strategy." Retrieved from the Web August 30, 2006. http://irvingwb.typepad.com/blog.2006/07/some_personal_r.html, www.globalinnovationjam.com, and http://domino.watson.ibm.com/comm/www_innovate.nsf/pages/ourselves.thinkplace.html.

vehicle for drumming up support and building a coalition is the business plan. We described an entrepreneur's business plan in Chapter 5. The major differences between an intrapreneurial business plan and an entrepreneurial one are:

1. The intrapreneurial plan does not have an ownership section detailing the conditions and requirements for selling shares because the corporation owns the venture—unless the proposal calls for a spin-off or a joint venture with another company.
2. The intrapreneurial plan does not seek outside financing. However, it does need to meet the corporation's internal financing and capital-budgeting criteria.
3. The intrapreneurial plan needs a section to describe the relationship (strategic, operational, financial, and marketing) between the corporation and the internal corporate venture.

The business plan helps the intrapreneur find a sponsor or set of sponsors who can help get resources and pave the way for political acceptance. This is crucial, because corporate managers and the bureaucracy often see these **internal corporate ventures (ICVs)** as threats to the current power structure and to the resource allocation process. Also, the sponsor will keep the intrapreneur objective about the prospects for success and failure. It is easy to lose objectivity when caught up in the excitement of creative innovation.

Tim O'Reilly, founder and CEO of computer publisher O'Reilly Media, says that the "architecture of participation" must be compelling to ensure coalition building. The Rite-Solutions stock market model described above make this architecture (buy-in) both professional and fun. With each employee getting $10,000 in opinion money to invest in ideas, employees can signal their favorites, share their enthusiasm, and best of all, indicate where they will be willing to volunteer their efforts. Volunteers get stock in the idea, which can have a real monetary payoff if the stock proposal becomes a profitable product.[33]

Resource Mobilization. Stage 3 calls for resource mobilization. The intrapreneur is looking for the same types of resources as the entrepreneur: physical, technological, financial, organizational, human, and reputational. To succeed, an internal corporate venture must be rare, valuable, imperfectly imitable, and without desirable substitutes. In the early stages of resource acquisition, the intrapreneur may be "borrowing" resources officially assigned to others in the corporation. As the project gains momentum and resource needs mount, the ICV needs official formal recognition. This will be given when the ICV passes the test of the corporation's internal capital market and receives its official budget.

One way to mobilize resources early in the process is to create a **skunk works**, an autonomous group with a mandate to find and develop new products outside the company's core competence.[34] One of the prime benefits of the skunk works is that it takes the development of the new venture out of the traditional corporate bureaucracy, governance structure, and decision-making process. The independence of the skunk works insulates it from company politics and from the sunk-cost thinking of incumbent managers.

Project Execution. Stage 4 is the actual execution of the ICV. It is parallel to an entrepreneur's official launch of a new venture, except that in this case there are multiple levels of managers with different degrees of experience.[35] When the time comes to execute the intrapreneurial strategy (see Chapter 4), the ICV must develop its entry strategy and determine its entry wedges. If it has first-mover advantage, it must employ isolating mechanisms to protect that advantage for as long as possible. It must assess the industry environment, both static and dynamic, and make appropriate operating and tactical decisions. It may be necessary to open the ICV to external influences and to recruit personnel and technology from outside.[36] Finally, the venture must adopt a strategic posture and put in place criteria for evaluating performance and strategy.

Venture Completion. Stage 5 is the venture-completion phase. If the ICV has been less successful, it can be dismantled and its resources reabsorbed by the corporation. If it has succeeded, it can be sustained and supported with additional investment. The more or less permanent position of the ICV in the organizational structure (see Chapter 9) should now be established. If for any reason (uncertainty, incentive alignment, opportunism) the agency problem has proven insurmountable, the ICV may become a spin-off—a completely independent company.[37] In such a case, the intrapreneurial managers can buy the assets from the corporation using a **leveraged buyout (LBO)**. A leveraged buy-out is a financing scheme whereby the purchasers of the assets put up very little equity and borrow most of the money for the deal. Sometimes the amount of leverage approaches 100 percent (very little equity). The lender takes the assets of the venture as collateral for the loans. After the LBO is executed, the new owners can keep and operate the new company or they can take it public. In this scenario the intrapreneurs' rewards are enormous since they have used almost none of their own money. The proceeds from the IPO pay off the loans and the founders now have piles of company stock. What did they do to earn it? They saw the opportunity, they put the deal together, and they absorbed the risks and uncertainty.

Even though they understand the process, recognize an ICV's potential benefits, and are well aware of the impediments to intrapreneurship, corporations nevertheless find the task daunting. They need to recognize that intrapreneurs and a viable intrapreneuring process are rare, valuable, imperfectly imitable, and nonsubstitutable resources. Thus, intrapreneurship is a source of sustainable competitive advantage.

Following a process in detail is not a recipe for guaranteed success. Sometimes the process goes wrong. Sometimes the process is discontinuous, with a lengthy time lag. On occasion, innovations originally designed for one purpose are used for something else. Failure is definitely a possibility. Street Story 10.2 tells the story of some failures and some delayed successes. It also shows that people can learn vital lessons from good failures.

The IDEO Method

One of the firms listed in Table 10.1 as a world class innovator is IDEO, but it plays a different role than the other firms in the list. IDEO is in fact a consultancy whose prime domain is corporate innovation and venturing. It has a unique perspective on the innovation process, one that deserves a more focused look. Steve Jobs has said, "When we

Discovering It's OK to Fail

Ford had the Edsel. McDonald's had the hulaburger, a slice of grilled pineapple topped with cheese for vegetarian customers. Coca-Cola had the New Coke. Lots of successful businesses have suffered failures and gone on to become even more successful.

Many experts advise that innovation requires risk taking, and that risks don't always succeed. Harvard Business School professor Stefan H. Thomke, author of *Experimentation Matters,* reports that when he speaks to business groups he often tells them that failure is not a bad thing. "I always have lots of people staring at me, [thinking] 'Have you lost your mind?' That's O.K. It gets their attention," he says. Jeffrey R. Immelt, Chairman and CEO of General Electric, apparently agrees. "If you try something and it fails but you went about it the right way and learned from it, that's not a bad thing," Immelt suggests.

Ford Motor Co. shut down production on the Edsel after about 2,800 cars were produced in 1960. But in the aftermath of that failure, the company's research on what consumers really wanted and what they were willing to pay led to the 1964 introduction of the Mustang, which sold 1 million units in the first 18 months of production. The 1962 failure of McDonald's hula burger spurred a franchise owner to suggest the Filet-O-Fish sandwich, which remains a staple on the fast food giant's menu. And when Coca-Cola stopped producing the New Coke after just 79 days in 1985, consumers who complained must have rediscovered original Coke, because sales of that product soared.

Intuit, the company that produces business and financial management software like QuickBooks and TurboTax, has found a way to institutionalize the process of learning from mistakes. Jane Eggers, head of the firm's Innovation Lab, hosts "When Learning Hurts" sessions at which blunders are dissected for insights. "It's only a failure if we fail to get the learning," notes Intuit Chairman Scott Cook.

There is a kind of six-step recovery program that can help companies spring back from missteps:

- First, schedule some time for reflection.
- Second, encourage everyone in the organization—especially managers—to share their own failures so employees will feel comfortable talking about their defeats.
- Third, bring in outsiders to evaluate a flop from their less emotional and more objective viewpoint.
- Fourth, celebrate smart failures and reward risk-takers who deserve it.
- Fifth, when you are ready to move on to the next innovation, be flexible in your goals so you don't get trapped by unrealistic expectations.
- Sixth, test your new innovation with an eye towards proving yourself wrong, not right.

Drug company Pfizer thought it had a loser when tests for Sildenafil showed the medicine wasn't effective for treating angina. But after reviewing patient reports, the company discovered that the drug had an unexpected side effect. Pfizer reintroduced it as Viagra. "Figuring out how to master this process of failing fast and failing cheap and fumbling toward success is probably the most important thing companies have to get good at," observes Scott Anthony, managing director at the consulting firm Innosight.

SOURCE: Adapted from Jena McGregor, "How Failure Breeds Success," *BusinessWeek,* July 10, 2006: 42.

have some wacko problem, chances are that someone at [IDEO] has the skills to take care of it."[38]

IDEO was created in 1991 as a merger of two firms: David Kelley Design and ID Two. In 1982 Kelley designed the first mouse for Apple Computer and ID Two designed the first laptop computer, so IDEO's roots are in the design industry. It has won many awards, and in 1996 even redesigned chocolate.[39] Kelley and the ID Two founder Bill Moggridge still manage IDEO, along with current CEO Tim Brown.

Over the years IDEO has become a force in the design industry and in the world of corporate innovation. It is huge for a design firm, with over 350 employees and revenues of $60+ million. The client list includes such Fortune 100 companies as Apple Computer, IBM, Hewlet-Packard, ATT Wireless, BBC, Samsung, and P&G. More than half the firm's turnover comes from overseas.

As IDEO has become the iconic innovation house, its methods have drawn increasing attention and, of course, imitation (the sincerest form of flattery). IDEO too has a five stage process:

1. Observation. IDEO consultants are psychologists, sociologists, anthropologists, engineers, graphic designers, architects, and other people with unusual (for a business consultancy) skills. When they observe, they see different things: They see relationships, networks, behaviors, and environments. Their job is to understand the consumer experience. Among the techniques IDEO uses are shadowing the customer, mapping the behavior in 3-D space, and storytelling.

2. Brainstorming. This technique has been employed by many businesses for over 50 years, but IDEO is a leader in its effective use. It sets a firm time limit of one hour per session. The rules are written on the walls and strictly enforced. Participants include the extremely diverse IDEO consultants and the client's people. Outside-the-box thinking is encouraged and there is an absolute "no criticism" rule. Frequently over a hundred ideas are generated in these sessions.

3. Rapid-prototyping. According to IDEO philosophy, it is easier to understand an innovation when you can see it than when it is just a concept. So they build models of products, environments, experiences, and technologies. Using cheap supplies (frequently just cardboard) and short movies, IDEO designs prototypes of the ideas generated in the brainstorming session. They move fast and without frills to see if it will work.

4. Refining. IDEO then helps clients winnow out the less valuable ideas and focus on a few big ideas. The consultants are disciplined in their selection and make hard choices. The process requires prioritization and resource calculations. Stakeholders must agree on the final list before the next stage. This is the buy-in.

5. Implementation. IDEO stays with the client throughout implementation. Its diverse workforce from over forty countries continues to provide input and creative thinking during the final stage.

In his book *The Ten Faces of Innovation* (2003), IDEO founder Kelley writes that "innovation is a team sport." His firm is unique for two reasons. First it has the most diverse team. IDEO divides the process participants into ten people-centric "personas," each with a role in the innovation process. When acting in a new persona, people see things differently and develop new insights. They are being innovation instead of simply observing it from a comfortable distance. There are no negative roles that focus on only the worst-case scenarios, as with a devil's advocate. This intellectual approach is part of IDEO's intellectual property and is difficult for imitators to copy. It is a source of SCA for IDEO. In Street Story 10.3, IDEO's creativity-promoting personas are summarized.

The second unique aspect of IDEO is its central position in the global network of innovation and venturing. Because of its long experience in the field, its prominent client list, and its stunning successes, IDEO has a unique historical place in the creativity universe. This is clearly rare, valuable, hard to copy, and non-substitutable.[40] In a strategy that helps IDEO maximize the value (versus the protection) of its intellectual property, IDEO's Kelley has made a founding donation to Stanford University's new Institute of Design. Information about the current projects and methods of the *d.school,* as it is known, can be found at http://www.stanford.edu/group/dschool.

INTRAPRENEURIAL STRATEGIES

Almost all large corporations now recognize the need for intrapreneurship and corporate venturing. They risk losing current markets if they don't exploit disruptive technologies. Still it is not an easy thing to do. If it were, all companies would do it successfully and it would be an advantage to none. The strategies employed for corporate venturing can make the difference. This section reveals how firms pursue technical innovation and presents a framework that enables companies to increase their odds of succeeding, the **Blue Ocean** strategies.

Technological Innovation

Technical innovation can be defined as the art of introducing a new device, method, or material for application to commercial or practical objectives.[41] A successful technical innovation gives a corporation new core competencies, new revenue streams, new entry barriers, and improved profitability.[42]

There exists a global network for technical innovation, a system that includes independent inventors, private not-for-profit research tanks, universities, government agencies, and both public and private firms. These actors engage in three activities:

- **Basic research** is the pursuit of scientific knowledge. Frequently, there is no particular commercial application in mind when the scientists begin basic research programs—for example, research on molecular biology and the genome. Governments, universities, and non-profits are most likely to deal in basic research since there may be no financial payoff for a long time, if ever.
- **Applied research** sets out to solve a problem or develop an application for the basic research. It aims to provide something useful for someone. Most pharmaceutical research into new compounds is applied research. Companies and inventors do this type of research.
- **Development research** leads directly to commercialization. The development of new drugs and the subsequent testing for safety and effectiveness is development research.

STREET STORY 10.3

The 10 Personas of IDEO

IDEO is a creativity and venturing consultancy. Part of its job is to encourage positive contributions to new initiatives and to avoid advocate negativity. Ten roles have been incorporated into their process, along with a brief description of each. Next time you work on developing something novel, especially in a team setting, assign some of these roles to participants and be sure that no one shoots down the ideas until they have been fully explored in a positive way.

The Learning Personas help acquire and generate new information and combinations:

- The *anthropologist* has insights about the way people behave, how they interact physically and emotionally. Keeps detailed notes of reality.
- The *experimenter* creates prototypes, continuously testing their characteristics. Engages in enlightened trial and error.
- The *cross-pollinator* takes ideas from other cultures, industries, and environments and applies them to the current situation. Creates innovative concept combinations.

The Organizing Personas deal with organizational politics and help reduce resistance and promote change.

- The *hurdler* overcomes barriers to intrapreneurship and corporate venturing. Knows the players and their hot buttons.

- The *collaborator* brings together groups whose own self-interest supports the innovation. Helps build consensus and majorities.
- The *director* assembles the cast of people who will promote and implement the venture. Gets the best performances from his players.

The Building Personas implement the innovation or venture by applying the insights offered by the earlier personas to the project.

- The *experience architect* designs compelling experiences for the new customers. Provides the link between the venture and the market.
- The *set designer* transforms the physical environment of the new venture to mold organization/employee performance and customer interface.
- The *caregiver* cares, supporting the venture's employees as they deal with the uncertainty of the new business. Caring about customers helps the venture exceed their expectations.
- The *storyteller* communicates the news about the venture, both internally and externally. Develops the narrative that can become the legend of the start-up.

SOURCE: T. Kelley and J. Littman, *The Ten Faces of Innovation* (New York: Doubleday, 2005).

Since all of these types of research are connected, **technology clusters** are sometimes created. These are groups of firms that do interrelated research and are located close to each other geographically. The clusters enable the scientists and businesspersons to interact easily and to share data, research results, and business opportunities. These clusters facilitate **technology spillovers**. Spillovers occur when an innovation can be used in multiple situations and serve multiple markets.[43]

Although this all seems quite rational when described in a textbook, the process is actually quite messy and risky, as illustrated by the **technology funnel**. For every 3000 raw ideas, corporate innovators will submit around 300 detailed proposals to top management. Of these, top management will fund about 125 demonstration projects. A demonstration project does just what it says: It attempts to demonstrate the benefits and features of the innovation. Only an estimated four demonstration projects of the 125 might be adopted by top management as a major new initiative. Of the four initiatives, two products will be launched and only one will succeed. The odds are 3000:1 against.[44]

To succeed, technological innovators need the same sort of incentives as innovators in other areas:

- They need the support and recognition of top management and an organizational culture that favors corporate entrepreneurship.
- They need slack resources like skunk works and time to develop and evaluate their projects.
- They need autonomy, as Christensen suggests, to make decisions free from the core rigidities of the organization.
- They need—whenever possible—financial incentives: promotions, stock ownership, and bonuses.[45]

Blue Ocean Strategies

A recently published book, *Blue Ocean Strategies* (2005), has both creatively summarized much of the previously understood ideas and actions about corporate venturing and offered important new insights. The book offers executives and intrapreneurs a set of tools and principles which clarify the content and process of creating internal corporate ventures.[46] More information about this book can be found at http://www.blueoceanstrategy.com/index.htm.

The title refers to the place where venturing should occur—in the **Blue Ocean**, the competitive area that has no competitors. It is open water, clear, pristine, and abundant with fresh opportunities. Compare this to the **Red Ocean**, which is bloody with the battles of competitors. The water here is crowded with predators and their prey. As the resources of the Red Ocean dwindle, the struggle for existence intensifies—and there are no winners. The Red Ocean strategy is "better, faster, cheaper," the race to lower levels of profitability for the venture. The Blue Ocean strategy is **value innovation**, the leap into uncontested space where utility is raised, price is lowered, and costs are reduced. This recalls the Innovator's Dilemma in which the disruptive technology comes to market with high utility and a lower price/cost ratio.

Tools of Analysis. Blue Ocean Strategy offers seven or eight tools, depending on how they are counted. These tools begin with understanding where the market is now, move on to aid analysis for finding Blue Ocean, and then implement the corporate venture.

1. The **strategy canvas** illustrates graphically the current state of the market. The authors of Blue Ocean strategy used the wine industry of the late 1990s as their example and discussed the launch of [yellow tail] wine. Figure 10.1 shows how the identification of market factors graphed against market segments (premium versus

budget) produces the initial canvas. Note that the factors are the same for each segment and so is the price/value ratio. Asked what they want, customers will respond, "More value for less price"—the equivalent of a faster horse.

2. The **four actions framework** gets away from simply offering more for less. In the case of the wine industry the question became: How do we get nonconsumers to drink wine? Instead of competing against other wine producers for the same customers, Australia's Casella Winery looked for an alternative—competing against nonconsumption of wine. The four actions are:

- **Elimination**: What factors can be done away with completely? The competitors assume these are important, but are they?
- **Reduction:** What factors can be lowered significantly without a loss of value for nonconsumers?
- **Raise**: What factors can be raised above industry averages to seduce the nonconsumer?
- **Creation**: What factors can be added to create value for the nonconsumer?

By applying these actions to the strategy canvas, the intrapreneur creates a new value curve as illustrated in Figure 10.2.

Figure 10.1   The Strategy Canvas of the U.S. Wine Industry in the Late 1990s

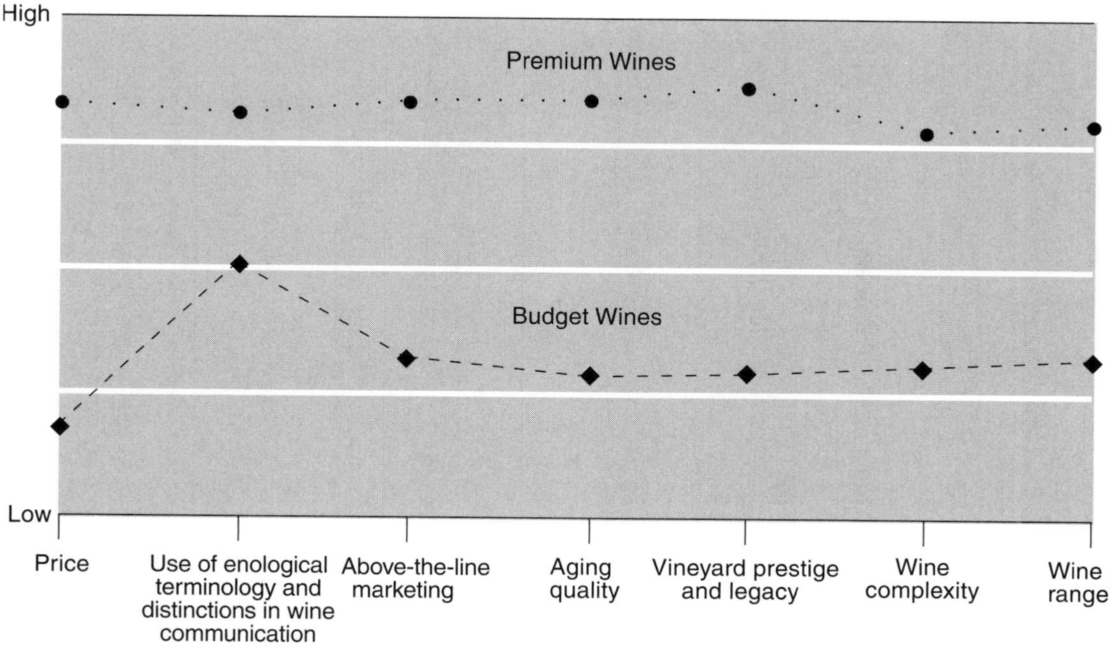

SOURCE: W. C. Kim and R. Mauborgne, *Blue Ocean Strategy* (Cambridge, MA: Harvard Business School Press, 2005).

FIGURE 10.2   The Strategy Canvas of [yellow tail]

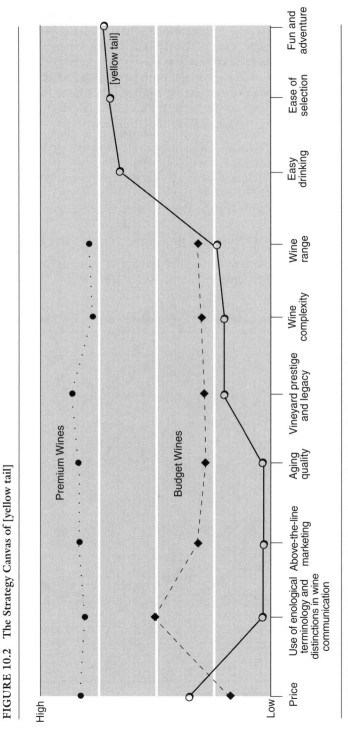

SOURCE: W. C. Kim and R. Mauborgne, *Blue Ocean Strategy* (Cambridge, MA: Harvard Business School Press, 2005).

3. The **ERRC grid** plots the four-action framework on a 2 x 2 grid. The Blue Ocean strategy example is Cirque du Soleil. This unique circus-based stage show entered the tired and very mature (Red Ocean) circus business in a new and exciting way. They eliminated star performers and animal acts, changed the fun and humor from slapstick to cool, and became a more serious and sensual show. They also raised the value of the venue. Instead of performing in a tent on a midway, they appear in high-end theaters and on stages like the Bellagio in Las Vegas. They created a themed circus in a refined environment, with multiple versions and artistic music and choreography.

4. The **six paths framework** offers ways to reconstruct market boundaries (Principle #1):

   - Look for *alternative* industries with different forms and functions, but the same purpose.
   - Look across *strategic groups* within an industry and capture the strengths of more than one (as in IDEO's cross-pollination).
   - Look across *chains of buyers* by shifting to a new buyer group.
   - Look across *complementary* products, services, and offerings to add value to the entire chain.
   - Look across *function and emotional appeal* to buyers and try to shift the emphasis from one to the other.
   - Look across *time* by envisioning how the industry and market will evolve—not just analyzing trends but projecting future scenarios.

5. The **visualization exercise** consists of a number of stages: *awakening, exploration, communication, and visualizing at the corporate level.* This process focuses attention on the big picture, not just the numbers (Principle #2). Recall that frequently new corporate venture markets are initially small, which can be a barrier to intrapreneurship. By visualizing the big picture, the intrapreneur can see bigger payoffs. Key to this tool is developing a compelling **tag line**. A tag line is a short saying that encapsulates the value of the new product or service. It is a version of an advertising slogan.[47]

6. The **portfolio tool** enables the corporate host to determine which corporate ventures are *pioneers, migrators, or settlers.* Pioneers are intrapreneurial efforts with high potential tomorrow. Migrators are middle producers with potential for high innovation and therefore have potential down the road. Settlers are the cash cows that produce good stable returns. Note the similarity to the Boston Consulting Group portfolio tools.[48]

7. The **buyer utility map** shows who buys and who doesn't and why. This helps top managers figure out how to change nonconsumption into a market (Principle #3). Tier 1 nonconsumers are at the edge of the market and may soon purchase. Tier 2 nonconsumers have deliberately chosen not to buy, so they must be lured by some new value. Tier 3 nonconsumers are not familiar with the product and are unexplored by competitors.

8. The **price corridor of the mass** identifies the majority (mass) of buyers and specifies the price level within the corridor, which is essentially a range. If intrapreneurs can protect their value with isolating mechanisms and discourage imitation (resource-based concepts), they can sustain higher prices.

Principle #4 is to get the sequence of strategy right. The correct sequence is:

Buyer Utility → Price → Cost → Adoption

This sequence brings us back to the strategy canvas and the new value curve. The first step is determining whether and how buyer utility has been increased. Next, the product is priced. This requires costing the product to determine projected margins. If they are acceptable (and economies of scale can generate increasing margins over time), the product can be adopted.

Principle #5 is to overcome organizational hurdles, and Principle #6 is to build execution into the strategy. These matters have already been covered—Innovator's Dilemmas, Innovator's Solutions, IDEO methodology, etc.

GUIDELINES FOR SUCCESS

Intrapreneurship does not work without radical changes in the thinking of corporate managers and their stockholders.[49] Even when these changes have been implemented, successful intrapreneurship can develop only after the corporation has gained some experience and learned some lessons from the market.[50] Top corporate executives must nurture the atmosphere and supply the vision necessary to encourage intrapreneurial activity.[51] A number of frameworks and processes offer guidelines for success, but the actual process is somewhat idiosyncratic. It is not the same everywhere and recipes cannot be too closely followed. Context counts. If successful intrapreneuring could be reduced to a formula, everyone would do it successfully. This would be the intrapreneurial paradox, paralleling the entrepreneurial paradox of Chapter 2. Guidelines, however, can help, and they come out of different sources and contexts.

Innovator Solutions

Christensen (1999) made a significant contribution by recognizing why large organizations were so poor at corporate venturing that entailed disruptive technology. They could not make decisions that seemed to go against the very factors that made them successful—listening to customers; improving products and services; selling better, cheaper goods faster to a growing mass of consumers. But in the *Innovator's Solution* (2003) he offers his most fundamental advice: Separate the corporate venture from the main body of the corporation. Keep it as a stand-alone entity. Take an equity position and/or find partners to help with financing and operations. Put the best innovators and intrapreneurs in the new venture and structure incentives that let them act as entrepreneurs. Of course, the corporation should also continue making sustaining innovations to their older products. The modern corporation needs to be good at managing both sustaining and disruptive change.

Freedom Factors

Intrapreneurs practically need a bill of rights to set them free and let them simulate the external entrepreneurial environment within the organization. These freedom factors, developed by Pinchot (1985), are:

1. *The right to appoint oneself an intrapreneur.* Intrapreneurs cannot wait for the corporation to discover them and put them in intrapreneurial positions. They must have the right to initiate.

2. *The right to stay with the venture.* Corporations often force the originators of ideas and projects to hand off their creations when they require additional resources and expertise and become bigger and better developed. Intrapreneurs need the right to see the project through.

3. *The right to make decisions.* Intrapreneurs need the right to make important decisions that affect the future of the venture. Pushing decision making up the hierarchy moves it away from people who know and care to people who don't.

4. *The right to appropriate corporate slack.* In large bureaucracies, managers control resources so tightly it is often impossible to redeploy them to more productive uses. Intrapreneurs need discretion to use a percentage of their budgets, time, and physical resources to develop new ideas.

5. *The right to start small.* Large corporations have a home-run philosophy. They prefer a few large, well-planned projects, but intrapreneurs need permission to create smaller, experimental ventures and let natural selection produce the winners.

6. *The right to fail.* Intrapreneurship cannot be successful without risk, trial and error, mistakes, and failures. False starts are part of the process. If intrapreneurs are punished for failure, they will leave the organization, and others will be reluctant ever to take chances.

7. *The right to take enough time to succeed.* The corporation cannot set unrealistically short deadlines for the success of intrapreneurial efforts. They must be patient with their investment.

8. *The right to cross borders.* Intrapreneurs often cross organizational boundaries to put together the resources and people needed for the project. Corporate managers resist incursions on their turf. Intrapreneurs need passports and the freedom to travel.

9. *The right to recruit team members.* Intrapreneurs need the freedom to recruit for the cross-functional teams they must assemble for the project. The team must be autonomous, and members owe their first allegiance to the team, not to their former department.

10. *The right to choose.* Independent entrepreneurs can choose among many suppliers, financial sources, customer groups, and personnel. The intrapreneur must not face internal corporate monopolists who constrain the choices for procuring resources. The intrapreneur needs the freedom to choose from external sources when they are superior.

Rules from Intrapreneurs

The *Innovator Solutions* advice is aimed at top corporate executives. The freedom factors are philosophical tenets. What practical advice can be offered to intrapreneurs in the trenches? Suggestions from practicing intrapreneurs can help.

For innovators, here are some lessons from a recent conference hosted by Jump Associates of San Mateo, California:[52]

1. Avoid using the term "innovation." It can ignite hostility from other departments and managers. If you appropriate the term innovator for yourself, what are the rest of the managers doing?
2. Use a buddy system. Find a partner, someone whose strengths match your weaknesses and vice versa. It is hard to change things by yourself.
3. Set the metrics in advance. You need different measurements than those used for the existing corporate products/markets. Get these approved before you begin.
4. Aim for early successes. Top executives often have short time horizons and lack patience. Quick wins will buy you time for longer-term processes later.
5. Get data. Intuition is useful and sometimes reliable, but back up your gut reaction with quantitative data to justify your decisions.

Lessons from the world's most creative companies:[53]

1. Bring together specialists in a cross-functional design, research, and innovation center. Cross-pollination will occur.
2. Think character as well as metrics. In evaluating innovators, look for courage and imagination.
3. Include subordinates in big decisions. The young guns below the top executives should be able to present their ideas along with senior management.
4. Preserve innovation values and practices. Use senior management to tell and repeat stories of intrapreneurs who succeeded at the company.
5. Get the CEO involved from the beginning. The innovation culture starts at the top.

Marissa Mayer is the vice-president for search products and user experience at Google. She works for one of the world's most innovative companies at the core of its innovation mission. She has nine ideas about what makes a great corporate venturer and intrapreneur.

1. Expect great ideas to come from anywhere—even finance!
2. Share ideas, information, and processes to stimulate thinking within the firm.
3. Favor intelligence and character over experience when hiring.
4. Approve slack time and resources (skunk works) for employees. Google gives employees a free day once a week, and half the new launches originate from this slack time.
5. Instant perfection is not possible. Innovate first, improve later.
6. Use data, not politics, to get your projects approved.
7. Creativity loves constraint. For every new idea, provide structure and guidance.
8. Simplify and make it easy to use. Money will follow.
9. Don't play the devil's advocate, wear the black hat, or kill projects. Morph, modify, alter, and evolve them into something better.

These recommendations and suggestions demonstrate that personal initiative, creative leadership, and corporate policies are all required for corporate venturing. No single prescription will always work, and context is critical.

SUMMARY

The modern large corporation needs intrapreneurs and corporate venturing in order to survive and grow. There are many similarities between entrepreneurial and intrapreneurial processes, and there are also significant differences. The primary difference is that the intrapreneur must always consider the corporate environment.

Intrapreneurship can be accomplished using variations of a simple five-step process. Companies like IDEO, while being creative and innovative themselves, help other companies by employing processes that bring new information and insights to the corporation. They use archetype personas to accomplish this.

The basic innovator's dilemma is that incumbent managers find it almost impossible to adapt to disruptive change and technology. From their perspective, the best use of the company's resources is sustaining change—making current products and services better. Doing things differently or doing different things fails to meet corporate standards and seems to cannibalize current offerings. The innovator's solution is to create stand-alone, independent venture units managed by intrapreneurs to promote the innovations. Many other guidelines for success are offered. The key is to recognize that the organization context will affect the intrapreneur's path.

KEY TERMS

Applied research
Basic research
Blue Ocean
Buyer utility map
Corporate entrepreneurship
Corporate venturing
Development research
Disruptive innovation
Elimination
ERRC grid
Four actions framework
Internal corporate ventures (ICV)
Intrapreneurship
Leveraged buy-out (LBO)
Portfolio tool
Price corridor of the mass

Red Ocean
Six paths framework
Skunk works
Strategy canvas
Sustaining innovation
Tag line
Technical innovation
Technology clusters
Technology funnel
Technology spillovers
Value innovation
Visualization exercise

DISCUSSION QUESTIONS

1. What benefits can corporations gain through successful intrapreneurship?
2. What are the important similarities and differences between entrepreneurship and intrapreneurship?
3. How is the intrapreneurial business plan different from the entrepreneurial business plan? Why is this so?
4. What impediments do large corporations impose on intrapreneurial efforts?
5. Explain the Innovator's Dilemma? What is it and how does it impede intrapreneurship?
6. How does IDEO's model promote intrapreneurial thinking and action? How is IDEO's approach unique?
7. What are the key aspects of technical innovation? How is it different from other types of innovation?
8. Why is a Blue Ocean strategy preferred to a Red Ocean strategy?
9. What are the Blue Ocean tools and principles? How do they work? Which seems the most critical to you?
10. How is innovation done at your company or university? What improvements in the process would you make?

EXERCISES

1. Choose a company from Table 10.1. Research the company's intrapreneurial experience, processes, and history. Evaluate its approach compared to that of its closest competitor.
2. Consider a company you work (or have worked) for. How was corporate venturing done at this firm? How were you and co-workers involved in the process? What recommendations would you offer to make this company more intrapreneurial?
3. Identify a product category that looks ripe for innovation. Use the Blue Ocean tools to reconfigure the market and find Blue Ocean space for a corporate venture.

Panera: Rising to the Challenge

The Panera restaurant chain has been lauded as a top contender in customer satisfaction by J.D. Power and Associates and is recognized as a leader in returns to shareholders by *The Wall Street Journal*. During the five-year period beginning in 2000, the company's sales rose 33 percent a year while its net income grew at an annual rate of 50 percent. During that same period the price of its stock quintupled. Now that growth has apparently hit a plateau. Increases in same-store sales have begun to dip, and there is some doubt about whether the Panera Bread Company has the innovative yeast to allow its growth and profits to keep rising.

Positioned as an alternative to what its CEO Ronald Schaich calls "self-service gasoline stations for the body," Panera specializes in breads baked daily at each of its locations and free of unhealthy transfats. The company motto is "A loaf of bread in every arm." The chain also makes bagels, muffins, and pastries; blends coffee drinks; serves homemade soups; and prepares salads and custom sandwiches from hormone-free chicken and other healthy ingredients. "It's food you crave, food you trust," explains Schaich. "People sense it."

Panera has much more panache than most fast-food restaurants. The food is served on china plates with stainless steel utensils. The tables and chairs are wood, the floors are carpeted, and there is free wireless Internet to lure patrons toting laptops. Those perks may explain why the average Panera customer spends $8.51 on lunch, almost twice the $4.55 industry average.

That lunchtime business is at the core of Panera's dilemma. While traffic and sales in the middle of the day are strong, morning and evening business is weaker. The chain introduced breakfast soufflés to help build its A.M.

business. Now it is reaching out to the after-work crowd by experimenting with drive-through lanes and by offering a flatbread pizza called crispani after 4 P.M. "It is a very upscale product, and the first salvo in our effort to boost sales during the evening," says Schaich. "It's a natural extension of our bread business."

Schaich has some experience with menu innovation. It was his idea to add salads to Panera's offerings when the low-carbohydrate diet craze hit in 2003. The chain continues to present a wide variety of vegetarian and low-fat dishes to suit shifting American tastes, and it keeps its menu fresh by seasonally rotating soups and sandwiches and rolling out new items.

Panera currently has over 930 bakery-cafés in 37 states, one-third company-owned and two-thirds operated as multiple-unit franchises. It is opening new stores at a rate of 100 to 150 a year and plans to expand into Canada shortly. Schaich believes Panera could someday have as many as 5,000 stores, and industry analysts seem to agree. But analysts also note that newer stores are doing less business than those opened before 2005, a not-uncommon problem for aggressively expanding restaurant chains. A study of the storefronts opened in 2005 showed that sales at franchise stores were 5 percent lower than sales at the company-owned stores.

While Panera has historically been suburban-based, it is beginning to expand into big cities. Panera CEO Schaich has some experience with that kind of location, too. Schaich was CEO and co-founder of Au Bon Pain, Inc., when the chain purchased the 20-unit St. Louis Bread Company and renamed it Panera Bread in 1993. When Schaich decided to concentrate on building Panera in

1999, he sold Au Bon Pan to outside investors because, ironically, he believed that chain's urban locations would limit future growth.

SOURCE: Adapted from Michael Arndt, "Giving Fast Food a Run For Its Money," *Business Week Online*, April 17,

2006. Retrieved from the Web May 15, 2007, http://www.businessweek.com/print/premium/content/06_16/b3980084.htm?chan=gl; adapted from Neil A. Martin, "Running Low on Yeast?" *Barron's Online*, July 17, 2006. Retrieved from the Web September 4, 2006, http://online.barrons.com/public/article/SB11529247138260 7621-CPfutFBbLVua_rW8k7jZsD1Lga8_20060817.html?mod=9 _0002_b_free_features, and www.panera.com.

Case Questions

1. Are Panera's new initiatives innovations, or are they simply line or brand extensions? Explain.
2. Are Panera's new strategies likely to find Blue Ocean or Red Ocean? Explain your choice.
3. If current customers are not a source of innovation, where should Panera look?
4. Do you think intrapreneurship can spur Panera's continued growth? Why or why not? What role do you think the franchisees can play?

APPENDIX

The Franchising Alerternative

Another way for a corporation to venture, expand its boundaries and the reach of its activities is through franchising. **Franchising** is a marketing system by which the owner of a service, trademarked product, or business format grants exclusive rights to an individual for local distribution and/or sale of the service or product. In turn, the owner receives payment of a franchise fee, royalties, and the promise of conformance to quality standards.[1] The **franchisor** is the seller of the franchise, and the **franchisee** is the buyer. To what extent is the franchisee an entrepreneur? Any distinction between franchisor and franchisee must focus on the concept of innovation. The franchisee creates an economic organization, perhaps a network of organizations. Gain and growth are clearly goals, and risk and uncertainty are ever-present. However, because the franchisee is contractually obligated to operate the business in a prescribed manner, he or she has little apparent room for innovation. Also, the franchisee does not usually have total control of the disposal of the business: Franchisors usually reserve the right to choose or approve the next franchisee. However, franchisees frequently do make innovations that are either tolerated by the franchisor or adopted and incorporated into the system. For example, some of McDonald's best new product ideas originated with franchisees eager to improve their sales.

Franchising is one of the fastest-growing forms of business and now represents a major share of all fast-food restaurants, auto parts dealers, and quick-print copy shops. Another group of franchise opportunities are automobile dealerships, major league sports teams, national and international real estate brokers, child-care centers, and accounting and tax services. A recent study by the International Franchise Association (IFA) indicates that franchising is booming.[2] Some highlights of the report are:

- There were over 2,500 franchising systems (companies that sell franchises) in the United States. Seventeen of eighteen categories grew in 2005.
- The largest categories of existing systems are fast food (20 percent, 500 systems) and retailing and services (both growing at 11 percent).
- The smallest category of existing systems is travel, and travel is the only category that decreased in 2005.
- Retail food is the fastest growing category with 67 percent growth in the period from 2003 through 2005.
- One-third of all franchise systems have 100+ units and nearly half have 50 units; 25 percent of all franchise systems have 10 units or less.
- Franchise sales topped $1.5 trillion dollars.
- Franchise systems employ over 18 million Americans.

Franchising is also one of the most prevalent corporate venturing strategies in international markets. For example, both McDonald's and Yum Brands (KFC) are in intense competition to expand their franchises in China. They want to attract the best entrepreneurs from the emerging Chinese entrepreneurial class. Yum is expected to launch over 300 new Kentucky Fried Chicken franchises a year for the next decade and McDonald's has a goal of over 1,000 units by 2008. Both companies offer intensive support to their franchisees. KFC requires thirteen weeks of training in a restaurant before it will consider an application, and McDonald's trains its prospects at the Hong Kong branch of Hamburger University.[3]

The fantastic success of franchising is one of the fundamental changes in business since World War II, but why is it so successful? How does it work?

Theoretical Foundations

Franchising is a method of implementing the growth strategy of the franchisor's venture. The successful franchisor possesses resources that are rare, valuable, imperfectly imitable, and nonsubstitutable. Usually these resources are a business concept, an operating system, a brand name, and an actual or potential national reputation. Franchising enables the franchisor to multiply the rents collected on the four-attribute resource through the franchise agreement. Each franchisee becomes an outlet for the value added by the special resource configuration. The basic assumption is that value has been created and captured through careful operation, testing, and documentation of a commercially viable idea.[4]

Franchising enables the franchisor's venture to grow using the franchisee's money, knowledge of the specific locale, and human resources. It also allows the franchisor to enjoy increasing economies of scale in purchasing, building development and improvements, and advertising and promotions. Finally, it enables the firm to enjoy two traditional strategic advantages at once: local control of costs through close supervision of the franchisee, and effective national or international product and service differentiation through the marketing efforts of the franchisor.[5]

However, there are times when the franchisor's desire for growth is a liability. Consider Boston Market. The company grew from 20 stores in the late 1980s to over 900 stores in the 1990s. They were making a high five-figure fee on each franchise unit opened, but the stores themselves were losing money. "If you are not making money at a single outlet, chances are pretty great that you're not going to make a lot of money at a lot of outlets," says Scott Shane, a management professor at Case Western. Boston Market eventually had to halt franchise sales, close 200 stores, and sell itself to McDonald's in 2000. Growth without prudent profitability proved their downfall.[6]

Organizational Boundaries

Franchising is a way of setting the boundaries of the organization. Businesses that can expand by opening individual units always have the choice of establishing a chain through company-owned units or franchising. In fact, most franchising systems contain a significant number of company-owned units in addition to the franchised ones. This enables the franchisor to conduct market experiments, gain knowledge of customer trends and changes, and maintain a solid understanding of procurement and operating costs. Frequently, the franchisor attempts to keep the best locations as part of the company-owned chain, even repurchasing them from franchisees who have made them successful.

Franchising is a hybrid form of organization and employs a hybrid mixture of capital and resources. The franchising agreement defines those boundaries by delimiting the organizational and financial constraints on the franchisor.[7] Therefore, it expands the organization's boundaries, which would otherwise be limited by resources and money.

Additionally, franchising is a way to balance the bureaucratic transaction costs of owning, monitoring, and controlling all the outlets or units of the venture (as a chain operation) with the market transaction costs of contracting with the franchisee.

The Agency Problem

The agency problem occurs when ownership and control are separated and the agent or manager substitutes his or her own goals and objectives for those of the owner. Because the franchisee is the owner/manager of the unit, the problems arising from the separation of ownership and control are greatly diminished. Because it would be difficult for the franchisor to monitor the quality and behavior of all the venture's outlets spread over the globe, the franchisor instead trusts that owners need much less monitoring than managers. Therefore, franchising is a partial solution to the agency problem.[8] A study using U.S. Census data on the food and motel industries found that franchising enables the franchisor to better control the most physically dispersed outlets and to protect the system's brand-name capital. The same study also indicated that franchising permits larger local outlets than using non-franchised operations.

However, franchising is only a partial solution because sometimes the owner of a franchise outlet hires managers to run the business and the agency problem recurs. Also, when franchisees serve a transient customer base, such as travelers on highways or in airports, they often let quality slip because they know there is little repeat business.[9] In summary, franchising enables the owner of a resource that is rare, valuable, imperfectly imitable (by outsiders), and nonsubstitutable to make perfect copies of the resource without lessening its rarity. To do this, the franchisor must grant exclusive *local* operating rights to the franchisee so that, from the point of view of the final customer, the product or service is locally rare and somewhat hard to get.[10] The franchisor must build a national reputation. As shown in Chapter 2, reputation is a resource that can possess the four attributes of sustainable competitive advantage. So what franchisors give up in the complexity of local organization and the proprietary nature of technology or physical resources, they attempt to overcome with reputation, high visibility, and a system-wide culture of high performance.

Franchisor Considerations

The primary form of franchising is the **business format franchise**. The franchisor grants the right to the franchisee to operate the business in a prescribed way. The franchisor can sell these rights one unit at a time or for a geographic territory. The one-at-a-time approach enables the franchisor to maintain close control over locations and the speed of growth. The geographic approach actually speeds growth, because it is usually in the interest of the franchisee to saturate the territory as quickly as possible. However, it enables some franchisees to become very large and powerful. This might be undesirable and risky from the franchisor's point of view because powerful franchisees can sometimes demand contractual concessions and resist royalty increases. In the business concept format, the franchisor is selling the business or the marketing system, not the hamburger or the quick-copy service. It is estimated that before the first franchisee is operating, the total costs for a franchisor of setting up these systems can run from as little as $5,000 to $1,950,000 or more. Table 10.1A shows the range of costs for the top 10 franchises and Table 10.2A shows the different cost drivers for the franchisor.

Franchising takes other forms in addition to the popular business format. A franchisor can grant an **exclusive right to trade**. For example, an airport or highway authority grants to specific companies the exclusive right to sell food and beverages in the airport or along the highway. A **distributorship** is also a form of franchise. Automobile dealers have a franchise to sell a particular make of automobile. A **registered trademark franchise** enables the franchisee to use a name with the expectation that it is recognizable to customers and that quality will be maintained. One example is the Best Western Hotel system. Each unit is independently owned and operated, but each uses the name Best Western and meets certain minimum standards.

In addition to different types of franchises, there are different types of franchise agreements. The simplest is the **individual franchise agreement** which allows the franchisee to open one store. **Area franchise agreements** enable the franchisee to operate a number of stores within a defined geographic area. A **master franchise agreement** authorizes the franchisee to grant franchise rights to other franchisees. It is like a sub-franchise agreement. Last, a franchisor can grant a **multiple unit franchise** which specifies exactly how many units the franchisee may open.

TABLE 10.1A   Top 10 Franchise Performers for 2005

Franchise Name	Minimum Investment*	Maximum Investment*	Years in Operation
Abbey Carpet Systems	$ 48,900	$ 108,100	35
Assist-2-Sell	$ 35,000	$ 62,000	16
Banfield, The Pet Hospital	$242,000	$ 443,000	8
Batteries Plus	$176,485	$ 327,485	14
CiCi's Pizza	$404,400	$ 646,400	18
Cruise Planners	$ 2,245	$ 20,440	12
Curves for Women	$ 38,425	$ 53,450	11
Del Taco	$272,000	$ 626,000	18
Domino's Pizza	$118,350	$ 450,100	39
Friendly's Restaurants	$498,500	$1,954,000	10

*From the Uniform Franchise Offering Circular. Does not include real estate costs.

SOURCE: *The Wall Street Journal Online Startup Journal* from FRANdata, Arlington, VA. Retrieved from the Web August 14, 2006

The Franchiseable Business

Certain types of businesses are appropriate for franchising. The first and primary requirement is a successful series of **pilot stores**, locations, or operating units. The franchisor bears the cost of developing the formula during the pilot period. The franchisor must learn enough about how to make the business a success to be able to train others to succeed. This means learning the key elements of accurate site selection, efficient operations, internal and external financial keys and ratios, operating cost control, a consistent and workable pricing policy, and training procedures for both potential franchisees and their employees. In addition to systematically perfecting each of these areas, the potential franchisor must be sure that after all costs are met, enough is left over for the franchisee to earn a respectable return and pay the royalty to the franchisor.

Table 10.2A summarizes the key cost drivers that a franchisor must consider.

Businesses suitable for franchising often have a number of common elements. They have a product or service that satisfies a continuing demand. Because it will take two or three years for both the franchisor and franchisee to see a return on their money, the franchise idea cannot be based on a fad or a quick make-a-buck opportunity.

The format of the franchiseable business must be simple and mechanical. A high degree of customized personal service or individual flair and skill are difficult for a franchisee to duplicate. Uniform standards of quality and appearance for the stores or outlets are important. This means that the franchisor must give serious thought to what quality means to the customer and be able to define and measure it accurately. The franchisor looks for a simple, easy-to-remember name for the business. Strong advertising and promotional support are crucial. The franchisee locations must be good enough to support the business but not so expensive that they absorb all the profits, which is why site selection criteria are vital.

The administration of the franchise system should be kept simple. The franchisor needs a way to ensure that sales and profits are reported accurately and royalty payments are correct and timely. If possible, the franchisor should arrange for a bank or financial syndicate to provide financial assistance to prospective franchisees.

Even the best business format franchise system cannot long endure if the original pilot oper-

---

TABLE 10.2A   Cost Drivers of Franchising

Research and Development Costs
Associated with the creation of the initial product, market research for the product and the franchise system, and the franchising blueprint.

Creation of the Franchise Package
Requires the hiring of a legal team to prepare the Uniform Franchise Offering Circular (UFOC) for the U.S. Federal Trade Commission. Franchisors are also highly regulated by state authorities.

Marketing the Franchise
Will cost money for advertising the franchise's availability, recruiting and selecting franchisees, further product and service development, and additional operational expenses.

Working Capital
For ongoing operations such as training franchisees, continued promotions, further development and refinement, and possible financial capital to help franchisees get started, plus some extra in reserve.

SOURCE: Adapted from R. Justis and R. Judd. Franchising (Cincinnati. OH: South-Western Publishing. 1989).

ations lack the resources to obtain sustainable competitive advantage. Barringer and Ireland (2006) offer these steps in the development of a successful franchise opportunity:[11]

1. Develop a franchise business plan (See Chapter 5).
2. Get professional advice. Franchise law is a highly specialized area.
3. Conduct an intellectual property audit: What do you control?
4. Develop the franchise documents and complete the UFOC.
5. Prepare the operating manuals for the prospective franchisees.
6. Plan your advertising strategy and franchise training program.
7. Put together a team for opening new units.
8. Design a strategy for soliciting, qualifying, and selecting new prospects.
9. Help franchisees with site selection, financing, and opening.

One of the more unusual franchise systems is Wild Birds Unlimited. It does not do things by the textbook. Street Story 10.4 offers details.

Competitive Issues

The franchise system engages in two simultaneous competitions: The franchisor competes to sell franchises, and the franchisee competes locally to sell the product or service. These are interrelated efforts. If the franchisee faces stiff competition and losses are accumulating, the franchisor will find it more difficult to sell franchises. Conversely, if the franchisor has trouble selling franchises, it decreases the brand value, name recognition, advertising support, and purchasing economies of scale that the franchisee relies on for marketing and operations.

The dependency can run in the other direction too. Franchisors depend on their franchisees for cooperation, so a franchisee rebellion can be a serious problem. The franchisor can discipline individual franchisees who fail to live up to quality standards or contractual agreements, but a system-wide rebellion can force the franchisor to negotiate or capitulate. Franchisee rebellions have occurred in some of the most famous and popular fast-food organizations, including Taco Bell, KFC, Holiday Inn, and Burger King. Still, for the most part, power is held by the franchisor who screens and selects franchisees, draws up the contracts, and collects the royalties.

One recent franchisee rebellion ended peacefully as the parties agreed to talk things through. Pop-A-Lock, Inc., had a fight on its hands. The franchisees of this car-unlocking and locksmith firm were fighting over franchisor support and training, and over the growth of the franchise system. Before the franchisees went so far as to sue, they sat down with a new CEO and hammered out a long-term agreement. Everyone embraced the deal and saved on legal fees. This is considered a good ending to the conflict.[12]

Because of the preponderance of power on the franchisor side, the government regulates the franchise industry primarily to protect franchisees. The franchising business is regulated both by individual states and by the Federal Trade Commission (FTC). Much of the regulation has to do with ensuring that franchisors provide franchisees with the information necessary to make informed decisions. Franchisees contend that these rules are widely abused or ignored.

Under the current rule, franchisors must disclose all financial terms and obligations of the franchisee. Franchisors do not have to state how much money franchisees can expect to make, but they must document their claims if they volunteer this information. Civil penalties of $10,000 can be levied for each violation. However, individual franchises cannot sue the franchisor under the FTC rule; only the FTC can bring action in federal court.[13]

Teaching Franchises to Fly

When Jim Carpenter opened his first retail store in 1981, he remembers some potential customers walking by without even glancing through his window. Carpenter claims he didn't care. "It's not like I gambled the farm," he says. "I took a one-year lease at $400 a month . . . If worst came to worst, I'd close up shop after the year and go back to working for someone else. Meanwhile, I would have fun spending time talking about birds."

But Carpenter got to have fun and remain self-employed. Not only was his first store in Indianapolis successful but now, thanks to franchising, there are more than 300 Wild Birds Unlimited stores in 43 states and 4 Canadian provinces.

From the beginning Wild Birds Unlimited has been a different kind of franchise operation. The franchise mission statement reads, "We bring people and nature together and we do it with excellence." Carpenter, who has a master's degree in ecological plant physiology, says his stores are more than a retail operation: He sees them as a community resource that provides valuable knowledge about the hobby of bird feeding. The stores don't all look the same, and the locations were all picked by the franchisees, not targeted by the franchisor.

Bird watching and bird feeding aren't everyone's hobbies, so Carpenter isn't catering to a broad market. And bird enthusiasts can purchase seed, feeders, binoculars, and other supplies at many other stores at lower prices. What Wild Birds Unlimited offers is a premium shopping experience with information and education for consumers, and custom products and seed blends. Owners are encouraged to develop a friendly relationship with their customers; at least one franchisee reports that 80 percent of her business comes from 20 percent of the people who walk through the door.

Carpenter became interested in franchising because his customers told him what he was doing "looked like fun," and his information for prospective franchisees still talks about the "adventure of retail" and the satisfaction of spending "days with nice people." Carpenter says, "I can't find owners for my franchises—they have to find me," and all but two of his storeowners did exactly that. "It's really important that our people both love what they do and want to be successful," he explains. "Our store is more about teaching than selling."

Wild Birds Unlimited has the same kind of relationship with its franchisees that it encourages them to have with their customers. New owners receive extensive training not only in business fundamentals, but also in whatever they need to become a bird authority for their area. Company representatives check in with every store once a week, and a Franchise Support Center staffed by 40 professionals is available to help owners during regular business hours. "It's really important to take care of the individual stores," says Carpenter. "The growth of the system depends on it." Franchisees obviously appreciate his commitment: A survey conducted by *Success* magazine named Wild Birds Unlimited first in franchisee satisfaction.

The network of Wild Birds Unlimited stores now has more than $100 million in annual sales, yielding the parent company $5.1 million in royalties and other revenue. "We have always taught our store owners that nature education provides its own rewards," says Carpenter. "It's very satisfying, it adds so much to customers' lives, and it comes back to you in your business."

SOURCE: Adapted from Victoria D. Williams, "Wild Birds Still Flying," *Indianapolis Business Journal*, July 24, 2006: 3; Geoff Pollack, "For the Birds: Seeds of Invention," *The College Magazine*, Indiana University, Summer 2001. Retrieved from the Web September 1, 2006. http://www.indiana.edu/~college/magazine/s2001.invention.shtml and www.wbu.com.

Despite regulation and potential problems, franchising remains popular because it enables businesses to expand quickly with other people's money and lets a self-motivated owner/manager control the operation. For franchisors to take advantage of these two benefits, they must be able to deliver a franchiseable product and business system.

Franchisee Considerations

Franchisees must be careful in evaluating franchise opportunities and choosing the best option. Potential franchisees are urged to examine their personal preferences for risk, autonomy, and hard work. They should consider how their talents and experience will contribute to making the franchise a success. Because of the constrained nature of the franchise agreement, franchising is not for every "wannabe" entrepreneur.

Franchisee Requirements

What are the most important things for franchisees to look for?

1. *Proven operating locations serve as a prototype for the franchisee.* This demonstrates do-ability to the customer. These stores have been tested and their operations refined. They are profitable, and the books should be open for qualified franchisees. The operation must be transparent enough for the franchisee to believe that he or she can manage it.
2. *A credible top management team demonstrates to franchisees that they will not be alone and that there is sufficient expertise at the franchisor level to handle any emergency or contingency.*
3. *Skilled field support staff will train the franchisee and communicate the franchisor's message to the units in the field.* They help the franchisee attain his or her goals.
4. *A distinctive and protected trade identity will enable the franchisee to use the trademarks, signage, slogans, trade dress, and overall image.* The franchisee should be concerned that quality, perceived or real, is similar throughout the system.
5. *A proprietary operations manual comprehensively explains the proven methods of operation and management.* It should be easy to read and understand.
6. *Training programs, both on-site and at headquarters, should be regularly updated, and available to franchisee staff and management.*
7. *Disclosure and offering documents that meet all federal and state regulations are required.* In addition, a franchise agreement that balances the needs of the franchisor and franchisee should be prepared.
8. *Advertising, marketing, public relations, and promotion plans should be prepared and available.* The franchisor should be ready to show how a national and regional product reputation will be developed for the benefit of the franchisee.
9. *A communications system should be established for ongoing dialogue between franchisor, franchisee, and the entire franchise network.* This includes meetings, scheduled visits, and attendance at association conferences, as well as random calls and inspections.
10. *Sufficient capital must be on hand to get the franchise system off the ground.* These substantial costs to the franchisor are described in Table 10.2A. The franchisee is responsible for due diligence before investing in any franchise operation. There are many horror stories of franchisees caught unaware and unprepared either by unscrupulous franchisors or by difficult economic times. Despite regulation, unprincipled dealers and susceptible buyers abound.

Table 10.3A summarizes the types of issues to be resolved in the contract.[14] Franchisees should retain competent counsel to advise them on all matters.

Franchisee Guidelines

The potential franchisee should investigate a franchise opportunity by doing the following:[15]

1. *Perform a self-evaluation.* Is franchising really for you? If you are very entrepreneurial, maybe not. Franchising requires discipline to operate under someone else's concept. But if you are just getting started and like the idea of owning your own business, franchising can give you some low-risk experience.

2. *Investigate the franchisor.* Visit other company stores and talk to other franchisees. Question earnings. Find out how the franchisor treats the franchisees in good times and bad. Pay particular attention to the extent to which the franchisor respects the franchisee's territory. You do not want to be in competition with your own franchisor.

3. *Study the industry and competition.* There are no sure things, and overall industry conditions and the nature of the competition will affect the individual franchisee. Also look at the degree of regulation in the industry. Many convenience store/gas station franchisees were stunned in the 1980s when they had to replace their underground gas storage tanks after the government mandated tighter environmental controls. Few were prepared for the expense.

4. *Study the Uniform Franchise Offering Circular (UFOC).* The UFOC is the document required of every franchisor by the FTC. It contains some 20 items, including the history of the franchise; the background of the franchisor(s); a description of the franchise, the financial obligations of the parties, territories and sales restrictions; and matters related to copyrights, trademarks, logos, and patents.

5. *Investigate the franchisor's disclosures.* The franchisor is obligated to report any "fact, circumstance, or set of conditions which has a substantial likelihood of influencing a reasonable franchisee or a reasonable prospective franchisee in the making of a significant decision

TABLE 10.3A   Issues to Be Addressed in a Franchising Agreement

Issue	Questions to resolve
Franchise fee	Amount? One time or per unit?
Royalties	Amount? As a percentage of net or gross? Sliding scale?
Quality control	Quality specifications? Inspections and monitoring? Rewards and sanctions?
Advertising	Fee? Local budget? National? Extensiveness and intensiveness? Messages and campaigns?
Offerings	Product line? Product mix? Required offerings? Alternatives? Franchisee-generated offerings?
Equipment	Required? Additional? Financing?
Location	Site selection requirements? Franchisor aid? Financing?
Operations	Signs? Hours? Maintenance? Décor? Personnel policies?
Reporting	Types of reports? Frequency? Auditing? Sanctions?
Dispute resolution	Methods? Equity? Arbitration?
Termination	Timing? Causes? Sanctions?

SOURCE: Adapted from R. Justis and T. Judd, *Franchising* (Cincinnati, OH: Southwestern Publishing, 1989).

related to a named franchise business or which has any significant financial impact on a franchisee or prospective franchisee."[16]

6. *Know your legal rights and retain counsel.*

Key Terms

Area franchise agreements
Business format franchise
Distributorship
Exclusive right to trade
Franchisee
Franchising

Franchisor
Individual franchisee agreement
Master franchise agreement
Multiple unit franchise
Pilot stores
Registered trademark franchise

Discussion Questions

1. Are franchisors entrepreneurs? Are franchisees entrepreneurs? Give reasons for your answers.
2. Why has franchising been so successful in the United States? Does it have the same potential worldwide?
3. Why is the pilot store so important for the potential franchisor?
4. What are the characteristics of a franchiseable business?
5. What is the nature of the dependency between franchisor and franchisee?
6. What should a franchisee look for in evaluating a franchise opportunity?

Exercises

1. Interview a local franchisee. Ask the franchisee about his or her relationship with the franchisor. What are the problem areas and the positive points? How does the future look? Find out whether the franchisee is satisfied and would do it again.
2. Request a package of material from a franchisor. Advertisements for these can usually be found in *Inc.* or *Entrepreneur* magazines, among other places. Evaluate the material. Does it answer the questions a potential franchisee will have? Follow up by calling the franchisor. What additional information can you obtain this way?
3. Evaluate your own business plan for its franchiseability. Does it meet the criteria for franchising? If so, develop a franchise plan.

Cases to accompany

ENTREPRENEURSHIP

Strategies and Resources

FOURTH EDITION

CASE 1

MedTrack

INTRODUCTION TO MEDTRACK

The capstone course at the Kelley School of Business's online MBA program is a course in entrepreneurship and new venture creation. Students are required to develop an idea into a business plan. They go through the following stages to reach the final plan:

1. Idea generation
2. Idea evaluation
3. Feasibility analysis including
   Market feasibility
   Financial feasibility
   Operational feasibility
   Strategic feasibility
4. Plan preparation
5. Plan presentation

Each of these steps is intended to give the students ample time to develop their ideas, strengthen their business model, and tighten their operational and financial grasp of the start-up of a new enterprise.

In late 2005 a group of students presented the MedTrack plan. The plan described an idea to use RFID technology to help hospitals keep better track of their equipment, drugs, movable utensils, and gear. The value proposition was that the adoption of their system by a hospital would make that organization more efficient, save it time and money, and most of all, save lives.

The students were all intending to continue in their current jobs (online students must be employed to enter the program) and careers now that they had their MBA degrees. But there was the nagging doubt in their minds that the business plan they prepared for class had more potential for them as a new venture than going back to their former positions. They felt that they had identified a significant value-added opportunity in the growing health-care and medical services industry. They could see that RFID technology was clearly both relatively simple to implement and very cost efficient. But because none of the students had direct access to professionals in the field or direct experience with either RFID technology or hospital administration, they did not know where to turn for the next step.

Should they:

- Quit their day jobs and work on this full time?
- Continue at their current jobs and use their spare time to see if the opportunity had legs?
- Pool their money to hire someone who could get the business off the ground?
- Forget about it and get on with their lives?
- Something else?

The plan for MedTrack is presented below with some editing for space considerations.

EXECUTIVE SUMMARY

Company: MedTrack
5555 Medvision Blvd
Cureonia, CA 75098, USA
Ph: (924) Med Track
Fax: (924) Med 9 Fax
Web Site: www.MedTrack.Com
Contact: Ivanette Bonilla

Type of Business

MedTrack designs, develops, and markets RFID solutions to hospitals to help hospitals track vital supplies and critical equipment.

Source: The research for MedTrack was performed by Ivanette Bonilla, Dan Fillenwarth, Sri Sampath, and Vassil Chalashkanov under the direction of Professor Marc Dollinger, Kelley School of Business. The material is used with their permission.

MedTrack will develop the software platform that will integrate the hardware components required to transpond, receive, and compile inventory data. The solution will be marketed to hospitals with at least 150-bed capacities.

Management

MedTrack is led by Ivanette Bonilla, who has an MBA and several years of experience in developing products. The rest of the founding team has several years of experience in marketing, finance, and operations. All the members of the management team also have MBA degrees.

Product and Competition

The overall outlook for MedTrack and RFID applications looks to be that of high growth as the industry is expected to grow rapidly to $3 billion in the next two years. The spectrum of existing firms offering RFID solutions ranges from small start-ups to industry giants such as Motorola, Siemens and Texas Instruments. However, only about four or five firms offer RFID solutions to hospitals. Research on these companies indicates less than a total of five RFID implementations in hospitals.

Funds Requested

MedTrack is requesting $5 million in cash funds in lieu of equity. Toward the end of the first year of operation, MedTrack will also attempt to borrow $4 million in fixed interest loans.

Use of Proceeds

MedTrack will invest approximately $3 million in the first year and about $5 million in the second year toward research and development of the product/service.

Exit

At the end of five years, the projected value of the business is $170 million. Based on the initial investment of $6 million, the terminal value of the business represents an IRR of 107 percent. Depending on the market conditions, an IPO of the business will be considered at the end of year five. Other scenarios of merger with an equivalent-sized company might also be considered if the market for IPO is not attractive.

BACKGROUND AND PURPOSE

History

Historically, hospitals have invested less in Information Technology (IT) than in other equipment. As a result they have failed to enjoy fully the benefits of technology and the information era. This has impacted the industry both financially and operationally.

Current Situation. Because their primary goal is to save lives, hospitals are not very efficient in inventory control, and write off at least 15 percent of inventory as lost or stolen. Furthermore, a hospital's inability to track its vital supplies and equipment can prevent it from providing timely care and treatment. In addition, most hospitals do not have tools to help prevent errors like administering the wrong medication to patients. Such errors cost as many as 100,000 lives a year in the United States.

EXHIBIT 1   Pro Forma Financial Projections

	Year 1	Year 2	Year 3	Year 4	Year 5
Total revenue	$ 1,000	$ 8,260	$27,498	$63,290	$116,074
Net income (loss)	(1,810)	(1,135)	6,483	17,344	32,678
Assets	8,310	7,651	16,996	38,907	74,786
Liabilities	4,895	6,338	8,417	13,465	17,146
Cash flow	7,970	4,651	7,579	17,382	34,402

MedTrack's goal is to provide hospitals with RFID systems that will help them eliminate inventory-related errors and save more lives through more effective and reliable tracking systems. To exploit this opportunity, MedTrack will develop and deliver a complete solution to hospitals that will consist of the RFID system and necessary software. The system will include the hardware and the software necessary to track any equipment, supply, or drug in a hospital. The offering will consist of (a) an RFID tag to be attached to supplies or equipment that need to be tracked, (b) RFID receivers that detect signals from devices, (c) a computer server for hosting the data base and application, (d) several client computers for users, (e) application platform/software, and (f) training, maintenance, and support. MedTrack also aims to partner with key medical equipment suppliers and drug distributors to deliver RFID-tagged supplies to the hospitals.

Resources

Financial. The four founding partners will provide some of the initial equity, with the majority provided by a participative venture capitalist. Growth projections indicate that additional financing will need to be secured by the end of the first year of operation. These will likely be borrowed funds rather than additional equity.

Human. The founding team has several years of experience in key entrepreneurial functions of the business such as marketing, sales, finance, operations, and IT. Initially, the primary gaps to fill will be IT (possibly the director of IT) and human resources. Ownership stakes will be offered to a few key individuals to round out the leadership team.

Technological. The core business will be to develop a high-tech application. The founding partners bring several years of experience as users and marketers of high-tech applications. MedTrack's greatest resource is the knowledge of its people and partners in RFID technology and software development. Gaps in development of technology will be quickly filled with dynamic individuals through part ownership in the venture. This strategy will ensure that the systems are unique and successful.

Organizational. MedTrack will be a flat organization driven by innovation, speed, and customer satisfaction. The entire organization will be fully engaged in delivering quality products and services on time and within budget. The founding partners have several years of corporate experience in Fortune 500 companies; this experience will be readily transferable to the organization. The team has strong insights, vision, and the drive to take this business to the next level and help hospitals save more lives.

OBJECTIVES

Short Term

MedTrack will develop and sell complete RFID systems to hospitals, which will provide the real-time location of all equipment and supplies identified in the system. The systems will be sold based on the premise that they will save more lives by being able to quickly locate medical equipment and ensure the accurate dispensing and administering of medication. However, the final decision to purchase will likely be based on the fact that the reduction in losses (due to the real-time location data) will more than offset the cost of the system. The first system's installation should be completed 12 months from the time of inception of MedTrack.

All hardware will be purchased with an emphasis on component standardization. The software will be developed and licensed by MedTrack. The initial hospital launch partner will be considered part of the R&D effort and will receive significant cost savings. This strategy should speed the completion of the first project and can be used in part in follow-on sales and marketing efforts.

Initial marketing efforts will be conducted in the Midwest through trade magazine advertising, trade shows, and personal contacts in the hospital administration arena. Initial launch partners will likely be found through personal contacts and may include government grant dollars.

Long Term

The key long-term objective will be to partner with the drug companies and the equipment suppliers so that the RFID tags are attached to the equipment and supplies when shipped by the manufacturers (an estimated three to five years). It is expected that this partnering will create a rapid acceptance of the technology as well as significant market opportunities. MedTrack will be positioned to capitalize on this opportunity via rapid deployment of reliable systems. Further objectives will be to integrate the value chain by partnering with suppliers of components and customers.

MedTrack will have a national presence in five years and become a global leader in RFID systems for hospitals in ten years. MedTrack will also investigate other markets for their potential as the health-care market adopts this technology throughout the next decade. Industries that employ high-dollar equipment or experience significant inventory losses are potential opportunities in the long term.

MARKET ANALYSIS

Overall Market

The overall outlook for MedTrack and RFID applications appears to be that of high growth. Propelled by aggressive plans of persuading retailing giants Wal Mart and Target to implement RFID, the RFID industry is expected to grow rapidly to $3 billion in the next two years. Software companies like Microsoft and Oracle are also racing with each other to develop middle-ware platforms to create RFID-based products and services.

Three different approaches[1] are evolving in company strategies to implement RFID: (1) slap and ship by vendors who have to comply with a mandate like Wal-Mart's, (2) closed-loop strategy that focuses within the company, and (3) supply chain strategy that focuses on supply chain integration with vendors and customers. Applications of RFID technology are being tried in a variety of industries such as (1) agriculture, where the USDA is tracking cows for mad-cow disease, (2) armored vehicles, which are being tracked by the Department of Defense (DOD), and (3) the airline industry, which is tracking luggage.

With such rapid interest and investment in RFID technology, the industry is expected to undergo rapid consolidation in the near term. Industry standards continue to evolve to create uniform and compatible RFID systems. Furthermore, a rapid drop in the prices of RFID components is expected as manufacture of the components shifts to Asia. In addition, as the industry rapidly evolves, many companies may prefer to be "late followers" rather than "early adopters," which could choke growth. The industry might also be affected by privacy-related concerns, as the growth of RFID is driven by the retail industry.

Specific Market

Saving Lives. It is estimated that as many as 100,000 patients die each year in hospitals due to the incorrect administration of medications. The RFID system will monitor exactly which drugs are in which patient's rooms, and sound an alarm at the nurse's station when a drug enters the patient's room that has not been prescribed by the doctor.

In addition, hospitals have difficulty keeping track of their mobile medical equipment, to the point of simply losing it altogether through theft. By installing sensors in the appropriate locations, hospital staff will know exactly where all equipment is located. Each piece of equipment will have an area in which it is required to reside (think of the system as an invisible fence), and if a piece of equipment leaves the area, an alarm will sound alerting hospital staff of the infraction. Knowing exactly where this equipment is at all times will help hospital personnel save time during crisis situations and react faster to emergencies, ultimately saving more lives.

Inventory Losses. Fraud examiners and investigators say that employee theft is out of control, citing recent U.S. Chamber of Commerce figures that employees steal approximately $400 billion from businesses each year, and an Ernst & Young survey showing that nearly 90 percent of organizations countrywide experienced some type of fraud in the 12 months prior to the survey. An additional undetermined amount is being reported lost because of external fraud committed by customers, vendors, and others having contact with a company or institution. Fraud experts note that all sectors are targets—including retailers, hospitals and health care, the hotel industry, schools, and college campuses.[2]

Pilferages of ordinary hospital supplies such as bed linens have been quite common. However, increasingly, hospitals report theft of expensive medical equipment as well. Such thefts create a financial loss to hospitals and the danger that some life-saving equipment will be missing when needed. More than 50 hospitals have been hit over the past 18 months.[3] The cost of replacing equipment such as wheelchairs is estimated at several hundred dollars, which makes hospitals eager to find more difficult ways for would-be thieves to steal essential equipment.[4]

Recently, pilferage of controlled substances has also increased. In a recent survey, 64 percent of hospitals reported at least one documented or suspected case of such pilferage in the past year. Drug diversion occurred in 76 percent of the hospitals with more than 100 beds, and in only 28 percent of the hospitals with less than 100 beds. About 75 percent of such theft was attributed to hospital employees, which has led to the conclusion that hospitals need more stringent methods of control and surveillance.[5]

When a hospital's top executives engage in fraud, theft, and embezzlement, these crimes can be among the most unobtrusive and damaging that a health-care institution can face. While, in the past, even incidents involving millions of dollars were covered up and often went unprosecuted, today the U.S. Attorney General is pursuing such crimes more vigorously because of the federal funds that may be involved.[6]

The specific markets for MedTrack are the hospitals with a capacity of at least 150 beds. American Hospital Association statistics show 5,764 registered hospitals in the United States with a total bed capacity of about 965,000. Of this number, community hospitals totaled 4,895 with a bed capacity of 813,000. Total hospitalization expenses were nearly half a trillion dollars, with community hospitals accounting for nearly 95 percent of this amount. Targeting the top 10 percent of this market provides a potential $50 billion market. A conservative estimate of 10 percent toward the cost of supplies and services (the Mayo clinic incurred 23 percent in 2004), implies a $5 billion industry for supplies and equipment.

EXHIBIT 2   Hospital Care Expenditure

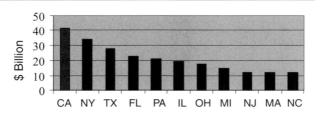

Competitive Factors

Bargaining Power of Buyers. MedTrack aims to target mid-sized hospitals with a capacity of 150 to 500 beds. The ability of such hospitals to invest a fraction of their revenues in MedTrack is expected to be significant. Although hospitals are free to buy the RFID devices off the shelf and have them deployed through their in-house IT group, traditionally hospitals have not built significant in-house IT capabilities for such purposes. A turnkey solution with system support is likely to be the main business model for hospitals in deploying RFID.

MedTrack's main strategy will be to differentiate itself with customized software and service to satisfy customers' complete needs. MedTrack's solutions will be scalable to suit medium- as well as large-sized hospitals. As economies of scale continue to lower the costs of RFID devices, MedTrack will further target small-sized hospitals, hospices, and small-business clinics.

MedTrack will aim to integrate its applications with industry standards followed by the suppliers and customers of hospitals, and will constantly strive to bring innovative solutions that meet the needs of the customer. By adopting a differentiated strategy on value-added services, combined with low-cost hardware supplies, MedTrack will aim to minimize the bargaining power of its customers.

Bargaining Power of Suppliers. MedTrack's suppliers will chiefly be manufacturers of RFID devices, computer workstations, and servers. In addition, MedTrack will depend on the availability of skilled software professionals whose expertise will be critical in developing, deploying, and maintaining the platform.

The high-tech manufacturing industry is very competitive, as most of the hardware products such as silicon chips have been commoditized. Much supply procurement is international and can now be performed over the Internet. This situation helps MedTrack take advantage of the lowest possible prices.

However, quality control of the suppliers may be difficult as the major manufacturing is expected to shift to lower-cost countries in Asia.

Supply of skilled software professionals that can not only be attracted to the venture but also be retained as the venture grows is the key to MedTrack's success. MedTrack's goal is to build a diverse, well-compensated workforce with a strong work ethic, professionalism, and respect for everyone's contribution.

Threat of Relevant Substitutes. In general, the use of RFID devices is expected to establish and improve the hospital's tracking and monitoring of supplies and equipment. It is mainly expected to replace bar-code-based technology to track goods and supplies. The advantages and value added from RFID technology appear compelling over the costs bar-code-based technology.

Although RFID applications have not been leveraged in the health-care industry, the technology has been applied in many other areas. The earliest implementations have been in toll roads, libraries, smart cards, and so on. Providers of such solutions can easily customize their solutions to target the health-care industry.

Threat of New Entrants. High-tech industry has been historically vulnerable due to the entry of new players. This has often led to overcapacity, a drop in prices, and a glut in the market. Successful high-tech companies have propelled themselves with a strong entry, and sustained their growth with rapid development and deployment of new products and constant innovation to stay in business.

RFID technology is likely to undergo a cycle similar to that of other high-tech products, such as mobile phones and communication devices. Although high entry barriers exist for providers of RFID during the infant stages of technology, it is expected that early birds such as MedTrack will reap the rewards of establishing a strong customer base.

Rivalry Among Existing Firms. The spectrum of existing firms offering RFID solutions ranges from small start-ups to industry giants such as Motorola, Siemens, and Texas Instruments. However, only about four or five firms offer RFID solutions to hospitals. These companies are privately held and appear to have started up or ventured into RFID recently. Research on these companies indicates less than a total of five RFID implementations in hospitals. Rivalry among these existing firms is likely to be less, as the market appears to be wide open to providers of RFID solutions. However, consolidation and acquisition of successful companies by large firms is a high possibility within the next few years. Acquisition of a small provider by a large company like Intel or GE could provide formidable challenges to MedTrack.

Macroenvironmental Influences

Political and Governmental. Raising health-care costs and their impact on the profitability of companies through employer-provided insurance have not gone unnoticed by the public and the government. The unveiling of the president's Health Information Technology Plan and the establishment of the Office of the National Coordinator for Health Information Technology (ONCHIT) under the U. S. Department of Health and Human Services in 2004 have resulted in a sharp focus on the use of IT as a means of improving health care. ONCHIT data indicate that while most industries spent about $8,000 per worker on IT, the health-care industry has invested about $1,000 per worker on IT, an investment level it hopes to increase. ONCHIT also estimates that Health IT can reduce health-care costs by about 20 percent,[7] which establishes a favorable climate for investment and development of technologies such as RFID.

Macroeconomic. The overall state of the U. S. economy appears to be improving steadily since the recession of 2002-2003.

Macroeconomic indicators, such as the unemployment rate, productivity, and interest rates show measured progress in the economy.

The Kaiser Family Foundation[8] reports that in FY 2000 total U.S. health-care costs were about $1.1 trillion. About 36 percent of this amount was directly spent on hospital care (see Exhibit 3 below) and another 8 percent was spent on nursing home care. Twenty-nine percent of this amount was estimated as having been spent on physicians and professional consultation services—most likely in clinics. Average health-care costs have been increasing at about 9 percent per year (see Exhibit 4) while inflation has been steady at or below 3 percent per year.

These factors are expected to play a favorable role in the growth of MedTrack for the next ten years.

Demographic Analysis. U.S. Census Bureau data indicate that approximately 11 percent of the population is 65 years or older and 54 percent of the population is between 19 and 64 years old. The demographics of the health-care industry are rapidly changing with the aging of the baby-boomer generation. Between the years 2000 and 2010, the size of the 45- to 64-year-old and 85-year-old-plus age groups is projected to undergo a large increase. The next decade shows a projected 40 percent increase in people between

EXHIBIT 3   Spending on Hospital Care

United States	Percent	Million $
Hospital care	36%	$ 413,131
Physician & professional services	29	328,983
Drugs & other medical nondurables	13	151,926
Nursing home care	8	95,296
Dental services	5	60,726
Home health care	3	31,616
Medical durables	2	17,750
Other personal health care	3	36,687
Total		$1,136,115

EXHIBIT 4   Average Annual Percent Growth in Personal Health Care Expenditures, FY1980-2000

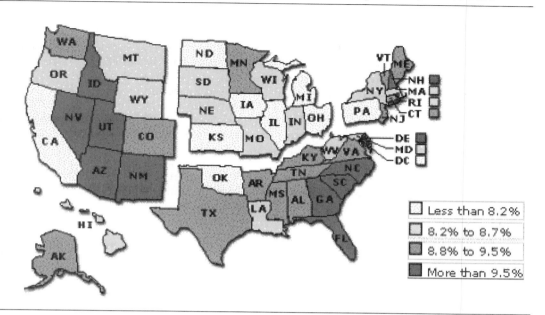

Less than 8.2%
8.2% to 8.7%
8.8% to 9.5%
More than 9.5%

EXHIBIT 5   Projected Population Change by Age, U.S. (Percent)

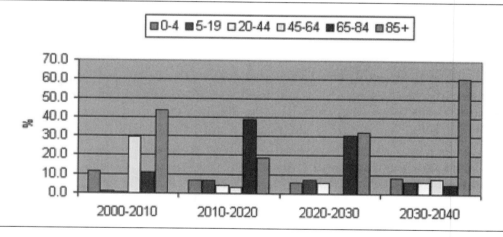

■0-4 ■5-19 □20-44 □45-64 ■65-84 ■85+

the ages of 65 and 84. Such a large shift in the demographics is expected to increase the burden on the health-care industry. In addition, the recent recession of 2002-2003 and the tech stock burst have depleted the retirement savings of many retirees and are expected to increase the burden on Medicare. Reduced profitability and an increase in cost control are likely results of these shifts. While MedTrack's RFID solutions may help reduce the costs of supplies and equipment for medical providers, hospitals are likely to encounter tight capital expenditures to launch such applications.

Technological Analysis. MedTrack's RFID solutions straddle the technology of semiconductors, communication equipment, computers, and software industries commonly known as the high-tech industry. The high-tech industry's growth has been quantified by Moore's law, which has become a self-fulfilling prophecy of a rapid drop in prices along with a rapid increase in capacity. Rapid advances in the high-tech industry have led to rapid growth and increase in productivity. However, such growth has also led to shorter life cycles, shorter boom-bust cycles, increase in burnout, and rapid consolidation. Although consumers eventually benefit from rapidly changing technology, start-up companies in nascent markets are often vulnerable to unpredictable forces.

Sociocultural Analysis. The high-tech industry's main challenge seems to be in maintaining a competent workforce in the face of rapid change, competition, development, and globalization. Globalization has not only shifted production of hardware to low-cost countries, but has also shifted value-added services like software development to countries such as India, Ireland, and Israel. Such a shift has caused strain on the availability of local skills for implementation and deployment of software solutions. Shifting of vital jobs and opportunities from the United States to off shore sites has the potential to produce a political backlash that might result in stifling software developmental efforts.

The software industry also faces the challenge of decreasing the digital divide (divide between developed nations and developing nations).

DEVELOPMENT AND PRODUCTION

Manufacturing and Production

The offering will consist of a combination of hardware devices, software platform and sup-

port, maintenance, and training. The manufacturing model will consist of outsourcing or contracting hardware components while developing the value-added software and application expertise in-house. MedTrack will broadly design the application/software platform and database, but they will be outsourced for development. In addition to customization and implementation of the solution, MedTrack will deliver customer training, support, and maintenance.

MedTrack's strategy toward successful start-up and launch of operations will heavily depend on applying the "Design for Six Sigma" methodology, which advocates prelaunch application of the six-sigma approach to designing a product that results in high quality standards, as opposed to quickly launching the product followed by user identification of glitches.

Advantages of Outsourcing. There are several advantages to contract manufacture of hardware components. MedTrack's hardware requirements are mainly semiconductor products such as computer servers, user workstations, and RFID transponders and receivers. The semiconductor industry undergoes rapid changes, as the life span of high-tech products averages around two years. This high-paced growth demands heavy capital investments, which MedTrack can circumvent by outsourcing. However, MedTrack will form strong and sustainable partnerships with suppliers of hardware components.

Design and development of software platform and applications were formerly done mostly by the firms launching such applications. However, the recent trend in the industry is toward outsourcing the development of these applications. The main advantage in outsourcing development of software is that MedTrack will be in a position to engage professional software programmers while keeping its head count low during its early growth.

Selection Criteria. MedTrack will aim at long-term partnerships with well-established hardware suppliers. The company may also use contracts and agreements when partnerships are infeasible. Because size is a big factor in reducing the costs in the high-tech semiconductor industry, MedTrack will seek to affiliate itself with a large distributor. Experience, stability, and reliability of supplies at a competitive cost will form the basis for establishing contractual agreements. In addition, MedTrack will use partnerships for strategic fit and synergic savings.

For the development of software, size of the developing company is usually not a critical factor. In fact, small and nimble companies often develop breakthrough technologies and are much easier to work with than large organizations. Outsourcing of software development also provides a range of business models, from U. S. contractual programmers to overseas developers. MedTrack will seek to engage low-cost developers from small and nimble firms that can not only develop high-quality products, but also provide background support if necessary. MedTrack will likely seek an established U. S. firm that is able to take advantage of low-cost development overseas. This model will enable MedTrack to gain vital interface in the United States on short notice while it takes advantage of low overseas development costs.

Resource Requirements

Because MedTrack plans to outsource most of the hardware and software, the resource requirements will be focused on successfully operating the core business. MedTrack's key strengths will be its intellectual and human resources, which will bring years of experience in the industry, a positive attitude toward customer service, and high ethical values. Each of MedTrack's founding partners has several years of experience in providing services to customers in a corporate environment. In addition, each brings experience in marketing high-tech products, development of solutions for the drug industry, continuous improvement based on Six Sigma, and managerial experience in an operating environment.

EXHIBIT 6 Manufacturing Model

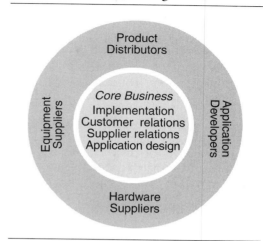

MedTrack estimates that early on it must fill specific skills in the design and implementation of software applications and in marketing-account managerial experience in hospitals. MedTrack's strategy for attracting talented candidates to fill these positions will be to provide adequate stock ownership while minimizing up-front expenses on salary and administration. A flat organizational structure that minimizes overhead and operational costs will be a key strategy.

Quality Assurance

MedTrack's quality assurance will be based on a preventative strategy rather than a corrective or reactive strategy. This means that MedTrack will increase the time and effort it will spend on the drawing board stages as opposed to the customer maintenance and support stages.

The main drawback in outsourcing development is the control of quality and stability of the platform. MedTrack aims to avoid the pitfalls by in-house design of the platform and close co-ordination with the developers of the application. Well-defined specifications and tightly established testing protocols will enable MedTrack to identify and eliminate bugs and software glitches before a product is released. MedTrack will embrace a total quality control approach such as TQM and Six Sigma not only for the manufacture and delivery of products and services, but also during the design stages. MedTrack will also aim to target and achieve ISO certification within five years of establishing itself as a growth-oriented firm that is measured by a metric such as two consecutive profitable quarters.

Because of the dependence of MedTrack on RFID and computer hardware, the partners and suppliers of these devices will be selected based on their existing quality control methodologies. Strong preference will be given to firms with a quality management program or certification.

MARKETING ORIENTATION

Marketing Segments

MedTrack identifies three customer segments among hospitals based on their size: large hospitals (500-plus beds), medium-sized hospitals (150 to 500 beds) and small hospitals (up to 150 beds). The specific needs of these segments vary according to the scale and scope of their operations and their annual expenditures for supplies, which are our primary tracking target. Based on detailed financial data on 468 California hospitals,[9] small hospitals' supply costs range on average between $1 million and $7 million per year, while the amounts for mid-sized and large hospitals go up to $38 million and $68 million, respectively. With regard to equipment, there is no clear positive correlation between hospital size and expenditures for equipment. Nevertheless, the amounts average from $3 million to $120 million per year per hospital. In addition to having large budgets, large and mid-sized hospitals manage numerous staff and have complex administrations. Hence, the larger the hospital, the more difficult it becomes to effectively manage its supplies and its equipment movement. Asset shrinkage can go up to 10 percent,[10] to millions of dollars per hospital. The goal of MedTrack

will be to reduce or eliminate shrinkage by reliably tracking valuable hospital assets most susceptible to theft or unauthorized "borrowing." In light of the significant costs of developing and implementing a tracking system, MedTrack's efforts should be directed toward larger hospitals where the organization is fairly complex and where the supplies and equipment budgets (and asset shrinkage) are sufficiently high to warrant the implementation of the system. On the other hand, implementing MedTrack in the largest hospitals would require significantly more financial and human resources due to the scale. Therefore, MedTrack will target the mid-sized hospital with somewhat complex administration, multimillion dollar supplies, an equipment budget, and a substantial asset shrinkage problem as its primary potential customer.

Marketing Strategy and Resources

Product. MedTrack is a complete tracking solution designed by professionals experienced in hospital administration and created by highly skilled programmers to respond to specific hospital needs and impact costs negatively. The product will add value by reducing asset shrinkage, assisting in inventory, staff, and patient management, and increasing hospitals' effectiveness in responding to emergencies, because hospitals will be able to locate their critical equipment and supplies at all times. MedTrack's greatest advantage will be its ability to offer a completely integrated system that replaces any legacy inventory management software and hardware.

The offering will consist of (a) an RFID to be attached to supplies or equipment that need to be tracked, (b) RFID receivers that receive signals from devices, (c) a computer server for hosting the data base and application, (d) several client computers for users, (e) application platform/software, and (f) training, maintenance, and support.

All hardware components will be outsourced. MedTrack will broadly design the application/software platform and database, but will outsource them for development.

While a standard low-end version of the application will be available for smaller hospitals, custom-built solutions will be developed for large and complex hospitals. MedTrack will also deliver customer training, support, and maintenance. MedTrack's team of professionals, in collaboration with strong partners in hardware and software and customization of solutions, will serve as a value-added component of the product/service.

Option 1. Turnkey system. The complete price of the system will vary according to the size of the hospital and the amount of hardware, the number of software modules, and the level of customization required. MedTrack will price its product at a premium as it will be the only provider, at least in the beginning, that will offer a complete solution that helps hospitals track and manage inventory, patients, and staff. Prices will typically range between $1 million and $3 million (1 percent of annual supply and equipment costs) per solution. Several pricing alternatives may be available to customers. The first will be for the customer to purchase a turnkey system. Assuming the system reduces the typical shrinkage of supplies and equipment by 20 percent (from 10 percent to 8 percent), this option will ensure a minimum ROI over the next five years of at least 200 percent.

Option 2. Lease option. Pursue five-year minimum leases, although shorter leases will be entertained. Leasing with the option to buy in the future will also be possible.

Option 3. Down payment plus a percent of the realized cost saving (reduction of write-offs). This is less desirable for MedTrack as the time associated with accurately determining the realized cost savings will likely be expensive. Lengthy legal contracts and difficult negotiations would accompany each invoice for the percentage of realized cost savings.

With all pricing options, MedTrack will pursue maintenance contracts based on time and material. (Flat-fee contracts based on customer insistence will be considered.) Some hospitals will be comfortable with this as a long-term arrangement while others will purchase this service for a specified time period while their own staff become sufficiently competent to no longer require MedTrack's maintenance services. This revenue stream will be critical to the startup of the business. It is recognized that customers will have a plethora of financing needs. The various pricing plans are designed to ensure maximum flexibility for the customer and to overcome possible budgetary constraints.

Distribution. MedTrack will subcontract regional software, equipment, and supplies to distributors with developed local field sales networks and preferably with connections in the medical sector. The distributors will approach hospitals, assess and qualify their needs, and present and sell the concept as a value addition to procurement of supplies. Technical experts from MedTrack will assist in closing the sale and then take over the implementation. MedTrack will offer above-average agent commissions to its distributors to ensure their commitment and motivation.

In addition to the distributor network, the in-house sales force will be comprised of high-caliber account executives and will be charged with identifying and approaching a list of specific medical institutions across the country classified as key accounts.

Advertising and Promotion. To build brand and product awareness, MedTrack will advertise in medical journals and other specialized periodicals and will sponsor medical training films, a TV series, and documentaries. MedTrack representatives will attend medical conferences and medical equipment exhibitions and fairs. They will hold press conferences and make presentations on the system launch and its further development. In addition, direct mailings of letters and advertising brochures will inform potential customers of the system's capabilities. A Web page will be developed to present the capabilities of the system. Members of the senior management team will network extensively among medical professionals and hospital administrators to ensure further exposure of the product.

Sales Forecasts

Of the 5,764 registered hospitals in the United States, approximately 40 percent (2,305) fall within the mid-sized target segment. With an average supplies and equipment budget of $45 million per mid-sized hospital and target revenue of 1 percent of that amount, the potential total market amounts to over $1 billion. Over the next five-year horizon, MedTrack's goal will be to capture 10 percent of that market or $100 million in revenue.

FINANCIAL PLANS

Financial Statements

The financial statements that follow are based in part on the following assumptions:

- Each individual sale will average $2MM.
- First installation will be complete in 12 months. This first installation will be at a reduced price of $1MM. This reduced price will aid in securing the first contract quickly.
- Progressive payments will be negotiated with customers for enhanced cash flow.
- MedTrack's revenue will exceed $100MM in year five.
- Three-year (average) maintenance contracts will be secured with 70 percent of the installations. Each maintenance contract will average $2MM annually.

Note that MedTrack will attempt to secure government financial assistance to aid in the startup financing, but no government funds have been included in the financial statements due to the uncertainty of the endeavor.

Financial Resources

The four equal partners will each invest $250,000 obtained through their own means. The four partners will also have resources beyond this initial investment such that they will require no salary in the first year of operation. For additional key personnel, reduced wages along with ownership stakes will be offered as a means to manage cash flow.

Financial Strategy

An initial investment of $6MM is required to begin operations. Beyond the $1MM invested by the four partners, an additional $5MM will be sought from a value-added venture capitalist who can contribute to the success of the business with connections, experience, and expertise.

After the first year, an additional $4MM is needed. A bond issue at 12 percent will be budgeted that can be called at the end of year. The venture capitalist will be asked to advise in this endeavor and there may be better alternatives to secure this additional $4MM.

Beyond the initial financing, MedTrack's fiscal strategy will promote the growth of the company. For example, MedTrack will invest heavily in R&D from the outset. In the first three years of operation, the R&D expenditure will be 38 percent of the entire operating budget. Then, beginning in year four, expenditures will be maintained at 10 percent of sales. This significant investment will be necessary to quickly launch the company and sustain a leadership role in the market.

MedTrack expects to achieve premium pricing on installations due to the value offered. While the hardware will be priced at a modest 10 percent markup (due to the commodity nature of the hardware business), the software, integration, training, and follow-on support will exhibit characteristics that position MedTrack for a sustainable competitive advantage. These resources are considered rare, valuable, and hard to copy.

Dividends will not be considered when organic growth opportunities exist. MedTrack will establish internal benchmarks for financial

EXHIBIT 7   Pro Forma Income Statement for MedTrack (U.S. $000s)

Year-by-Year Profit and Loss Assumptions	Year 1	Year 2	Year 3	Year 4	Year 5
Annual cumulative price (revenue) increase	—	2.0%	4.0%	6.0%	8.0%
Revenue	Year 1	Year 2	Year 3	Year 4	Year 5
Systems revenue ($2MM avg. per sys.)	$1,000	$8,160	$27,040	$61,480	$111,240
Maintenance rev. (5% of prev. 3 yrs. sys. rev.)	0	100	458	1,810	4,834
Total revenue	$1,000	$8,260	$27,498	$63,290	$116,074
Operating expenses					
COGS (20% of revenue)	$ 200	$1,652	$ 5,500	$12,658	$ 23,215
Selling (10% of systems revenue)	100	816	2,704	6,148	11,124
Administration	50	400	800	2,000	3,000
Salaries (15% of sales beg. yr. 2)	200	1,239	4,125	9,494	17,411
R & D (outsourced)	3,000	5,000	4,000	6,329	11,607
Lease costs (office, autos, equip)	30	245	541	1,230	2,225
Depreciation (minimal cap. invest. early)	5	50	87	175	329
Interest ($4MM bond @12%)	0	480	480	480	480
Total operating expenses	$3,585	$9,882	$18,236	$38,513	$ 69,391
Operating income before taxes	($2,585)	($1,622)	$ 9,262	$24,777	$ 46,683
Income tax expense (assumed 30% of IBT)	(776)	(487)	2,778	7,433	14,005
Net income (loss)	($1,810)	($1,135)	$ 6,483	$17,344	$ 32,678

performance comparable to those of similar public companies.

ORGANIZATION AND MANAGEMENT

Key Personnel Resources

The founding management team is composed of four very dedicated, knowledgeable, and diverse people with great determination to make MedTrack a winning company. The areas of focus will be the following:

- Ivanette Bonilla: CEO and R&D manager
- Dan Fillenwarth: Operations manager
- Sri Sampath: CFO
- Vassil Chalashkanov: Marketing and sales manager

The qualifications of the management team are outstanding. They include the following:

Ivanette Bonilla:

- Developed new batch records, implemented many process improvements, and organized justification for funding of new encapsulation equipment in the manufacturing area of the Procter & Gamble (P&G) pharmaceuticals plant in Puerto Rico.
- Executed technical and consumer research for comparison testing of several absorbent core materials in the feminine care business of P&G Cincinnati.
- Initiated execution of consumer purchase panel for product acceptance testing and purchase intent analysis.

EXHIBIT 8   Pro Forma Balance Sheet for MedTrack (U.S. $000s)

Assets	Initial Balance	Year 1	Year 2	Year 3	Year 4	Year 5
Cash and short-term investments	$6,000	$7,970	$4,651	$ 7,579	$17,382	$34,402
Accounts receivable (25% of sales)		250	2,065	6,875	15,823	29,019
Total inventory (2% of sales)		20	165	550	1,266	2,321
Prepaid expenses		0	0	0	0	0
Total current assets	$6,000	$8,240	$6,881	$15,004	$34,470	$65,742
Machinery and equipment		75	825	2,134	4,754	9,690
Less: Accumulated depreciation expense		5	55	142	317	646
Net property/equipment	0	70	770	1,992	4,437	9,044
Deferred income tax	0	0	0	0	0	0
Long-term investments	0	0	0	0	0	0
Deposits	0	0	0	0	0	0
Other long-term assets	0	0	0	0	0	0
Total assets	$6,000	$8,310	$7,651	$16,996	$38,907	$74,786
Liabilities						
Accounts payable (25% of expenses)	$ 0	$ 895	$2,338	$ 4,417	$ 9,465	$17,146
Accrued expenses	0	0	0	0	0	0
Capital leases	0	0	0	0	0	0
Total current liabilities	$ 0	$ 895	$2,338	$ 4,417	$ 9,465	$17,146
Long-term debt	0	4,000	4,000	4,000	4,000	0
Other long-term debt	0	0	0	0	0	0
Total debt	$ 0	$4,895	$6,338	$ 8,417	$13,465	$17,146
Other liabilities	0	0	0	0	0	0
Total liabilities	$ 0	$4,895	$6,338	$ 8,417	$13,465	$17,146
Equity						
Owner's equity (common)	$1,000	$1,000	$1,000	$ 1,000	$1,000	$1,000
Paid-in capital (Venture Capitalist)	5,000	5,000	5,000	5,000	5,000	5,000
Preferred equity	0	0	0	0	0	0
Retained earnings	0	(2,585)	(4,687)	2,578	19,442	51,640
Total equity	$6,000	$3,415	$1,313	$8,578	$25,442	$57,640
Total liabilities and equity	$6,000	$8,310	$7,651	$16,996	$38,907	$74,786

- Led tested product-making efforts and developed a questionnaire for several consumer tests.

- Designed new feminine protection pad product prototype for consumer test in focus group.

EXHIBIT 9   Pro Forma Cash Flow for MedTrack (U.S. $000's)

	Year 1	Year 2	Year 3	Year 4	Year 5	Total
Operating activities						
Net income	($1,810)	($1,135)	$6,483	$17,344	$32,678	$53,560
Depreciation	5	50	87	175	329	646
Accounts Receivable	(250)	(1,815)	(4,810)	(8,948)	(13,196)	(29,019)
Inventories	(20)	(145)	(385)	(716)	(1,056)	(2,321)
Accounts Payable	895	1,443	2,079	5,047	7,681	17,146
Deferred Income Taxes	(776)	(487)	1,262	0	0	0
Total operating activities	($1,955)	($2,089)	$4,718	$12,902	$26,436	$40,012
Investing activities						
Capital expenditures	($75)	($750)	($1,309)	($2,620)	($4,936)	($9,690)
Other investing cash flow items	0	0	0	0	0	0
Total investing activities	($75)	($750)	($1,309)	($2,620)	($4,936)	($9,690)
Financing activities						
Long-term debt/financing	$ 4,000	($480)	($480)	($480)	($4,480)	($1,920)
Preferred stock	0	0	0	0	0	0
Total cash dividends paid	0	0	0	0	0	0
Common stock	0	0	0	0	0	0
Other financing cash flow items	0	0	0	0	0	0
Total financing activies	$ 4,000	($480)	($480)	($480)	($4,480)	($1,920)
Cumulative cash flow	$ 1,970	($3,319)	$2,929	$9,802	$17,020	$28,402
Beginning cash balance	6,000	7,970	4,651	7,579	17,382	
Ending cash balance	$ 7,970	$4,651	$7,579	$17,382	$34,402	

Dan Fillenwarth:
- Led a team that effectively doubled the capacity of the EBPVD Praxair Surface Technologies plant in Indiana over the past four years.
- Implemented a series of engineering improvements to equipment in the plant that have increased output of current capital by 30 percent..
- Created and implemented a scheduling program that significantly improved communications throughout a 24/7 operation.

Sri Sampath:
- Developed a new design for a baby-care product that would combine the features of different products. Currently under prototype development.
- Developed conceptual design of a new exercise/therapy product for foot mas-

sage/exercise based on Asian therapeutic techniques.
- Developed conceptual design for a hair-care appliance.
- Partly financed several entrepreneurial ventures. One of the ventures was in the production of a mass-media product in India. Financed two other ventures in information technology development for the health-care industry. Of these two, one is an information-technology consulting firm in India that specializes in products and applications in medical-imaging technology. The other provides services to the health-care industry.
- Cofounded a community organization of volunteers to share Indian cultural heritage with local elementary school kids. This organization is currently evaluating proposals for creating a venture to build a local gathering place.

Vassil Chalashkanov:

- Designed, tested, and implemented a sales script aimed at introducing a standard selling method and increasing the effectiveness of sales efforts throughout all company-owned retail outlets in Bulgaria. Using the script ensures that all elements of the effective sales approach are used.
- Introduced new services to the market that required expanded facilities, and negotiated the rental contract and set up the warehouse space in a way that complies with the customs requirements for a bonded warehouse. Ensured the on-time licensing of the facilities to launch the new products sooner.
- Initiated a service center expansion project at DHL in 1998. The expansion was necessary to address the problem of insufficient geographic service coverage and imperfect performance indicators in same-day shipment departures and deliveries. Created partnerships with small, local service companies who had excess capacity and were willing to start delivering and collecting shipments on DHL's behalf in their area. Doubled the number of service centers in one year. Coverage and same-day performance improved dramatically.
- Worked closely with the CEO of the largest gasoline importer in Bulgaria and the regional chief of customs, who supported projects on several occasions by ensuring the speedy processing of licensing documentation.

Organizational Plan and Human Resource Strategy

MedTrack's Purpose. To significantly improve the quality and lower the cost of health care by enabling medical providers to accurately track medicines and equipment 100 percent of the time. To help hospitals save more lives.

MedTrack's Values (CRISP).

- Customer Focus—We are dedicated to exceeding the expectations of our stakeholders.
- Results Driven—We have a sense of urgency. We confront and overcome obstacles to achieve our objectives.
- Integrity—We will earn trust by honest and ethical business practices.
- Safety—We are committed to providing reliable tracking systems to ensure patient health and safety.
- People Driven—We enable our customers to keep patients safer. We will value our employees by providing them a safe and innovative environment.

MedTrack's Mission. MedTrack will eliminate deaths related to preventable tracking errors in hospitals by supplying an accurate and efficient tracking system. The system will provide value to hospitals and increase patient satisfaction. The goal is to make incorrect administration of medicine and patient wait for life-saving equipment a thing of the past.

MedTrack's Goal. MedTrack's Goal is to establish itself in hospitals throughout the 50 states in five years and become the largest provider in the world of medicine-tracking systems within ten years.

Organizational Plan. The organization will be built on a commitment to provide a safe, equitable, and innovative workplace environment with an emphasis on valuing people. MedTrack's core values and strong commitment to human resources will enable the company to not only attract talented individuals, but also retain them. In addition, this will enable MedTrack to change the focus from a compensation-based organization to an organization that values people and their contributions, thereby providing better motivation and satisfaction to employees.

The initial organizational plan will be to

staff the R&D department, as R&D will be a key platform for building growth, and to hire experienced ERP implementation project managers to help minimize the risks involved in these types of projects. In addition, MedTrack will be building its marketing and distribution network, thereby ensuring that distributors and in-house sales force are equipped to provide all the necessary information hospitals will need to make their purchasing decisions. Initial management of human resources (HR) will be shared by the other managers. As MedTrack continues to grow, it will staff a separate HR department to manage employee relations and a purchasing department to manage relationships with suppliers. Particular emphasis will be provided to customer service and training. The customer service department will be state of the art, as it will have an area that will be dedicated to providing excellent training to customers and another that will focus on ensuring proper functionality of all systems. MedTrack will also strengthen its R&D department by hiring the best software developers and an IT manager who will help guide the continuous improvement of all systems. Through marketing research, MedTrack will always be in tune with the customer's needs. Furthermore, the company will continuously focus on the development and training of all employees because this will be critical in maintaining competitive advantage.

MedTrack will reward people who respect the company's purpose and values and who work toward the company's goals.

OWNERSHIP

Form of the Business

The most appropriate legal form of the business is a C corporation. That form will ensure the limited liability of the owners, as well as the continued life of the firm after its founders withdraw from the business. The drawback is the "double taxation" of profits at the corporate and personal income tax levels. However, the effect of this shortcoming will be mitigated by the plans of the founders not to take salaries for the first year, and compensated by the ability of the corporate legal form to participate easily in an IPO.

Equity Positions

The founders plan to retain 87 percent of initial equity and use the remaining shares to finance the venture. Further dilution of the founders' equity is expected as additional management staff is hired. In order to benefit from the experience of its investor(s), MedTrack will look for a value-added VC with experience in the high-tech sector and RFID in particular. The projected five-year cash flows have been estimated based on a 40 percent IRR for the VCs, which is comparable to existing VC expectations.

The founders have a total of $1 million of personal funds to invest. The remaining $5 million of the $6 million initial investment will be obtained through a VC firm. Allocating 13 percent of the total cash flow to the repayment of the VC's investment will give MedTrack an IRR of 40 percent.

CRITICAL RISKS AND CONTINGENCIES

The risks associated with the critical success factors for this new venture are important insofar as they could jeopardize the entire endeavor. There are several critical success factors that will determine the course of the enterprise. The first is defining and sticking with the firm's core competence. MedTrack's strategy will be to differentiate itself by offering a complete tracking solution that fits customers' needs, rather than simply providing the RFID technology.

MedTrack's core competence will be its ability to understand hospitals' tracking needs better that any of the direct competitors or other providers of RFID technology, and to design the system that meets these needs. To that end, MedTrack's strategy will

EXHIBIT 10.   Deal Structure (U.S. $000s)

	Year 0	Year 1	Year 2	Year 3	Year 4	Year 5
Investment	($6,000)					
Cumulative cash flow		$1,970	($3,319)	$2,929	$9,802	$ 17,020
Terminal Value						170,204
Net cash flow	($6,000)	$1,970	($3,319)	$2,929	$9,802	$187,224
Source of Investment						
Founders' savings	($1,000)	$1,712	($2,884)	$2,544	$8,517	$162,670
Venture Capitalist(s)/ Banks	(5,000)	258	(435)	384	1,286	24,554
Remaining	$ 0	$ 0	$ 0	$ 0	$ 0	$ 0

be to keep the design of the software and architecture of the system in-house, but to outsource its development, manufacturing, and sales. The relevant risk associated with this core competence is failing to bring the right people on board. Getting the right kind and caliber of professionals into the organization will be important for bringing the idea to life. MedTrack must employ people with significant hospital management experience who are software design professionals as well as astute business managers.

Making the right partnerships will be another important success factor. Regardless of how well designed the product is, its execution will depend entirely on other companies' abilities. The product can fail due to badly written software, defective hardware, or inept distribution efforts. To control any of the numerous risks, MedTrack must have a stringent supplier selection process and such selection criteria that will ensure the firm's partners are of the highest quality and reputation.

While getting the product right will be important, there will be the risk of waiting too long before its release to such an extent that rival companies will have already made a significant head start in filling market demand. Even though the specific hospital market is still wide open, MedTrack should work on a tight schedule in the development and release of its first system in order to take advantage of the opportunity. Seizing opportunities in its market should become another competence for MedTrack. As its rivals mul-

tiply and become stronger and more focused, the only way for MedTrack to stay ahead will be by taking its offering one step further through innovation.

Research suggests that a significant portion of enterprise-wide ERP implementations fail because of mistakes such as delay in implementation, cost overruns, or both. MedTrack's implementations carry the same kinds of risks as ERP implementations. A disappointing implementation will incur additional costs and damage its fragile reputation in its initial development stages. Hiring experienced implementation project managers as well as focusing on quality will minimize those risks.

Discussion. This schedule is aggressive. Prior to the legal start of MedTrack, the founding partners will be engaged in identifying key staff members and beginning the marketing that will result in the launch hospital.

Many operational elements will overlap to provide the launch system on a compressed time scale:

- Based on MedTrack marketing knowledge, we will develop most of the software prior to securing the first contract. After the launch contract is complete, software customization can be completed as needed.
- MedTrack will procure limited materials prior to contract completion. Some risk attaches here.

EXHIBIT 11   Scheduling and Milestones

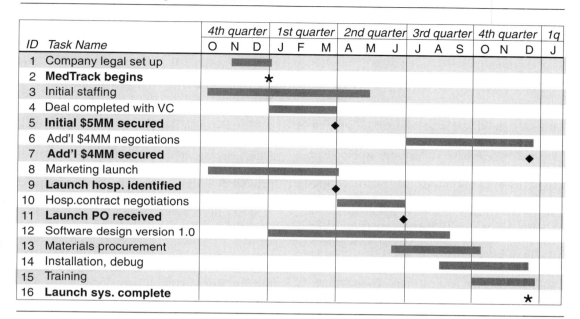

- Installation will be ongoing while materials are received.
- Training on the system basics will begin approximately 10 weeks prior to system completion. Several different training modules will be provided for the various system users.

Two contracts will be secured near the end of year one and two contracts early in year two to meet the sales forecast for year two.

SUMMARY AND CONCLUSIONS

MedTrack believes that RFID technology is poised for replacing the decades-old bar-code technology. This transition will lead to an exponential growth in RFID applications. The health-care industry and hospitals in particular will have significant opportunities to not only save on the cost of supplies and equipment, but also to provide better quality care and treatment to their patients. As an early entrant to tap this market, MedTrack will have a big opportunity to establish, grow, and become a trailblazer. MedTrack's strong business plan supports this vision.

NOTES

1. http://knowledge.wharton.upenn.edu/index.cfm?fa=viewArticle&id=1161
2. *Hospital Security and Safety Management* 21, no. 10, February 2001: 5-8.
3. *Hospital Security and Safety Management* 19, no. 7, November 1998: 5-9.
4. *Hospital Security and Safety Management* 11, no. 7, November 1990: 5-8.
5. *American Journal of Hospital Pharmacy* 38, no. 7, July 1981:1007-1010
6. *Hospital Security and Safety Management* 15, no. 10, February 16, 1996: 5-10.
7. http://www.hhs.gov/healthit/
8. www.statehealthfacts.org
9. http://www.oshpd.cahwnet.gov/HQAD/Hospital/financial/hospAF.htm.
10. Maureen Glabman, "Room for Tracking RFID." http://www.hospitalconnect.com.

CASE 2

Rubio's: Home of the Fish Taco (A)

FOUNDING AND EARLY YEARS

Rubio's Restaurants Inc., formerly known as Rubio's Deli-Mex, was founded as a family-owned and operated Mexican restaurant located in southern California. Rubio's specializes in authentic, fresh-tasting Mexican food using authentic Mexican recipes. Rubio's is best known, however, for its fish tacos, which were relatively unknown in San Diego prior to Rubio's entry in 1983. Although Rubio's is known as the "Home of the Fish Taco," the menu also offers a variety of other, more traditional Mexican favorites such as burritos and carnitas. Designed as a fast-food restaurant, Rubio's gives its customers the options of ordering the food for consumption on the premises or ordering it for carryout. Rubio's offers an alternative to the full-service Mexican restaurant without sacrificing quality. The success of this concept has been phenomenal. After opening in 1983 with one location near Mission Bay, Rubio's grew in just 9 years (1992), to 12 restaurants extending from San Diego to Orange County.

HISTORY

The concept for Rubio's restaurants was first developed in the late 1970s during one of Ralph Rubio's camping adventures in San Felipe on the Baja peninsula, Mexico. According to the legend, it was on one of these excursions that Ralph observed numerous American tourists lined up to purchase fish tacos from the San Felipe beach vendors.

Source: This case was prepared in 1992 by Professor Kenneth E. Marino of San Diego State University with the assistance of graduate student Linda Kelleher Carter. It is intended as a basis for class discussion rather than to illustrate effective or ineffective handling of an administrative situation.

Over the years, taco stands proliferated in San Felipe. Ralph figured that fish tacos would be as popular in San Diego as they were in the Baja. He solicited one of the veteran beach vendors, "Carlos," to move to San Diego and open a restaurant that featured these tacos. Although Carlos declined, he provided Ralph with his "secret family recipe" for fish tacos. Ralph carried this recipe with him for five years after his 1978 graduation from San Diego State University. Armed with his liberal arts degree, eight years' experience in the restaurant industry, and $30,000 from his father, Ralph opened the first Rubio's on January 25, 1983. It was located on East Mission Bay Drive in the Pacific Beach area of San Diego, California, on the site of a previously failed hamburger restaurant. Despite Ralph's lack of a menu just two days before the restaurant's scheduled opening, the first week's sales averaged $250 a day and the restaurant was packed. Within three years, sales at the restaurant grew to $2,000 a day. Based on the success of the first restaurant, in March 1986 a second location was opened on College Avenue near San Diego State University. Shortly thereafter, in August 1987, Rubio's opened its third location near Pacific Beach. Rubio's expansion has continued at a rapid rate. Rubio's now has 12 locations from as far south as Chula Vista to as far north as Irvine.

THE FAST-FOOD INDUSTRY (1991)

The United States food service industry estimated its 1991 sales at $248.1 billion. The second-largest category of restaurants in the food service industry is the limited-menu outlets, which consist largely of fast-food restaurants such as Rubio's. Sales in this category of food providers are estimated for 1991 at $74.1 billion. According to the National Restaurant Association (NRA), fast-food restaurants have enjoyed rapid growth. In fact, from 1970 to 1990, sales in these limited-menu restaurants have increased at an estimated 12.9 percent compound rate, compared with 7.9 percent for the remainder of the U.S. food service industry.

The success of the fast-food industry, a relatively mature, highly competitive business, is believed to be the result of changing demographics and lifestyles. Over the past several decades, more Americans have been turning to restaurants for their meals. Dual-income families made the option of dining out a necessity because of the families' lack of spare time. At the same time, additional income made dining out more affordable. The fast-food industry has also managed to sell its customers on the value and convenience their products and services offer. This perception has been enhanced by the addition of drive-through windows, which enable customers to order and be served in their cars. Restaurants have further catered to customers' idea of convenience by adding delivery to the current list of services offered. Despite these positive indicators, Rubio's faced several challenges at that time. The relatively weaker economy of 1991 and 1992 led to higher unemployment and an increase in meals prepared and consumed in the home. The fast-food industry was also threatened by several other factors, including environmental pressures, increased nutritional awareness, the AIDS scare, and governmental legislation. As a player in the fast-food industry, Rubio's monitored the arena in which it participated and responded to the following opportunities and challenges.

Changing Demographics

Aging Population. The United States is simultaneously experiencing a rise in life expectancy and a decline in the number of people ages 15 to 34. The net effect of these trends is an aging U.S. population. This change in demographics is likely to have a significant impact on the fast-food industry. First, as the population of consumers grows older, it is likely their tastes will shift toward midscale restaurants and away from the fast-food industry. In fact, according to a 1988 study conducted by the NRA, customers ages 18 to 24 eat out at fast-food restaurants 79 percent of the time; individuals ages 45 to 54 eat out at fast-food restaurants only 60 percent of the time. The difference between these age groups is allegedly the result of older patrons' higher disposable income and their desire for additional amenities.

The Baby Boomers. The second impact of the changing demographics results from the rise in birth rates. Although double-income families have less time for food preparation, baby boomers started having families of their own by the early 1970s. As a result, there are more households with small children who are less likely to dine out. Instead, these families are utilizing such conveniences as microwaves and take-out and delivery services.

The Decline in Teenagers. Finally, the decline in the birth rate in the early 1970s has resulted in a decrease in the number of youths between the ages of 16 and 20. The fast-food segment of the restaurant industry has traditionally relied on this category of individuals as its main source of labor. As a result, fast-food restaurants have had a harder time attracting and retaining employees. This has, to a degree, been alleviated by the vast amount of unemployment resulting from the 1991-1992 recession. However, the overall change in demographics is forcing the fast-food industry to adjust accordingly.

Nutritional Concerns

In addition to the changes associated with an aging population, the fast-food industry must also respond to changes in customers' needs and concerns. Baby boomers are becoming preoccupied with healthier eating, and fast-food restaurants are responding accordingly. Individuals are now concerned not only with value and convenience, but also with the fat and cholesterol content of the items offered by fast-food restaurants. As a result, restaurants are changing their menus and product offerings to emphasize, or deemphasize, the benefits of their products.

In an effort to lure customers, McDonald's launched the new McLean Deluxe, a burger that boasted only 9 percent fat because of the use of seaweed substitutes. Although purportedly healthier, the new item costs the consumer a $0.20 premium over the usual quarter-pounder, which has twice the fat. McDonald's also followed the lead of other fast-food restaurants by switching to 100 percent vegetable oil from a blend containing beef tallow for cooking fries and hash browns. Encouraged by consumer acceptance of these products, McDonald's replaced its ice cream with low-fat yogurt, introduced low-fat milk shakes, and even added cereal and bran muffins to its menu. In June 1991, McDonald's introduced, as limited time promotional items, a 90-calorie Diet Coke float and a 275-calorie grilled chicken sandwich. Other fast-food restaurants, such as Burger King and KFC, have also changed their product offerings to cater to consumers' health concerns. These changes reflect the need of fast-food restaurants to change in response to the needs and concerns of a changing population.

Governmental Legislation

Teen Labor Laws. The fast-food industry must also deal with changes in the legislation that affect it. One such area of legislation is teen labor laws. Current legislation prohibits 14- and 15-year-old persons from working on school nights after 7:00 p.m., a time when restaurants usually need a full staff to deal with the dinner crowd. Representatives in the industry have been advocating changes in these restrictions to permit teenagers (1) to work a maximum of four hours on days before school days, one hour more than currently allowed, and (2) to work until 9:00 p.m. on school nights, two hours past the current restriction. Industry advocates are also seeking an extension of the cooking and baking activities these workers are legally

permitted to perform. These proposed changes would help ease the pressures on restaurant managers who are attempting to deal with the limited workforce. However, the industry's lobbyists met much resistance. In fact, several legislators were seeking to enact certain bills that would increase the pressures on the fast-food industry's hiring practices. One proposed bill would substantially increase penalties for serious infractions of federal teen labor laws to include prison terms for employers whose willful violations resulted in the serious injury of a teenage employee. Another provision of the bill sought a requirement that all applicants under the age of 18 secure a state-issued work permit if they do not possess a high school diploma. Industry representatives believed that regulations such as these would decrease the number of teenagers hired, thereby hurting the exact individuals whom the laws were designed to protect.

Federal Minimum Wage Hike. Legislation in other areas may also affect the fast-food industry. On April 1, 1991, the federal minimum wage rose from $3.80 to $4.25, with a subminimum exception for persons who have never before held a job. Payroll expenses generally account for 26 percent of all sales dollars. According to a survey conducted by Oregon State University, fast-food outlets were relatively unscathed because the majority of their employees already earn between $5.50 and $6.00 an hour. Although full-service restaurants were hit the hardest by this legislation, labor is the second-biggest cost for all restaurant operators.

Mandated Health Plans. The food service industry also faces an increase in labor costs from legislation related to mandated health plans. Legislators are pushing for a bill that would require employers to provide all their employees with health insurance or face a special payroll tax of 7 percent to 8 percent. The special payroll tax would then be used to fund a federally administered insurance program for low-income Americans. If enacted, the industry feared that many small restaurant operations would be forced out of business by the expensive plan. As an alternative, industry advocates are seeking tax breaks and other incentives designed to encourage restaurant owners to voluntarily provide health insurance to employees.

Discrimination in the Workplace. The fast-food industry is also monitoring proposed legislation intended to curtail job discrimination by allowing workers the right to have juries decide lawsuits against employers suspected of discrimination in the workplace. The act would permit the victims of discrimination to seek both compensatory and punitive damages, an option previously restricted to persons charging racial discrimination. Industry advocates contend that this legislation would shift the burden of the culpability test to require a business to prove its innocence rather than requiring the plaintiff to prove its guilt. As such, restaurants would be forced to resort to hiring persons because of their demographic traits rather than their abilities. Although the original form of the act would not have passed, proponents have negotiated a compromise with the White House guaranteeing its passage.

AIDS, *E. coli*, and Customer Health. The fast-food industry cannot escape the effects of the AIDS controversy. According to the executive vice president of the NRA, Bill Fisher, a number of restaurants are identified as employing individuals either suffering from AIDS or infected with HIV. Once identified, the restaurants suffer a rapid decline in business and are often forced to close. As of July 1990, food service lobbyists were attempting to revive the Chapman Amendment (as it was known in the House), a measure that would exempt food service operators from providing employees with AIDS the same rights and privileges as their healthy peers. Employers would then be able to reassign infected employees to positions of comparable salary that did not involve any food handling. Contrary to the food industry's desires, the Senate enacted the Hatch Amendment, which is similar to the

Chapman Amendment with one added qualification. It provides that the secretary of the U.S. Health and Human Services Department specify annually the diseases that can be transmitted through food. The Hatch Amendment further provides that only persons with a designated illness may be reassigned. According to Dr. Louis Sullivan, former secretary of the U.S. Health and Human Services Department, AIDS cannot be spread through food or beverages. The net effect of enacting this law is that food handlers with AIDS may retain their posts, and restaurants are virtually defenseless against consumers' fears.

The winter of 1993 saw an outbreak of illness caused by *E. coli* bacteria infection. A total of 475 cases of illness and three deaths were reported in the West, predominantly in the state of Washington. The cause has been attributed to tainted hamburger meat served at fast-food establishments operated by Foodmaker, Inc. (Jack in the Box). Review of meat vendor qualifications and cooking procedures was immediately undertaken, but a precipitous decline in sales could not be avoided. It was not known whether Foodmaker would survive or what kinds of federal legislation might follow.

Environmental Pressures

The fast-food industry was also facing increasing pressure from environmental groups to become more concerned over the ecological effect of its products and packaging. According to these environmental groups, chlorofluorocarbons (CFCs) used in the production of the plastic packaging used by the fast-food industry are responsible for damage to the ozone layer, which protects life on earth from the harmful effects of the sun's ultraviolet rays. Environmentalists also contend that the plastic packaging made of polystyrene foam takes up valuable space in landfills, takes decades to decompose, and has no viable recycling market. Despite some studies that indicated that the packaging is environmentally sound, McDonald's, the world's largest restaurant chain, began replacing plastic packaging in favor of paper. Although the paper is not recyclable and requires tremendous chemical and industrial processes to create it, it is biodegradable if composted and requires less space than foam packaging when discarded. McDonald's explained some of the factors leading to its switch, citing its lack of success at recapturing the packaging that leaves its restaurants and the lack of an infrastructure in the plastics-recycling industry. However, the company's 1990 annual report explains the real impetus for McDonald's change: "Although scientific studies indicate that foam packaging is sound, customers just don't feel good about it." Several other fast-food companies have also initiated environmental policies that involve recyclable polystyrene and biodegradable paper and plastic. McDonald's plan, however, was the most sweeping in the industry. The company replaced its large white take-out bags with brown recyclable ones, converted to smaller napkins, installed stainless steel condiment dispensers to eliminate the need for packets, composted eggshells and coffee grounds, and tested starch-based spoons, knives, and forks as substitutes for current plastic versions. The company further challenged its vendors to recycle and required periodic progress reports that evidence the suppliers' use of recycled material in containers.

Suppliers

Food and beverage suppliers to the fast-food industry exert power on the participants by raising prices or reducing the quality of their products and/or services. One way a restaurant may deal with its suppliers is through backward integration. McDonald's entertained such a move and entered the business of raising cattle. Naturally, the environmentalists who condemn the use of plastics also condemn the raising of cattle—their grazing habits cause erosion and their waste pollutes the ground and air.

Rivalry among Competitors

As a member of the fast-food industry, Rubio's competes with numerous types of restaurants, ranging from individual independent operations to franchises and chains. Rivalry among competitors results from a number of factors, including fixed costs. Fixed costs in the restaurant industry, which include labor costs, utility bills, and the interest expense on buildings, land, and equipment, are quite high. Restaurants have developed a variety of alternatives to compete by reducing their fixed costs.

Contract Services. PepsiCo Inc.'s Taco Bell has adopted one way to reduce high fixed costs. Since the mid-1980s, Taco Bell shifted as much of the food preparation to outside providers as possible. By contracting with these outside suppliers, Taco Bell reduced not only labor costs but kitchen space as well. This reduction in fixed costs has allowed Taco Bell to slash its menu prices, thereby attracting 60 percent more customers and reaching sales of $2.6 billion, a 63 percent increase.

Robotics. The desire of fast-food restaurants to reduce their labor costs has resulted in several more imaginative alternatives. Taco Bell investigated whether robotics in the kitchen would increase savings by reducing space and labor requirements. Within two years, they expected to adopt automatic taco makers and soft-drink dispensers. Carl Jr.'s restaurant is utilizing an automated ordering system, dubbed "Touch 2000," which allows customers to enter their own selections on a touch-sensitive countertop menu. The menu is connected to an IBM computer that checks the order and prompts the customer for more specific information if it is not satisfied. When satisfied, the computer relays the order automatically to the kitchen and the cashier. Burger King evaluated the system as well. Although robotics reduce labor costs, increase productivity, and virtually eliminate boring jobs, not all fast-food restaurants are converting to their use. The economy made human labor more available, reduced restaurant profits, and forced cutbacks in spending on research and development.

Reduced-Sized Restaurants. Restaurants were also developing downsized units in an effort to reduce costs and gain access to towns that were previously dismissed because of their inability to generate sufficient sales to sustain a full-size outlet. McDonald's new prototype, called the "Series 2000," was 50 percent smaller and cost 30 percent less to build. These units seat 50 patrons and employ only 20 persons per shift. McDonald's traditional units seat twice as many customers and require, at a minimum, 40 employees per shift. These downsized units not only allowed the chain to enter small towns, but also allowed the company to secure locations in congested markets that were previously inaccessible because of the limited size of available sites.

Value Menus. Fast-food restaurants have also explored a variety of strategies to attract customers during hard economic times. In an attempt to compete for the consumer's dollar, Red Lobster, a dinner house, launched a value menu that boasts numerous entrées for less than $10. In addition, the chain upgraded its china, uniforms, and napkins to enhance its image of providing the customer with value. Although fast-food restaurants must proceed cautiously to ensure that the customer's need for quick service is satisfied, many fast-food restaurants are also opting for expanded menus to attract customers. McDonald's has also unveiled new menu selections designed to boost sales. Of particular concern to Rubio's is the addition of two Mexican items, the breakfast burrito and the chicken fajita. McDonald's is also testing turkey and pizza as other menu options. McDonald's U.S. president, Ed Rensi, does not anticipate that the addition of these new products will dilute the company's concept of serving hot fast food in a pleasant environment at a low cost. In fact, new technology should enable McDonald's to broaden its menu while maintaining good service times. Other fast-food restaurants have responded to this threat by promoting time-intensive products on a limited basis only.

Taco Bell, the nation's leading Mexican fast-food restaurant, is credited with having started these discount wars with the addition of its 59-cent and 39-cent value menu items. As operating profits for the third quarter of 1991 decreased, analysts wondered whether Taco Bell's value menu had discounted the chain out of a profit margin. However, according to Taco Bell president John Martin, the chain will not need to raise prices for at least five years because of its systemic restructuring and cost-saving technological changes in operational methods.

Marketing Strategies. Restaurants have also explored other marketing strategies in an attempt to attract customers. Burger King developed a Kids Club to capitalize on the power of children to influence the purchases of their parents. Burger King entices its 2.7 million members with six newsletters "written" by well-known cartoon characters. The members also receive iron-on T-shirt logos and activity booklets. Burger King analysts credit the club for a recognizable increase in the chain's business. Burger King is also investigating other marketing alternatives to increase consumer spending. To further reach its teenage market, Burger King bought time on Channel One, a satellite service that beams 12 minutes of programming and commercials each day into school classrooms. It is believed that a 30-second commercial on Channel One reaches 40 percent more teens than a commercial on MTV. Finally, Burger King is spending a portion of its advertising budget on local tie-ins to help build traffic at its franchises.

Delivery Service. Fast-food restaurants such as Burger King are also attempting to prod the dinner crowd, which would ordinarily select a midrange restaurant, by offering limited table service during the dinner hour. Customers place their orders at a walk-up counter, serve themselves a drink, and select a seat. When ready, their order is served to them at their table. Although Burger King does not intend to raise its prices as a result of this new service, the effects remain to be seen.

Acknowledging that the 1990s were a decade dedicated to convenience, pizza restaurants were not alone in their home delivery service. Although KFC franchisees were reluctant and anticipated operational difficulties, KFC was planning to add delivery service to all 500 of its domestic units. Because no other chicken segment player offered home delivery, it was an opportunity to preempt its competitors and gain a competitive edge.

Payment Convenience. Fast-food restaurants were also experimenting with the use of bank cards and ATM cards as alternative methods for payment. MasterCard, which wants people to use its card for everyday transactions, estimates that 70 percent of the people who eat at fast-food restaurants have a bank card. Arby's tested the system and discovered that bank card transactions exceed cash purchases by 30 percent to 60 percent. As a result, Arby's installed the system in all company-owned stores. McDonald's was also experimenting with a McCharge card for use in its outlets.

Expanding Distribution Channels. In addition to expanding product lines, restaurants are also looking for new points of distribution. Aided by new technology, fast-food restaurants have moved into many nontraditional outlets. PepsiCo, which owns Taco Bell, Pizza Hut, and KFC, will expand into any outlet where it may tempt hungry consumers. As a result, PepsiCo's food service brands may now be seen in supermarkets, convenience stores, movie theaters, student unions, amusement parks, fairs, hospitals, airports, and sports arenas. Taco Bell is also entertaining the possibility of selling packaged meals on supermarket shelves, a potentially lucrative market given that a quarter of the people aged 35 to 44 are single.

THE RUBIO'S FOUNDING CONCEPT

Product Line

Rubio's main draw was its $1.49 fish tacos. A fish taco consists of a soft corn tortilla, pieces of deep-fried fish fillet, salsa, white sauce, cabbage, and a lime. The white sauce is made up of a mixture of mayonnaise and yogurt. Although the basic ingredients in the fish taco are known, because of local taco wars, Rubio's batter for the fish remains a company secret. As a result, the batter was packaged at a location other than the individual restaurants. Rubio's also offered a fish taco *especial*, which cost a little more but was prepared with such extras as guacamole, jack and cheddar cheese, cilantro, and onion. For those patrons who do not savor the idea of a fish taco, Rubio's menu offered such other traditional Mexican favorites as burritos, tostadas, nachos, and nonfish tacos. Consistent with the company's desire to satisfy the needs of its customers, menu items have been added or modified in response to customer input. All these items, including the fish tacos, are prepared to order using authentic Mexican recipes and fresh ingredients. A copy of Rubio's 1991 menu is attached as Exhibit 1.

In addition to providing authentic, fresh-tasting Mexican food, Rubio's differentiated itself by offering a cold food menu, enabling customers to purchase select ingredients to prepare their own meals at home. In essence, customers may purchase the makings for almost every item on the menu.

Facilities

Rubio's original restaurant locations were selected based on Ralph Rubio's knowledge of the areas and characteristics of their population. Although Rubio's target market varies to some extent by store location, on the whole its market consists of young and middle-aged upscale professionals and students. Members of these groups typically value their health and enjoy such social activities as the beach, athletic competition, musical entertainment, and dining out. As a result, the facilities are typically located in fast-growing retail areas with high traffic and visibility. Rubio's also considers the land use mix within a three-to-five-mile radius. As a result, the restaurants are located in areas with high percentages of residential and office or industrial uses. Unlike the typical inaccessible mall location, these locations provide a greater number of customers with the characteristics of Rubio's target market and more flexible operating hours.

Under the Rubio family's direction, the exterior style and interior design of each of Rubio's restaurants is consistent throughout their 12 locations. The typical unit features a walk-up order counter with a large red-and-white-lettered menu behind it. Paper menus, which detail the company's phone-in order policy, are also provided. The units' decor is contemporary, with light wood, green wallpaper, color framed prints, and Mexican tile tables. A mural of the company mascot, Pesky Pescado, usually appears on one wall. (Pesky is an animated fish, standing upright on his tail, with a taco shell wrapped around his body.) The typical unit also features decorations that emphasize a beach theme, including surfboards, palms, green-and-white walls, ceiling fans, and beach scenes. This upscale atmosphere is further enhanced by a sound system that plays authentic mariachi music.

Although the units vary slightly by location, most have 2,200 square feet, with a cooking area, a dining area for approximately 50 people, and an outdoor patio. Each restaurant features an area where customers may purchase deli items and/or a variety of promotional items, such as T-shirts, bumper stickers, and decals. All units, other than the original one near Mission Bay and the SDSU location, have beer and wine licenses, a feature intended to strengthen Rubio's image as a fast-food alternative to fine Mexican restaurants. Consistent with the company's emphasis on service and convenience to the customer, one restaurant site also features a drive-through facility.

Each Rubio's location also has a designated receptacle for recycling bottles and cans used in the restaurant. Given that there is no consensus on whether plastic or paper is better for the environment, Rubio's continued to use clamshell containers, which have better thermal retention. Rubio's did, however, switch to tray service to reduce the amount of paper used in each facility. Therefore, each facility also has an area des-ignated for tray storage. As the recycling infrastructure grows, Rubio's continues to monitor plastic recycling. Once the decision to recycle is made, each facility must also designate space for plastics recycling.

In addition to these 12 restaurant locations, in April 1990 Rubio's joined the concession lineup at Jack Murphy Stadium. By May, Rubio's had expanded to the plaza level in an effort to meet the enormous demand at the stadium for its product. More recently, Rubio's joined the concessions at the Irvine Meadows Amphitheater.

Unit Operations

The typical unit has 15 to 25 employees, depending on the amount of customer traffic. Each unit has one general manager, two assistant managers, a cashier, an expediter, a prep clerk, four line clerks, a shift leader, and a customer service employee. To ensure uniformity throughout its facilities, the company has developed job descriptions for each of these positions. A sample of these descriptions is contained in Exhibit 2.

Despite the increase in the federal minimum wage rate, Rubio's employees have not been affected. On average, the employees make an hourly wage that already exceeds the new federal minimum. Unit structure and wage scales are presented in Exhibit 3.

In addition to a higher minimum wage, full-time employees are also offered various benefits, such as health insurance. Although Rubio's offers its full-time employees health insurance, only 30 percent currently take advantage of this benefit. Rubio's believed that this may be a result of cultural differences. As a result, Rubio's engaged in direct marketing of its health insurance plan to its employees in an effort to increase participation rates to 70 percent. Rubio's made this effort despite the anticipated increase in costs to the company.

Marketing Strategy

Despite the fact that San Diego shares a border with Mexico, Ralph Rubio recognized that no other restaurant in the area was serving authentic Mexican food. By offering fresh-tasting, authentic Mexican food in a contemporary, clean atmosphere, Rubio's targeted a key segment of the market: young, upscale professionals and students, ages 18 to 49, with a taste for better food. Rubio's success is, therefore, the result of carving out a special niche in an otherwise crowded fast-food market.

During its first couple of years of operation, Rubio's rarely advertised. Instead, early efforts were concentrated on ensuring that the total concept, from the menu to the decor, was designed to satisfy the customer's needs and desires. Yet despite this lack of advertising, Rubio's was attracting new and repeat customers. Rubio's promoted its business in at least three media—print, radio, and television—that appeal to consumers within its targeted market. Rubio's is currently investigating the idea of poster panels and billboards as an additional medium to access its target market. Advertising objectives and strategies were:

Advertising Objectives:
- Increase "trial" visits to Rubio's within target audience, adults 18 to 49.
- Encourage repeat visits to Rubio's.
- Increase overall awareness of Rubio's.
- Generate awareness of Rubio's new location(s).

Advertising Strategies:
- Implement a consistent, chain-wide media plan in San Diego that will effectively reach the target market.
- Execute local store marketing efforts in San Diego for grand openings and locations with special needs.
- Implement a localized media and promotions plan in Orange County with emphasis on the Irvine location.
- Administer sales promotion during heavy advertising periods.

As in the past, Rubio's used local cable television channels and radio stations to promote its products. Although the commercials were relatively simple, they were designed to increase consumer awareness of Rubio's products. By tying the commercials to specific promotions, the effect was to increase regular foot traffic in Rubio's facilities as well as to attract first-time customers unfamiliar with fish tacos. Current advertising also seeks to generate awareness not only for Rubio's products but for its new locations as well.

Rubio's also used direct mail to attract customers. With direct mail, Rubio's was able to identify potential customers within a five-mile radius of a new or existing restaurant. Rubio's believed that if it were able to persuade potential customers to try its product once, they would become repeat customers.

In addition to direct promotions, Rubio's participated in numerous indirect promotions. Rubio's sponsored local athletic events such as the San Diego International Triathlon. Rubio's also sent a 15-foot inflatable version of Pesky Pescado to local parades, sporting events, and restaurant openings. Pesky, Jr., an inflatable human-sized costume, also makes local appearances. These marketing efforts represent 2.5 percent of sales, or $256,000. As Rubio's expanded throughout southern California, it continued to educate its potential customers through the use of these media and promotions.

Management

Despite its growth from one small restaurant in 1983 to over 12 locations throughout southern California, Rubio's remained a closely held corporation with ownership split among the family members. Ralph and Ray Rubio (Ralph's father) are the founders and majority stockholders. Ralph Rubio was acting president of the company. Ralph's brothers and sister filled the other key positions in the company: Robert was vice president of operations, Richard was vice president of expansion, and Gloria was vice president of training. The youngest Rubio, Roman, assisted Gloria at corporate headquarters with training. Although Rubio's brought in outside people to fill management positions, the family intended to maintain ownership and control for as long as possible.

As a relatively young, family-owned

organization, Rubio's was characterized by centralized management and control. The company offered extensive training programs for its managers and employees to ensure efficiency and standardization in the production of its products. This policy was evidenced by its thorough and detailed operations manual. As the business expanded, managers were provided with a sufficient degree of flexibility to handle day-to-day operations tailored to the needs of each individual store. Ultimate authority, however, remained with the Rubio family.

Finances

As a privately held company, the majority of Rubio's growth has been achieved with funds generated from within. Early expansion was also assisted by bank financing. The company's growth was relatively slow and cautious. Sales, however, have not been slow. The combined sales from the 12 restaurant locations averaged over 10,000 fish tacos per day. Including sales of other menu items, the average Rubio's store had sales of $700,000 during 1991. This figure represents a decline from 1990, when the average store had sales of $745,000. Each store unit is, however, designed to handle $1 million in annual sales, leaving plenty of opportunity for an increase in sales. Rubio's goal for the next several years is to increase the average store's sales to over $800,000.

Even with the current decrease in sales, the stores are quite profitable. To break even, the typical store must achieve monthly sales of approximately $30,000 to $35,000. The main cost difference among Rubio's facilities results from different lease costs. Labor and material costs remain the same across facilities. Food ingredients represent about 16 percent of the sales price of menu items. The ingredients breakdown for the fish taco and the fish taco *especial* are presented in Exhibit 4.

A LOOK TO THE FUTURE

Ralph's belief that the fish taco would be as popular in San Diego as it was in the Baja was correct—and judging from the amount of sales and the number of imitators, it is here to stay. Although Rubio's already has 12 restaurant locations, its goal is 50 company-owned restaurants in southern California averaging sales of $40 to $50 million annually. Fast-food industry figures also show that the Mexican food segment is still experiencing lucrative growth nationwide. Therefore, Rubio's plans to continue its expansion into new geographic markets. Although Rubio's has already expanded into Orange County, it will continue its investigation of northern California.

Yet as Rubio's approached its tenth anniversary, the company faced many decisions and challenges that would affect its future. First, the company must determine issues related to future expansion:

1. Is there a market on the east coast or in the mountain states for fish tacos?

2. Is international expansion a viable alternative? Assuming that such expansion is feasible, the company must then determine how to establish operations in distant locations.

3. Should the company consider franchising, licensing agreements, partnerships, or even joint ventures?

4. Should the company attempt to remain a closely held, family organization? Alternatively, Rubio's may focus its attention on expanding its distribution channels.

5. Should Rubio's manufacture its fast-food products for distribution in nontraditional outlets?

6. Should Rubio's offer a packaged version of its product in supermarkets and grocery stores? Moreover, given the importance of limiting or reducing costs, Rubio's must also consider the feasibility of assorted cost-saving investments.

7. Should Rubio's centralize the preparation of some or all of its food products once the company reaches a specified number of outlets?

8. Should Rubio's integrate into its own sources of supply?

EXHIBIT 1 Rubios's Menu (1992)

Menu...

Welcome to Rubio's... Home of the Fish Taco! Founded in January of 1983, we have since served over 6 million of our delicious San Felipe style fish tacos to happy customers all over San Diego. Our philosophy is to provide delicious Mexican food served in a clean attractive atmosphere, while maintaining that original Baja flavor. Please enjoy your visit and come back soon!

¡Hasta Luego!

Los Otros

QUESADILLA we spread guacamole on your flour tortilla, sprinkle with cheddar cheese and top it with salsa, we fold it, then heat until it's hot and melted.................... **$2.09**

TAQUITOS three tacos deep-fried and topped with guacamole, salsa and cheese **$1.79**

NACHOS REGULAR our own homemade chips topped with a melted jalapeno cheese sauce.. **88¢**

NACHOS GRANDE the mas mucho o' nachos. over a bed of chips, you'll find cheese sauce, beans, salsa, guacamole, sour cream, and a black olive at the very top....... **$2.95**

CHIPS a bag of our fresh tortilla chips, we cut them and fry them right here, every day.... **60¢**

BEANS a plate of our spicy delicious baked pintos, sprinkled with cheese.............. **75¢**

PALETAS frozen fruit sticks.............. **75¢**

CHURROS .... **75¢**

Combinations

all served with homemade chips and beans

#1 any two tacos
beef carnitas or fish......................... **$2.29**

#2 chicken burrito, beef taco......... **$3.89**

#3 carnitas, burrito, fish taco......... **$3.00**

#4 beef burrito, carnitas, taco......... **$3.70**

#5 fish burritos, fish taco............ **$3.27**

NEW **#6** carne asade, burrito, fish taco..... **$3.89**

PESKY COMBO two fish tacos especiales with beans and chips......................... **$2.09**

Tacos

FISH TACO ESPECIAL for the supreme of fish tacos we provide one of our regular fish tacos dressed with guacamole, cheddar cheese and cilantro/onion. go ahead try one....................................... **$1.79**

SHREDDED BEEF in a soft-shell corn tortilla with guacamole, salsa, cilantro/onion and shredded with lettuce........................... **$1.59**

CARNITAS shredded pork, served on a soft-shell corn tortilla with salsa, cilantro/onion and lettuce............................. **$1.94**

FISH tacos san tempe-style, a strip of fish battered and deep-fried then placed in a soft-shell corn tortilla with salsa, our special white sauce and cabbage, add a squeeze of lime and you have an authentic fish taco........ **$1.00**

NEW **CARNE ASADA*** marinated chunks of steak, seasoned, skillet-seared and placed in a soft-shell corn tortilla with guacamole, salsa, cilantro/onion and cabbage, es deliciosa... **$1.34**

Burritos

BEEF a soft flour filled tortilla with guacamole, beans, spicy shredded beef, salsa, cilantro/onion and a little lettuce. Moo-y delicious..... **$2.49**

CARNITAS shredded pork on a flour tortilla with beans, salsa, cilantro/onion, and lettuce. one of our specialties......................... **$2.44**

CHICKEN chicken simmered in a spicy tomato sauce with onions and peppers, then served on a flour tortilla sprinkled with cheddar cheese, cilantro/onion, and lettuce **$2.49**

FISH a local favorite. fish filets in a flour tortilla and guacamole, beans, salsa, white sauce, cilantro/onion and cabbage. so mucho tasty....................................... **$2.54**

BEANS AND CHEESE beans on a bed of cheese with salsa and cilantro/onion..... **$1.09**

MACHACA our shredded beef and egg with salsa and cilantro/onion, a great way to start the day...................................... **$1.98**

CHORIZO mexican pork sausage scrambled in egg with cilantro/onion and salsa, good and spicy.. **$1.98**

NEW **CARNE ASADA*** from the streets of Mexico City, a recipe that includes tasty chunks of steak marinated and skillet-seared served on a flour tortilla with beans, slasa, cilantro/onion and guacamole.. **$2.55**

Tostadas

BEEF a deep-fried tostada shell covered with beans, salsa, lettuce, chopped tomato, onion, cheese, sour cream, and garnished with a black olive.................................. **$2.18**

CHICKEN our shredded chicken on a bed of beans, salsa, lettuce, chopped tomato, onion, cheese, sour cream and an olive...... **$1.05**

BEAN beans cover the tostada shell and are then topped with salsa, lettuce, chopped tomato and onion, cheese and an olive......... **$1.49**

SALAD MEXICANA our spicy shredded chicken on a bed of fresh lettuce and tortilla chips covered with chopped tomatoes, jack cheese and sour cream. add our special salsa dressing and you have a light tasty meal that is "mucho" healthy!.............. **$2.95**

Drinks

pepsi. diet pepsi. rootbeer. orange slice. slice. iced tea. coffee. lowfat milk. big kahuna fruit juice.

cerveza available at most locations

EXTRA ITEMS guacamole, cheese or sour cream on any item............................ ...**25¢**

■ all orders packaged to go
■ phone in orders welcome

Cold Food Menu

Corn Tortillas	.80 Doz
Flour Tortillas	1.20 Doz
Beans	1.00 Pt 1.80 Qt
Taquitos	1.00 set (3)
Guacamole	3.75 lb
Cilantro & Onion	1.00 lb
Shredded Beef	3.75 lb
Carnitas	3.75 lb
Chicken	3.75 lb
Shredded Cheese (Jack Ched)	3.00 lb
Shredded Mexican Cheese	3.00 lb
Chips	1.75 lb
Quesadillas	2.09 each
Salsas	1.60 Pt 3.00 Qt

Note: We do not sell our cold food products in increments less than a pound, pint or dozen.

CALL – IN ORDER POLICY

■ Please call in your orders before 1:30 am. No call-in orders will be accepted between 11:30 am and 1:30 pm.
Note: No call-in or pick-up orders between 11:30 am and 1:30 pm at our Kearney Mesa and University City stores.
■ Be aware of our two locations in Pacific Beach to avoid misplaced orders
■ Customer phone numbers will be required on all orders over $10.00
■ When picking up your order, please stand and pay in the cashier line.
■ Please allow 24 hours notice for any large deli orders over $25.00

Thank you, Rubio's

Locations

MISSION BAY 4504 Mission Bay Dr 272-2801	CHULA VISTA 789 N. El Camino Ave 427-3811
S.D.S.U. 5187 Collan Ave 206-3844	ENCINITAS 481 Hemingway St. 632-7395
PACIFIC BEACH 925 Grand Ave 270-4800	EL CAJON 298 Magnum Ave 440-3326
POINT LOMA McCloud & Vista Blvd 223-2631	KEARNEY MESA 1420 Cameron Mesa Blvd 268-6770
SAN MARCOS Vine & Mesa Way 745-2962	UNIVERSITY CITY 8936 Towne Center Rd 463-1606

Our Fish Tacos are now featured at JACK MURPHY STADIUM!

Now in Tustin & Irvine

*Available all stores June 15 Prices may vary according to location and are subject to change without notice

Home of the Fish Taco.

EXHIBIT 2   Rubio's Job Descriptions

Prep	Responsible for prepping all the food product, cleanliness, and organization of walk-in, and care of equipment.
Line 3	Under the direction of Line 1; Line 3 heats tortilla, fries fish, taquito, and churrose, and cooks machaca and chorizo.
Line 2	Under the direction of Line 1; Line 2 works the condiment table, wraps the food, and keeps the condiment table stocked and the area clean.
Line 2B	Works alongside Line 2; responsibilities are mainly the wrapping of food to help expedite the food more quickly. This position is implemented during peak hours.
Line 1	The "Quarterback"—sets the pace in the kitchen, reads the ticket, works the steam table, and gives direction to Line 2 and Line 3. Line 1 is directly responsible for how smooth the shift goes. He or she is the leader.
Expediter	Responsible for bagging orders correctly and putting out orders. Responsible for restaurant cleanliness. Restocks throughout the day. Always says "thank you" to customers. Must wear the tag provided by the company.
Cashier	Greets the customer, takes the order, and cashiers throughout the day. Responsible for the cash drawer. Keeps area clean and, along with the expediter, helps clean the dining area. If there is time, helps put out orders. Must wear the name tag provided by the company.
Shift Leader	Responsible for upholding the company's standards and procedures to the highest possible level in every aspect of the restaurant operations. Responsible for the maintenance of the restaurant's operations while under the direction of the management crew. Shift leaders will adhere to the management demeanor and dress policies.
Customer Service Employee	Hired by special service organizations for the disabled to meet the needs of our customers during the busy lunch period. Employee of our customers. Responsible for bussing, wiping tables, restocking, sweeping, getting napkins and utensils for customers already seated, and any other duties specified by the particular store.

EXHIBIT 3 Typical Rubio's Store Structure

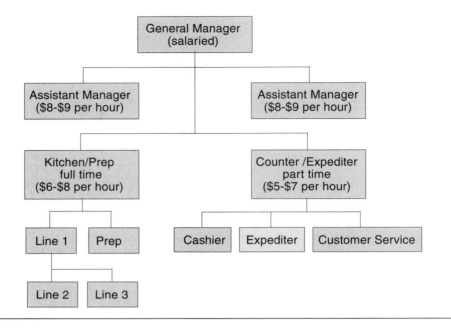

EXHIBIT 4   Menu Recipe File

Fish Taco

Ingredients	Portion	CPU	Cost
Fish (pollack)	1.25 oz	$0.1031250	$0.1289063
White sauce	0.50 oz	0.0215625	0.0107812
Cabbage	0.75 oz	0.0133547	0.0100160
Limes	1.00 slice	0.0069179	0.0069179
Corn tortilla	1.00 each	0.0291667	0.0291667
Fish batter	0.75 oz	0.0218750	0.0164063
Salsa	0.75 oz	0.0227422	0.0170566
		Cost	$0.2192510
		Menu price	$1.44
		Item cost (%)	15.226%
		Gross profit	$1.2207490

Fish Taco Especial

Ingredients	Portion	CPU	Cost
Corn tortilla	1.00 each	$0.0291667	$0.0291667
Fish (pollack)	1.25 oz	0.1031250	0.1289063
Fish batter	0.75 oz	0.0218750	0.0164063
Salsa	0.75 oz	0.0227422	0.0170566
White sauce	0.50 oz	0.0215625	0.0107812
Cabbage	0.75 oz	0.0133547	0.0100160
Guacamole	0.50 oz	0.0641875	0.0320937
Cheese	0.50 oz	0.0812500	0.0406250
Cilantro/onion	0.25 oz	0.0248750	0.0062187
Limes	1.00 slice	0.0069179	0.0069179
		Cost	$0.2981885
		Menu price	$1.79
		Item cost (%)	16.659%
		Gross profit	$1.4918115

CASE 3

Rubio's: Home of the Fish Taco (B)

THE GROWTH YEARS

By 2000, Rubio's enjoyed significant growth and development. Rubio's Restaurants Inc. had become a publicly held corporation that owned and operated 128 high-quality, quick-service Mexican restaurants in California, Arizona, Colorado, Nevada, and Utah. Known for its Baja-style Mexican food and signature fish tacos, Rubio's had undergone phenomenal growth in the past 10 years, from 12 stores in 1992 to a planned 138 stores by 2002, and the company franchised another 14 stores. Rubio's focuses on offering a high-quality product at the price and speed of a fast-food restaurant, and its success has been phenomenal, as is evident in its growth both in number of stores and sales. Since opening in San Diego County in 1983 as a family-owned restaurant, Rubio's has helped define the quick-service Mexican food segment of the restaurant industry. Management intends to continue doing so at a national level well into the future.

THE RESTAURANT INDUSTRY

The restaurant industry, which is defined by the National Restaurant Association (NRA) as encompassing all meals and snacks prepared away from home, including all takeout meals and beverages, was expected to achieve sales of $399 billion in 2001. This represents an increase of 5.2 percent over 2000 sales and marks the tenth consecutive year of real sales growth for the industry. Sales at quick-service (fast-food) restaurants alone were forecast to reach $112 billion, or 28 percent of total restaurant industry sales.

With sales projected to equal 4 percent of the U.S. gross domestic product (GDP), the restaurant industry is a cornerstone of the nation's economy, employing 11.3 million people (making it the largest employer in the country outside the government). In close to 30 years, the number of locations that offer food service has nearly doubled, from 491,000 in 1972 to 844,000 in 2000. This phenomenal growth has been parallel to the growth of the restaurant industry's share of the food dollar, which has risen from 25 percent in 1955 to 45.8 percent in 2000. (The average annual spending on food away from home was $2,030 per household, or $812 per person.) In addition, it is projected that by 2010, 53 percent of the food dollar will be spent on food away from home. This industry growth has been driven by the growth in the number of higher-income households and the rising need for convenience and value. On the other hand, the large growth in sales has helped foster a fiercely competitive environment, consisting of 844,000 dining locations. As a result, restaurant owners are focusing on the physical settings of their facilities (i.e., design, decor, and atmosphere) as a basis for differentiation, rather than on food and service (as has been the focus in the past).

In addition to a highly competitive environment, restaurant owners have several other challenges to address. Labor, purchasing, and operational costs have continued to rise, and energy costs, especially in California, have soared. Workplace safety has become increasingly important, as labor laws have become more stringent, and worker's compensation insurance has become more costly. Use of technology has become widespread in ordering supplies, processing transactions, and providing information (via Web sites) to suppliers and customers. As a partic-

Source: This case was prepared in 2001 by Jennifer Quinnet (MBA) under the direction of Professor Kenneth Marino, Department of Management, San Diego State University.

ipant in the fast-food segment, Rubio's must monitor its competition and face these challenges in order to remain successful in this competitive environment.

Regional Trends

Western Region. Although total employment, disposable personal income, and population growth was higher than the national average in 2000, the region's economy is predicted to slow simultaneously with the nation's economy. However, at the state level, California is expected to continue leading the nation in total sales volume and total employment in the restaurant industry. Unfortunately, California is quickly becoming saturated by full-service and quick-service restaurants, and other states may provide more opportunities to new businesses.

Mountain Region The mountain region achieved the strongest national growth in total employment and total population in 2000, as well as a higher than average growth in disposable personal income. At the state level, Nevada and Colorado are expected to lead not only the region but also the nation in eating-place sales growth in the future.

Central Region. In the midwestern and central regions, the economy, total employment, disposable personal income, and population growth increased at a rate well below the national average. Furthermore, the region is expected to continue with these trends, posting the lowest restaurant industry sales growth in the nation.

Eastern Region. Economic growth in the mid-Atlantic and New England regions of the eastern part of the nation slowed in 2000, while the South Atlantic region posted economic growth well above the national average. In fact, at a regional level, the South Atlantic is expected to lead the nation in restaurant sales in the future. New England's eating-place sales are expected to increase at the national rate, with New Hampshire and Rhode Island leading the way for the region.

Major Market Trends

Education. Food and drink sales by contract food-service providers at educational institutions are expected to increase in the future as a consequence of the continued increase in academic enrollment. The higher education sector of the educational market is expected to increase at the fastest rate.

Recreation. Food and drink sales at recreation and sports centers are projected to increase at a higher rate than sales in the educational sector due to increased event attendance and the growth in the number of higher-income households. For example, attendance at spectator sports such as ice hockey and baseball is increasing, and attendance at theme parks is up as a result of new and improved attractions and repeat visitors.

Transportation. The transportation market is expected to experience the highest increase in food and drink sales. Railroad depots are projected to post the largest sales increase due to increased passenger traffic, especially for short trips. Airports provide another venue where substantial numbers of travelers seek preflight and between-flight meals.

Lodging Places. Although food and drink sales at lodging places are expected to grow, the increase is expected to be less than in other markets due to the slower growth in personal and business travel. This will be most evident in the hotel-restaurant segment.

Business Places. Sales by contract food-service providers are predicted to increase slightly at commercial and office buildings. The growth rate is equivalent to the expected employment growth in areas such as finance, insurance, real estate, and government.

Economic Trends

Sales at quick-service restaurants are expected to reach $112 billion in 2001, which is a 4.4 percent increase over the segment's 2000 sales of $107 billion. When adjusted for inflation, (real) sales are actually increasing at a rate of 1.8 percent in 2001, slightly less than the 2.1 percent growth in 2000. This decrease in the growth rate of real sales is a result of a slower growth in the national economy, as well as slower unit growth within the quick-service segment. Slower unit growth is believed to be the result of a move toward franchise-owned versus company-owned stores and a trend toward co-branding or multiconcept branding at a single establishment (e.g., Carl's Jr. with The Green Burrito, and KFC with Taco Bell).

Unemployment. Although the restaurant industry as a whole continues to benefit from the nation's steady economic growth, individual restaurant owners are finding it difficult to attract and retain employees during this prosperous time when the employment rate has reached a 30-year low. Furthermore, high turnover rates plague the restaurant industry. In fact, in 1998, fast-food restaurants reported a median annual turnover rate of 117 percent. Additionally, the median tenure for workers in food-service occupations is 1.3 years, well below the median of 3.6 years for all wage and salary workers in the nation. Because of low unemployment and high turnover rates, restaurant operators believe that recruiting and retaining employees will continue to be one of the top challenges their businesses face. As a result, many employers are devoting more time and money to employee development by expanding overall training programs and implementing cross-training programs. In addition to training, it is equally important for employers to communicate the career paths available to employees in the restaurant industry. If workers can begin to see their jobs as part of a longer career path in the restaurant industry, they may be more inclined to remain in a particular job and loyal to a single organization.

Labor Force

Labor Statistics. According to the Bureau of Labor Statistics (as reported in a March 2000 article in *Restaurants USA Magazine*), 4 percent of all employed men, 6 percent of all employed women, and 20 percent of all employed teenagers worked in food-preparation and food-service jobs in 1998. Furthermore, the number of total workers in the restaurant industry is projected to reach 12.5 million by the year 2008 (an increase of nearly 15 percent from 1998). According to the Restaurant Industry Employee Profile (a National Restaurant Association instrument), the typical employee in a food-service occupation is:

- High school graduate or less (71 percent)
- Single (71 percent)
- Living in a household that includes:
  a. relatives (82 percent);
  b. two or more wage earners (80 percent);
  c. average U.S. household income
- Part-time employee working an average of 25.5 hours per week
- An individual with relatively short job tenure

Women in the Workforce. The number of women in the workforce has steadily been increasing over the last two decades and is expected to continue to outpace growth in male employment. With regard to employment, the restaurant industry is more likely than other businesses to hire women. As an illustration of this trend, in 1998, women made up 46 percent of the total employed labor force, and they constituted 58 percent of those employed in food-service occupations. Furthermore, women dominated men in a majority of positions: supervisors, wait staff, kitchen workers, and (front) counter staff. However, women are less likely than men to be employed full time, as is evident in 1998, when 66 percent of all part-time employees were female.

Minorities in the Workforce. As minority populations continue to grow in the United States, so does the number of minorities working in the restaurant industry. In 1998, Hispanics accounted for 17 percent of all persons employed in food-service occupations, and African-Americans accounted for 12 percent. As a basis of comparison, Hispanics comprise 10 percent of the national population of employed persons, and African-Americans represent 11 percent. In terms of staffing positions, both minority groups are more likely than average to be employed as cooks and miscellaneous food workers, and Hispanics are also more likely than average to be wait-staff assistants.

Job Growth.

Although the employment rate in the food-service industry has been increasing annually for nearly a decade, it has been lagging in comparison to the nation's overall growth rate for the past three years. However, the industry continues to be a major job provider, creating more than 1.5 million jobs during the 1990s, making it the third-largest private-sector job creator.

Consumer Needs and Lifestyles

Consumers' need for convenience continues to increase as employment increases, leaving little spare time to prepare meals at home. In 1999, a typical person (age eight and older) consumed an average of 4.2 meals prepared away from home per week. Therefore, quick-service restaurants are increasing their efforts to provide fast and easy service to customers in order to keep up with their busy lifestyles. According to the 2000 Consumer Survey conducted by the NRA, 47 percent of adults between the ages of 18 and 24 reported that takeout food is essential to the way they live. Furthermore, 77 percent of adults, ages 18 to 24, indicated that consuming takeout or delivery meals allowed them more time to spend on other activities.

Along with increased convenience, restaurant owners are continually trying to meet the changing tastes and preferences of their customers. In fact, 76 percent of quick-service operators reported that they introduced new food items in 2000, and 66 percent stated that they intend to do the same in 2001. In addition, because customers are seeking more value for their dollar, many restaurants offer a variety of promotions throughout the year, such as weekly or monthly specials, as well as bundled meal discounts. Promotional offerings are determined largely by the type

of customer quick-service restaurants are trying to attract. Quick-service operators indicated that the following customer groups are the most important (in order of significance): (1) businesspeople, (2) teenagers, (3) senior citizens, and (4) tourists and parties that include children.

Ethnic Cuisines. During the 1990s, the market for ethnic cuisines grew with consumers' desire to experience menus based on different cultures. In fact, the growth was so widespread that Italian, Chinese, and Mexican restaurants, which are the most popular, have become mainstream rather than exotic and new. Many ethnic foods have become more readily available and are offered at "nonethnic" restaurants. Therefore, ethnic restaurants can no longer rely solely on their menus to attract their target consumers, who are typically younger and living in major metropolitan areas. Service, value, and atmosphere are as significant for ethnic eateries as they are in any restaurant.

Seafood. Seafood consumption has been on the rise, as consumers are looking for healthier and more innovative alternatives in restaurant menus. Customers have indicated the primary reason for eating seafood is the taste, followed by health, diet, and caloric reasons. Most people perceive seafood to be healthful, more so than beef and pork products. However, consumers are more likely to order seafood at a fine-dining or casual restaurant than at a fast-food establishment due to concerns regarding freshness, limited preparation options, and a preference for hamburgers or chicken when eating fast food. In fact, the most common reasons for not eating seafood include lack of convenience or availability, dislike of the taste, high prices, and food-safety concerns.

Restaurant Setting. The physical setting in which customers dine is becoming a more integral part of the restaurant experience, as well as a basis on which to compete. Design, decor, and atmosphere have become the focus of many restaurant owners and managers. In the NRA's Restaurant Settings

2000 Survey, approximately 66 percent of the respondents reported using the services of an interior designer, and 75 percent worked with an architect in the design of their restaurants. Restaurant owners are particularly interested in keeping their settings modern yet timeless.

Of course, customer satisfaction with food and service has been and continues to be of utmost importance to restaurant owners, which is why most of their time is still devoted to these areas; if food and service are unsatisfactory to the customer, physical setting is likely to be insignificant in the overall dining experience. Once food and service needs are met, restaurant owners can focus on the physical environments of their restaurants, giving attention to the type of experience the customer is seeking. However, in general, the physical setting is often less important at midscale restaurants where patrons spend less time and are usually interested in just getting something to eat quickly. In contrast, the physical setting becomes integral to upscale restaurants where consumers are looking for a complete dining experience.

External Pressures

Energy Costs. As energy prices continue to soar, restaurant owners look for new ways to maximize their energy usage and subsidize their rising costs, One way of handling this problem is to raise menu prices. California businesses are not only facing doubled energy costs, but also rolling blackouts, which shut down a business's energy for a minimum of one hour, causing a loss in business and often product when the refrigeration system does not work. As energy prices and blackouts continue, many businesses will be forced to close their facilities and move to places where traffic and costs allow them to operate.

Workplace Safety. Improvements over the last decade in workplace safety, along with more stringent requirements regarding worker's compensation insurance, have successfully reduced occupational injuries and illnesses in the restaurant industry. Lower rates of injury and illness have helped restaurant owners maximize labor productivity while, at the same time, managing heath-care expenses.

Technology. Technology has become prominent in every facet of business. In the restaurant industry, technology is used for a variety of tasks, both at the corporate and store levels. Examples may include (1) ordering and purchasing supplies from vendors, (2) maintaining computerized accounting systems, (3) taking customer orders electronically, and (4) designing and hosting a Web site. The Internet has become a competitive business tool in every industry, and approximately half of the respondents to the NRA's 2000 Table Service Operator Survey reported that they have a Web site. Restaurant Web sites are typically informational, providing consumers with information such as locations, menu items, and promotions. Other more technologically advanced restaurants offer online reservations and online ordering capabilities. Regardless of its use, technology is taking over business and being used to increase efficiency while decreasing long-term costs.

Competition. Competition in the quick-service segment of the restaurant industry is stronger than ever, not only from other quick-service restaurants, but also from other food-service providers and segments of the restaurant industry that offer takeout menus. Some of the key competitive factors in the restaurant industry are food quality, price and value, service quality, restaurant location, and the dining atmosphere.

THE RUBIO'S CONCEPT

Product Line

Rubio's menu features burritos, soft-shell tacos, quesadillas made with marinated char-grilled chicken breast and lean steak, and seafood such as char-grilled mahi mahi, sautéed shrimp, and their signature Baja-style fish taco. All items are made-to-order, and side items such as chips, rice, and beans are made fresh daily. Rubio's restaurants offer a self-serve salsa bar where customers can choose from three freshly made salsas. Prices for menu items range from $1.89 for the signature fish taco to $6.29 for a Lobster Combo. Most of the individual establishments also offer a selection of imported Mexican and domestic beers, along with a variety of soft drinks.

Most restaurants also offer a HealthMex menu and Kid Pesky meals for children. The HealthMex items are designed for the nutritionally conscious consumer; less than 20 percent of their calories are from fat. The Kid Pesky meals offer a choice of a fish taco, chicken taquitos, quesadillas, or a bean burrito served with a side dish, drink, churro, and toy surprise.

To add variety, Rubio's occasionally offers limited-time promotional menu items, such as the tequila shrimp burrito. However, most of these items are not permanently added to the menu due to the seasonality and limited availability of the product.

Facilities

Rubio's targets high-profile, major metropolitan areas that offer appealing demographic characteristics such as high traffic patterns; high density of white-collar families; medium-to-high family incomes; high education levels; a large concentration of daytime employment; residential, retail, and entertainment developments; and limited competition. The senior management team is actively involved in selecting new markets, and each new site must be approved by the Rubio's Real Estate Acquisition Committee. Once the site is approved, Rubio's leases rather than purchases the appropriate facility space in order to minimize the cash investment associated with each unit.

Historically, the typical restaurant size has been 1,800 to 3,600 square feet, but future sites are expected to range from 2,000 to 2,400 square feet. On average, the total cash investment required to open an individual restaurant is $380,000 to $450,000, not including preopening expenses of $19,000 to $25,000.

Once the space is leased, construction begins to design the interior and exterior according to Rubio's usual specifications. Some of the design elements include colorful Mexican tiles, saltwater aquariums with tropical fish, beach photos, surfboards, and authentic palm-thatched patio umbrellas. The intent of the decor is to create a relaxed and casual environment in which customers can enjoy an authentic Baja Mexican meal.

Unit Operations

The typical restaurant employs one general manager, one to two assistant managers, and 18 to 22 hourly employees, 60 percent of whom work full time. All employees working over 30 hours per week are eligible for health-care benefits, and employees over 18 years of age that work more than 20 hours per week are eligible to participate in Rubio's 401(k) plan. In addition, managers are offered performance-based cash incentives that are tied directly to sales and profitability, and they have the option to buy shares of common stock when hired or promoted.

Besides unit management and employees, Rubio's also employs district managers, each of whom reports to a regional manager and is responsible for all phases of restaurant operations as well as opening new units.

Marketing Strategy

As Rubio's has grown to 128 stores in 5 states over 18 years, it has built upon its original "fish taco" concept to expand its menu and position itself between the quick-service and casual-dining segments of the restaurant industry. The key elements of Rubio's market positioning are:

- Distinctive, fresh, high-quality food
- Casual, fun dining experience
- Excellent dining value

To achieve its positioning goals during its first 18 years of operation, Rubio's advertising had been handled in-house. However, as of January 2001, Team One Advertising was hired to help build the Rubio's brand, develop promotional advertising, increase awareness, and generate trial in new markets. In addition, Rubio's plans to hire local public relations firms to help establish brand awareness in the new markets.

Broadcast advertising, both television and radio, coupons, and in-store point-of-purchase displays have been used as marketing tools to increase brand awareness, attract new customers, and build customer loyalty. The promotional theme is designed to portray Rubio's as a high-quality, quick-service Mexican food restaurant, as well as to publicize special offers.

All of the marketing strategies employed are designed to help accomplish and reinforce the business objective of becoming the "leading high-quality, quick-service Mexican restaurant brand nationwide" (Rubio's 10-K, 2000).

Competition

The restaurant industry is fiercely competitive and segmented, based on the type of service, food, and price being offered. In the quick-service, high-quality Mexican food segment, Rubio's direct competitors include Baja Fresh, La Salsa, and Chipotle (see Exhibit 3). Rubio's indirect competitors include full-service Mexican restaurants such as Chevy's and El Torito, as well as fast-food restaurants, especially those concentrating on Mexican food offerings such as Taco Bell and Del Taco. Although Rubio's is able to compete favorably in the restaurant market, many of its competitors are better established nationwide with greater financial, marketing, and management resources.

Franchise Opportunities

To enhance the company's expansion strategy, Rubio's implemented a franchising program in 2000 (see Exhibit 4). Management and financial resources will be provided by Rubio's to build the infrastructure of the newly franchised units, and franchisees will in turn pay area development fees, new store-opening fees, and royalties to Rubio's. As of February 2001, Rubio's had two signed franchisee agreements, one to open eight units and the other to open six.

Financials

Exhibit 1 reports the financial highlights for 2000 and prior years. Rubio's had 90 units open the entire year, which generated an average sales per unit of $896,000, an average operating income per unit of $130,000 (14.5 percent of sales), and an average cash flow per unit of $166,000 (18.6 percent of sales). Comparable restaurant sales (for units open and operating over 12 months) increased 0.6 percent in 2000, much lower than the 6 percent increase from the previous year. Overall sales increased 40.9 percent over 1999 sales, an increase that is partially a result of the opening of 36 new restaurants in 2000. Of the 90 units open the entire year, 22 are located outside of California. Those 22 units generated an average sales per unit of $733,000, an average operating income per unit of $36,000 (4.9 percent of sales), and an average cash flow per unit of $75,000 (10.3 percent of sales).

In May 1999, Rubio's made an initial public offering in order to raise capital for the operation and expansion of the business, yet does not anticipate paying any cash dividends in the foreseeable future. Unfortunately, although restaurant revenues have continued to increase, Rubio's stock price has been spiraling downward (see Exhibit 2 below).

Rubio's attributes the depressed stock price to higher labor, energy, and food costs, which have led to a number of underperforming restaurants

A LOOK TO THE FUTURE

Although Rubio's has been reasonably successful thus far in the highly competitive restaurant industry, the company has some challenges to face in the near future. The company already plans to raise menu prices and focus its marketing efforts to improve sales in order to offset some of the cost pressures. Although the long-term plan is to grow to nearly 2,000 restaurants nationwide, Rubio's is slowing store growth in the immediate future in order to preserve capital and focus on operational excellence.

Although Rubio's management is taking steps to overcome the challenges they face, there are a number of issues to be considered regarding current strategy and future growth:

1. Is Rubio's expansion plan feasible?
2. Is the Rubio's concept transferable to other regions of the country? If yes,

where should expansion efforts be focused?

3. What other markets and distribution channels could Rubio's penetrate? (For example, university campuses, frozen foods in grocery stores, etc.)

4. Is franchising a good option?

5. What are other possible solutions to offset the drop in stock price?

EXHIBIT 1   Abbreviated Annual Financials

Income Statement (in millions except per-share amounts.)	Dec-00	Dec-99	Dec-98
Revenue	$ 95.7	$ 67.9	$ 44.5
Cost of goods sold	$ 32.6	$ 23.0	$ 15.0
Gross profit	$ 63.1	$ 44.9	$ 29.5
Gross profit margin	65.9%	66.1%	66.3%
SG&A expense	$ 61.9	$ 42.0	$ 28.8
Operating income	$ 1.2	$ 2.9	$ 0.7
Operating margin	1.3%	4.3%	1.6%
Total net income	$ (0.2)	$ 1.7	$ 0.9
Net profit margin	—	2.5%	2.0%
Diluted EPS ($)	$(0.03)	$ 0.20	$ 0.14

Balance sheet (in millions)	Dec-00	Dec-99	Dec-98
Cash	$ 1.3	$ 3.5	$ 0.8
Net receivables	$ 1.4	$ 0.8	$ 0.3
Inventories	$ 2.0	$ 0.6	$ 0.4
Total current assets	$12.1	$12.9	$ 4.5
Total assets	$52.3	$50.0	$25.8
Short-term debt	$ 0.0	$ 0.0	$ 0.7
Total current liabilities	$ 7.7	$ 5.8	$ 5.9
Long-term debt	$ 0.0	$ 0.0	$ 1.1
Total liabilities	$ 9.3	$ 6.9	$ 7.8
Total Equity	$43.0	$43.1	$17.9
Shares Outstand.(mil.)	8.9	8.9	1.0

SOURCE: Information from www.hoovers.com.

EXHIBIT 2   Rubios Historical Stock Price

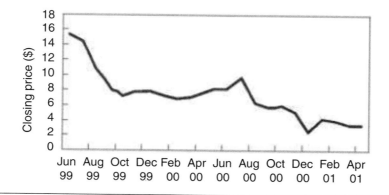

EXHIBIT 3   Competitive Analysis (2002)

Locations	Rubios Baja Grill	Chipotle	La Salsa Fresh Mexican Grill	Baja Fresh Mexican Grill
	Arizona	Arizona	Arizona	Arizona
	California	California	California	California
	Colorado	Colorado	Colorado	Colorado
	Nevada	Illinois	Connecticut	Illinois
	Utah	Kansas	Indiana	Maryland
		Maryland	Nevada	Nevada
		Minnesota	Ohio	Ohio
		Missouri	Puerto Rico	Oregon
		Ohio	Texas	Texas
		Texas	Utah	Virginia
		Washington DC		
Menu Offerings	Tacos Burritos	Tacos Burritos	Tacos Burritos	Tacos Burritos
	Combination Platters	Fajita Burritos	Combination Platters	Combination Platters
	Side Dishes	Side Dishes	Side Dishes	Salads
	HealthMex Menu	N/A	Party Packs	Side Dishes
	Baja Bowls		"Grande Trays"	Party Packs
	Kid Pesky Meals		Catering	
	Party Packs			
	Catering			
Fish Tacos	Original Fish Taco		Baja Style Fish Taco	Baja Fish Taco
	Grilled Mahi Mahi Taco		Sonora Style Fish Taco	Baja Style Shrimp Taco
	Shrimp Taco		Baja Style Shrimp Taco	
Price Range	$1.89–$6.29	$4.55–$5.25	$2.35–$7.45	$1.85–$6.95
Web site	www.rubios.com	www.chipotle.com	www.lasalsa.com	www.bajafresh.com
Franchising	Yes	No	Yes	Yes
Public/Private	Publicly Held	Privately Held	Publicly Held	Privately Held
Ticker symbol	RUBO	N/A	SBRG	N/A
Planned expansions	24 units	Unknown	3 units	10 units
Areas of expansion	None	N/A	None	Washington, DC

EXHIBIT 4   Franchise Opportunities with Rubio's Baja Grill

WELCOME TO RUBIO'S FRANCHISE PAGE
AND THANK YOU FOR YOUR INTEREST!

This is the beginning of an exciting period for Rubio's, because we are franchising for the first time in our 17 year history!

We are seeking experienced, well-capitalized partners that have the financial and operational wherewithal to develop multiple locations within a given market area.

We have a minimum financial requirement of a net worth of $500,000, with liquid assets of $250,000. Based on the number of restaurants to be built as part of the area development agreement, we will require that you have the financial capability to meet the development objectives. If you meet our minimum financial requirements and would like some additional information, please contact us at:

e-mail:
Franchisedepartment@rubios.com
Facsimile: (760) 929-8203

Corporate Address:
Rubio's Restaurants, Inc., 1902 Wright Place, Suite 300, Carlsbad, CA 92008
Attn: Franchise Department

Thank you again for your interest.

Rubio's Baja Grill Restaurant franchises are available only in certain states. We do not offer any franchises in jurisdictions where we are not yet registered (or otherwise qualified) to make offers or sales. The information on this Web site is not an offer to sell or solicitation of an offer to buy a Rubio's Baja Grill Restaurant franchise. An offer for a Rubio's Baja Grill Restaurant franchise is made by prospectus only.

SOURCE: Information found at www.rubios.com.

CASE 4

Rubio's Restaurants, Incorporated (C)
Troubles and Turmoil (2006)

In May of 1999, Rubio's Restaurants issued an IPO and became a public company. The decision to go public was made so that the chain could raise the money needed for future growth. The IPO also enabled the Rubio family to become more liquid, to have a way to exchange their shares for cash, and to allow them to diversify their personal holdings.

At the time of the IPO, Rubio's had 67 company-owned units operating primarily in the southwestern region of the United States.

The IPO was for 3,150,000 shares and was priced at $10.50 per share. Of the total made available to the public, 2.25 million shares were offered by the company and 900,000 were offered by the family. The stock trades under the ticket symbol RUBO on the NASDAQ national market. The lead underwriter was Thomas Weisel Partners LLC, and the comanagers were Dain Rauscher Wessels, a division of Dain Rauscher Inc., and U.S Bancorp Piper Jaffray. The underwriters were granted a 30-day over-allotment option to purchase an additional 472,500 shares. If the over-allotment shares were to be purchased, the total number of shares outstanding would be 9,078,122.

Thus began the big expansion of the Rubio chain and its franchising efforts. The expansion plans were ambitious and "in a move expected to pave the way for continued growth," the company hired a new president. On September 9, 2002, the company announced that it had hired Sherri Miksa as its new president and chief operating officer.

Ralph Rubio made the announcement and he retained his positions as chairman and CEO of Rubio's.

Ralph said that "Sheri's proven restaurant experience in key management, operations, and marketing roles will serve Rubio's well, helping to move the company to the next level as we accelerate growth in the coming year." Sherri was quoted in the company press release: "Rubio's is poised to enter into a new phase of its growth. I am excited about the fast-casual category and this company's potential. I look forward to leading the team to the next level."

SHERRI MIKSA: NEW LEADERSHIP

The new president of Rubio's had an impressive resume. She received her MBA from the Stanford Graduate School of Business. She began her career in food and beverage and hospitality, working in management or marketing positions at Aspencrest Hospitality, Inc., Sceptre Hospitality Resources, Inc., Frito-Lay, General Foods Corporation, and Atlantic Richfield Company. She also worked as vice president of operations for LSG Sky Chefs, a leading airline catering company.

It is likely that Miksa's last two positions were what made her look so good to Rubio's. She spent a number of years in leadership and operational roles at YUM! Brands, Inc., where she had increasing P&L responsibility for over 200 Taco Bell Corporation units. (Taco Bell is a subsidiary of YUM!) Her last position before joining Rubio's was as COO with the Seattle Coffee Company (a subsidiary of AFC Enterprises, Inc.). Seattle Coffee is a parent company of Seattle's Best Coffee®. At Seattle's Best, Miksa had responsibility for the profitability and strategic direction of all company and franchise

Source: This case was prepared in 2007 by Marc Dollinger from public sources.

operations, marketing and product development, and development and systems support.

Miksa made a smooth transition to Rubio's and had considerable early success. In a feature article in *Chain Leader* magazine (October 1, 2004), she and Ralph discussed the company's success and future.

> Miksa: [When I was with Taco Bell] "I always found it interesting to talk to people who went to Rubio's," Miksa recalls. "They talked about the food in such reverential tones." Her verdict when she finally tried Rubio's? "I loved it," she says. "I was so intrigued by the unique flavors."
>
> Miksa also recalled her days running a 2,000-person food-service and hospitality operation on the Alaskan pipeline at Prudhoe Bay, Alaska: "I had all these people 'living in my house,'" she says. "I was responsible for food, maintenance, and operations. The experience taught me that I could do anything if I put my mind to it," she adds.
>
> Rubio: "We want to improve sales within existing restaurants, become more profitable and establish the company to grow again at a rapid pace."

Miksa was right on target in 2004. She slashed the cost of goods sold by 2 percent and launched a new menu with bundled

EXHIBIT 1   Snapshot of Rubio's 2003-2004

(Sales and profits in millions)

Units	151
2003 systemwide sales	$124.8
2004 systemwide sales	$130.0
Unit volume average	$929,000
Average check	$7.50-$8.00
Expansion plans	5-8 units
2003 loss	$1.90
2004 profit (6 mos.)	$1.76

meals at low, nonsale prices. She had to hire a new CFO and a new VP of marketing, both of whom she poached from Taco Bell. She also put the company on the road to profitability. A snapshot of the company's results reports this growth (see Exhibit 1). Despite its growth the company lost $1.9 million on sales of $125 million in 2003. Exhibit 2, however, illustrates the problems of fast and aggressive growth. Even as revenue was growing, net income became unpredictable, and stock price fluctuated widely and trended lower.

To implement her cost cutting, new

EXHIBIT 2   Problems with Fast and Agressive Growth

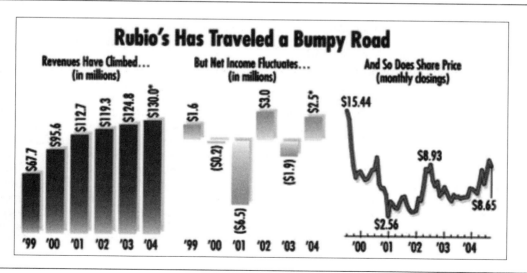

SOURCE: Company reports, Chain Leader estimate.

menu, and other innovations, Miksa used a management philosophy based on the "4 Ms": measure, meet, manage, and motivate. She met with managers weekly, reviewing unit scorecards and results.

> "You've got to talk to your guest, formally or informally," Miksa says. "That's how we learn and get better, not by doing things that won't improve the guest experience. We look at the restaurants as individual profit centers."

Miksa returned the company to its "Baja inspiration" roots. She rolled out a new menu and redesigned the physical menu to be brighter and easier to read. Sales rose for the chain and for comparable stores. Transactions increased by 5.9 percent but average check amounts remained about flat.

The company's quick expansion after the IPO underwent its bumps and setbacks. Rubio's lost $6.5 million in the two years after going public and had to close 11 stores. Miksa's plans for the future include expansion but she was reticent to discuss specific opportunities. She does not rule out franchising, although there are now only four franchised units in Nevada. Rubio's is currently debt-free and has financed expansion in the past with cash from operations. The company receives inquiries about franchising, and considers this interest good news. But as Miksa says, Rubio's must find partners "who share the passion for the brand, the focus on quality and who really understand the uniqueness. With the right franchisees, it could be a good thing."

The article in *Chain Leader* also contained some commentary from restaurant consultants and business analysts. A sampling of these comments is provided in Exhibit 3 below.

COMPETITIVE AND FRANCHISING ISSUES

The competitive factors stand out as a serious hurdle for Rubio's. The fast-casual segment of fresh Mexican food is heating up. In a *Wall Street Journal* article (January 4, 2005), the problems faced by the segment and specifically Wendy's Baja Fresh chain were highlighted.

Wendy's International purchased Baja Fresh in 2002 for $270 million in an attempt to break into the fast-growing fast-casual segment. Rival McDonald's had already bought a stake in Chipotle. At the time of the Wendy's purchase, Baja was the industry leader.

But the investment in Baja has not paid off. In December 2004, Wendy's wrote off almost $100 million of its Baja investment. They closed over 20 stores and announced they would focus new units only on the east and west coasts. Baja, with about 300 units, is no longer the industry leader. Chipotle has over 400 stores and Moe's is growing so quickly that it could have about 400 units by 2006.

How does a success become a problem so quickly? Conjecture was that it was a result of poor site selection, increased complexity in cooking and food preparation, rising commodity and labor costs, and the perceived resistance to Mexican food in the conservative Midwest. But not all chains had all these problems. Janice Meyer, an industry consultant, concluded that, "They just didn't run as tight a ship from the operations standpoint. And when you have a broad menu, it's easy to get your operations mucked up."

Bill Moreton, the new CEO brought in for the turnaround adds, "As you put new items on the menu, you ask, 'does it fit with the concept and the brand? How does it affect operations?' "

But streamlining Baja will take some effort. Chipotle has a Subway-type assembly line process that is faster—even faster than Taco Bell's. Chipotle is less expensive on an item-by-item basis for comparison. Steve Ells, cofounder of Chipotle, is proud of his creation. "What is appealing about Chipotle is it isn't mysterious food. It's not concocted in the back. It's prepared in front of the customer. That lends realness," he says. And Chipotle has been growing in the Midwest too.

EXHIBIT 3   Sample Comments

Gary Dollarhyde, consultant and former CEO of Baja Fresh Mexican Grill	There is significant competition from Baja Fresh, Chica Grill, Moe's Southwest, and Sharky's to name a few. "The big brands have returned in the past year and a half." Subway and Quiznos are "nipping away at quick casual too."
Tony Brenner, analyst, Roth Capital Partners	"Rubio's is still a regional company, and I think they have to work on expanding the concept outside southern California." But "[the menu] is something that Rubio's needed to make itself more portable."
Julie Stewart, former Taco Bell executive, current CEO of IHOP Corp.	"I thought her qualities were unique and unusual." She "had to manage, lead, and think outside the box to get ordinary people to do extraordinary things. She's done a nice job of working with the founder, which is never easy, and driving the business along and helping re-engineer the brand."

SOURCE: Lisa Bertagnoli, "Revving Up Rubio's," *Chain Leader,* October 1, 2004. Retrieved from the Web September 20, 2006. http://www.chainleader.com/archives/2004/10/rubios.asp.

EXHIBIT 4   Mexican Fast-Casual Segment

	2003 U.S. Sales (in millions)	Percent Change from 2002	2003 U.S. Stores	Percent. Change from 2002
Chipotle	$321.0	42.7%*	305	31.5 %
Baja Fresh	312.5	25.5	283	34.8
Rubio's	130.2	5.9	148	3.5
Qdoba	86.7	33.1*	126	48.2
Moe's	71.0	86.8	105	111.0
La Salsa	70.5	13.1*	100	1.0
Taco Del Mar	26.0	8.3	72	10.8
*Estimated				

SOURCE: "Technomic Inc." From Steven Gray, "Wendy's Stumbles with Baja Fresh," *The Wall Street Journal*, January 4, 2005: B7.

Exhibit 4 provides a glimpse of the segment as of the end of 2004.

In addition to the problems that parts of the segment were having in 2004, the franchising systems were also having issues. Rubio's in particular had hoped to open dozens of franchised units in the western states over the period 2002-2004. But only a handful of the proposed units opened, and sales in these units were sluggish. Even fish tacos were not selling well. One Rubio's franchisee defaulted in just months. The compa-ny halted its franchising efforts at that point—before things got worse.

"We outgrew ourselves. We thought we had a prototype such that we could just franchise it, but it wasn't working," Ralph Rubio concluded.

Scott Shane of Case Western Reserve University said, "It's definitely possible to kill off a good concept by trying to grow too fast. Any franchisor has to be especially careful in the beginning to evaluate growth. If you are not making money at a single outlet,

EXHIBIT 5 Rubio's Financial Results for the Period Ending June 25, 2006.

RUBIO'S RESTAURANTS, INC.
CONDENSED CONSOLIDATED STATEMENTS OF OPERATIONS
(in thousands, except per share data)
(unaudited)

	For the Thirteen Weeks Ended		For the Twenty-Six Weeks Ended	
	June 25, 2006	June 26, 2005	June 25, 2006	June 26, 2005
RESTAURANT SALES	$ 37.068	$ 35,964	$ 72,095	$ 69,663
FRANCHISE AND LICENSING REVENUES	84	71	140	129
TOTAL REVENUES	$ 37,152	$ 36,035	$ 72,235	$ 69,792
COST OF SALES	$ 10,363	$ 9,597	$ 19,900	$ 18,707
RESTAURANT LABOR	11,867	11,527	23,420	22,744
RESTAURANT OCCUPANCY AND OTHER	8,869	8,540	17,424	16,326
GENERAL AND ADMINISTRATIVE EXPENSES	3,584	3,240	6,903	6,182
DEPRECIATION AND AMORTIZATION	2,069	1,911	3,929	3,847
PRE-OPENING EXPENSES	15	0	48	49
STORE CLOSURE REVERSAL	(247)	0	(247)	0
LOSS ON DISPOSAL/SALE OF PROPERTY	60	0	74	3
TOTAL EXPENSES	$ 36,580	$ 34,819	$ 71,451	$ 67,858
OPERATING INCOME	$ 572	$ 1,220	$ 784	$ 1,934
OTHER INCOME	130	113	231	196
INCOME BEFORE INCOME TAXES	$ 702	$ 1,333	$ 1,015	$ 2,130
INCOME TAX EXPENSE	263	424	384	732
NET INCOME	$ 439	$ 909	$ 631	$ 1,398
NET INCOME PER SHARE:				
Basic	$ 0.05	$ 0.10	$ 0.07	$ 0.15
Diluted	$ 0.05	$ 0.09	$ 0.01	$ 0.14

[continued on next page]

EXHIBIT 5 (continued) Rubio's Financial Results for the Period Ending June 25, 2006.

	Percentage of Total Revenues For the Thirteen Weeks Ended		Percentage of Total Revenues For the Twenty-Six Weeks Ended	
	June 25, 2006	June 26, 2005	June 25, 2006	June 26, 2005
TOTAL REVENUES	100.0%	100.0%	100%	100%
COST OF SALES[1]	28.0%	26.7%	27.6%	26.9%
RESTAURANT LABOR[1]	32.0%	32.1%	32.5%	32.6%
RESTAURANT OCCUPANCY AND OTHER[1]	23.9%	23.7%	24.2%	23.4%
GENERAL AND ADMINISTRATIVE EXPENSES	9.6%	9.0%	9.6%	8.9%
DEPRECIATION AND AMORTIZATION	5.6%	5.3%	5.4%	5.5%
PRE-OPENING EXPENSES	0.0%	0.0%	0.1%	0.1
STORE CLOSURE REVERSAL	(0.7%)	0.0%	(0.3%)	0.0%
LOSS ON DISPOSAL/SALE OF PROPERTY	0.2%	0.0%	0.1%	0.0%
OPERATING INCOME	1.5%	3.4%	1.1%	2.8%
OTHER INCOME	0.3%	0.3%	0.3%	0.3%
INCOME BEFORE INCOME TAXES	1.9%	3.7%	1.4%	3.1
INCOME TAX EXPENSE	0.7%	1.2%	0.5%	0.5%
NET INCOME	1.2%	2.5%	0.9%	2.0%

1. As a percentage of restaurant sales

CONDENSED CONSOLIDATED BALANCE SHEETS
(in thousands)

	June 25, 2006 (unaudited)	December 25, 2005
CASH AND SHORT-TERM INVESTMENTS	$ 11,436	11,071
OTHER CURRENT ASSETS	4,135	5,426
PROPERTY—NET	32,233	30,601
LONG-TERM INVESTMENTS	3,052	3,675
OTHER ASSETS	8,510	7,818
TOTAL ASSETS	$ 59,366	58,591
CURRENT LIABILITIES	$ 11,612	11,958
OTHER LIABILITIES	5,183	5,668
STOCKHOLDERS' EQUITY	42,571	40,965
TOTAL LIABILITIES AND STOCKHOLDERS' EQUITY	$ 59,366	58,591

chances are pretty great that you're not going to make a lot of money at a lot of outlets."

The archetypical case in point was Boston Market. It grew from 20 stores in the late 1980s to more than 900 franchises by 1998. Costs rose significantly and stores could neither pay their bills nor repay their debt to the franchisor. In 1998 the chain declared Chapter 11 bankruptcy, closed over 200 stores, and looked for a buyer. McDonald's absorbed the company in 2000.

RECENT EVENTS

Sherri Miksa was honored when the *Chain Leader* 2004 cover story appeared. Her performance was lauded and the challenges she faced were described. At the time the company's sales were increasing 5 percent per year and its stock was at a five-year high. But the challenges proved to be too much to overcome. On December 20, 2005, less than a year later, Miksa was replaced. She might have quit or been fired; it has never been formally revealed. But on December 21, 2005, the *San Diego Union-Tribune* reported that Rubio's suddenly announced her resignation and Ralph Rubio, founder and chairman of the board, retook the operational reins. A search for a successor to Miksa was announced as well.

Maybe it was not surprising that Miksa was pushed out. Performance for 2005 was way below expectations. The third quarter of 2005 showed a deep decline in profitability and flat sales. The company's stock was down over 20 percent.

The analysts and pundits pounced. They reported dissatisfaction with marketing efforts and investor relations. Brand positioning was also called into question. The menu had become decidedly "value oriented," which means many items were in the $1 to $1.50 range. This occurred while Rubio's was positioning for a more upscale niche. Fast food and an upscale brand do not yet go together in the public's mind.

But all was not negative in the news story announcing the transition. The stock analysts were still bullish. According to Ian Corydon, an analyst with Los Angeles-based B. Riley, "The stock is cheap and the balance sheet is OK. I think they have good growth opportunities."

The financial results for the latest period appear in Exhibit 5.

In the August 2, 2006, conference call for the public and analysts, Ralph Rubio, still interim CEO, John Fuller, CFO, and Larry Sink, VP of Marketing, described Rubio's latest plans and took questions from the audience.

Ralph Rubio began the conference with a review. He said that current sales initiatives were focused on improving the guest experience. Recent past initiatives might have been inconsistent, he said. The new focus is on the quality product, the freshness of the ingredients, and the healthy nature of many of the offerings. A survey of the quick-casual segment showed that the fish taco, burritos, and salads were clear winners. But Rubio acknowledged the need for better service. He had commissioned three organizations to do real-time research to find ways to improve service levels: Kurt Salmon Associates, the premier service operations consulting firm; Technomics, a high-tech consulting firm; and IBM Web services.

In addition to the focus on the guest experience, Ralph promoted the company's store design and development program. The new reimaged units were producing above-average unit sales. They had a colorful and new look. But the expansion was on hold. This year they had opened only one new store, one new franchise store, but had repurchased the four Las Vegas franchises. They also closed one store. Basically, the net was zero.

John Fuller presented next. He reviewed the financial results and provided these helpful hints:

- Net income for the quarter was $439,000 versus $909,000 for year over year.
- Earnings per share were $.05 versus .09 year over year.

- For the six months ending June, 2006, net income was $631,000 versus. $1.398 million.
- Revenue, however, was up 3.1 percent versus last year at $72.2 million.

Fuller also commented on the wage and hour lawsuit that the firm was defending. This was a class action suit claiming that restaurants in California did not properly pay workers for their lunch hours and their required work breaks. All the other restaurants named in the suit have already settled, but Rubio's appears ready and willing to go to trial. The expense of defending the company and going to trial would be significant and could hurt future earnings, according to Fuller.

Larry Sink discussed the marketing efforts of the company. He was quite critical of past efforts. He had four primary reasons for the ineffectiveness of the marketing:

1. Inconsistent brand identity—caught between low prices and high quality
2. Uneven advertising—$1 menu did not match store image
3. Poor in-store promotions—too many and too confusing
4. High fuel prices—reduced customer driving

He reported that the new plan was to emphasize quality food, friendly and efficient service, fun, and reasonable (but not low) prices. Rubio's had just hired a new advertising agency, Grant, Scott & Hurley of San Francisco, to emphasize the good taste of the food.

Ralph Rubio concluded the presentation with a look toward the future. He assured the audience that sales would continue to grow at 3 percent. He vowed to renew the firm's new-product development efforts and take the fish taco to places it had not been before. Stores would relaunch their take-away business. Advanced menu analysis would improve profitability with a mixture of reasonably priced and upscale items. The reimaging program would improve the look and feel of the stores. And better human resource policy and training would improve management and the service team members.

During the Q & A session, people asked questions about the poor financial performance, the wage and hour lawsuit, and the CEO search. The executives repeated the answers to the first and second questions, and Ralph said that the CEO search was approaching the critical stage and he could not comment. There would be no announcement until the deal was done.

Finally, one securities analyst commented as follows: It appeared that the enterprise value of each store (market value divided by number of stores) was $350,000 each. But the cost to open a new store was around $500,000. Maybe opening new stores was not a good use of the company's cash! Perhaps the company should buy back its own stock and focus on getting the stock price up to the value of the stores.

But Ralph Rubio said he didn't believe this focus on stock price was the best way to go. He said they needed to grow again and that Rubio's story was not yet finished. He would use cash for growth and all the initiatives he had earlier described. Besides, he added, there was not enough stock float out there to make much of a difference with a stock re-purchase program.

EPILOGUE

On August 22, 2006 (less than a month after the conference call), Rubio's announced that its new president and CEO would be Daniel Pittard. The search for Miksa's replacement had taken almost a year.

Pittard, 56, said that he would try to take the company into a pricier, more upscale segment. The days of the $1 special appear to be over. Pittard said that Rubio's would try to attract customers from restaurant chains like Chevy's and On the Border. These sit-down restaurants have more offerings in the casual than in the fast-casual segment.

Pittard has no prior restaurant experience. He is a former Pepsico and Amoco executive and oversaw Amoco's 8,000-plus gas station and convenience store operations. He also has been an angel investor and a managing partner at IdeaEdge Ventures of San Diego. He worked for McKinsey & Company, a management consulting firm, for 12 years where he was a partner. In 1992 he went to Pepsico and managed new ventures for Frito-Lay. He helped place Taco Bell products into supermarkets (Frito-Lay owns Taco Bell).

And what did the pundits think of the appointment? Generally they liked the move.

Mark Smith, who covers Rubio's for Sidoti and Co., New York, said, "I would have loved to see somebody with restaurant experience, but they needed someone who can take a turnaround company and make it into a growth company." He added that he liked the alliance that Pittard put together with McDonald's while he was with Amoco.

Ken Dunkley of Quick Food Consulting, La Jolla, said, "They want someone who can look at the company's business structure and financial strategy." He noted that previous initiatives outside California had not fared well. He offered that the plan to take business away from pricier competitors might work because, in tough times, customers sometimes trade down a bit. And it is good to avoid fast-food price wars.

The stock rose 20 cents on the news.

Pittard is optimistic. "I asked my friends to name their favorite restaurants and Rubio's was on almost everyone's list—many said it was their favorite. I wouldn't have come in if I hadn't seen substantial upside growth potential."

Additional information on Rubio's, its financial results, menu, community events, and marketing promotions can be found at http://www.rubios.com

NOTES

1. "Rubio's Restaurants Announces Initial Public Offering of Its Common Stock." Company press release, 1999.
2. "Sheri Miksa Named President and Chief Operating Officer of Rubio's Restaurants, Inc." Company press release, 2002.
3. L. Bertagnoli, "Revving Up Rubio's," *Chain Leader*, October 1, 2004. Retrieved from the Web September 20, 20006. http://www.chainleader/com/ archives/2004/10/rubios.asp.
4. S. Gray, "Wendy's Stumbles with Baja Fresh," *The Wall Street Journal*, January 4, 2005: B7.
5. K. Spors, "Not So Fast," *The Wall Street Journal*, September 19, 2005. Retrieved from the Web February 22, 2006. http://online.wsj.com/article/SB112671792850740632.html
6. D. Washburn, "Rubio's Top Exec Leaves Company," *San Diego Union Tribune*, December 21, 2005. Retrieved from the Web September 21, 2006. www.signonsandiego.com/uniontrib/20051221/news_1b21rubios.html
7. Conference call retrieved from Vcall, accessed through Rubio's Web site, August 3, 2006.
8. F. Green, "Rubio's Employs New CEO, Strategy," *San Diego Union Tribune*, August 22, 2006: B1.

CASE 5

Stamps.com: Maintaining a Leadership Position

INTRODUCTION

Jim McDermott, Ari Engelberg, and Jeff Green are legends at UCLA's Anderson School of Management because the company they created while they were MBA students there in the late 1990s quickly became a resounding success. A mere two years after the trio graduated, their Stamps.com attracted over $55 million dollars in its IPO. Since that time the company has been a dominant player in online postage, cornering as much as 80 percent of the market. But the company will face many new challenges in the next few years, including new forms of PC postage, new competitors, and old competitors with a revamped strategy. Can Stamps.com maintain its leading edge?

WHO IS STAMPS.COM?

Company History

In the spring of 1996 Jim McDermott, an MBA student at the University of California, Los Angeles, happened to run out of stamps in the middle of the night while he was preparing to send out resumes for a job search. Even though McDermott lived across the street from a post office, he was stuck. In 1996 there was no way for an individual or even a business to purchase postage outside of regular business hours. Further, there was no way to buy stamps or refill a

Source: By Mimi Dollinger, Marc Dollinger, and Christopher Tucci. This case is based on a case prepared by MBA candidates Ping Chen, Beth Flom, Rachel Glube, Margot Krikorian, and Karen Rothenberg under the supervision of Professor Christopher L. Tucci, distributed by the Berkley Center for Entrepreneurial Studies at the Stern School of Business, New York University. The earlier version appeared in Marc J. Dollinger's *Entrepreneurship: Strategies and Resources,* 3rd. ed. (NJ: Pearson Education, Inc., 2003.)

postage meter without going to the post office and standing in line.

The next day McDermott shared his frustration with fellow students Ari Engelberg and Jeff Green, and the three of them started brainstorming. Why wasn't it possible to purchase and print postage using a PC and an Internet connection? With a little research they discovered that the U.S. Postal Service (USPS) had already had the same thought. The USPS had recently established the Information Based Indicia Program (IBIP) to test PC Postage™. The program planned to use an Information Based Indicia (IBI), or multidimensional bar code, that could be printed on envelopes or labels. These indicia would contain information such as the amount of postage, zip code of origin, destination, mail class, and weight.

Later that year, McDermott, Engelberg, and Green formed StampMaster, Inc. and enrolled that company in the IBIP. In the fall of their second year in the MBA program, the three nascent entrepreneurs wrote a business plan for their company, envisioning a venture that would develop software which would enable customers to print postage in their homes or offices if they had a computer, an ordinary laser or ink jet printer, and an Internet connection. They submitted their plan to 25 venture capital firms without success. The potential funders were reluctant to bankroll a start-up that was dependent upon the Post Office granting a license. Further, they would have to compete against Pitney Bowes' postage meter system. But after nine months the three partners finally secured $6 million in financing from three venture capital (VC) firms, which allowed them to assemble a technology team and start developing the software for their company.

In August 1998, the new venture received USPS approval to beta test their software by distributing it to a limited audience to discover errors or bugs. Shortly thereafter, they also found a way to make their postage printable in Microsoft Word, which made their service more accessible.

In December 1998, with their software virtually in place, the three cofounders decided to change the name of their company to Stamps.com because they believed it was a stronger and more recognizable brand name.

In spring 1999, Stamps.com received $30 million in private equity funding from three VC firms. Galileo International, a leading provider of electronic distribution services to travel agencies, and the Intel Corporation also made investments in the fledgling company. In June of 1999, the Stamps.com IPO issued 5 million shares at the price of $11 per share. Then, in August of 1999, Stamps.com received approval from the USPS to commercially distribute its software-based indicia. By the end of October 1999, within ten weeks of its launch, Stamps.com had over 90,000 subscribers paying a monthly fee to download and use the company's software.

Early Management

In August 1998 John Payne, a former president and CEO of two software companies, was recruited to bring his management and technical experience to Stamps.com as the company's CEO. In February 1999, a former postmaster general, a former chief marketing executive for the USPS, and the founder and chairman of GeoCities, Inc. (a sponsor of Web pages and blogs), were added to the board of directors. The president and CEO of Hewlett-Packard was recruited to the board later that spring.

In December 1999, McDermott, Engelberg, and Green, the company's three cofounders, left Stamps.com in what was described as an amicable separation following the company's successful IPO and service roll-out. In Spring 2000, the three of them founded Archive.com, a data-storage software company. That company was sold in 2002. At least two of the three partners remain active in entrepreneurial activities.

McDermott is a managing partner in U. S. Renewables Group, a private investment company that acquires, develops, and operates renewable power generation and clean fuel assets, while Engelberg is a founding partner of the Los Angeles Social Venture Partners. Engelberg is also a history teacher and part-time basketball coach at the Los Angeles high school he once attended.

John Payne stepped down from his positions with the company in October 2000. Ken McBride, the company's CFO, was named Payne's successor, and served in that capacity for a number of years.

Early Competition

On the same day that Stamps.com received USPS approval for its software system, a competitor named E-Stamp Corporation was also authorized to distribute electronic postage. E-Stamp used a different model; its customers had to purchase a starter kit with a CD-ROM and a hardware device known as a postage vault or doggle in order to use its service. While E-Stamp customers accessed postage online, they printed their stamps and labels offline. Many customers found their system awkward and inefficient. E-Stamp exited the online postage market in November 2000, and Stamps.com acquired that company's name and patents in April 2001.

Two other IBIP participants also competed against Stamps.com from the beginning. Pitney Bowes, the postage meter giant, introduced an offline postage-printing program with a postage "bank" that could be refilled by phone or via the Internet. In 1999, Pitney Bowes sued Stamps.com for patent infringement, and in 2001, Stamps.com sued Pitney Bowes for the same. All suits were settled in 2003.

The other company was Neopost, the leading supplier of mailroom equipment in Europe. Neopost also introduced a competing postage program that customers printed offline with special labels and a Neopost "stamp dispenser."

Both then and now, Stamps.com aims

most of its competitive ammunition against traditional postage meter companies like Pitney Bowes and Neopost. The company claims its service is much more economical because it doesn't require additional hardware like a postage meter or scale (Stamps.com regularly supplies a free postal scale with payment for the first month of service), and because its monthly fee is generally lower than the cost of renting or purchasing a postal meter. While digital postage, accessed with either a phone or computer, makes it unnecessary to lug a postage meter to the post office for loading, Stamps.com points out that its service requires no additional fees for resetting, printing company logos or messages with the postage, or purchasing special ink cartridges. Stamps.com also advertises that customers can cancel their service at any time, unlike the long-term leases usually required for postage meter rentals. These factors, along with the ability to print the mailing address and postage in one step, verify addresses and zip codes online while the postage is being computed, track expenditures through cost center reports, and other features, have given Stamps.com a considerable competitive edge against these more traditional postage approaches.

Milestones

During its early years Stamps.com experimented with expanding its business with two enhancements it ultimately rejected. In October 1999, the company acquired iShip, an online shipping company. iShip was sold to the United Parcel Service (UPS) in May 2001. In February 2000 Stamps.com formed a wholly-owned subsidiary called EncrypTix to provide online event ticketing as well as travel and financial services. EncrypTix ceased operations in March 2001.

However, the company's core business continued to prosper during this time. In April 2002, Stamps.com printed its 100 millionth Internet postage stamp, and in September 2003 the company printed its 200 millionth Internet postage stamp.

Beginning in 1999, the company also formed alliances with a number of partners, including American Online, IBM, Office Depot, Microsoft, and Quicken.com, to reach more consumers and specifically target the Small Office/Home Office (SOHO) market.

In October 2004, Stamps.com announced it had achieved its first profitable quarter (third quarter 2004). Recent performance metrics are reported in Exhibit 1.

INDUSTRY OVERVIEW

Current Competition

Stamps.com has managed to eliminate two of its early competitors; the E-Stamp Corporation ceased operations in November 2000, and Neopost now relies strictly on a telephone system to refill their postage meters.

The USPS currently lists five vendors as authorized online postage providers: Stamps.com, Pitney Bowes Inc., eBay, Endicia™, and Click-N-Ship®. The eBay program is essentially a service provided to customers who sell items on eBay's Internet auction site, and is limited to those transactions. Endicia is a company that was founded in 1982 to develop software products for address verification and mail management. They began offering Internet postage in 2000. In October 2002 the U.S. Postal Service introduced its PC postage program, called Click-N-Ship.

The chart comparing the services offered by the five providers demonstrates their similarities and differences. All five providers allow customers to refill their postage "bank" and print postage 24 hours a day and seven days a week. They all calculate postage accurately for various weights and classes of mail at their homes or offices, which was not possible prior to online postage. All five providers also allow users to print an address label with postage in one step, and all can be used for domestic first-class postage for parcels. Therefore, all five current providers meet the basic goals that online postage was

EXHIBIT 1   Stamps.com Performance and Metrics

	2005					2006				
	Q1	Q2	Q3	Q4	Total	Q1	Q2	Q3	Q4	Total
Service Revenue	$ 9,100	$10,438	$10,945	$11,907	$42,390	$13,457	$13,628	$13,057	$13,685	$53,827
Product Revenue	1,885	1,826	1,766	1,889	7,366	2,393	1,980	1,924	2,399	8,696
Other Revenue	813	800	777	865	3,254	832	805	780	846	3,262
Total PC Postage	11,797	13,064	13,488	14,661	53,010	16,682	16,413	15,761	16,930	65,785
PhotoStamps Revenue	0	1,159	1,785	5,957	8,901	3,860	3,747	3,148	8,045	18,801
Total Revenue	$11,797	$14,223	$15,273	$20,618	$63,912	$20,542	$20,160	$18,909	$24,975	$84,586
Prior Quarter Paid Customers [1]	285,558	291,104	299,708	293,471		299,432	324,316	326,753	310,501	
New Paid Customers [2]	46,482	54,775	41,798	50,331		69,612	61,733	50,763	57,019	
Lost Paid Customers [3]	(40,936)	(46,171)	(48,035)	(44,370)		(44,728)	(59,296)	(67,015)	(48,294)	
Current Quarter paid Customers [1]	291,104	299,708	293,471	299,432		324,316	326,753	310,501	319,226	
Paid Customer Cancel Rate [4]	4.1%	4.4%	4.7%	4.3%		4.0%	5.1%	5.9%	4.4%	
Total Subscriber & Related Revenue ($000) [5]	$11,338	$12,601	$13,035	$14,205		$16,228	$15,954	$15,307	$16,476	
Avg. Monthly Subscriber Revenue Per Paid Customer [6]	$ 12.98	$ 14.01	$14.81	$ 15.81		$ 16.68	$ 16.28	$ 16.43	$ 17.20	
PC Postage Customer Acquisition Spend [7]	$ 4,423	$ 4,807	$ 4,453	$ 4,321		$ 5,316	$ 4,935	$ 4,965	$ 4,937	
Cost Per Gross New Registered Customer [8]	$ 58	$ 73	$ 80	$ 51		$ 54	$ 57	$ 59	$ 57	
Customer Postage Printed ($000)	$44,948	$44,951	$45,939	$52,804		$57,280	$54,691	$54,783	$62,429	
PhotoStamps Sheets Shipped (000)	0	68	105	345		210	210	176	464	
PC Postage Gross Margin	73.4%	75.4%	78.4%	81.8%	77.5%	79.0%	80.8%	80.9%	79.3%	80.0%
PhotoStamps Gross Margin	NA	34.1%	33.6%	40.7%	38.4%	37.3%	36.5%	33.8%	41.2%	38.2%
Total Gross Margin	73.4%	72.0%	73.2%	69.9%	71.8%	71.1%	72.6%	73.1%	67.0%	70.7%
GAAP Net Income ($000)	$1,640	$2,121	$ 2,565	$ 4,103	$10,429	$ 3,357	$ 4,160	$ 4,263	$ 4,684	$16,464
Non-GAAP Net Income ($000) [9]	$1,640	$2,121	$ 2,565	$ 4,103	$10,429	$ 4,151	$ 4,856	$ 4,982	$ 5,112	$19,101
Non-GAAP EPS [10]	$ 0.07	$ 0.09	$ 0.11	$ 0.17	$ 0.44	$ 0.17	$ 0.20	$ 0.21	$ 0.22	$ 0.79

(Definitions and notes presented on next page)

EXHIBIT 1 (continued)   Stamps.com Performance and Metrics

Definitions and Notes

1. Unique customers successfully billed at least once during the quarter.
2. Customers who were successfully billed for the first time during the quarter.
3. Customers who were successfully billed in the previous quarter but not successfully billed in the current quarter, less any recaptured paid customers from prior quarters.
4. Monthly cancellation rate calculated as [(Lost Paid Customers)/(Prior Quarter Paid Customers + New Paid Customers)] divided by 3.
5. Subscriber and Related Revenue include PC Postage Service Revenue, Product revenue, and package insurance (under Other Revenue); it excludes license fees and all PhotoStamps revenue.
6. Average monthly subscriber revenuer per paid customer

calculated as [Total subscriber revenue for the quarter/Current Quarter Paid Customers] divided by 3.
7. A non-GAAP measure of PC Postage total sales and marketing expenses plus PC Postage promotional costs (under Cost of Revenues), excluding all SFAS-123R expenses starting in fiscal 2006; for reconciliation between GAAP and on-GAAP sales and marketing and cost of revenues, see the Company's prior 8K filings.
8. PC Postage Customer Acquisition Spend divided by Gross New Registered Customers (signed up for Stamps.com account & provided a verifiable billing method) acquired during the quarter.
9. A non-GAAP measure excluding all SFAS-123R expenses starting in fiscal 2006; for reconciliation to GAAP see the Company's prior 8K filings.
10. Non-GAAP Net Income divided by the fully diluted weighted average share outstanding.

intended to meet. A competitive matrix is shown in Exhibit 2.

But beyond the basic services, some differences emerge. Stamps.com currently offers the most comprehensive list of services, with the greatest versatility and options for customization. However, both Endicia and Pitney Bowes offer only slightly fewer services, so these companies may be just as appropriate for many customers. eBay and Click-N-Ship are even narrower, but again, may be sufficient for many customers.

The actual cost for postage from all five providers is the same, and is also identical to the postage charge if a customer uses an offline postage meter or takes a letter or package to the post office.

But in addition to that postage cost, Stamps.com, Endicia, and Pitney Bowes all charge a monthly fee for their service, which essentially is a charge for accessing their software. Stamps.com and Endicia currently have essentially the same charge ($15.99 for Stamps.com, and $15.95 for the expanded Endicia service that most closely matches Stamp.com), while Pitney Bowes currently charges $18.99 per month. All of the paid services offer a free 30- or 60-day trial, and include promotional deals where new customers can get a scale or other items. The services are all on a month-to-month basis, and can be cancelled—or switched—at any time. Neither eBay nor Click-N-Ship charge

beyond the actual postage cost for their more limited services.

According to a company presentation posted on the Stamps.com Web site, the company currently has 85 percent of all online postage subscribers.

New Product Challenge

In 2004 Stamps.com received approval from the USPS to conduct a market test of Photostamps™, a new Internet postage product that allowed customers to upload photographs or other digital images from their personal computers to the Stamps.com site, select a color border and postage amount, and then have sheets of 20 of those custom stamps delivered to their homes or offices by mail. Photostamps were the first customized postage product ever sold in the United States. The product was heralded as a way for consumers to personalize their greeting cards, invitations, birth announcements, and other mail, and as a tool that businesses could use to create a customized identity and attract more attention with their mailings.

The test program was a big hit with customers; more than 2.75 million Photostamps were purchased during the initial trial period. But there were some problems. Photo stamps received negative publicity when customers ordered stamps displaying images of convicted spies Ethel and Julius Rosenberg, Yugoslavian war criminal Slobodan

EXHIBIT 2   Stamps.com Competitive Matrix

	Stamps.com	Endicia	Pitney Bowes Shipsteam Manager	eBay Shipping Manager	USPS Click-N-Ship
Prints and/or refills postage 24 hours a day, 7 days a week	Yes	Yes	Yes	Yes	Yes
Calculates accurate postage	Yes	Yes	Yes	Yes	Yes
Prints address label and postage in one step	Yes	Yes	Yes	Yes	Yes
Prints domestic first-class postage for parcels	Yes	Yes	Yes	Yes	Yes
Uses USPS database to verify delivery address and zip code	Yes	Yes	Yes	No	Yes
Imports addresses directly from other software (such as MS Outlook)	Yes	Yes	No	Yes - (from Ebay sales)	No
Offers comparisons for different USPS delivery methods	Yes	Yes	Manually	Manually	Yes – limited options
Prints domestic shipping for letters	Yes	Yes	No	No	No
Prints international postage	Yes	Yes	No	No	No
Prints other domestic mail classes for letters	Yes	Some	No	No	No
Prints customized domestic first-class postage for letters	Yes	No	No*	No	No
Provides Delivery Confirmation™, insurance, Certified Mail®, and tracking information	Yes	Some	Yes	Some	Some
Allows customer to print custom envelopes and labels with logos or personal graphics	Yes	Yes	Yes	No	No
Generates e-mail to notify customer shipment is on its way	Yes	Yes	No	Yes	No
Presorts periodicals and bulk mail for mailing	Yes	No	No	No	No
Charges monthly fee for either service or software	Yes	Yes	Yes	No	No
Requires purchase or rental of hardware other than computer, printer, and Internet connection	No**	No	Yes	No	No

*Stamp Expressions' custom postage machine available separately for purchase and monthly fee.
**Digital scale provided free of charge with purchase of one month of service.

Note: This information is accurate as of February 27, 2007.

Milosevic, and the stained blue dress made famous during President Bill Clinton's impeachment hearing. Stamps.com said it had rejected approximately 9 percent of 83,000 images that were submitted during the test due to issues of taste or copyright infringement. While the USPS abruptly terminated the test after just seven weeks, they later announced that controversial images did not disturb them as much as it seemed. Nicholas F. Barranca, vice president of product development for the Postal Service, claimed "We don't think that's really our role, as an arm of the federal government, to get involved in censorship." The post office insisted they were more concerned about the potential for fraud with the new stamps, and worried that their machines were having trouble recognizing the photo stamps as valid postage.

In May 2005 the USPS authorized Stamps.com to continue marketing photo stamps in a one-year test program, followed by a second one-year test, with a possible extension for a third year (which would end in May 2008). Two other vendors, Endicia and Zazzle (a joint venture with Pitney Bowes) are also involved in the test program.

Stamps.com currently markets its Photostamps through a unique Web site (www.photo.stamps.com). The current content restrictions published on that Web site give the company the sole discretion to determine what is an appropriate image, and authorize it to charge a $10 processing fee for any image it rejects. The Stamps.com policy further states that the company will reject any images it considers to be obscene, offensive, pornographic, deceptive, vulgar, or violent, along with any image that depicts a celebrity, politician, government leader, or convicted criminal, or any image that infringes on the copyright, trademark, or other intellectual or moral right of any individual or corporation. Technically, even an innocuous family photo can be rejected for a photo stamp if a person cannot prove that he or she owns the rights to the photo. The company also offers a library with the logos

of 32 NFL teams, 60 colleges and universities, selected NASCAR drivers, and photographs from designer Anne Geddes for customers to use on their Photostamps. The cost of the stamps, which are sold in sheets of 20 with varying postage amounts, is approximately $10 over the value of the postage.

Despite the price and the restrictions, digital image stamps are popular with consumers; Stamps.com reports it sold over 21 million photo stamps through February 2007. The company is also a leader in this business, reporting that they garnered 78 percent of the customized postage sold in the third quarter of 2006.

Stamps.com is now hoping to expand its marketing of Photostamps to businesses. The company reports that 18 percent of its photo stamp sales in the third quarter of 2006 were made to businesses. It appears to be an attractive market; the USPS estimates that businesses mail over 8.6 billion pieces of first-class mail to consumers each year.

THE FIGHT TO STAY ON TOP

Stamps.com has performed well in the past few years. Total revenue has grown from $16.2 million in 2002, to $21.2 million in 2003, to $38.4 million in 2004 and $61.9 million in 2005, with estimated revenue of $83.5 million in 2006. A company presentation from November 2006, posted on the Stamps.com Web site, states it has a strong financial position with $116 million in cash and investments with no debt, and that it has achieved a solid financial model with a stable and predictable revenue model and good growth prospects. Stamps.com also reports it has a strong U. S. patent portfolio, with 53 patents issued and 77 pending. This strong financial and technological position, along with the company's reputation and name recognition, will definitely help it to stay on top.

However, there are some areas for future concern. Despite its leadership position in PC postage and custom stamps, the company is locked in battle against two tenacious competitors, Endicia and Pitney Bowes, in both areas. It is important to point out that Stamps.com is dependent on licensing by the U.S. Postal Service: Its photo stamps program is currently operating on a trail basis, and the USPS terminated that trial program unexpectedly once before.

The company's financial report also shows that while Stamps.com was able to enroll approximately 41,000 to 69,000 new paid customers during each quarter of 2005 and 2006, it also lost approximately 40,000 to 67,000 paid customers during the same quarters. Retaining more customers will undoubtedly be important to both future growth and profitability. Financially (completely separate from the cost of the Stamps.com service), the price of U. S. postage is rising, which may motivate more individuals and businesses to find cheaper alternatives to mail.

Bibliography

DeWeese, Chelsea. "Zazzle, a Seller of Custom Goods, Gets Venture-Capital Backing." Retrieved from the Web July 18, 2005. http://www.online.wsj.com/article_print/0,,SB112164185982687851,00.html.

Dow Jones Newswires. "UPDATE: Stamps.com Up: Net Jumps As PhotoStamps Rise." Retrieved from the Web February 21, 2006. http://online.wsj.com/article_print/BT-CO-20060208-007296.html.

Mintz, Jessica. "Your Face on a Stamp Again? Custom Photo Postage Is Back," *The Wall Street Journal*, April 27, 2005: B1.

Selected Stories, *UCLA* Magazine, Summer 2000. Retrieved from the Web February 20, 2007. http://www.magazine.ucla.edu/year2000/summer00_03_09.html.

Smart Computing. "Buying Postage Online," 2000. Retrieved from the Web February 20, 2007. http://www.smartcomputing.com/editorial/article.asp?article=Articles/Archieve/G0801/15x01/44g01.asp&guid=

The Smoking Gun. "Stamps of Approval," 2004. Retrieved from the Web February 2, 2007. http://www.thesmokinggun.com/archive.0831041_photostamps_1.html.

Social Tech. Interview with Jim McDermott, cofounder of Stamps.com, 1999. Retrieved from the Web February 20, 2007, http://www.socialtech.com/fullstory/0001406.html.

Web Sites for Additional Research

www.stamps.com
www.usps.gov
www.endicia.com
www.pb.com
www.eBay.com
www.zazzle.com

CASE 6

Suzy's Zoo

INTRODUCTION

Suzy's Zoo, a closely held greeting card company located in San Diego, California, is now

Source: This case was prepared in 1992 by Professor Kenneth E. Marino of San Diego State University with the assistance of graduate student Terry Wittbrot. It has been updated for this edition by Mimi and Marc Dollinger from public sources of information. It is intended as a basis for class discussion rather than an illustration of effective or ineffective handling of an administrative situation.

approaching its 40th year of operations. Owner and Chief Executive Officer Suzy Spafford is the creative and driving force behind the menagerie of characters that make up Suzy's Zoo. In its early years, the company managed to secure a profitable and safe niche with a devoted following among its customers. The "Zoo" features a happy and colorful group of cartoon animals who live in the imaginary town of Duckport, including

Suzy Ducken, Jack Quaker, and Dooley Stegasouposaurus.

In 1996, Suzy was recognized for her outstanding creations by the National Cartoonist Society when she was awarded its top annual award for greeting cards. In 1999 the company introduced Little Suzy's Zoo, geared to infants and toddlers, which features a baby duck named Witzy and the creatures that inhabit his backyard. Little Suzy's Zoo is a success beyond anything the company had previously achieved. The company's newest characters are Wags and Whiskers, which are dogs and cats with names like Dottie Dachshund and Simone the Perfect. Each character has a distinctive personality, and characters are eventually retired when they lose their appeal in the marketplace.

The company and its products are conservative, appealing to middle-American, homespun tastes. As Spafford would say, "Suzy's Zoo cards are G-rated." Spafford does all she can to maintain the wholesome midwestern image she has created (she was born in Ohio). She is a member of many San Diego and southern California boards, including: Sharp Memorial Hospital Foundation, Rees-Stately Research Foundation, the San Diego Rotary Club, and the San Diego Hall of Champions. She gives generously of her time and money to support charitable causes. Spafford is a very visible person in the San Diego community.

Through licensing agreements, the characters appear on classroom supplies, fabric, plush animals, disposable diapers, wallpaper, infant and toddler apparel, and other items. Suzy's started licensing its designs and characters in the mid-1970s. Throughout the 1980s and 1990s its licensing income grew slowly but surely. During this time the company also expanded into international markets; currently, Suzy's Zoo products are sold in 40-plus countries worldwide.

Over the first 20 years of its existence, the firm grew to be a typical small business operation. With its comfortable market niche and philosophy of slow growth, Suzy's Zoo was always operated profitably. But changes in greeting cards, and in the way those greetings are delivered, present operational and competitive challenges. With its founder and chief designer now approaching retirement age (Suzy was born in 1946), the company must also make plans for future transitions. And the launch of Little Suzy's Zoo led to explosive growth and changed the nature of the business and organization.

EARLY HISTORY OF SUZY'S ZOO

Suzy's Zoo founder and President Suzy Spafford started the business in the mid-1960s when Spafford was working toward her bachelor of fine arts degree at San Diego State University. She recalled that she had always had a knack for drawing animals, going back to her childhood days in Ohio. To earn extra money for school, she worked summers and weekends at local art marts creating colorful pastel and water-color drawings, particularly cartoon characters custom-designed to buyers' tastes. She sold her drawings for $3 apiece, generating $3,000 to $4,000 per summer. During her senior year in college (1967), Bill Murr, a Berkeley, California, medical instrument manufacturer, saw Spafford's work at an art mart in San Diego. He proposed that the two of them team up and start a small greeting card business. Murr provided $600 in funding, and Spafford created eight card designs and agreed on a 90 percent (Murr) to 10 percent (Spafford) split. Suzy's Zoo was officially launched.

Spafford worked out of her home, creating designs that were shipped to Murr in Berkeley, who supervised the printing, then boxed and distributed the cards to local stationery stores. The cards immediately sold well in the Bay Area and on a smaller scale in Washington and Oregon. Within two years, the cards were selling throughout California. Sales increased steadily through the first several years. In the early 1970s, Murr decided he no longer wanted to handle the day-to-day operations. Spafford bought Murr's inventory and reversed the financial arrangement, with Murr retaining 10 percent owner-ship and no involvement in the actual running of the company. Suzy's Zoo was incorporated in 1976.

Spafford believes that the key to her early success was keeping the company small enough to produce on demand. No warehousing costs and low overhead allowed Suzy's Zoo to completely turn its inventory three to four times per year, a routine the company still tries to practice.

By the mid-1970s, Suzy's Zoo cards were being distributed nationally, and her characters were appearing on novelty items such as calendars. Over the years new products were gradually added to the Suzy's Zoo line, including invitations and boxed cards, gift wrap and party goods, Mylar balloons, and stickers and scrapbook supplies. In the late 1980s, Suzy's Zoo expanded into the international arena through European and Far Eastern licensing arrangements. The company has also begun to distribute a limited number of its greeting card designs electronically through partnerships with American Greetings, Blue Mountain, and eGreetings.

In the early years, Suzy's Zoo depended solely on Spafford for character and product design. For many years Spafford felt that maintaining the company as a one-artist operation was central to its success. However, the company has now added a number of artists, including trained illustrators. These artists work with Spafford in conjunction with additional designers who work with computers on licensing, marketing, and scrap-booking products. Suzy's daughter, Kerstyn Lott (SDSU class of 1997), joined the art department after her graduation.

In 1976, the year Suzy's Zoo was incorporated, total sales were $600,000. In 1992, total sales exceeded $6 million. Over these years, total sales increased 4 percent to 5 percent annually. Approximately 85 percent of Suzy's Zoo's annual revenues came from sales to U.S. retailers, 10 percent from licensing agreements, and almost 5 percent from export sales shipped directly from the Suzy's Zoo warehouse. Exhibit 1 shows sales data for the early years. Suzy's Zoo is a privately held company and financial information for the company, other than general sales data, is extremely difficult to come by.

THE GREETING CARD INDUSTRY

The greeting card industry generates $7.5 billion in U.S. retail sales each year. According to the Greeting Card Association (www.greetingcard.org), 90 percent of American households purchase at least one greeting card per year, and the average household purchases 30 cards per year. The industry is dominated by two giants: the privately held Hallmark Cards, which has an estimated 50 percent of the market, and the publicly traded American Greetings Corporation, with an estimated 36 percent of the market. American Greetings acquired Gibson Greetings, previously the third market leader, in 2000. Approximately 3,000 greeting-card publishers divide the remaining

EXHIBIT 1   Sales Figures for Suzy's Zoo

Year	Total Sales ($000)	Sales to U.S. ($000)	Percent of Total	License Income ($000)	Percent of Total	Export Sales ($000)	Percent of Total
1989	$5,350	$4,775	89.2%	$475	8.9%	$100	1.9%
1990	5,650	4,977	88.1	500	8.8	173	3.1
1991	5,900	5,090	86.3	550	9.3	260	4.4
1992	5,950	5,083	85.4	600	10.1	267	4.5

Note: Suzy's Zoo fiscal year ends June 30.

EXHIBIT 2   Greeting Card Industry: Market Share Comparison

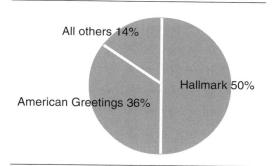

14 percent of the market among themselves (see Exhibit 2).

Ninety percent of all card purchasers are women. Unit sales growth in greeting cards has been 1 percent to 3 percent per year. However, this is a maturing market that recently has been threatening to stop growing for the first time since 1945.

The effect of this division is that two levels of competition operate. The two big card companies are competing against each other on one level, and all the rest of the card companies are competing with each other on another level—but the small companies are not really competing against the big companies.

The late 1980s saw vicious price wars in the greeting card industry. Retailers perceived greeting card companies as all alike; every big card manufacturer's profitability suffered in a discounting frenzy. Greeting card companies, therefore, had to develop new strategies to maintain their share, or get a large piece of a pie that is not growing.

Explosive growth in electronic technology, and burgeoning consumer use of the Internet gave birth to the electronic greeting card, or e-card, in the late 1990s. The development of this entirely new medium for card sending served to further expand the industry, producing new e-card publishers as well as e-greeting product offerings by traditional publishers.

The greeting card market is made even more competitive because barriers to entry are very low. This means that it does not take too much to get into the greeting card business. Anyone with an idea, some talent, and a little start-up money can give it a try. This makes for high turnover, as companies enter the market, fail, exit the market, and are replaced by other newcomers. It should be noted that this information pertains to entry into that 14 percent share of the market where the smaller card companies compete; barriers to entry into the arena where the two large card companies compete are very high.

In an effort to maintain their market share or boost sales in this static environment, the two big competitors have come up with a variety of strategies. Hallmark is trying to persuade today's too-busy-to-write Americans to let greeting cards express their sentiments for them. Midway between Father's Day (in June) and Halloween (October 31) is the worst time of year for American publishers of greeting cards. Retailers sell fewer cards at this time than at any other time of the year.

Trying to boost sales during this dry spell gave birth to the "nonoccasion" card. Hallmark has produced a series of 500 nonoccasion cards for adults and has a line of adult-to-child cards, "To Kids with Love," to help children ages 7 to 14 and their parents cope with growing up. Nonoccasion cards now account for more than 10 percent of the 7 billion greeting cards sold in America each year.

American Greetings has on staff a psychiatrist and various other experts to help come up with new products. The psychiatrist is good at identifying stressful situations in which people have a "psychological need for a card." To further enhance its competitive position and increase declining earnings, American Greetings instituted a cost-cutting program and improved its customer service. Unprofitable subsidiaries and excess costs were trimmed. Just-in-time (JIT) processes in manufacturing and card development allowed American Greetings to reduce inventories and decrease the time it takes to bring cards to market. As part of its emphasis on customer service, American Greetings established its Retail Creative Services Department. This unit emphasized working with customers to create seasonal displays designed to boost store traffic. American Greetings also formed its Information Services Department to develop software to analyze retailers' sales patterns and track inventories for many different products. Apparently these innovations paid off; sales of American Greetings cards and related products such as wrapping paper grew 10 percent, while Hallmark reported only a 1 percent increase in revenues for the same goods during this period (1992).

New technology has had some impact on the greeting card industry. Today the cards sold in more than 100,000 U.S. retail outlets play music when you open them, or even play a brief recording of the sender's voice. Even more significantly, cards have gone "virtual," with greetings sent electronically to computers or cell phones. It is presumed these innovations appeal to nontraditional card buyers such as men and younger people, as well as attracting the growing number of "wired" consumers. The two giants in the greeting card industry are pursuing these new products aggressively, and projections indicate that technology may absorb a significant portion of the greeting card industry in the future.

For smaller greeting card companies, other strategies have been useful. Finding a niche in the market is one way to compete. The goal is to develop a unique concept or style that will appeal to a wide segment of the buying public without disappearing into the shadows of the giants. For example, use of a distinctive sense of humor, stylized artwork, or messages that appeal to specific groups such as college students could establish a marketing niche.

Many small card makers have found that it is very important to listen to their retailers and sales representatives. To compete in an industry dominated by the big companies, the smaller companies have to be better, turn over more quickly, and be more profitable for the retailer.

SUZY'S GREETING CARD BUSINESS

One of Suzy's most important resources for marketing greeting cards is its network of independent sales representatives. These individuals are in continued contact with retail store owners, who can provide the most accurate information on consumer preferences. An early decision was made to go with the mom-and-pop shops as the stores of trade, and to stay away from the large, department-store business. These smaller stores have been Suzy's Zoo's bread and butter; they place their orders and pay their bills. According to Spafford, "It's a clean business and we make a better profit that way."

Some of the larger independent card companies are now encroaching on Suzy's Zoo shelf space in these stores. Some smaller independent card companies have merged to compete against the big companies. Suzy's Zoo maintained a simplified merchandising policy for sales—no fancy displays, no giveaways, "just simple, plain, honest business," Spafford says. In today's environment, continuing to operate under this policy is becoming more of a challenge. Retailers expect deals, discounts, merchandising, and guarantees from the manufacturer to take back unsold stock. If Suzy's Zoo does not offer some sort of consideration to the marketplace, maintaining shelf space may become more difficult.

Within the United States, manufacturers' representatives sell Suzy's Zoo merchandise to retailers. These representatives operate on a nonexclusive basis, getting standard commissions of 20 percent on the sales they make. Suzy's Zoo does not employ an in-house sales force. Its products are sold internationally through international licenses, international distributors, and direct sales.

Marketing strategies have had to change over the years to keep up with growth. The cards have been a boutique item, but other

EXHIBIT 3 Suzy's Zoo Greeting Cards: Organizational Chart

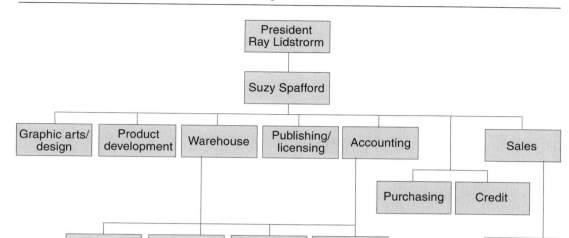

products such as tablecloths, invitations, cups, and plates are mass-marketed in high-volume stores. Revenues from cards have plateaued, and the overall increases in revenues can be attributed to other products. If people do not want to buy cards with cute images anymore, Suzy's Zoo will put the artwork on other products that people will buy—that is why it is found on items like children's sleepwear and baby products.

As consumer consciousness has been raised, recycled paper products have become more important. Some consumers will not buy paper goods without the recycling code. Another change in recent years is that all Suzy's Zoo products are bar-coded, which has allowed Suzy's Zoo merchandise to be sold in some of the larger retail outlets.

OPERATIONS

The company is a nonunion operation with approximately 50 employees. Spafford makes many of the major decisions regarding the company except for personnel and financial matters. Her husband, Ray Lidstrom, serves as company president and takes the lead in

those areas. The organizational chart for Suzy's Zoo Greeting Card division is illustrated in Exhibit 3.

Suzy's Zoo operates out of a two-story, 55,000-square-foot warehouse and office suite in the Sorrento Valley area of San Diego. The company moved into this facility in February 1990. Operations include product design, marketing, warehousing, and shipping. No manufacturing is done on-site; rather, manufacturing is accomplished through subcontractors.

The facility is set up to ensure the efficient flow of products through the warehouse (see operations diagram, Exhibit 4).

Shipments of manufactured goods arrive at the receiving dock from various locations via common carrier on palletized boxes and in cartons. The boxes are placed into a racked bulk-storage area adjacent to the receiving dock. Hand trucks and forklifts are used to move stock.

As product is needed, cartons are broken down, and the shelves are stocked in the "picking" area. The picking area consists of merchandise organized by product number on a shelving system, where pickers fill orders

EXHIBIT 4   Suzy's Zoo: Warehouse and Order Assembly Plant Layout

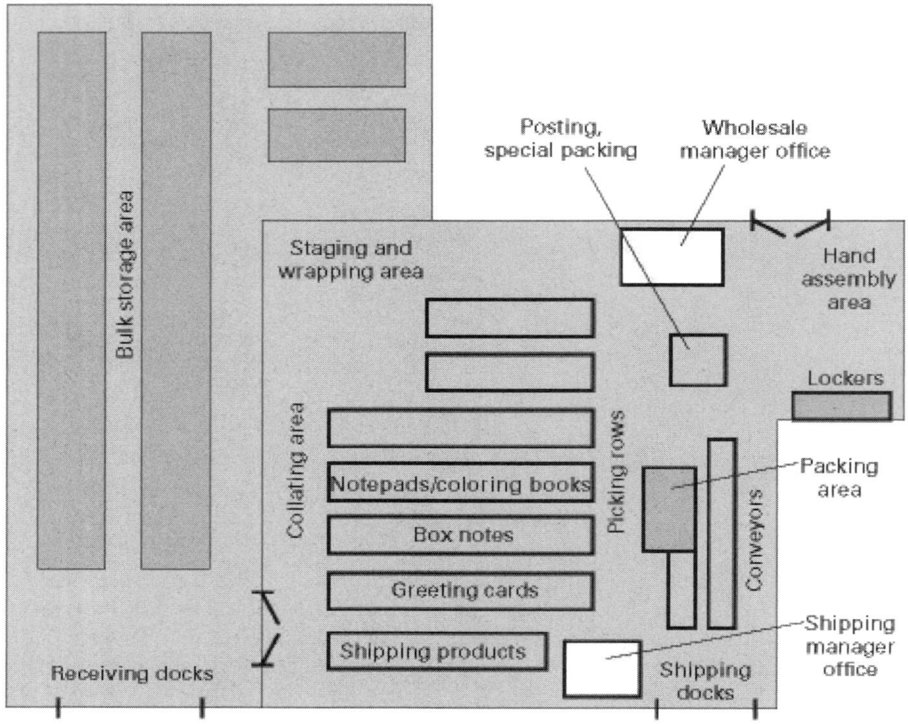

by progressing up and down the aisles pulling items called for in the order. Product is stocked from the backside of the shelves (the alleys) so that workers stocking product do not interfere with workers filling orders. As orders are retrieved, they are placed in cardboard cartons, sealed (shrink-wrapped), labeled, and shipped by common carrier to customers' locations. Machinery used in these operations consists of a counter/collator and a shrink-wrap oven.

An office staff of approximately 12 is maintained for accounting, purchasing, credit, marketing, and customer service functions.

Although the vast majority of sales are wholesale, a small showroom/retail outlet is operated at the front of the building for walk-in traffic. The receptionist performs office duties from the sales counter, and rings up the sales.

RECENT AND CURRENT DEVELOPMENTS

Spafford has remained very involved in product development, and many of her ideas come, as they always have, from her customers. Greeting cards are still a significant part of Suzy's Zoo sales. The Suzy's Zoo line has expanded to include almost anything that can be imprinted with an image of an animal and is in keeping with the company's values. This has been accomplished with licensing agreements.

Licensing allowed Suzy's Zoo to penetrate new markets that it could not enter in other ways, without assuming much of the risk.

No one knows in advance if a new product will sell, and with licensing, the licensee assumes the costs of manufacturing and getting the product to the marketplace. The major disadvantage of licensing, from Spafford's point of view, is the loss of creative control. She has admitted to the need for many compromises in this area. In addition to licensing images for nonpaper products, Suzy's Zoo images were also licensed to other manufacturers of greeting cards, such as Current, a large mail-order house based in Colorado.

Licensees are renting the artwork for a stated period of time so that they can apply Suzy's Zoo character images to their own products, such as mugs and T-shirts. A typical Suzy's Zoo license had a three-year term with an option to renew for an additional two years. The licensing fee was calculated as a percentage of sales and ranges from 3 percent to 6 percent. International licensees pay higher fees (10 percent to 12 percent), but this is split between Suzy's Zoo and its international broker. A list of Suzy's Zoo international brokers, the products they license, and their territories can be seen on the company's Web site at http://www.suzyszoo.com. The company's wholesale Web site is located at http://www.suzyszooshowroom.com.

But now, something major and in some ways unanticipated is underway for this company. The introduction of the Little Suzy's Zoo line in 1999 was hailed as an "unparalleled mass-market retail success story."[1] Created with the same look and feel as the original Suzy's Zoo, Little Suzy's Zoo was aimed at infants and toddlers. The characters were drawn to appear very young to capture the interest of the babies and their parents.

In the early years of the twenty-first century, licensing had grown so important that Suzy's had reorganized itself into two divisions. Suzy's Zoo Greeting Cards continues to offer stationary and printed products, keepsakes, and scrap-booking items and memo pads. Suzy's Zoo Studios was established to develop designs and artwork for the purpose of licensing. There are licensing style guides for each brand. Little Suzy's Zoo characters are the mainstay of this division. Spafford continues to have an active role and works with licensees on designs and prototypes. She has the final review and decision before a license can go forward.

Eventually licensing revenue grew beyond the capabilities of Suzy's Zoo Studios to manage. In April 2005 Suzy's entered an agreement with Earthworks Brand Management. Earthworks Brand Management was chosen to represent worldwide licensing for Suzy's branded products. Incredibly, Little Suzy's Zoo sales had risen to $100 million dollars by this time!

Both Spafford and the CEO of Earthworks entertainment issued statements when the agreement was announced.

Suzy: "We are delighted to name Earthworks Entertainment as licensing representatives for Little Suzy's Zoo. Both Peter Keefe and Cathy Malatesta (head of global licensing and marketing) are highly regarded by the licensing and entertainment industry for their innovative and successful programming and licensing achievements throughout their distinguished careers. We look forward to a long and successful association with this outstanding team."

Peter Keefe: "We have been fans of Suzy Spafford and the charmingly precious world of the Little Suzy's Zoo franchise since the company launched their marvelous Little Suzy's Zoo brand. It is with a special and heartfelt joy that we begin our representation of this absolutely splendid franchise to the licensing and merchandising community. We believe that this brand is now perfectly poised to gain a huge share of the global infant and toddler marketplace in the key categories ranging from books to apparel to toys."

In November 2005, Earthworks had its first major breakthrough in representing Suzy's Zoo. It announced that it had licensed the rights to Suzy Zoo brands to Sony Plaza Ltd. Sony Plaza is the retail sales and merchandising arm of Sony Inc. Sony Plaza planned to begin to produce and distribute products first in Japan, its home country. The Japanese have a taste for American culture and images and there is a vast market in Japan for "cute" products, like Hello Kitty.

Malatesta made the following comments at the Sony Plaza announcement: "The massively popular Suzy's Zoo line has over 200 whimsical characters and accounts for over $100 million in annual sales in the U.S.A. in categories ranging from apparel to toys to greeting cards. It is an ever-green, marvelously entertaining brand with millions of loyal fans. The Sony Plaza distribution arrangement signifies the initial success of our campaign to aggressively position this world-class property in the global marketplace. This is the first of what we believe will be many retails sales deals throughout the world."[2]

Would the Japanese take to Suzy's characters and products? The Suzy's products were introduced into Plaza stores at the beginning of June 2006. Sony Plaza offered 50 new products in its chain of over 100 retail stores. Within two weeks, Sony Plaza announced that it was doubling its sales projections for the Suzy line. No one knows how long the success will last, but Hello Kitty has been an icon of Japanese merchandising for over 30 years.

THE FUTURE

The company philosophy remains, as always, to "give them what they want at a reasonable price," says Spafford. This philosophy has given Suzy's Zoo a great reputation in the card industry. Spafford envisions constant growth. Her goal is to keep turning out cards and products people can relate to.

Suzy's Zoo will never become a giant in the greeting card industry. "We can't compete with Hallmark or American Greeting Cards, nor do we want to." Changes in the structure of the industry have turned in favor of Big Box retailers like Wal-Mart and away from independent stores. Greeting cards, however, will continue to make up a significant percentage of the product line.

But the recent licensing tidal wave that Suzy's has experienced has made the company a worldwide phenomenon. More success has followed. Spafford has turned some of the characters from Suzy's Zoo into storybook characters. In fact, Suzy has a publishing contract with Scholastic Inc. (the same company that publishes Harry Potter) and has produced over a dozen titles. These children's books give Spafford the opportunity to develop her characters within a fictional world where they have names, personalities, and even their own dwelling places, thus allowing endless possibilities for stories. Spafford originally envisioned a series of children's classics similar to *Winnie the Pooh*, and she has published a series of nine board books for toddlers, and four easy readers for primary-grade youngsters. Some of her earliest books are now out of print, but she continues to experiment with new titles, including *My Little Book of Prayers* illustrated with Suzy's Zoo characters.

After books, Spafford wants to try animation. The plans in this area are still vague, but Spafford hopes to create video either for television broadcast, such as a Saturday morning children's cartoon show, or a DVD for direct sales to video stores. Her ambition is to attract the attention of the Disney Company for a possible joint project. If animation becomes a reality, then, of course, this would necessitate the addition of other artists to create this specialized form of drawing. She is also unsure whether the company will create a book and video division or whether the characters will be licensed to an outside video production company.

While the company has continued to produce a steady stream of new stickers, scrapbooking supplies, photo albums, brag books, and other paper goods, along with its core greeting cards, to date Suzy's Zoo has had only limited involvement with the digital-card market, and with the high-tech gadget kind of greeting cards favored by its large competitors.

In addition to these product development ideas, nurturing and growing the greeting card business and responding to changes in retail requirements are also priorities. Internal issues of succession, organization, design, and management development have been highlighted by the continued growth of the business.

In any event, the company hopes that books and video will have a circular effect on Suzy's Zoo business, as the increased recognition that will come from these higher-profile exposures will boost sales for all products sporting the Suzy Zoo's character images.

Spafford concluded a recent SDSU alumni article interview by noting, "It's not the same world as it was. I feel like I was very lucky to get into it when I did. If I had to do it over again today, I think I would find it to be much more of a challenge." And there are still challenges ahead.

NOTES

1. *Business Wire:* "Earthworks Appointed Merchandising and Licensing Rep for 100 Million Dollar Little Suzy's Zoo Property," April 25, 2007. Retrieved from the Web March 8, 2007, from HighBeam Encyclopedia Web site.

2. *Business Wire,* "Sony Plaza to Sell Earthworks Entertainment Suzy's Zoo Property in Over 100 stores in Japan," November 15, 2005. Retrieved from the Web March 8, 2007 from the HighBeam Encyclopedia Web site.

CASE 7

Tellme Networks: Dial Tone 2.0? (Revised)

It was close to midnight on a brisk night in November 2000, and Mike McCue, co-founder and CEO of Tellme Networks, was on yet another recruiting mission.[1] His targets: top computer-engineering students at Stanford University. His secret weapon: free pizza. McCue planned to personally deliver pizzas to the Stanford computer lab in hopes of convincing a handful of top students to quit school and join Tellme, the leading provider of Web content that could be accessed using simple voice commands over a regular telephone. The now 32-year-old McCue had skipped college and joined IBM as a graphics specialist.[2] As CEO of Tellme, McCue spent about 60 percent to 80 percent of his time recruiting employees. "It's not hard to get money these days," he claimed. "It's getting the right people that's difficult."[3]

Indeed, it had not been hard for Tellme to win over financial backers. In fact, its success at raising money—an astounding $238 million as of the end of 2000[4]—made the voice portal war Tellme's to lose. Its list of backers was a virtual Who's Who of the venture capital world. Tellme had raised $125 million in October 2000 despite immense volatility in the stock markets and the general downturn of technology stocks.[5] The substantial investments—not to mention an alliance with

telecommunications giant AT&T—gave Tellme a significant leg up on the competition. Still, the company faced increasing pressure to deliver on its ever-evolving business plan.

"Our long-term goal is to create Dial Tone 2.0," McCue said, envisioning a future when users would not even need to dial Tellme. Instead of getting a dial tone when they picked up the phone, users would be connected directly to their personal Tellme virtual assistant, ready at their disposal.[ii] Would Tellme succeed in becoming the Yahoo! of the voice portal market? How would the company capture and sustain profits in this rapidly evolving market?

COMPANY BACKGROUND: "NETSCAPEES"

McCue got involved with computers at a fairly young age. He wrote several video games in high school, and after graduating he joined IBM as a graphics specialist.[6] In 1989, he left IBM and founded Paper Software, which went on to develop 3-D Internet software that enabled Netscape Navigator to display complex graphics. In February 1996, McCue sold his company to Netscape Communications for an estimated $20 million and joined the firm as vice president of technology. After America Online acquired Netscape in 1998, McCue, like dozens of Netscape's other top engineers and middle managers, left the company to start his own venture.

In January 1999, McCue and 22-year-old computer whiz Angus Davis, a fellow "Netscapee," founded Tellme Networks in Mountain View, California. McCue also quickly brought on one-time arch nemesis

Hadi Partovi, formerly the group program manager for Microsoft's Internet Explorer, as part of Tellme's founding management team, which consisted of several other Netscapees. (See Exhibit 1 for details on Tellme's 2000 management team.) In July, former Netscape CEO Jim Barksdale and former Microsoft Senior Vice President Brad Silverberg, along with Tellme's roughly 20 employees, contributed $6 million as seed money for Tellme.[7]

Thanks to the pedigree of its founders and management team, Tellme raised an additional $47 million in December 1999 from leading venture capital firms, Benchmark Capital and Kleiner Perkins Caufield & Byers. (See Exhibit 2 for details on Tellme's advisers.) In May 2000, AT&T invested $60 million in Tellme as part of a strategic relationship in which Tellme would use AT&T networking services and collaborate with AT&T to develop business and consumer applications. In October, Tellme raised an additional $125 million in financing from a group of well-known technology institutional investors. (See Exhibit 3 for a company timeline.) With its more than 250 employees, the company expected that the latest round of financing would carry it through to profitability.[8]

"TELLME MORE"

Tellme offers Web content via a toll-free number (1-800-555-TELL). Users can call Tellme and access news, weather forecasts, sports scores, stock quotes, traffic reports, horoscopes, and movie and restaurant listings using simple voice commands, such as "Tellme news" or "Tellme more." Users can also set "Tellme Favorites," including specific cities for weather forecasts and different types of news through Tellme's Web site. In addition, Tellme can connect users to major airlines and a local taxi service anywhere in the country. Within the industry, this type of service is known as the "directory business."

"Simple, everyday tasks for simple, everyday people on simple, everyday devices—

telephones," explains, McCue, who wanted to create something as attractive to consumers as the Web without a technology barrier.[9] "Everyone from my grandmother to my baby brother can understand this," he says. "Nothing to buy, download, install, or set up—just pick up the phone and dial." There are only a couple of hundred million Web-enabled devices in the world today, but there are 1.5 billion telephones.[10] With Tellme, anyone with access to a phone can access Web-based content without any additional hardware.

Industry experts are calling this interplay of Web-based content and the telephone a voice portal, much like a Yahoo! except via phone. Tellme began a nationwide three-month trial of its free voice portal service in April 2000 and officially launched its service in July after completing 1.6 million calls during the test period. Through the trial, the company increased its voice-recognition accuracy to an average of 95 percent. This is considered the minimum acceptable level for effective communication.

DEVELOPMENT OF TELLME

Although its service relies heavily on advanced voice-recognition software, Tellme actually outsources the technology, and licenses it from companies such as Nuance and Lernout & Hauspie. Tellme combines the voice-recognition technology with proprietary user interface tools and a new programming standard called VoiceXML (VXML) to encode Web content in such a way that a voice browser can automatically recognize and retrieve information.[11] McCue equates Tellme to "radio on demand," a combination of a speech-recognition portal and search engine designed to save time and money.

Tellme sells advertising and charges an undisclosed fee to list companies on its 1-800 directory. The company also makes money as an application service provider (ASP) by hosting applications for existing Internet sites.

"The real money is in the ASPs," says Yankee Group analyst Megan Gurley. "The e-commerce and advertising revenue will be chump change."[12] Eventually, Tellme plans to offer ecommerce as well, which would allow users to order items and services from e-tailers such as Amazon.com using just a telephone. The idea is that Tellme would take a cut of every order placed using its service. "It's about hearing a song on the radio, and being able to call Tellme and buy it," McCue says.[13]

After its most recent round of financing, Tellme recently began emphasizing professional services for building phone sites and providing other voice-enabling services to businesses. The company receives a professional services fee for developing the customized site and per minute hosting charges. In the industry, this is known as the "network business." Tellme offers businesses a technology called Tellme Studio (studio.tellme.com) that is free and offers extensive tools necessary to get a simple phone site up and running using a Web browser and an ordinary phone. Since Tellme Studio uses familiar Internet standards such as HTML, HTTP, JavaScript and SSL, companies can use their existing Web sites and Web technologies to build their phone sites. Once the phone sites are built, Tellme offers additional services, for a fee, to further improve these sites.

"This is all about recreating the Web phenomenon on the telephone network," says McCue. "By bringing the Internet's open standards to the phone, we expect to see the creation of thousands of compelling phone sites linked together to form a 'phone Web' that can be used by nearly anyone, anywhere."[14]

OVERVIEW OF THE VOICE PORTAL MARKET

Voice portals allow callers to use toll-free numbers to access the Internet from a telephone without an Internet connection. (See Exhibit 4 for an illustration of how a voice portal works.) Forrester Research estimates that voice-driven e-commerce could reach and exceed $450 billion in revenue by 2003, which is three times the projected revenue for online retailing.[15] Market research firm Kelsey Group projects that more than 18 million U.S. consumers will use a voice portal service by 2005.[16]

While mobile professionals are the likely target market for voice portals, other potential customers include commuters needing traffic updates, consumers wanting local information via audible yellow pages, disabled individuals who cannot utilize a keyboard but can access information audibly, and the estimated 55 percent of U.S. homes still without Internet access.[17]

Existing Web portals expect voice portals to be popular with regular Web users, who would hopefully log on more often if they could do so using their cell phones. They also anticipate tapping a vast and entirely new audience of users who do not own PCs, which amounts to about half of all U.S. households.

COMPETITION

Tellme faces roughly 30 to 35 start-up competitors in the voice portal market. Many players in this market are focusing on distinct services, such as providing driving directions or reading the user's e-mail out loud, or on specific markets, such as those outside of the United States, as a means of differentiation.

There are four types of competitors plus the potential competition from telecoms. These are:[18]

1. Voice portals of the directory type
2. Voice ASPs which are transaction based
3. Speech recognition software providers
4. WAP services that run the mobile internet

While competition among voice portal start-ups is already intense, established technology and Internet companies have also started to get in the mix. America Online recently took a small stake in Speechworks International, a Boston-based voice recognition software maker, and acquired voice portal Quack.com.[19]

Tellme's key competitive advantage may not be its technology or toll-free service offerings, but rather its seasoned management team, its blue-chip investors—including Kleiner Perkins and Benchmark Capital—its strategic alliance with AT&T, and its $238 million war chest. That is significantly more money than all of its rivals combined.[20]

Some of Tellme's competitors are also its suppliers. (See Exhibit 5 for a list of infrastructure companies supporting the voice portal market).

TELLME ALLIANCES

As a voice portal, Tellme needs content providers such as CNN Radio and *The Wall Street Journal* to feed news reports. However, Tellme's most important alliance has been its deal with telecom giant AT&T. Both AT&T and Tellme are gambling that consumers will want Web access when there is no good Web connection available.

For Tellme, AT&T's $60 million investment gave the start-up much-needed validation and credibility in the eyes of consumers—not to mention the much-needed cash. The alliance also solidified Tellme's leadership position in the voice portal market, and gave Tellme access to a wide range of advanced networking capabilities, a scalable infrastructure, networking management, professional services, and Internet hosting. In short, AT&T brought McCue & Co. one step closer to replacing the dial tone.

For AT&T, the deal gave the telecom giant a foothold in the voice portal market, putting it first in line to reap any benefits if voice portals really take off. In essence, AT&T was able to outsource its research and development (R&D) in this area to Tellme. In addition, AT&T stood to benefit with increased phone traffic as more and more consumers started using voice portals.

THE CHALLENGE FOR TELLME 2000

The day after McCue's latest pizza delivery/recruiting mission at Stanford, Tellme held a staff meeting that was part company meeting and part evangelical revival.[21] McCue sent out a rallying cry: "The next few months are the most important we've had—perhaps we'll every have—at Tellme. We need to stand and deliver now!"

After the meeting, McCue wondered how Tellme would maintain its lead in the voice portal market in the face of increasing competition to eventually become Dial Tone 2.0. The company's latest round of investors had very high expectations and wanted Tellme to push ahead in offering more business-to-business services. McCue asked himself: Should Tellme continue to build out its consumer-based Web site, or should it concentrate on increasing revenues from business customers? Could it do both? Or would Tellme be spread so thin that it would never become the Yahoo! of the voice portal market?

UPDATE: TELLME IN 2007

In the seven years since the founding of Tellme, the company has undergone many changes. The first was the bursting of the Internet business bubble in 2001. Many of the companies that were financed in the late 1990s and early in the twenty-first century did not have sustainable business models. They could not generate revenue, profits, or both. And these firms folded. Billions of dollars in risk capital were lost and many paper millionaires in Silicon Valley and on Wall Street found their net worth considerably diminished.

Tellme survived, though the experts disagreed on what the future held. In 2005 the Kelsey Group estimated that over 45 million people had registered on a voice portal.[22] This number exceeded earlier estimates, but had not yet been reached. In fact, instead of the $450 billion market forecasted earlier, the new estimates for the industry were $12.3 billion in revenue ($5.7 directory; $6.6 networking).[23] And while Jupiter Communications remained bullish on technological advances, Forrester Research predicted that both the technical and human limitations for Tellme's technology had been reached. Forrester felt that only a small set of firms would eventually need these services.[24]

The network business turned out to be the more lucrative and stable for Tellme, which claims the largest and most reliable VoiceXML platform in the world. (see Exhibit 6). As it developed, directory technology led to significant networking improvements. The software and technology constituted a complex bundle with important overlapping applications. Also, Tellme's clients spent about 30 cents to 50 cents per minute in total professional service fees and charges to use the voice network. If these clients had used human beings to answer the phones, the costs were estimated to be between $2 and $5 per phone call. As the average phone call lasted four minutes, the spread was high, as was the resulting savings to clients. Therefore, this is the direction that the business took. More information on the current Tellme can be found at its Web site: http://Tellme.com

But not all is settled and certain for the company as it faces the future. Demographic differences indicate that the use of the phone is changing. A Harris Interactive® survey commissioned by Tellme indicates varied needs and tastes in the use of directory assistance (411 calls). Some of these results are presented in Exhibit 7. Tellme management has to make sense of these data and develop new products, services, networks, and alliances.

Another issue facing the company now is whether to go public and sell stock in an initial public offering (IPO). Tellme might have gone public early in 2001 or 2002 if the stock-market Internet bubble had not burst and the IPO market had not tanked. Now, half a decade later, there is a good deal more rationality among investors and underwriters. Tellme has reached sales of more than

$100 million. It has 340 employees and that number is expected to increase by 30 percent this year. The company is now established and has proven it can handle large corporate accounts as well as manage the directory business. Voice recognition is now accurate to 99.4 percent.

There is still competition from companies like BeVocal, Intervoice, and Voxeo. And other firms like Convergys, Avaya, and Nortel are moving into voice applications. Nuance Communications owns the leading computer speech recognition product, Naturally Speaking. But Tellme is now considered the leader in voice ASPs.[25]

However, new initiatives are being launched all the time. On January 10, 2007, Steve Jobs of Apple, Inc. announced the introduction of the iPhone.[26] In a partnership with AT&T's Cingular cellular carrier, the iPhone may threaten Tellme's success. The iPhone is able to search the Web, customize dialing and settings, provide data services, and offer e-commerce and downloading capabilities; it also has a user-friendly touch screen. The phone is being called visual voice mail. Apple is hailing the product as being on a par in importance with the Macintosh computer and the iPod. It estimates sales of 10 million units by 2008 at $499 to $599 per unit. Other potential partners for the iPhone are Viacom and Disney for movie downloads, and Motorola for hardware.[27]

Perhaps Tellme will find its opportunities broadened by the iPhone and the imitators that are sure to follow. In May 2006, Tellme announced that Avadis Tevanian had retired from Apple and was joining the Tellme board. Tevanian was the software whiz behind Apple's OS 10 operating system and is considered a business and technology genius. "I believe their technology could revolutionize the way we use telephones. My goal is to really take the company to the next level in terms of revenue growth and their profits," said Tevanian.[28] In fact, Tellme already works with Cingular by providing it with automated voice directory assistance. Could Tellme be part of the alliance network

EXHIBIT 1   Tellme Management Team 2000

Mike McCue

CEO, chairman and cofounder, formerly vice president of technology at Netscape, Mike McCue played a leading role in establishing product, technology, and business strategy for the company's client, portal, and server businesses. Prior to Netscape, McCue was founder and CEO of Paper Software, which won nearly 80% market share in 3-D Internet software from competitors SGI and Microsoft. Netscape acquired Paper Software in February 1996. McCue left Netscape to cofound Tellme Networks in January 1999. At Tellme, he is responsible for the overall leadership and direction of the company.

Angus Davis

Director of production and cofounder. Formerly communicator product manager at Netscape, Davis was responsible for Netscape's next-generation browser technology. He coauthored "Netservices," a plan to transform Netscape from a software company to a services company, and worked on early strategy planning for Netcenter, the portal Web site. Having joined Netscape in 1996 when he was only 18, Davis was for some time the company's youngest employee. At Tellme, Davis helps develop corporate business strategies and strategic partnerships, and guide the future direction of the company.

Hadi Partovi

Vice president of production, board member. Formerly the group program manager for Microsoft's Internet Explorer, Partovi had broad responsibility for product strategy, design, and project management on the Internet Explorer team, where he helped direct four major releases of the browser software. Partovi left Microsoft to join his former arch-enemies from Netscape as part of Tellme Network's founding management team. At Tellme, he is responsible for delivering the consumer service that will bring the power of the Web to the telephone network. Partovi graduated from Harvard University with M.S. and B.A. degrees in Computer Science.

John Giannandrea

Vice president of platform development, CTO, and board member. Formerly chief technologist and principal engineer in the browser group at Netscape/AOL. Giannandrea led the development of many important Web browser technologies and contributed to many of today's Web standards and protocols. At Netscape, Giannandrea was involved with every release of the Navigator product, from the first beta of 1.0 through 4.5. Prior to Netscape, he worked on the Telescript and MagicCap technologies at General Magic. As vice president of platform development and chief technology officer at Tellme, Giannandrea is responsible for all technical aspects of Tellme's service offerings.

Charles Moldow

Senior vice president of business development and sales. Prior to joining Tellme, Moldow was general manager of MatchLogic, Excite@Home's digital marketing technologies and solutions company. Before the merger with Excite in January 1999, he was vice president of @Media Sales and Marketing. Previously, Moldow was vice president of business development for @Home Network, where he managed all facets of the company's development and deal efforts. Before joining @Home Network, Moldow worked at TCI, founded two companies in the marketing/publishing industries, and spent four years at Merrill Lynch in the mergers and acquisitions practice.

Andrew Volkmann

Vice president of finance and administration. Volkmann comes to Tellme from Netscape, where he spent 3.5 years in various financial roles. As the senior director of finance, he was responsible for the financial planning and analysis for Netscape's Netcenter division. Prior to the Netcenter position, Volkmann served as the director of finance for Netscape's enterprise software research, development, and marketing groups. Prior to Netscape, he served as a product line finance manager at National Semiconductor and as worldwide planning manager at Hitachi. At Tellme, Volkmann is responsible for all general and administrative functions.

SOURCE: Tellme Web site, 2000. http://tellme.com

EXHIBIT 2   Tellme Advisers 2000

Jim Barksdale, *Board Adviser*

Barksdale is managing partner at The Barksdale Group, a full-service investment advisory firm he founded in April 1999. Before that, Barksdale was president and CEO of Netscape Communications.

Peter Currie, *Board Member*

Currie is a partner at The Barksdale Group. Before that, he served as executive vice president and chief administrative officer of Netscape Communications. From April 1989 to April 1995, Currie held various management positions at McCaw Cellular Communications.

John Doerr, *Board Adviser*

Doerr is currently a partner at venture capital firm Kleiner Perkins Caufield & Byers, where he has sponsored a series of investments (Compaq, Cypress, Intuit, Macromedia, Lotus, Netscape, Sun Microsystems, and Symantec) that led to the creation of over 30,000 jobs.

Kevin Harvey, *Board Member*

Prior to founding Benchmark Capital in 1995, Harvey started two successful software companies: Styleware, which pioneered integrated software for the Apple II personal computer and was ultimately purchased by Claris Corp., and Approach Software, the first easy-to-use client/server database for Windows. Approach was acquired by Lotus Development in 1993.

Mike Homer, *Board Adviser*

Homer is currently a senior vice president at America Online. Prior to Netscape's acquisition by AOL, Homer held various executive positions at Netscape Communications, including exec-utive vice president and general manager of Netscape Netcenter.

Chip Pitts, *Board Adviser*

Pitts formerly worked at Nokia, where he negotiated key transactions and disputes, and also helped develop and implement Nokia's Internet strategy. Prior to Nokia, Pitts was a partner at Baker & McKenzie, the world's largest law firm, where he assisted many businesses in protecting and exploiting their intellectual property globally.

Brad Silverberg, *Board Member*

Silverberg is currently a founding member of the venture-holding firm Ignition, investing in wireless and other technology start-ups. He was formerly a senior vice president at Microsoft, where he served as a member of Microsoft's nine-person executive committee, its top decision-making body. Silverberg ran the Windows business from 1990 to 1995, and then directed Microsoft's Internet turnaround.

Jaleh Bisharat, *Board Adviser*

Bisharat was most recently vice president of marketing for Amazon.com. At Amazon.com, she oversaw customer acquisition and retention, brand marketing, public relations, market intelligence, and the customer experience group.

Scott Bedbury, *Board Adviser*

Bedbury has established himself as one of the world's most successful brand architects, helping Nike make "Just Do It" part of the global lexicon and fueling Starbucks' drive to reinvent a 900-year-old commodity. Bedbury directed Nike's worldwide advertising efforts from 1987 to 1994 and later served as Starbuck's chief marketing officer.

SOURCE: Tellme Web site, 2000. http://tellme.com

that will propel the iPhone to market dominance? And how much more would Tellme's IPO be worth if all of these speculations came to fruition?

NOTES

1. Based on an actual account, T. McNichol, "Capturing Eardrums," *Wired*, May 2000. Retrieved from the Web. http://www. wired.com

2. Ibid.
3. Ibid.
4. S. Silverman, "Tellme Announces New Funding and Focus," *Redherring.com,* October 4, 2000. Retrieved from the Web. *www.redherring.com.*
5. E. Nee, "Who Wants to Talk to the Web?" *Fortune,* November 13, 2000: 317.
6. McNichol, May 2000.
7. D. Kalish, "Former Netscape and Microsoft Execs in Unusual Internet Collaboration," *Associated Press,* July 18, 1999.
8. Silverman, 2000.

EXHIBIT 3   Tellme Company Timeline

January 1999: Tellme Networks, Inc., founded by Mike McCue, former vice president of technology at Netscape, and Angus Davis, former communicator product manager at Netscape. McCue brings on Hadi Partovi, former group program manager for Microsoft's Internet Explorer, as part of Tellme's founding management team.

July 1999: James Barksdale, former CEO of Netscape, and Brad Silverberg, former senior vice president and member of Microsoft's executive committee, along with Tellme's employees, invest $6 million in Tellme. Silverberg and Peter Currie, former executive vice president and CFO of Netscape and a partner at The Barksdale Group, join the company's board of directors.

December 1999: Tellme raises $47 million from leading venture capital firms Benchmark Capital and Kleiner Perkins Caufield & Byers. Seed-round investors, The Barksdale Group and Brad Silverberg also participate in this round of financing. Kevin Harvey, a founding partner at Benchmark, joins the company's board of directors.

April 2000: Tellme begins nationwide trial of its free voice portal service. Users can call a toll-free number and access news, weather forecasts, sports scores, stock quotes, traffic reports, horoscopes, and movie and restaurant listings using voice commands.

May 2000: AT&T invests $60 million in Tellme as part of a strategic relationship in which Tellme will use AT&T networking services and collaborate with AT&T to develop business and consumer applications based on Tellme's Internet platform and delivered over AT&T's network.

July 2000: Tellme officially launches 1-800-555-TELL, ending a three-month trial in which the company completed 1.6 million calls and brought its voice-recognition accuracy to an average of 95 percent.

October 2000: Tellme raises an additional $125 million in financing from institutional investors, Attractor, Amerindo Investment Advisors, Bowman Capital, Essex Investment Management, Ignition, Van Wagoner, and others including original investors Benchmark Capital, Kleiner Perkins, and The Barksdale Group.

SOURCE: Tellme Web site, 2000. http://tellme.com

9. M. Madeo, "Tellme Something New," *Business 2.0,* March 1, 2000. Retrieved from the Web. www.business.com/content/magazine/filter/2000/03/01/11097
10. J. Swartz, "Tellme Networks Want to Reinvent the Telephone," *Forbes,* March 21, 2000. Retrieved from the Web. http://www.forbes.com/2000/03/21/feat2.html
11. Nee, 2000.
12. P. Patsuris, "The Latest Web Gadget May Be the Phone," *Forbes,* July 28, 2000. Retrieved from the Web. http://www.forbes.com/2000/07/28/feat.html
13. P. Kapustka, "Big Fish: Calling Mike McCue CEO," *Redherring.com*, July 26, 2000. Retrieved from the Web. http://www.redherring.com
14. "Tellme Introduces the World's First Open Platform for the Telephone Network," *Wireless Developer Network Daily News,* June 14, 2000. Retrieved from the Web. http://wirelessdevnet.com/news/2000/166/news7.html
15. "The Value of Voice Portal Solutions." Retrieved from the Web in 2000. http://www.intel.com/eBusiness/products/momentum/voice.html
16. Ibid.
17. Ibid.
18. T. Eisenmann and N. Tempest, *Tellme Networks,* HBS 9-801-319, revised November 15, 2005.
19. S. Cleary, "Speak and You Shall Receive," *The Wall Street Journal* September 18, 2000: R 25.
20. A. Reinhardt, "The Good Ole Telephone Becomes a Hot New Web Tool," *Business Week,* April 24, 2000. Retrieved from the Web. http://www.tellme.com/newsclips/ bizweek4.html
21. McNichol, May 2000.
22. Eisenmann and Tempest. 2005: 7.
23. Ibid.
24. Ibid.
25. O. Kharif, "Tellme's Naughty Schoolboy," *Businessweek Online*, March 13, 2006. Retrieved from the Web. http://www.businessweek.com/technology/content/mar2006/tc20060313_91313 6.htm?chan=search on March 21, 2006.
26. N. Wingfield and Y. Li, "Apple's iPhone: Is It Worth It?" *The Wall Street Journal,* January 10, 2007: D1.
27. O. Kharif, "Tellme Bulks Up," *Businessweek Online,* May 9, 2006. Retrieved from the Web http://www.businessweek.com/technology/content/may2006/tc20060509_253957.htm?chan=search on January 11, 2007.
28. Tellme Web site, 2000. http://tellme.com
29. Ibid.

EXHIBIT 4 How a Voice Portal Works

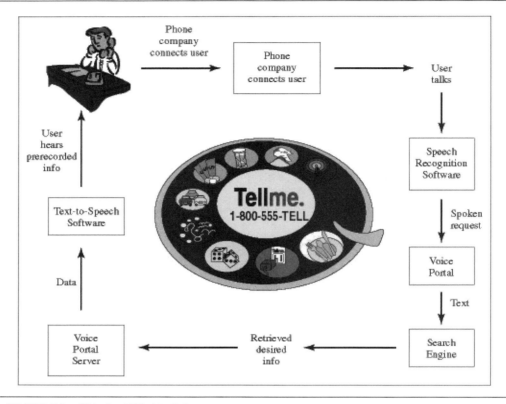

SOURCE: Tellme Web site, 2000. http://tellme.com

EXHIBIT 5 Infrastructure Companies Supporting the Voice Portal Market (2000)

Nuance Communications. Creates speech-recognition software. Used by Tellme and BeVocal.

Lernaut & Hauspie. Creates speech-recognition and translation software. Used by Tellme.

Speechworks International. Creates speech-recognition and translation software. Used by Quack.com. Also, Yahoo! plans to use Speechworks' software to convert text messages (e-mail) into voice. AOL holds minority stake in the company.

Phone.com. Merged with Software.com and renamed Openwave Systems, Inc., in November 2000. Openwave serves over 150 communications service providers with an aggregate of over 500 million subscribers. The new firm's portfolio of products includes wireless Internet infrastructure and browsers, unified messaging, mobile e-mail, directory services, voice processing, synchronization, and instant messaging.

Lucent (MCS). Creates a voice platform believed to be more scalable than competitors. Used by Phonerun.

EXHIBIT 6   The Tellme Platform

The largest and most reliable VoiceXML platform in the world.

Flexibility, scalability and reliability are the hallmarks of the Tellme platform, the world's largest open standards platform for the phone. Creating a bridge between the phone and the Internet, it is the first platform to allow a caller to search for what they want from any phone, simply by using their voice.

Want to trade a stock? Find your package? Be notified when your flight is delayed? Order a pizza? With some of the largest companies in the world using Tellme, millions of people get answers to these daily questions when they call any of the 3,000 different applications running on Tellme's platform.

Flexibility
The Tellme platform is based on open standards like VoiceXML, CCXML, and VoIP, making it incredibly flexible. This allows any of our 20,000 developers to quickly add new services to Tellme and enables our partners to build a broad array of applications for their customers.

Scalability
    35 million unique callers per month
    Over 10 billion utterances per year
    Over 2 billion calls per year
    The world's largest recorded audio library
Reliability
    Networkwide upgrades with zero downtime
    A bulletproof 99.995% network
    Three multitiered, carrier-grade, redundant data centers

EXHIBIT 7   Generational and Gender-Specific Behaviors When Calling 411 to Search for a Business

Which of the following business listings have you requested in the past year?

	All Adults	Millennials	Gen Xers	Boomers	Women	Men
Restaurants & bars	43%	50%	46%	39%	43%	43%
Retail stores	36%	33%	42%	34%	42%	30%
Hotels/lodging	24%	11%	19%	31%	20%	28%
Movie theaters, amusement, & recreation	20%	25%	21%	18%	22%	19%
Transportation: Taxis & airlines	10%	5%	11%	12%	7%	13%

When you've needed a phone number or address while in the car or "on the go," which of the following have you done instead of calling 411?

	All Adults	Millennials	Gen Xers	Boomers	Women	Men
Called a family member	58%	63%	65%	52%	64%	53%
Called a friend	46%	56%	52%	37%	49%	43%
Stopped at a phone booth	29%	19%	27%	35%	26%	31%
Called a colleague	27%	20%	32%	27%	23%	30%
Tore page from phone book	7%	7%	9%	6%	6%	9%
Booted up computer in the car	7%	6%	7%	7%	4%	10%
Driven to wireless "Hot Spot"	5%	6%	7%	3%	3%	6%
Person or people most frequently called for number		Mom: 38%	Spouse or Significant Other: 39%	Spouse or Significant Other: 37%	Mom: 21%	Spouse or Significant Other: 37%

SOURCE: Tellme press release. "The 411 on 411: New Study Uncovers Key Generational and Gender-Specific Behaviors When Calling 411 to Search for a Business," August 21, 2006. http://www.tellme.com/press-10092006.html.

CASE 8

Master International Franchising in China: The Athlete's Foot, Inc.

by Ilan Alon and Amber Xu

PART A

One day in late 2001, Rick Wang, the managing director of RetailCo Inc., the master franchisee for The Athlete's Foot in China, was reviewing the most recent sales report of his company. He found that the sales volume for the past six months had declined precipitously, down almost one-third from what it had been only one year ago. Inevitably, Wang was concerned.

RetailCo Inc. had enjoyed a banner year in 2000; however, the company had experienced a cascade of problems beginning in 2001. At the start of that year, the company was forced to deal with pressure due to a supply shortage of major products, which could deal a deathblow to any small retailer. In quick succession, financial crises and sales problems related to the lack of product created a systemic disaster. Unless Wang acted quickly and decisively, RetailCo.

Source: Amber Xu prepared Part A of this case under the supervision of Professor Ilan Alon solely to provide material for class discussion. The author does not intend to illustrate either effective or ineffective handling of a managerial situation. The author may have disguised certain names and other identifying information to protect confidentiality.

might not survive this confluence of major problems.

RICK WANG AND RETAILCO INC.

Rick Wang was a typical American-born Chinese, able to speak both American English and Chinese. His parents had immigrated to Taiwan and then America when they were fairly young; regardless of their geographic location, however, the family maintained strong cultural ties to its homeland. Wang was raised in a traditional Chinese family in the United States. After graduating from the University of Southern California with a degree in communications, he began his career as an account director at Lintas, a well-regarded international advertising agency. He then transferred to Foremost Dairies Ltd., a leading manufacturer of milk and ice cream in Taiwan, as its marketing director, and thus gained experience in short-shelf-life consumer goods.

In 1992, he moved to his parents' hometown, Shanghai, and worked for Shanghai Fuller Foods Ltd. as vice president of marketing. He assisted in the building of the company's factory in Jinqiao district and developed new brands of Fuller milk and ice cream. Under Wang's leadership, the brands "Qian Shi Nai" (milk) and "San Marlo" (ice cream) quickly achieved market leadership in the area, known by almost all the residents in Shanghai. In late 1997, Shanghai Fuller Foods Ltd. was sold to Nestle; Wang decided to strike out on his own.

As a result of a chance encounter, Rick Wang became acquainted with the athletic footwear industry and became a retailer. Wang retains a vivid memory of the day he was introduced to the possibilities of this retailing niche:

One day, when I was playing softball with a bunch of my American friends who then worked at Nike, one of them said to me, "Rick, since your ice-cream business has been sold, what do you want to do now?" I said, "I don't know yet. Maybe I'll go back to San Francisco, or back to Taiwan." He said, "Why don't you consider overseeing our Nike stores in Shanghai?" I asked, "Nike stores? Can I make money?" And he replied immediately, "Sure, they can make a lot of money!" I asked for the financial statement, which he showed me the next day. After looking carefully I said, "OK. Let's do it."

Rick Wang, at that time, had no experience in either the sports footwear industry or any direct knowledge of in-store retailing, but he was very excited about his new business venture. RetailCo Inc. was established with the intention of managing the retail realities of athletic footwear sales.

His optimism notwithstanding, Wang's hasty involvement and lack of experience in the footwear retailing industry led to the poor performance of his stores. In the six months after the company was established, no profit was made. As the situation worsened, Wang anxiously sought expert advice. He began by educating himself on the Internet, searching terms such as "athletic footwear retail," "sport retail" and "sports shoes retail." Surprisingly, he found that almost every page of his searches revealed one American company: The Athlete's Foot, Inc. Like many entrepreneurs, Wang recognized the value inherent in modeling his own activities on those of an industry leader.

THE ATHLETE'S FOOT, INC.

The Athlete's Foot, Inc., based on Kennesaw, Georgia, in the United States, was the world's foremost franchisor of athletic-footwear operations. It grew from a small, family-run store to an international retailer in three decades. The Athlete's Foot owned about 800 corporate and franchise stores in more than 40 countries (see Exhibit 1).

The history of the growth of The Athlete's Foot was a model of aggressive business behavior. In 1971, Robert and David Lando opened the world's first athletic-footwear specialty store, named The Athlete's Foot, on Wood Street in Pittsburgh, Pennsylvania. The very next year, The Athlete's Foot, Inc., began franchising its business model domestically. The first franchise agreement was signed by Killian Spanbauer, who opened a store at the Sawyer Street Shopping Center in Oshkosh, Wisconsin. After that, The Athlete's Foot began a period of focused expansion: by 1976 there were more than 100 stores; only two years later (1978), there were more than 200 Athlete's Foot outlets in America.

That same year, the company began to internationalize its franchising efforts; in 1978, the first of what was to become many international franchises opened, at 16 Stevens Place, in Adelaide, Australia. This milestone event encouraged The Athlete's Foot to franchise an additional 150 stores in international markets by 1979.

After a decade of successful market penetration, The Athlete's Foot, in its second decade, began a period of adjustment. In the early 1980s, Group Rallye purchased The Athlete's Foot from the Lando family. This buyout provided crucial financial support to the company at a time when it needed to pay more attention to product design and customer service, rather than focusing exclusively on expansion. For example, the company inaugurated a system-wide commitment to customer service. In order to help customers to find the "right" footwear, or at least to help to determine the proper fit, sales associates underwent training at "Fit University," introduced by The Athlete's Foot Wear Test Center to provide education on the physiology and anatomy of the feet and to enable sales associates to properly fit athletic footwear. This focus on educating its sales force—who, in turn, educated customers about the value of relying on The Athlete's Foot as a consumer-oriented facility—paid almost immediate dividends.

In the 1990s, The Athlete's Foot consolidated its market standing even as it continued its enviable international growth. The

Athlete's Foot changed its name to The Athlete's Foot, Inc. and moved its headquarters to Kennesaw, Georgia, after Euris purchased Group Rallye in 1991. The company's structure was reorganized into two divisions as a result of this change in ownership: a marketing team serviced the franchises, and a "store team" operated the company-owned stores. The marketing team did an impressive job in the years following the reorganization. The Athlete's Foot, Inc. grew to more than 650 stores worldwide in 1997 and was named the number-one franchise opportunity by *Success* magazine that same year. After a dynamic new chief executive officer (CEO), Robert J. Corliss, joined the company in 1999, the company experienced a record growth year—opening 37 corporate stores in six countries and 87 franchise stores, the most franchises in company history. The other division, the operations' team that managed company stores, also achieved significant success during this period. The company launched a new store design featuring an innovative, customer-oriented technology called the FitPrint System.[1] This innovation was to lead to a competitive advantage for The Athlete's Foot, Inc. As a result of franchise oversight and marketing innovations, the company was awarded the "Trendsetter of the Year" award by the sporting goods community for 1999 and 2000.

The growth story of The Athlete's Foot became a model for franchising even as it successfully continued its almost 30-year tradition of domestic and international expansion. Many would-be entrepreneurs were drawn to the company, for reasons linked to the company's focus points: customer service, aggressive marketing and control of the pipeline from production to point-of-sale. Comments from franchisees illustrate the company's magnetic effect on franchisee development. Jaclyn Hill from Auburn said that her "decision to join The Athlete's Foot was based primarily upon them having an established, customer-service focused program to sell athletic shoes." Powell's Kyle H. Johnson commented:

The Athlete's Foot was my choice when I decided to enter the retail industry for several reasons. Some are obvious such as access to vendors, reasonable franchise fees, and fair royalty rates. Beyond that, they offer a tremendous amount of support.[2]

AN ATHLETE'S FOOT MASTER FRANCHISEE IN CHINA

Rick Wang was one of many entrepreneurs interested in pursuing business opportunities in the footwear retailing sector; Wang, however, had not followed the less risky entrepreneurial path of franchising, but had struck out on his own, with problematic results. His research on the successes of The Athlete's Foot's management model led him to contact that company. At that time, Wang had little knowledge of how franchising worked, or what potential benefits he might realize. In fact, his ostensible reason for contacting the company was his belief that he might pick up some pointers from this more experienced retailer:

> I was not a believer in franchising. I did not believe in franchising because I did not believe in paying so much money to buy somebody's brand and then putting more money in to build it. I can do that by myself. But I decided to contact The Athlete's Foot because I really knew that I needed help.

Rick Wang decided to fly to Atlanta, to view the company's headquarters and evaluate the company and its team. This trip was fruitful. As a potential Chinese partner, Wang received a warm welcome from the CEO and the entire management team during his visit. Among his stops, he was especially impressed by the inventory control system in the merchandize department. Wang recalled:

> I wasn't very excited until I walked into the merchandize department and I saw their buying team, how they bought products. I saw how intensively they controlled the inventory system, using a very high-tech system. And then I started to learn the science behind the retailing. And I started to realize perhaps I need to pay the tuition to learn this. It's

always the case: if you want to dance, you have to pay the band.

After Wang returned to China, he immediately started his franchise and retail plan. He first persuaded the board of RetailCo. to agree to his idea of becoming the master franchisee of an Athlete's Foot structure in China. Second, he efficiently worked out a negotiations' plan with the U.S. franchisor on the subjects of sales territory and royalty fees. He suggested separating the huge Chinese market into three regions: East China Area, North China Area and South China Area. The region of East China, stretching to the cities of Chengdu and Chongqin, was the biggest and potentially the most important market in China; it was in this area that Wang planned to focus his efforts. The region of North China, including Beijing, although a potentially lucrative market, was to be a secondary consideration. Last, development of the South China Area was to be delayed until after the first two regions were penetrated; the proximity to Hong Kong, with its history of appropriating brand names and flooding the market with cheaper copies, made immediate consideration of this region a risky and ambiguous proposition.

In terms of royalty fees, Wang fortunately negotiated a fairly good deal with The Athlete's Foot, Inc. The monthly royalty was to be 2.5 per cent of net sales. Other initial-area development fees—including franchising fees, fees for additional stores, purchasing a management information system (MIS), an employment-control system, etc.—totaled a few thousand dollars per store. In addition, Wang requested discounts related to any future fees for local marketing. All the funds for initiating business were to be self-financed.

When the deal was made, Wang, together with his six colleagues, went to Atlanta for "New Owner Training" at Athlete's Foot's, Inc. Within six weeks, they had completed their "On Site Training" and had practiced operating the business: they worked in a store, sold shoes, helped people with their fit-tings and even worked in the warehouse, experiencing first-hand the realities of inventory control. They also learned how to work internal-control systems and marketing procedures. Overall, their training covered issues related to marketing, merchandizing, operations management and employee sales training. Wang commented: "It was just fascinating, like going back to school. It was very enjoyable."

Their efforts paid off. In September 1998, the first store of the nascent master franchisee's China operation was opened in the Parkson Department Store on the Huaihai Road in Shanghai, in the East China Area. Parkson was the most popular department store with an ideal demographic: the youngest customers between the age of 20 to 35—those considered most devoted to brand names and most style conscious—shopped on fashion-oriented Huaihai Road. Therefore, the first store was actually in the fashion center amid a favorite venue of young consumers. The store was opened on the ground floor of Parkson's with the same store design and equipment as those in the United States. Beautiful store design and abundant/diverse name-brand products made the store attractive to customers.

Wang achieved success in starting his retail franchising at a time when the franchise concept in the Chinese market was new and innovative, and the sports footwear market was underdeveloped. His business instincts, his knowledge of the Shanghai market and his training at Athlete's Foot, Inc.'s headquarters combined to initiate a signal success in what was then a relatively new entrepreneurial concept.

BUSINESS CONTEXT

Franchising in the Chinese Market

The franchise concept first entered the Chinese market in the early years of the 1990s with the emergence of reputable international franchising companies, such as KFC and McDonald's. They originally entered

China in the early 1990s, building corporate stores first. After having achieved steady sales volumes and sufficient economies of scale, they cautiously but aggressively expanded. These pioneer global franchisors included dominant players in the fast-food industry and various master franchisors in other industries, such as 7-Eleven convenience stores, 21st Century Real Estate, EF education, Avis auto rental, Kodak film developing and Fornet laundry service. These firms contributed to China's franchising market development and created an awareness among an increasingly entrepreneurial class that franchising held substantial positive outcomes for those able to enter into such relationships.

Overseas franchisors tended to adopt one of two approaches when operating in the Chinese market: the franchise of a product or trade name (product name franchising) or the franchise of a particular business model in exchange for fees or royalties (business format franchising). Corporations that had a strong capital background, such as McDonald's and KFC, would choose an off-shore franchise retail model (see Exhibit 2) to ensure effective control over product quality and company operations. Small- and medium-sized franchisors would often choose direct franchising by seeking a local franchisee. Franchisors, licensing to local partners, could take advantage of local knowledge, saving the costs resulting from distance—both in terms of logistics and culture.

Since the end of the 1990s, franchising had become a mature, steady growth opportunity in China. By the end of 1997, there were just more than 90 franchisors in China and about 30 franchise stores. One year later, however, the number had grown to more than 120 franchisors with sales volume of more than 50 million RMB (US$6.05 million), of which 40 percent were franchise stores.[3] By 2000, the number of franchisors approached 600. The sales volume also increased dramatically, jumping about 80 per cent from 1999 to 2000.[4] This remarkable growth (at the time of this article, franchising was growing at a high double-digit growth rate) continued in the years that followed.

Franchised businesses in China varied along a wide spectrum of business sectors. Companies in more than 30 industries had chosen franchising as a business model to sell their products and expand in this market. Retail and food/restaurant operations had always been the dominant franchising industries, accounting for 35 percent and 30 percent of total franchisors[5] respectively. Other segments experiencing significant growth included education, business services, auto services, interior decoration, beauty and health, and laundry. The service sector had also grown in importance in recent years.

Market Environment

In the late 1990s, as many in the global market were aware, China was becoming the land of opportunity. China's strong and steady growth, proven by 10 years of continual gross domestic product (GDP) increases, seemed unstoppable. Economic growth led to an increase in personal incomes, especially in larger cities. The emergence of a large middle class, often consisting of well-educated professionals, added to the consumer demand for globally recognized, quality products.

Domestically, the Chinese government made great efforts to regulate the market and standardize the business environment. To facilitate access to the World Trade Organization (WTO), China committed itself to removing more market-entry barriers, which created a more open market for international investors. The laws and regulations governing franchise businesses were, thus, improved. On November 14, 1997, the Ministry of Internal Trade published and released the very first Chinese franchise law, *The Regulation on Commercial Franchise Business (for Trial Implementation)*. Afterwards, the Regulation was revised and improved several times: in 2005, *The Law on Commercial Franchise Business Administration* was eventually released as a basic rule for franchise operations in China.

Market competition in China was less rigorous than that in the United States. In the athletic footwear retailing industry in China, for example, there were few capable players in the early to mid-1990s. Meanwhile, the demand for high-quality athletic footwear increased as consumers' incomes increased (see Exhibit 3). Market research for 1998 indicated that people in Shanghai owned only one pair of athletic footwear. By 2005, they had, on average, three pairs. In terms of style, people's preferences changed from choosing footwear for functional purposes to opting for fashion. Athletic footwear retailers selling name-brand shoes had what seemed to be a promising future.

THE GLORIOUS AGE

The success of his first store encouraged Wang to open more stores, more quickly than he had initially planned. In the months following his franchise premiere in Shanghai in 1998, Wang adopted an aggressive expansion strategy, opening a new store every 22 days. After spreading the business to the North China region, the company opened 40 corporate stores in seven other Chinese cities. The company realized a profit in its second year of operations, reaching a sales volume of US$14 million in 2000.

Every one of RetailCo's stores acted in accord with the standard of global Athlete's Foot, Inc. The stores, equipped with indoor music, sports videos and fashionable designs, established a pleasant atmosphere for shopping. All stores provided the best possible service for their customers. The service staff in every store were trained before they began their work—also in accordance with the model that Wang and his team had seen in Atlanta. In addition, every store was equipped with computers for billing and inventory control. In fact, the inventory-control system was an advantage that distinguished Wang's stores from other retailers. By adhering to strict, computerized tracking

of product, store managers were able to react promptly to shortages or excesses of inventory. The company used the franchisor's proprietary pricing model by utilizing aggressive price reductions to manage inventory excesses. More important than the store brands that the store marketed were the famous internationally branded sports goods, such as Nike, Adidas and Reebok, which were available at the stores. A pioneering store atmosphere, an excellent inventory-management model and the availability of famous brands quickly made The Athlete's Foot a premier competitor in the Chinese sports retailing industry.

Domestic promotion of The Athlete's Foot brand name was also managed aggressively. Besides media advertising, the company put more emphasis on direct and in-store marketing. It organized three-on-three street basketball games and tournaments to grab the attention of young sports lovers. The company also sponsored high-school basketball teams to further inculcate brand-name recognition of both the stores and their products among teenagers. In-store marketing activities included cooperation with the fast-food giant, McDonald's; monthly newsletters advertising The Athlete's Foot were distributed in McDonald's stores. Nevertheless, the brand-building process was not as successful as it had been in the United States. People responded to the brands of products more than to the retail brand itself: consumers visited stores because they could find internationally known products, not necessarily because they were drawn to The Athlete's Foot as a brand. This customer motivation would lead to substantial problems for Wang in future years.

In 2000, Wang started, cautiously, to seek appropriate franchisees in an attempt to expand the business. Wang selected one sporting goods franchising exhibition in Beijing as the venue for promotion of his franchise opportunities. Almost 500 applicants applied for franchises in one day, far exceeding Wang's expectations. Some applicants even came with large amounts of cash as testament to their financial abilities (and solvency). Wang was concerned, however, about the values of the applicants; he wanted to ensure that the selected candidates were service-oriented and fully understood the partnership requirements related to franchising. Carefully vetting all of the applicants, Wang short-listed 20 candidates. These finalists had strong financial capabilities as well as fine educational backgrounds; they could understand the vital realities involved in franchising partnerships. RetailCo invited these 20 candidates to come to the Shanghai Office for face-to-face meetings with the board. Finally, one—out of 500—was signed with RetailCo to be the first sub-franchisee of The Athlete's Foot, Inc. Later, using the same careful scrutiny, 12 additional sub-franchisee stores were developed in second- and third-tier cities, such as Nanjing, Wuxi and Ningbo.

SIGNS OF PROBLEMS

In 2001, in spite of—or possibly due to—its rapid growth, the company gradually felt pressures related to cash flow, marketing and supply. The first "pressure" came from the need to commit large amounts of capital to obtaining retail venues. Since the location of retail stores was related to sales performance, gaining a quality location was crucial. Wang's good fortune in being able to open his first store at a high-traffic, upscale shopping area in Shanghai was often difficult to replicate at equally moderate rental rates. Obtaining a quality retail space in China usually requires at least a 24-month leasing commitment; in some department stores, a 36-month rental agreement was the norm. To lock in quality locations in this competitive retail real-estate market, the company signed long-term contracts, looking to best competitors by securing desirable locations. This laudable approach to ensuring franchisee success, however, required an immense commitment of up-front capital. RetailCo took over prime spaces in department stores, but the cost of

doing so was great. Unfortunately, when market conditions changed and sales decreased, the pressure caused by an insufficiency of ready reserves of cash inevitably increased.

A second pressure was related to a problem many "breakthrough" franchisors experience in new markets: since 2001, The Athlete's Foot had started to lose its "first-mover" advantage. China began in 2000 to finalize preparations for entry into the WTO. The global financial community was increasingly convinced by then that the immense potential of the Chinese market was soon to become a reality. As a result, the athletic footwear market—along with every other foreign franchise business—underwent major changes, and foreign direct investment (FDI) increased.

In department stores, the space for sporting goods enlarged dramatically from 300 square meters to 700 square meters, then 1000, 1500, and finally to an average of 3,000 square meters. This growth spurt meant that franchising space allotted to The Athlete's Foot was, as a percentage of total space, gradually diminished. More footwear retailing players joined the industry; for example, Quest Sports started to open stores in China in 2001. Competition also came from local players, who were able to insinuate themselves in this market due to competitive pricing, enhanced customer service and increased product quality. In other words, these local competitors learned from Wang's Athlete's Foot franchises what Wang had learned from the franchisor. A final concern occurred when individual brands opened more of their own stores.

As a result of its success in the market—partly related to the improved business climate in China as a whole—RetailCo/The Athlete's Foot was, paradoxically, losing its competitive advantage. In 1998, the size of an Athlete's Foot store was almost 100 square meters, often occupying one-third of the total size of the sporting goods section of a large department store. The typical store was supplied by several world-famous

EXHIBIT 1   Countries Where the Athlete's Foot Stores Are Located

Antigua	China	Greece	Kuwait	Poland
Argentina	Costa Rica	Guadeloupe	Malaysia	Portugal
Aruba	Curacao	Guatemala	Malta	Republic of Palau
Australia	Cyprus	Hungary	Martinique	Reunion Island
Bahamas	Denmark	Indonesia	Mexico	St. Kitts/ St. Nevis
Barbados	Dominican Republic	Italy	New Zealand	St. Maarten
Canada	Ecuador	Jamaica	Panama	South Korea
Cayman Islands	France	Japan	Peru	United States
Chile	French Guyana	Jersey Island	Philippines	Venezuela

SOURCE: www.theathletesfoot.com

EXHIBIT 2   Offshore Franchise Retail Model

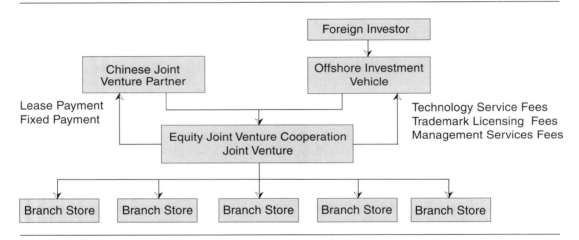

SOURCE: Fraser Medel, " Legal Issues Related to Franchising in China," *Franchising in China,* November 2003.

EXHIBIT 3   Consumption of Recreation Goods in Entertainment and Sports Sector, 1997–2003

	1997	1998	1999	2000	2001	2002	2003	2004
	Per Capital Annual Disposable Income of Urban Households							
Income	5160.3	5425.1	5854.0	6280.0	6859.6	7702.8	8472.2	9421.6
	Per Capital Annual Living Expenditures for Consumption in sector of Education, Culture, and Recreation Service							
Consumption	448.38	499.39	567.05	669.58	736.63	902.28	934.38	1032.80

Source: China Statistics Yearbooks (various years)

EXHIBIT 4 Franchise Structures of The Athlete's Foot in China

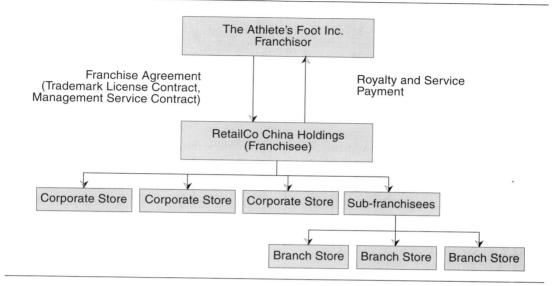

brands, such as Nike, Adidas and Reebok. The rest of the sporting goods space was devoted to selling locally branded products and sports equipment: footballs, basketballs, tennis rackets, etc. Although the goods sold in an Athlete's Foot store were exclusive and superior to others, the above-mentioned changes led to a ten-fold increase in the amount of store space devoted to sporting goods. Athlete's Foot did not and could not grow as fast, now (post-2001) occupying merely one-fifteenth of the total space devoted to sporting goods in a large department store. Size and visibility matter: the "idea" of Athlete's Foot became increasingly insignificant in customers' minds.

Worse, for Wang, was the fact that his suppliers—the producers of the often-popular styles and models his growing customer base demanded—began to increase their own penetration of what had previously been a fairly wide-open market. The Athlete's Foot multi-brand approach was forced to compete directly with brand-name suppliers who opened their own outlets in direct competition. Inevitably, Wang found it difficult to get the most desirable brand-name products for his stores; the home office—although committed to Wang's status as the master franchisor—was unable to put enough pressure on producers to stem the tide. Wang's stores were unable to keep current inventory of the most recent styles and most in-demand products.

With declines of comparative store size and product varieties, and increases in competition from local and brand-specific market entrants, The Athlete's Foot found itself squeezed out of high-value department store venues. Department stores welcomed the single-brand retailers because they were content with the smaller ratios of retail space; besides, grouping single-brand retailers together made a department store one, huge multi-brand store. The Athlete's Foot had to move to street-front locations that commanded higher rents and were less popular with the purchasing public. Thus, costs increased but revenue decreased.

WHAT SHOULD WANG DO?

Rick Wang realized the company was in risk of bankruptcy if he did not immediately address the radically changed demands of the marketplace.

PART B

In a quickly changing market, Rick Wang and his Athlete's Foot stores encountered a series of problems that threatened his company. Increased competition, in what had heretofore been an "open" market, forced Wang to work out a number of strategies so that his franchise plans could survive. After evaluating and implementing a number of strategies, Wang made a difficult decision. The available options and Rick Wang's actual decisions are discussed in the following case study.

A STRUGGLE FOR SURVIVAL

After being squeezed out of department stores by his competitors, Wang had to relocate his business to "the street" or to less-desirable, lower-traffic shopping malls in order to adhere to a certain economy of scale. However, the consequences of his decision to relocate led to higher rents and lower sales. Wang was forced into a string of strategic decisions, all related to stricter competition from better-positioned competitors. In fact, Wang faced a retailer's worst nightmare: higher costs and lower profits. Worse still,

Source: Professor Ilan Alon and Amber Xu wrote Part B of this case solely to provide material for class discussion. The authors do not intend to illustrate either effective or ineffective handling of a managerial situation. The authors may have disguised certain names and other identifying information to protect confidentiality.

Ivey Management Services prohibits any form of reproduction, storage or transmittal without its written permission. Reproduction of this material is not covered under authorization by any reproduction rights organization. To order copies or request permission to reproduce materials, contact Ivey Publishing, Ivey Management Services, c/o Richard Ivey School of Business, The University of Western Ontario, London, Ontario, Canada, N6A 3K7; phone (519) 661-3208; fax (519) 661-3882; e-mail cases@ivey.uwo.ca.

Copyright © 2006, CEIBS (China Europe International Business School), Version: (A) 2006-09-18

the more stores he had, the worse his bottom line fared. This, despite the fact that rapid franchise growth had been his key strategy before competitors emerged in his market. Ultimately, Wang had to close stores to preserve the financial balance of his over-extended empire.

When Wang looked for alternative retailing methods, ones which would complement his established but faltering on-site retailing outlets, he opted for e-commerce. He wondered if selling shoes in a virtual store would lead to increased profits and act as a magnet for his brick-and-mortar operations. He "opened" an online shoe booth aimed at reclaiming and increasing consumers' brand-loyalty to his product.

Unfortunately, the online booth did not succeed in attracting customers. E-commerce, at that time, was in its infancy in China, though it was booming in most Western countries. Limited by uncertain internet access and restrained by a lack of credit, consumers in this section of the Chinese market were not (yet) comfortable with internet retailing. Additionally, Chinese consumers were culturally attuned to the physical act of "trying and buying." And, since Wang's products were quite expensive when compared to local athletic shoes, he also had to overcome a cultural distaste for purchasing items by virtue of appearance alone. Even major international suppliers of competitors' footwear brands had rejected online marketing, so Wang's choice—although a forward-looking one—was not something that more experienced retailers had found useful.

In athletic footwear retailing, having the most fashionable and trendy supply is essential. Wang turned to his franchisor, The Athlete's Foot Inc., to help him with local supply-chain problems. He assumed that his franchisor, with its 30-year history of international experience (including stores in over 40 countries) would help him to overcome his lack of leverage over reluctant suppliers. He assumed incorrectly.

The franchisor was simply not as well-informed and powerful in this market as Wang had hoped. The Athlete's Foot Inc. had been successful in the American domestic market, and had also done well in Australia and parts of Europe; however, it had almost no substantive experience in or knowledge of the Chinese market. The Athlete's Foot Inc. did support Wang by providing an efficient business model, a superior operations system, and some basic retailing knowledge, but this was all they could offer. The Athlete's Foot Inc. did not have corporate stores in China, nor did it have any other experience in the Chinese market. Wang and his company would have to bear the sole responsibility for success in this immense and uncertain business environment.

Ironically, even while Wang's local branch stores in Shanghai were losing revenue, his sub-franchisees, mostly in smaller cities like Nanjing, Wuxi, etc., were still doing quite well. They were making profits and enjoying the results of increased customer traffic and brand-consciousness. This disconnect was primarily due to a lag in the maturation of their different sub-market niches. Major brands were, at that time, focusing on building market share in the larger cities, and what would come to be called the "single-brand trend" had not yet extended to those smaller cities. As was the norm in other international markets, market transformation in smaller cities tended to be 18 to 24 months behind that in the largest cities. It was for this reason that Wang's franchisees were thriving even as he faltered.

On the other hand, even as his franchisees celebrated their survival in these smaller Chinese cities, they were becoming aware—through Wang's experience—that they faced an uncertain future once the single-brand giants came to compete with them in these less-mature markets. It was likely that these profitable franchisees would come to face the same problems that Wang was encountering in his more-mature market. Current success does not guarantee future survival, so even these franchisees had an interest in Wang's strategies.

TRANSFORMATION

Wang's attempts to rescue his Athlete's Foot stores from crisis had failed. To avoid bankruptcy, Rick Wang eventually made a painful decision: he would terminate his contract with the franchisor. He recalled: "I took a gamble, and I decided that we would restructure our company." He chose to convert his retailing stores from the Athlete's Foot to Adidas, from a franchising structure to a "pure" retailing operation. He chose to concentrate on single-brand rather than on multi-brand retailing, following what he perceived as structural changes in the marketplace.

His decision was painful as well as adventurous. The termination of the franchising relationship could lead to costly legal action if he could not negotiate with the Athlete's Foot Inc. He understood the need for extreme caution at this point; otherwise, the company would be beaten down before it could be rebuilt.

Calmly and carefully, Wang began the process of exiting the franchise relationship by communicating with the franchisor—always professionally—about the intricacies of the crisis facing the sports footwear market in the current Chinese environment. Wang tried to convince the franchisor that great efforts had been made to build and maintain the brand; the Athlete's Foot *could* succeed *if* there were no changes to the market that they had entered together. However, as the market changed, the retailer was forced to change its marketing strategy to deal with these changes. Wang specifically pointed to the franchisor's inability to corral suppliers, which ultimately deprived him of a responsible way to address change and guarantee the survival of The Athlete's Foot in China.

As he considered his exit strategy, Wang also communicated with his own franchisees, hoping to have them join him as he transformed his company. He made clear to the franchisees the problems he was facing—and those that they, too, would soon face: changing market trends, the reluctance of big-brand suppliers to commit, and the weaknesses of The Athlete's Foot as a franchisor. "If you want to continue with multi-brand, we will do our best to help. But you probably will not get some big brands to fully cooperate," Wang said to them. He welcomed those who committed to his future plans, and he committed himself to a parenting role as they made the move with him. Instead of royalties and operations fees—such as those they would expect to have to pay in a standard franchising format—Wang promised to adopt a direct operational model: those stores would become more like sub-dealers, buying the latest supplies from Wang and paying him a small commission derived from their sales volumes. In this way, supply chain problems could be managed, and franchisee costs would not be fixed if sales volumes dropped. For those who were unwilling to follow, Wang chose to take over their stores, paying fair compensation in each case. Wang agreed to subsidize their depreciated inventory costs and refund them some of the money they had paid for their franchises.

Wang's openness and fairness avoided legal disputes and, even better, won the trust of most of his sub-franchisees. They converted themselves to Adidas retailers, demonstrating their full confidence in Wang's leadership as together they made the transition from multi-brand to single-brand retailing.

Gradually, Wang and his company recovered from hardship: sales volumes increased continuously and he found himself setting new sales records. Although he was no longer operating under the franchise model, Wang credits his experience with The Athlete's Foot Inc. as a core part of his current success, saying, recently:

I still believe in the franchising model—it is a very good growth model. When it plays out properly, you can grow your business tremendously. It is regretful that changes in the market hurt my operation, and these changes prevented the system from sustaining profitability.

NOTES

1. According to Athlete's Foot, Inc., the FitPrint System is a proprietary state-of-the-art computerized technology that measures pressure points at different phases of a customer's gait.
2. www.theathletesfoot.com, accessed July, 2005.
3. Ye-Sho Chen, "Franchise China: She is Ready, Are You?," http://isds.bus.lsu.edu/chen/Franchise.htm, accessed July 2005.
4. *Franchise: The International and Management of Franchise,* Xinhua Press, Beijing, 2003, pp. 181.
5. Ibid.

CASE 9

Biocon Ltd.: Building a Biotech Powerhouse

by Alson Konrad, Charlene Nichols-Nixon, and R. Chandrasekhar

INTRODUCTION

In November 2005, Biocon Ltd. was the largest biotechnology enterprise in India and the 14th largest biotechnology company globally (see Exhibit 1). Kiran Mazumdar-Shaw, chairman and managing director, was excited about her goals for the future: to achieve annual revenues of $1 billion[1] and to secure a place among the top 10 global biotech firms by 2015. Based on the sales turnover of $167 million for the year ending March 2005, achieving these goals would mean generating a six-fold increase within the next decade. To this end, Mazumdar-Shaw envisioned building a vertically integrated biotechnology enterprise with a strong discovery orientation.

Since Biocon's inception in 1978, Mazumdar-Shaw had been pursuing a sequential growth strategy, adding businesses that were interlinked and progressively more complex. Each business—enzymes, biopharmaceuticals, research services and, of late, drug development—provided a stepping stone toward her vision of making Biocon a biotechnology powerhouse. Under her leadership, Biocon had consolidated its core skills in enzymes (known to be the building blocks of biotech), established a footprint in biopharmaceuticals (which helped generate regular cash flow), and partnered with global firms (serving as launching pads for drug development). Now, she believed that Biocon was ready to take the leap into the far riskier, and potentially far more rewarding, realm of drug discovery. Yet she knew that the board of directors of the company, whose consensus was crucial, was anxious to realize the vision without jeopardizing the financial viability of Biocon.[2]

Said Mazumdar-Shaw:

> The risk in drug discovery for a company is the risk of failure. Only one in 5,000 molecules reaches the clinical trials stage. Only one in 500 undergoing clinical trials reaches the commercial stage. We have nine molecules today at Biocon in various stages of development. All these are based on partnerships with global companies. Some have reached clinical trials. They will all hopefully reach commercialization stage by the end of the decade. But, there are no certainties. The variables are many.
>
> Biocon has been using a de-risked business model since the beginning. As we make a transition from drug development to drug discovery, we must learn to manage risks. This requires a change of mindset. It is like the difference between gambling in a casino within a fixed budget where you know how much you would lose and any gain would therefore be treasured, and gambling with large sums in order only to win. Managing infinite risk has not been part of the traditional mindset at Biocon.

A meeting of the board of directors, already convened, was less than a week away.

Source: R. Chandrasekhar prepared this case under the supervision of Professors Alison Konrad and Charlene Nichols-Nixon solely to provide material for class discussion. The authors do not intend to illustrate either effective or ineffective handling of a managerial situation. The authors may have disguised certain names and other identifying information to protect confidentiality.

Mazumdar-Shaw anticipated some sharp questions about the viability of expanding the company's drug discovery activities and the action plan for managing this transition. She needed to build a strong case for continuing along this trajectory when so much was at stake.

GLOBAL BIOTECH INDUSTRY

The discovery of recombinant DNA technology, in 1973, marked the beginning of modern biotechnology. Since then, the range of applications of biotechnology covered agriculture (as in genetically modified foods), industry (bio-fuels and bio-enzymes), and medicine (diagnosing diseases and designing new drugs). The use of genetic engineering in developing health care products had brought about a paradigm shift in the global pharmaceutical industry. Drug manufacturing processes based on chemistry were gradually giving way to those based on biology. It was estimated that by 2025, bio-drugs would replace 70 per cent of conventional therapies.[3] "Designer drugs" based on biotechnology were expected to gain ground. They were considered more effective than one-size-fits-all synthetic drugs because they attacked the underlying genetic cause of a disease.

There were 4,416 biotech companies worldwide in 2004 (see Exhibit 2). Although Europe had the largest number of biotech companies, 78 per cent of global biotech revenues were generated in the United States. The global biotech sector employed 183,000 professionals and had revenues of $54.6 billion in 2004.

INDIAN BIOTECH INDUSTRY

The turnover of the Indian biotechnology industry had crossed the $1-billion landmark in March 2005. The top 20 Indian biotech firms had a combined turnover of $641 million, amounting to about 64 percent of the country's industry sales (see Exhibit 3).

Nearly 60 percent of India's biotechnology products were exported. There were 280 biotech companies in India in 2003, employing 11,800 scientists. The Indian biotech companies fell into three categories: those building on bedrock biotech products, such as enzymes, to move into molecules (e.g. Biocon); migrants from related sectors, such as pharma; and start-ups occupying niche spaces based on a specific skill set. A bulk of their revenues came, as in Biocon, from generics.

A generic drug was the equivalent of an originator pharmaceutical product, differing only in price. It contained the same active pharmaceutical ingredient (API) as the original and was manufactured to the same standards of quality, safety and efficacy in plants approved by regulatory bodies. A generic drug, however, typically cost 20 percent to 80 percent less because the product was not burdened with legacy expenses of research, development, clinical trials and marketing. Using less expensive alternatives of both non-active ingredients (such as colorings, starches and saccharoses) and packaging materials, a generics maker could also reduce prices by leveraging process efficiencies and low-cost advantages.

The Indian generics market consisted of more than 10,000 small companies producing less expensive copycat versions of patented drugs and selling them both locally and in countries that had limited patent protection. An industry analyst observed:

> All drug companies, big and small, use the generics platform to move into drug discovery. The generics platform provides a steady stream of revenue with which to finance drug discovery. The main lure of generics is the ready market and instant cash gratification it provides.

Biocon was among the 74 manufacturing facilities in India certified by the U.S. Food and Drug Administration that together sold more than $1-billion worth of generics per annum in the competitive and regulated U.S.

and European markets. With $82-billion worth of global blockbusters facing patent expiry by 2006, the generics industry was set to grow. India's share of the global generics market was expected to increase to about 33 percent in 2007, from four percent in 2004, according to a study by London-based Global Insight.[4] The economics of the market were so attractive that every biotech player—big and small—was seeking a foothold in generics. The biopharmaceuticals space, in which Biocon had built a niche, was thus becoming more crowded and competitive day by day. Low prices, integral to a generic's business, made it impossible for Biocon to secure revenue breakthroughs, in tune with its global aspirations, through the generics route alone.[5]

Moreover, the regulatory environment that had made generics such an attractive sector in India was also changing. The government of India had introduced a full-fledged patents regime in compliance with the World Trade Organization agreement on intellectual property.[6] In the past, the Indian government had granted patents for the process of manufacturing a drug, not for the drug itself. Process patents (as opposed to the product patents prevalent in North America) had allowed Indian companies to produce generic versions of drugs patented in other countries. Having found a profitable revenue stream in producing copycats while the patents were still running their course elsewhere in the world, the Indian drug companies had prospered. But under the new regime, manufacturing and marketing a patented drug was prohibited. A generic version was allowed only after the expiry of the product patent, typically after about a decade.

While the generics space was becoming more competitive, new opportunities were opening for Indian firms interested in drug discovery. With all major drug companies under pressure to drive down costs,[7] the major players were looking to specialist firms located in India and China, such as Biocon, as economical sources of input for research and clinical development.

BIOCON AND MAZUMDAR-SHAW

Kiran Mazumdar set up Biocon in 1978. After receiving a postgraduate degree in zoology from Bangalore University in 1972, she went to Balart College of Melbourne University of Australia for a diploma in Malting and Brewing. When she returned to India in 1975, she found, to her dismay, no employment prospects for a female brewer. A few years into contractual jobs, she secured a referral to the founder of Ireland-based Biocon Biochemicals Limited (BBL), a manufacturer and exporter of enzymes for the brewing industry worldwide. Joining the company as a one-person affiliate based in Bangalore and upgraded later as a minority stockholder, Mazumdar-Shaw observed BBL being acquired successively by Unilever plc and ICI Ltd. Unlike her Irish partner, she held onto her stock until she branched out on her own in 1978, forming Biocon India. During the first decade and a half, Mazumdar-Shaw focused on building a core competence in the largely neglected area of solid state fermentation. Under her leadership, Biocon secured a U.S. patent for a reactor it developed, known as plafactor. The patent gave the company exclusive global rights to use and license the technology for the manufacture of drugs involving genetically engineered micro-organisms in a solid-state fermenter.

Mazumdar-Shaw (who preferred to be addressed as "chairman" in all business correspondence, instead of the politically correct "chairperson"), offered the following reflection on her career path:

> I did not, like most professional women executives, run into a glass ceiling. I started right at the top—or was it the bottom?—as an entrepreneur. What I ran into was a concrete ceiling. No man was willing to work for me. My accountant left at the first sign of another job because he presumed that a woman

would not be a dependable employer. No banker was keen to talk to me across the table for a line of credit. As a businesswoman, I was a risk. I got the financing only after I met a member of the tribe at a friend's wedding. No property owner in Bangalore was willing to rent office space for me. I was not reliable. All these I could take in my stride. It was while dealing with raw material vendors that I faced the cutting edge of gender bias. Some of them said that should I hire a male manager with whom they could deal directly! At Biocon today, 30 per cent of employees are women. We have women at senior management levels.

From the company's origins making enzymes for the breweries industry, Biocon had expanded and diversified into related fields during the next two decades. By 2005, Biocon had achieved revenue of $167 million (see Exhibit 4) and was the market leader in Indian biotech. It had issued an initial public offering (IPO) in March 2004 which valued the company at $1.1 billion. Biocon specialized in four broad areas: enzymes, biopharmaceuticals, custom research, and clinical research (see Exhibit 5 and Exhibit 6). In order to become an integrated biotech enterprise, the company needed a portfolio of drug development candidates.

Enzymes

The global enzymes market generated $3.7 billion per annum in 2004 and was forecast to grow at 6.5 per cent over the next five years. It had three broad segments: Industrial enzymes (used in detergent, starch, fuel, textile, leather and alcohol industries) comprising 55 percent of demand, food enzymes (used in manufacture of wine, juice, beer, bread, alcohol and cheese) comprising 35 percent, and feed enzymes (used in animal feeds) comprising 10 percent of demand. Two European players—Novozymes and Danisco, both based in Denmark—together held more than 70 percent of the global market share. Biocon was a relatively small player, with less than one percent global share. Its

main competitors included niche players, such as Shin Nihon Chemical Company Ltd. of China.

The importance of enzymes for Biocon lay in the fact that the business was a springboard for one of the company's competitive advantages. Fermentation was a core skill that offered Biocon a leverage in stage 3 of the value chain of biopharmaceuticals (see Exhibit 7). The company's fermenting capacity gave it both the ability to scale up an industrial process and the platform on which to pursue discovery-led growth. The company had earmarked $100 million towards expansion of fermentation facilities in 2005/06. The proportion of Biocon's revenue generated by enzymes was likely to remain at between 13 and 15 percent for the foreseeable future.

Biopharmaceuticals

The global generics market was set to grow as dozens of blockbusters were slated to come off-patent over the next few years. Moreover, governments, insurers and health care organizations in developed countries were actively promoting generics as part of an initiative to reduce the cost of health care. An even more important trigger, from Biocon's perspective, was that global drug companies were outsourcing many parts of the value chain to low-cost producers, such as India and China. Biocon was expanding its biopharmaceuticals capacity at a capital cost of $35 million.

Biopharmaceuticals represented 80 percent of Biocon's turnover, with the production of APIs for statins accounting for 45 percent of revenue. Statins would lose patent protection in 2008 in the United States. As a result, the dollar value of the global market for statins would shrink from $22 billion to $3 billion. There were also pricing pressures from low-cost Chinese competitors.

Said Mazumdar-Shaw:

> Beginning 2008, we will have to look for new markets, outside of the U.S. and Europe, for statins. Even through the market will

shrink in value, it will continue to grow in volume. Biocon will differentiate itself from competitors in the making of APIs by continuing to deploy our core skills in fermentation (unlike our competitors taking the synthetic route). We will also move beyond making APIs to supplying formulations to innovator companies. The turnover from biopharmaceuticals segment (comprising statins, immunosuppressants and insulin) should progressively move up to $600 million by 2015.

An industry analyst confirmed the strength of Biocon's approach:

> Most aspiring entrants into drug discovery have core skills in synthetic chemistry. Biocon is at the recombinant protein end. Its core competence is molecular biology. It is equally involved in synthetic chemistry but its competence in molecular biology is a big differentiator. A biological process of manufacture ensures that the end product is less intrusive, when embedded within a biological system, ensuring seamless delivery. The risk of failure of clinical study is lesser for a biological drug than for a synthetic drug. It also costs less to manufacture.

Clinical Trials

Biocon's clinical trials were handled by Clinigene, a subsidiary set up in 2000. Clinigene was leveraging the country's large population and its low-cost pool of qualified medical and scientific professionals to provide quality clinical research services at attractive prices and to facilitate rapid establishment of trial groups. Biocon was focused on providing Phase I to Phase III clinical trials for new drug molecules. The cost of clinical trials comprised about 70 per cent of the total development costs. According to a McKinsey report, up to 30 percent of global clinical trials were to take place, by 2008, outside the United States and Western Europe. India was the preferred destination because of two advantages: speed of patient enrollment and shorter timelines.[8]

The market for clinical trials in India was valued at $70 million in 2002 and growing at 20 percent per annum. There were 30 clinical research organizations (CROs) in India. They had developed capabilities across a wide spectrum of the research and development (R&D) value chain, offering cost efficiencies, high rates of patient recruitment, and documentation quality to global clients. The rapid proliferation of CRO units had created intense competition in this space, with the possibility of a shakeout in the near future, leading to consolidation. The top three players were Quintiles India with revenues of $18 million, SIRO Clinpharm with revenues of $10 million, and iGate Clinical Research with revenues of $7 million. Clinigene, with revenues of less than $0.5 million, was yet to build up its capability as a CRO.

Custom Research

In 1993, Biocon had formed a subsidiary, Syngene, to capture the growing business of research process outsourcing (RPO). The RPO business was driven by a compulsion among drug companies to reduce R&D costs and shorten product evaluation times. In a competitive space comprising full-service global drug development companies, in-house R&D divisions of pharmaceutical and biotechnology majors, universities and teaching hospitals, Syngene had positioned itself as a provider of RPO in two areas: synthetic chemistry (where it was partnering with established pharma companies in their search for new chemical entities) and molecular biology (where it was involved, in partnership with biotechnology firms, in the search for novel therapeutic agents in disease segments, such as cancer, arthritis, and AIDS). Its main competitors were newer, smaller entities with a specialty focus, aligned to a specific disease or therapeutic area.

Drug Discovery

Typically, the route to drug discovery consisted of three sequential stages: research, development, and commercialization.

Research. Syngene and Clinigene were already leading the research endeavors at Biocon, providing a valuable platform on which to move progressively into drug discovery. Clinigene had acquired competencies in stages 7, 8 and 9 (see Exhibit 8). While stages 5 and 6 were being outsourced by Biocon because it did not have the necessary in-house skills and because it cost less, the company was building up competencies in stages 10, 11 and 12. Syngene had so far acquired only the basic skills in stages 1, 2, 3 and 4 of the drug development cycle. Biocon was also in the process of building up manufacturing capacities for industrial scale-up.

The company had an in-house R&D team, set up in 1984, to complement its biopharmaceuticals business. It comprised 98 scientists and technologists who had filed several patents. Biocon was investing between 10 percent and 15 percent of turnover on in-house research. The company had also launched a biodiversity program in 1995, with the mandate to collect, catalogue and conserve rare and diverse species of indigenous bacteria, yeast and fungi. The program had identified and characterized more than 3,000 unique microorganisms of Indian origin, several of them with novel traits. The collection was seen as a valuable tool in discovering new biotech products.

Partnerships with biotech start-ups were also seen as a key element of the company's strategy because they further helped Biocon to integrate backward into discovery research.

Said Mazumdar-Shaw:

> Biocon is committed to finding biotechnology solutions in global health care. In our pursuit of therapeutic areas for drug discovery, we have identified two focal points of disease research: diabetes and cancer. The numbers are compelling. There are 177 million diabetics in the world. One in four of them is an Indian. Nine million new cancer cases are diagnosed every year worldwide, of which over half are fatal. The highest incidence is of head and neck cancer. Biocon has developed oral insulin, which will go on Phase I trials in early 2006. Biomab, an antibody for head and neck cancer, will hopefully be the first molecule off the block from Biocon in terms of market entry. It should generate annual revenues of $250 million for the company in the next few years if we get the necessary approvals and market it well.

Development. Building on its capabilities in clinical trials, Biocon had taken tentative steps toward involvement in the development stage of drug discovery. The company had limited its activities to known targets and known molecules. It also relied upon partnerships with global biotech firms (see Exhibit 9), as a way of sharing development costs. For example, the antibody that Biocon was developing with CIMAB, its Cuban partner, was for head and neck cancer, a known target. The new delivery technology it was developing was for insulin, a known molecule.

Said Mazumdar-Shaw:

> Many international venture capitalists are beginning to see an "India strategy" a powerful way to de-risk their own investments. Risk capital has been drying up in the U.S., of late. The probability of funding increases with the progress of drug development—the farther along a drug is, the more likely someone is to fund it. Since venture capital commitment is greater after proof-of-concept, valuations increase exponentially along the development curve. Proof of concept is when the lead compound has been identified. Partnering with India is, for many companies, a fast-track way to climb the valuation chain. The platform technologies for the nine molecules, which Biocon has taken on for development, were built by our individual partners who invested in drug research. They have partnered with us to take the drug development process forward. Biocon saves costs on drug research. Its partners save costs on drug development. It helps both ways.

Commercialization. Relative to the company's other activities, Biocon had the least expertise in this final stage of drug discovery and development. Investments were being made in creating the manufacturing capacity for industrial scale-up. Commercialization would also require compliance with manufacturing standards, deployment of a sales force, and development of expertise in marketing and promotions aimed at physicians and end-customers.

STRATEGIC CONCERNS IN NOVEMBER 2005

Mazumdar-Shaw was confident that she could turn Biocon into a top-10 biotechnology firm, with sales exceeding $1 billion per annum, by 2015. To this end, the company was involved in a number of activities ranging from enzyme production to drug discovery. As Mazumdar-Shaw contemplated these activities, she knew that there would be some questions about whether the company was spreading its resources too thinly across different stages in different sectors.

Mazumdar-Shaw also knew that in order to generate a major percentage of Biocon's revenues from proprietary drugs, she would have to stretch or build the company's capabilities. Biocon had operated for a long time in the realm of commodities, characterized by business-to-business sales. Making the transition to drug discovery and development would involve developing competence in several key areas: building a portfolio of promising drug candidates to move through the development pipeline, project management skills to facilitate this process, regulatory compliance, manufacturing, and marketing. The need to develop capabilities in these areas would place greater demand on Biocon's financial resources, yet without these investments it was unlikely that Mazumdar-Shaw would realize her vision of building Biocon into a top-tier biotechnology company. Said Mazumdar-Shaw:

> A biotech business is a marathon race in which a CEO manages potential more than performance. Balancing the demands of research with the demands of the bottom line . . . that is the challenge for a CEO.

As she contemplated this challenge and the upcoming board meeting, she began to think about the pros and cons of her aggressive vision for Biocon and the action plan that she would need to present to the board in order to sustain their support for her vision.

NOTES

1. All dollars in U.S. currency.
2. The Indian biotechnology ambience, characterized by low availability of venture capital (VC), made it imperative for entrepreneurs to sustain business risks entirely on their own. It was unlike the situation in North America, for example, where entrepreneurial risk was minimal, and a dedicated VC firm would often fund several start-ups, betting on one of them becoming a blockbuster.
3. Supriya Bezbaruah, "Seeds of a Revolution," *India Today,* August 9, 2004.
4. Manjeet Kripalani, "India: Bigger Pharma," BusinessWeek online, April 18, 2005, www.businessweek.com/magazine/content/05_16/b3929068.htm, referenced December 25, 2005.
5. In spite of being the world's fourth largest drug producer by volume, India's pharma revenues were low because of low-end prices. For example, the total value of India's drug sales (including exports) was $6.5 billion in 2004, less than the $8 billion revenue received by Pfizer from a single blockbuster product, Lipitor, in the same year.
6. The Patents (Amendment) Act 2005 was enacted by the federal government on April 5, 2005.
7. Richard Balaban et al., "Beyond the Blockbuster," a research report prepared by Mercer Management Consulting, www.amanet.org/PharmaFocus/good_company/mar_04.htm, referenced October 19, 2005.
8. Rolly Dureha, "Trailblazing Trials," *Biospectrum,* January 6, 2005, www.biospectrumindia.com/content/careers/10501061. asp, referenced December 26, 2005.

EXHIBIT 1 Top 20 Global Biotech Firms

Rank	Company	Country	2004 Sales (US $million)
1	Amgen	USA	10,600
2	Genentech	USA	4,620
3	Biogen Idec	USA	2,200
4	Genzyme	USA	2,200
5	Applied Biosystems	USA	1,740
6	Priority Healthcare	USA	1,740
7	Chiron	USA	1,700
8	Accredo Health	USA	1,500
9	Gilead Sciences	USA	1,300
10	Medimmune	USA	1,120
11	Biovail	Canada	886
12	Millenium Pharmaceuticals	USA	448
13	Imclone Systems	USA	389
14	Biocon	India	165
15	Nektar Therapeutics	USA	114
16	Caliper Life Sciences	USA	80
17	Celera Genomics	USA	60
18	Diversa Corp	USA	58
19	Exelixis	USA	53
20	Incyte	USA	14

SOURCE: Received from editor of *Biospectrum Magazine.*

EXHIBIT 2 GlobalBiotech Firms: Number, Revenue, Income, and Employment By Region, 200₄

Region	No. of Listed Firms	No. of Private Firms	Total no. of Biotech Firms	Revenue ($ million)	R&D Costs ($ million)	Income/(Loss) ($ million)	Employment (Number)
United States	330	1,114	1,444	42,740	15,701	(4,317)	137,000
Europe	98	1,717	1,815	7,729	4,151	(484)	25,640
Canada	82	390	472	2,091	782	(408)	7,370
Asia-Pacific	131	554	685	2,052	253	(94)	13,410
Total	641	3,775	4,416	54,612	20,887	(5,303)	183,820

SOURCE: Ernst &Young's "Beyond Borders: Global Biotechnology Report 2005," www.epraire.com/news/vnews, referenced July 29, 2005.

EXHIBIT 3 India's Major Biotech Firms, Ranked by Biotech Sales, 2004–2005
(in US$ million)

Rank	Company	2005 $ million	2004 $ million	Rank	Company	2005 $ million	2004 $ million
1	Biocon	145.8	113.3	11	GlaxoSmithKlein	17.5	13.8
2	Serum Institute of India	127.4	124.1	12	Indian Immunologicals	16.3	12.8
3	Panacea Biotec	49.0	33.7	13	Shantha Biotechnics	15.8	9.0
4	Venkateshwara			14	Novozymes	15.6	11.9
	Hatcheries	42.4	19.8	15	Eli Lilly & Co.	15.4	15.2
5	Mahyco Monsanto	37.5	12.2	16	Wockhardt	15.1	9.0
6	Novo Nordisk	30.4	24.8	17	Bharat Immunological	12.0	4.8
7	Rasi Seeds	19.6	–	18	Bharat Biotech	9.3	8.1
8	Aventis Pharma	19.0	16.4	19	Advanced Biochemicals	8.9	6.8
9	Bharat Serums	18.3	18.0	20	Biological E	8.2	8.6
10	Chiron Behring Vaccines	17.6	15.1			641.1	477.4

SOURCE: Biospectrum Magazine.

EXHIBIT 4   Biocon Financials, 2004–2005

Statement of Revenue For the year ending March (US$ million)	2005	2004
Revenue		
Sale of products	148.18	113.19
Contract research services	15.18	8.74
Other income	3.46	1.86
	166.82	123.79
Less:		
Cost of goods sold	89.72	66.84
Cost of contract research services	7.70	5.17
Gross Profit	69.40	51.78
Less:		
Research & Development expenses	3.36	2.98
Selling, general and admn. expenses	10.91	8.43
Depreciation	5.04	3.58
Interest	0.44	0.33
Income tax	5.67	5.96
Net Income	43.98	30.50
Balance Sheet		
Assets		
Current Assets		
Cash and cash equivalent	0.45	0.34
Investments in marketable securities	49.79	4.99
Restricted time deposits	0.23	71.13
Trade receivables	41.83	26.80
Inventories	16.92	19.32
Others	3.44	5.05
Fixed Assets		
Goodwill	0.50	0.50
Property, plant and machinery	128.61	48.28
Other investments	4.11	–
Loan to joint venture company	2.35	–
Other assets	0.85	0.39
Total Assets	249.08	176.80
Liabilities and stock equity		
Liabilities		
Accounts payable	47.23	27.06
Advance from customers	1.57	0.83
Short-term borrowings	11.47	10.71
Deferred taxes	15.54	9.78
Stockholders' equity		
Common stock	11.46	11.28
Authorized paid-up capital	76.93	75.69
Others	0.35	(0.97)
Retained earnings	84.53	42.42
Total Liabilities & Stock Equity	249.08	176.80

SOURCE: Biocon Ltd. files.

EXHIBIT 5 **Biocon: Product and Service Offerings**

Products		Services	
Enzymes	*Biopharmaceuticals*	*Custom Research*	*Clinical Research*
Amylases	Anti-Diabetic Agents	Small Molecule Synthesis	Clinical Trials
Cellulases	Anti-Hypertensive Agents	Medicinal Chemistry	Phases I – IV
Esterases	Anti-Inflammatory Agents	Library Synthesis	Patient databases in select
Glucanases	Antioxidants	Solution Phase	disease segments (dia-
Hemicellulases	Cardiovascular Agents	Solid Phase	betes, oncology, lipidemia
Xylanases	Digestive Aid Enzymes	Custom Synthesis - GMP	and cardiovascular)
Oxidases	Haemostatic Agents	Process Chemistry	Clinical Studies
Pectinases	Hepatoprotective Agents	Molecular Genetics	Bioavailability & Bio-equiva-
Proteases	Immunosuppressants	rDNA /cDNA/gDNA	lence
Tannase	Nutraceuticals		Novel Biomarkers via
			Proteomics & Data-mining

SOURCE: Biocon Ltd. files

EXHIBIT 6 **Segment-wise Profitabiltiy (U.S. $thousands)**

	Enzymes		Bio-pharma		Clinical Research		Custom Research		Total	
	2005	2004	2005	2004	2005	2004	2005	2004	2005	2004
Revenue	20,560	15,249	127,621	99,809	317	298	14,860	8,587	163,358	123,943
% of total revenue	12.58	12.30	78.12	80.53	0.20	0.24	9.10	6.93	—	—
Cost of sales	10,269	9,222	82,465	60,768	985	724	7,697	5,076	101,416	75,790
Operating income	10,291	6,027	45,156	39,041	(657)	(391)	7,152	3,476	61,942	48,153
% of total operating income	16.61	12.52	72.90	81.08	(1.05)	(0.83)	11.54	7.23	—	—

SOURCE: Biocon Ltd. files.

EXHIBIT 7   Lab-to-Market Value Chain (for a Bio-pharmaceutical Product)

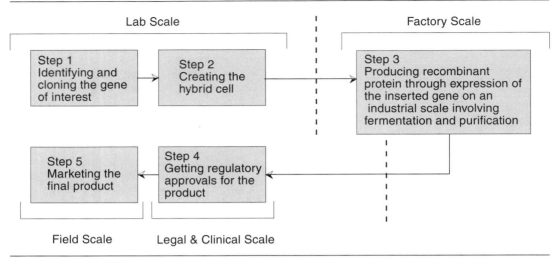

SOURCE: Joel Ruet et al., Biotechnology in India, Les biotechnologies en Inde, 2001, www.cerna.ensmp.fr/Documents/
AM-JR-MHZ-BiotechReport.pdf.

EXHIBIT 9   Biocon's Partnerships: Feeding the Discovery Pipeline

Year	Partner	Objectives
2003	CIMAB Cuba	Develop monoclonal antibodies and cancer vaccines
2004	Vaccinex USA	Focus on antibody products directed at cancer, inflammation and auto-immune diseases Identify promising antibody candidates and move them rapidly into clinical development Discover and co-develop at least four therapeutic anti-body products
2005	Nobex Corp USA	Develop an oral peptide product for the treatment of cardiovascular diseases Jointly develop an oral insulin for treating diabetes on a global scale

SOURCE: Biocon files.

EXHIBIT 8   Drug Discovery and Development Cycle

1. Target identification
Drugs usually act on chemicals in the body—known as targets—which are believed to be associated with a disease under investigation. A variety of techniques are used to identify and isolate a target.

2. Target validation
Researchers analyse and compare each drug target to its counterparts based on their association with a specific disease and their ability to regulate biological and chemical compounds in the body.

3. Lead identification
A lead compound is one that is believed to have the potential to treat the disease. Laboratory scientists compare known substances with new compounds to determine their likelihood of success. Leads are also sometimes developed as collections—known as libraries—of individual molecules.

4. Lead optimization
It compares the properties of various lead compounds and provides information to help select the compound with the greatest potential to be developed into safe and effective medicines.

5. Pre-clinical studies
Laboratory tests document the effect of the investigational drug on animal models (in vivo) and on cells in a test tube (in vitro).

6. Pharmaceutics
The results of pre-clinical testing are used to determine how best to formulate the drug for intended clinical use. Pharmaceutics consists of two phases—pharmacological tests to determine the effects of the candidate drug on the body and toxicology tests to identify risks to human body.

7. Phase I clinical studies
Designed to verify safety and tolerance of the drug in humans, phase I studies take, typically, between 6 and 9 months. A small number of healthy volunteers, from 20 to 100, take the investigational drug for short periods of time.

8. Phase II clinical studies
Designed to determine the effectiveness and safety of the drug in humans, they take from 6 months up to 3 years for completion. Testing is done on several hundred patients suffering from the conditions that the drug is designed to treat. Phase II study also establishes the minimum and maximum effective dosage.

9. Phase III clinical studies
They provide expanded testing of the safety and effectiveness of an investigational drug usually in randomized and blinded clinical trials. The time span is between one and four years. Phase III trials are conducted with several hundreds to thousands of volunteer patients suffering from the condition the drug is designed to treat.

10. New Drug Application
Filed with the regulatory bodies for approval (the Food and Drug Administration in the US), NDAs document the safety and efficacy of the drug providing all the information collected during drug development process. Obtaining approvals takes between 6 months and 2 years.

11. Phase IIIb/IV studies
They expand the testing of a proven drug to broader patient populations and compare the long term effectiveness and cost of the drug to other drugs available in the market to treat the same condition.

12. Post–marketing studies
They test a marketed drug in new age groups and patient types.

SOURCE: www.ppdi.com/PPD_U7.htm, referenced February 19, 2006.

Software Innovation Inc.

by James E. Hatch and Teddy Rosenberg

It was early 2005, and Jeff Park, the senior vice-president of Covington Capital Corporation (Covington), had a decision to make. For almost a year, he had been following the progress of Software Innovation Inc. (SI), talking with its management and learning about its business. The time had come to decide whether Covington should make an investment in the company or move on to other opportunities. Park was intrigued by the product category—project collaboration software—and the company's success in working with a marquee customer. But he kept thinking: "This company is at an awfully early stage. How much upside is there really? And how long is it going to take us to realize it?"

JEFF PARK AND COVINGTON CAPITAL

Jeff Park had been with Covington since 1998. He had started as the lowest of the low—an analyst—but had worked his way up to vice president and was now one of the three senior partners who were the key man-

agers of the firm. He had a solid track record but the technology and venture capital markets had been so painful over the past few years that Park, like most venture capitalists (VCs), was a little shell-shocked. Venture investing had been very depressed since the technology bust of 2000, but it appeared that investors were beginning to have more confidence in the investment market.

Covington Capital Corporation was the investment manager for five Ontario-based Labour Sponsored Investment Funds (LSIFs) with combined assets of approximately $600 million. LSIFs were similar to venture capital funds with the exception that government legislation imposed several constraints and restrictions on the nature and timing of the investments in order to protect investors and ensure that the government's goals of job development and local investment were met.

Park felt that Software Innovation was a good candidate for several of the Covington Funds. (It was possible for Covington to spread an investment among several of its funds.) Covington had a number of general funds into which SI could fit, and Park thought that SI could be particularly interesting for the new Strategic Capital Fund. This fund was started in December 2004 in conjunction with Microsoft Corp., Hewlett-Packard Corp and systems integration partners, such as Deloitte Consulting. The fund's intent was to invest in technology companies where these partners could validate the technology and market opportunity and, after investment, could potentially work with the companies to develop their businesses. However, this fund was small—with only $5 million in capital—and new—with only two prior investments.

In large funds, it was possible to "play the

averages," expecting a few big returns to make up for a handful of complete write-offs. In a smaller fund, Park knew he had to be more cautious since a single write-off could drastically affect the returns of the fund. Yet, Park felt that by using his strategic partners to validate the technology and market potential for Software Innovation, he could hedge his risk and accelerate the company's growth to meet a reasonable exit timeframe.

In any event, for each of the Covington Funds that might participate in an investment in SI, Park knew he had to make a solid case for a compounded return of 35 percent. He also knew that an exit was essential in no more than five years because Covington needed to constantly demonstrate returns to keep the flow of new capital coming in. Park also knew from the experience of the past difficult years in the venture business, it was helpful to have a like-minded partner putting money into any investment alongside Covington.

The Approach

Park first learned of SI through its chief executive officer (CEO) and major investor, Randall Howard, with whom Park had sat on the board of another software company. That was almost a year ago. Howard had indicated a fairly wide range in both the valuation he was looking for as well as the amount the company proposed to raise. Howard told Park that the company was willing to take a maximum dilution in this round of 35 to 45 percent and that the company wanted to raise $7 million to $10 million. These numbers implied a pre-money valuation ranging from $8.5 million to $19 million. This wide range was troubling: what did the company really want? Even at the low end, Park was concerned by the proposed valuation. At the high end, he thought the numbers were more reminiscent of the technology boom than the current state of the market. Yet Park also knew that for a good company with a strong management team it was worthwhile to stay in touch and to see whether, over time, their views on value and investment size might

converge. And for the next nine months that's what Park did.

SOFTWARE INNOVATION INC.

Software Innovation provided project collaboration software to the $3 trillion[1] capital projects market. The software, branded "Coreworx," was targeted at large-scale and complex, billion-dollar construction projects. These mega-projects included the development of new power plants, oil platforms and chemical plants. SI sold to owner-operators and engineering, procurement, and construction companies (EPCs). Owner-operators such as ExxonMobil and Dow Chemical were organizations that owned and operated a facility or capital project. EPCs were organizations such as market leaders Fluor and Bechtel that could be contracted by an owner-operator to manage the creation or upgrade of a capital project facility. Coreworx enabled collaboration among the involved parties at every stage of the capital project, from initial concept and specification, through front-end engineering and design, procurement, construction, commissioning/handover, and extending into the ongoing maintenance and operations cycle.

SI had evidence that it was addressing a critical market need. The National Institute of Standards and Technology (NIST) in the United States had released a study titled "Cost Analysis of Inadequate Interoperability in the U.S. Capital Facilities Industry." The report estimated that inadequate interoperability was costing the industry $15.8 billion per year. Highlighted inefficiencies included manual re-entry of data, duplication of business functions, and a reliance on paper-based information systems. All of these problems were addressed in the Coreworx product.

The company, based in Toronto, Ontario, had gone through three changes in ownership to reach its current state. The company began on February 3, 1997 as Software Innovation Inc., a wholly owned subsidiary of Software Innovation ASA (SI ASA), a Norwegian software company whose shares traded publicly on the Norwegian stock exchange (symbol: SOI). Its operations were funded completely by SI ASA, to the tune of approximately $3.5 million until a management buyout on November 1, 2001. At that time, SI's CEO, Finn Backer, bought 81 per cent of the company, and SI ASA retained 19 per cent of the company.

From 1997 to the buyout in 2001, SI was a software distribution and services company selling and supporting the products developed by SI ASA into the North American market. These products included a customer relationship management product, a business intelligence product, and two document management products. Revenue in this period was made up of license sales, professional services, and support and maintenance revenue, all related to this product set, and fluctuated between $1 million and $2 million per year.

In 2001, Finn Backer saw an opportunity in a project developing with Fluor Corporation, the world's largest publicly held engineering consulting company. The project, originally driven by a document management sale, expanded into an extended opportunity for enterprise-wide project document management and collaboration. SI acquired the rights to an existing solution from SI ASA and worked to customize it to meet Fluor's needs for project collaboration. At the same time, Backer recognized the potential for productizing and selling the application as built for Fluor to others in the project management space.

The Fluor project started in June 2001. By October 2001, the project scope had increased to encompass a global license for a secure project collaboration product (that would become SI's Coreworx product). At the same time, SI ASA had responded to investor pressure to limit its exposure outside its core Nordic market by reducing its interest in SI to 19 percent, which marked the beginning of SI's transition into an independent software development company from a distribution and services firm. Although SI had exclusive North American distribution rights for SI ASA's continuing product mix, the future of SI was becoming focused on developing its own products.

The Fluor project was a success. SI's revenues in 2002 were $3.1 million, of which Fluor accounted for the vast majority. The final delivery to Fluor took place in 2003. In that year, Fluor made up $1.35 million of SI's total revenue of $1.65 million. This revenue was primarily in the form of funded development.[2] Through 2003 and early 2004, the company focused on ensuring a highly successful implementation of the solution at Fluor, recognizing that this customer would be the beachhead into the project collaboration market.

Despite this success Backer decided he wanted to return to Norway. On May 11, 2004, Backer sold his 81 per cent ownership. His payment for the sale was structured such that he would receive approximately $2.5 million in a series of payments, some of which were dependent on company performance, over the period October 2004 to December 2008. This transaction was effectively a leveraged buyout in which the payments to Backer would be made out of the company's cash flow.

Backer's position was purchased by Verdexus, a boutique investment firm. Verdexus was founded in 2001 by technology entrepreneurs to provide management and financial services, focusing on management buyouts and corporate divestitures.

SI was the first venture in which Verdexus invested. The Verdexus partners, all seasoned operators, became the senior management team at SI. Immediately following the buyout, Verdexus and SI management and employees committed to an investment round to provide additional working capital to the company. Finally, Verdexus and management invested $300,000 in a convertible debenture in December 2004. The debenture was convertible into common shares at the price set by the next round of financing.

The capitalization table at January 2005 was as follows in Exhibit 1.

EXHIBIT 1 Capitalization, January 2005

Shareholder	Shares	% Ownership
Verdexus	2,027,150	74.7
Employees	45,500	1.7
SI ASA	287,850	10.6
Total Common Shares Outstanding	2,360,500	87.0
Options	354,075	13.0
Fully Diluted Shares	2,714,575	100.0

Coreworx

SI's flagship product was Coreworx, a Web-based application that enabled everyone connected to a capital project, be they engineers, architects, subcontractors, or others, to gain immediate, secure access to key documents, drawings, the project calendar and other information. The product was designed in conjunction with Fluor to ensure it met real-world requirements.

Coreworx incorporated a range of tools, including document management, workflow, mark-up and access control. The basic structure was proprietary to SI, as were a number of key application modules. In addition, Coreworx had been or could be integrated with other critical software used by owner-operators or EPCs, including enterprise resource planning (ERP) systems from SAP and Oracle, computer-aided design (CAD) systems such as Autodesk, and other document management systems from vendors such as Documentum and OpenText. Coreworx also included some software applications acquired on an original equipment manufacturer (OEM) basis from other software developers (such as the ProArc document management system from SI's former parent, SI ASA).

Competition

SI faced competition on a number of fronts. Historically, software spending in the capital project market had been in four silos of technology: enterprise resource planning (ERP)

or accounting software, project management (PM) software, engineering and computer-assisted design (CAD) tools, and document management (DM). Each represented critical information and functionality for the capital project market, and each had some claim to the market space inhabited by Coreworx. Although ERP vendors, such as SAP and Oracle, provided the means to track accounting and related information at a corporate level, these vendors did not typically function well on a project level. CAD tools from vendors such as Autodesk, Intergraph and Dassault Systèmes were the key applications that did the actual drawings and blueprints needed by engineers, architects and designers for large capital projects, but these CAD tools did not focus on facilitating the exchange of these documents with other users.

Competition also provided Park with a way of thinking about the valuation he might place on SI. Exhibit 4 provides valuation metrics for both competitors and related companies.

Daratech Inc., a leading market researcher, forecasted approximately $3.8 billion in technology software and services spending by EPCs and owner-operators in 2004. This number encompassed all of these silos of technology as well as the emerging project collaboration functionality. It was noted that as some of these silo vendors attempted to extend their footprint within their customers, they might wish to move further into SI's project collaboration space.

SI also faced competition from smaller vendors specifically focused on the project collaboration space. Most significant among these were the following:

> Citadon: Formed in late 2000 through the merger of two other companies, Citadon was a child of the technology bubble and had tens of millions of dollars sunk into it. It remained a private company; nevertheless, it shared many of the same features as Coreworx and targeted the same cus-

tomers. Notable among its customers were Bechtel, the Chicago Transit Authority and Halliburton. Equally notable was Citadon's failed project at Fluor that led to SI's engagement there.

Skire: Skire was a private company founded in 1988. Its Unifier product was well-regarded and very similar in functionality to Coreworx. The product and company focused primarily on owner-operators and was less appropriate for EPCs. Customers included Amgen, Baxter, Chiron, Bayer, Genentech, Hyundai and Motorola.

As the following chart illustrates (Exhibit 2), the company believed Coreworx to be the strongest product in the market landscape.

Market Engagement Strategy

SI intended to focus initially on four of the owner-operator verticals: oil and gas, process/power, pharma, and industrial. Government, aerospace/defense, and other vertical markets would follow. SI planned to pursue an aggressive growth strategy, expanding sales efforts through regional offices in key markets. Initially the company would pursue strategic accounts in the targeted verticals with a direct sales organization, migrating to a channel focus over 24 months. Within 48 months, the target was to achieve 50 percent of revenue through partners/channels.

SI realized that the sales cycle would be a long one: up to two years. Buyers in this space were notoriously conservative. In addition, SI felt that its product was most competitive when applied to very large and complex projects. With these factors in mind, the company expected the sales cycle in a given customer to progress from:

- $100,000 to $250,000 in initial projects wherein the product and concept were proven with a live project in a controlled environment, leading to
- $1 million in divisional sales where multiple projects within a vertical seg-

EXHIBIT 2   Market Landscape

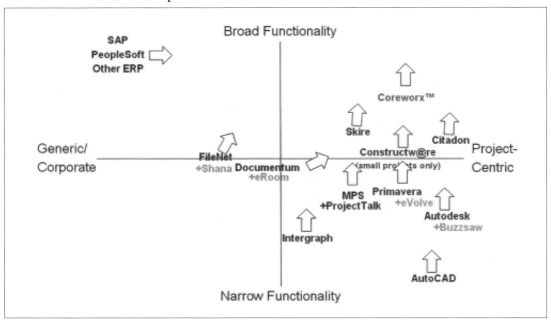

ment or business unit were managed with Coreworx, followed by

- $4 million+ in enterprise license sales.

Based on its success with Fluor and a proven customer return on investment (ROI) for the product, the company felt it could penetrate a small number of new customers each year, while adding users and modules, and hence earning additional revenue from existing customers.

SI envisioned a partner strategy that would embrace technology vendors, such as Microsoft, HP and Adobe, as well as complementary product providers, such as Documentum, Primavera and Intergraph. SI also planned to use systems integrators (e.g. Deloitte, Sapient and others) who served the target market.

Management

Park first learned of SI from its CEO, Randall Howard. Howard had formed Verdexus along with Waqar Zaidi and Ray Simonson. Each had significant experience as operators in high-tech companies, although they had not worked together previously. The Verdexus partners viewed SI as their stepping stone in establishing their boutique investment firm.

The partners formed the senior management team at SI, with Howard as CEO, Zaidi as chief operating officer (COO), and Simonson as chief technical officer (CTO). Park felt comfortable that the team had extraordinary experience. Howard was a founder and former CEO of MKS, and had led it through its listing on the Toronto Stock Exchange (TSX) and for three years thereafter. MKS provided software application lifecycle management solutions to enterprise customers. Simonson founded BlueGill, which was subsequently acquired by CheckFree, a NASDAQ-listed company that provided financial electronic commerce services and products. Other key roles that had been filled were chief financial officer (CFO), vice-president operations and development, and director of marketing.

Financial Plan. Park had received the projected financial statements seen in Exhibits 5 and 6. In light of his past experience with early stage companies, he felt that the financial statements might be optimistic. Sales estimates made by the company could be as much as double what could be expected. Gross margins were also forecast by the company to improve considerably over the planned time period. The company expected to be EBITDA[3] negative through 2006, explaining the need for the planned round of financing.

The financial forecast seen in Exhibits 5 and 6 was built on some key assumptions:

A three-stage sale to global customers:
Initial deployment project expected to total $250,000 plus the expenses associated with annual maintenance and support to comprise:
$175,000 license revenue
$75,000 consulting services
$35,000 annual maintenance and support
One-third of initial deployment projects progress to divisional sales expected to total $920,000 and to comprise:
$600,000 license revenue
$200,000 consulting services
$120,000 annual maintenance and support
Global sale totally $3,480,000 a year after the divisional sale to comprise:
$2,400,000 license revenue
$600,000 consulting services
$480,000 annual maintenance and support
Additional revenue from maintenance, support, and additional services generating 35 percent of license revenue on an annual basis.

Additional sales offices as follows:
2005: Houston
2006: Calgary
2007: Europe

Revenue per sales staff projected at $2.4 million

Continuing product development to add modules to Coreworx and reduce reliance on OEM products incorporated into Coreworx.

Research and development (R&D) costs targeted at roughly 10 percent of revenue for 2009 reflecting a mature software product.

SI at January 2005

As Park contemplated an investment in SI, he knew that the company had a marquee customer in Fluor. Coreworx was live and in use by more than 10,000 users on more than 55 projects in 25 countries. It was demonstrably enterprise-grade software built on robust technology. If Fluor wasn't proof enough, Park also had validation from technical evaluations done by Microsoft and Deloitte Consulting.

In addition, the company had an impressive sales pipeline comprising Chevron, ExxonMobil, Dow Chemical, Bechtel and British Petroleum. The pipeline illustrated one of the valuable features of this market: its interconnectedness; that is, many potential SI customers were already customers of Fluor. Yet this was the same prospect list Park had seen when he first met the company in April 2004. The company had made no sales since Fluor.

The company expected to continue to burn through cash for at least the next couple of years. At the moment, Verdexus and some members of management were funding the company directly, as evidenced by the recent convertible debenture.

As Park considered the investment in SI, he believed that the company had another financing alternative in the form of a group of high net worth individuals. They appeared less valuation-sensitive than Covington but they were only willing to put up about $1.5 million.

Park stood at his office window, viewed the sometimes calm and sometimes choppy Lake Ontario and wondered: "Should we make this investment? And if so, how should we structure it to take its unique characteristics into account?"

NOTES

1. All dollar amounts are in US$ except for references to the Covington Funds.
2. "Funded Development" means that Fluor paid SI for the development of the product that became Coreworx.
3. EBITDA is earnings before interest, taxes, depreciation, and amortization.

EXHIBIT 3

	Company	Project Revenue$	Expected Project Sales 2005	Expected Divisional Sales 2005	Notes
1	Chevron Texaco Pilot	250,000	Q2	Q4	Fluor customer.
2	ExxonMobil Pilot TX	250,000	Q2	Q4	Fluor customer.
3	ExxonMobil Pilot VA	100,000	Q2	Q4	Requirement agreed by management. Fluor customer. Probably Q1 06. RFI to be submitted in Jan/Feb, Demo done.
4	Dow Chemical Pilot	150,000	Q3	Q4+	Fluor customer.
5	Bechtel Pilot	250,000	Q2	Q4	Demo done. Fluor competitor.
6	BP Pilot	250,000	Q3	Q4+	Probably Q1 06. Fluor customer.

EXHIBIT 4   Valuation Metrics

Selected Software M&A Transactions

Date Announced	Effective Date	Acquiror	Target	Transaction Value $MM	LTM Sales $MM	TV/LTM Sales	Consideration
Apr-04	Pending	Sybase	XcelleNet	$ 95.2	$ 30.0	3.2x	Cash
Mar-04	Pending	SS&C Tech	OMR Systems	20.0	20.0	1.0x	Cash
Jan-04	3/1/2004	Vignette	Tower Technology	125.0	40.0	3.1x	Cash & Stock
Dec-03	Mar-04	The Sage Group	ACCPAC	106.2	88.7	1.2x	Cash
Oct-03	Dec-03	Macromedia	eHelp	65.7	25.0	2.6x	Cash & Stock
Oct-03	Pending	Open Text	IXOS	239.0	136.6	1.8x	Cash & Stock
Oct-03	Dec-03	EMC	Documentum	1,700.0	274.7	6.2x	Stock
Sep-03	Sep-03	Lawson Software	ClosedLoop	$4.2	1.8	2.3x	Cash
Jul-03	Dec-03	Business Objects	Crystal Decisions	820.0	270.0	3.0x	Cash & Stock

Selected Publicly Traded Software Companies as of mid-June 2004

Sector	Company	Enterprise Value	EV/2004 Revenue	P/E est. 2005
ERP	Oracle	$52,983.0	4.6x	18x
	Sybase	1,129.0	1.4x	15x
	SAP	47,398.0	6.3x	8x
	Peoplesoft	5,232.0	1.8x	18x
	Sage Group	2,422.0	3.5x	16x
	Lawson	459.0	1.2x	32x
Do./Content Mgt	Open Text	$1,000.0	2.7x	22x
	FileNet	872.0	2.1x	35x
	Vignette	246.0	1.3x	43x
Technical	Dassault	$4,555.0	5.8x	31x
	Autodesk	4,007.0	3.6x	23x
	Parametric	875.0	1.3x	19x

SOURCE: Internal company files

EXHIBIT 5 Income Statement US$

	2004A	2005P	2006P	2007P	2008P	2009P
Revenue						
Licenses	$ 52,304	$2,075,000	$4,750,000	$10,525,000	$18,075,000	$26,750,000
Services	97,645	775,000	1,550,000	3,675,000	6,575,000	10,200,000
Maintenance & Support	234,094	385,962	660,000	2,683,000	6,086,400	9,704,120
Interest Income						
Total Revenue	$ 384,043	$3,235,962	$6,960,000	$16,883,000	$30,736,400	$46,654,120
Cost of Sales						
Cost of Licenses	$ 30,465	$ 360,188	$ 629,375	$ 1,026,188	$ 1,129,688	$ 1,203,750
Cost of Services - Staff	100,742	428,488	1,145,342	2,180,386	3,325,789	4,300,117
Cost of Mtce - Staff	30,662	43,125	105,350	307,098	557,388	758,522
Cost of Mtce - Royalty	73,507	96,680	118,800	375,620	608,640	776,330
Total Cost of Sales	$ 235,376	$ 928,481	$1,998,867	$ 3,889,292	$ 5,621,505	$ 7,038,719
Gross Profit	$ 148,667	$2,307,481	$4,961,133	$12,993,708	$25,114,895	$39,615,401
% Gross Margin	39%	71%	71%	77%	82%	85%
Research & Development						
R&D Staff Costs	$ 264,735	$ 652,480	$923,081	$ 1,883,707	$ 3,142,034	$ 4,859,001
Sales & Marketing						
Sales Staff	$ 129,900	$ 941,000	$1,835,269	$ 3,139,560	$ 4,444,616	$ 5,988,474
Marketing Staff	76,979	359,594	583,341	1,234,273	2,023,905	2,757,583
Travel	28,812	230,000	497,778	977,778	1,400,000	2,106,667
Other	74,629	385,167	674,065	1,041,556	1,636,056	2,141,130
Consulting		75,000	100,000	120,000	140,000	160,000
Total Sales & Marketing	$ 310,320	$1,990,761	$3,690,453	$ 6,513,167	$ 9,644,577	$13,153,854

(continued on next page)

EXHIBIT 5 (continued)

	2004A	2005P	2006P	2007P	2008P	2009P
General & Administration						
Executive Remuneration	$ 334,466	$ 956,152	$1,226,215	$ 1,754,260	$ 2,157,023	$ 2,522,825
G&A Staff	127,428	210,069	471,649	642,934	906,203	1,175,200
Other Staff Expenses	26,432	24,552	28,519	35,667	42,519	49,000
Consultants		569,074	255,170	415,657	55,556	240,000
Rent - Head Office	95,912	136,296	202,963	237,037	237,037	237,037
Other Occupancy Costs	58,782	69,018	91,613	115,246	140,140	166,568
Other Offices		40,000	201,667	409,306	556,632	695,790
Travel & Entertainment	65,634	157,278	233,889	446,667	546,667	546,667
Professional Fees	47,249	33,333	55,556	64,815	85,185	122,222
Bank Charges & Forex	16,036	3,889	4,741	5,815	6,889	7,778
Total G&A	$ 771,939	$2,199,661	$2,771,982	$ 4,127,404	$ 5,233,851	$ 5,763,087
		0.68	0.40	0.24	0.17	0.12
EBITDA	($1,198,327)	($2,535,421)	($2,424,383)	$ 469,430	$ 7,094,433	$15,839,459
Other Income & Expenses						
Other Income/(Expenses)	$79,039	($ 41,433)	($ 41,433)	($ 41,433)		
Amortization - Dev. Costs						
Amortization - Capital Assets	(54,807)	(389)	(27,133)	(56,479)	($ 63,228)	($ 67,800)
Total Other	24,232	(50,822)	(68,566)	(97,912)	(63,228)	(67,800)
Net Income (Loss) Before Tax	($1,174,095)	($2,586,243)	($2,492,949)	$ 371,518	$ 7,031,205	$ 15,771,659
Tax	235,256	517,248	498,589	(74,304)	(2,158,024)	(5,993,231)
Net Income (Loss) Before Tax	($938,839)	($2,068,995)	($1,994,360)	$ 297,214	$ 4,873,181	$ 9,778,428

EXHIBIT 6   Balance Sheet (US$)

	2004A	2005P	2006P	2007P	2008P	2009P
Current Assets						
Accounts Receivable	$ 23,140	$ 960,000	$2,338,000	$2,387,900	$1,975,320	$4,070,256
Employee Advances	1,481	1,481	1,481	1,481	1,481	1,481
GST Receivable	12,084	12,084	12,084	12,084	12,084	12,084
Income Tax Receivable	234,819	752,067	1,250,657	1,176,353		
Prepaids - Current Portion	53,638	24,423	24,423	24,423	24,423	24,423
Total Current Assets	$ 325,162	$1,750,055	$3,626,645	$3,602,241	$2,013,308	$4,108,244
Capital Assets						
Hardware	$ 201,991	$ 201,991	$ 201,991	$ 201,991	$ 201,991	$ 201,991
Software	6,004	12,004	24,004	42,004	66,004	96,004
Furniture & Fixtures	171,142	203,625	240,376	291,375	348,375	400,876
Leaseholds	122,109	142,109	262,109	282,109	282,109	282,109
Less: Amortization	(481,608)	(490,997)	(518,130)	(574,609)	(637,837)	(705,637)
Total Longterm Assets	$19,638	$ 68,732	$ 210,350	$ 242,870	$ 260,642	$ 275,343
Other Assets						
Financing Costs	$ 135,168					
Development Costs	124,299	$ 82,866	$ 41,433			
Goodwill	148,037	148,037	$48,037	$ 148,037	$ 148,037	$ 148,037
Prepaids - Longterm	47,100					
Total Other Assets	$ 454,604	$ 230,903	$ 189,470	$ 148,037	$ 148,037	$ 148,037
Total Assets	$ 799,404	$2,049,690	$4,026,465	$3,993,148	$2,421,987	$4,531,624

(continued on next page)

EXHIBIT 6 (continued)

	2004A	2005P	2006P	2007P	2008P	2009P
Current Liabilities						
Bank Debt	$154,332		$2,360,991	$1,956,982		
Accounts Payable/Accrueds	139,771	$ 268,137	485,744	565,765	$ 616,168	$ 838,321
Payroll Liabilities	19,751	19,751	19,751	19,751	19,751	19,751
Capital Leases - Current	8,790	8,790	6,545			
Accrued Revenue	89,472				981,671	5,011,560
Total Current Liabilities	$412,116	$ 296,678	$2,873,031	$2,542,498	$1,617,590	$5,869,632
Longterm Liabilities						
Capital Leases	$15,335	$ 6,545				
Total Longterm Liabilities	$15,335	$ 6,545	$0	$0	$0	$0
Shareholders' Equity						
Class A Shares	$1,190,260	$1,190,260	$1,190,260	$1,190,260	$1,190,260	$1,190,260
Retained Earnings/(Deficit)	(818,305)	(2,887,300)	(4,881,660)	(4,584,446)	288,735	10,067,163
Total Shareholders' Equity	$371,955	($1,697,040)	($3,691,400)	($3,394,186)	$1,478,995	$11,257,423
Total Liabilities &						
Shareholders' Equity	$799,406	($1,393,817)	($818,369)	($851,688)	$3,096,585	$17,127,055
Cash Need or Surplus (-)		$3,443,507	$4,844,834	$4,844,836	($674,598)	($12,595,431)

Notes

Chapter 1

1. Quoted in Patricia B.Gray, "Do You Need School to Succeed?" *Fortune Small Business,* CNN Money.com. Retrieved from the Web March 1, 2006. http://money.cnn.com/magazines/fsb/fsb_archive/2006/03/01/8370301/index.htm.

2. "Know Your Future, *Economist*, Special section on "A Survey of the Young," December 23, 2000: 6-9

3. "It's a Great Time to Be an Entrepreneur." Retrieved from the Web April 28, 2006. http://bnoopy.typepad.com/bnoopy/2005/06/its_a_great_tim.html.

4. "Know Your future," 2000.

5. As students and teachers, we need to give more thought to this phenomenon. If the trend continues, there will be the need for lifelong learning as entrepreneurial skills and environments may change many times over the course of any individual's career.

6. "Know Your Future," 2000

7. "Know Your Future," 2000.

8. "Know Your Future," 2000.

9. "Know Your Future," 2000.

10. "Know Your Future," 2000.

11. " It's a Great Time to Be an Entrepreneur," 2006.

12. F. DiMeglio, "The B-School Route to Career Change," *Business Week Online,* special report, "Second Acts," January 19 2006.

13. Gray, 2006.

14. One model of lifelong entrepreneurial education is being pursued by the Consortium for Entrepreneurial Education at http://www.entre-ed.org/. The consortium introduces the subject and experience in secondary schools.

15. J. Boyette and H. Conn, *Workplace 2000* (New York: Dutton, 1991).

16. S. Perman, "Act II: A Biz of One's Own." *BusinessWeek Online,* special report, 2006. Retrieved from the Web January 17, 2006.

17. M. Mangalindan, "And the Opening Bid Is . . . " *The Wall Street Journal Report: Encore,* September 26, 2005: R9.

18. M. Low and J. MacMillan, "Entrepreneurship: Past Research and Future Challengers." *Journal of Management* 14, 1988:139–161.

19. The term *network* was added here to anticipate the possibility of the entrepreneur creating a "virtual" organization. This is an organization that employs other organizations almost exclusively to carry out the functions that are ordinarily thought of as being performed within the enterprise.

20. J. Schumpeter, *The Theory of Economic Development* (Cambridge, MA: Harvard University Press, 1934).

21. Although one can argue that the origins of the theory can be claimed by E. Penrose in her book, *The Theory of the Growth of the Firm* (New York: Wiley, 1959), it really was not until the mid-1980s that the resource-based theory of sustained competitive advantage began to be explored and developed in management terms. Two particularly salient articles are: J. Barney, "Firm Resources and Sustained Competitive Advantage," *Journal of Management* 17, 1991: 99–120; and K. Conner, "A Historical Comparison of Resource-Based Theory and Five Schools of Thought Within Industrial Organization Economics: Do We Have a New Theory of the Firm?" *Journal of Management* 17, 1991:121–154. Barney and Conner make the initial claim that this theory may supersede others as a theory of the firm. A solid bibliography of RBV articles can be found at http://www.istheory.yorku.ca/rbv.htm. New work is being published all the time.

22. B. Wernerfelt, "A Resource-Based View of the Firm," *Strategic Management Journal* 5, 1984: 171-180.

23. J. Barney, "Is the Resource-Based View a Useful Perspective for Strategic Management Research? Yes," *Academy of Management Review* 26, no. 1, 2001: 41-56.

24. M. Morris and F. Jones, "Entrepreneurship in Established Organizations: The Case of the Public Sector," *Entrepreneurship: Theory and Practice* 24, no. 1, 1999: 71–91.

25. W. Baumol, *Business Behavior: Value and Growth* (New York: Harcourt Brace, 1967).

26. J. Carland, F Hoy, W. Boulton, and J. Carland, "Differentiating Entrepreneurs from Small Business Owners: A Conceptualization," *Academy of Management Review* 9, 1984: 354–359.

27. Walden Kayaks closed down in late 2004, but it survives as http://www.waldenkayak.com/.

28. E. Penrose, *The Theory of the Growth of the Firm* (New York: John Wiley, 1959): 55-57. This book was the precursor to the development of the resource-based theory that is the foundation for this text.

29. J. McMullen, and D. Shepard, "Entrepreneurial Action and the Role of Uncertainty in the Theory of the Entrepreneur," *Academy of Management Review* 31, no. 1, 2006: 132-152.

30. The study can be found in papers collected at www.aeaweb.org.annua._mtg_papers/2006 papers.html. Retrieved from the Web April 28, 2006. T. Astebro, "The Return to Independent Invention," *Economic Journal*, 2003. The quote by Baumol is from "Economic Focus: Searching for the Invisible Man," *Economist*, March 11, 2006: 68.

31. S. D. Sarasvathy, "Entrepreneurship as Economics with Imagination," *Business Ethics Quarterly*, The Ruffin Series #3 on Entrepreneurship and Business Ethics, 2002: 95-112.

32. G. O'Driscoll, K. Holmes and M. Kirkpatrick, "Who's Free, Who's Not," *The Wall Street Journal,* November 1, 2000: A26.

33. M. Jordan, "How One Woman Stormed Vietnam to Realize a Dream," *The Wall Street Journal,* May 5, 1994: 1.

34. J. Vitullo-Martin, "Moscow Entrepreneurs Seize Golden Opportunity," *The Wall Street Journal,* January 20, 1997: A11.

35. A. Grimes, "A Liberal Entrepreneur Finds Room to Grow; Then Politics Intrude," *The Wall Street Journal,* October 5, 2000: A1.

36. T. Richman, "Creators of the New Economy," *Inc.'s* "The State of Small Business," 1997: 44–48

37. This is another factor contributing to the definitional confusion.

38. D. Birch, J. Gunderson, A. Haggerty, and W. Parsons, *Corporate Demographics.* (Cambridge MA: Cognetics, Inc., 1999).

39. R. Lesonsky, "Ahead of the Pack," *Entrepreneur.* Retrieved from the Web January 25, 2007. http://www.entrepreneur.com/article/printthis/171824.html.

40. Richman, 1997.

41. Richman, 1997.

42. In fact, one professor of entrepreneurship referred to the teaching and taking of entrepreneurship courses as an oxymoron—the juxtaposition of two incompatible ideas.

43. These terms will be defined and their meanings elaborated in the next chapter.

44. Conner, 1991.

45. R. Holcombe, "The Origins of Entrepreneurial Opportunities," *Review of Austrian Economics* 16, no. 1, 2003: 25-43.

46. P. Drucker, *Innovation and Entrepreneurship* (New York: Harper & Row, 1985).

47. L. Carrel, "After a Dubious Movie Moment, 'Coyote Bar' Concept Shines," *The Wall Street Journal,* November 16, 2004:B1.

48. Drucker, 1985.

49. W. Gartner, "A Conceptual Framework for Describing the Phenomenon of New Venture Creation," *Academy of Management Review* 10, 1985: 696–706.

50. This brief discussion owes its genesis to Chris Argyris' discussion of the ethics of a consultant in *Intervention Theory and Method: A Behavioral Science View* (Reading, MA: Addison Wesley, 1973).

51. S. Caminiti, "A Payoff from a Good Reputation," *Fortune,* February 10, 1992: 74–77. This is a quote from Laurel Cutler.

52. D. Garvin, *Managing Quality* (New York: Free Press, 1998). See chapters 3 and 4 for a detailed discussion. This is one of the seminal books that launched the "quality" revolution in the United States.

53. Garvin, 1998.

54. Garvin, 1998.

55. Rather than repeating the four desirable attributes of resources constantly throughout the book, we will adopt the convention of calling them "the four attributes" of the resource-based model or "VRIN" (valuable, rare, imperfectly imitable [hard to copy], and nonsubstitutable).

56. First attributed to the VRIN comedian, Groucho Marx.

57. J. Bain, "Economies of Scale, Concentration, and the Conditions of Entry in Twenty Manufacturing Industries," *American Economic Review* 44, 1980: 15 - 39. M. Porter, *Competitive Strategy* (New York: Free Press, 1980).

Chapter 2

1. J, Barney, "Strategic Factor Markets: Expectations, Luck and Business Strategy," *Management Science* 32, 1986: 1231–1241.

2. B. Peabody, *Lucky or Smart? Secrets to an Entrepreneurial Life* (New York: Random House, 2004).

3. Recently, a new debate has been opened that considers whether or not the resource-based view of the firm is a complete theory. See the following for the details. J. Butler and R. Priem, "Is the Resource-Based 'View' a Useful Perspective for Strategic Management Research," *Academy of Management Review* 26, no.1, 2001: 22–40—Yes; J. Butler and R. Priem, "Tautology in the Resource-Based View and the Implications of Externally Determined Resource Value: Further Comments," *Academy of Management Review* 26, no. 1, 2001:57–66. In fact, this book generally adopts Barney's approach to the problems and issues of entrepreneurship, and although I agree that Butler and Priem's work adds to the dialog, in the end I believe that Barney's arguments carry the day.

4. A seminal work in the development of the RBV is B. Wernerfelt, "A Resource-Based View of the Firm," *Strategic Management Journal* 5, 1984:171-180. This original work presented the theory in the context of corporate diversification. The question addressed was: Which resources does a firm need to acquire, in what sequence, and from what source (an acquisition or a partner)? The goal of the corporation is to create a situation that makes it difficult for another organization to catch up.

5. Here is a personal example: Two business professors teaching in Hong Kong, one an expert in management, the other in marketing, have endlessly discussed how to make money in China. After all, the rumor is that everyone is getting rich in China, and these two professors are smart, talented, and even speak Chinese. But in spite of the myriad of opportunities available to them, the professors are unable to create a new venture. Why? Because they have no resources and all they know how to do is teach class and write academic papers.

6. S. Winter, "Knowledge and Competence in Strategic Assets." In D. Teece (ed.), *The Competitive Challenge* (Cambridge: Ballinger, 1987).

7. Wernerfelt, 1984.

8. D. Miller and J. Shamsie, "The Resource-Based View of the Firm in Two Environments: The Hollywood Film Studios from 1936-1965," *Academy of Management Journal* 39, no. 3, 1996: 519-543.

9. Collins, 1994.

10. D. Collins, "Research Note: How Valuable Are Organizational Capabilities?" *Strategic Management Journal* 15, 1994: 143-152.

11. History is often not studied in social sciences such as psychology and sociology and even, to some extent, economics. One of the finest works in management and organization theory is a set of histories by A. Chandler, *Strategy and Structure* (Cambridge, MA: MIT Press, 1962); and entrepreneurial histories abounded as an early form of study. See Section II. H. Livesay "Entrepreneurial History." In C. Kent, D. Sexton, and K. Vesper (eds.), *Encyclopedia of Entrepreneurship* (Upper Saddle River, NJ: Prentice-Hall, 1982). To understand how history and science are related, see any works by Stephen Jay Gould.

12. Barney, 1986.

13. C. Bowman and V. Ambrosini, "Value Creation versus Value Capture: Toward a Coherent Definition of Value in Strategy," *British Journal of Management* 11, 2000:1-15.

14. From Valuebasedmanagement.net. Retrieved from the Web on January 31, 2007. http://www.valuebasedmanagement.net/methods_barney_resource_based_view_firm.html.

15. J. Barney, "Firm Resources and Sustained Competitive Advantage." *Journal of Management* 17, 1991;99–120.

16. Some recent formulations (if you google-search "VRIO" you will see it) of the RBV have adopted a VRIO set of qualities instead of the VRIN espoused here. The difference is that in the new formulation, *nonsubstitutability,* is included in Imperfect Imitability and the *O* stands for organizational ability. However, I would disagree with the new format. The VRIN rubric describes categories of qualities of resources. Organizational ability is a type of resource and is therefore different. I include organization in the PROFIT model instead.

17. J. Timmons, *New Venture Creation.* (Homewood, IL: Irwin, 1990). Timmons uses these three general criteria for assessing the worthiness of an entrepreneurial effort. We will discuss the evaluation of business opportunities and business plans in more detail in this and later chapters.

18. J. Schumpeter, *Capitalism, Socialism and Democracy,* 3rd ed. (New York: Harper & Row, 1950). Schumpeter first coined the phrase "destructive capitalism" in his description of entrepreneurship as the force that initiates change in capitalistic systems.

19. M. Kakati, "Success Criteria in High-Tech Ventures," *Technovation* 23, no. 5, 2003: 447.

20. I. Grousbeck, M. Roberts, and H. Stevenson, *New Business Ventures and the Entrepreneur* (Homewood, IL: Irwin, 1989). See, especially, chapter 1.

21. See, for example, A. Strickland and A. Thompson, *Strategic Management: Concepts and Cases.* (Homewood, IL: Irwin, 1992).

22. J. Barney, 1986. Barney also makes a case that luck plays a much larger role in entrepreneurship and business success in general. This view may also explain why there is incongruence between "rich" and "smart."

23. http://en.wikipedia.org/wiki/Bertrand_competition. Retrieved from the Web, January 30, 2007.

24. Barney, 1991.

25. Barney, 1991.

26. For more on culture and its effects, see C. Enz, *Power and Shared Values in the Corporate Culture* (Ann Arbor: UNI Research Press, 1984); and G. Hofstede, *Culture's Consequences: International Differences in Work-Related Values* (Beverly Hills: Sage Publications, 1984).

27. There is now a fairly large literature on institutional theory. A good summary article is A. Kondra and C. Hinings, "Organizational Diversity and Change in Institutional Theory," *Organizational Studies*, Winter 1998. Retrieved from the Web May 10, 2006. http://www.findarticles.com/p/articles/mi_m4339/is_5_19/ai_65379676. An article that tries to integrate the two approaches is C. Oliver, "SCA: Combining Institutional and Resource-Based Views," *Strategic Management Journal* 18, no. 9, 1997: 697-713.

28. Barney, 1991.

29. H. Neck, G. D. Meyer, B. Cohen, and A. Corbett, "An Entrepreneurial System View of New Venture Creation," *Journal of Small Business Management* 42, no. 2, 2004: 190-208.

30. M. Dollinger, P. Golden, and T. Saxton, "The Effects of Reputation on the Decision to Joint Venture," *Strategic Management Journal* 18, no, 2, 1997: 127–140. See also C. Fombrun and M. Shanley, "What's in a Name? Reputation Building and Corporate Strategy," *Academy of Management Journal* 33, 1990: 233–258.

31. Hamel and Prahalad refer to organizational resources, particularly those that confer strategic advantage on the firm, as "core competencies." See G. Hamel and C. Prahalad, "The Core Competencies of the Organization," *Harvard Business Review*, May–June 1990: 79–91.

32. G. Huber, "The Nature and Design of Post-Industrial Organizations," *Management Science* 30, 1984: 929–959. This article takes a futuristic approach to organizational design and is still ahead of its time.

33. Huber, 1984.

34. C. Brush, L. Edelman, P. Green, and M. Hart, "Resource Configurations over the Life Cycle of New Ventures," *Frontiers of Entrepreneurship Research*, 1997 edition, Babson College, Arthur M. Blank Center for Entrepreneurship, Wellesley, MA. Retrieved from the Web. http://edu/entrep/fer/papers97/brush/bru1.htm.

35. R. Grant, *Contemporary Strategy Analysis* (Oxford, UK: Blackwell, 1992).

36. J. Freear and W. Wetzel, "The Informal Venture Capital Market in the 1990s." In D. Sexton and J. Kasarda (eds.), *The State of the Art of Entrepreneurship* (Boston: PWS-Kent, 1992): 462-486.

37. Grant, 1992.

38. We qualify this a bit when we say "on a strictly financial basis." Clearly, money raised from organized crime activities is neither morally nor contractually equivalent to a loan from the local commercial bank.

39. R. Baron and G. Markham, "Social Skills and Entrepreneurs' Financial Success: Evidence that the Ability to Get Along with Others Really Matters," *Frontiers of Entrepreneurship Research*, 1998 edition, Babson College, Arthur M. Blank Center for Entrepreneurship, Wellesley MA. Retrieved from the Web. http://edu/entrep/fer/papers98/IV/IV_B/IV_B.html.

40. O. Richard, "Racial Diversity, Business Strategy and Firm Performance: A Resource-Based View," *Academy of Management Journal* 43, no. 2, 2000: 164–177.

41. Sometimes relational capital is referred to as "networking." For more information, see S. Birley, "The Role of Networks in the Entrepreneurial Process," *Journal of Business Venturing* 2, 1985: 155–165; M. Dollinger and P. Golden, "Interorganizational and Collective Strategies in Small Firms: Environmental Effects and Performance," *Journal of Management* 18, 1992: 696–717. For alliance information, see J. Baum, T. Calabrese, and B. Silverman, "Don't Go It Alone: Alliance Network Composition and Start-Ups' Performance in Canadian Biotechnology," *Strategic Management Journal* 21, 2000: 267–294.

    For the use of outside consultants, see J. Chrisman and W. McMullan, "A Preliminary Assessment of Outsider Assistance as a Knowledge Resource: The Longer Term Impact of New Venture Counseling," *Entrepreneurship: Theory and Practice* 24, no. 3, 2000: 37–53.

42. J. Dyer and H. Singh, "The Relational View: Cooperative Strategy and Sources of Interorganizational Competitive Advantage," *Academy of Management Review* 23, 1998: 660-279.

43. Barney, 1991.

44. A. Bharadwaj, "A Resource-Based Perspective on IT Capability and Firm Performance: An Empirical Investigation," *MIS Quarterly* 24, no. 1, 2000: 169-196.

45. C. Crossen, "The Last Laugh," *The Wall Street Journal, The Journal Report: Small Business,* May 9, 2005: R 10.

46. W. Boulton, J. Carland, and F. Hoy, "Differentiating Entrepreneurs from Small Business Owners: A Conceptualization," *Academy of Management Review* 9, 1984: 354–359.

47. D. McClelland, *The Achieving Society.* (Princeton, NJ: D. Van Nostrand, 1961).

48. See R. Brockhaus, "The Psychology of the Entrepreneur." In C. Kent, D. Sexton, and K. Vesper (eds.), *Encyclopedia of Entrepreneurship* (Upper Saddle River, NJ: Prentice Hall, 1982): 39-71.

49. J. Rotter, "Generalized Expectancies for Internal Versus External Control of Reinforcement," *Psychological Monographs* 80, Paper 609, 1966.

50. Brockhaus, 1982,

51. "Optimism-Pessimism," 1998. Retrieved from the Web February 1, 2007. http://www.macses.ucsf.edu/Research/Psychosocial/notebook/optimism.html.

52. M. Puri and D. Robinson, *"Who Are the Entrepreneurs and Why Do They Behave that Way?"* Unpublished manuscript, 2006. Retrieved from the Web February 1, 2007. http://www.lse.ac.uk/collections/RICAFE/pdf/Puri_Manju.pdf.

53. A. Cole, "Definition of Entrepreneurship." In J. Komives (ed.), *Karl A. Bostrum Seminar in the Study of Enterprise* (Milwaukee: Center for Venture Management, 1969): 10 – 22.

54. J. Baum, M. Frese, and R. Baron, *The Ppsychology of the Eentrepreneur* (Mahwah, NJ: Lawrence Erlbaum Associates, 2006).

55. A. Shapero and L. Sokol, "The Social Dimensions of Entrepreneurship." In C. Kent, D. Sexton, and K. Vesper (eds.), *Encyclopedia of Entrepreneurship* (Upper Saddle River, NJ: Prentice Hall, 1982): 72-90.

56. R. Amit, " 'Push' and 'Pull' Entrepreneurs," *Frontiers of Entrepreneurship Research,* 1994 edition. Retrieved from the Web at http://www.babson.edu/entrep/fer/papers94/amit.htm.

57. Professor Pyong Gap Min, quoted in D. Lorch, "Ethnic Niches Creating Jobs that Fuel Immigrant Growth," *New York Times,* January 12, 1992.

58. Based on a story by Timothy Noah that appeared in *The Wall Street Journal,* August 2, 1992.

59. Noah, 1992.

60. Noah, 1992.

61. S. Birley, "The Role of Networks in the Entrepreneurial Process," *Journal of Business Venturing* 1, 1985: 107–118.

62. For a discussion of this and other background characteristics, see chapter 3 of R. Hisrich and M. Peters, *Entrepreneurship* (Homewood, IL: Irwin, 1991).

63. This is not an uncommon situation, but it is a difficult one. Consider the employee (for example, an accountant, salesperson, or consultant) who serves a customer, after which the customer encourages the employee to go into business for himself. The promise implicit here is that the customer will switch his business to the new entrepreneur. This is a common situation. But is it ethical? Does the employee have a responsibility to an employer not to steal the customer? Should

the employee report the offer and try to do a better job servicing the customer within the current employment relationship? There is an economic side here as well. A firm with a single customer is vulnerable. The customer may feel the entrepreneur is in some way obligated to give the customer the best deal because of their history together. The new firm's employees will, of course, know the circumstances of their firm's founding and may replicate it when the time comes.

64. Much of the discussion on spin-offs is adapted from D. Garvin, "Spin-Offs and the New Firm Formation," *California Management Review 25*, l983: 3–20.

65. U. Gupta, "Blending Zen and the Art of Philanthropic Pastry Chefs," *The Wall Street Journal,* January 2, 1992.

66. A. Singh, "Out of the Office, Into the Classroom," *The Wall Street Journal*, March 7, 2006: B5.

67. Shapero and Sokol, 1982.

68. Grousbeck et al., 1989.

Chapter 3

1. From Sharon M. Oster, *Modern Competitive Analysis* (Oxford University Press, UK: l994): 124.

2. J. McMullen and D. Shepherd, "Entrepreneurial Action and the Role of Uncertainty in the Theory of the Entrepreneur," *Academy of Management Review* 31, no. 1, 2006: 132-150.

3. The model has antecedents in the work of many industrial organization economists, but it was Michael Porter's book that made the analysis compulsory for noneconomics majors in all business schools. See M. Porter, *Competitive Strategy* (New York: Free Press, 1980).

4. L. Fahey and V. K. Narayanan, *Macroenvironmental Analysis for Strategic Management* (St. Paul, MN: West Publishing, 1986).

5. Focus groups are small panels of experts or interested individuals who have special knowledge of the problem at hand.

6. K. Alexander, "From Google to Noodles: A Chef Strikes Out on His Own," *New York Times*, 2005. Retrieved from the Web September 20, 2005. http://www.nytimes.com/2005/09/20/business/business.

7. K. Alexander, "From Google to Noodles: A Chef Strikes Out on His Own," *New York Times*, 2005. Retrieved from the Web Spetember 20, 2005. http://www.nytimes.com/2005/09/20/business/business.

8. J. Pearce and R. Robinson, *Strategic Management*, 4th ed. (Homewood, IL: Irwin, 1991).

9. M. Bhave, "A Process Model of Entrepreneurial Venture Creation," *Journal of Business Venturing* 9, 1994: 223-242.

10. L. Buchanan, "Bringing Back a Classic," *Inc.*, August 2003: 46.

11. "Japanese Business Methods," *Economist,* April 4, 1992: 19–22.

12. S. Munoz, "Court Denies Smucker Patent Bid," *The Wall Street Journal,* April 11, 2005: B5.

13. J. Hookway, "A Paradox for Poor Nations," *The Wall Street Journal*, May 9, 2005: A20.

14. Fahey and Narayanan, 1986.

15. E. Olson, "After the Flood, Free Advice for Entrepreneurs in Need," *New York Times*, February 21, 2006. Retrieved from the Web February 25, 2006. http://www.nytimes.com/2006/02/21/business.

16. This section is largely derived from Fahey and Narayanan, *Macroenvironmental Analysis,* 1986.

17. J. Surowiecki, "Printing Money," *New Yorker,* April 3, 2006. Retrieved from the Web May 15, 2006. http://www.newyorker.com/talk/content/articles/060403ta_talk_surowiecki.

18. J. Goldenberg, D. Lehmann and D. Mazursky, "The Idea Itself and the Circumstances of its Emergence as Predictors of New Product Success," *Management Science* 47, 2001: 69-84.

19. B. Wattenberg, "America by the Numbers," *The Wall Street Journal*, January 3, 2001: A11.

20. J. Millman, "'El Gringo Malo' Wins Fans Airing Spanish Baseball," *The Wall Street Journal,* September 14, 2004: B1. Also see the Web site at http://www.sbnbeisbol.com/.

21. Retrieved from the Web May 16, 2006. http://geography.about.com/cs/worldpopulation/a/mostpopulous.htm.

22. C. Kluckhorn, "Values and Value-Orientation." In T. Parsons and E. Shils (eds.), *Toward a General Theory of Action* (Cambridge: Harvard University Press, 1962): 338-433.

23. *Distributive justice* refers to the desirable distribution of the wealth of society among its members.

24. The World Commission on Environment, 1987. Retrieved from the Web February 6, 2007. http://www.wsu.edu:8080/~sus-dev/WCED87.html.

25. Comments by Frank Popoff, CEO and chairman of Dow Chemical Company, at the Graduate Business Conference, Indiana University, Bloomington, Indiana, April 3, 1992,

26. "General Electric and Dow Jones Announce Winner of Economics: The Environmental Business Plan Challenge Award: Recipient Received $50,000 for Innovative Environmentally Friendly Plan," 2006. Retrieved from the Web May 10, 2006. http://online.wsj.com/.

27. The story is an old one and often makes the rounds in graduate economics classes. However, I was reminded of it by reading S. Oster, *Modern Competitive Analysis* (New York: Oxford University Press, 1990).

28. A frequently heard question when one is challenging a new venture opportunity is: If this is such a good idea, why has not someone already done it? As we can see, this is actually an economic question in sheep's clothing. The correct answer to this line of questioning is: Because no one else has been smart enough, until now.

29. C. Montgomery and B. Wernerfelt, "What Is an Attractive Industry?" *Management Science* 32, 1986: 1223–1230.

30. These three strategies are known as *generic* strategies because other strategies derive from them. Porter originally argued that a firm must choose to pursue one of the three strategies because it could not adhere to more than one strategy within a single market. He called this being "stuck in the middle." Empirical research has demonstrated that sometimes firms can achieve differentiation and the low-cost position simultaneously. C. Hill, "Differentiation Versus Low Cost or Differentiation and Low Cost: A Contingency Framework," *Academy of Management Review* 13, 1988: 401–412; A. Murray,, "A Contingency View of Porter's Generic Strategies," *Academy of Management Review* 13, 1988: 390–400; P. Wright, "A Refinement of Porter's Strategies," *Strategic Management Journal* 9, 1980: 93–101.

31. This is the model developed and popularized by Michael Porter in his two books, *Competitive Strategy* (New York: Free Press, 1980), and *Competitive Advantage* (New York: Free Press, 1985). Although this chapter borrows heavily from these two books and uses the Porter analysis to examine the problems of new venture creation, there is really no substitute for reading the originals.

32. We often hear the argument that quality improvements pay for themselves, either by increasing customer loyalty or increasing the customer base. This argument may be true if the increased loyalty leads to more price elasticity of demand, and if the cost increases can be passed on to the new customers.

33. There are some interesting counterexamples, however. When competition heats up in the automobile industry, factory rebates (price concessions from manufacturers), plus the normal bargaining process within the dealerships, can produce final sales prices lower than the average variable cost for the combination of manufacturer and dealer. In an overheated housing market, buyers often bid up the price of the house against each other instead of bargaining for lower prices. Such bargaining may occur even if the supply of houses is greater than the demand. It is the inflationary expectations that drive this process. People feel that the prices will be even higher if they do not buy quickly. Of course, this is a self-fulfilling prophesy for the group of buyers, even if it benefits a particular buyer.

34. This is especially true when a third party is paying for the airline ticket (for example, an employer), but the flyer receives private credit for the miles.

35. See Porter, 1980.

36. The presence of entry barriers is *prima facie* evidence that perfect competition does not exist. But does actual entry have to occur to keep incumbents from earning above-normal returns? It can be argued that the threat of entry is itself sufficient, as long as that entry is relatively costless and irreversible. This theory, the contestability theory, makes a distinction between competitive markets, where actual entry enforces price discipline, and contestable markets, where the threat of entry enforces discipline even though the industry looks like an oligopoly. See W. Baumol, J. Panzer, and R. Willig, *Contestable Markets and the Theory of Industry Structure* (New York: Harcourt, Brace, Jovanovich, 1982).

37. The general model to determine if entry will

be profitable can be written as an equation where the sum of all future discounted cash that flows from the new venture is set against the sum of the direct investment attributable to the new venture, plus the sum of the expenses related to overcoming the structural barriers, plus the sum of the expenses related to retaliation costs (such as price concessions, marketing, and legal expenses). All too often, when entrepreneurs make their calculations, they include only the direct-investment costs (property, plant, equipment, and initial organization costs). An opportunity that looks profitable based on direct costs might not be profitable when the barrier and retaliation costs are factored in.

38. Retrieved from the Toys "R" Us Web site February 6, 2007. http://www.toysrus.com/helpdesk/index.jsp?display=safety&subdisplay=terms&clickid=botnav_terms_txt.

39. Exit barriers are those structural impediments that prevent inefficient firms from leaving an industry even when the firms are unprofitable and have little prospect of achieving profitability. Examples of exit barriers are psychological commitment by the firm's owners, specialized assets, fixed costs of exit (e.g., labor agreements), and government policy (e.g., Chrysler and Lockheed in the United States).

40. Porter, 1980: 18–20.

41. The Federal Trade Commission maintains a classification scheme for all businesses. It is known as the Standard Industrial Classification code, or SIC for short. All products and services are assigned codes that range from two to seven digits. Two- and three-digit SIC codes are too broad and general to identify competitors, and five- through seven-digit codes may be too narrow. The four-digit SIC code is the one that is generally accepted for current and potential competitor analysis.

42. See Chapter 2 for complete definitions and descriptions of the resources and their attributes.

43. Included in the general term *strategy* here would be such elements as the firm's goals and future goals, its assumptions about itself and its industry, and its own assessment of its strengths and weaknesses

Chapter 4

1. There are a number of fine textbooks on the subject of strategic management. The following list is not meant to be complete or exclusive: G. Dess and A. Miller, *Strategic Management* (New York: McGraw-Hill, 1993); H. Mintzberg and J. Quinn, *The Strategy Process* (Upper Saddle River, NJ: Prentice Hall, 1991); J. Pearce and R. Robinson,. *Strategic Management: Formulation, Implementation and Control* (Homewood, IL: Irwin, 1992); A. Strickland and A. Thompson, *Strategic Management: Text and Cases* (Homewood, IL: Irwin, 1992).

2. D. Hambrick, "Some Tests of the Effectiveness of Functional Attributes of Miles and Snow's Strategic Types," *Academy of Management Journal* 26, 1983: 5–26.

3. Probably the second-most important core decision that an entrepreneur and the top management team can make (after the choice of product or service) is customer and market selection. Who are you going to sell to and in what channel(s)? See J. Magretta, "Why Business Models Matter: The Difference between Business Models and Strategy," *Harvard Business Review* 80, no. 1, May 2002: 86-87; Magretta says a strategy is a summary of its intended and preferred modes of accomplishing its goals. This differs from our own definition given above.

4. D. Hambrick and J. Fredrickson, "Are You Sure You Have a Strategy?" *Academy of Management Executive* 15, no. 4, 2001: 48-59.

5. The strategy diamond was suggested as a useful tool by George Norman of Tufts University. I thank Professor Norman for his valuable input.

6. R. Amit and C. Zott, "Value Creation in E-business," Strategic *Management Journal* 22, 2001: 493-520.

7. K. Kafner, "Wary of a New Web Idea That Rings Old," *New York Times,* March 24 2006. Retrieved from the Web March 24, 2006. http://www.nytimes.com/2006/03/24/technology/24venture.html.

8. The original concept and description of entry wedges was developed by Karl Vesper. See K. Vesper, *New Venture Strategies* (Upper Saddle River, NJ: Prentice Hall, 1980). Rev. ed. 1990.

9. Vesper, 1990.

10. P. Drucker, *Innovation and Entrepreneurship* (New York: Harper & Row, 1985).

11. Drucker, 1985.

12. A. Morse, "An Entrepreneur Finds Tokyo Shares Her Passion for Bagels," *The Wall Street Journal,* October 18, 2005: B1.

13. The actual license agreement can be found at http://www.java.com/en/download/license.jsp. Retrieved from the Web February 8, 2007.

14. Sun Microsystems, Inc. press release. Retrieved from the Web February 8, 2007. http://www.sun.com/smi/Press/sun-flash/2004-09/sunflash.20040914.1.xml.

15. J. Emshwiller. "Federal Research Labs Can Help Small Firms Compete," *The Wall Street Journal,* December 9, 1992: B2.

16. L. Busenitz, R. Hoskisson, and M. Wright, "Entrepreneurial Growth through Privatizations: The Upside of Management Buy-outs," *Academy of Management Review* 25, no. 3, 2000: 591–601.

17. S. Lippman and R. Rumelt, "The Payments Perspective: Micro-Foundations of Resource Analysis," *Strategic Management Journal* 24, no.10, 2003: 903-927.

18. J. Mahoney and J. Pandian. "The Resource-Based View within the Conversation of Strategic Management," *Strategic Management Journal* 13, 1992: 363–380.

19. S. Lippman and R. Rumelt, "A Bargaining Perspective on Resource Advantage" *Strategic Management Journal* 24, 11, 2002: 1069-1093.

20. J. Dyer and H. Singh, "The Relational View: Cooperative Strategy and Sources of Interorganizational Competitive Advantage," *Academy of Management Review* 23, no. 4, 1998: 660-679.

21. These rewards can rightly be characterized and defined as entrepreneurial rents, the difference between a venture's *ex ante* cost (or value) of the resources combined to form the venture. See R. Rumelt, "Theory, Strategy and Entrepreneurship." In D. Teece (ed.), *The Competitive Challenge* (Cambridge: Ballinger, 1988).

22. J. Doh, "Entrepreneurial Privatization Strategies: Order of Entry and Local Partner Collaboration as Sources of Competitive Advantage," *Academy of Management Review* 25, no. 3, 2000: 551–571.

23. M. Lieberman and D. Montgomery, "First-Mover Advantages," *Strategic Management Journal* 9, 1988: 41–58.

24. Winter, 1987.

25. Winter, 1987.

26. Lieberman and Montgomery, 1988; R. Rumelt, "Theory, Strategy and Entrepreneurship" In D. Teece (ed.), *Competitive Strategic Management* (Upper Saddle River, NJ: Prentice Hall, 1998): 556-570.

27. M. Lieberman and D. Montgomery, "First Mover (Dis)advantages: Retrospective and Link with the Resource-Based View," *Strategic Management Journal* 19, no 11, 1998:1111-1125.

28. This section follows Mahoney and Pandian, 1992.

29 Quoted in Mahoney and Pandian from W. Starbuck, 1985. "Organizational Growth and Development." In J. March (ed.), *Handbook of Organization* (Chicago: Rand McNally, 1992):451-533.

30. E. Penrose, *The Theory of the Growth of the Firm* (New York: John Wiley, 1959).

31. For more information, see Wikipedia at http://en.wikipedia.org/wiki/Total_Quality_Management. Retrieved from the Web February 8, 2007.

32. W. Deming, "The Roots of Quality Control in Japan." *Pacific Basin Quarterly*, Spring 1985: 3–4.

33. This study was conducted over a three-year period by Ernst & Young and the American Quality Foundation. Five hundred and eight firms participated. The findings reported here are taken from two secondary sources: *Business Week,* November 30, 1992, and *The Wall Street Journal,* October 1, 1992.

34. C. Shapiro and H. Varian, *Information Rules: A Strategic Guide to the Network Economy* (Boston: Harvard Business School Press, 1999).

35. Amit and Zott, 2001.

36. S. Birley and P. Westhead, "Growth and Performance Contrasts between 'Types' of Small Firms," *Strategic Management Journal* 11, 1990: 535–557.

37. For example, the production function or product life-cycle curve.

38. M. Porter, *Competitive Strategy* (New York: Free Press, 1980). See chapter 10.

39. Drucker, 1985. The examples are taken from chapter 19.

40. E. Eisenhardt, K. Lyon, and C. Schoonhoven, "Speeding Products to Market: Waiting Time and First Product Introductions in New Firms," *Administrative Science Quarterly* 35, 1990: 177–207; K. Eisenhardt and L. Bourgeois, "Strategic

Decision Processes in High-Velocity Environment: Four Cases in the Microcomputer Industry," *Management Science* 34, 1988: 816–835.

41. M. Werner, "Planning for Uncertain Futures: Building Commitment Through Scenario Planning." *Business Horizons,* May–June 1990: 55–58.

42. In the short run, firms can survive if price is less than average *variable* cost, but in the long run, negative contribution margins cannot be sustained. In the long run, price must be sufficient to cover average *total* costs.

43. M. Feldman, M., Hatch, J. Martin, and S. Sitkin. "The Uniquenes Paradox in Organizational Stories." *Administrative Science Quarterly* 28, l983: 438–453.

44. C. Baden-Fuller and J. Stopford, *Rejuvenating the Mature Business.* (London: Routledge, l992).

45. Porter, 1980.

46. Adapted from W. Bulkeley. "Maturing Market: Computer Startups Grow Increasingly Rare," *The Wall Street Journal,* September 8, 1989: 1, 16.

47. Bulkeley, 1989.

48. M. Porter, "How to Attack the Industry Leader," *Fortune,* April 29, 1985: 153–166.

49. P. Audia, E. Locke, and K. Smith, "The Paradox of Success: An Archival and a Lab Study of Strategic Persistence Following Radical Environmental Change," *Academy of Management Journal* 43, no. 5, 2000: 837-853.

50. M. Selz, "Small Companies Thrive by Taking Over Some Specialized Tasks for Big Concerns," *The Wall Street Journal,* September 11, 1992: B1–2.

51. Porter, 1980. See chapter 12.

52. H. Green, "Great Online Expectations," *Business Week,* February, 20, 2006: 86.

53. P. Gogoi, "Startup Secrets of the Successful," *Business Week Online.* January 18, 2006. Retrieved from the Web January 24, 2006. http://www.businessweek.com/smallbiz.

54. Porter, 1980. See chapter 9.

55. These examples are from Porter, 1980.

56. S. Galante, "Venture Firms Are Foraying into Fragmented Industries," *The Wall Street Journal,* October 6, 1986.

57. A Bhide, "How Entrepreneurs Craft Strategies That Work," *Harvard Business Review*, March-April 1994: R-94202.

58. R. Grant, "The Resource-Based Theory of Competitive Advantage: Implications for Strategy Formulation," *California Management Review* 34, 1991:114–135.

59. These capabilities have, at various times, been described as "distinctive competencies" or "core competencies" by other authors. See L. Hrebiniak and C. Snow, "Strategy, Distinctive Competence and Organizational Performance," *Administrative Science Quarterly* 25, 1990: 317–336; G Hamel and C. Prahalad, "The Core Competencies of the Organization," *Harvard Business Review*, May–June 1990: 79–91.

60. R. Rumelt, "Evaluation of Strategy." In D. Schendel and C. Hofer (eds.), *Strategic Management* (Boston: Little, Brown, 1979): 196-210.

Chapter 5

1. Of course the formulation and implementation of a new venture plan frequently do not proceed consecutively. There is usually considerable overlap. The very act of collecting information often puts prospective entrepreneurs in contact with other businesspeople, creating a network for the new venture, a process that could be considered implementation. The distinction simply divides analysis from action.

2. E. Barker, "The Bullet Proof Business Plan," *Inc.* 2001. Retrieved from the Web June 6, 2006, http://www.inc.com/magazine/20011001/23484.html.

3. B. McWilliams, "Garbage In, Garbage Out," *Inc.,* August 1996. Retrieved from the Web June 5, 2006. http://pf.inc.com/magazine/19960801/1764.html.

4. D. Gumpert, *Burn Your Business Plan,* (Needham MA: Lauson Publishing Co., 2002).

5. Retrieved from the Web February 12, 2007, http://en.wikipedia.org/wiki/Bootstrapping_%28business%29.

6. R. Hisrich and M. Peters, "Chapter 5," *Entrepreneurship* (Homewood, IL: Irwin, 1992).

7. K. Andrews, *The Concept of Corporate Strategy* (Upper Saddle River, NJ: Prentice Hall, 1980).

8. A. Cooper, W. Dunkelberg, and C. Woo, "Entrepreneur Perceived Chances for Success," *Journal of Business Venturing* 3, 1989: 97–108.

9. "Full material disclosure" is a legal concept. It means that people who rely on the document for information regarding the business's prospects are entitled to the full facts as they are known to the entrepreneur, or as they should be known to a reasonable person.

10. C. Bamford, T. Dean, and P. McDougall, "Initial Strategies and New Venture Growth: An Examination of the Effectiveness of Broad Versus Narrow Breadth Strategies." *Frontiers of Entrepreneurship Research*, 1997 edition, Babson College, Arthur M. Blank Center for Entrepreneurship, Wellesley, MA.

    Retrieved from the Web, http://www.babson.edu/entrep/fer/papers97/bamford/bam.htm; G. Hills and R. Schrader, "Successful Entrepreneurial Insights into Opportunity Recognition." In *Frontiers of Entrepreneurial Research*. Retrieved from the Web 1998, http://www.babson.edu/entrep/fer.

11. J. Bailey, "Successful Start-Ups and Other Problems," *New York Times,* February 21, 2006. Retrieved from the Web February 25, 2006.

12. Bailey, 2006.

13. C. Schwenk, and C. Shrader, "The Effects of Formal Strategic Planning on Financial Performance in Small Firms: A Meta-Analysis," *Entrepreneurship: Theory and Practice* 17, 1993: 53–64. A meta-analysis is a statistical analysis of a group of other research reports—a study of studies. Another recent study showed that for young firms, planning that involves financial projections is positively related to both profits and financial strength. G. Hills, G. Lumpkin, and R. Schrader, "Does Formal Planning Enhance the Performance of New Ventures?" In *Frontiers of Entrepreneurial Research,* 1998. Retrieved from the Web, http://www.babson.edu/entrep/fer.

14. K. Vesper, *New Venture Mechanics* (Upper Saddle River, NJ: Prentice Hall, 1993): 330.

15. D. Shepard, "New Venture Entry Strategy: An Analysis of Venture Capital Decision Making," *Frontiers of Entrepreneurial Research*, 1997. Retrieved from the Web http://www.babson.edu/entrep/fer.

16. W. Sahlman, "How to Write a Great Business Plan," *Harvard Business Review,* July/August 1997: 98-108.

17. For a book-length treatment of the essentials of the business plan, see D. Gumpert and S. Rich, *Business Plans That Win $$$*. (New York: Harper and Row, 1987); and D. Gladstone, *Venture Capital Handbook* (Upper Saddle River, NJ: Prentice Hall, 1988). For a detailed outline in article form, see W. K. Schilit, "How to Write a Winning Business Plan," *Business Horizons* (July–August, 1987): 13–22.

18. See chapter 10 of Vesper, 1993.

19. Vesper, 1993.

20. The summary outline presented here is adapted from Gladstone, 1988: 26–27.

21. When talking about an accounting concept like gross margin, remember that the terms high and low are relative to what is achieved (and achievable) by other firms in the industry.

22. Total quality management is an organizing system that emphasizes benchmarking (determining the ideal levels of achievable quality), teamwork and participation, and the dedication of the company to continuous and ceaseless improvement of product and service quality. It is embodied in the work of W. Edwards Deming, the American productivity expert who introduced the system to Japanese industry after World War II. See chapter 4.

23. Some venture capitalists believe that the deal structure is *their* field of expertise and that the business plan should not contain a specific structure because venture capitalists who are interested in the proposal will offer the deal they want. On the other hand, it can be argued that the entrepreneur is the one with something to sell (equity in the new venture) and has the obligation to set the initial price.

24. The term *unit* is used because sometimes shares are combined with various other rights, such as warrants or options.

25. *Dilution* refers to the phenomenon that occurs immediately after the financing. The new investor's shares are diluted after the offering when the new investor has paid more than the average price paid by the founders. This is the usual case. Dilution will be covered in chapter 8.

26. Adapted from Schilit, 1987: 13–22.

27. See chapter 4 of Gladstone, 1988

28. Rich and Gumpert, 1987.

29. Vesper, 1993.

30. Excerpted from E. Roberts, "Business Planning in the Start-up High-Tech Enterprise." In R. Hornaday (ed.), *Frontiers of Entre-*

preneurship Research, 1983 edition, Babson College, Arthur M. Blank Center for Entrepreneurship, Wellesley MA: 107.
31. Roberts, 1983.
32. McWilliams, 1996.

Chapter 6

1. G. Hills and R. LaForge, "Research at the Marketing Interface to Advance Entrepreneurship Theory," *Entrepreneurship: Theory and Practice* 16, no. 3, 1992: 33-59.
2. G. Hills and R. LaForge, "Marketing and Entrepreneurship: The State of the Art." In D. Sexton and J. Kasarda (eds.), *The State of the Art of Entrepreneurship* (Boston: PWS-Kent, 1992).
3. Many fine marketing textbooks offer detailed descriptions and models of much of what we attempt to cover in this single chapter. Among the best for additional readings are:

• P. Kotler, and G. Armstrong, *Principles of Marketing,* 11th ed. (Upper Saddle River, NJ: Prentice-Hall, 2005).
• W. Bearden, T. Ingram, R. LaForge, *Marketing: Principles and Perspectives,* 4th ed. (New York: McGraw Hill/Irwin, 2003).

4. R. Peterson, "Small Business Adoption of the Marketing Concept versus Other Business Strategies," *Journal of Small Business Management* 27, 1989: 38-46.
5. See http://www.benjerry.com/our_company/our_mission/index.cfm.
6. See http://www.thebodyshopinternational.com/web/tbsgl/values.jsp.
7. D. Aaker, V. Kumar, G. Day, *Marketing Research,* 8th ed. (New York: J. Wiley, 2003). R. Kaden, "Guerilla Marketing Research: Marketing Research Techniques That Can Make Any Business More Money" (London UK, Koren.Page, 2006). G. Churchill, and D. Iacobucci, *Marketing Research: Methodological Foundation* (Belmont CA: Southwestern Pub, 2004).
8. However, there is evidence that entrepreneurs shy away from conducting detailed market research and that many do not prepare detailed marketing plans. See D. Andrus, D. Norvell, P. McIntyre, and L. Milner, "Market Planning, in *Inc.* 500 Companies," in G. Hills (ed.), *Research at the Marketing/ Entrepreneurship Interface* (Chicago: University of

Illinois at Chicago, 1987): 163-171; D. Spitzer, G. Hills, and P. Alpar, "Marketing Planning and Research Among High Technology Entrepreneurs," in G. Hills, R. LaForge, and B. Parker, (eds.), *Research at the Marketing/Entrepreneurship Interface* (Chicago: University of Illinois at Chicago, 1989): 411-422.
9. S. McDaniel and A. Parasuranam, "Practical Guidelines for Small Business Marketing Research," *Journal of Small Business Management* 24, 1986: 1-8.
10. McDaniel and Parasuranam, 1986.
11. P. Gogoi, "Steering Patients through the System," *BusinessWeek,* February 27, 2006: 80. See also http://www.quantumhealthllc.com/.
12. Quoted in M. Mayer, "Creativity Loves Constraints," *BusinessWeek,* February 13, 2006: 102.
13. E. Rogers,, *Diffusion of Innovations* (New York: Free Press, 1983).
14. Additional information can be found at http://www.anu.edu.au/people/Roger.Clarke/SOS/InnDiff.html. Retrieved from the Web February 23, 2007.
15. R. Gibson, "Location, Luck, Service Can Make a Store Top Star," *The Wall Street Journal,* February 1, 1993: B1.
16. Gibson, 1993.
17. R. Peterson, "Small Business Usage of Target Marketing," *Journal of Small Business Management,* October 1991: 79-85.
18. Some industries have added their own specific "Ps" to the traditional 4-P frameworks. For example, in the travel and hospitality industry, there are four additional "Ps": packaging, programming, people, and partnerships. Every marketing strategist should design specific policies to meet specific industry requirements.
19. The following relies primarily on R. Lindberg and T. Cohn, *The Marketing Book for Growing Companies that Want to Excel* (New York: Van Nostrand, 1986).
20. "Signaling" is discussed in more detail in M. Porter, *Competitive Analysis* (New York: Free Press, 1980).
21. This definition and those following are from *Marketing Definitions: A Glossary of Marketing Terms* (Chicago: American Marketing Association, 1960).
22. S. Vranica, "Where Ad Dollars Go," *The Wall Street Journal Online,* May 6, 2006. Retrieved

from the Web, May 8, 2006, http://online.wsj.com.

23. Vranica, 2006.

24. Recommended readings for additional advertising information are *Advertising Age* and the *Journal of Advertising Research*.

25. See the following references for a more detailed discussion: G. Churchill Jr., N. Ford, and O. Walker, *Sales Force Management*, 4th ed. (Homewood, IL: Irwin, 1993); W. Stanton, R. Buskirk, and R. Spiro, *Management of a Sales Force*, 8th ed. (Homewood, IL: Irwin, 1991).

26. J. Borzo, "New Services May Bring the End of Cold Calling," *The Wall Street Journal Startup Journal* Retrieved from the Web, http://www.startupjournal.com, June 16, 2006. The lists of Web sites that follow are also from this article.

27. S. Needleman, "Accidentally Stumbling on Viral Marketing," *The Wall Street Journal Startup Journal*. Retrieved from the Web, June 16, 2006, http://www.startupjournal.com.

28. J. Bosman, "Advertising Is Obsolete, Everyone Says So." *New York Times,* January 23, 2006. Retrieved from the Web, http://www.nytimes.com/2006/01/23/business/media/.

29. M. Mandel and R. Hof, "Rethinking the Internet," *BusinessWeek*, March 26, 2001: 117-22.

30. H. Rosenberg, "Student Power, Part 2," *BusinessWeek,* June 20, 2000. Retrieved from the Web February 23, 2007.

31. J. Matthews, "Threatened by eBay?" Retrieved from the Web February 23, 2007, http://siliconvalley.internet.com/news/article.php/48914.

32. See http://www.pwc.com/extweb/pwcpublications.nsf/docid/FA564C927B0E4D3480256CC300514CB3. Retrieved from the Web February 23, 2007.

33. Useem, "Dot-Coms: What Have We Learned?" *Fortune,* October 30, 2000: 82–104.

34. G. Bounds, "For One Domain Shopper, Haggling Pays Off," *The Wall Street Journal,* May 9, 2005: R8.

35. D. Kesmodel, "When the Cookie Crumbles," *The Wall Street Journal,* September 12, 2005: R6.

36. B. Elgin, "Keywords for Ad Buyers: Pay Up," *BusinessWeek,* February 21, 2006: 40.

37. R. Richmond, "Web Ads Present a New Front in Hacker Wars," *The Wall Street Journal*, June 15, 2006: B3.

38. L. Flynn, "Like This? You'll Hate That Not All Web Recommendations Are Welcome," *New York Times,* January 23, 2006. Retrieved from the Web, http://www.nytimes.com.

39. K. Spors, "Small Talk," *The Wall Street Journal,* April 25, 2006: B8.

40. From an interview with Jason Calacanis conducted by Alan Meckler, "Can Bloggers Make Money?" *The Wall Street Journal Online,* April 19, 2006. Retrieved from the Web, http://www.wsj.com/online.

41. D. Kesmodel, "More Marketers Place Web Ads by Time of Day," *The Wall Street Journal,* June 23, 2006: B1.

42. See K. Marino, *Forecasting Sales and Planning Profits,* (Chicago: Probus, 1984).

Chapter 7

1. *The Wall Street Journal,* October 16, 1992: R7.

2. For example, the lessons of portfolio theory require that a portfolio exist. The business is the major, if not the only, asset of many entrepreneurs,. Similarly, many of the assumptions of the capital asset pricing model do not hold true for small, new, privately held firms.

3. Basic accounting textbooks include J. J. Wild, *Fundamentals of Accounting* (New York: McGraw-Hill, 2007); and C. Stickney and R. Weil, *Financial Accounting: An Introduction to Concepts, Methods, Uses.* (Cincinnatti: Southwestern Publishing, 2002). There are also good online sites for quick review. http://www.bizzer.com/images/Financial/ http://www.bizzer.com/images/Financial/ http://www.allbusiness.com/accounting-reporting/reports-statements/1259-1.html

4. This is for firms with total investments under $10 million. U.S. Bureau of the Census, *Quarterly Financial Report: Manufacturing, Mining and Trade Corporations, 4th Quarter, 1983* (Washington, DC: U.S. Government Printing Office, 1983): 65, 130, 135.

5. This section follows J. Petty and E. Walker, *Financial Management of the Small Firm,* 2nd ed. (Upper Saddle River, NJ: Prentice Hall, 1986): chapter 6.

6. Adapted from D. Bonder, D. Garner, and R. Owen, *Arthur Young Guide to Financing for*

Growth (New York: John Wiley, 1986): 231-33.

7. In addition to the books mentioned in notes 5 and 6, see B. Mavrovitis, *Cashflow, Credit and Collection* (Chicago: Probus, 1990); L. Masonson, *Cash, Cash, Cash* (New York: Harper, 1990); B. Blechman and J. Levinson, *Guerrilla Financing* (New York: Houghton-Mifflin, 1991): chapter 5.

8. A. Bhide, "Bootstrap Finance: The Art of Start-Ups," *Harvard Business Review*, November-December 1992: 110-17.

9. "What Is Mezzanine Financing?" Retrieved from the Web February 27, 2007, http://www.wisegeek.com/what-is-mezza-nine-financing.htm.

10. J. Fraser, "Capital Steps," *Inc.*, February 1996: 42–47.

11. H. Sapienza and J. Timmons, "Venture Capital: The Decade Ahead." In J. Kasarda and D. Sexton (eds.), *The State of the Art of Entrepreneurship* (Boston: PWS-Kent, 1992): 402-437.

12. Lee Gomes, "The Angels Are Back and This Time They Have a Trade Group," *The Wall Street Journal*, April 11, 2005: B1.

13. State laws are known as blue sky laws. Federal laws are primarily those of the U.S. Securities and Exchange Commission (SEC) that regulates private offerings. It is imperative that any entrepreneur navigate these waters with the aid of experienced legal counsel.

14. J. Freear and W. Wetzel, "The Informal Venture Capital Market in the 1990s." In D. Sexton and J. Kasarda (eds .), *The State of the Art of Entrepreneurship* (Boston: PWS-Kent, 1992): pp. 462–486; and Wetzel, 1992.

15. I. Grosbeck, M. Roberts, and H. Stevenson, *New Business Ventures and the Entrepreneur,* 3rd ed. (Homewood, IL: Irwin, 1989).

16. D. Enrich, "Lessons from a Lender," *The Wall Street Journal*, May 8, 2006: R6.

17. W. Bygrave, "Venture Capital Returns in the 1980s." In J. Kasarda and D. Sexton, eds., *The State of the Art of Entrepreneurship* (Boston: PWS-Kent, 1992): 438-61.

18. J. Solomon, "Intelligence Investing," *The Wall Street Journal*, September 12, 2005: A4.

19. J. Emory, "The Value of Marketability as Illustrated in Initial Public Offerings of Common Stock," *Business Valuation Review,* December 1990: 114–16.

20. See http://www.grameen-info.org/# for more information about the bank. Retrieved from the Web February 27, 2007.

21. Adapted from J. Timmons, *New Venture Creation*, 3rd ed. (Homewood, IL: Irwin, 1990).

22. Adapted from A. Mamis, "Can Your Bank Do This?" *Inc.*, March, 1996: 29–38.

23. P. Singer, "Capital Ideas," *The Wall Street Journal*, May 8, 2006: R6.

24. Singer, 2006.

25. L. Berton, "Asset-Backed Loans Aid Cash Strapped Entrepreneurs," *The Wall Street Journal*, November 28, 1989: B2.

26. In chapter 5, we suggested that unless good business reasons suggested otherwise, a valuation could be calculated at the end of a five-year period of projections.

27. They may also be bargaining over a host of other issues. These will be discussed in the next chapter.

28. Of course, historical returns are no indication of future returns. This is boilerplate language that all who solicit investments must use. Statistically the best prediction of future returns is past returns, but this may be a misuse of statistics.

29. The government is paid first (taxes), then employees. Creditors are paid next, followed by equity investors, first preferred stockholders, and finally common stockholders.

30. Arbitrage occurs when an asset (or business) has different prices in different markets. For example, for a very short period of time (because of the speed of information), a stock can be selling for more in Tokyo than in London. Why? Because news affecting earnings (in this case positively) is released in Tokyo first due to the time difference. An arbitrageur can profit briefly by buying the stock in London and selling it in Tokyo. Because the price difference will be small and the window of opportunity very narrow, only very large transactions make sense.

31. This discussion follows Stevenson et al., 1989.

32. A "pure play" is a firm that is undiversified and operates in a single line of business. Because most new ventures operate as pure plays and very few ongoing larger firms do, it is difficult to get comparable capitalization rates.

33. Of course, the actual amount of equity the investor will own is subject to negotiation and many other variables. These will be dis-

cussed in the next chapter. This example is simplified for computation purposes.

34. R. E. Silverman, and T. Herman, "IRS Steps Up Scrutiny of Family Partnerships," *The Wall Street Journal,* January 25, 2006: D1.

35. Retrieved from the Web July 17, 2006, http://www.sec.gov/info/smallbus/qasbsec.htm.

36. As used in Section 2(15)(ii) of the Securities Act of 1933 shall include the following persons:

(a) Any savings and loan association or other institution specified in Section 3(a)(5)(A) of the Act whether acting in its individual or fiduciary capacity; any broker or dealer registered pursuant to Section 15 of the Securities and Exchange Act of 1934; any plan established and maintained by a state or its political subdivisions, or any agency or instrumentality of a state or its political subdivisions, for the benefit of its employees, if such plan has total assets in excess of $5 million; any employee benefit plan within the meaning of Title I of the Employee Retirement Income Security Act of 1974, if the investment decision is made by a plan fiduciary, as defined in Section 3(21) of such Act, which is a savings and loan association, or if the employee benefit plan has assets in excess of $5 million or, if a self-directed plan, with investment decisions made solely by persons that are accredited investors;

(b) Any private business development company as defined in Section 202(a)(22) of the Investment Advisers Act of 1940;

(c) Any organization described in Section 501(c)(3) of the Internal Revenue Code, corporation, Massachusetts or similar business trust, or partnership not formed for the specific purpose of acquiring the securities offered, with total assets in excess of $5 million;

(d) Any director, executive officer, or general partner if the issuer of the securities being offered or sold, or any director, executive officer, or general partner of the issuer;

(e) Any natural person whose individual net worth, or joint net worth with that person's spouse, at the time of the purchase exceeds $1 million;

(f) Any natural person who had an individual income in excess of $200,000 in each of the two most recent years or joint income with that person's spouse in excess of $300,000 in each of those years and has a reasonable expectation of reaching the same income level on the current year;

(g) Any trust, with total assets in excess of $5 million, not formed for the specific purpose of acquiring the securities offered, whose purchase is directed by a sophisticated person as described in Rule 506(b)(2)(ii); and

(h) Any entity in which all of the equity owners are accredited investors."

37. These observations are from comments made by Stephen J. Hackman, Esq., in a talk entitled "Financing Entrepreneurial Ventures" at the Indiana Entrepreneurial Educational Conference, Indianapolis, Indiana, March 1, 1991.

38. See E. Altman, R. Haldeman, and P. Narayanan, "ZETA-Analysis: A New Model to Identify Bankruptcy Risk," *Journal of Banking and Finance,* June 1977: 29–54.

39. Retrieved from the Web July 18, 2006, http://www.law.cornell.edu/wex/index.php/Bankruptcy.

Chapter 8

1. H. Stevenson, I. Grosbeck, M. Roberts, *New Business Ventures and the Entrepreneur,* 3rd ed. (Homewood, IL: Irwin, 1989): chapter 6.

2. This follows Stevenson et al., 1989.

3. D. Cable, and S. Shane, "A Prisoner's Dilemma Approach to Entrepreneur-Venture Capitalist Relationships," *Academy of Management Review* 22, no. 1, 1997: 142-76.

4. H. Sapienza and M. Korsgaard, "Procedural Justice in Entrepreneur-Investor Relations," *Academy of Management Journal* 39, no. 3, 1996: 544-574.

5. This follows J. Timmons, *New Venture Creation* (Homewood, IL: Irwin, 1990).

6. Kauffman Foundation, http://www.kauffman.org/. Reported in R. Breeden, "Family, Friends Can Offer a Strong Financial Base," *The Wall Street Journal.* Retrieved from the Web August 23, 2003, http://wsj.com.

7. L. Napoli, "Giving Start-Ups a Leg Up, for a Slice of the Pie," *New York Times,* September

20, 2005. Retrieved from the Web September 20, 2005, http://www.nytimes.com.

8. N. Heikens, "Software Firm Bets Future on Artificial Intelligence," Indianapolis Business Journal, October 11–18, 1993; A. J. Schneider, "CID Cashes In Again; New Firm Goes Public," *Indianapolis Business Journal*, March 27–April 2, 1995.

9. These are based on the research of T. Tyebjee and A. Bruno, "A Model of Venture Capitalist Investment Activity," *Management Science* 30, no. 9, 1984: 1051–66. Others have confirmed these findings, most notably: I. Macmillan, R. Siegal, and P. N. Subba-Narasimha, "Criteria Used by Venture Capitalists to Evaluate New Venture Proposals," *Journal of Business Venturing* 1, 1985: 119–28; C. Hofer, W. Sandberg, D. Schweiger, "The Use of Verbal Protocols in Determining Venture Capitalists' Decision Processes," *Entrepreneurship: Theory and Practice* 13, no. 2, 1988: 8–20; R. Hisrich and A. Jankowicz, "Intuition in Venture Capital Decisions: An Exploratory Study," *Journal of Business Venturing* 5, 1990: 49–62.

10. Hisrich and Jankowicz, 1990. In a study employing a small sample, it was found that management was the most important of three factors. The others were opportunity and return.

11. Jack Gill, personal conversation and class presentation, November 2002.

12. See chapter 3 of R. Alterowitz and J. Zonderman, *New Corporate Ventures* (New York: John Wiley, 1988).

13. Timmons, 1990.

14. Adapted from V. Fried and R. Hisrich, "Venture Capital Research: Past, Present and Future," *Entrepreneurship: Theory and Practice* 13, no. 1, 1988: 15–28.

15. L. Bransten, "Venture Capitalists Find Cash, But Few Great Ideas," *The Wall Street Journal*, October 22, 2000: C18.

16. The most comprehensive directory is in S. Isenstein and J. Morris, eds., *Pratt's Guide to Venture Capital Sources* (New York: Thompson Financial, 2003).

17. A. Lashinsky, "Bright Lights, Big Money," *Fortune*, March 6, 2006: 49.

18. R. Buckman, "Silicon Valley Start-Ups See Cash Everywhere," *The Wall Street Journal*, March 20, 2006: C1.

19. R. Buckman, "How Venture Capital Is Trying to Get Down with Young CEOs," *The Wall Street Journal*, July 8, 2006: A1.

20. This section follows J. Blakey and H. Hoffman, "You Can Negotiate with Venture Capitalists," *Harvard Business Review* 65, no. 2, 1987: 7–11.

21. H. Landstron, S. W. Manigart, C. Mason, and H. Sapienza, "Contracts Between Entrepreneurs and Investors: Terms and Negotiation Processes," *Frontiers of Entrepreneurship Research* (Wellesley, MA: Babson College, 1998).

22. "Note on Financial Contracting," 1987. *Harvard Business School Publishing* reprint 9-288-014. Revised June 22, 1989.

23. This example was suggested by Stevenson et al., 1989.

24. Bank lending on cash flow is improbable without collateral, a guarantor, or a relative on the bank's board of directors. Therefore, this example should be considered hypothetical.

25. J. Barney, L. Busenitz, J. Fiet, and D. Moesel, "Factors Underlying Changes in Risk Perceptions of New Ventures by Venture Capitalists," *Frontiers of Entrepreneurship Research*. (Wellesley, MA: Babson College, 1996).

26. To see this, discount the total cash flow line by 50 percent. This figure is approximately $2,510,000. Divide the $2 million needed by this figure for 79.9 percent.

27. The source of this example is W. Sahlman, "Aspects of Financial Contracting," *Journal of Applied Corporate Finance*, 1988: 25–36.

28. This example follows the one provided in the Duncan Field case (9-392-137) by R. O. von Werssosetz and H. I. Grousbeck, and accompanying Teaching Note (5-385-074) by M. Roberts (Cambridge, MA: Harvard Business School, 1982).

29. D. Gullapalli, "A Piece of the Action," *The Wall Street Journal*, November 29, 2004: R10.

30. The field of negotiations and negotiating strategy has many good books and materials for the entrepreneur. For example: "Harvard Business Essentials Guide to Negotiation," Harvard Business School Publishing, 2003; R. Lewicki, D. Saunders, and B. Barry, *Negotiation*, 5th ed. (New York: McGraw-Hill/Irwin, 2005); R. Fisher, B. Patton, and W. Ury, *Getting to Yes: Negotiating Agreement Without Giving In* (Boston: Houghton-Mifflin, 1992).

31. J. Wall, *Negotiations: Theory and Practice* (Glenview, IL: Scott, Foresman and Company, 1985).

32. J. Wall and M. Blum, "Negotiations," *Journal of Management* 17, 1991: 273-303.

33. C. Perrow, "Power in Organizational Analysis: Illustrations, Summary and Conclusions." In *Complex Organizations: A Critical Essay* (New York: McGraw-Hill, 1986): 258-78.

34. Fisher, Ury, and Patton, *Getting to Yes,* 2nd ed. (New York: Penguin Books, 1991).

35. "Last offer" arbitration means that the arbitrator can choose only between the two last offers of the parties. In the case of the baseball negotiations, it is the choice between the last offer the team makes for the player's salary and the last offer the player makes to play for that team. The arbitrator hears evidence supporting each side's offer and then must pick. No splitting the difference is allowed.

36. E. Glenn, D. Witmeyer, and K. Stephenson, "Cultural Styles of Persuasion," *Journal of Intercultural Relations,* Fall 1997: 52-66.

37. L. Pye, "The China Trade: Making the Deal." In *The Art of Business Negotiation* (Cambridge, MA: Harvard Business Review Publications, 1997).

38. These tactics are suggested by Lewicki and Letterer, 1985.

Chapter 9

1. J. C. Collins and J. I. Porras, *Built to Last: Successful Habits of Visionary Companies* (New York: HarperBusiness, 1997).

2. R. S. Kaplan and D. P. Norton, The *Balanced Scorecard: Translating Strategy into Action* (Boston: Harvard Business School Press, 1996).

3. M. Tushman and B. Virany, "Top Management Teams and Corporate Success in an Emerging Industry," *Journal of Business Venturing* 1, 1986: 261–74.

4. A. Bruno and T. Tyebjee, "A Model of Venture Capitalist Investment Activity," *Management Science* 30, no. 9, 1984: 1051–66.

5. B. Bird, *Entrepreneurial Behavior* (Glenview, IL: Scott, Foresman, 1989).

6. D. Krueger, A. McCarthy, and T. Schoenecker, "Changes in Time Allocation Patterns of Entrepreneurs," *Entrepreneurship: Theory and Practice* 15, 1990: 7–18.

7. S. Birley and D. Norburn, "The Top Management Team and Corporate Performance," *Strategic Management Journal* 9, 1988: 225–37.

8. K. Andrews, *The Concept of Corporate Strategy.* (Upper Saddle River, NJ: Prentice Hall, 1986).

9. J. Katzenbach and D. Smith, "The Discipline of Teams," *Harvard Business Review,* March–April, 1993: 111–20.

10. Katzenbach and Smith, 1993.

11. J. Kamm and A. Nurick, "The Stages of Team Venture Formation: A Decision-Making Model," *Entrepreneurship: Theory and Practice* 17, 1993: 17–27.

12. P. Dvorak and J. Badal, "Relative Problems," *The Wall Street Journal,* July 24, 2006: B1.

13. J. Menkes, *Executive Intelligence: What All Great Leaders Have* (New York: Collins, 2005).

14. See K. Bantel and M. Wiersema, "Top Management Team Demography and Corporate Strategic Change," *Academy of Management Journal* 35, 1992: 91–121; K. Bantel and S. Jackson, "Top Management and Innovations in Banking: Does Composition of the Top Team Make a Difference?" *Strategic Management Journal* 10, 1989: 107–124.

15. S. Finkelstein and D. Hambrick, "Top Management Team Tenure and Organizational Outcomes: The Moderating Role of Managerial Discretion," *Administrative Science Quarterly* 35, 1990: 484–503.

16. Kamm and Nurick, 1993.

17. A. Murray, "Top Management Group Heterogeneity and Firm Performance," *Strategic Management Journal* 10, 1989: 125–41.

18. "The Melting Pot Bubbles Less," *The Economist,* August 7, 1993: 69.

19. K. Kumar, L. Michaelsen, and W. Watson, "Cultural Diversity's Impact on Interaction Process and Performance Comparing Homogeneous and Diverse Task Groups," *Academy of Management Journal* 36, 1993: 590–602.

20. "Melting Pot" 1993.

21. "Melting Pot," 1993.

22. J. Timmons, *New Venture Creation,* 3rd ed. (Homewood, IL: Irwin, 1990).

23. J. Carey and J. Hamilton, "Gene Hunters Go for the Big Score," *Business Week,* August 16, 1993: 44.

24. Timmons, 1990.

25. For in-depth treatments of the research on

groups in general and work groups in particular, see J. R. Hackman (ed.), *Groups That Work (and Those That Don't)* (San Francisco: Jossey-Bass, 1990); M. Shaw, *Group Dynamics: The Psychology of Small Group Behavior,* 3rd ed. (New York: McGraw-Hill, 1991); J. Simpson, W. Wood, and S. Worchel (eds.), *Group Processes and Productivity* (Newbury Park, CA: Sage 1991).

26. G. Dess, "Consensus on Strategy Formulation and Organizational Performance: Competitors in a Fragmented Industry," *Strategic Management Journal* 8, 1987: 259–77.

27. J. Covin and D. Slevin, "Creating and Maintaining High Performance Teams." In J. Kasarda and D. Sexton (eds.), *The State of the Art of Entrepreneurship* (Boston: PWS-Kent, 1992): 358–86.

28. G. Parker, *Team Players and Teamwork: The New Competitive Business Strategy* (San Francisco: Jossey-Bass, 1990).

29. R. Black, L. Michaelson, and W. Watson, "A Realistic Test of Individual versus Group Consensus Decision Making," *Journal of Applied Psychology* 74, 1989: 834–39.

30. See S. Robbins, *Organizational Behavior,* 6th ed. (Upper Saddle River, NJ: Prentice Hall, 1993): chapter 10.

31. Bird, 1989.

32. Timmons, 1990.

33. Robbins, 1993.

34. See C. Leanea. "A Partial Test of Janis' Groupthink Model: Effects of Group Cohesiveness and Leader Behavior on Defective Decision Making," *Journal of Management,* Spring 1985: 5–17; J. Montanari and G. Morehead, "An Empirical Investigation into the Groupthink Phenomenon," *Human Relations,* May 1986: 339–410.

35. N. Kogen and M. Wallach, "Risk Taking as a Function of the Situation, the Person and the Group." In *New Directions in Psychology,* vol. 3 (New York: Holt, Reinhart and Winston, 1967).

36. An excellent Web-site discussion of the formation of boards and management of top executives can be found at http://www.managementhelp.org/boards/boards.htm. Retrieved from the Web March 5, 2007.

37. C. McCabe, "Entrepreneur's Notebook: The Value of Expert Advice," *Nation's Business,* November 1992: 9.

38. A. Bruno, W. Bygrave, J. Rothstein, and N. Taylor, "The CEO, Venture Capitalists and the Board," *Journal of Business Venturing,* March 1993: 99–113.

39. K. Scannell and D. Reilly, "Small Firms' Sarbanes Suffering?" *The Wall Street Journal,* April 6, 2006: C1. Also for a full report see the SEC's Web site. For the accounting profession's requirements, see http://www.kpmg.de/library/pdf/040413_SOX404_PCAOB_Requirements_en.pdf.

40. Collins and Porras, 1997. This section will apply the book's results to new venture issues and rely on the Collins and Porras text.

41. M. Meyer, "Here's a 'Virtual' Model for America's Industrial Giants," *Newsweek,* August 23, 1993: 32.

42. A. Byrne, "The Virtual Corporation," *Business Week,* February 8, 1993: 98–102.

43. "Virtual Corporations: Fast and Focused," *Business Week,* February 8, 1993: 134.

44. M. Granovetter, "Economic Action and Social Structure: The Problem of Embeddedness," *American Journal of Sociology* 91, 1985: 481–510.

45. H. Aldrich and P. Dubini, "Personal and Extended Networks Are Central to the Entrepreneurial Process," *Journal of Business Venturing* 6, 1991: 305–313.

46. We use the terms *networking, partnering, joint ventures,* and *alliances* interchangeably to make the text more readable. Sometimes distinctions are made between these different forms based on ownership, control, number of participants, and other factors.

47. K. Harrigan, *Managing for Joint Venture Success* (Lexington, MA: Lexington Books, 1986).

48. B. Wysocki, "U.S. Incubators Help Japan Hatch Ideas," *The Wall Street Journal,* June 12, 2000: A1.

49. Aldrich and Dubini, 1991.

50. Aldrich and Dubini, 1991.

51. A. Hirschman, *Exit, Voice, and Loyalty* (Cambridge: Harvard University Press, 1972).

52. M. Granovetter, "The Strength of Weak Ties," *American Journal of Sociology* 78, 1973: 1360–80.

53. S. Birley, "The Role of Networks in the Entrepreneurial Process," *Journal of Business Venturing* 1, 1985: 107–117; B. Johannison, "New Venture Creation: A Network Approach," *Frontiers of Entrepreneurial Research* (Wellesley, MA: Babson College, 1986).

54. Aldrich and Dubini, 1991.
55. M. Dollinger, "Environmental Boundary Spanning and Information Processing Effects on Organizational Performance," *Academy of Management Journal* 27, 1984: 351–68.
56. Granovetter, 1973.
57. From E. Carlson, "Outside Directors Are an Asset Inside Small Companies," *The Wall Street Journal,* October 30, 1992.
58. Quoted in J. Saddler, "Electronic Bulletin Boards Help Businesses Post Success," *The Wall Street Journal,* October 29, 1992.
59. D. Krueger, A. McCarthy, and T. Schoenecker, "Changes in the Time Allocation Patterns of Entrepreneurs," *Entrepreneurship: Theory and Practice* 15, 1990: 7–18.
60. G. Astley and C. Fombrun, "Collective Strategy: Social Ecology of Organizational Environments," *Academy of Management Review* 8, 1983: 576–87.
61. M. Dollinger, "The Evolution of Collective Strategies in Fragmented Industries," *Academy of Management Review* 15, 1990: 266–85.
62. P. Coy, "Two Cheers for Corporate Collaboration," *Business Week,* May 3, 1993: 34.
63. M. Selz, "Networks Help Small Companies Think and Act Big," *The Wall Street Journal,* November 12, 1992: B2.
64. M. Geringer, *Joint Venture Partner Selection* (New York: Quorum Books, 1988).
65. I. Macmillan, and J. Starr, "Resource Cooption via Social Contracting: Resource Acquisition Strategies for New Ventures," *Strategic Management Journal* 11, 1990: 79–92.
66. Geringer, 1988.
67. M. Casson, *Enterprise and Competitiveness.* (Oxford: Clarendon Press, 1990).
68. A. Chandler, *Strategy and Structure: Chapters in the History of American Industrial Enterprise* (Cambridge: MIT Press, 1962).
69. Chandler, 1962.
70. Kaplan and Norton. This section draws on the concepts of the balanced scorecard and applies them to entrepreneurial ventures.
71. J. Cornwall and B. Perlman, *Organizational Entrepreneurship* (Homewood, IL: Irwin, 1990): chapter 5.
72. B. Marsh, "Dance, Damn It," *The Wall Street Journal Special Small Business Report,* November 22, 1991: R4.
73. B. Bowers, "Ommmmmmmmmmmm," *The Wall Street Journal Special Small Business Report,* November 22, 1991: R4.
74. E. Carlson, "What If You Just Ate a Pizza?" *The Wall Street Journal Special Small Business Report,* November 22, 1991: R4.
75. "Inventor of the Laser," Retrieved from the Web. http://lala.essortment.com/history-laserin_rnxv.htm, May 14, 2007.
76. Quoted on page 51 in J. Seglin, *The Good, the Bad, and Your Business: Choosing Right When Ethical Dilemmas Pull You Apart.* (New York: John Wiley, 2000).
77. For standard treatments of human resource theory and personnel practice, see the following texts: J. Boudreau and G. Milkovitch, *Human Resource Management,* 6th ed. (Homewood, IL: Irwin, 1991); W. Cascio, *Applied Psychology and Personnel Management,* 4th ed. (Upper Saddle River, NJ: Prentice Hall, 1991); K. Davis and W. Werther, *Human Resources and Personnel Management,* 4th ed. (New York: McGraw-Hill, 1993).
78. These examples are drawn from *Inc.* magazine's July 1993 issue on the best small businesses to work for.

Chapter 10

1. B. Dumaine, "Closing the Innovation Gap," *Fortune,* December 2, 1991: 56–62.
2. Adapted from R. Hisrich, R. Nielsen, and M. Peters, "Intrapreneurship Strategy for Internal Markets: Corporate, Nonprofit and Government Institution Cases," *Strategic Management Journal* 6, 1985: 181–89.
3. A. Delbecq and J. Pierce, "Organizational Structure, Individual Attitudes and Innovation," *Academy of Management Review* 2, 1976: 27–37.
4. Some of the best full-length treatments for this topic are: C. Christensen, *The Innovator's Dilemma: When New Technologies Cause Great Firms to Fail* (Boston: Harvard Business School Publishing, 1999);
   C. Christensen and M. Raynor, *The Innovator's Solution: Creating and Sustaining Successful Growth* (Boston: Harvard Business School Publishing, 2003); W. C. Kim and R. Mauborgne, *Blue Ocean Strategy: How to Create Uncontested Market Space and Make the Competition Irrelevant* (Boston: Harvard Business School Publishing, 2005); D. Kuratko and R. Hodgetts, *Entrepreneurship: Theory, Process, Practice* (Mason, OH: Thompson-Southwestern, 2004).
5. R. Burgelman, "Corporate Entrepreneurship

and Strategic Management: Insights from a Process Study," *Management Science* 29, 1983: 1349–64.

6. C. Christensen, 1999.

7. S. Zahra, "Predictors and Financial Outcomes of Corporate Entrepreneurship: An Exploratory Study," *Journal of Business Venturing* 6, 1991: 259–85.

8. A. Barrett, "J&J: Reinventing How It Invents," *BusinessWeek Online* April 17, 2006. Retrieved from the Web April 9, 2006, http://www.businessweek.com.

9. Barrett, 2006.

10. J. Dean, "Intel Capital Funds Four Chinese Firms," *The Wall Street Journal,* June 27, 2006: C4.

11. E. Neuborne, "Pepsi's Aim Is True," *Business Week e.biz,* January 22, 2001: 52.

12. D. Kiley, "Advertisers, Start Your Engines," *BusinessWeek,* March 6, 2006: 26.

13. The information on 3M is extracted from P. Drucker, *Innovation and Entrepreneurship* (New York: Harper & Row, 1985).

14. D. Henry, "Creativity Pays. Here's How Much," *BusinessWeek Special Report,* April 24, 2006: 76.

15. This discussion follows Pinchot, 1985.

16. I. Hill, "An Intrapreneur-Turned-Entrepreneur Compares Both Worlds," *Research Management* 30, 1987: 33–37.

17. R. Knight, "Technological Innovation in Canada: A Comparison of Independent Entrepreneurs and Corporate Innovators," *Journal of Business Venturing* 4, 1989: 281–88.

18. J. Butler and G. Jones, "Managing Internal Corporate Entrepreneurship: An Agency Theory Perspective," *Journal of Management* 18, 1992: 733–49.

19. This discussion follows Pinchot, 1985.

20. T. Heller, "Loosely Coupled Systems for Corporate Entrepreneurship: Imagining and Managing the Innovation Project/Host Organization Interface," *Entrepreneurship: Theory and Practice* 24, no. 2, 1999: 25–31.

21. Z. Block and H. Sykes, "Corporate Venturing Obstacles: Sources and Solutions," *Journal of Business Venturing* 4, 1989: 159–67.

22. Block and Sykes, 1989.

23. H. Geneen, "Why Intrapreneurship Doesn't Work," *Venture* 7, 1989: 46–52.

24. R. Kanter, "The New Workforce Meets the Changing Workplace: Strains, Dilemmas, and the Contradictions in Attempts to Implement Participative and Entrepreneurial Management," *Human Resource Management* 25, 1986: 515–37.

25. Mimi Dollinger, Book Review: "Innovator's Dilemma," *Business Horizons* 50, no. 1, January 2007, 85-87. (Bloomington, IN: Elsevier, 2007).

26. J. Cornwall and B. Perlman, *Organizational Entrepreneurship* (Homewood, IL: Irwin, 1990).

27. These sources are suggested in P. Drucker, 1985.

28. Drucker, 1985.

29. Drucker, 1985.

30. N. Byrnes, "FAO Schwarz's Toytown Tryouts," *BusinessWeek Online,* March 21, 2006. Retrieved from the Web March 24, 2006, http://businessweek.com.

31. J. Surowiecki, The *Wisdom of Crowds: Why the Many Are Smarter Than the Few and How Collective Wisdom Shapes Business, Economies, Societies and Nations* (New York: Doubleday, 2004).

32. W. Taylor, "Here's an Idea: Let Everyone Have Ideas," *New York Times Online,* March 26, 2006. Retrieved from the Web March 26, 2006, http://nytimes.com.

33. Taylor, 2006.

34. K. R. Allen, *Launching New Ventures: An Entrepreneurial Approach* (Boston: Houghton-Mifflin, 2006): 16-17. The term has an interesting derivation.

Wikipedia reports that the term "Skunk works" came from the then-popular Al Capp comic strip Li'l Abner, which was popular in the 1940s. In the comic, the "Skonk Works" was a backwoods still operated by Big Barnsmell, known as the "inside man at the Skonk Works." In his secret facility, he made "kickapoo joy juice" by grinding dead skunks and worn shoes into a smoldering vat. The original Lockheed facility, during the development of the P-80, was located downwind of a malodorous plastics factory. According to Ben Rich's memoir, an engineer showed up to work one day wearing a Civil Defense gas mask as a gag. To comment on the smell and the secrecy the project entailed, another engineer, Irving Culver, referred to the facility as "Skonk Works." One day, when the Department of the Navy was trying to reach the Lockheed management for the P-80 project, the call was accidentally transferred to Culver's desk. Culver answered the phone in his trademark fashion of the time, by picking up the phone and stating "Skonk Works, inside man Culver." "What?" replied the voice at the other end. "Skonk Works" Culver repeated. The name stuck. Culver later said in an interview conducted in 1993 that "when Kelly [Johnson] heard about the incident, he promptly fired me. It didn't really matter, since he was firing me about twice a day anyways." At the request of the comic strip copyright holders, Lockheed changed the name of the advanced development company to "Skunk Works" in the 1960s. The name "Skunk Works" and the skunk design are now registered trademarks of the Lockheed Martin Corporation." Retrieved from Wikipedia August 2, 2006, http://en.wikipedia.org/wiki/Skunk_Works.

35. R. Burgelman, "Strategy Making as a Social Learning Process: The Case of Internal Corporate Venturing," *Interfaces* 18, 1988: 74–85.

36. R. Garud and A. Van de Ven, "An Empirical Evaluation of the Internal Corporate Venturing Process," *Strategic Management Journal* 13, 1992: 93–109.

37. D. Garvin, "Spinoffs and the New Firm Formulation Process," *California Management Review* 25, 1983: 3–20.

38. A. Hargadon, "Are You Looking in All The Wrong Places?" Retrieved from the Web August 2, 2003, http://www.darwinmag.com. Excerpt reprinted from *How Breakthroughs Happen: The Surprising Truth About How Companies Innovate* (Boston: Harvard Business School Press, 2003).

39. Chocolate lovers will want to know how they did this and what the result actually was. From their own Web site comes this description:

The unique properties of chocolate presented a wealth of rich material for eleven designers to explore, inspiring new modes of manufacturing and eating and creating a collection with an emphasis on ritual, delight, inquiry, and surprise. Six concepts, brought to life by Chocolates a la Carte, are shown here:

1. A chocolate with a removable top, it easily reveals its center and prevents the tragedy of the half-eaten chocolate.

2. These bundled strands give the chocolate lover a choice of two sensations, to eat it slowly strand by strand or chomp it all at once.

3. This chocolate's center can be reached only by licking or by breaking off the petals one at a time. She loves me, she loves me not.

4. An olive-like chocolate that is worn on the finger. Since chocolate melts at 96° F, it can be used to finger-paint—and cleanup will be delicious!

5. This chocolate hides its secret only a little: a cherry, still sealed in a plastic pouch, creating a moment's delay before eating.

6. A translucent corn-starched candy holds a rich French brandy, which continues into the chocolate half. Stirring it into coffee melts the chocolate and releases the liquor."

   (Retrieved from the Web September 6, 2006. http://www.ideo.com/portfolio/re.asp?x=50084)

40. This section on IDEO has relied on a number of sources. They include: B. Nussbaum, "The Power of Design," *BusinessWeek Online*, May 17, 2004. Retrieved from the Web March 30, 2006, http://www.businessweek.com; Hargadon, 2003; T. Kelley and J. Littman, *The Ten Faces of Innovation: IDEO's Strategies for Beating the Devil's Advocate & Driving Creativity Throughout Your Organization* (New York: Currency Books, 2005); IDEO's Web site: http://www.ideo.com.

41. M. Shilling, *Strategic Management of Technological Innovation* (New York: McGraw-Hill Irwin, 2005).

42. Allen, 2003.

43. Shilling, 2005.

44. G. Stevens and J. Birley, "3000 Raw Ideas Equals 1 Commercial Success," *Research and Technology Management* 40, no. 3, 1997: 16-27.

45. R. Dorf and T Byers, *Technology Ventures: From Ideas to Enterprise* (New York: McGraw Hill Higher Education, 2005).

46. Kim and Mauborgne, 2005.

47. Examples of classic tag lines:

- "I'm Going to Disney World!"—The Walt Disney Company during and after the Super Bowl
- "Let your fingers do the walking."—Yellow Pages, 1964, Geers Gross
- "I'm lovin' it"—McDonald's
- "Must See TV"—NBC, late 1990s
- "The First Kid's Network"—Nickelodeon
- "Breakfast of Champions"—Wheaties, 1935, Blackett-Sample-Gummert (later "The Breakfast of Champions" into the 1990s)
- "Bet you can't eat three"—Shredded Wheat
- "Where Do You Want To Go Today?"—Microsoft, 1990s
- "Intel Inside"—Intel
- "Can't Get Enough of That Golden Crisp"
- "Getting There Is Half The Fun"—Cunard Line

- "Leave the driving to us"—Greyhound Lines
- "What can brown do for you?"—UPS
- "Exceedingly Good Cakes"—Mr Kipling Cakes
- "Doing what we do best" and later "Something special in the air"—American Airlines
- "Were Not All There"—Ireland
- "Make it happen"—Royal Bank of Scotland
- "Do the right thing—buy a Chicken Wing"—Petey Pablo
- "Circle—It's a style"—Nike
- "Because you're worth it"—L'Oréal
- "Have it your way"—Burger King
- "Think outside the bun"—Taco Bell
- "Think different"—Apple Computer, Inc. (after IBM's internal slogan "Think!")
- "The champagne of ginger ales"—Canada Dry, 1970s
- "Think small"—Volkswagen, for the Type 1 Beetle

(Retrieved from the Web, http://en.wikipedia.org/wiki/Advertising_slogan).

48. The BCG matrix has four types and is a 2 x 2 grid. It has stars (pioneers), question marks (migrators), cash cows (settlers), and dogs (divestitures). More on the BCG and other portfolio approaches can be found at http://www.valuebasedmanagement.net/methods_bcgmatrix.html. Retrieved from the Web August 3, 2006.

49. J. Duncan, P. Ginter, T. Jacobs, and A. Rucks, "Intrapreneurship and the Reinvention of the Corporation," *Business Horizons* 31, 1988: 16–21.

50. Z. Block, I. MacMillan, and P. Narasimha, "Corporate Venturing: Alternatives, Obstacles Encountered and Experienced Effects," *Journal of Business Venturing* 1, 1986: 177–91.

51. J. Quinn, "Managing Innovation: Controlled Chaos." Reprinted in *Entrepreneurship: Creativity at Work* (Cambridge: Harvard Business Press, 1985).

52. D. Patnaik, "Founder of Jump Associates Offers Five Key Strategies for Managing Change," *Across the Board,* June 2006: 32.

53. J. McGregor, "The World's Most Innovative Companies," *BusinessWeek*, April 24, 2006: 67.

Company and Name Index

Subject Index